Working Smart

A Union Guide to Participation Programs and Reengineering

by Mike Parker and Jane Slaughter

with

Larry Adams	Alan Benchich
Ellis Boal	Stephanie Pearson Breaux
Madelyn Elder	Jon Gaunce
Martha Gruelle	Lars Henriksson
Mary Hollens	Nancy Jackson
John Kobler	Dan La Botz
Rick McKim	Ed Miller
Kim Moody	Greg Poferl
John Price	Trudy Richardson
Roberta Till-Retz	Laura Unger
Ben Watanabe	

A Labor Notes Book
Detroit • 1994

A Labor Notes Book
Copyright © 1994 by the Labor Education and Research Project
First printing: November 1994

About the publisher:
Labor Notes is a monthly magazine of labor news and analysis intended to help activists "put the movement back in the labor movement." It is published by the Labor Education and Research Project, which holds a biennial conference for all labor activists, acts as a resource center, and puts on schools and workshops on a variety of topics. See the advertisement at the end of the book for more information on Labor Notes publications.

Design by David McCullough and Jim West.

Library of Congress Catalog Card Number: 94- 73182
ISBN #0-914093-08-8

Contents

Acknowledgments

We have a lot of people to thank for their help on this book. In many ways it is a collective effort.

We are very proud that so many other authors contributed chapters; they are listed on the cover and the title page. We owe them a great deal, since their stories make the subject come alive. Many of them improved the book in other ways as well, with information and analysis, by helping at our team concept schools, and by tossing around ideas.

In addition to the chapter authors, other people wrote smaller pieces of the book, and we thank them as well: Bruce Bernard, Dave Binns, Mike Drake, Jim Green, Ernie Hite, Norm Kujawa, Eric Parker, Charley Richardson, Jim Turk and Jean Unda, Ed Vandenberghe, Kathy Wood, and Dave Yettaw. And of course, Bob Wages, for writing such a spirited Foreword. These writers and the chapter authors come from 17 different unions.

The cartoons are always an especially popular part of our books; we see them reprinted in union newspapers all around the country. We thank Estelle Carol and Bob Simpson, Al Chase, Don Frank, Judy Horacek, Gary Huck, Mike Konopacki, Ted Rall, Debra Rooney, and Don Stone for permission to use their work. By their initials ye shall know them. We especially thank Ricardo Levins Morales, who whipped up cartoons specifically for this book. Ricardo's drawings feature the Smile-Face Manager; we hope this idea will spread.

Two people helped us with editing: Dianne Feeley and Ilene Winkler. We especially appreciate their willingness to dig up additional information on their own and to work with authors to get the tough questions clear. The editor's job is usually unsung, so we're singing it loud and clear here.

Two Labor Notes interns spent untold hours at the computer getting the manuscript in shape for lay-out and doing various research chores: Emily Citkowski and Steve Hinds. Their good cheer at doing this often-tedious work made us feel less guilty at handing it off. David Mc-Cullough designed the inside of the book (as he has all Labor Notes' books). Jim West did all the lay-out, much of it as chapters were still being written. We thank him for putting up with this unorthodox procedure (at least the book is up-to-date).

We owe a particularly big debt to the Labor Notes staff: Martha Gruelle, Mary Hollens, Yolanda Holmes, Mary McGinn, Kim Moody, Simone Sagovac, and Jim West. Besides their encouragement, patience, and contribution of ideas, they shouldered Jane's work so that she could work on the book. In particular, Simone took over as director for a summer that stretched far into the fall.

We have enjoyed working with Mary Hollens on all the work related to cooperation/lean production that Labor Notes does, but in particular the team concept schools. Mary has added immensely both to the schools and to our understanding. We are not aware of any other writing on the impact of participation programs on women and people of color.

Similarly, Ellis Boal has added both his legal mind and his political thinking to our own, taking on the Dunlop Commission with both written and oral arguments. It has been very gratifying to have two more co-workers, Mary and Ellis, to shoulder part of the work.

We want to thank all the union members who helped us with this book—by providing information, by commenting on chapters, by contributing to our thinking over the years. From some of you, your help was in thoughtful criticism. This list is necessarily incomplete, but we thank:

Richard Aguilar, Robin Alexander, Judy Ancel, Garret Anglin, Steve Babson, Helen Bamford, Steve Barnes, Sherry Baron, Dean Braid, Harry Brighouse, Amy Bromsen, Anne Burger, Jim Campana, Mike Cinal, David Cohen, Kevin Corrigan, Brian Daley, Jean-Pierre Daubois, Warren Davis, Frank DePirro, Galen Devoe, Jed Dodd, Greg Drudi, Bill Dunham, Enid Eckstein, Bob Ehinger, Frank Emspak, Rod Estvan, Dianne Feeley, Sandy Felder, Sergio Ferreira, Warren Fretwell, Sam Gindin, Mike Griffin, Peter Grossi, Tom Grygorcewicz, Bill Hanline, Al Hart, Steve Hinds, Wayne Horman, Bob Hull, Nick Karras, Phil Keeling, Elly Leary, Mike Leslie, Nelson Lichtenstein, Caroline Lund, Dora Mack, Annette Maloney, Brad Markell, Rocky Marsh, Ron Maxwell, Bruce May, Gordon McClelland, Dave McCullough, Randy McSorley, Marybeth Menaker, Pete Mortaro, Phyllis Ohlemacher, Bill Parker, Bob Parker, Melva Parker, John Persico, Peter Rachleff, Victor Reuther, Martha

Roberts, David Robertson, Selwyn Rogers, Terry Rogers, Herman Rosenfeld, Gary Saganski, Laura Sager, Bill Scheuerman, John Schmidt, Mark Serafinn, Bob Sermak, Len Shindel, Sid Shniad, Tony Smith, Hal Stack, Don Stone, Paul Swanson, Wendy Thompson, Steve Tormey, Hideo Totsuka, Chris Townsend, Jerry Tucker, Bill Urman, Don Wells, Ilene Winkler, Dave Yettaw and all those interviewed for the chapters.

There is also the matter of money. Even with all the publishing work we do in-house and with extensive use of volunteer labor, there is still a daunting (for us) amount of money required for the initial print run and distribution of this book.

We asked all *Labor Notes* readers to donate for the book, along with the other work we do. They responded very generously, and their names are too many to list here. We thank all of you very much.

The following unions and individuals made substantial contributions specifically for the initial printing of this book:

American Federation of Grain Millers Local 154
American Postal Workers Union, Albany,
    New York Local
Stephanie Pearson Breaux
Brotherhood of Maintenance of Way Employees
Canadian Auto Workers
Canadian Auto Workers Local 88
Canadian Media Guild
Communications, Energy, and Paperworkers
    Local 855
Communications Workers of America Local 1168
Communications Workers of America Local 9510
International Association of Machinists Lodge 2740
Oil, Chemical, and Atomic Workers Local 4-620

Mary and Ben Parker
United Auto Workers Local 599
United Paperworkers Local 9
United University Professions
Michael L. Walsh

Mike wants to thank Margaret Jordan and Johanna Jordan Parker for their assistance, advice, and most of all for their support.

Jane thanks Peter Landon and Simone Landon for their patience and support, and Simone for the cover design she suggested:

Foreword

President
Oil, Chemical and Atomic Workers International Union

OUR HISTORY IN NORTH AMERICA is one of hostile labor-management relations. Those relations have always been marked by conflict and by the employers' fundamental unwillingness to respect unions. Yes, strikes are less frequent these days than in the past, but that is due to the sophistication of the workplace, to the large number of non-union employees on site, and to workers' fear of being permanently replaced, not because of any success in lowering the level of employer hostility.

The employing class as a whole has a fundamental contempt for unions as representatives of their employees.

Yet today an effort is under way to convince workers that we all must view our future in the context of the "Workplace of the Future," or some other moniker that reflects the ruminations of a group of people who have never worked a day in their lives, yet feel compelled to convince us that what is good for corporate America is good for us all.

Cooperation, increased productivity, and competition in the global economy are frequently discussed all in the same breath. Indeed, President Clinton appointed the Dunlop Commission last year with the mission of examining how to increase productivity and create a less litigious employee-employer problem-solving process.

Thus the pitch to workers to embrace jointness and cooperation is the usual corporate mantra about "competitiveness."

In OCAW, our experiences with employee involvement point to a very different "high-performance workplace of the future" than that envisioned by Secretary of Labor Robert Reich. We think corporate America envisions a workplace in which *flexibility* is the central objective. It requires a workforce that can be adjusted with ease. That means the unbridled use of temporary workers and subcontracted workers who can be pulled in when needed and discarded when not needed. It means minimizing the number of permanent workers and maximizing their interchangeability.

Groups of workers are expected to exert pressure on their peers to "rise to the occasion," all in the name of profit.

Corollary measures include involvement schemes (feedback circles to capture the workers' knowledge of their jobs), training to instill cooperationism, and the organization of self-directed work teams to eliminate intermediate and first-level supervisors (termed "right-sizing").

Add other trends such as periodic "performance testing," which can eliminate older and/or injured workers, and the high performance workplace of the future begins to look like a nightmare for workers. Only the youngest, healthiest (and hungriest) workers will be employed there.

In short, whether we are talking about oil refineries or government offices, hospitals or the local diner, the workplace of the future embodies the management-by-stress production system that is described so well in this book.

A SINGLE INTEREST

Apparently, in the view of the Clinton team (which reflects the prevailing view of Corporate America), in the workplace of the future, workers will, or should, subordinate all their other interests to a single goal: that the company should thrive and survive so that they can hold on to their jobs. In that light, they will not need or want an adversarial organization. And since the key strategy for job security is cooperation, workers might even be willing to accept a company-dominated organization to "represent" them.

Such a view is unrealistic, not to mention absurd. First of all, even in the workplace of the future, workers will have other interests that are just as important as job security. They include an independent voice, dignity, and recognition of long-standing service. Voice and dignity cannot be bestowed by the company—they can only arise from an independent workers' organization.

Furthermore, all the evidence indicates that the workplace of the future greatly *increases* job insecurity.

Employees are courted to embrace cooperation with the pronouncement that job security lies in the success of the enterprise. This is pure bull. Profitable facilities are sold off, and the employees with them, where a facility does not fit with a corporate decision to "downsize" or "reconfigure" to match the market. Almost daily we hear reports of thousands of workers being laid off, as yet another corporation marches dutifully along the downsizing road toward the high performance workplace of the future. Some of these employees are even terminated and then invited back to their old positions as temporary "consultants" or part-timers or independent contractors. Many of the facilities involved have been showcases of employee involvement and cooperation: GM, AT&T, Kodak, Ameritech—the list goes on.

OUR EXPERIENCE

OCAW *has* had some interesting experiences with cooperation. At the Texaco Chemical Company's Port Arthur, Texas plant, the turn-around actually saved the facility. But Texaco Chemical Company has been sold, because apparently it does not fit into Texaco, Inc.'s long-term plans.

Similarly, Mobil has engaged our union in a discussion on cooperation and has had some success at its large Beaumont, Texas complex. Yet at its Chalmette, Louisiana refinery, it has fought the union tooth and nail over our efforts to represent five technical employees.

This anomaly has a rational explanation. Cooperation is okay where corporate interests are satisfied; employee involvement is okay so long as it goes no further than flexibility of assignment and increased productivity, and does not intrude into broader corporate decisions that affect workers' lives; jointness works so long as control of the joint decision is vested in the corporation.

My purpose is to sound a warning to fellow union members: WATCH OUT. Just because there is a Democrat in the White House doesn't mean that policies will be worker- and union-friendly; just because the boss buys you donuts and asks for your opinion doesn't mean you will have a job next year; just because your firm is

more profitable than it's ever been doesn't mean it'll stick around...

In the United States, we remain the champion among industrialized countries in the brutalization of workers for the sake of the bottom line. I am not referring to enterprises going over the edge, but about sacrificing workers to marginally improve the bottom line, in order to look good to investors.

American workers are working, on the average, one month more in a working year (173.3 hours) than they did in the 1960s—and more members of the worker's family must be employed these days. Real wages are down 19 percent, while productivity is up 25 percent since 1972.

More and more workers have become "benefits slaves," unable to look for a better job because of the necessity to hang on to health care benefits at all costs.

And the Clinton Administration is looking for a way to encourage labor-management cooperation. But the fact is, we already have such an institution—it's called collective bargaining. Negotiations are the means by which opposing interests are mediated; that is, collective bargaining is the means by which adversaries cooperate.

How must the trade union movement respond to these circumstances?

This book helps us on two counts. First, it is solidly grounded in the outlook, the commitment to unionism and workers' welfare as paramount, that must be our starting point. Second, it distills lessons from dozens of workplaces and helps us learn from the successes and the mistakes of others.

Upholding unions as the independent voice of workers must remain paramount. Whether it's the companies or the Clinton Administration approaching us with "come along, git along" programs, our first question should be: How will this program affect the union—will it make it stronger or weaker?

[signature]

October 1994

Introduction

"Work smarter, not harder." How many workers of the 1990s have heard their managers explain a new participation program that way? The new way of working will be win-win, we're told. We'll get to do things right, without any extra effort—except perhaps mental effort to plan the new way of working, and that will make us feel good. Involved.

It's appealing; every worker can point to ways of doing things—usually insisted upon by management—that are just plain stupid. How often have we chafed under the knowledge that our suggestions on how to work smarter will be ignored?

But management's definition of "smarter"—like everything else in the workplace—turns out to be different from the worker's definition. The time-study man says it's smarter to fill up every second of available time with "value-added work." The reengineering consultant says it's smarter to have one person do the work of three. The worker, meanwhile, thinks it would be smart to save her back by taking time to stretch, and even smarter not to destroy the jobs people need to live.

Over and over, in writing *Working Smart*, we ran up against contradictions between management definitions and union ones. We've explored them in detail, and tried to get across this message: even though all the experts, all the media, sometimes even our own union leaders, seem to rule the day with their own definitions, we must rely on our common sense and our union-bred notions of what's right. If we let the other side set the ground rules, we've already lost the game.

Working Smart brings together our writings about labor-management cooperation and management-by-stress under one cover. Chapters 4-7 are reprinted from *Choosing Sides: Unions and the Team Concept*, and chapters 13-14 contain bits of *Choosing Sides* and *Inside the Circle: A Union Guide to QWL*. The rest of the material is new. *Working Smart* is meant to be used in conjunction with our shorter pamphlet, *A Union Strategy Guide to Labor-Management Participation Programs*.

Choosing Sides is now out of print. *Inside the Circle* is still available, and still a good, in-depth guide to participation programs. See the ad at the end of this book.

Much of what went into this book we learned through teaching seven Labor Notes "team concept schools" between 1990 and 1994, along with Labor Notes staffers Mary Hollens and Kim Moody and attorney Ellis Boal. The thick workbooks we prepared for those schools and the experiences of the union members there have been turned into much of the advice in sections III and VI.

HOW TO USE THIS BOOK

We urge the reader who's in a quandary over a participation program not to turn immediately to the Strategies section. You will get more out of the strategies if you've read the background material first.

We've written summaries at the beginning of every chapter (the paragraph in italics), to help you figure out whether that chapter contains what you're looking for.

It was difficult to decide where to place the various case studies by other authors, since they contain so many overlapping lessons. Chapter 21, for example, illustrates well the trajectory of management's interest in participation programs—but it also tells how the local fought QWL. In fact, nearly all the case studies are about "the solution" as well as "the problem." You will find much helpful information in the case studies that is not repeated in the other chapters.

Chapters 13-16 and 32 contain exercises for use in union education about participation programs. We strongly urge unions to use them; people learn more by doing than simply by listening or reading. They happen to be fun too.

When we began studying labor-management cooperation programs in the early 1980s, they were a sideshow to the main event in the labor movement—the employers' assault on unions in the quest for concessions. Now, a dozen years later, "jointness" has become the dominant way of thinking at some levels of the labor movement itself.

We wish it were otherwise. We wish there were no need for this book. But since it is necessary, we hope that *Working Smart* will be passed from hand to hand, photocopied, reprinted, and used to fight the smart fight.

Mike Parker and Jane Slaughter
Detroit. October 1994

Chapter 1

From QWL to Reengineering: How We Got Here

Participation programs help employers to implement management-by-stress. The history of these programs shows a progression in employers' sales pitches: from some emphasis on workers' input and interests to open admission that the programs are about management control and job cuts. The push for "flexibility" in the workplace is only one aspect of employers' drive for deregulation of all aspects of corporate conduct.

IN THE 1980S, CHANGE IN THE WORKPLACE WAS FAST AND CONFUSING. On the one hand, "respect for the worker" and "worker participation" became the new watchwords of management, from manufacturers like General Electric and General Motors to service providers such as hospitals and the federal government.

On the other hand, workers in many industries complained of job overload and a general tightening of the screws, from attendance policies to nonreplacement of retiring workers. Repetitive stress injuries became widespread. And hanging over almost every workplace was a cloud of insecurity, as workers wondered if they would be lucky enough to keep their jobs.

In 1988 we argued in *Choosing Sides* that these two seemingly contradictory phenomena were in fact two sides of the same coin. Management did want workers' ideas—and would use them to institute speed-up and tighter management control as well as to cut jobs.

Change proceeded at different paces in different industries, but by 1990—with fits and starts, detours, and some dead ends, all of these programs—from Total Quality Management to self-directed work teams to New Work Systems to Dr. Deming's Fourteen Points—seemed to end up with management-by-stress.

It helps to think of the whole phenomenon as made up of two parts: participation programs and management-by-stress.

1) *Participation programs* involve special events away from the job: meetings of quality circles, task forces, joint labor-management committees, and the like. (In the *Strategy Guide* that accompanies this book we call these the "cooperation apparatus.") These circles brainstorm ideas about productivity, quality, and/or working conditions, and almost always include both workers and members of management.

The cooperation apparatus includes new positions such as full-time facilitators and trainers. It involves a new set of management policies, including particular definitions of "quality," "competitiveness," the "needs of the customer," and worker participation and dignity.

The birth of the program is usually accompanied by a propaganda offensive: promises to change old management attitudes and exhortations to save jobs by beating the competition. Signs and slogans featuring the letter "Q" may appear throughout the workplace (CQI, TQM, QFD); fans of "Sesame Street" will recognize the technique. Workers usually get hours of training, often by outside consultants. Both the new committees and the attitude training are pretty much outside the regular work process. Participation programs are discussed in Section III.

2) *Management-by-stress* (more commonly called "lean production" by those who promote it) involves changes in the way work is done. Both the way workers do their jobs every day and their rights on the job are affected. Management-by-stress can include deskilling, strict standardization of the way jobs are done, extensive contracting out, and feedback systems so that management can monitor every worker. It is discussed in Section II.

The function of participation programs is to introduce management-by-stress. This has become increasingly true over the years. Chapter 14 describes how even the question of quality—and management's peculiar definition of quality—is related to management-by-stress.

Management is notorious for being unable to see past the end of its collective nose. In most cases, the personnel departments (renamed human resource departments) that began Quality of Work Life or Employee Involvement programs in the early or mid-1980s were not already plotting the introduction of management-by-stress. Perhaps many well-meaning managers sincerely believed that their feel-good programs would benefit both employees and management—the famous "win-win" model. Billions of dollars were spent—much to the delight of the mushrooming consultant industry—to teach the seven steps of problem-solving, effective listening, trust, and cost/benefit analysis.

But these sorts of programs were overshadowed by the urgent push to "get competitive." Competition from overseas, in particular from Japan, put the heat on American manufacturers to improve quality. As profit margins fell, management searched for ways to restore them.

The pressures were felt first and most strongly in the auto industry, which was already the leader in launching the cooperation-type programs.

Competitiveness became the buzzword of the 1990s throughout industry and government, with myriads of councils and study groups set up to come to the same conclusion: American management needed to tighten up and bear down, *with the enthusiastic cooperation of American workers*. This consensus of the elite culminated in President Clinton's appointment, in 1993, of the Commission on the Future of Worker-Management Relations (the Dunlop Commission). This group, mostly academics, was mandated to investigate:

> What (if any) new methods or institutions should be encouraged, or required, to enhance workplace productivity

How Widespread Are Participation Programs?

Many surveys have tried to answer this question, and it is a difficult one. One reason is the wide variety of programs, practices, and opinions on what "workplace innovation" or "high performance" consists of.

The consensus of the surveys, however, is that participation programs are spreading to more and more workplaces. (Of course, as your Aunt Mabel might say, "Any fool could have told you that.")

Two authors analyzed the surveys done by various researchers, consultants, and government agencies.[1] Among the Fortune 1000 companies, the percentage of firms with at least one employee involvement practice increased from 70 percent in 1987 to 85 percent in 1990.

However, the "employee involvement practices" asked about included everything from soup to nuts: group decision and problem solving, just-in-time delivery, flex benefits, employee surveys, stock ownership, team incentives, monitoring the cost of quality, and more.[2] Other surveys indicated a similar jumbling of those features usually associated with employee involvement, those associated with quality programs, and those associated with lean production, or management-by-stress. This indicates that the U.S. government and the academics and consultants who try to shape policy in this area share the same perception of these practices that we argue in this chapter—that is, that they are all part of the same ball of wax.

Researchers Eileen Appelbaum and Rosemary Batt point out that the surveys they analyzed shared three sorts of bias. First, companies that have introduced new practices are the most likely to respond to surveys about such practices, so such firms may be overrepresented. Second, most surveys focus on very large firms, which are probably more likely to have made such changes. Third, usually only managers and executives were interviewed. Only one of their surveys looked as far down the food chain as line managers. None included workers.

> Often...the manager interviewed for the survey was responsible for the program or practice. Such individuals...may be overly optimistic in assessing the incidence and results at their companies.[3]

The Commission on the Future of Worker-Management Relations (Dunlop Commission) summarized the results of several surveys in its May 1994 Fact Finding Report. The studies the Commission cited gave wide-ranging estimates of the extent of employee participation:

• 36 percent of the workforce works in organizations with some type of employee involvement program, and 23 percent have been personally involved (1985).

• among large manufacturers, 31 percent of employees are in programs where they make decisions and 69 percent in ones where information is shared (1994).

• 80-91 percent of 51 large firms have committees dealing with safety and health, productivity, or quality (1993).

• 64 percent of workplaces with 50 or more employees have over half their core employees in one or more employee involvement activities (1991).

Taking all this evidence together, the Commission estimates that between one-fifth and one-third of the workforce is covered by some form of employee participation, but only a small fraction of these efforts merit the label "high-performance workplace."[4] One expert who testified before the Commission, Jerome Rosow of the Work in America Institute, pegged the high-performance figure at two percent.[5]

Not too impressive. But looking at one of the same surveys the Commission did (1991, cited above), the National Center for the Workplace concluded that 37 percent of all workplaces with more than 50 employees are "transformed."[6]

On the one hand, this sort of guesswork should be embarrassing. On the other hand, it's inevitable, partly because of the confusion about what's what, discussed above.

through labor-management cooperation and employee participation?

What (if any) changes should be made in the present legal framework and practices of collective bargaining to enhance cooperative behavior, improve productivity and reduce conflict and delay?

Let's step back for a minute and review briefly the participation/management-by-stress trajectory that began in the 1980s. Many union members look at the profusion of programs cynically as a "flavor-of-the-month" phenomenon—and they are mostly right. But we can see a change in management's thinking over the years and a change in the rhetoric that accompanied the various programs.

HOW THE PROGRAMS EVOLVED

Quality of Work Life programs came on the scene late in the 1970s. A small group of managers, a few union leaders, and some academics concluded that workers might work better if given more responsibility and more interesting jobs.

This thinking was a response to the sudden discovery of worker alienation, the "blue collar blues." The 1972 strike at General Motors' Lordstown, Ohio plant, in particular, set the pundits and the media talking about the need to humanize work. These strikes were led mostly by young Vietnam vets who did not want to put up with the numbing tedium of the assembly line—especially after GM increased the line speed to 100 Vegas per hour.

The idea behind these first QWL programs was that if you improved the conditions of work, absentee problems would decline, quality would improve, and companies would be more profitable. But the focus was to be on improving work life. Productivity and profits were a by-product. Indeed, both company and union proponents warned that any attempt to organize around productivity would doom the programs. As Irving Bluestone, one of the early union proponents of QWL put it:

> Workers should be assured that their work pace will not be increased by reason of the introduction of the QWL process...The process should be honestly designed to enhance workers's satisfaction and provide a vehicle for the realization of self-worth and self-fulfillment. It must not be simply a management "gimmick" to increase productivity at the expense of the worker.[7]

With the recession of the early 1980s, there was a shift toward the terms *Employee Involvement* or *Employee Participation*, to get away from the expectation that the focus should be on improving working conditions. AT&T and the U.S. Postal Service are two employers who jumped on the bandwagon at this time. Workers were encouraged to get beyond the belittling "creature comfort" issues (fans, water fountains), and move on to the more challenging questions of improving productivity and quality.

Programs negotiated at this stage tended to be accompanied by concessions. Union leaders and journalists often spoke of the new "power" unions had won in exchange for giving up money or work rules. In some workplaces management renamed workers "associates" and declared them to be "our most important asset."

Later in the 1980s, *Team Concept* carried this notion further: we—management and workers—were all in the competitiveness rat-race together. The auto companies were pioneers of team concept; the steel industry used Labor-Management Participation Teams; at Xerox it was Commodity Study Teams. "We want your brain as well as your muscles," management stroked us. "We want you to work smarter—not harder." We all had to take responsibility for productivity increases, and apply peer pressure if our co-workers were not pulling their load.

A hallmark of this phase was the definition of a "team" as a group of interchangeable workers. Competition among teams, or departments, or plants was encouraged.

However, the concept of "teamwork" was often attached to *Lean Production*, the system we have called *Management-by-Stress*. Lean production included elimination of classifications (to make team members interchangeable), just-in-time delivery, and "continuous improvement," or continuous speed-up. The bible for this phase, a book called *The Machine that Changed the World* from the Massachusetts Institute of Technology, treated unions as either an obstacle or irrelevant.

None of these 1980s fads did workers any good. But at least management claimed to believe in the value of employees and their ideas. Employers said that their programs were the road to job security. There was even talk that lean production should include Japanese-style lifetime employment.

The attention to workers' needs began to fade with the rise of *Total Quality Management* in the 1990s. TQM was straightforwardly a method of managing, a way for management to insure that the whole organization worked more effectively for the goals of the company. The emphasis was on top management setting the course; "strong leadership" became the rage again, rather than the softer consensus style of the 1980s.

The job of strong leadership was to organize the workplace so that decisions would "cascade down." The role for employees was to bring their activities into alignment with the organization's overall goals and eliminate any variation (judgment) they might introduce into the process (see chapter 14).

Since management viewed TQM as a matter of management method, employers tended to installed TQM

Latecomers

Ironically, it was not till February 1994—when management was well past the most worker-friendly stage of participation programs—that the AFL-CIO Executive Council endorsed a model of union-management partnership. Previously, the de facto position of the Federation had been a mixture of wariness, defeatism, support, and avoidance.

programs unilaterally. They wanted union cooperation, but that was not their starting point.

Looking forward to the present, perhaps unions might have taken consolation in the fact that TQM was a moderate approach; it claimed to take the organization as it was and improve it. Some TQM advocates (notably the late W. Edwards Deming) even talked about "driving out fear" from the workplace, with the implication that management should offer job security. Of course, "driving out fear" was not the point that most managers emphasized. But at least unions had some pegs to hang a union approach from.

Today, the latest buzzwords are *Reengineering* and *Reinventing*. At their most developed, these techniques would presumably lead to *Agile Institutions* and *Virtual Corporations*. Management is reengineering white-collar and service jobs with a vengeance —areas that were often bypassed when the focus was on lean production and manufacturing. The *Wall Street Journal* warns, "Much of the huge U.S. service sector seems on the verge of an upheaval similar to that which hit farming and manufacturing, where employment plunged for years while production increased steadily."[8]

Reengineering revisits a management theme of the 1980s: use technology to eliminate unnecessary work and workers. In factories, "lights out" production was the goal: automation would be so advanced that people were no longer necessary and the machines could work in the dark. The "paperless office" would use computers for direct transactions both within and between companies.

Ten years ago these strategies pushed the limits of available technology. As a result some flops were spectacular: robots painting themselves and computer failures shutting down entire companies or losing millions of dollars. (Remember how often you heard "the computer is down—we can't help you"?) Technology seemed to introduce more expense and labor than it saved. As a result, many companies downplayed the technology approach, and interest shifted to the success of lean production methods.

The emergence of reengineering in the 1990s, with once again a prominent role for technology, is partly because the technology itself has greatly expanded and improved. And the techniques of lean production have provided an important benchmark for guiding the use of technology: how many jobs did you erase?

"A common misperception," according to the two consultants who popularized the term, "is that [reengineering] is the same as Total Quality management...TQM is about improving something that is basically okay, and reengineering is about taking something that is irrelevant and starting over."[9]

This clean-sheet-of-paper approach counsels management not to reform its work processes, but to "obliterate"

Employee Participation in the 1920s and 1930s

In testifying before the Dunlop Commission, labor historian Jim Green noted that some academics who advocate employee participation have pointed to the management-created employee representation plans of earlier this century as a positive example. These people ask, said Green, "Is not some form of worker representation, even in employer-dominated forms, better than nothing at all? And wouldn't some form of representation open the way to new unionization as it did in the 1930s, when the Steelworkers 'took over' the company unions?"

Green looked at history to answer these questions. Following is a summary of one part of his testimony:

The first government-sanctioned "shop committees" were established during World War I, as part of the "Rockefeller plan." In 1918 the National War Labor Board established 86 shop committees in the railroad, fuel, and clothing industries. Few of these committees exerted any real influence over questions of factory discipline, hiring, firing, promotions, or apprenticeship rules. From management's standpoint the councils were most useful when they focused on reducing turnover and waste.

At first, the unions did not formally oppose these shop committees and councils. Some unionists thought they could be an opening wedge for worker control on the shop floor. When the employers began imposing wage cuts after the war, the committees endorsed the cuts. And in 1919, the AFL convention condemned the Rockefeller plan of employee representation as "a snare and a delusion." The AFL's resolution seemed ratified by events during the 1920s, as company unions grew and unions declined.

In 1933 the National Industrial Recovery Act stimulated a wave of union organizing. In response, more employers set up employee representation plans. By November 1933 over 600 such plans existed in manufacturing and mining.

At U.S. Steel, the CIO's Steel Workers Organizing Committee gained substantial control over the employee representation plans in many mills. Management finally recognized the Steel Workers there without a strike, in 1937. But in other steel companies and at General Electric, Westinghouse, and RCA, independent unions had to be organized *against* the company unions.

At Ford and at smaller steel companies, the company unions were part of the companies' effective resistance to unionism until 1941-42. At Jones & Laughlin Steel in Aliquippa, Pennsylvania, for example, the union was unable to capture the company union. Only after the Supreme Court ruled in 1937 that company unions were illegal did the Steel Workers strike against J&L and the company union—and win. (This story was told in the PBS series "The Great Depression.")

as many as possible. Right now, reengineering consultants are pushing certain notions: break down job classifications; one person handles a task from beginning to end; build the organization around generalists; contract out for specialized work.

Fortune magazine describes reengineering:

> It is occurring in a dramatically altered competitive landscape; it is a major change, with big results; it cuts across departmental lines; it requires hefty investment in training and information technology; and layoffs result.[10]

Fortune recounts how GTE reengineered its telephone operations: The company started with repair clerks, whose job had been to take down information from a customer, fill out a trouble ticket, and send it on to other workers who tested lines and switches and fixed the problem. GTE wanted that done while the customer was still on the phone. So they moved the testing equipment to the repair clerks' desks and trained them how to use it.

The next step was to link sales and billing with repair, so customers could have one-stop shopping. With new software, operators can now handle virtually any customer request.

In the process, says GTE, "we eliminated a tremendous amount of work—in the pilots, we've seen a 20 or 30 percent increase in productivity so far."[11]

The reengineering gurus stress that top management will have to be strong and powerful to break the resistance that is sure to come from middle managers and workers afraid for their jobs. Their imagery is macho and violent:

> The way that you have to deal with this resistance is a combination of relentless communication, support incentives, and a bloody ax.

> We are going on a journey. On this journey, we will carry the wounded and shoot the stragglers.

> You either get on the train or we'll run over you with the train.

> Nuke it.[12]

> To succeed at reengineering, you have to be a visionary, a motivator, and a leg breaker.[13]

We have only to look at the notions of *Agile Institutions* and *Virtual Corporations* to see where all of this is heading.

Agile Production is promoted by the (Lee) Iacocca Institute at Lehigh University and has the enthusiastic backing of the federal government. The Defense Department has sought bids for $30 million in projects that incorporate

agile manufacturing.[14]

An agile system, we are told, can respond rapidly to changes in the market, new customer requirements, and business opportunities. The agile corporation is able to shift quickly from one task or process to another.

To do this the company has to be freed from commitments to particular factories, processes, or machines, and therefore freed of commitment to the workers whose jobs depend on these expendable elements of profit making.

General Motors is teaming with the public school system in Genesee County, Michigan (that's Flint) to form a 21st Century Agile Manufacturing Academy. The idea is to prepare children for the workplace of the future. Kindergartners build hamburgers to learn the difference between mass production and lean production. Teams of fourth-graders build "products" out of Legos to compare the old methods with "just-in-time."[15]

The *Virtual Corporation* provides maximum agility. It keeps only that which is central to the corporation: its profit center. For continuity, the corporation maintains its top management, the key idea people, the organizers, and the brokers. As much as possible everything else—manufacturing, services, clerical work, communications—is sourced out. Every project is temporary.

Robert Reich, now Secretary of Labor, explained the concept in his 1991 book, *The Work of Nations*:

> In the high value enterprise.... all that really counts is rapid problem-identifying and problem-solving, the marriage of technical insight with marketing know-how, blessed by strategic and financial acumen. Everything else—all of the more standardized pieces—can be obtained as needed. Office space, factories, and warehouses can be rented; standard equipment can be leased; standard components can be bought wholesale from cheap producers (many of them overseas); secretaries, routine data processors, bookkeepers, and routine production workers can be hired temporarily.
>
> In fact, relatively few people actually work for the high-value enterprise in the traditional sense of having steady jobs with fixed salaries.[16]

Reich cites a Hollywood production to illustrate "pure brokering." The studio contracts on a project by project basis with the producer, director, writers, actors, and technicians. When the movie is in the can, everyone returns to the marketplace, waiting to be called for the next project.

Another image that comes to mind, however, is the day labor markets on the street corners of Los Angeles, where contractors bring their pick-up trucks and immigrants line up to compete for a day's work.

Frightening? Yes. On the agenda? In most cases, not in full form. Big manufacturing can't achieve the full virtual model, but companies can aim to reduce their built-in capability as much as possible to "fast assembly" operations.

Agile institutions cannot be dismissed as merely the current fad. The trend is solidly in place and growing, in the form of contracting out.

Paradoxically, the more work is contracted out, the greater management's control, because the easier it is to jump from one product or project to another, without the bother of fixed assets or employees. The other advantage is getting rid of the types of work that are hardest to standardize and speed up, such as janitorial or repairs, leaving management to extract maximum efficiency from those left working.

Reengineering and agile institutions mean that long-term commitments to employees ("our most important asset") hit the trash bin, along with decent jobs and strong unions. Contractual and moral commitments are collapsing around the world, in Japan and Europe as well as in North America.

The emperor of cooperation has no clothes: if workers have no job security, then all the earlier talk of

---

War Zone

In 1994 workers in the industrial city of Decatur, Illinois designated their town a "war zone." No longer the "Pride of the Prairie," two factories were on strike, and a third was locked out. Workers at Caterpillar, Bridgestone/Firestone, and A.E. Staley fought union-busting contracts that, union members said, would have rolled back gains they had taken half a century to win.[17] Just one example of company demands: at Staley, 12-hour shifts at straight time, three days on and three off, rotating from days to nights.

It is no accident that all three of these companies pushed participation programs in the years right before the open warfare. Union members now feel that by participating in management's programs, they set themselves up.

At Caterpillar, management seemed to make an 180-degree turn-around after a long strike in 1982-83. The company actively sought to mend fences, set up a QWL program, and got union members to contribute thousands of suggestions. The company passed out jackets with both the company and union logos. Productivity rose 30 percent between 1986 and 1992.[18]

In the Decatur plant, the union agreed to reduce the 232 classifications to 80. By 1992, 2,000 workers were producing what 4,500 had in 1979. Local President Larry Solomon said, "They made millions and now they've turned vicious and say you're not entitled to the product of what you've helped save." Solomon feared the company saw cooperation as a sign of weakness, then decided to launch "class war" against its employees.[19]

The United Rubber Workers, on strike at Bridgestone/Firestone (BFS), call themselves a union "known for fostering labor-management cooperation." In the 1980s, BFS set up quality circles and talked of lifetime employment. The company even allowed the URW to organize its new plants. But the union intercepted a memo indicating that, a year before the contract expired, the company was planning to force a strike in 1994. BFS demanded a two-tier wage, a 12-hour day, substitution of productivity pay for COLA, continuous operations (a seven-day week with no premium pay).

"It simply became impossible to cooperate when the companies tried to tear apart contracts which took nearly 60 years to build," said Kenneth Coss, URW president.

At Staley, the company used "union-management cooperation groups" and "socio-technical systems." Local 837 member Mike Griffin wrote, "We endured nearly ten years of participation...Our plant went from 1,600 employees to 750. Since our lock-out, the Staley Co. has told us they are going to reduce the workforce to 450. The jobs are there. They are simply outsourced to scabs, contracted, or moved to management positions."[20]

Art Durning recalled, "Eighteen out of 36 people in my department were on committees of some sort. After the company vacuumed all our gray matter, they ended the program."

partnership, empowering the workforce, and investment in people is a fraud.

WHO BENEFITS?

Who benefits from all this increased speed and efficiency—if in fact, those are the results? (Never underestimate management's incompetence in implementing even its own most cherished desires.) Clearly the corporations do. The gains show up in the profit column, with no guarantee of being translated into benefits for the consumer. For workers, of course, these concepts are a boon only to those who have no interest in job security, or in a job they can grow old in.

We are not knocking efficiency, or the idea of designing jobs or products or processes so that they're easily done. Any worker can tell you that many of the old ways of doing the work of the world are broke and badly need fixing. In most industries, mismanagement is a way of life. The problem is the assumptions that are the basis of reengineering.

Management's assumptions are that the primary goal is to obliterate jobs, that management has no responsibility beyond pleasing the shareholders, and that the marketplace, or society, or your family, or someone else will absorb the consequences.

The union starting point, on the other hand, has to be the right to work at a decent job. Reengineering to do our current work in less time could be a worthy activity—if it meant a shorter work week and not a smaller workforce. We discuss a union vision further in chapter 3.

A MULTI-PRONGED STRATEGY

From QWL to reengineering, management's offensive at the workplace did not take place in a vacuum. Changes in the workplace itself are only one part of a grander strategy. In the 1970s, American managers decided that they had been soft too long, and launched a multi-pronged drive to increase corporate power and weaken everyone else's.

Much of this drive took place under the heading of "deregulation." At first glance, deregulation may sound appealing—as an individual, who wouldn't like to put up with fewer rules and regulations in our lives? But in the context of the 1980s, deregulation meant the employers' push to undo all sorts of government controls on corporate behavior that had previously been won by the unions and other social movements.

Working people had fought long and hard to force governments to put restrictions on corporations' ability to function however they chose. Unions fought for the right to collective bargaining, a minimum wage, health and safety regulations. Anti-trust laws, anti-discrimination laws, consumer protection, affirmative action, environmental controls: all of these were things that corporations would never have done on their own. They had to be forced by government—which in turn was compelled to

act by the pressure of the union movement, the civil rights movement, the women's movement, the environmental movement.

The Reagan-Bush years saw the undoing of many of these gains. Business and its allies in government told us that prosperity was possible only if we gave corporations a break and let the magic of the market do its work. OSHA enforcement was gutted; affirmative action became a dead letter. Whole industries—trucking, airlines, railroads, banking, telecommunications—were deregulated. In each case the result was business failures, job loss, wage cuts, and de-unionization.

The whopper deregulation, of course, is represented

The Government Likes It

Labor-management cooperation was promoted to some degree under the Reagan and Bush administrations, through the Labor Department's Bureau of Labor-Management Relations and Cooperative Programs. But government involvement really got a boost when Bill Clinton was elected.

It's worth recalling that while he was campaigning, Clinton referred approvingly to workers at a Texas GM plant that was locked in battle with a Michigan GM plant over which one would be picked to remain open. Clinton said,

> ...a General Motors plant in Texas is saving the jobs because the workers said no to the bosses of their own union. And they said, 'We are going to scrap these work rules. We are going to be flexible. We are going to change our jobs. We are going to save our jobs by having the courage to change.' And that's what we are all going to have to do.[21]

Clinton appointed Harvard professor Robert Reich as Secretary of Labor—a man with virtually no ties to workers or unions, but with lots of ideas. Reich revamped the Bureau to become the Office of the American Workplace, pumped up its staff and budget, and set out to take an activist role in spreading the gospel of cooperation.

Reich wrote, "I pledge that President Clinton and I, in partnership with Commerce Secretary Ron Brown, will do all we can to accelerate the pace of workplace change."[22] In December 1994, for example, the Office co-sponsored a conference for employers "dedicated to improving your ability to compete." Amidst many workshops devoted to "team-based workplaces," "leveraging diversity for innovation," and "giving up control: the changing role of managers," one stood out: "Managing Change in Difficult Times: Saying Goodbye, Letting Go and Moving On."

State governments jumped on the cooperation bandwagon as well. Minnesota, for example, set up a series of Total Quality workshops for small public and private employers, and offered to pay half of participants' fees.[23]

by NAFTA and GATT (the General Agreement on Tariffs and Trade, now called the World Trade Organization). These two treaties are about removing any "barriers," in the form of laws passed by national governments, that would make it more expensive to do business in one country than another. The idea is for laws, taxes, social programs, and regulations (or the lack thereof) to be levelled to the lowest common denominator.

Here's an indication of what NAFTA will promote: in September 1994, NAFTA's National Administrative Office sponsored a trinational conference. The topic: "Labor-Management Cooperation: Legal, Social, and Productivity Dimensions."

Thus it is no accident that management-by-stress arose in the 1980s, the decade of deregulation. Management-by-stress can be seen as the workplace version of deregulation. Over the years, unions won restrictions on management's absolute right to jerk workers around: seniority rules for transfers and promotion; classifications to keep management from piling work on without limit. Under the new regime, these are referred to as "outmoded work rules." Management-by-stress seeks to erase these union-won regulations, returning the workplace to a regime closer to that of a non-union shop.

Under NAFTA, Mexico will be an investor's paradise. Under management-by-stress, the deregulated workplace is the foreman's dream. All in the name of "flexibility," from the shop floor to the world market.

The wonder is that so many people have bought the deregulation argument: that our lives will be better if corporations are left to their own devices than if we have some control over their behavior.

As we believe will be amply demonstrated in the rest of this book, the bottom line for all the labor-management programs is improving "competitiveness." In the next chapter, we discuss what's wrong, from a union member's point of view, with the competitiveness contest.

Notes

1. Eileen Appelbaum and Rosemary Batt, *The New American Workplace: Transforming Work Systems in the United States*, ILR Press, Ithaca, New York, 1994. Chapters 5 and 6 and Appendixes A and B present the authors' review of surveys and case studies of employee participation.

2. Appelbaum and Batt, Appendix A.6, listing the results of a survey by Edward E. Lawler III, Susan A. Morhrman, and Gerald Ledford, *Employee Involvement and TQM: Practice and Results in Fortune 1000 Companies*, Jossey-Bass, San Francisco, 1992.

3. Appelbaum and Batt, p. 62.

4. Pp. 34-36.

5. Testimony at the Commission's September 15, 1993 hearing. Cited in Ellis Boal, "The Dunlop Commission Fact Finding Report: Analysis and Comment," Labor Notes, Detroit, 1994, p. 2.

6. The survey is by Paul Osterman, "How Common Is Workplace Transformation and Who Adopts It?" *Industrial and Labor Relations Review*, Vol. 47, No. 2, January 1994, pp. 173-188. It is described in the Center's newsletter, Issue No. 2, Spring 1994. The Center is at the University of California at Berkeley.

7. Irving Bluestone, Address to the Society of Automotive Engineers, Detroit, 1981.

8. Joan E. Rigdon, "Technological Gains Are Cutting Costs, and Jobs, in Services," February 24, 1994, p. A1.

9. Interview with Michael Hammer and James Champy, *Across the Board* magazine, June 1993. Hammer and Champy are authors of *Reengineering the Corporation: A Manifesto for Business Revolution*, HarperBusiness, 1993.

10. Thomas A. Stewart, "Reengineering: The Hot New Manag-

ing Tool," *Fortune*, August 23, 1993, p. 42.

11. Stewart.

12. All above quotes from *Across the Board* interview.

13. Michael Hammer, quoted in Stewart.

14. John Holusha, "Industry Is Learning to Love Agility," *New York Times*, May 25, 1994, p. C5.

15. Drew Winter, "Agile Manufacturing: Can it really make big operations nimble?" *Ward's Auto World*, April 1994, pp. 40-44.

16. Robert B. Reich, *The Work of Nations: Preparing Ourselves for 21st-Century Capitalism*, A.A. Knopf, New York, 1991, p. 90.

17. For more information about these three struggles, which attracted a great deal of support from the labor movement in the Midwest, see *Labor Notes'* coverage beginning in January 1992 (Caterpillar), December 1992 (Staley), and October 1994 (Bridgestone/Firestone).

18. Kevin Kelly, "This Brawl Could Cost Cat a Couple of Its Lives," *Business Week*, March 23, 1992, p. 82.

19. David Moberg, "Caterpillar bulldozes union relations," *In These Times*, April 1-7, 1992, pp. 3, 11.

20. "We Have Not Yet Arrived," *Labor Notes* No. 176, November 1993, p. 10.

21. Remarks to Hillsborough County Retired Teachers Association, March 6, 1992, carried on C-SPAN March 8.

22. "The New American Workplace," *American Workplace*, Vol. 1, Issue 1, September 1993, p. 4.

23. "Grants offered for total quality workshops," *Union Advocate*, November 1, 1993.

Working Smart:
A Union Guide to Participation Programs and Reengineering
Labor Notes • 7435 Michigan Ave. • Detroit, MI 48210 • (313) 842-6262

Chapter 2

The Competitiveness Game: They Win, You Lose

"Competitiveness" = profitability. When unions embrace competitiveness, they only help to cut jobs and make the remaining jobs worse. Competitiveness is not "win-win" for companies and workers. The existence of highly-skilled workers will not bring about high-skill or high-pay jobs.

U.S. companies do not compete with companies in the Third World. Rather, those Third World companies are the subcontractors for U.S. corporations. Because of this, American workers are being forced to compete with Third World workers. Though American wages are declining, U.S. corporations are not concerned about losing a market for their products. They are turning instead to the richest 20 percent of the population worldwide.

Businesses must compete to survive. To survive, workers must not compete against each other. Instead they must attempt to "take labor out of competition," by standardizing wages across each industry. Business and labor struggle over these two conflicting imperatives. Unions can force employers to compete by means other than workers' wages.

by Kim Moody

EVERY NEWSPAPER, EVERY POLITICIAN, every corporate executive, every manager, and many labor leaders—all talk about "competitiveness." Improving America's competitiveness, or their firm's competitiveness, is *the* goal of the 1990s. Bill Clinton took office determined to be the "competitiveness President."

But what does this buzzword really mean? The book *Unions and Economic Competitiveness*, from the union-backed Economic Policy Institute, defines it as "the ability of domestic producers to succeed in international markets."[1]

Just how does a firm "succeed"? In the business world, "success" is not measured by the quality of your product, or by the size of your market share, or even by the productivity of your workforce. In the business world there is only one measure of a firm, and that is its profit rate. And not just any profit, but a profit large enough to satisfy stockholders, and make them want to invest in your firm rather than some other.

All the other things companies do—from applying for

the Malcolm Baldrige Quality Award to moving a plant to Mexico to managing by stress—are means toward that end.

It's only natural that the gurus of competitiveness—from Bill Clinton and Robert Reich to Lee Iacocca and Lane Kirkland—prefer that term to "profitability." Somehow it wouldn't come off so well for the President to say that the American people must sacrifice in order to restore "America's profitability."

WRONG STARTING POINT

Throwing themselves into the competitiveness race is exactly the wrong place for unions to start.

1. No finish line. As has been amply demonstrated over the last 15 years, once workers get into competition with each other, there is no sure finish line, no place where the union can stop the merry-go-round and get off.

Auto workers are a well-known example. In 1979 (and again in 1980 and 1981), Chrysler workers took concessions because Chrysler was losing money. The competition, although this was not mentioned often, was Ford and GM. A little later in the decade, with wages falling behind inflation, all Big Three workers were asked to sacrifice; this time the competition was "the Japanese." In the

---

Kim Moody is a staff writer for Labor Notes, the author of An Injury to All: The Decline of American Unionism, *and co-author of* Unions and Free Trade: Solidarity vs. Competition.

1990s, after NAFTA, it appears the competition comes from Mexico. But no one argues that American workers can compete with Mexican wage levels.

2. Cuts jobs. The motivation for unions to join the drive for competitiveness is to save jobs. But if there is one tactic that is essential to employers' plans for competitiveness, it is getting rid of good jobs.

By early 1994, U.S. corporations were cutting more than 3,100 jobs each business day, even though the U.S. economy had officially been in a recovery for two years. They were re-engineering to become competitive.

Contracting out is *the* corporate strategy of the 1990s. Temporary employment grew 13 times faster than overall employment between 1980 and 1994. Taken together, temporary, contract, and part-time workers now make up a quarter of the workforce.[2]

BankAmerica Corp., the nation's second-largest bank, is an example of what competitiveness means for jobs. In 1983, most employees were full-time. But in 1993, the bank planned to cut full-timers to 19 percent of the workforce. Nearly 60 percent would work fewer than 20 hours a week and receive no benefits.

The *Wall Street Journal* said, "BankAmerica reported record profits in each of the past two years. It says it is taking these steps to improve profits even more…"[3]

WALL STREET TELLS ALL

In a remarkable article, the *Journal* summed up the consequences of "the re-engineering movement":

> Some estimates call for it to wipe out as many as 25 million jobs; the private sector today encompasses roughly 90 million jobs….
>
> 'We can see many, many ways that jobs will be destroyed, but we can't see where they will be created,' says John Skerritt of Andersen Consulting….
>
> Re-engineering can be great for the performance of individual companies [that is, for their competitiveness], but what about the economy as a whole? Virtually all economists agree than re-engineering ultimately should bring about faster economic growth…and improved living standards….
>
> The bad news comes in the dislocation of all those people whose current jobs will disappear….With millions being laid off, nearly everyone may feel threatened, and with good cause. For most workers, job security will be the most tenuous since the Depression….
>
> Re-engineering could knock out between a million and two-and-a-half million jobs each year for the foreseeable future.
>
> The new job shrinkage should not be confused with [the recent layoffs by IBM, GM, Boeing, and Sears. Those] reflect shrunken demand for the companies' output.
>
> Productivity-related job losses are of a distinctly different variety. They are staff reductions made by healthy [i.e., competitive] companies…"[4]

It used to be that many workers expected to have a job when the economy was in good shape, or their employer was, and to lose out when either went sour. In the re-engineered present and future, you lose your job even in a healthy company.

3. Bad jobs. Not only are there fewer jobs in a company bent on competitiveness, the remaining jobs are lousy—harder, faster, more regimented. And, as the chart below shows, the new jobs that are being created pay less.

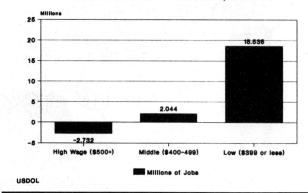

JOB LOSSES & GAINS BY WAGE LEVELS
PRIVATE SECTOR PRODUCTION &
NONSUPERVISORY WORKERS, 1979-93

HIGH-SKILL, HIGH-PERFORMANCE

Some economists, academics, and labor officials try to sugar-coat competitiveness. They say it can be a win-win situation for workers and employers. All we need is to convince employers to adopt a different competitiveness strategy that will benefit both sides.

Ray Marshall, the former Secretary of Labor and a member of the Dunlop Commission, is a prominent advocate of this strategy. He promotes a high-wage, high-productivity, high-skills model. Irving Bluestone, retired vice president of the UAW, and Barry Bluestone, co-authors of *Negotiating the Future: A Labor Perspective on American Business*, tell us that we can be competitive and have good jobs too.

The AFL-CIO Executive Council embraced the win-win idea in its February 1994 report *A New American Workplace: A Labor Perspective*. The report calls for a "new labor-management partnership" to create "high skill, high wage" jobs, and assumes more than a little good will and honesty on management's part.

These proposals are worth examining. Here's a summary of what Marshall, writing in *Unions and Economic Competitiveness*, says about "high performance systems":

> Mass production is no longer the most competitive way to organize work. More flexibility, quality, and productivity are required. Companies must use leading-edge technology and organize work to reduce waste: better inventory control, the efficient use of labor, quality controls. The system requires better educated, skilled workers who are less tolerant of monotonous work and authoritarian management.
>
> Workers must be willing to learn and to be flexible. They must take responsibility for decision-making, as layers of managers are eliminated. They must be willing to go "all out" to raise productivity. Their incentive is that they have job security.
>
> Unions are necessary because workers need someone to represent their interests, and because you can't have a

cooperative relationship between parties with greatly unequal power. Unions and companies can cooperate to make
the pie bigger, and then bargain over how to split it.[5]

This would sound great, if we weren't already
familiar with what these terms mean in real life.

Inventory control = just-in-time. Efficient use of
labor = speedup. Flexibility = no classifications = do
whatever management tells you to do. Waste = you.[6]

Edward Lawler, director of the Center for Effective
Organizations at the University of Southern California
says, "The high-performance work system does not solve
the problem of job creation." He points out that when a
conventional company converts to a high-performance system, job loss is automatic unless the company expands its
markets dramatically.[7]

But in a competitive world, not every company can expand dramatically. There's the rub.

Jack Gordon, who interviewed Lawler, is editor of
Training magazine. Surely a magazine devoted to this buzzword of the 1990s, Robert Reich's cure-all for what ails
the American worker, would be on the high-skills, high-
performance bandwagon. That's where its advertising dollars come from, after all.

But Gordon's research convinced him that the next
twenty years will be "a rough ride for an awful lot of the
American people." He cites the loss of high-wage jobs,

the growth of temps, and asks, "Can training really help?"

For one thing, Gordon says, high skills will not necessarily mean high pay. He cites the case of Carrier Corp.,
which opened a new 150-worker factory in Arkadelphia,
Arkansas in 1992. Before they were even guaranteed a
job, applicants took six weeks of training in blueprint reading, math, statistical process control, computer skills, and
interpersonal communication. This sounds like a high-performance workplace if there ever was one. Workers are
"empowered," too, ordering their own supplies and
granted the ability to stop the production line.

The salaries of these skilled, responsible employees:
$16,000-$17,000 a year.

"In the recession of the early '90s," Gordon notes,
"veteran workers and managers aged 35 to 54 have been
hit with layoffs at double the rate of recessions in the
1970s. Companies getting rid of their most experienced
employees are not looking for higher skills. They're looking for younger people who'll work cheaper."

Second, most of the new jobs being created in the
U.S. economy are low-skill service jobs. If highly trained
workers take these jobs, will their skills make a difference?

Finally, there is the question of whether "high skills,"
in the current definition really *are* high skills. Just working with sophisticated equipment—computers, for example—doesn't make the operator sophisticated.

The National Association of Manufacturers has chosen a machinery producer called Universal Dynamics as one of its favorite high-performance companies. The *Washington Post* described Universal's attitude toward high skills:

> One key to its success: the use of sophisticated equipment by hourly factory workers who need no more than an eighth-grade education and few language skills to do the job. Some of [the company's] best workers, operating computerized equipment using statistical process controls, are immigrants who speak very little English...
>
> [Company President Don] Rainville said that with the increased use of computers to run machines, it now requires much less skill to operate even the most sophisticated equipment. As with the instructions on the machines his own firm makes for worldwide distribution, Rainville said the written word is being replaced by pictures very much like those on the cash registers at a fast-food restaurant.
>
> If anything, Rainville sees less of a need for further education as companies turn increasingly to automation. "I see the trend going the other way," Rainville said. Rainville concedes that higher education is still very much needed for engineers and other technicians, but not on the factory floor. "What I'm looking for is enthusiasm," he said.[8]

Jack Gordon concludes that it still makes sense to "skill up" the workforce, "even though we know that unless a lot more companies start finding ways to make productive use of people with higher skills, we'll just be training smarter workers for dumber jobs."

THEIR COMPETITION

The editors of *Business Week* connect the "high wage, high productivity" approach to the transformation of unions into partners with employers. They say, "America needs unions, but not the kind it has now." Drawing on a particularly outdated stereotype, *Business Week* writes:

> "Forget the Teamster goons and the picket lines.

Under the new model, unions raise output, cut wasteful work practices, and help the U.S. stand up to global rivals."[9]

But in reality, most business rivals are not "global" at all. Most U.S. companies compete with other U.S. companies right here at home.

The increased openness of the world market has contributed to the intensification of competition, as new norms of efficiency are set globally. But direct foreign competition in imports and exports is still the exception, not the rule, in the U.S. economy.

Almost 90 percent of the goods and services we consume are produced in the U.S. by American workers, although some of the companies may be foreign-owned.[10] And a good deal of the imports that compose the remaining 10 percent are not from "competitors" at all, but from subcontractors, suppliers, and subsidiaries of U.S. companies.

To make the competitiveness (profitability) agenda seem more palatable, however, or even patriotic, "rivals" are usually described by business writers and politicians as "global," i.e., foreign.

To make it all even more ominous, they imply that these rivals are in the Third World, working for peanuts.

But the real competition in the world market today is not between companies based in the rich countries and new, upstart companies in the Third World. Rather "global competition" is primarily between companies based in the 25 wealthy industrial countries of North America, Europe, and the Pacific Rim. Measured in dollars, the enterprises based in these countries produce about 80 percent of the manufactured goods in the world. They account for 70 percent of the world's $4 trillion in international trade.[11]

About two-thirds of the value of all U.S. imports is from companies in these industrial countries or the OPEC

Competitiveness: It Ain't Necessarily So

Although the rhetoric of "competitiveness" seems to be universally accepted, one aspect is easy to refute. Paul Krugman, a mainstream economist at MIT, did so in several articles published in 1994.[13] Although Krugman is a liberal and a Clinton backer, he took particular aim at the competitiveness rhetoric of the Clinton Administration and some of its economists, including Robert Reich. Krugman quotes Bill Clinton saying that each nation is "like a big corporation competing in the global marketplace"—and then proceeds to rip that concept to shreds.

"People who believe themselves to be sophisticated take it for granted...that the United States and Japan are competitors in the same sense that Coca-Cola competes with Pepsi," Krugman says. In reality, "competitiveness is a meaningless word when applied to nations." Companies, not nations, sell products in markets. Companies can go out of business if they lose to the competition, nations cannot.

"Moreover, countries do not compete with each other the way corporations do. Coke and Pepsi are almost purely rivals...So if Pepsi is successful, it tends to be at Coke's expense.

"But the major industrial countries, while they sell products that compete with each other, are also each other's main export markets and each other's main suppliers of useful imports. If the European economy does well, it need not be at U.S. expense; indeed, if anything a successful European economy is likely to help the U.S. economy by providing it with larger markets... International trade, then, is not a zero-sum game...the major nations of the world are not to any significant degree in economic competition with each other."

The point that American business is not the same thing as the United States is one worth remembering. What's good for GM *isn't* always good for America. However, as Krugman points out, political leaders find "the competitive metaphor extremely useful as a political device."

oil producers. And most of what U.S. firms sell abroad is sold in these same developed industrial countries.[12]

Thus, the reality of international competition is that it goes on between the big corporations in countries with living standards comparable to those in the U.S. and Canada.

When we are asked to "get competitive," then, the implication is that U.S. labor costs are too high compared to those of European or Japanese workers, that U.S. labor is more costly or less efficient.

This might have been the case several years ago, but today it is simply not true.

In manufacturing, U.S. and Canadian labor costs per hour are less than those of Japan or Western Europe. In services, no one in an industrial country works cheaper than U.S. workers.

Total Hourly Labor Costs In Manufacturing, 1993

Country	Hourly Cost
U.S.	$16.79
Canada	16.36
Japan	19.20
Germany	25.56
Europe Average	18.67

Source: U.S. Department of Labor, USDL-94-261, May 25, 1994.

In terms of productivity, or output per worker, U.S. manufacturing workers produce 20 percent more each year than their counterparts in Japan and 25 percent more than those in Germany, the two countries usually held up as productivity models. Germany consistently falls behind the U.S. in productivity. In some industries such as auto and steel the Japanese are ahead, in others such as computers and food the U.S. is ahead. The Japanese advantage, however, is canceled out by the high dollar value of labor costs there.[14]

The bottom line in comparing the economic performance of industry in different countries is to put these two measures—labor costs and productivity—together. That measure is called "unit labor costs," and means real hourly labor costs adjusted for productivity. On this measure, U.S. workers are a bargain, compared to those in other developed nations.

Put crudely, U.S. workers have high productivity plus modest wages—the best of all possible worlds for employers. The U.S., in fact, is the only developed nation whose unit labor costs have fallen in recent years. As the figure below shows, U.S. unit labor costs took a nosedive in the mid-1980s and have been dropping ever since, in relation to those of *all* the industrial nations whose corporations compete with one another.

OUR COMPETITION

With comparable wages and productivity prevailing in most developed industrial countries, the corporations can no longer compete on the basis of different labor costs among these countries.[15]

So, for over a decade they have turned toward low-wage countries for their labor needs, through subcontracting and outsourcing of all kinds.

Business writers and management operatives frequently perform a little sleight of hand by talking about how "we" now face competition from countries like Mexico or Indonesia. But the operations in the Third World that export to the U.S. are not competitors of U.S. companies; they are suppliers. They are typically either subsidiaries or subcontractors of big transnational corporations.[16]

In other words, U.S. corporations compete with their corporate counterparts in Europe and Japan, while forcing American workers to compete with our worker counterparts in the Third World.

Dan Gallin, general secretary of the International Union of Food and Allied Workers Associations (the international federation of unions in food-related industries), put it well:

> This global economy has created a global labor market where European, North American, Japanese or Australian labor is in direct competition with the labor force of countries where labor costs are kept 10 to 20 times lower.[17]

And U.S. companies win two ways when they move work to low-wage areas abroad: not only do they save on immediate labor costs, they can also force your wages down by threatening further outsourcing if you don't become "competitive."

This set-up means that we compete with the world's poor. Whether they work in sweatshops, as part-timers, temps, or industrial homeworkers at home or abroad, or in Third World "office parks" or "industrial zones," it is they we are to "beat."

Of course, these workers, whether they live in East L.A. or East Asia, are no more our "enemy" than the person who works next to us every day. They have nothing to say about corporate investment, outsourcing, or other business decisions that adversely affect workers in the U.S. or Canada.

Besides, we couldn't compete with the wages of

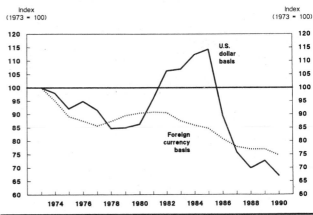

**U.S. Manufacturing Unit Labor Costs
Relative to 12 Competitors, 1973-90**

Index (1973 = 100)

Source: U.S. Department of Labor, USDL 92-752, Dec. 2, 1992.

workers in the Third World if we wanted to, because we couldn't live in the U.S., Canada, Europe, or Japan on so little money.

To put it bluntly, we are being asked to help keep the poor poor and to reduce our own living standards to near or actual poverty: the near poor fighting the desperately poor. "Competitiveness" is not about maintaining high wages in the U.S., but about forcing them down. All in the cause of higher profitability and greater dividends for the rich and shameless.

Are the Suits Shooting Themselves in the Foot?

For decades many unionized workers in the U.S. believed that their relatively high wages were the backbone of America's mass consumption economy. We buy what we make.

But what happens when the high-wage jobs are gone? Who will buy the U.S. economy's still growing output of goods and services if the majority of working people get too poor? Isn't business shooting itself in the foot?

Clearly, business doesn't see it this way. They are looking to markets abroad instead.

HAVES AND HAVE-NOTS

The U.S. is becoming a nation of haves and have-nots. The majority of Americans are getting poorer each year.

• Real weekly earnings of production and non-supervisory workers have been falling faster and faster since 1980: by 0.5% a year in 1980-85, by 0.8% a year in 1985-90, and by 1.2% each year in 1990-93.

• Real average family income fell by 6% from 1989 through 1992.

• Average family net worth (homes, cars, savings, investments) fell by 12% from 1988 through 1991.

• The official poverty rate rose from 12.8% in 1989 to 14.5% in 1992, bringing the total to 37 million people. For Blacks it rose from 30.7% to about 33% and for Latinos from 26.2% to about 29%.

On the other hand, a minority of Americans are getting richer.

The share of U.S. income of the top 20% of families rose from 41.7% in 1979 to 44.2% in 1991. This may sound small, but it represents a transfer of over $100 billion in household income from the majority to the wealthy.

The share of net worth that the top 20% of households own was 84.3% in 1989, leaving only about 15% of all personal wealth to be shared by the rest of us.

The bottom 60% of U.S. households own—together—only 3% of all personal wealth. In this have-not majority, nearly a third are people of color and a fifth are female-headed households.

Obviously, the wealthy have a very personal stake in the shift to low-wage disposable workers.

But they still need to sell the consumer goods and services that spin out of their low-wage, high performance workplaces. Not even the rich can buy them all. Who can?

GLOBAL CONSUMER ELITE

The answer is the bloated globe-trotting business elite that runs the international production systems, world-wide financial markets, and global retail chains. It includes not only capitalists and what they buy for production purposes, but also managers, certain types of professionals, government officials, financial speculators, and other well-paid hangers-on able to buy western-style consumer goods.

We're talking about, say, the top 20% of individuals in the poor countries of the world. This top 20% earns 67.5% of all income in Brazil and 56% in Mexico, for example.

In all, this represents some 900 million people in poorer countries who are able to join in the upscale consumer binge. In effect, they are able to stand in as consumers for millions of North American and European workers with declining incomes.

This global consumer elite is today's solution to the problem of who will buy what we make. It is one more reason why open markets in the Third World are so important to U.S. corporations.

WILL IT WORK?

Will this export-driven, global consumer strategy work? For now it will work for some companies and not for others. Every firm makes its production and marketing decisions separately. They tend to adopt similar strategies to stay competitive, but, unless they're forced to, they don't worry much about the overall social or economic consequences.

If the American working class sinks past the point where we can call ourselves "the middle class"—hey, it's not their problem.

So Toyota produces more and more upscale Lexus models and loads up the formerly cheap Corolla. Bennetton opens stores in the ritzy neighborhoods of Rio and Hong Kong, not in downtown Detroit; U.S. workers can buy Asian-made clothes at K-Mart.

The dismal conclusion for workers in the U.S. and other industrial countries is that capital is not shooting itself in the foot, it is shooting workers in the back and getting away with it.[18]

Not such a pretty picture of "making America competitive," much less a convincing scenario for job security or "high wage, high productivity" employment.

WHO BENEFITS?

Yet, each and every day, corporate America says, "It works for me."

As the chart below shows, while real wages have fallen 10 percent since 1980, real incomes derived from capital have risen at a handsome clip. The top 10 percent of U.S. families, who own about 90 percent of the stocks and bonds from which interest and dividends are drawn, have been the winners in the war of competitiveness all along.[19]

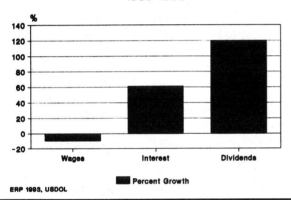

GROWTH OF REAL WORKER & CAPITAL INCOME 1980-1993

ERP 1993, USDOL

As their reward for this continuous improvement in stockholders' incomes, the CEOs, those "fellow employees" who say they are in the same boat as you, saw their salaries increase by 15 times from 1960 through 1993, while wages grew by only four times. By 1993, the CEO's average salary was 149 times the average worker's wages.[20]

If the outcome of the competitiveness game is judged by results, it is win-win for those who own and run big business and lose-lose for those who produce this wealth through their labor.

FIRST LITTLE PIGGY TO MARKET

Business competition has always been about profits and more profits. But it seems that we hear far more about that competition today. And today's competitive situation *is* different from the situation of 25 years ago.

First, the fight over market share and profits is more intense today than it used to be, because neither the national nor the world economy is expanding at the rate they once did. Markets tend to be saturated by corporations producing similar products. Hence, the fight over market share is far more acute than when these markets were growing rapidly, as in the 1950s and 1960s.

Second, NAFTA and the General Agreement on Tariffs and Trade (GATT), signed in 1994, both mean sweeping deregulation of corporate activities. Both limit the ability of governments to control economic activity within their borders. They grant more power to the transnational corporations to carry on trade and investment exactly as they see fit.

The corporations' new-found "freedom," however, sharpens the fight for profits and market share. Speed and flexibility in production are a priority because the first to market reaps the biggest gain.

If your company is the first with the latest you have no real competition—no one else offers the features or services you do. With little or no competition, you can set the price and reap a bigger profit than if you had to compete. You earn what economists call a "monopoly profit."

Of course, this first-to-market advantage doesn't last long. The next company will come up with its own new improved version. So the whole process must be repeated. In this kind of world, work organization must be fluid and the worker pliable, ready to work long hours or as disposable as temporary help.

Third, ironically, all the investment in new technology over the last few decades has made it harder for corporations to make the same return on investment they once did. The total profits are much larger, but so is the accumulated amount of capital invested. Adjusted for inflation, the value of assets owned by corporations for each U.S. manufacturing worker rose from $9,300 in 1963 to $26,000 by 1987.[21] So, as the graph below shows, the *rate* of profit has been dropping for over two decades. The "rush to market" strategy is a way of trying to compensate for this drop by increasing the early profit made on a new product.

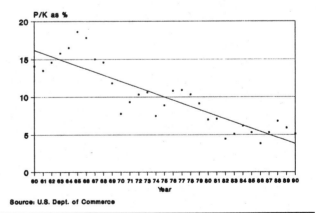

RATE OF PROFIT (P/K) U.S. 1960-90 Trend

Source: U.S. Dept. of Commerce

ECONOMICS 101

The conflict of interest between labor and capital has been so universally recognized for so long that it was written into the basic law governing labor relations in the U.S., the National Labor Relations Act.

In a 1960 decision upholding this obvious truth, the National Labor Relations Board reaffirmed, "[Labor and management] still proceed from contrary and to an extent antagonistic viewpoints and concepts of self-interest."[22] This, by the way, was under the Republican Eisenhower Administration.

There is, for example, the conflict over where the lion's share of the wealth produced by labor goes—to worker wages and benefits or to profits, dividends, and executive salaries. There is the age-old conflict over the speed and intensity of work, and so on. But there is also a basic conflict over competition itself.

Business competition is, of course, a reality. It is in the nature of a market-based capitalist economy that individual enterprises in the same line of business compete. They compete to increase both the amount of their profits and their profit rates (the return on their total investment). One way for a business to increase its profits is to increase its share of the market. To increase the rate of profit, businesses usually invest in technology to improve productivity.

To further increase their competitive advantage and to help pay for the new investment, they seek to reduce other costs: raw materials, components, rent and other overhead, and labor costs. Labor is the only "factor of production" not controlled by another business and, hence, a logical choice for cost reduction. Business competition, then, always creates pressure to reduce labor costs—by cutting wages and benefits or by dumping workers.

Workers, on the other hand, must not compete among themselves if they are to survive economically. If workers enter the labor market as individuals, they are completely subject to the competitive demands of business. If they allow the employers' competitive needs to dictate the level of wages and benefits, worker income will always decrease.

So, historically, workers have banded together in unions (and frequently in political parties) to raise the price of labor. They do this primarily by standardizing (that is, equalizing) wages, benefits, and conditions for all those performing the same work in the same industry or product market.

Economists call this union practice "taking labor out of competition"; it is central to unionism. The standardization of wages and benefits through national or "pattern" contracts prevents the (unionized) employers from pitting one group of workers against another. To put it another way, such standard agreements restructure the competitive workings of the labor market to be somewhat more favorable to labor.

So, in any capitalist economy workers and employers have conflicting economic needs and imperatives. Each of these economic imperatives is real. Each draws on certain facts about the workings of the market economy. Each is achieved at the expense of the other.

COMPROMISE THROUGH STRUGGLE

How is this conflict of economic imperatives resolved? Usually, in normal times, it is resolved through a compromise. Labor and management agree that neither side will take the whole economic surplus that workers create; they will split it. How they split it—who gets what share—has often been the subject of fierce struggle—lockouts, strikes, injunctions, fines, violence.

This compromise is embodied in union contracts. The compromise that prevailed in North America from World War II to the late 1970s was a trade-off. Unions won the ability to set standard wages and benefits in unionized industries. In return, unions gave the employers the right to control the organization of work, to introduce technology, to change the product, and to accumulate capital through growing profits. Unions agreed to keep wage increases within the bounds of productivity increases. Thus, the workers got increased income and the employers got the ability to increase productivity and profits.

Even under a contractual compromise, of course, the conflict of interest goes on. For example, inflation spurs workers to fight for higher wages regardless of productivity levels. Also, the effects of management control and new technology force workers to resist speed-up and other erosions of working conditions, sometimes with unofficial actions.

Conversely, as we know, employers routinely attempt to break one or another clause in the contract to cut costs or weaken the union.

In times of economic crisis, the employers resist compromise. For example, as the U.S. economy moved in and out of depressions in the 1880s and 1890s, the employers moved to smash the unions of that time. The employers won at the expense of the workers.

Again, during the Depression employers were forced to compete more fiercely. The brutal decline in living standards, on the other hand, forced workers to take action too. Before there could be a compromise, there was a historic confrontation: the mass union organizing battles of the 1930s. The workers won a major victory at the expense of the employers.

Under the unequal power relations of a capitalist economy, a union "victory" is always within the framework of compromise. And the employers win when they prevent unions from imposing standards.

The fact that employers can compromise with unions in both good economic times (1945-1978) and bad ones (1934-1939) proves that unions can force employers to compete by other means than through workers' wages. Businesses will always compete. The question for workers is, on what basis?

Indeed, competition can be a reason for giving in to union demands, if a strike means losing market share or profits. Businesses must weigh these conflicting pressures, just as workers must weigh the long-range and short-range costs of a strike to them.

In other words, contrary to the current received wisdom, the fact that businesses compete is not an absolute, unchangeable determinant of wages or working conditions.

NOT A FORCE OF NATURE

Of course, the spokespersons of business talk as if competition were a force of nature, akin to the weather. But competition is structured by human-made institutions—corporations and government agencies that barely existed in their current form 50 years ago. Far from a force of nature, they are run by human beings and changeable by human beings.

These institutions make rules governing business prac-tices. But today, business is changing the rules and too many political leaders are simply going along.

NAFTA and GATT are examples of business reshaping the forces of competition in business's favor, by changing the rules of international trade and investment.

Sixty years ago, American workers began changing some of the rules in favor of working people. It is time we took on that job again. To do that, we need to remember who we are.

Notes

1. Lawrence Mishel and Paula B. Voos, eds., *Unions and Economic Competitiveness*, M.E. Sharpe, Inc., Armonk, New York, 1992, p. 2.

2. Clare Ansberry, "Workers Are Forced To Take More Jobs with Few Benefits," *Wall Street Journal*, March 11, 1993, p. 1.

3. G. Pascal Zachary and Bob Ortega, "Workplace Revolution Boosts Productivity at Cost of Job Security," *Wall Street Journal*, March 10, 1993, p. 1.

4. Al Ehrbar, "'Re-Engineering' Gives Firms New Efficiency, Workers the Pink Slip," *Wall Street Journal*, March 16, 1993, p. 1.
This article and the two cited above are part of a series the *Journal* ran titled, "Down the Up Escalator: Why Some Workers Are Falling Behind." Together, these articles contain a wealth of facts, statistics, and analysis of corporate downsizing and re-engineering. Coming from the mouthpiece of corporate America, they belie the notion that structural changes are "win-win." Here's a sample quote, from the Zachary and Ortega article: "Many labor specialists fear that the four horsemen of the workplace—global competition, technology, downsizing and the growth of the contingent work force—will cause wages to continue to fall, creating a nation increasingly divided into haves and have nots."

5. "Work Organization, Unions, and Economic Performance," in Lawrence Mishel and Paula B. Voos, Eds., *Unions and Economic Competitiveness*, M.E. Sharpe, Inc., Armonk, New York, 1992, pp. 287-315.

6. The first part of this chapter, up to this point, comes mostly from Jane Slaughter, "Should We All Compete Against Each Other?" *Labor Notes* No. 170, May 1993, pp. 7-10.

7. Quoted by Jack Gordon, "Into the Dark: Rough Ride Ahead for American Workers," *Training*, July 1993, pp. 21-29.

8. Frank Swoboda, "Manufacturing Success," *Washington Post*, April 11, 1994.

9. "Why America Needs Unions, But Not the Kind It Has Now," *Business Week*, May 23, 1994, pp. 70-82.

10. *Washington Post National Weekly Edition*, April 11-17, 1994.

11. United Nations Commission on Trade and Development, *World Investment Report 1993*, New York, 1993; World Bank, World Development Report 1990, Washington, DC, 1990.

12. Council of Economic Advisers, Economic Report of the President 1994, Washington, DC, 1994.

13. Quotations are from Paul Krugman, "Competitiveness: A Dangerous Obsession," *Foreign Affairs*, March/April 1994.

14. *The Economist*, April 2, 1994.

15. U.S. Department of Labor, "International Comparisons of Manufacturing Productivity and Unit Labor Cost Trends, 1992," Washington, D.C., December 2, 1992.

16. Even firms based in the famous Asian Tigers (Taiwan, South Korea, Hong Kong, and Singapore) account for less than one percent of what is purchased in the U.S. The largest exporter of goods to the U.S. is Canada.

17. Dan Gallin, "Inside the New World Order: Drawing the Battle Lines," *New Politics*, Vol. V, No. 1, Summer 1994.

18. This box was taken from a longer article: Kim Moody, "When High Wage Jobs Are Gone, Who Will Buy What We Make?" *Labor Notes* No. 183, June 1994, pp. 8-9, 13.

19. Lawrence Mishel and David M. Frankel, *The State of Working America 1992-93*, Economic Policy Institute, Washington, D.C., 1993.

20. Richard Barnet, "The End of Jobs," *Harper's*, September 1993, p. 52.

21. U.S. Department of Commerce, *Statistical Abstract of the United States 1993*, Washington, D.C., 1993, p. 742.

22. Quoted in Ellis Boal, "The Independence of Labor: A Critique of S 669 and HR 1529, the Proposed Teamwork for Employees and Management Act," Labor Notes, Detroit, 1993.

Working Smart:
A Union Guide to Participation Programs and Reengineering
Labor Notes • 7435 Michigan Ave. • Detroit, MI 48210 • (313) 842-6262

Chapter 3

A Union Vision

To employers, good jobs are nothing but barriers to competitiveness; the union vision makes good jobs the goal. Our society is wealthy enough that productivity need not be the only aim. The human needs of the employees are at least as important as the customer's needs. The union vision of good jobs includes not only working conditions but power and freedom from fear.

Each firm pursuing its own competitive ends adds up to a harsh vision for the society as a whole. Unions must go beyond challenging management-by-stress in the workplace to challenging it as social policy.

WORK IS AT THE CENTER of all human societies. Work creates the wealth of societies. The way work is organized is at the root of much of the social structure of society and determines who will benefit most. It is no wonder that the nature and organization of work are debated and fought over again and again in human history.

One of these great battles was over industrial labor itself. In England, the lower classes of the early nineteenth century fought to keep their way of life as free farmers and not to be herded into the "Satanic mills" of the day. In the United States, a bloody war was fought over slavery: was it a moral and an efficient way to organize society?

Today the debate over work has been initiated by the corporate elite. They say that the old assumptions about work are over. Something new is needed. Unions and workers have joined that debate—but at a great disadvantage. The terms of the debate have been set from above.

Much of this book is about details: discussions about classifications, job assignments, how many seconds to do how many tasks. These are the stuff of day to day working life. These are the issues unions deal with every day.

But at bottom, this book is not about the details. It's about a conception of good jobs and the role of a union in winning them. Taken all together, the details determine our lives. But how we approach the details and how we understand them flow from our vision of what we're working for.

The various visions of work have often masqueraded as scientific truth. In the early 20th century Frederick W. Taylor presented his ideas about how work should be organized as "scientific management." Now the high priests of management theory from academia claim statistical

proof that lean production is what should be and will be running our lives. Technology requires this; competition demands that; scientific study has proven that X is the most efficient way. Yet, on examination, the management science of today is no more scientific than the scientific knowledge that the earth was flat, that human beings could not fly, or that blood-letting cured disease.

Similarly, what is considered normal and acceptable in society changes as well. It was only 150 years ago that Americans were locked in debate over whether slavery was more moral than capitalism. Only 100 years ago, child labor was widespread. Today, a debate over the merits of these practices seems absurd.

THE CORPORATE VISION OF WORK AND SOCIETY

Just like older forms of work organization—such as slavery and child labor—the conception of work in the 1990s rests not on science but on a particular vision of society. Those who benefit from participation programs and from management-by-stress push not only the new programs themselves, but also the vision on which they depend. To the extent that we accept the vision, we also accept its consequences, with minimum protest.

The corporate vision is simple: Put the needs of business at the center of society, because what's good for business is good for society. Faster for some, slower for others, the proceeds of successful business will trickle down to the rest of us. Since the bottom line of business is making a profit, what's good for profitability is good for all.

The mechanism that makes this all work is competition. Survival of the fittest—and therefore "best"—com-

GLOBAL SOLIDARITY

panies results in efficiency and quality products. Competition is the natural way of the world. Or so the story goes.

Like raw materials and electricity, workers are viewed as a "factor of production." What we cost is balanced against what we contribute to the bottom line, and that contribution is then compared against other factors. Does it make more sense, for example, to use low-paid workers and low technology, or to replace workers altogether with automation?

As recently as 20 years ago, the powers that be assured us that if we accepted this vision and worked within its strictures, the reward would be a high standard of living (higher for some than for others, but let's not quibble...). But today, workers are not even promised prosperity in return for productivity. Survival, not increased prosperity, is at stake. No president is telling you that "you have nothing to fear but fear itself." In the 1990s, you have everyone to fear—the Japanese, the Mexicans, workers in competing companies, those in the next department, the next generation.

The future is represented in war-like language about global winners and losers. The very idea of a steady job is being replaced with that of a predatory labor market in which only the educated, smart, and nimble survive. Either you get with the program, or you fall into the ranks of the low-paid and partially employed.

The corporate vision is illustrated by the following exchange:

Gerald Greenwald, new chairman of United Airlines, has called a meeting with his employees, who are now, thanks to an employee buy-out, "owners" of the airline. A mechanic at Dulles Airport, Fotios Lekas, challenges Greenwald. How can he justify his million-dollar signing bonus and $665,000 salary, when the employee-owners have taken pay cuts of 8.25 to 23.5 percent?

Greenwald says his own salary reflects the market value for industry executives.

Then he informs Lekas that the mechanic has three choices. He can continue to complain and get in the way of progress. Suck it up and work like hell to make his equity stake worth something. "Or vote with your feet. Go out and find your own market value, my friend."

The crowd explodes into applause.[1]

If anyone, say the labor movement, challenges the rules of competition and maximizing profitability, we are told that along the way lies economic decay and loss of liberty.

This pro-business vision is promoted not only by the business elite themselves, but also by politicians (Bob Dole and Bill Clinton spring to mind), in the media (which are corporations themselves), and in the schools. Business has the power to shape ideas through its control of money. It's the modern-day form of the golden rule: he who has the gold makes the rules. We're told that the two-party system is the American way. But as the Labor Party Advocates slogan puts it: "The bosses have two parties. We should have at least one."

Understanding the corporate vision, as described in the previous chapter, is essential for union members who are trying to respond to management's initiatives in the workplace. But it is just one vision, after all, and one that serves only the interests of the few.

OUR VISION

We need our own vision to provide direction and guideposts as we make our way through the complicated questions of participation and lean production.

Here we discuss our assumptions about what work should be—our vision—and compare this to the management vision. If you search labor history and if you look at the thousand instances of solidarity, large and small, that make life in the late twentieth century bearable, you will find that this vision is and has been shared by millions of other working people. But it is often obscured by the dominance of the other vision and the focus on what is demoralizing, alienating, and downright evil in our society.

I. Most people work because they have to: to support themselves and their families, to afford to enjoy their time off, to see that their children get an education, to cover medical bills, to participate in community activities, from church to ball teams to computer clubs. In other words, we "work to live" rather than "live to work."

II. Our time on the job dominates the time we're awake (at least for those of us who still have full-time jobs). And we are identified to society primarily by our jobs—"what do you do?" doesn't mean "what's your hobby?"

Only a few of us are lucky enough to have jobs that are a goal in and of themselves and rate our primary commitment. Some health care professionals, some academics, some scientists, some journalists, some artisans, some skilled workers are lucky enough to have jobs that are intrinsically interesting and satisfying. And most people take pride in doing their work well even if the job itself seems

remote from their own values and interests.

Given how important our work is to our whole lives, it should be a goal of society to make work more satisfying—work with some control over what goes on, a job that sparks your interest, work you can take pride in, a job that is more than a necessary evil.

For the last 50 years we have spent so much time working to buy the things that will make our lives comfortable outside of work, that we have neglected that huge component of our lives that is work. It is one of the tragedies of our decade that we feel more powerful as consumers—individuals—than as workers, collectively.

We try to make ourselves feel good by buying—whoever has the most toys wins—to make up for the lack of control and self-esteem we're allowed to feel at work. After all, as consumers we got Coca Cola to bring back Coke Classic, while as workers we couldn't get the anti-scab bill past a filibuster.

There must be a special rung of hell reserved for union officers who tell members, "You're lucky to have a job." Unions were formed not to help employers grant any old jobs to grateful workers, but to make those jobs into good jobs. We should see good jobs not as a luxury, not as a memory from the good old days, but as a right. Not

"But it IS finished."

only for ourselves but for our children's children.

III. Not all jobs can be made interesting. For the foreseeable future, many will remain boring or unpleasant.

If we accept this fact, then we look for ways to make such jobs bearable—in particular shorter work time.

This is preferable to pretending that it's possible to make assembly line work creative, as some of our best-paid academicians do[2] (see chapter 8).

Wouldn't it be more rational to create some trade-offs? The jobs that are worst in and of themselves—on an assembly-line, say, or data entry—could be part-time, by choice, with full benefits. Conditions would be decent, but the idea would be to do the job and get it over with. People could choose to do the more interesting jobs full-time, especially if our definition of full-time were a lot shorter than it is now: a short work week for everyone. There is clearly enough work to go around.

Some people would choose to take a creative job at less pay over a boring job at more pay. Others would choose the opposite. Maybe they'd trade off at different times of the year. The idea would be that individuals could choose what was best for them at different points in their lives.

IV. Our society is enormously productive, and much of our capacity is not being tapped—millions of un-employed people, thousands of shuttered factories. Given our great collective wealth, we can afford to make human beings the priority *even if we don't achieve maximum productivity*. Or profitability.

Heresy though it may sound, productivity need not be God. Even concern for the quality of the product should not override concern for workers' conditions. If our over-all goal is to build a society of "quality," then surely the quality of the time we spend at work is a major ingredient.

V. Power is a human value. Feeling in control of our circumstances and of the decisions that affect our lives is a legitimate human aspiration. This fact is recognized by the participation gurus, but the "empowerment" they offer through their programs is not power.

Union power is a means to better income and benefits, but it is also valuable in and of itself. The knowledge that we, collectively, have won a strike, or the reputation that our team doesn't take any bull; these are worth something.

VI. The only way that most working people can have any real power at work is through their union. Individual rights at work only mean something insofar as there is col-lective power to back those rights up. Promotions may go by seniority—but not if the union fails to enforce the con-tract.

What we are learning, as unions struggle with the new forms of work organization, is that how management or-ganizes the workplace is not the only question. In the long run, what makes the difference between a livable workplace and a sweatshop is not simply whether clas-sifications exist or the union's formal rights in the con-tract. What makes the difference is the shop floor strength of the union and the consciousness of the membership:

their willingness to stand up for themselves.

Which is better: to work in a non-union shop that, be-cause of inept management, has a more relaxed pace, or to work in a lean production shop with a strong union? Under the pressures of competition and without a strong union, the jobs that are tolerable today are bound to be sped up. Any "rights" workers have enjoyed will soon dis-appear. On the other hand, even in the leanest workplace, a strong union can create rights and push for more breath-ing room. As described in chapters 30 and 36, this is just what some unions have done—to the chagrin of the managers-by-stress.

In other words, part of our vision is workers acting like a *real* team, on their own behalf. This is sort of "team-work" is intrinsic to unionism: "What force on earth is weaker than the feeble strength of one? But the union makes us strong."

VII. A basic element of a good job is freedom from fear. It's not a good job if you dread losing it so much that you will kiss up to keep it. No matter how well paid, it's not a good job if you fear your carpal tunnels won't last till retirement.

IT ALL ADDS UP

All the work reorganization programs add up. Each company or government agency, each pursuing its own competitive ends—together they add up to a prescription for the society as a whole.

Analysts keep saying with some surprise that even in a recovery, the U.S. economy is not creating enough jobs. Is it any wonder, when lean companies hire as few people as possible, and then meet their expansion needs with over-time, ten-hour days, and temporaries?

The much-praised productivity and cost savings of management-by-stress at the plant level are achieved by shifting the costs to others. Job security and high wages are promised to a few at the top of the pyramid, which is maintained by those on the bottom: low-wage suppliers, temporaries, part-timers without benefits, and full-timers hired after the job security pledge was made.

Certainly individual companies can get higher produc-tivity through elaborate screening of applicants, plus inten-sified work that pushes aside those who can't keep up. But the end result is that as a society, we have fewer people working and more unemployed. The social costs that result from unemployment, poverty-level jobs, and little hope for a decent life all have to be carried by the declin-ing numbers of those who still have decent-paying jobs.

The ultimate irony: the city of Detroit, home of the productivity advances that have cut union auto worker jobs in half, is reduced to futile attempts to invent jobs by build-ing casinos.

When management-by-stress increases an industry's productivity, it simply worsens the problem of over-capacity that already exists in many industries. The num-ber of goods is increased, without a corresponding increase in the market of people able to buy them. The corporations then deal with overcapacity by closing plants—thus increasing instability in the economy and in society.

DOES THIS MAKE SENSE?

Step back for a moment and ask yourself if you want a society in which:

• Big corporations dump 2,000-3,000 workers each business day to get competitive.

• Almost 80 percent of the new jobs are in the two lowest-paying, lowest-skilled categories—retail trade and services. The numbers of working poor are on the rise.

• In one industry after another, the 10-hour day is reintroduced so employers can use their capital round the clock with fewer workers. The average person spends the equivalent of one month more a year on the job than in 1969.[3] As a result family and social lives are ripped apart.

• Management-by-stress makes fewer people produce (more efficiently) the goods and services—while the unemployment and welfare lines stretch to the horizon. With millions unemployed or working part-time, auto workers in the midwest work 58-hour weeks to make the Big Three competitive.

• The age bubble in the population chart is approaching its fifties, but the acclaimed forms of work organization make it harder for older people to do the jobs.

• The system discards older workers in the hopes that younger ones will make a cheaper, more compliant workforce. A *Newsweek* reporter spells it out: "After all, when pushing the frontiers of technology, going where no one has gone before, experience doesn't count for a lot."[4]

• Repetitive strain injuries are epidemic in offices and stores as well as factories.

• New consumer products pour out at an astounding rate. We work more and more overtime to afford what the neighbors have and our teenagers demand, yet nobody seems any happier. Life feels like a treadmill...

• Demagogic politicians take advantage of our alienation and whip up outrage over scapegoats—from "welfare cheats" to "teenage mothers" to "illegal aliens."

• For millions of schoolchildren, violence is a fact of life.

• The gap between the haves and the have-nots grows wider and wider and as hopelessness grows, so do racial tensions.

Welcome to the 1990s.

A DIFFERENT STARTING POINT

The corporate vision starts with the needs of the corporation in a competitive world economy and demands that our values, our eduction system, and the organization of work all fall into line. We are asked to embrace values that see dog-eat-dog competition as good. Everyone for themselves. It's no surprise that the competitiveness consultants love games and socio-dramas in which we learn to compete against fellow workers. Even when we form teams, it is to defeat another team.

The corporation starts from the premise that there are too many workers making too high wages. It wants to "slim down," become "lean and mean."

But unions have a different starting point. We start with human values and needs, and work from there. Yes, we live in a society where the competitors have the power and make the rules. But we make a mistake when we accept those rules as given, and make no effort to impose our own rules—our own values—on the decision-makers. Our goal has always been to force corporations and governments—as much as we can, usually one step at a time—to fall in line with union values, not the other way around.

Using human values as a starting point, any new work organization plan would be evaluated with criteria like these:

• Do workers have satisfying jobs?

• Can workers choose the job that best suits them?

• Does training lead to skills that can be transferred to other workplaces or other areas of life?

• Are stress-related illnesses and injuries on the decline?

• Is it possible for workers to remain in the workforce until they are ready to retire?

• Do workers have the opportunity to produce good quality?

• Is there a simple and speedy way to resolve grievances or other workplace problems?

• Do workers have the right to speak up, to complain?

• Do workers have the right to determine when they need to take time off?

• Most important, do workers have a sense of collective power—that if any of the above conditions are not being met, they can act to change them?

In other words, in our model of society, the human needs of the employees are at least as important as the customer's needs, and more important than the company's profits. Jobs with decent wages and working conditions should be seen as fixed inputs; management has to work within those parameters.

To employers, good jobs are nothing but barriers to competitiveness.

For years unions and other movements have fought to curb the competitors' arbitrary power, both through bargaining and through legislation. On many fronts, they won. Some principles formerly denounced as "uncompetitive" are now commonly accepted and embedded in laws. It is illegal for companies to boost their competitiveness by using child labor, sub-minimum wages, hazardous working conditions, unfunded pensions, discrimination, or slavery.

All these laws interfere with management's flexibility. But they were insisted upon by movements that were not afraid to intrude on the sacred rights of corporations, and enacted by governments afraid to say no.

NOT ECONOMICS BUT POWER

President Clinton's economists are full of explanations for why the budget deficit must be cut, and why working people will have to sacrifice to do it.

Here's a dissident view: *the question is not economics, but power.* If working people and social movements were in the streets, supporting each other's causes; if unions dared to use their economic power to show who really keeps the country running; if we formed a new political party and succeeded in capturing Congress and the White House—ways would be found to produce full employment, a short work week, race and sex equality, a humane education system, homes for everyone, and national health care.

The wealth is there. It's just in the wrong hands. The richest one percent of households in the U.S. own half again as much wealth as the bottom 90 percent.[5] Tax laws make sure it stays that way. If that doesn't anger you, consider that these same wealthy families make billions of dollars off the interest on the federal debt they complain so much about.

Then, too, much of the nation's wealth is used for the wrong things. For example, U.S. corporations spent $12 trillion on mergers and buyouts from 1985 through 1990. That's the equivalent of about two years of the country's gross domestic product and almost three times the total federal debt. Then, of course, there are the yet-to-be-totalled hundreds of billions of taxpayer dollars spent on the savings and loan bailout.

Where does it end? It ends where and when we put a stop to the subordination of labor to corporate priorities. Elites never end a system of work from which they benefit. As Frederick Douglass put it, "If there is no struggle, there is no progress. Power concedes nothing without a demand. It never did, it never will." The slave owners would never have ended slavery if the Union army, which included tens of thousands of former slaves, hadn't defeated them. The captains of industry would never have given up child labor if unions and other social movements had not forced them to. Today is no different.

Unions must go beyond challenging management-by-stress in the plant or office to challenging it as social policy. Unions' vision and struggle for a workplace of dignity, skill, and worker control are necessary not just for union members but for the whole society.

Notes

1. Marla Dickerson, "Heat's on Greenwald to keep United airborne," *Detroit News*, August, 7, 1994, p. 3D.

2. "Lean production offers a creative tension in which workers have many ways to address challenges." James P. Womack, Daniel T. Jones, and Daniel Roos, *The Machine that Changed the World*, Rawson Associates, New York, 1990, p. 102.

3. Juliet Schor, *The Overworked American: The Unexpected Decline of Leisure*, Basic Books, 1991.

4. July 11, 1994.

5. In 1989, the richest one percent of households owned 38.3 percent of all households' net wealth, and the bottom 90 percent owned 24.3 percent. Lawrence Mishel and David M. Frankel, *The State of Working America,* Economic Policy Institute, Armonk, New York, 1991, p. 162.

Working Smart:
A Union Guide to Participation Programs and Reengineering
Labor Notes • 7435 Michigan Ave. • Detroit, MI 48210 • (313) 842-6262

Chapter 4

Management-by-Stress: Management's Ideal

Each aspect of the management-by-stress system (also called lean production) depends on the other aspects. Speed-up, just-in-time, "multi-skilling," intensified Taylorism, and workers' right to stop the assembly line combine to create a system where any mistake has consequences that are visible to all—as is any idle time. The lack of slack means each worker must exert extra effort to keep the system functioning. This stress is deliberate, and designed to keep all working at the top of their capabilities. Workers' dignity is presumed to come from striving for management's goals.

DURING THE 1980s, WHILE THE U.S. auto industry was in a tailspin, several Japanese automakers established factories in the United States: Honda in Ohio, Nissan in Tennessee, Mazda in Michigan, Mitsubishi in Illinois, and Toyota in California. These plants achieved stellar productivity and quality figures using management techniques imported from Japan. Toyota accomplished these numbers in a joint venture with General Motors, using a former GM plant and a United Auto Workers workforce; the joint venture is called New United Motors Manufacturing Inc.—NUMMI. More than any other single plant, NUMMI became the one for U.S. management to watch.

Although management uses the term "synchronous production" to describe this model, we have coined the term "management-by-stress," because it highlights the way stress serves as the force that drives and regulates the system. This chapter examines the principles and underlying philosophy of the management-by-stress model.[1] Chap-

ters 5-8 provide more details of its functioning.

It is impossible to understand how a management-by-stress system works without seeing all of its features as interrelated and dependent upon each other. The remarkable productivity figures achieved by NUMMI cannot be attributed to any single policy. Instead management's success story results from a combination of the following:

1. Speed-up—ways for workers to do more work in less time
2. Just-in-time (JIT) organization of inventory and production
3. Extensive use of outside contracting
4. Technology designed to minimize indirect labor
5. Design-for-manufacture—products specifically designed to reduce labor costs
6. Methods to reduce scrap and rework
7. Tighter management control.

As we will see, the approach in each of these areas depends on a corresponding approach in the other areas.

SPEED-UP: STRESSING THE SYSTEM

Management-by-stress goes against many traditional U.S. management notions. It even seems to go against common sense. Isn't it logical to protect against possible breakdowns and glitches by stockpiling parts and hiring extra workers to fill in for absentees?

Instead, the operating principle of management-by-stress is to systematically locate and remove such protections. The system, including its human elements, operates in a state of permanent stress. Stressing the system iden-

Chapters 4-7 are reprinted from *Choosing Sides: Unions and the Team Concept*, published in 1988. They describe the NUMMI and Mazda factories, and also General Motors' Fairfax plant in Kansas. They portray those plants as they were at the time, but much has changed since then—see chapter 36. Chapter 8 also contains a great deal of new information.

We are reprinting chapters 4-7 because they give a good picture of management-by-stress before unions have had a chance to respond to it. They are a purer version of management-by-stress: the employers' ideal.

tifies both the weak points and those that are too strong. The weak points will break down when the stress becomes too much, indicating that additional resources are needed. Just as important, points that never break down are presumed to have too many resources, and are thus wasteful.

The *andon* board illustrates how management-by-stress works. Andon is a visual display system, usually including a lighted board over the assembly line that shows each work station. In one variation of the andon board, the status of each station is indicated with one of three lights:

GREEN—production is keeping up and there are no problems;

YELLOW—operator is falling behind or needs help;

RED—problem requires stopping the line.

In the traditional U.S. operation, managers would want to see nothing but green lights. They design enough slack into the machinery and procedures so that an operation almost always runs in the green. Individual managers try to protect themselves with excess stock and excess workers to cover glitches or emergencies. CYA (cover your ass) is considered prudent operating procedure.

But in the management-by-stress production system, "all green" is not a desirable state. It means that the system is not running as fast or efficiently as it might. If the system is stressed (for example, by speeding up the assembly line), the yellow lights go on and the weakest points become evident. A few jobs will go into the red and stop the line. Management can now focus on these few jobs and make necessary adjustments.

A NUMMI manager explains the process to workers by comparing it to their experience when the plant was run by General Motors:

> Ever shut the line down? What happened? Everything broke loose. The plant manager, the plant superintendents, assistant superintendents, foremen, general foremen,

everybody became unglued. We don't get unglued here. It's a different world. It's okay to shut the line down. It's okay to make a mistake. It's okay to cause a problem because that's an opportunity for us to change something and do something just a little better the next time around.[2]

Once the problems have been corrected, the system can then be further stressed (perhaps by reducing the number of workers), and then rebalanced. The ideal is for the system to run with all stations oscillating between green and yellow.

Stressing the system can be accomplished by increasing line speed, cutting the number of people or machines, or assigning workers additional tasks. Similarly, a line can be balanced by decreasing the resources or increasing the work load at those positions which always run in the green. In management-by-stress systems, extra resources are considered as wasteful as producing scrap.

There is an elegance to the idea that the system "equilibrates" or drives towards being evenly balanced. The logic of the system itself is to move towards what management considers perfection, by constantly readjusting and rebalancing to be ever more efficient. After years of observing waste in traditional plants, some people (workers, as well as management) are attracted to this vision of a smoothly functioning, rational, efficient system. In engineering terms, it could be described as a tighter control system with "fast response inner loops." The only problem is that human beings are the cogs in the system, not transistors, computers, and motors.

JUST-IN-TIME

Just-in-time (JIT) is a "demand-pull" approach to production. This means that an operation does not produce until its product is called for by the next operation. A material handler does not replace stock until the line operation signals that it needs more. A department does not

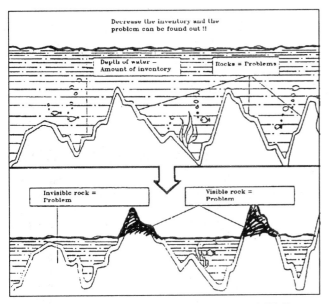

Mazda manual illustrates some of the advantages of JIT. The headline reads: "Decrease the inventory and the problem can be found out!!"

produce until it is signalled from the following department that more is needed. Just-in-time is best known because it allows (or requires) drastic cuts in inventories. Instead of stockpiling parts at various points in the production process, management attempts to reduce stockpiles as nearly as possible to zero, and to organize production so that parts will arrive just as they are required.

There are several well-known savings with just-in-time:

1. Interest costs on the value of capital tied up in inventory. Depending on current interest rates, this amounts to between five and fifteen percent of the value of the material in inventory.

2. The cost of warehousing and storing the inventory. This includes the cost of the warehouse space, labor, management, and record keeping, as well as the cost of damage and losses that take place during warehousing. Savings are even higher when delivery is directly to the assembly line, rather than to a receiving dock.

3. Quality control is easier because there are fewer parts in the pipeline. When a part supply runs two days ahead of actual use, if a problem is discovered at the point of use, this means that two days' worth of parts will have to be repaired or discarded. But if parts production is running only minutes ahead of use, a problem can be corrected almost instantly.

By themselves these are powerful reasons for management to adopt JIT. But what about the traditional reasons for inventory? By maintaining inventories or banks, one part of the production system is cushioned from problems in another part—the "just-in-case" method. There is time to fix a problem before it affects the next section of the plant.

Consider an assembly operation under JIT. If a station in the middle stops, downstream operations must quickly stop because they have no supply. Less obvious is that upstream operations must also stop, because the finished products have no place to go. Even if there were some place to stack parts, it is a violation of the operating principles of JIT to produce when there is no immediate demand.

These seemingly negative features of JIT become positive under a management-by-stress system. When a single point experiences trouble of any kind—whether difficulty meeting production or quality—there is no hiding. It becomes instantly apparent to all and is likely to affect operations far beyond the immediate trouble spot. Management at all levels will focus attention on the weak spot.

But how to deal quickly with problems allowed to surface through JIT? One option is to add resources to the weak spot. The production system could be designed with "flying squads," available to come to the aid of workers having a problem.

But the characteristic response under management-by-stress is very different: pressure is allowed to transmit through to production workers, team leaders, and lowest level management by making *them* solve the problem and catch up. There is no external assistance until management

is satisfied that extraordinary efforts and all the resources available to the team have been used. And, as with the andon board, management can use JIT to identify those departments which never have a problem, and then trim their resources or add work until problems do start showing up. "Cushions" have no place in management-by-stress.

The system assumes that pressure is the most effective way to motivate workers. For example, a Mazda manual describes a situation where a tire assembly station builds up a large supply of tires between itself and the installation point on the main line. What seems to be an advantage—that the main line will not have to stop if the tire assembly machine has a problem—is really a disadvantage. The manual explains that with the buffer there is not enough pressure on the operator: "When the trouble which occurred at the tire assembly station is found and corrected, the pressure to find the true cause of the situation is weakened."[3]

Stress, rather than management directives, becomes the mechanism for coordinating different sections of the system. The stress throughout tightly links the different parts to make the system "self-regulating" for management's purposes.

Ideally this means that top management only needs to make a few key decisions about the output required and the system will automatically adjust to produce that output to specifications as efficiently and cheaply as possible. Top management does not have to constantly monitor and direct specific production schedules in every department. Instead management only has to let the entire plant know the general level of planned production. As Monden says of the Toyota system: "Only the final assembly line needs to be notified of changes in sequence for the entire plant's production to be modified accordingly."[4]

But this can only work if the material handler, supplier department, and supplier company are all firmly committed to deliver just-in-time despite any obstacles. In order to maintain this commitment over a long period of time there are penalties for failure. In the case of supplier companies, the penalties are financial. In the case of individual workers, the penalties include attention and pressure from management, reduced perks, undesirable new assignments, and possible discipline. That is why personal stress as well as system stress is required for management-by-stress to keep running smoothly. A relaxed attitude—"I am just doing my job, I don't need to pay attention to anyone else's job"—makes the system inoperable.

That is also why management-by-stress relies so heavily on visual displays of the production system. When everyone can see who is responsible, more pressure can be brought to bear on those who fail to respond to the demands of the system. As Toyota managers put it:

> In the just-in-time production, all processes and all shops are kept in the state where they have no surplus so that if trouble is left unattended, the line will immediately stop running and will affect the entire plant. The necessity for improvement can be easily understood by anyone.[5]

Similarly, equipment breakdowns are clearly of greater consequence under JIT. One result is that there is a much greater emphasis on preventive maintenance. But when breakdowns do occur the system makes them highly visible, and tremendous pressure is put on maintenance workers to make repairs as quickly as possible, sometimes neglecting safety procedures. While this pressure also exists in traditional plants, in management-by-stress plants the reduced number of maintenance workers, the change in job duties, the blurring of lines of demarcation, and the demands of JIT increase the frequency and stress level of "crisis" jobs.

Set-up jobs under JIT also become crisis jobs. Following the principles of JIT means that only small lots are produced at one time. This particularly affects stamping plants, where relatively few large presses produce many different parts—but only one kind at a time. Under older systems it might require 24 hours to change a die in a press. Then the press would stamp out a part supply for a week or more before the die was changed for another part. But with the small batches required by JIT, many more die changes are necessary and the pressure is on to reduce the time per change.

There are amazing results. *Automotive Industries* magazine runs an annual die change contest. In 1987 the fastest team used two minutes and 28 seconds from the time the last of the old parts came off the press to the time the first good new part came off. The fastest teams were at the Nissan and Honda plants. Much of this swiftness is accomplished with design changes—major and minor alterations in the presses, dies, parts, and tools. But part of the speed comes from pressure to work quickly.

TAYLORISM AND SPEED-UP

At the turn of the century Frederick W. Taylor championed "scientific management," symbolized by the time-and-motion study "expert" with the stopwatch. Since then, management has sought ways to break jobs down to their smallest elements, examine each work element, determine the fastest method to perform an operation, and instruct workers to use those methods. At the same time, unions have found that decent working conditions required limiting Taylorism.

Most of the current industrial relations literature portrays team production, including the versions which depend on management-by-stress, as a humanistic alternative to scientific management. *Business Week* editorializes:

> Such team-based systems, perfected by Japanese car makers, are alternatives to the "scientific management" system, long used in Detroit, which treats employees as mere hands who must be told every move to make.[6]

This is part of the fantasy being constructed around the new system. In fact, the tendency is in the opposite direction—to specify every move a worker makes in far greater detail than ever before. The bottom line: far from a repudiation of scientific management, management-by-stress intensifies Taylorism.[7]

In management-by-stress plants, as in traditional plants, team members have very little control over the basic design of their own jobs. Management chooses the processes, basic production layout, and technologies to be used. These in turn largely determine job requirements and design. For example, when GM opened its Fairfax II plant under a new team agreement, workers thought they were going to have input into their job designs. They were surprised when they got called back to find that management had already selected their team leaders, who (with industrial engineers) had already broken the jobs down into basic elements and laid them out.

While the jobs are in fact designed by "teams," most of the original members of these teams are engineers, supervisors, and management-selected team leaders. They "chart" the jobs, that is, they break every job down to its individual acts, studying and timing each motion, adjusting the acts, and then shifting the work so that jobs are more or less equal. The end result is a detailed written specification of how each team member should do each job. Jobs are "balanced" so that the difference between *takt* time (number of seconds the car is at each work station) and the job cycle time (number of seconds for a worker to complete all assigned operations) is as close to zero as possible. (See chapter 5 for a more detailed discussion of work standards.)

As production increases and bugs are worked out, there are fewer changes made in job operations. Workers who are brought onto the team are expected to follow detailed procedures that have been worked over and over to eliminate free time. The team member is told exactly how many steps to take and what the left hand should be doing while the right hand is picking up the wrench.

Jobs are to be done in precisely the same way every time by every worker. If the charting calls for holding the part with your right hand and tightening with your left, that is how it must be done. The worker may not change the procedure without permission from a supervisor. The company explains that this is how quality is maintained. Why even chance a possible variation that might result from holding and tightening with opposite hands?

While this may be logical from an engineering point of view, it can be hard on the human element. Short people may find it easier to do a job differently from tall people. Sometimes it is desirable to change the way one is doing a job in the middle of the day to give some muscles a chance to relax and use others. The very rigidity of the system is illustrated by one Mazda team leader's notion of flexibility: "We make allowances for people who are left-handed."

But no matter how well workers learn their jobs, there is no such thing as maintaining a comfortable work pace. There is always room for *kaizen*, or continuous improvement. Whether through team meetings, quality circles, or suggestion plans, if you don't kaizen your own job someone else is likely to. The little influence workers do have over their jobs is that in effect they are organized to time-study themselves, in a kind of super-Taylorism.

MANAGEMENT CONTEMPLATES THE "PERFECT WORKER"...

© 86 Huck ue
AFTER ROBERT MINOR

APPROPRIATING WORKERS' KNOWLEDGE

Contrary to his current-day image, Frederick Taylor realized that workers do have minds and valuable knowledge. He insisted that the first duties under scientific management were

> the deliberate gathering in on the part of those on the management side of all the great mass of traditional knowledge, which in the past has been in the heads of the workmen and in the physical skill and knack of the workmen which they have acquired through years of experience.[8]

Management-by-stress seeks to utilize a worker's sense of observation, recognizing a valuable tool that should not go to waste. Like Taylor, managers-by-stress seek to harness that brain power by asking or even demanding that workers make available their thoughts about the production process. Workers make suggestions, and management may or may not accept those suggestions. But once the suggestion is made, the knowledge becomes part of management's power to control every worker on the line.

Management-by-stress does differ from Taylorism in one regard. Taylor thought that he could discover production workers' secret knowledge of the manufacturing process all at once, and that workers would then revert to being nothing but hired hands. Today's managers, on the other hand, know that since workers continue to actually do the work, they continue to have knowledge about it that management observers do not enjoy—and therefore some power over production.

So the formula is not to try to take all decision-making power off the shop floor, but to shift that small amount that workers do have to lower-level management or to those workers who identify with management. There

are several elements to this:

1. Lower-level management knows the production process because group leaders (first-line supervisors) regularly work the line—something forbidden by union practice in traditional auto plants.[9] (Taylor also advocated that management work on the floor with semi-skilled and skilled workers, in order to develop cooperative relations.)

2. Team leaders, who rotate through all jobs and are union members, are often effectively incorporated into management. At NUMMI some 900 workers have taken the 30-hour (no pay) training course to qualify for a team leader position.[10] Except for the fact that they lack formal powers of discipline, team leaders may have a full range of supervisory responsibilities and often come to think like supervisors. A key part of their jobs is to document worker knowledge for use by the actual supervisors.

3. Within the limits of the basic process and technology used, group leaders have the main responsibility for designing jobs and adjusting them. At NUMMI there is no separate industrial engineering or time-study department. The group leaders and their team leaders have a vested interest in seeing that the initial job design and charting they did during trial-build succeeds, and they are in a position to monitor the work continually.

4. Through charting, jobs are very tightly defined, and workers are not allowed to alter the way the job is done. A worker who believes she knows an easier or better way to do a job must share that knowledge with the team or group leader in order to get the group leader's approval. Similarly, job rotation under these circumstances

forces workers to share their job knowledge with each other and with management. In traditional plants workers often share information with each other voluntarily. The fact that this sharing is voluntary is a source of dignity and satisfaction. Further, having the choice when and when not to share information with management provides the worker with some bargaining ability. The choice to share with fellow workers allows peer group pressure against those who would be rate-busters.

While there is worker resistance to the tight control over jobs, without union support it is not very powerful. Thus in the management-by-stress system management can gather to itself the information about how things actually work in production—information often denied traditional management by its self-imposed or union-imposed isolation from the shop floor.

This added knowledge allows management to increase its control over the finest details of production. Without this detailed knowledge, attempts by management to exert exact control over the work process just couldn't work; the results would be laughable.

Lacking detailed knowledge of the shop floor, traditional management has to back off and allow workers some flexibility in how they do their jobs if anything is to be produced. This is not to imply that workers have much flexibility in traditional plants. Rather, management-by-stress seeks to squeeze the tiny amount of worker autonomy and flexibility out of an already rigid system.

ABSENTEEISM

Another key element in maintaining a taut system is the policy toward absenteeism. At NUMMI and Mazda, there are no extra workers hired as absentee replacements. A team consists of four to eight workers plus a team leader. The team members all have full jobs carefully assigned through the charting system. There is no slack. The team leader has no regular production job but performs an extensive list of assignments, some of which would be handled by the supervisor in a traditional plant. The team leader keeps track of absenteeism and tardiness, distributes tools and gloves, deals with problems of parts supply, and trains team members on new jobs. In addition, the leader helps out when a team member is having difficulty with a job, and fills in when someone needs relief or must go to the repair area to correct a defect.

If a member is absent, normally this means the team leader has to do the production job of the missing member. Then if team members need relief or help, they must depend on the group leader (who supervises two to four teams), either to fill in directly on the job or to assign a leader or member from another team to help out.

Again, stress keeps the system functioning. All the difficulties of someone's being absent fall on those who are in daily contact with the absentee—the co-workers and immediate supervisor. The problems are not shifted upstairs by having the Personnel Department hire and maintain a "redundant" workforce to cover for possible absences. No

department's budget is hurt by absenteeism; only the absentee's peers suffer.

Other team members find it is harder to get relief when they need it. Because of the way jobs are set up, if the person covering the absentee's job has difficulty it will interfere with the pace of the other jobs. As a result, team members tend to resent the absentee who, given the assumptions of management-by-stress, seems to be the cause of the problem.

The team leader also has limited sympathy for the absent worker, because he or she has to replace the absentee in addition to trying to keep up with normal team leader responsibilities. And, an absent worker results in major changes for the group leader, who must now fill in on the line, shuffle people around, and/or lose the services of the team leader.

The system is set up so that any variation in the company-determined operating arrangements places additional stress on those at the bottom. Because the jobs are already hard, survival and self-preservation produce enormous peer pressure against absenteeism. Several workers interviewed at NUMMI commented that they would like to have people who were absent too much removed from their group.

Peer pressure can be a powerful force in the workplace. Most of us have strong needs to be accepted and respected by the people we regard as our peers. In a factory where the discipline of the line increases alienation and a sense of powerlessness, the threat of losing this acceptance and respect is even more compelling. The harder the job is, the more workers depend on one another for even small instances of informal cooperation: moments of relief, humor, psychological support, watching your back, physical assistance, and information.

Management well understands the power of peer pressure and directs it to their own ends. Maintaining a macho atmosphere so that workers are made to feel like wimps for enforcing health and safety standards is one example. Of course, using peer pressure in this way is not new to management-by-stress. Many piece-rate systems were set up so that workers would get angry at an absent group member because the replacement was not as fast and therefore held back the pay of the whole group. Under management-by-stress, the stakes are raised from bonus payments to being able to survive on the job.

The pressure against absenteeism is reinforced during the hiring process. An applicant's attendance record is one of management's most important considerations. NUMMI's application form requires workers to specify the number of days missed each year for the previous five years and to give reasons for any absences over ten per year. A strict disciplinary procedure with harsh penalties further inhibits absenteeism.

The total system is successful in enforcing attendance. GM claims around two percent unscheduled absenteeism for NUMMI, compared to 8.8 percent for the whole corporation.[11]

STOPPING THE LINE

"Workers can stop the line." This promise is the single feature that has come to symbolize the difference between the new production system and "the old way of doing things." The companies present this power as the foundation of their policy of respect for the humanity of workers. Monden says, "It is not a conveyor that operates men, it is men that operate a conveyor."[12]

Exactly how a worker goes about stopping the line differs from plant to plant and even within plants. At NUMMI, for example, "pulling the cord" results in distinctive chimes and flashing lights on the andon board. If the cord is not pulled again within a set time to cancel the warning (usually one minute), then the line will stop. In other versions, the worker may have a choice of buttons: yellow to sound the call for help, and red to stop the line. In some variations the worker can restart the line, while other variations require a supervisor to restart it.

The ability to stop the line is powerfully attractive. In the Big Three, a worker did not stop the line unless someone was dying. It didn't matter if a worker couldn't keep up or if scrap was going through. You tried to get the foreman's attention, and he could decide whether to stop the line (rarely) or leave the problem to be repaired further on (usually). Stopping the line without a really good cause meant discipline. The decision to stop the line represented the boundary between the judgment of workers and the judgment of management.

The right to stop the line is supposed to substitute for the cumbersome system of establishing work standards used in traditional auto plants. In traditional plants, the company industrial engineers or time-study experts determine the particular operations and time allotments for each job. The union contract requires employees and union to be notified when a job is to be time-studied, and prohibits management from setting standards under exceptional circumstances or by using exceptionally young, strong, nimble, or well-trained workers. Work standards, once established, cannot be changed arbitrarily except by repeating the contractual procedure. The union has the right to grieve work standards, and these are among the few issues that can be struck over during the life of the contract.

The contract specifies that when a tool, process, or part is changed, the old standards do not apply. Consequently, many jobs are operated without formal production standards. Even then, the worker has more protection than in a management-by-stress plant, because the contract language states that management cannot discipline workers for failing to keep up as long as they are working at a "normal pace." Under these circumstances, management pressures to force higher production could be resisted by the union as "harassment."[13]

"But with the stop cord, why have all these bureaucratic procedures?" the argument goes. There is no need for contractual arrangements to change line speed or the number of tasks on a job, if you have a system that trusts the worker. If the worker is making a genuine attempt, but cannot keep up, he just pulls the stop cord. There is—supposedly—no penalty.

This arrangement is written into the NUMMI contract:

> Employees are expected to use their best efforts in performing the job within the *takt* time [production time per vehicle] and to alert their Group/Team Leader of production and quality problems. If the problem in production or quality is such that they cannot complete their tasks in the proper manner, they are expected, without being subject to discipline, to pull the cord or push the button to sound the alarm, and ultimately stop the line, alerting a Group/Team Leader of the problem. If the problem is of a recurring nature, the employees will work together to kaizen the operation....[14]

The NUMMI contract specifically allows for easy change of production standards by the group leader. The union is not involved in the initial setting of such standards. Production standards are specifically not grievable but use a different procedure: if a worker is dissatisfied with a production standard, the first step is to try to work it out with the group leader. If this fails the worker can appeal to the Standardized Work Committee, composed of two management and two union representatives.

During trial-build and training periods the cord seems to work for everyone. It helps workers get assistance when problems come up, and it helps keep quality high even through all the problems of establishing a new line. It aids management in identifying problems so they can be quickly resolved.

However, once the job is well defined and most of the bugs are worked out, the cord can become oppressive. As the line is sped-up and the whole system is stressed, it becomes harder and harder to keep up all the time. Once the standardized work—so painstakingly charted, refined, and recharted—has been in operation for a while, management assumes any problem is the fault of the worker, who has the burden of proof to show otherwise. NUMMI rules provide for warnings, suspensions, and firing for "failure to maintain satisfactory production levels based on Company performance standards." Stopping the line means the chimes and lights of the andon board immediately identify who is not keeping up. The pressure is also on the supervisor.

As a NUMMI manual explains:

> The role of the supervisor is to go to the trouble spot as soon as the *andon* displays the problem and find out what happened. If the line is stopped and there is no safety problem, the supervisor's first priority is to get the line back into operation as fast as possible. Then it is the supervisor's responsibility to find out the real cause of the problem, and take counter measures to make sure that the same problem cannot happen again.[15]

There is good reason for this pressure. An idle assembly line represents enormous costs in equipment and labor. Just-in-time can multiply these costs many times over. The system cannot achieve its legendary productivity if the line is stopping frequently. Thus once the line is up to full operating speed, supervisors do become "unglued" when the line actually stops.

A worker who is having trouble keeping up has four immediate choices, none of them good:

1. He can stop the line. This is likely to attract immediate and unhappy attention from the group leader.

2. He can work "into the hole"—farther down the line from his assigned position—to try to catch up. But it's hard to catch up when you're already working at maximum speed. And, like everything else in management-by-stress, the system uses peer pressure against working in the hole. Because jobs are so tightly charted, a worker who keeps working into another person's area may throw off that worker's pacing.

3. He can signal the team leader for help. But if the team leader has to spend all her time helping one worker to prevent the line from stopping, then that leader is not available for other workers who might need to go to medical or just need temporary assistance—creating peer pressure again.

4. He can let the job go through uncompleted. Again the system works against it. Workers downstream are certain to pull the cord if they spot an incomplete job from a previous station. Not only does management teach workers over and over that this is their responsibility, but this is one instance when pulling the cord may get the downstream workers a breather at no cost to themselves. And attention is once again drawn to the unfortunate worker who has fallen behind—and compounded his error by letting unfinished work go through.

Therefore, under the assumptions of management-by-stress, the only solution is for workers to keep up with the line speed with no errors.

Reluctance to pull the cord thus translates into pressure to keep up with the job whatever it takes. Some NUMMI workers use part of their breaks or come in early to "build stock" or get ready for their jobs. When asked why they do it, they insist that there is no management pressure on them. The breaks are their time and they feel better using breaks to make their jobs bearable. But as this practice spreads, and the union does nothing about it, more and more workers will be forced by the system to use personal time to keep up. Thus the high productivity figures are partly the result of effectively forcing workers to work overtime for free.

Others just try to work harder. Some work "in the hole" in hopes of catching up later. A Mazda worker describes the Catch 22 in which a co-worker found herself:

> She had a hard time one day and pulled the stop cord several times. The next day management literally focussed attention on her. Several management officials observed and they set up a video camera to record her work. She found herself working further into the hole. She worked into the hole too far and fell off the end of the [two-foot] platform and injured her ankle. They told her it was her fault—she didn't pull the stop cord when she fell behind.

Management is aware of workers' reluctance to pull the cord, although it provides a different explanation. Monden describes a situation in Japan:

> Because the workers' morale is so high, they often fail to stop the line when they should and even enter the next

process to complete their assigned operations; i.e. they force themselves to finish their jobs in spite of the supervisors' instructions to stop the line if they are delayed or become tired.[16]

Toyota installed photoelectric cells in some stations to check for failure to complete all operations in the allotted time. Other checking devices include floor mat sensors that are triggered if an operator moves too far from the as-

---

Some New Terms

A number of Japanese terms have become part of the daily language in management-by-stress plants.

Andon A system of visual displays. The *andon* lighted display board over a work area shows which work stations are not keeping up.

Jikoda Sometimes used to refer to automation generally, or more specifically to automation that checks for defects and automatically stops the process. Sometimes called "autonomation."

Kaizen Constant improvement. Sometimes used as a verb—to solve a problem or to fix, as in "we have to *kaizen* that machine."

Kanban The cards attached to parts in Toyota's just-in-time "demand-pull" system. As the parts are used or transferred, the *kanban* are removed and used to request (order) replacements. The term is sometimes used to refer to the whole just-in-time system.

Three M's:

Muda Waste. Scrap production, overproduction, idle time, wasted time, inefficient process.

Muri Overburden. Overloading a piece of equipment or a person.

Mura Unevenness. Inconsistent use of a person or machine.

Four S's:

Seiri Removal of unnecessary material and equipment.

Seiton A place for everything and everything in its place.

Seiso Cleaning the equipment and area.

Seiketsu Practicing the above three to keep the workplace neat and clean.

Takt time Effectively, the amount of time the vehicle is at each operator's station. More generally, calculated by taking number of minutes the line or process is running and dividing by the total production planned. Usually measured in minutes or seconds per unit, it is the inverse of the more traditional measure of line speed in units/hour. Example: if a line is to produce 500 vehicles in a 450-minute (7.5 hour) work day, the *takt* time would be .9 minutes, or 54 seconds per unit. The line speed in this case would be just under 67 units per hour.

The Five Why's: Asking "why" at least to five levels to get at the root cause of problems in order to correct them.

signed position. These automatically shut down the line. Initially, workers did not appreciate this further limit on their own autonomy and

> resisted such limited forms of automatic controls because they were forced to complete their jobs within the assigned cycle time. [But after supervisors explained why these controls were necessary] the workers fully accepted the system, quality control improved, and the total time consumed by line stoppages was actually reduced.[17]

Thus with a fairy tale explanation, management installs electronic supervisors and electric tethers and automates the very item—the cord—that was supposed to symbolize workers' power over production.

THE MULTI-FUNCTIONAL WORKER

Everything in the management-by-stress system is tied together. A principle of just-in-time is that a worker never produces for stock even if there is nothing else to do. Stock is waste, and besides, there is no place for it to be stored and no procedure to handle it. It is better for workers and machines to stand idle than to produce in excess of what is immediately needed.

Yet management also cannot allow idle time to be part of the system. Idle time reduces labor productivity. The system is designed so that any idle time is a visual indication that something needs to be adjusted. For example, a worker who can shave a few seconds from his or her cycle time should not take the initiative to help out fellow workers or find some task to be done. It is better to stand idle so that management and team members can see that there is some free time that can be assigned a regular task. If management allowed JIT to result in idle time as a normal situation, the value of idle time as a visual indicator would disappear.

If JIT forbids producing in advance, but idle time cannot be tolerated, the only way that the system can work is if production is organized so that jobs can be shifted and adjusted easily without disrupting the production process itself. This is particularly important in the auto industry, where both the number of vehicles to be built and the model mix can vary considerably and quickly.

For example, one way to adjust production in a sales downturn is to slow down the speed of the assembly line. Slowing the line creates idle time for each worker. But if management can remove some workers and redistribute the tasks to the workers remaining in the team, most idle time can again be eliminated. The ease and speed with which management can redistribute tasks determines how responsive the plant can be to shifting demand. While all auto plants do this to some extent, the high responsiveness of management-by-stress plants is a major contribution to their high productivity.

This management flexibility to easily redistribute tasks and eliminate idle time requires that:

1. Tasks must be broken down into the smallest units possible.

2. Each task must be well defined so it can easily be reassigned.

3. The skill level required for each task must be as low as possible.

4. Workers must be able and willing to do any task assigned.

5. Tasks must be arranged close together and in a way that decreases non-productive time walking between tasks.

One approach is to mix subassembly jobs with jobs on the main line. An arrangement such as shown here allows workers to move from task to task in a circular pattern, reducing non-productive walking time. It also makes it easy for management to shift a task from worker A to worker B for line balancing, or to eliminate one worker and redistribute the tasks to those remaining.

Most significant is the requirement that workers be *able to do and movable to* any job management wishes. Management calls it "multi-skilling," but this is a misleading term.

The *abilities* required to do several very short jobs which have been carefully broken down by the charting process are manual dexterity, physical stamina, and the ability to follow instructions precisely. Even here management is careful to design jobs not to require exceptional amounts of any of these, because they want to be able to assign workers interchangeably. These are not "skills" in the usual sense of requiring training and specialized knowledge. The essence of "multi-skilling" is actually the *lack of resistance*, on the part of the union or the individual worker, to management reassigning jobs whenever it wishes, for whatever reason.

During hiring, management-by-stress plants have shown little interest in applicants' skills acquired from previous work and much more interest in attendance records, ability to follow directions, physical stamina, and general attitude toward management. Once hired, the worker does not benefit by learning more marketable skills. Instead, she learns how to carry out a large number of extremely job-specific tasks. Each such task requires little training in the sense of learning new skills—rather they require practice in order to learn to do them quickly enough. Multi-skilling thus has less to do with training than with overcoming any barriers such as union contract provisions, classifications, or traditions that prevent workers from doing more than one job. What training there is focuses more on company procedures and values than on marketable technical skills.

OUTSOURCING

The UAW-NUMMI contract specifies that the company will take "affirmative measures," including "assigning previously subcontracted work to bargaining unit employees capable of performing this work," before laying off any employees. This arrangement, a variant of the system used in Japan, is being interpreted in this way: as long as the company guarantees the jobs of all regular workers, the union will not object to outside contracting (employees of an outside firm do work in the plant, such as cleaning) and outsourcing (parts are bought from outside firms). Outside contracting and outsourcing are extensive at both NUMMI and Mazda.[18]

The deal seems to provide job security, but in reality the job security is less than if the work were not outsourced and the plant had traditional seniority protections during layoffs. Say the management-by-stress assembly plant has 1,000 workers, and there are 200 workers at a supplier company nearby making seat cushions. If sales decline, which would normally cause the layoff of, say, 200 assembly workers, the assembly plant is committed to bringing the seat cushion work into the plant, in order to keep those 200 assembly workers on the job. (Whether management would actually follow through on this commitment during a downturn, given the investment required, is another question.) The 200 cushion workers at the supplier company would all lose their jobs, in favor of the assembly workers.

Now let us look at the same situation in a traditional assembly plant of 1,200 workers. This plant includes a cushion room because the union was able to prevent the company from outsourcing the cushion work. When sales decline, the lowest 200 or so workers are laid off, plantwide. There are still 1,000 workers on the job and 200 on the street—but the laid-off workers have recall rights to their union plant.

The 1,000 management-by-stress workers, who supposedly received job security in exchange for outsourcing, have not gained any more job security in comparison with the 1,000 highest-seniority workers in the traditional plant. All these workers have achieved is to isolate themselves from the cushion workers, who now work for a different company for lower wages and with less job security.

Thus the job security that the deal provides is of the "see no evil" variety. Management divides workers into two tiers—those at the main plant, protected by the union and the paternalism of the company, and those at the supplier plants, usually non-union, who have no protection from layoffs and no sup-

plementary unemployment benefits as the unionized workers do.

In the long run, of course, jobs are lost by attrition even at the main plant.

Union endorsement of this kind of arrangement gives substance to the charge that unions attempt to protect the elite few at the expense of poorer, less protected, workers—who also turn out to be disproportionately women and minorities. Such a policy also makes it all the more difficult for unions to organize the increasing number of non-union supplier plants.

Outsourcing accounts for some of the supposed savings of just-in-time. The assembly plant gets rid of the costs of holding inventory, but the supplier company is forced to maintain inventory (even renting warehouses near the JIT customer) so it can supply exactly when the assembly plant "pulls." Mazda, for example, has plans to rent warehouse space on its Flat Rock, Michigan site to suppliers. The supplier must also inspect its products and bear the costs of delivery directly to the line. Thus inspection, material handling, rework, and clerical jobs are all still being performed. But the work is removed from the bargaining unit and contracted out to the lower-paid, typically non-union suppliers.

INDIVIDUALS CAN BE EASILY HANDLED BY THE SYSTEM

COLLECTIVELY, THE SYSTEM BECOMES MORE VULNERABLE

Ted Rall

Often the only economic pressure constraining management to produce subassemblies in-house is the need to control them very closely. For example, most assembly plants used to have their own cushion rooms for seat upholstery partly because of the need for the right color and style to go in the right car. With greater main plant control over suppliers, the trend in recent assembly plants is to outsource the cushion work. At NUMMI, for example, Hoover Universal delivers the proper color and style seat seats every few hours. As the procedures for JIT deliveries direct to the line are improved, more and more subassemblies will be outsourced.

Similarly, because management-by-stress is built on standardizing and regularizing all work, jobs that do not neatly fit this pattern, like construction work and landscaping, are contracted out.

USE OF NEW TECHNOLOGY

NUMMI management points with pride to the fact that it has succeeded without the most advanced technology. This has led many, both in management and in the union movement, to see in NUMMI an alternative to the high-tech approach to productivity.

At NUMMI Toyota chose a conservative approach to technology because it was dealing with its first plant in the U.S. and a special relationship with General Motors and the United Auto Workers. Even so, while the plant does not represent the cutting edge in new technology, it is not far behind. Mazda is even more modern. In 1986 Nissan management claimed that its Smyrna, Tennessee facility had more robots than any other U.S. assembly plant.[19] Honda has announced elaborate plans to install a new system in its Ohio plant that is supposed to automate 80 percent of vehicle assembly and triple productivity.[20]

Management-by-stress systems have a coherent approach to technology. Automation is not done for its own sake. Labor is divided into two kinds. On the one hand is direct or "value-added" labor. This is direct work on or assembly of materials which increases the value of the product. On the other hand, almost everything else is "non-value-added" or indirect labor. This includes material transfer and handling, most inspection, maintenance, and cleaning. There is a heavy emphasis on reducing non-value-added labor.

Since the focus is on simplifying, standardizing, and regularizing work, any technological change that essentially replaces a production worker with an indirect, non-value-added job is rejected. For example, a machine that replaces one production worker but requires an additional electrician to be in the area is a bad idea. Secondly, the automation must increase management flexibility, not decrease it. The approach can be seen in Monden's warning about possible problems with automation:

> Even if the introduction of an automatic machine reduces manpower by 0.9 persons, it cannot actually reduce the number of workers on the line unless the remaining 0.1 person...can be eliminated...
> [Automation] often has the undesirable effect of fixing

the number of workers who must be employed at a given workplace...regardless of production quantity...
> In both respects the introduction of [automation] may actually eliminate the ability to reduce the number of workers—a matter of some concern, since it is always essential to reduce the workforce, especially when demand decreases.[21]

The emphasis, then, is on small automation which improves the functioning of the system—*jikoda* or "autonomation," as it is called at NUMMI and Mazda— rather than on sweeping changes that transform basic manufacturing methods. These terms refer especially to technology that is used to detect production problems and that automatically stops operations. Plant engineers, then, concentrate on such changes as installing a photoelectric cell that shuts the line off if a part is not installed properly.

At the same time, management-by-stress also makes it easier to introduce larger technologies, in two ways. First, by requiring workers to do jobs in very exact machine-like ways, management uses workers as prototype automation. Second, since management can flexibly assign workers to new duties and the system forces cooperation, many of the usual problems of introducing automation are reduced.

Thus, management-by-stress plants are not likely to be an alternative to high-tech plants. While they may not install unproven technologies that require highly skilled operators and maintenance back-up to overcome "bugs," management-by-stress plants will very quickly install and modify technologies once they are proven elsewhere.

DESIGN-FOR-MANUFACTURE

It used to be that cars and other products were designed with only the market in mind. Once designed, it was the engineer's job to figure out how to mass produce the design as cheaply as possible. Now the idea is to design the product from the very beginning with an eye toward decreasing production costs and minimizing labor required. How the product is designed in large part determines how it is produced.

One German estimate is that 70 percent of the cost of the automobile is already determined at the design phase, and only a 10 percent variation is possible through the whole production phase.[22]

Management-by-stress fits particularly well with design-for-manufacture. The detailed charting process provides design engineers with the kind of data they need to calculate production time into their designs. Similarly, the high degree of flexibility management has in determining exactly how production will be carried out allows for better integration of design and production.

Product design is one of those so-called management rights which unions have rarely challenged but must begin to do so. From a worker's vantage point it makes little difference whether a job is lost after production begins, when management designs a robot that can weld two pieces together, or whether a design changes eliminates the need to put those pieces together in the first place.

TIGHTER MANAGEMENT

In business circles, proponents of the team concept emphasize that one of its principles is to push decision making and responsibility to the lowest levels of the organization. As we have seen, responsibilities (in the sense of demands on the individual worker) are pushed down as far as possible to the workers on the line. But the power and control that determine how these demands are to be met are pushed down only to the group leader level. Thus it is the group leader who controls the detailed setting of work standards to which the hourly worker must adhere.

Keeping the system stressed is the key to tighter managerial control with fewer managers. If a worker is off the job, slows down, falls behind, or does something incorrectly, the tightness of the system itself makes the lack obvious, even faster than in a traditional plant. Less supervision is needed because management observers are not required to identify trouble spots; the system does this either through visual indication or by breaking down. Management can concentrate on dealing with the trouble spots. As Toyota managers put it:

> Control of abnormality becomes easy. It will only be necessary to make improvements by directing attention to the stopped equipment and the workers who did the stopping.[23]

Further, a supervisor gets less interference from the union than under a traditional contract. In the management-by-stress system, job standards are not protected or policed by the union; supervisors can change work standards or work assignments at will. In a traditional plant workers sometimes protest by working to the letter of the rules. There can be no "work to rule" when all the rules are made by the supervisor.

AND WHAT ABOUT TEAMS?

In management and union circles, as well as the press, the system we have described as management-by-stress is referred to as the "team concept." Yet we have made few references to the functioning of teams. In the actual operation of the plant—as opposed to the ideological hype—the main significance of teams is that they are simply the name management gives to administrative units. For the most part, if we substituted "supervisor's sub-group" for team and "sub-group leader" for team leader, understanding of management-by-stress would not suffer at all.

There is, however, some reality to the widespread notions about teams. Some teams meet and discuss real problems. When the lines move slowly enough, workers can and do help each other out. But this is most likely during initial start-up, when the "teams" often consist mainly of supervisors, engineers, and team leaders. Once the line is up to speed, jobs are specified in detail and each worker can barely keep up with his or her own job, let alone help someone else out. Besides, the system does not like uncharted actions on the line.

When the system is running at regular production speed, team meetings tend to drop in frequency. Some workers at NUMMI complain that months pass between team meetings. In other cases team meetings are nothing more than shape-up sessions where quality or overtime information is transmitted to the workers or a supervisor announces changes in assignments.

When management talks to itself about what makes the system work, teams, in the sense of teamwork or team meetings, are rarely mentioned. In his description of Toyota, considered *the* reference by many NUMMI managers, Yasuhiro Monden does not use the term "team" at all. He does describe the mandatory Quality Control Circles made up of "a foreman and his subordinate workers." In the entire 230-page book explaining the production system, discussion of these circles totals seven pages, and much of this discussion covers the suggestion system and its rewards.

Similarly, John Krafcik, an MIT researcher and a former quality control engineer at NUMMI, lists teams as one of the reasons for NUMMI's success. But in describing them, Krafcik discusses only the supervisory duties of the team leader ("although a UAW member") and the peer pressure against absenteeism, not any supposed team powers or problem-solving functions.[24]

THE UNION

Management-by-stress is truly a lean and mean system. In tightly connecting all operations, consciously seeking to strip out all protections and cushions, and making all parts of the system almost instantly responsive to change, management-by-stress becomes a highly efficient system for carrying out management policy.

But these same strengths also create a potential Achilles heel for management. The responsiveness of the system to basic management decisions means that a single miscalculation outside a limited range can bring the system down.

Many of the new management techniques to increase productivity also make unions *potentially* more dangerous. If workers *collectively* take certain actions, the system becomes extremely vulnerable. One industry publication contains the warning that with just-in-time, "unions have a lot more power than they did before."[25] The action of workers in one department can immediately affect the entire operation, both upstream and downstream. The visibility used by management to maintain stress also becomes the way that workers throughout the plant know that something is up.

The key word is "collectively." The system easily handles individuals and small groups who resist. The visual display techniques, combined with the appropriation of worker knowledge, the detailed charting of all jobs, the multi-skilling, the role of team leaders, and the fact that supervisors regularly work the floor, make it relatively easy for management to identify and replace "troublemakers."

But suppose everyone starts pressing the stop button, in an organized campaign to let management know that the line speed is too fast or that they need absentee replacements. It is no longer a case of isolated troublemakers, and management can no longer contain the problem. An organized slowdown, sick-out, or other job action affecting a sizable minority in a department can disrupt the entire plant. If team members are unified and refuse to cooperate with a management-appointed team leader, the team can effectively force management to appoint a leader of the team's choosing. And if union consciousness is strong and the union backs the team leader, the team leader and team meetings can be used to organize for workers' demands.

While collective action gives power to workers in both traditional and management-by-stress plants, the latter are particularly vulnerable to workers' small-scale shop floor actions. But collective action of this kind takes organization—the kind provided both formally and informally by unions.

In management-by-stress plants the union's relationship with management must be settled from the beginning. The system operates by putting stress on workers. It cannot operate for long with a union that fights stressful jobs and organizes its members to challenge management on the shop floor. For management there are two alternatives: either prevent unionization in the first place, or keep a subdued union which helps prevent any collective action and defuses any sense of solidarity and militancy on the shop floor. There is no room in management-by-stress for a union that actively organizes its members in their own interests.

PERSONAL STRESS

Applied to the world of inanimate objects, the word "stress" simply means pressure or force. It is neither good nor bad. Increasing stress will tend to cause a piece of metal to deform or break—a desirable result if the metal is being stamped into a fender, but undesirable if the metal is a bridge support. In most mechanical situations, stress can be continuous as long as it is below a certain point.

But stress is much more complicated in human beings. Some forms of stress contribute to a person's health. Aerobic activity, such as running, conditions skeletal and heart muscles by subjecting them to small doses of stress followed by periods of relaxation. The stress response also helps the body to deal with emergencies. The cascade of physiological changes that takes place when a person is faced with a dangerous situation is often called the "flight or fight" reaction. The increased production of certain hormones allows for exceptional effort, including seemingly superhuman feats such as lifting a truck off a trapped co-worker.

Yet stress can also kill. Continued long-term stress over which the individual has no control, when the high hormone levels and other physiological changes become the body's normal state, has well-established links to heart disease, asthma, ulcers, diabetes, depression, drug abuse, and alcoholism. Research on animals has shown a direct relationship between "inescapable stress" and suppression of the immune system cells involved in fighting cancer.[26] The primary hormone released in response to stress, cortisol, suppresses the immune function generally and kills certain brain cells.[27]

Chronic stress contributes to accidents and family problems. Continued high stress levels can be particularly dangerous because a person can believe that he or she has gotten used to stressful environments, even while the body maintains its high reaction to stress.[28]

What kind of jobs generate the greatest stress? Researchers have found that the combination of high job demand and low job control produces the maximum stress.[29] Contrary to the popular belief that stress is the burden of top executives, studies have shown that the most stressful jobs include inspectors of manufactured products, material handlers, public relations workers, laboratory technicians, machinists, laborers, mechanics, and structural-metal craftspersons.[30]

It is not just the work itself that creates stress in management-by-stress plants. For all the public talk about their job security, interviews with NUMMI workers reveal that fear of a plant closing is uppermost in their minds, and often justifies everything that happens in the plant. The fact that the system is so inflexible when it comes to workers' personal needs also generates stress. (What kind of job could I do in this plant if I were injured? How do I get time off for a personal problem?)

Management-by-stress plants often deal with some of the causes of stress through such things as paying attention to tool design. They may also have individual counseling and exercise programs to help relieve some of the symptoms of stress. (Such programs also, of course, contribute to a "blame the victim" outlook.)

But overall, the system itself multiplies personal stress by continually increasing the demands on the individual while reducing personal control.

RESPECT AND DIGNITY FOR THE INDIVIDUAL

Toyota and NUMMI claim that respect and dignity for the individual are key to their management theory. Toyota managers describe the system as the "respect-for-human" system. Evidence of this respect certainly exists. Visitors to the NUMMI plant are struck by the plant's atmosphere. Workers are addressed using courteous language. The plant is clean and well lit and seems like a nice place to work.

At the same time, operation of the plant indicates a very peculiar notion of humanity—that human fulfillment is achieved only by striving for management's goals. Monden gives one example of this management mentality:

Reductions in the workforce brought about by workshop improvements may seem to be antagonistic to the worker's human dignity since they take up the slack created by waiting time and wasted action. However, allowing the worker to take it easy or giving him high wages does not necessarily provide him an opportunity to realize his worth. On the contrary, that end can be better served by providing

Other Views

This chapter paints an unlovely picture of life in a management-by-stress plant. It contradicts most of what is said in the glowing accounts of the team concept in the popular media. Where do those accounts come from?

Many stories about how workers feel about life in management-by-stress plants are based on reports of company officials, union officers, or consultants who have some vested interest in the programs' being declared a success. Some very positive descriptions are based on interviews at the time the plant was starting up.[31] As we have described earlier, the conditions, the role of teams and teamwork during the start-up period are transformed by the time the lines reach full production speed. Some reports are based on testimony by workers specially selected by the company to meet reporters. The distortions are then compounded by authors who know little about what life is like in a factory.

There is certainly a minority of workers in management-by-stress plants who claim to love their work situations. There are even workers for whom the discipline, regimentation, and hard physical labor of management-by-stress plants fit their personal needs. There are also some workers who have received or hope to receive perks such as trips to Japan or promotions.

But there are several reasons why these views do not provide an accurate picture of the views of most workers in the plants. And they mean even less about how the system would be accepted if spread to still more plants and more workers.

1. Most of the new management-by-stress plants were able to select their workforces from a huge pool of applicants. Over 130,000 applied to Nissan and 96,000 to Mazda. (NUMMI had a much more restricted pool but was as selective as possible.) The companies screened carefully, so that the workers at these plants are not a representative sample of working people.

2. The number of active supporters will probably decline as the plants get older. Experience with Quality of Work Life programs shows that in the early stages of these programs workers are usually positive about them and tend to give management the benefit of the doubt, because workers would like to believe the promises of participation and respect.

3. Many workers privately admit to the pressures and the difficult pace—"eight hours of aerobic exercises," some have called it.[32] But they defend the company because it provides them with the only decent-paying job they are likely to get. While many fear they will not be able to keep up with the pace when they grow older, they fear even more losing their jobs immediately. They accept the view that if the company were not run essentially the way it is, there would be no jobs at all. They also believe that public criticism of the company will hurt sales and threaten their jobs.

4. The sense of fear in management-by-stress plants is striking. The power exercised by supervisors, combined with little sense of either union presence or individual rights, chills the desire to criticize a plant where company loyalty is a priority. Many NUMMI workers have declined to be interviewed by reporters about their experiences in the plant, citing responses of management and fellow workers to previously published interviews.

the worker with a sense that his work is worthwhile and allowing him to work with his superior and his comrades to solve problems they encounter.[33]

In management-by-stress plants, workers are expected to believe that personal illness or family needs must take second place to perfect attendance. Personal time is at the beck and call of the company. Mazda tells its workers to arrange their personal lives so they can work ten hours every day although management may only assign them eight.[34] Workers' human qualities are manipulated so that peer pressure works to achieve management's ends.

The view that a paternalistic management endows workers with dignity by reducing the workforce and increasing the workload of those remaining may be a convincing rationalization for the managerial mind. But unions have different goals and need a different definition of human dignity.

Notes

1. We have drawn heavily on the views of Toyota management as described in *Toyota Production System* by Yasuhiro Monden, an industrial engineering book endorsed by senior Toyota managers (Yasuhiro Monden, *Toyota Production System: Practical Approach to Production Management*, Industrial Engineering and Management Press, 1983). We have also used documents and videotapes developed by General Motors for internal management use, as well as training materials developed by NUMMI and Mazda. Finally, and most importantly, we have looked at the day-to-day operation of NUMMI and Mazda by interviewing workers from those plants.

2. General Motors Technical Liaison Office, *"This Is NUMMI,"* videotape for GM Managers, 1985.

3. MMUC *Production System: Concept and Outline*, Mazda Motor Manufacturing (USA) Corporation, 1986.

4. Monden, p. 65.

5. Y. Sugimori, K. Kusunoki, F. Cho, S. Uchikawa, "Toyota

Production System and Kanban System," 1977, reprinted in Monden, p. 211.

6. *Business Week*, August 31, 1987.

7. Two excellent pieces with analyses similar to that presented here are Knuth Dohse, Ulrich Jurgens, and Thomas Malsch, "From 'Fordism' to 'Toyotism'? The Social Organization of the Labor Process in the Japanese Automobile Industry," *Politics and Society,* Vol. 14, No. 2, 1985; and Peter J. Turnbull, "The Limits of Japanisation—Just-In-Time, Labor Relations and the UK Automotive Industry," to be published Autumn 1988 in *New Technology, Work, and Employment,* Vol. 3, No. 2.

8. "Testimony to the House of Representatives Committee, 1912" in Frederick Taylor, *Scientific Management*, Harper and Brothers, New York and London, 1917.

9. The actual NUMMI contract language on supervisors working is not that different from that in traditional contracts. Both reserve bargaining unit work for bargaining unit members. Both have exceptions and loopholes. Although the loopholes are bigger at NUMMI, the main difference is past practice and union enforcement. The result is that supervisors seldom work very long on bargaining unit jobs in traditional plants. When they do the union files a grievance and often a penalty is paid to union members. This policy was traditionally considered a point of union honor because it protects union jobs and gives workers some small power over management. It is common in management-by-stress plants, however, to see supervisors and even higher management working the line, and to do so is even a matter of company pride.

10. Tetsuo Abo, "The Application of Japanese-Style Management Concepts in Japanese Automobile Plants in the U.S.A.," WZB Conference, Berlin, November 1987.

11. *Detroit Free Press*, January 25, 1988.

12. Sugimori, p. 211.

13. See, for example, *Agreement Between Chrysler Corporation and the United Auto Workers*, Production and Maintenance, Section 44, October 26, 1985.

14. *Agreement between New United Motors Manufacturing, Inc. and the UAW*, July 1, 1985, XXVII(1.2).

15. *Toyota Production System 2*, Toyota Motor Corporation, June 1984, p. 52.

16. Monden, p. 144.

17. Monden, p. 145.

18. For international trends in outsourcing see Michael A. Cusumano, *The Japanese Automobile Industry: Technology & Management at Nissan & Toyota*, Harvard University Press,

Cambridge, 1985, p. 189.

19. David Kushma, "East Meets West on the Line," *Detroit Free Press*, November 2, 1986.

20. *Detroit Free Press*, December 30, 1986; Louise Kertesz, "More U.S. Hondas Due for Dealers," *Automotive News*, May 18, 1987.

21. Monden, p. 124.

22. Wolfgang Reitzle, cited in Ulrich Jurgens, Knuth Dohse, Thomas Malsch, "New Production Concepts in West German Car Plants," WZB, Berlin, December 1984, p. 5.

23. Sugimori, p. 210.

24. John Krafcik, "Learning From NUMMI," Internal Working Paper, International Motor Vehicle Program, Massachusetts Institute of Technology, September 15, 1986.

25. *Manufacturing Week*, August 3, 1987.

26. L.S. Sklar and H. Anisman, "Stress and Coping Factors Influence Tumor Growth," *Science*, August 3, 1979. pp. 513-515.

27. R. Sapolsky, Glucocorticoids and Hippocampal Degeneration, Abs., 69th Annual Meeting of the Endocrine Society, Indianapolis, June 1987, p. 9.

28. Communications Workers of America, *Occupational Stress: The Hazard and the Challenge*, Instructor's Manual, 1986; National Institute for Occupational Safety and Health, U.S. Department of Health and Human Services, *Stress Management in Work Settings*, May 1987.

29. "Jobs Where Stress is Most Severe: Interview with Robert Karasek," *U.S. News and World Report*, September 5, 1983; *Also* Lee Shore, "Occupational Stress: A Union Based Approach," Institute for Labor and Mental Health, Oakland, California;
Also John Holt, "Occupational Stress," in Leo Goldberger and Shlomo Breznitz, *Handbook of Stress*, The Free Press, New York, 1982.

30. *Psychology Today*, January 1979.

31. Jeff Stansbury, "NUMMI, a New Kind of Workplace," *UAW Solidarity*, August 1985.

32. John Junkerman, "Nissan, Tennessee," *The Progressive*, June 1987. This expression or a variation is also used at the NUMMI and Mazda plants.

33. Monden, p. 131.

34. Louise Kertesz, "Team Concept Makes Mazda Flat Rock a Different Plant," *Automotive News*, February 29, 1988, p. 36.

Working Smart:
A Union Guide to Participation Programs and Reengineering
Labor Notes • 7435 Michigan Ave. • Detroit, MI 48210 • (313) 842-6262

Chapter 5

Standardized Work: Time-Study with a Vengeance

Under management-by-stress, work is standardized so that every second of a worker's time is spelled out and accounted for. Workers learn to time-study each other and are encouraged to submit suggestions for streamlining their work further. Decisions on work design and changes, however, remain with management.

IN EVALUATING THE MODERN workplace, it is easy to look at the frills instead of the essence. Workers may get to park and eat alongside their supervisors. Management may call workers "associates," in tones of respect. Team meetings may be stimulating sessions. All of these things can affect how workers feel about their jobs and themselves.

But team meetings last only a half hour per week. Ultimately any work organization system must be judged on what workers actually do during the eight to ten hours per day, five to seven days per week, that they spend working.

In traditional auto plants most production workers are paced by machines. The assembly line is the clearest example, but increasingly automation determines the pace of all kinds of machines and their human operators. Management time-study experts analyze each job and instruct the operator on what actions to take. Management is constantly looking for ways to correct the workers' motions or the physical arrangement of the machines to require less operator time, resulting in either the operator doing more jobs or the same number of jobs at a faster pace. The time-study approach is commonly identified with Frederick Taylor and "scientific management." When it is combined with mass production and machine pacing many observers refer to it as "Fordism."

A big misconception about the team concept is that it represents an alternative to telling workers every move to make.[1] The media image is that management relinquishes control to workers, who plan their own jobs. By getting rid of narrow classifications and using job rotation, work is organized around workers' brains, we are told, rather than their arms and legs. Workers can use their "creative and managerial" skills, according to GM advertisements. Workers now consider their labor a craft.[2]

If we look at the two team concept plants being used as the model for the rest of industry, NUMMI and Mazda, we find no repudiation of Taylorism or Fordism. Instead there is an intensification of both in these management-by-stress plants. In fact, the specific methods used under management-by-stress are not new. What is new is that management now wants workers to cooperate in the use of old methods.

In this chapter we will describe the methods used at NUMMI, Mazda, and the General Motors Fairfax II plant in Kansas. NUMMI and Mazda use Japanese terms for various problems and processes. Fairfax relies on U.S. industrial engineering jargon.

STANDARDIZED WORK

In all three plants the end result is a "standardized work sheet." The job functions are broken down into "transferable work components," as they are called at Fairfax. Such a component is defined as the smallest practical combination of "acts" that can be transferred from one worker to another.

For example, installing a piece of trim would be a transferable work component. It might include three acts: getting the trim, applying the glue, and pressing the trim into place. It would probably not make sense to assign these three acts to different people. But the whole task of installing the trim could readily be shifted from one worker to another.

For each worker, two, three or four "transferable work components" make up the total job.

LINE BALANCING

One of the reasons management wants to specify every motion and operation is to make it easy to rearrange job assignments, or rebalance the line. If the line speed is cut because sales are slow, it becomes possible to remove one worker and shift her operations to the remaining operators. If ways are found to cut out specific operations, the remaining operations can be shifted around so that a worker is eliminated. The philosophy of management-by-stress plants is explicit. The goal is *not* to ensure that work is evenly distributed among all workers at all times. Rather it is to try to organize the work so that as many operators as possible are working every second of the *takt* time (time that the car is at each operator's station). If this leaves one operator with little to do temporarily, that is okay, because the obvious idle time will serve as a motivation to eliminate her job altogether.

The ability to shift operations around in this manner requires both a "multi-functional" workforce and a physical arrangement which puts jobs very near each other. One approach is mixing off-line subassembly operations with assembly line jobs.

A similar approach is to use U-shaped lines, as illustrated.

Just-in-time applied to machining operations requires reducing the time that parts spend waiting for their next operation. Consider a situation where an engine part requires work by four different machines, say a cutter, a rough grinder, a boring machine, and a finish grinder. Assume each worker, being multifunctional, can operate all four machines. There are four of each machine. A traditional layout would assign a different worker to operate all four cutters or all four grinders, etc.

But such a layout would not allow management to vary the number of parts produced without causing idle time. If the production quota is cut 25 percent, then all four workers are idle 25 percent of the time (or additional work of some sort must be found for them).

A more ideal layout would be to have four operators each operate four different machines. One advantage is that there is no accumulation of parts between stations—a definite just-in-time plus. Also, if production is reduced by 25 percent, it is a simple matter to remove worker A while keeping the others working with no idle time. If the reduction is by ten percent, then it is only necessary to find additional tasks for one of the workers, rather than all four.

WHO DESIGNS THE JOBS?

One of the most prevalent myths about team concept plants is that team members get to design their own jobs. In fact, jobs are defined long before most operators are assigned to them. At Fairfax jobs are designed by the group leaders and team leaders, who themselves work within very restricted conditions. The technology, layout of the line, and product design have already been determined. And additional conditions are imposed:

> The primary task presented to Group and Team Leaders is that given various job functions and a pre-determined amount of manpower to complete these functions, [to] assign jobs to operators in such a way as to create a balanced and efficient operation.[4]

The initial "transferable job components" and the standard time allotted to each are not even devised at the plant itself but come from corporate headquarters. The times attached may be modified by the local industrial engineer or the group leader, however.

The group and team leaders write up initial job descriptions. They then run these through a computer to check for balance. The leaders then fill out several reports, draw up flow diagrams of each job, create transparencies for use in instructing the operators, and assign the operators.

Now the operators get involved:

> When the Group and Team Leaders have decided on a final operation layout and all operator assignments appear to be functioning properly, each operator should then complete a manual describing his operation in detail. This is done so that any worker previously unfamiliar with the operator's

ACT BREAKDOWN

Study File No. __A469__ Date __7-29__
Oper. Name-Equip. Description __Gas Tank__
__Solder Machine Auto Apply Solder__

Tools Used __Solder Pot Brush__

Standard Time __.80 Min. (48 Sec.)__
Analysis By __Mike Gonz__

Step No.	LEFT HAND			P R O	RIGHT HAND		
	DESCRIPTION	OBJECT	ACT	ACT	OBJECT	DESCRIPTION	
1	From Bench	Tank	G	G	Tank	From Bench	
2	To Fixture	Tank	P	P	Tank	To Fixture	
3		Fuel Tubes	G	G	Tank		
4	Bend Tubes For Clearance	Tubes	P		Tank	Hold	
5		Palm Button	G	G	Palm Button		
6		Palm Button	P	X P	Palm Button		
7	Wait			G	Solder Pot		
8	From Pot	Brush	G	P	Pot	Toward L. Hand	
9	To Tube	Solder	P		Pot	Hold	
10	To Pot	Brush	P		Pot	Hold	
11	Wait			P	Pot	To Holder	
12	From Bench	2nd Tank	G	G	2nd Tank	From Bench	
13	To Fixture	Tank	P	P	Tank	To Fixture	
14		Fuel Tube	G	G	Tank		
15	Bend Tubes For Clearance	Fuel Tube	P		Tank	Hold	
16		Palm Button	G	G	Palm Button		
17		Palm Button	P	X P	Palm Button		
18	Wait			G	Solder Pot		
19	From Pot	Brush	G	P	Pot	Toward L. Hand	
20	To Tube	Solder	P		Pot	Hold	
21	To Pot	Brush	P		Pot	Hold	
22	Wait			P	Pot	To Holder	
23	From Fixture	First Tank	G	G	First Tank	From Fixture	
24	To Finish Bench	Tank	P	P	Tank	To Finish Bench	

"Act Breakdown Analysis" sheet from Fairfax II. This is part of a training example describing how to eliminate waiting periods.[3]

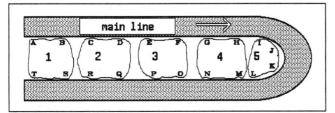

Subassembly jobs mixed with line jobs. Each letter represents one transferable work component and each circled area represents one operator's total job. Instead of speeding up the line, work can be sped up by withdrawing one of the workers in diagram #1 and redistributing the work components to those remaining, as illustrated in diagram #2.

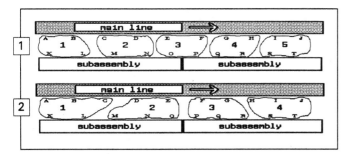

U-shaped assembly operations allow easier rebalancing.

particular assignment would gain a relatively good understanding of the work assignment by reading the manual.[5]

At NUMMI, Production Control establishes a target time for each operation. The procedure is in the union contract: "Team Leaders and Group Leaders discuss and develop each suggested standardized work. The Manager approves the suggested standardized work.[6]

FINE-TUNING THE SYSTEM

Once the basic system has been put in place and is operating, workers are encouraged to make suggestions to improve the system. Here is where management-by-stress differs from Taylorism. For Taylor, it was the job of the industrial engineer to continue studying time and methods to make work more efficient and reduce required labor time. Management-by-stress, on the other hand, shifts responsibility for this kind of industrial engineering work to the group leader, the level of management closest to the production process, although he or she does not have formal training in it. Management-by-stress also includes both inducements and pressures to get workers to help time-study themselves (see chapters 4 and 8).

Involving workers in self-time-study can generate many suggestions valuable to the company. At least at the beginning, it also helps give workers the illusion that they have some say over their jobs. The idea is that they will then offer less resistance when the leaders continually rebalance the lines.

The Fairfax manual explains:

> Once a team's operation is well under way and functioning, it still is subject to review and testing...Constant improvement in team operations is the direct responsibility of Group and Team Leaders. They should encourage sugges-

tions from Team Members to enlist better and more efficient production practices.[7]

But workers' involvement is only in the form of suggestions. The decisions are to be made by the group leader. A worker is never to simply try a slightly different way of doing things to make work more comfortable, or move an item to make work more efficient. All the manuals stress this. A Mazda training manual explains:

> For all work we perform in the workshop, a work procedure sheet has been provided....If the operator changes the work procedure at his discretion, he may put the processes before and after that process in jeopardy, or increase the cost though the quality is improved. Therefore the operator should always observe the specified work procedure sheet faithfully. If you have any doubts, you may propose a change to the team leader and should never change the work procedure at your discretion.[8]

Another Mazda manual is quite specific: "Team members do not on their own judgment decide on different locations for parts other than the counts and locations already established.[9]

At NUMMI standardized work charts are supposed to be posted at each work site "so that the supervisors can regularly check the actual work against the standardized work.[10] Note that here the supervisor is not checking to see that the *results* are as specified. The supervisor is policing to make sure that the job is being performed exactly the same as the written instructions.

There is some worker resistance to such an inflexible system, as there is on every rigid assembly line. Even the most elementary preferences can put a worker at odds with the system: someone with a sore shoulder might prefer to take more steps and have less distance to reach, for example. And most would like to find ways to shave their operations to create more breathing space. The degree to which workers can get away with varying from the standardized work sheet depends in part on whether the team leader identifies with management and whether the union will back the worker.

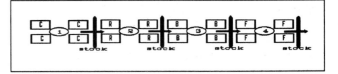

In a traditional layout, each operator, represented by circled numbers, operates only one type of machine.

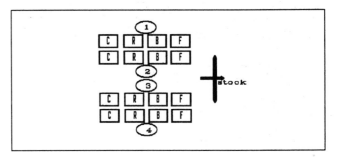

In the preferred layout, each operator operates four different machines plus possibly jobs in the adjoining area.

TIME AND MOTION STUDY

The time-study techniques used in management-by-stress plants are not new. Management teaches workers time-study, including the use of the stopwatch and various recording techniques. Mazda video tapes workers as they work so that they can analyze their own motions.

One of the key questions in time-study is how to establish a standard time for an operation, since people differ in how they do things and in their natural pace of work. The UAW-Ford contract specifies that

> Such production standards shall be fair and equitable and shall be set on the basis of normal working conditions, the quality of workmanship, and the normal working capacities of normal experienced operators, with due consideration to fatigue and the need for "personal" time.[11]

Compare this to the assumptions used at the Fairfax plant: "Operator performance is always 100%. No learning or fatigue effects are considered.[12]

But what about the problem of determining who is the "normal" operator? The Fairfax plant uses GM's usual method: in order to set the standard for how long the job must take to complete, the time-studier multiplies the actual time he measures as he observes the worker by another figure—an "operator performance rating" which can range from zero to one hundred percent. In other words, the expert judges how much effort the operator is putting out as compared to some "standard" worker in the time-studier's mind. The expertise to arrive at this percentage is, we are told, "accomplished after years of experience in time-study... [and is] a very subjective process because the analyst must judge the operator's speed.[13]

Thus the supposed science of time-study is reduced to one management-paid expert's judgment of how fast someone else should be working. This is one of the reasons that unions have long fought to put restrictions on time-study.

NUMMI establishes work standards by choosing as the "normal" operator an experienced worker who likely aspires to management. Again, this is written into the contract:

> Time-study on a pilot vehicle: Group Leader and Team leader evaluate each suggested standardized work [suggested by Production Control] by having a Team Leader who does not always work on the actual operation try it out.[14]

Time-study training shows how management uses numbers to give the appearance of science to what is actually the time-study expert's subjective judgment about what is a reasonable amount of work. The Fairfax training, for example, includes precise details on the operation of the stopwatch to record the smallest work elements to the nearest hundredth of a minute. It goes on to explain how to make this measurement more accurate by averaging it out over many operations.

Mazda provides video tapes of what management considers a normal, fast, and slow work pace for use as standards. Workers training in time-study watch the video tapes and record their own ratings. They then compare their ratings of the taped workers to management's (called the "actual ratings"). Workers practice with the video tapes until their ratings approximate the "actual."

So this is science; how can anyone object to it? Picture yourself as the scientific worker studying another worker. You time a job very carefully, taking many samples under many different conditions. You average them out and come up with the precise figure of .55 minute for the time it takes to complete the job. Then you need an "operator performance rating." You say to yourself:

> Let's see, when I was training with the video tapes I was always rating too high. I'd better put down something on the low side. Shall I give him a 50 percent rating or an 80 percent? Let's split it down the middle and give him a 65 percent.

So you multiply your very precise .55 by your thoroughly subjective .65, and come up with a "scientific" .35 minutes (or 21 seconds) as the standard time for this job.

Although the standard work time includes a large component of subjective judgment, it is difficult to challenge it. The group leader is the lowest level with authority to adjust a standard. Since both the group leaders and the team leaders participated in establishing the standard they are likely to defend it. Since workers are "multifunctional" and many can be assigned to any job, it is likely that management can find a worker who will do the job (at whatever the cost to his popularity with his fellow workers).

Management's desire for interchangeable workers does limit the top pace that it can establish as "standard." The work standard has to be do-able by most of the workers who might be assigned to a particular job. Taking this into account, the end result is a still a very fast pace. Those who can't keep up use their break time to catch up, or they are forced to quit.

In traditional Big Three plants, disputes over work standards, including the pace of the line and the number of operations required of an operator, can be taken to the grievance procedure. Since they are not covered by arbitration, these issues are also strikable during the term of the contract.

At NUMMI, on the other hand, "problems" with standardized work are taken through their own special procedure and are not strikable. Each step in the procedure is ruled upon by a joint company/union committee, presumably operating by consensus. While the contract language is vague, it would appear that unless a higher level of management was willing to reverse a lower level's decision, that lower level's specifications for what is "standard" would hold.

TIPS FOR EFFICIENT WORK

All the training programs contain many tips for making work easier and faster. The idea is to eliminate all forms of "waste," which is broadly defined to include anything that lowers productivity (see box on "The Three Evil M's").

One tip from Mazda management is to reduce the

The Three Evil M's

Muda: Waste. The Mazda manual gives some examples:

"Waiting *muda*: if you are standing in front of your machine doing nothing, you yourself are not gaining respect as a human being. And, moreover, because this results in higher costs of the car, the customer will not buy the car."

"Operational *muda*: If you are walking around looking for a component or tool, time is being wasted."

"Conveyance *muda:* If you move components from a large pallet to a small pallet, and then from that to the workbench, this piling and re-piling is eventually becoming an increase in costs."

Other forms of MUDA include inferior goods production, over-production, and too much inventory.

Mura: "Irregular or inconsistent use of a person or a machine in such a way as to cause inconsistent results. For example, making two trips carrying two boxes the first time and four boxes the second, not doing the job continuously the same way."

Muri: "Working a person, machine, or tool beyond capacity."[15]

number of hand motions by using the feet. An example is foot-operated electrical switches to start the machine moving. "Not that you must constantly use your feet, but it is worthwhile to consider if you can freely use your feet."[16]

Building a special fixture to hold the parts may make an assembly operation quicker. Redesigning a tool or hanging a tool from overhead with a counterweight may make a job easier. Rearranging the work may reduce walking by five steps per operation. Five steps per operation, of the size specified at Fairfax of 2.5 feet/step, add up to more than a mile per day. Management encourages ideas like these. But again, we need to remember the context:

1. Once lines are up to full speed there is normally no time during regular work to engage in even the most minor experiments.

2. Whatever ideas an operator may have are supposed to be approved by a supervisor before they are tried out, and approved again before they are adopted.

3. Standardized work is just that. In theory there is no room for operators on different shifts doing the same job to do it slightly differently from the standard or from each other.

4. While it may be called "working smarter, not harder" to eliminate five walking steps from an operation, the savings do not go to the operator in the form of some breathing space. Management will fill up the time saved by providing the operator with another operation. For management, the question whether this productive operation is harder on the worker than walking the five steps is not an issue.

★   ★   ★

See chapter 8 for some recent examples of standardized work.

Notes

1. See for example the editorial in *Business Week*, August 31, 1987.

2. Ad in *Business Week*, April 20, 1987.

3. *Fairfax Industrial Engineering Training Program: Team Leader/Group Leader Edition*, General Motors Fairfax, Kansas plant, no date (about 1986), chapter 4, p. 14.

4. Fairfax...Training Program, Chapter 10, p. 1.

5. Fairfax...Training Program, Chapter 10, p. 3.

6. Contract dated July 1, 1985, Appendix C.

7. *Fairfax ...Training Program*, Chapter 10, p. 3.

8. *Quality Control In Which All Employees Will Participate In and Help Advance*, Mazda, 1986, p. 20.

9. *MMUC Production System: Concept and Outline*, Mazda, 1986, p. 17.

10. *Toyota Production System 2*, Toyota Motor Corporation, manual used in NUMMI training, June 1984, p. 35.

11. *Agreements Between the UAW and Ford Motor Company*, Volume 1, 1987, p. 18.

12. *Fairfax...Training Program*, Chapter 8, p. 1.

13. *Fairfax...Training Program*, Chapter 6, p. 7.

14. Contract dated July 1, 1985, Appendix C.

15. *Kaizen Simulation*, Mazda Motor Manufacturing (USA) Corporation, no date (about 1986), p. VI-2.

16. *Kaizen Simulation*, p. V-12.

Working Smart:
A Union Guide to Participation Programs and Reengineering
Labor Notes • 7435 Michigan Ave. • Detroit, MI 48210 • (313) 842-6262

Chapter 6

NUMMI: First Model of Management-by-Stress

Because of its high productivity and quality, the NUMMI plant became a model for the rest of industry, both auto and others. The plant embodied the principles of management-by-stress: one classification for production workers; no absentee replacements; heavy workload including both on-line and off-line work; no more "good jobs"; appointed team leaders; little union control and no right to strike over work standards; management flexibility (favoritism); little union presence. Management's commitment to avoid layoffs made the workforce willing to put up with conditions they would not have tolerated when they were General Motors workers.

TATSURO TOYODA, PRESIDENT OF NEW UNITED MOTORS MANUFACTURING INC. and grandson of the founder of the Toyota Corporation, addressed 1,200 production workers at the dedication of the NUMMI plant on April 4, 1985. During his ten-minute speech, Toyoda was interrupted seven times by loud applause, cheers, and shouts of *"Itchi bon!"*—Japanese for "We're number one!"[1]

NUMMI is a joint venture of General Motors and Toyota. The new corporation operates an assembly plant in Fremont, California which was shut down by GM in 1982. GM claimed that the Fremont plant was unprofitable, but it was reopened two years later employing many of the former Fremont workers and using much of the old GM layout and track.

In its first two years of operation NUMMI had such high productivity and quality figures that the plant became the model for the rest of the U.S. auto industry. Here we take a look at the operation of the plant.

The NUMMI plant is strikingly clean. No coffee cups, newspapers, cigarette butts, or fast food wrappers litter the floor. In fact, no smoking, eating, drinking, or reading are allowed except in specified break areas. All workers keep their areas clean.

"Just-in-time" (JIT) parts delivery adds to the feeling of spaciousness. Only the parts needed for a few hours are stacked by the line. Mostly these require small cartons rather than the large storage bins that clutter traditional plants.

Hourly and salaried workers and top management all use the same cafeterias and parking lots. All workers and supervisors are issued a uniform of gray pants and blue shirts; about two-thirds wear it.

The number of robots in the plant—about 170 during the first stages—is more than many older assembly plants, but short of the 300 to 400 in newer plants. NUMMI has also built a 200,000-square foot stamping plant with five press lines to directly feed the assembly line with major body panels and selected small stampings.

NUMMI takes a conservative approach to technology. It is modern, but it is not the cutting edge of technology. There are no automatic guided vehicles (AGVs); the just-in-time inventory system relies primarily on paper cards called *kanbans* rather than on bar code readers and computer terminals. Almost all the automation was designed and tested by Toyota in Japan and then shipped to the U.S. for installation. The plant sports Komatsu stamping presses, Hitachi robots, and Toyopuc programmable controllers (computers that control the lines and other automation).

The job security provisions at NUMMI have attracted much attention, although the contract stops short of providing job guarantees. It states:

> The Company agrees that it will not lay off employees unless compelled to do so by severe economic conditions that threaten the long term financial viability of the Company.
>
> The Company will take affirmative measures before laying off any employees, including such measures as, the reduction of salaries of its officers and management, assigning previously subcontracted work to bargaining unit

employees capable of performing this work, seeking voluntary layoffs, and other cost savings measures.[2]

PRODUCTIVITY AND QUALITY

As the first unionized Japanese-managed auto plant in the U.S., NUMMI has attracted much interest. This interest has been magnified by the high productivity and quality ratings the plant has achieved in only two years of operation.

NUMMI's productivity statistics are indeed impressive. A 1986 GM internal report shows that NUMMI's Nova required 21.2 hours of direct and indirect labor per car, compared to an average of 37 hours at the three GM J-body (Cavalier) assembly plants.[3] The raw figures would give NUMMI a 90 percent productivity advantage, but this figure should be reduced to account for differences in the car and in the manufacturing method. The report also broke the production process down into departments, giving the highest ranking for each department to the plant that used the least labor. NUMMI ranked first in all areas except inspection, where it ranked 14th out of 20.

A study conducted at the Massachusetts Institute of Technology compared the NUMMI plant to the GM Framingham plant, which builds the Celebrity and the Ciera. This study attempted to adjust for factors such as automation, number of welds, contractual relief time, and the size and complexity of the car. The study concluded that NUMMI has about a 50 percent productivity advantage—operations on a car that take 20 hours at NUMMI would take slightly more than 31 at Framingham. The same study found that labor productivity at NUMMI is only slightly less than at the Toyota plant in Takoara, Japan.[4]

One reason for the high productivity is NUMMI's extensive outsourcing and outside contracting. Seat cushions, for example, are made by an outside firm and delivered to the plant only hours before installation. (There are also some jobs at NUMMI which, until recently, have not been part of traditional assembly plants. For example, NUMMI does major stampings in its own highly efficient press room.)

Outside contracting substitutes for much of the indirect labor needed in the plant. NUMMI's policy is to use skilled trades workers only for preventive and minor maintenance and to contract out all major maintenance and construction. NUMMI also contracts out truck driving, landscaping, cleaning, accounting, data processing, and security. While these show as reduced labor costs for NUMMI, no figures are available to show how much this outside contracting actually reduces bottom line costs.

NUMMI has consistently achieved high quality ratings. According to the MIT study, NUMMI rated 135-140 out of a perfect 145 compared to Framingham's 125-130. On an owner satisfaction survey scaled 0-100, NUMMI scored 91-94, compared to Framingham's 85-88.

The just-in-time system contributes to quality because there are no long pipelines full of bad parts. While there are repair areas in the plant, there are very few specialized repair workers. NUMMI's technology and training are designed so that inspection is ongoing, and as many problems as possible are caught immediately. If a defect is found, it is corrected by someone from the area that did the job originally; the team leader or a team member will either follow the car down the line or go to the repair area.

NUMMI workers feel genuine pride in producing a high quality product. One NUMMI worker said, "It's nice to be at a party and know you won't be embarrassed when someone says they own a Nova."[5] Workers also hope that quality translates to job security.

In fact, NUMMI workers' concern for quality is one of the sources of their criticisms of management. Once production reached full speed and the pressure was on, many workers felt harassed when they stopped the production line, as they had been instructed to do if there was a problem. More defects began to get through. Similarly, when there was a breakdown in parts supply management was less inclined to stop the line, instead tagging the cars to have the part installed later. Around the end of 1986 normally unused areas of the plant were filled with assembled cars awaiting missing parts.

Ultimately the defect is repaired or the missing part installed, but both management and workers understand that when this happens, quality suffers. When a job is done "in station," the right tools apply the proper torque to fasteners; already installed parts do not have to be removed or forced aside. While workers insist that during this period NUMMI maintained high quality by careful inspection and repair, management was clearly back-sliding from "doing the job right the first time." The fact that management tried to maintain full production with missing parts and unsolved problems was a symbol that perhaps NUMMI was not so different from traditional U.S. auto plants after all, where "making production" justifies anything.

MANAGEMENT STRUCTURE

GM describes NUMMI as having three levels of management (with managers and assistant managers counted as one level). The lowest level supervisor, the group leader, is in charge of two to six teams, collectively called a "group." A team consists of four to eight workers plus an hourly team leader. Group leaders report directly to assistant managers of sections or departments (stamping plant, body shop, assembly, etc.). The section managers report to the general manager of manufacturing or his assistants.

While group leaders are responsible for disciplining workers, many of the other responsibilities of traditional first-level supervision are delegated to team leaders. The group leaders do much of the work of industrial engineers in traditional plants, such as enforcing and changing the work methods and work standards. Group leaders have veto rights in hiring new workers for their teams, and the group leader's assessment during probation usually determines the outcome.

Approximately 40 team meeting rooms are scattered around the plant. Each ceilingless room contains desks for the group leaders and team leaders, bulletin boards, blackboards, and tables for team meetings. Outside of the room is a bulletin board with production charts, quality charts, and absentee records.

TEAM LEADERS

Team leaders are key to the functioning of the NUMMI system. They are members of the union, but they have a number of critical supervisory responsibilities. They are carefully selected by the company. The first team leaders were chosen from hourly applicants and given an extensive orientation. They were sent to Japan for up to three weeks to learn methods there.

During this evaluation period some were screened out for having the wrong attitude. One was a black worker with 20 years and a good record at GM who was enthusiastic about the NUMMI system, but had been an active unionist and expressed doubts that U.S. workers would be willing to work as fast as their Japanese brethren.[6]

Toyota Is In Charge

The initial capital investment in NUMMI, estimated at $300 to $400 million, was split evenly between GM and Toyota. The $120 million value of the old Fremont plant was included as part of GM's share.[7] NUMMI's eight-person board of directors is evenly divided between Toyota and GM.

But the participation and interest of each of the corporate partners is very different. GM gets the right to study the plant and rotate a few managers through it. Toyota runs the plant.

Initially, General Motors assigned 16 management people to NUMMI for a three-year rotation. In 1985 two of these were on the general manager level. Already several of these NUMMI-trained managers have been distributed over the GM system to help "diffuse the process," including at the Van Nuys, California plant, the Saturn project, and the Ellesmere Port, England Vauxhall plant. GM has also established a "Technical Liaison Office" which coordinates GM contacts with NUMMI. This office has produced video tapes, training materials, and a computer database on NUMMI methods, all available to managers throughout the GM system.

The GM employees who are section managers work under a "double management system" with a "coordinator" from Toyota, who "assures that the manager's decisions fall within the guidelines of the Toyota Production System."[8]

Toyota is experimenting with NUMMI, using it to learn how to deal with American suppliers, legal structures, and workers. Many of the managers from Toyota are being trained for non-union Toyota operations in Kentucky and Ontario.

Now that the plant has reached stable operation, openings for team leaders are posted. Since one of the qualifications for the position is to be able to do all jobs on the team, applicants usually come from the team or at least the group which has the opening. Applicants must attend, on their own time, three-hour classes, two nights a week, for six weeks. The classes emphasize communication skills and use role playing for problem solving. For example, "John always comes to work with alcohol on his breath. As his team leader, what do you do?" It is common for management "assessors" to come to the classroom and observe the applicants.

The instructor's evaluation, an in-plant test on problem solving, and the group leader's evaluation determine which applicants get the team leader positions.

The team leader is paid an additional 50 cents an hour and has a range of responsibilities:

• Filling in on the line for workers who are absent, tardy, seeking medical attention, or on bathroom breaks
• Training new workers in their jobs
• Assisting workers who are having difficulty
• Keeping attendance, tardiness, and off-the-job records
• Assigning work when the line stops
• Minor maintenance and housekeeping
• Assessment of new team members
• Leading *kaizen* (continuous improvement) or quality circle sessions
• Organizing social events outside the workplace.

Many NUMMI workers say they would never want the team leader job because there are too many demands and the team leader always gets caught in the middle. As workers describe it, some team leaders serve as buffers between the workers and unreasonable management pressure. Others see the team leaders as management's spies who, in addition to gathering vital production information, are emotional gauges to assess how far the workers can be pushed. Most workers we interviewed felt that the personality and role of the team leader was the single most important factor in determining how bearable work is. As one put it; "If he's good, it'll be okay. If he's bad, you're f-----." For example, in a team that rotates regularly, a "bad" team leader will cover for an absence by taking the softest job on the team, rather than the job vacated by the absent worker.

The recruitment and training of new team leaders has become an important vehicle for management to convince a key section of the workforce to adopt its goals and implement its programs. Not only do all applicants go through the management-designed training course, they must also attempt to prove their abilities while they are still team members. According to one study, 900 workers have been through the team leader training program.[9] There is no official union input into the selection or training process.

There are usually many applicants for each team leader opening. While the company was hiring and the need for team leaders was expanding, significant numbers of workers could reasonably believe that they had a chance for advancement. But once the workforce stabilized, that hopefulness was replaced by frustration and resentment as people realized they might never achieve team leader. Many workers, including strong advocates of the team concept, expressed the view that the selection process is subject to favoritism (and in some cases union deals)—"just like it was at GM"—rather than merit. Further, as management stabilized, the team leader job became less attractive because advancement to group leader was harder.

TEAM FUNCTIONING

Team meetings are of two kinds. Team leaders hold very brief meetings at the work location just as the line is starting up to make announcements, distribute work gloves, or survey for overtime. These are similar to daily preparations in many traditional plants.

The group leader usually schedules a more formal team meeting during lunch, before work, or after work. The group leader is usually present during the meeting and turns in members' time cards for overtime pay for the length of the meeting. Occasionally, a group leader may call a team or group meeting when the line is down.

The frequency of formal meetings varies considerably. Some teams meet weekly for an hour or more. Some meet monthly, and some less than that, or on an as needed basis. Meetings occur more frequently when there are production problems to be worked out, as the line was being brought up to speed, for example, or when production of the Corolla FX16 began. Once the lines were running smoothly and the jobs were balanced, group leaders were less inclined to call meetings.

In addition, teams are encouraged to hold team-building activities after work, such as sports and parties. NUMMI's conception of teams explicitly involves building a web of personal relations among team members, the group leader, and the team leader. "P.T." (for "personal touch") guidelines are specified for team and group leaders. For example, one management hand-out lists "Facts a Group Leader Must Know" about team members:

- Is the member married?
- Does the member have children? What ages?

A NUMMI Chronology

March 1982—General Motors closes the Fremont assembly plant.

February 17, 1983—Toyota and General Motors announce plan for joint venture.

September 21, 1983—Letter of intent signed with United Auto Workers specifying that a "blending of American and Japanese production methods" will be used in the plant and that a majority of workers will be laid-off GM Fremont workers.

March 30, 1984—Former Fremont workers invited to start application process.

December 10, 1984—First Chevrolet Nova rolls off production line.

June 25, 1985—First three-year contract signed. Contract endorses production system, including commitments to team concept and continuous improvement process, and includes job security. Wages equal or exceed those in Big Three contracts.

December 1985—Second shift in operation, plant now fully staffed, with about 2,200 UAW members.

April 1986—Line running at full speed.

January 1987—Stories about problems at NUMMI begin appearing in press.

December 1987—Continued Nova sales slump. Line speed cut to a low of 45 per hour. No layoffs.

June 1988—Close union elections following a bitter campaign. Incumbents charge that People's Caucus victory would cause plant to close. Incumbent Administration Caucus maintains presidency and shop chair (5 of 7 top union positions). People's Caucus wins heavily among district committeepersons and union coordinators.

April 1989—Toyota announces it will install new truck line at NUMMI.

June 1991—Close elections, again following a bitter campaign with same themes. People's Caucus wins a majority on executive board and bargaining committee. This causes considerable concern within UAW and Toyota, which calls Human Relations VP Bill Childs to Japan to explain. But People's Caucus winning candidate for President, Charlie Curry, goes over to Administration Caucus, returning majority of both committees to that group.

1992-1993—Major dispute over company's desire for Alternative Work Schedule (3 shifts, 10-hour day, 4-day week). Although most of union leadership supports plan, membership votes it down overwhelmingly in June 1993. Union leaders campaign for revote, implying Toyota might pull out and assuring members that AWS would be only for volunteers in Stamping and Plastics Parts sections. Revote gives union leaders permission to discuss AWS at table.

January 1993—Cal-OSHA cites NUMMI for extensive ergonomic hazards.

June 1994—Close elections again; same theme. Administration Caucus wins majority of leadership bodies. But People's Caucus leader Richard Aguilar defeats long-time Shop Chair George Nano.

August 1994—Brief strike; company informs members how to resign from union and cross picket lines. Union defeats AWS and company demands on breaks and attendance penalties. But economic take-aways patterned after Big Three cause membership dissatisfaction. Contract ratified by 60 percent.

- Birthday
- Anniversary
- Hobbies
- Work experience
- Other interests.[10]

Team members are encouraged to help each other deal with personal problems.[11]

Every six months, the company provides each group with P.T. funding—$15 per member—for use in whatever after-work activity the group chooses (subject to group leader approval). Common activities are pizza and beer parties or Mexican dinners.

JOB ROTATION

Management's stated desire is for each worker to learn all the jobs in the plant. The most obvious advantage for management is that it can then easily shift workers in response to production problems, or to handle changes in production quantities and mix. Management claims other benefits from rotation as well. First, rotation allows workers to have a thorough understanding of the whole plant, to see how their job fits with other operations and how a mistake in one place can affect a job elsewhere. Also, by knowing many operations a worker will more likely notice defects in other jobs and call attention to them.

Furthermore, rotation is supposed to be the antidote to alienation. One group leader explained:

> Now we are multi-functional—we no longer feel like robots doing the same thing over and over again. We do many things...fixing our own machinery, quality of the car, working out problems between team members. Now we do everything as a team.[12]

The amount of actual job rotation varies considerably from team to team. When the line started up, management seemed to favor a six-month rotation so that the job would not always be done by a novice. Management clearly wants every worker to be able to do all the jobs in the team and, if possible, the group. Management does not seem to favor any more rotation than necessary to accomplish this.

Decisions about rotation are generally left to the group leader, although some teams have successfully exerted pressure to change the rotation time period. Most teams rotate jobs on a monthly or weekly basis. A few teams rotate within a shift. In one case—installing seats—the team rotates every two hours because the job is so physically wearing.

Management expects all production workers to be "multi-functional." There is no pay-for-knowledge. Under the 1985 contract, after 18 months all production workers make a base rate of $13.28 per hour plus cost of living and shift premiums. This is 10 to 30 cents higher than assembler wages at traditional GM plants and roughly the same as GM's other team concept plants.

STANDARDIZED WORK ON A FAST LINE

When a new model is introduced at NUMMI, group leaders and team leaders break tasks down to the smallest possible units and enter them on "standardized work" charts. The charting is refined when production starts, and suggestions from team members are considered. When the line is up to speed, it is "balanced" so that every worker is fully utilized. If there are eight workers on a team and each has about 15 percent idle time, one worker can be removed and the tasks divided among the remaining seven. But the system depends on workers being "multi-functional" or "interchangeable" so that tasks can be shifted without causing problems in production. Standardized work procedures are described in Chapter 5.

One result of standardized work is that NUMMI has eliminated virtually every job that production workers traditionally have regarded as easy, good, or preferred. Because job balancing often mixes on-line and off-line work, there are few specialized jobs. Many jobs considered highly desirable, like landscaping, are contracted out.

Custodial jobs in other auto plants are usually considered desirable. Although they pay slightly less than other jobs, there is less pressure, and workers can pace themselves. Many workers bid for cleaning jobs as they grow older or develop physical difficulties. NUMMI has eliminated custodial jobs as a category. Some cleaning tasks are done by production workers when the line has stopped. Others are done by outside contractors which pay their workers several dollars per hour less than NUMMI.

In most plants, material handling is a desirable job because it is not paced by the assembly line. But at NUMMI, just-in-time has changed that. Steve Bera, a production control supervisor, explained the change from a management perspective:

> The best job used to be material handling. Because what did you do when you walked in the morning. The first thing you do...is stop at the newspaper stand and pick up a paper, right? Then you get on your truck and you scout the line and you look for a place to stack material. And you put on eight hours, 16 hours, if you could put on 16 *days* of material you would do it— because what's the next thing you do when you stack the line? You went to the satellite area, got a coffee, and you read your newspaper and you didn't have to do anything anymore.
>
> What does this plant do? Every 60 minutes we are stocking the line. The people who are in material handling now—they are working eight hours a day.[13]

A good job in stamping plants is metal finishing, which entails repairing imperfections, dents and dings in parts that will go on the outside of the car. At NUMMI, metal finishing is only one of the many duties of a press operator. The list includes:

- Inspecting quality of finished parts
- Doing minor maintenance
- Housekeeping the area
- Participating in changing dies
- Ordering of dies and blanks

- Metal finishing of defective panels
- Keeping production records.

In most traditional plants inspection jobs are highly desirable, but at NUMMI the workload for inspectors has increased dramatically. Arlene Diamond explained:

> We work hard, we sweat, it's very physical. We are not lifting anything except for our pens, but there is a lot of bending, a lot of pulling, a lot of testing, a lot of reclining [testing seat backs] and then sit-ups.
>
> It's not easy any more; it's not what it used to be. When we were starting up, people would put in requests for transfer to inspection. They would come down and watch us work, and they would withdraw their transfer request. They thought they could get something easy, and it's just not...
>
> Now there are very few transfers to get into our department.

In 59 seconds, inspector Richard Aguilar has to get in and out of the car and check to make sure each contains the items specified on a form for that particular car. Each item is also checked to see that it operates correctly. The list includes checking the headlights, high beams, turn signals, back lights, side marker lights, parking lights, radio, speakers, heater, air conditioner, dome lights, air ducts, steering wheel, console, dash, shift lever, the upholstery for its color, cleanliness, tightness, and damage, the headliner for its tightness and damage, and the garnishes (moldings which cover joints).

It is possible to do these jobs. They may not even look difficult to the touring visitor who has never worked in a factory. But keeping up this kind of job, car after car, day after day, takes its toll when you are at your best, let alone when you are feeling slightly ill or worried or have missed a good night's sleep. One worker says that a cold requiring him to blow his nose regularly puts him too far behind to catch up.

Because most assembly line jobs are so demanding in traditional auto plants, workers look to the off-line desirable jobs as a form of job security. If they cannot keep up the pace when they get older, they can hope that they will have enough seniority to select a job that matches their capabilities. At NUMMI, these jobs do not exist. Because the jobs are so difficult and require so much stamina, many NUMMI workers wonder how they will make it when they grow older.

ABSENTEEISM

One of the reasons that NUMMI achieves such high productivity is because of the heavy pressure on workers to be punctual and to achieve perfect attendance. In traditional plants, workers are expected to be on the job at starting time, but the job may be five minutes away from the time clock. A worker who is occasionally late to the job but has punched in on time usually is not penalized financially, although the supervisor will not be pleased. At NUMMI there is no need for time clocks. At starting time, workers are expected to be at their work stations, in work clothes, optional exercises completed, ready for the line to start. The team leader keeps lateness and absence records.

In traditional plants, at the end of the day workers line up at the time clock, waiting to punch out. At NUMMI, there is no clean-up time. The line runs until the last minute. If a worker is in the middle of a job when the line stops, the job must be finished.

GM claimed that one of the problems in its Fremont plant was that during lunch, particularly on payday, workers would go out to their cars or to local bars or decide to celebrate a nice day. They would return late or not at all. NUMMI has solved this problem by paying workers for an extra half-hour for their lunch period. Workers are permitted to leave the plant at lunch time, but if they do, even to go to the parking lot, they lose the extra pay. In addition, the gates closest to the parking lot are locked so that anyone who leaves has to go the long way around through the guarded main gate.

Applicants at NUMMI are carefully screened for poor attendance records. Although they had access to GM's records, NUMMI required all applicants to fill out forms explaining their absences while working at GM.

If a worker is late or leaves early, the group leader talks to him or her and gives a written warning (which does not go on the record). If this happens three times in 45 days it constitutes an offense on the worker's company record. Four such offenses in one year, and the worker is fired.

NUMMI has what it likes to call a "no-fault" absence policy—all absences except those contractually allowable (bereavement, military, jury duty, vacation, and approved leaves) are counted in the disciplinary procedure. Personal illness or illness in the family is not an allowable reason for absence. Normally a three-day absence counts as three separate absences, but if the company accepts the employee's doctor's note, it is only counted as one. Approved leaves may be granted for extended illnesses. Three absences in a 90-day period equal an "offense." Four offenses in one year result in firing.

There are additional offenses related to absence. These include failure to report an absence at least 60 minutes before the start of the shift (twice in 90 days equals an offense) and failure to report an absence before start of the shift (one offense each time). Any combination of four tardy or absence offenses also results in firing. A GM official estimates that two to four NUMMI workers are discharged for absenteeism each month.[14]

A worker who has more than ten days of unallowable absences in a year forfeits 20 percent of vacation time. A year's perfect attendance yields one bonus vacation day.

Team and group leaders have considerable discretion in dealing with both tardiness and absenteeism. Team leaders fill in for tardy workers. If a favored worker arrives late, the team leader, who also keeps the time records, need say nothing. Similarly, while the "no-fault" absentee policy is usually strictly enforced, the system allows the group leader the flexibility to grant retroactive leaves. This flexibility can be extremely powerful given the heavy emphasis upper management places on absenteeism and tardiness. Many workers complain of favoritism.

To generate peer pressure against absenteeism, management has waged an intensive ideological campaign about how fellow team members are hurt by it. Absence records are displayed prominently on the bulletin board outside each team room: yellow for vacation, orange for emergency, and red for no excuse. A worker must fill out a special explanation form for every absence, with copies to the group leader's and department manager's files. Explanations for absenteeism may be discussed at team meetings. The union has participated in maintaining peer pressure; issues of the union newspaper have devoted one-fourth of their space to recognition of those with perfect attendance, complete with pictures.

But the most effective pressure against absence is the way the jobs are structured. There are no regular absentee replacement workers, so the team leader usually fills in for an absent worker. But the team leader is supposed to be responsible for other relief and assistance, so one person's absence makes all team members' lives more difficult—because management has organized it that way.

All of these factors—the hiring process, strict enforcement of rules, public visibility of any absence, and peer pressure—have reduced NUMMI's absenteeism to exceptionally low levels. In 1985 management claimed to have only 1.5 percent absenteeism.[15] This figure is remarkably low. It means that workers miss on the average only three days per year due to illness or any other "unallowed" reason. More recently management uses a figure of about two percent.

One might think that with such a low rate, absenteeism would hardly affect working conditions. But because management runs the system so tightly, even a few absentees produce enormous pressure. The absentee replacement policy has become a major issue; many workers want it changed. In February and March 1986 more than a thousand workers signed a petition:

> We, as concerned New United Motors Team Members, are requesting to Human Resources and the UAW to help us solve the absentee problem we are currently experiencing.
>
> If it means that we must redesign our attendance policy in order to effectively resolve this problem, and assure quality and job security, let's not hesitate to do so.
>
> The burden placed on our teams, due to absenteeism, is an unnecessary one.

Workers who circulated and signed the petition believed that they were politely asking for management to provide replacement workers, at least for long term absences. Instead, the company and the union established an hourly Attendance Coordinator who mainly counsels absentees on overcoming *their* problems.

When the line speed was decreased in the summer of 1986, the pressure caused by absenteeism declined. A decrease in line speed and a cut in the number of workers on the line should not affect how hard each individual's job is, since "rebalancing" will increase the number of tasks each worker must do. But it does makes a difference in the overall pressure level. First, there is still one team leader per team. If the size of the team is reduced, then the relief and assistance provided by the leader for each

member is increased. Secondly, since there are now "excess" workers, management is willing to use them as replacements for those on leaves of absence.

In the fall of 1986 the pressure built again because of higher line speeds, compounded by the introduction of a new model, parts delivery problems and quality problems. The company refused to hire additional people, instead relying on overtime and using team and even group leaders to work the line. Some team leaders worked line jobs continuously for weeks at a time to substitute for workers on personal leaves.

In the spring of 1987 poor sales of the Nova caused management to drop the line speed again. The sales slump continued throughout that year, and line speed was eventually reduced to about 45 per hour. While the no-layoff policy was maintained, management also refused to allow reduction of workloads. Instead teams were rebalanced and the "excess" workers were assigned to training programs (one-day training in problem solving) and to special project *kaizen* teams. Some *kaizen* teams prepared for the 1989 model. Others were assigned to observe and *kaizen* those still working on the line. Still others appeared to be doing nothing but wandering around the plant. Needless to say, those still working at full production pace felt some resentment towards those who got the soft jobs.

SKILLED TRADES

NUMMI has two skilled trades classifications: about 200 workers are "general maintenance" and about 25 are "tool and die," who work mainly in the stamping area. Those tool and die tradespeople who qualify as "die-try-out" receive an additional 40 cents per hour.

General maintenance workers are supposed to be able to do all jobs, but they are often known and assigned by their "strong points," that is, as electricians, pipefitters, millwrights, etc. Roughly every six weeks maintenance workers go for a two-week, two hours per day cross-training course to learn another trade. Gradually the "strong points" shift; a tradesperson will be considered an electrician, for example, when he or she understands and can adjust the Toyopuc programmable controllers used on most of the automation.

Maintenance forces are kept small and busy. In the entire assembly area, the maintenance group on one shift consists of 22 tradespeople, three team leaders, a group leader and a clerk dispatcher (a salaried clerk-typist job). Lights on a master console track the six main lines. When a light indicates a problem, such as a stopped assembly line, the clerk or a leader dispatches a maintenance team immediately. The first defense against breakdowns is two mobile maintenance vehicles, each staffed by one electrician and one pipefitter or millwright. The clerk can call the maintenance shop for additional help if required.

The organization of maintenance is one area that poses contradictions for the NUMMI system. Management tries to eliminate idle time by assigning maintenance workers to preventive maintenance (PM) programs. But management's aversion to idle time can be counterproductive. When a major breakdown occurs, maintenance workers may not be immediately available. Large numbers of production workers stand idle, and the problem is compounded by just-in-time. The pressure to get the line started up again is enormous.

NUMMI also wants maintenance workers to take initiative "above and beyond" to get things moving. Often speedy repairs or efficient maintenance require a tradesperson to work through a scheduled break. But if the worker tries to make up the break during a non-scheduled time, a supervisor— trained to see red at any idle time—may try to assign other work or initiate disciplinary action.

As a result management vacillates between regularizing preventive maintenance and finding ways to have maintenance people available at the first instance of trouble—without, of course, increasing the number of skilled workers. The very slow production during 1987 and into 1988 provided a temporary solution: assign all preventive maintenance to the graveyard shift and absorb idle time during other shifts with special projects. But the dilemma will resurface once production returns to capacity. The same problem exists in traditional plants, but it is intensified at NUMMI because of just-in-time and management's zealous ethic about idle time.

NUMMI management is trying to get tighter control over maintenance by keeping track of how long jobs take. The time that the line stops and starts is automatically logged on chart recorders, and the time that maintenance workers are dispatched is noted. Some maintenance teams have posted charts indicating the measures taken and the length of time to correct each breakdown.

Many NUMMI maintenance workers, particularly those who did not previously work for GM, like the single classification system. "If your field is a wide field you just learn more," one said. Some point to the satisfaction of being able to complete an entire job. Those who worked at GM are most critical of this system and believe that their crafts are being destroyed—"Jack of all trades, master of none."

Through cross-training, NUMMI maintenance workers are definitely learning skills that they would not in a traditional classification system. At the same time, the range and depth of skills within particular trades is more limited. Few tradespeople get experience in major construction or major repairs since these jobs are contracted out. Repair of most electronic equipment is taught at the level of "board swapping." Training barely touches on board repair or circuit analysis. Few electricians know how to use an oscilloscope.

UNION STRUCTURE

The contract provides for an in-plant union structure with a full-time chairperson, five district committeepersons on the day shift, and three to five on the night shift. There is no separate skilled trades representative.

Four hourly employees appointed by the International Union are assigned to the company Human Resources Department to work in health and safety, benefits, employee assistance, and apprentice/cross-training. In 1986 the union and company established a union attendance coordinator.

The "union coordinator" is the first level of union representation in the plant. The contract specifies one coordinator for every two groups (each group consisting of those teams under a group leader), but the practice seems to be one coordinator for each group leader.

Union coordinators are elected in in-plant elections every three years. They work full-time at production jobs and get an additional two hours pay per week from the company.

At most auto plants, union representatives deal with problems during regular working hours, but NUMMI's union coordinators are expected to handle all union business on lunch time, breaks, or before and after work. If the union coordinator has rapport with the group leader, or if an issue is tense, or there is a lot of pressure from the workers, a coordinator may be permitted to handle union business during work time. But this is the exception because there is usually no one available to take the coordinator's place on the line.

GRIEVANCE PROCEDURE

The word "grievance" is not used in the NUMMI contract. There are only "problems." The very language represents a subtle but important shift. A "grievance" implies that the worker finds fault with the system or its implementation. But to say the worker has a "problem" suggests there is something the worker needs to correct. The four-step "problem resolution procedure" is as follows:

1. The employee must discuss any problem with the team leader or group leader. The contract says:

> If the problem is not settled to the satisfaction of the employee, he may discuss the problem with the union coordinator during the period when there is clearly no interference with their job duties such as lunch, break period, etc.[16]

Some group leaders have used this clause as the basis for objecting to workers even talking to coordinators before approaching the group leader. In fact, as some observers describe it, the union coordinator "does not assume an active role in workshop affairs until discussion with the group leader reaches an impasse."[17] Thus, usually a worker with "a problem" must take the first steps in dealing with management by him or herself.

If the problem is not resolved after discussion among the worker, union coordinator and group leader, the union's district committeeperson and the company's human resources representative will be called in. They share the same office and usually work together to investigate and solve problems.

2. If the matter is unresolved the committeeperson can submit the problem to the Labor Relations Department on a "Problem Notice Form," which most workers refer to as a grievance. The union chairman and the manager of Labor Relations attempt to resolve the issue at this step.

3. At the third step different forms are used and the problem goes to the Joint Union/Management Committee. The union is represented by the International representative, the president, and the chairman. The company members are the general manager of Human Resources, the manager of Labor Relations, and a general manager related to the problem. If this committee cannot resolve the problem, then the company makes the decision.

4. The union can appeal the company's decision by taking the issue to arbitration. In the standard UAW/Big Three contracts, health and safety, work standards, and outside contracting are strikable between contracts and do not go to arbitration. There are no strikable issues in the NUMMI contract. Work standards are resolved through a separate, but similar, problem-solving procedure.

In practice, at least in the initial period, the system seems to solve small problems fairly successfully. When asked how the NUMMI problem-solving procedure compared to GM's grievance procedure, none of the workers we interviewed wanted to go back to GM's procedure. At GM, they said, once the grievance was written, you never heard again...the grievance took forever...it just got kicked upstairs...general supervisors would always back the foremen...you never won...if you won it was too late to do any good.

At NUMMI the rank and file worker participates more in the process. Often the solutions are not in favor of one side or the other, but involve some compromise or third option, which the worker might be involved in formulating. Although the approach is patience and letting things cool down, many problems are solved within a few days. In fact, management truly seems to practice the idea that it is better to solve small issues quickly and at the bottom than to let them fester and build up. To give an example: management agreed to pay a worker whose street clothes were ruined by grease where there should not have been any.

NUMMI's style is to avoid public rebuke and humiliation. When a department manager overrules a group leader or rules against a worker, it is usually done with a few days' consideration and then presented as a solution to a problem rather than as one side winning and the other losing.

Richard Aguilar, who is the union coordinator for his group, points out that the patient approach is fine until you get to something that has to be solved quickly—where working for two or three more days under the same circumstances imposes hardship.

One of the reasons that NUMMI management can afford to be more flexible than traditional management about small issues at the lower level is that it starts from a position where it has more authority and workers have many fewer specified rights. There are not many issues that a worker has a chance of winning if pushed to a formal complaint. Workers who are upset about favoritism in the assignment to *kaizen* groups find that their complaints don't go anywhere. As one put it:

> When the good jobs were bid by seniority at least you knew where you stood. Now when they give the good jobs by favoritism you call the committeeman and he says there is no grievance here, nothing he can do because there is nothing in the contract against it.

On the other hand, the contract does give management language it can use. Individual workers and the union are contractually obligated to "promote *kaizen*," achieve quality goals, support the team concept, and "assist the company in meeting production goals and scheduling." Workers who fail to meet these vague requirements are subject to management discipline.

Also, since the contract is clear that anything settled at the first step has no significance as precedent or "past practice," any concession made by management does not limit its future flexibility.

Even where a worker does have a right, he or she may decide not to pursue it very far. Because the supervisor has so much authority to determine whether one's work day is comfortable or unbearable, it may not be worthwhile to challenge a supervisor who takes losing badly.

The atmosphere of cooperation tends to discourage workers from asserting their rights. The story of one skilled tradesperson illustrates this: J had some problems

with his supervisor so he put in for a transfer to another department. For family reasons he needed to work days and had the seniority to hold days. But the manager of the department said he would only accept J's transfer if J worked graveyard shift for six months. Co-workers told him the company couldn't do that and that he should take it to the union. J's response:

> I already have one group leader pissed at me. If [the department manager] wants to do this to me and I fight him, I am no better off there than I am here. I am not going to bother the union to force me into a department.

ROLE OF THE UNION

There is no consensus among workers on what the role of the union should be at NUMMI. The union leadership is sharply divided. The leadership of the opposition People's Caucus, Financial Secretary Bob Fernandez and Committeeperson Bob Silva, are careful to point out that they support the team concept. The issue, Fernandez and Silva say, is whether workers get representation and respect through their union in dealing with the real problems in the plant.

The union does not seem to have much of a presence in the plant. One indication is the fact that a thousand people signed the very cautiously worded petition on ab-senteeism, which was directed to both the company and the union. In most traditional plants, workers would think first of going to the union and getting the union to take action.

Few workers we interviewed mentioned the union unless asked. Most spoke about the union as the officers, and saw it as a continuation from the GM operation, since most of the current officers are the same as when GM closed the plant. Many noted a change in the union's attitude. Some charge that the union is in bed with the company and that the officers "back management more than they back the people."

On the other side, some workers dismiss "complainers" as being "just hard-core union." One said:

> Those people were always the ones who wanted to do less for more. They don't believe in helping other people if it's not their job....The union used to protect the wrong people. Now it is not like that; [the company] gives people the benefit of the doubt but if they don't work, they are out the door.

Many workers view the union coordinator as a traditional steward whose job it is to represent the worker in dealing with management. They complain about coordinators who try to act as mediators between the worker and management or even "act like supervision." One said:

> He tells me that other people can do this job—why not

me? I say I can do it, but I shouldn't have to run. He says that with my attitude the place will close again.

But others think that union coordinators should try to look at issues from the overall company view as well as the worker's. Although their official name is *union* coordinators, many workers refer to them as *team* coordinators. In several instances, team leaders are also union coordinators. NUMMI management is proud of this fact,[18] and most workers do not see anything wrong with it in principle. Even many who are critical of the union as too cozy with management do not object to the practice.

The problem-solving procedure at step two and above is not used as much as the grievance procedure is in other plants. During the first year and a half of the contract at NUMMI fewer than 100 problems reached this stage. There are several possible explanations: 1) problems are solved at step one; 2) workers don't expect anything to come of pushing things to a higher level so why bother? or 3) the union actively discourages filing problem notices. The People's Caucus believes the last explanation is the most important one. Supporters of the union leadership seem to share the company's aversion to grievance writing—one gave as evidence for labeling Committeeperson Bob Silva a militant that "he writes grievances."

No one accuses the present leadership majority of being too militant. The most common defense of the leadership is that it is "realistic...they have learned from the GM experience that if you push the company to the wall you lose." As another worker put it: "If I got involved [in the union] I would be with the Administration [majority leadership] Caucus because I am for the company."

Dan Simons strongly approves of the NUMMI philosophy and also considers himself a good union person. Yet, he says, "It feels like when I worked in a non-union place. The union just isn't there." After showing up three times for monthly union membership meetings which could not get a quorum, Simons gave up. In fact many workers have given up. There was not a quorum for a membership meeting in almost two years.

A VISION AND JOB SECURITY

The vision that NUMMI tries to project is one of cooperation, participation, harmony, respect, fulfillment, and job security. Many workers started at NUMMI with high hopes. Dan Simons described his initial feelings:

> At my old job, if the boss didn't take a liking to you, you had a problem. When I came to work for New United Motors I sighed with thanks—"at last I finally have a home."

But some of the promises are wearing thin. Simons, like many others, is concerned that "old ways are creeping back here," particularly among some of the first-line supervisors. Others point to the constant pressure, the job overloading, the feeling of being pushed to the breaking point on the line. "It turns out that this is like every other plant—they want production and if something gets in the way, too bad."

Despite all the talk of equality, there are clear differences between bosses and workers even on small issues not immediately connected to production roles. One worker, for example, considers it degrading that he may not post anything on a bulletin board without his group leader's permission.

Whatever the criticisms, nobody says they want to return to the days when GM ran the plant. Most workers see the core of the problem in the way the system has been implemented. Bad apples, individual selfishness, and "thinking the old way" are commonly cited. Most workers seem to have high respect for the top management and focus the blame on group leaders or union leaders. When you have a problem, according to skilled tradesman Mike Condon, it is because

> the top Japanese who know how the program should be run are not involved. I'm dealing with ex-GM supervisors who don't play the game...don't follow [team concept] and don't understand it.[19]

In its management training video, "This Is NUMMI," management stresses that NUMMI is a system where everything fits together. However, few workers link the problems in the plant to the NUMMI Production System (what we call management-by-stress).

When problems come up they are often dismissed as bad communication. Teddy Holman, a standardized work trainer, wrote in the local union newspaper:

> We not only don't hold enough Team, Group, and Section meetings with each other, we don't communicate between shifts when we do standardized work and strive on each shift for constant improvements...
>
> We also hear that there are places in the plant that we don't have a say in the way standardized work is set up and/or carried out...
>
> We hear talk of the old GM and Ford ways and how they are on their way back...Yes, it is easy to fall back into the old ways, and we really need to get a handle on it, and we can do this through better communication and proper use of our system. Believe me, it does work, all we have to do is get involved.[20]

Why do workers see the team concept as a good system marred by individuals who fail to carry it out properly, rather than as a system with fundamental defects?

First, working for General Motors was no picnic either. NUMMI workers very much want to hold on to management's promises of job security and dignity and respect as long as they have the slightest credibility.

Second, the two years between the closing of GM-Fremont and hiring at NUMMI was for most workers truly a "significant emotional event" (GM Vice President Al Warren's phrase for a condition that gets workers to accept major concessions). When unemployment compensation and Supplemental Unemployment Benefits began to run out, workers were forced to choose between moving to plants in Kansas or Oklahoma or being dropped from safety net programs. High-paid industrial jobs on the West Coast were disappearing. The former GM workers were faced with the prospect of a vastly reduced standard of living. When the letter from NUMMI arrived in the mailbox inviting them to apply for a job, it was the miracle hand reaching from the sky just when they were going down. It is understandable that the former Fremont employees are born-again workers who see NUMMI as a second chance for life.

Everything else, at least for a while, is reduced to this one issue. Bert Wright, a production worker, said:

> I've had as many problems in the plant as any of you guys. But we have production, we have quality, and we have jobs. Under the old system they didn't have production, they didn't have quality, and we eventually lost the jobs. If anything else needs to be said you better think about that first.[21]

Despite the formal job security provisions in the contract, the atmosphere is one of insecurity. Every discussion almost always returns to the same theme. Describing the role of the committeeperson in the problem-solving procedure, Cheryl Franklin concludes:

> They do not have time and we do not have time for the little petty stuff. The main thing we are concerned with is keeping our jobs.[22]

Third and most important, NUMMI's is a sophisticated and complicated system. Criticizing the system and finding alternatives to it requires leadership, resources, and organization—normally roles of the union. But well

before the plant opened, most of the respected local union leaders from GM-Fremont were brought into line by the company, which methodically convinced these people to commit themselves to the NUMMI system in exchange for maintaining the union structure. Perks, such as trips to Japan, buttressed the argument and promises. When the plant opened, union leaders were in place who saw their main responsibility as making the NUMMI system work.

It takes time to convert vague discomfort and gripes into realistic alternatives. It is especially difficult when everyone—from the media to your union leadership—tells you the only alternatives are far worse. One worker summed up the hope, frustration, and fear which all exist at the same time:

> The team concept is a great idea—the problem is that some group leaders are taking advantage of it. But sometimes, deep down, I get this feeling that it is a form of union busting.

★   ★   ★

For up-to-date information on developments at NUMMI, see chapters 8 and 36.

Notes

1. Described in speech by Dennis Cuneo, NUMMI management representative, May 1, 1985, San Francisco, California.

2. *Agreement Between New United Motor Manufacturing, Inc. and the UAW*, July 1, 1985, III.

3. General Motors, *D-150 Labor Performance* Report—Passenger Assembly, week ending 5/11/86, No. 36.

4. John Krafcik, "Learning From NUMMI," Internal Working Paper for the International Motor Vehicle Program at Massachusetts Institute of Technology, September 15, 1986. Krafcik is a former NUMMI quality control engineer.

5. Note on sources: Unless otherwise specified, quotations are from our interviews. Many of the NUMMI workers we interviewed did not wish to be identified. In a few instances, situations have been slightly disguised to honor those wishes. See also KQED Television, *Express*, program of interviews and discussion with NUMMI workers, March 4, 1987; Tim Wise, "Life on the Fast Line," *Dollars and Sense*, April and May 1987.

6. *Oakland Enterprise*, February 13, 1985.

7. *Automotive Industries*, May 1983.

8. General Motors Technical Liaison Office, "This Is NUMMI," videotape for GM managers, 1985.

9. Tetsuo Abo, "The Application of Japanese-Style Management Concepts in Japanese Automobile Plants in the USA," WZB Conference, Berlin, November 1987, p. 6.

10. General Motors Technical Liaison Office, "Team Concept," November 26, 1984, description of NUMMI.

11. See, for example, Jeff Stansbury, "NUMMI: A New Kind of Workplace," *Solidarity*, August 1985.

12. "This Is NUMMI."

13. "This Is NUMMI."

14. *Detroit Free Press*, January 25, 1988.

15. "This Is NUMMI."

16. *Agreement, July 1, 1985*, Section X.2.1.

17. Abo, p. 7.

18. "This Is NUMMI."

19. Videotape interviews, January 21, 1988.

20. *Local 2244 Labor News*, August 1987.

21. KQED Television, *Express*.

22. Videotape interviews, January 21, 1988.

Working Smart:
A Union Guide to Participation Programs and Reengineering
Labor Notes • 7435 Michigan Ave. • Detroit, MI 48210 • (313) 842-6262

Chapter 7

Mazda: Choosing Workers Who Fit

The new Mazda plant in Michigan had its thousands of applicants undergo a strenuous screening procedure, designed to find workers likely to develop company loyalty. Exercises probed what applicants would do about fellow workers who were not keeping up the pace. Once hired, orientation gave the message that workers would control and structure their jobs—an expectation dashed once production began.

OFFICIALLY, THE NEW MAZDA plant in Flat Rock, Michigan was not a joint venture. But Ford owned 25 percent of the Japanese parent company of Mazda Motor Manufacturing (USA) Corporation (MMUC). The new assembly plant, located 30 miles south of Detroit, was on the site of Ford's former Michigan Casting Center.

MMUC President Osamu Nobuto said that MMUC and Ford were "freely providing the opportunity to observe each other's plants."[1] Ford would purchase 60 percent of the production of MMUC and would market the car as a Ford Probe.

Because of its ties to Ford and its location in the center of U.S. auto production, the Flat Rock plant set strong precedents for the rest of the auto industry.

MAZDA GOES UNION

The deal to bring Mazda to Michigan was constructed in 1984. The state of Michigan put together a package of inducements totalling more than $120 million. This included $16 to $18 million for job training, $30 million in funds for improvements to roads, railway spurs and other infrastructure, and about $80 million in tax abatements from Flat Rock and Wayne County.

But Mazda was not about to open its first U.S. plant in the Detroit area, home of the United Auto Workers, and face an all-out struggle with the union. Before the Michigan deal could be consummated, the company required that the union issue be settled. According to the *Detroit Free Press*, "State officials worked directly with the UAW on the job training program and on concessions sought by Mazda on work rules and job classifications."[2]

A "letter of intent" between Mazda and the UAW was drafted in September 1984. They agreed on recognition of the UAW, hiring preference for laid-off Ford workers, and some points to be contained in a future collective bargaining agreement:

> The Collective Bargaining Agreement will provide for the Union's long term cooperation in the recognition and commitment to the principle of flexibility that the company must have to maintain and improve quality and efficiency and to the implementation of work practices and production systems similar to those used by Mazda in Japan. This flexibility includes, among other things, a minimal number of job classifications, flexibility in job assignments and job transfers, employee training, the performance by employees of different jobs, an effective cooperative work relationship among the employees, the use of the team concept, and an active and meaningful employee involvement program.

The union made major concessions on seniority language. For example, management would have the right to designate the departments from which new job openings would be filled rather than allowing plant-wide bidding. Layoffs and recalls would give "consideration to such factors as employees' abilities, qualifications, experience, physical capacity, and length of service." The understanding also included a wage structure with starting pay at 72 percent of Big Three wages, increasing to 85 percent after 18 months. The letter contained a commitment to raise the pay scale to the level of the Big Three during the course of the first three-year contract.

No formal signing of the letter of intent was ever announced. Suits by the anti-union National Right-to-Work Committee over terms in the UAW-GM Saturn contract forced the UAW to be more cautious about pre-production agreements. No UAW or Mazda spokesperson would comment on the letter. But in public statements made in 1986,

UAW officials clearly regarded the plant as organized.[3]

Some provisions of the letter were not carried out. A special letter was sent to all laid-off Ford employees inviting them to apply. But as a group it does not seem that they were given preference over other applicants. A Mazda spokesperson declared that the number of previous Ford employees was "proprietary information,"[4] but workers estimated the figure at about ten percent in early 1988.

On the other hand, Mazda adhered to the wage structure in the letter, and the UAW never challenged management's flexibility or work arrangements. Mazda publicly announced a policy of strict neutrality on whether its workers joined the union. The UAW, although not formally recognized, did participate in new-hire orientation sessions.

Throughout the start-up period, the UAW got workers to sign authorization cards. To help avoid challenges, the company and the union agreed to a secret ballot election conducted by the American Arbitration Association. The UAW magazine *Solidarity* described the election campaign as a "low key, word-of-mouth effort describing the benefits of unionization."[5] Announcements of the election were posted in the plant, but there was no campaign literature either pro or con. On September 11, 1987 the vote for union representation was 717 to 92.

Following the election the local began to hold union meetings. Several hundred attended the first meeting, which included dinner, and large numbers attended the next two. The meetings provided many members with their first opportunity to get questions answered. How were the appointed local officers selected? What could they do about how team leaders were selected? What was the relationship of the local to Ford workers? UAW Regional Director Ernie Lofton reassured anxious workers that if there was a Ford strike, Mazda workers would not go out with Ford workers, despite the fact that the Mazda plant's main product would be sold by Ford.

The union representatives include a benefits representative, a health and safety representative, five committeepersons, and a president, all appointed by the UAW regional director. Workers complain that they do not get to talk privately to their committeepersons unless they insist. The committeepersons share offices with their management counterparts, and in some departments they respond together on problems or grievances.

NO BURNED OUT BULBS

The atmosphere and organization of the plant are much like NUMMI's. Like NUMMI, the plant is strikingly clean. Those who have worked in other auto plants comment that oil leaks or burned-out light bulbs are taken care of right away. The plant is modern, with about 350 robots and some automatic guided vehicles (AGV's) in the stamping operation.[6] MMUC President Nobuto says, "Yes, we'll have some robots and state of the art machinery but it won't be space age equipment that requires a lot of ex-

perimentation."[7]

There are 15-minute mass relief breaks in the morning and afternoon and a 40-minute lunch time (ten minutes paid). There is a single production worker classification and no pay-for-knowledge.

Teams consist of four to eight members. Management selects the team leaders, who are paid an additional 42 cents an hour. Team leaders keep track of attendance, provide relief, replace absentees, train new members, help establish programmed work standards, and so on.

The lowest level supervisor is called the unit leader, who is in charge of two to four teams. The original unit leaders and team leaders were sent to Mazda's plant in Hofu, Japan for training.

Team meetings are scheduled regularly. Production workers gather every morning before the start of the shift for ten minutes (unpaid) of exercise and meeting. Once a week the team meets for a half hour. In addition there are periodic department or "town meetings."

Weekly "diagonal slice" meetings with the plant manager involve about 20 people, including managers of different levels and selected team members (different people each time). The meetings are mainly for workers to raise problems directly to the highest levels of management. Most of these problems are usually referred to departmental management, but workers speak positively about the meetings.

The diagonal slice approach apparently was an important part of Plant Manager Dennis Pawley's popularity in the plant. Workers comment that Pawley, with his earthy language and knowledge of the shop floor, was one of the few managers comfortable "not wearing a tie" and was very approachable.

Skilled trades for the entire plant, including tool and die makers, are in a single classification referred to as maintenance. The total skilled trades force at full staffing is planned at 180-200, less than half the number at a traditional assembly plant of this size. It is especially low given the amount of technology and normal start-up problems.

This low number is achieved in several ways. Everyone in the maintenance classification is cross-trained. Work traditionally done by such trades as glaziers and carpenters is contracted out. Production workers perform some traditional skilled jobs, such as replacing weld tips, changing hoses, and reprogramming robots. Construction and maintenance jobs that require more than a few hours are assigned to outside contractors. Furthermore, management attempts to apply the principles of standardized work to maintenance procedures, especially preventive maintenance.

Maintenance teams meet every morning for 10 to 45 minutes. Often the meetings are brief, taking up only team leader reports and the day's assignments. But frequently maintenance teams will have discussions about problems with specific machines, safety problems, or company policies like lack of adequate tools.

CULTURES MIX

When the Flat Rock plant started, Mazda brought from Japan 500 "dispatchees"—engineers and advisors. The plan is to slowly phase out all but a few of them. Most of the U.S. workers seem to enjoy the contact with a different culture. Many of the workers recently moved to the area, and there is a fair amount of social contact outside the plant between the U.S. workers and the dispatchees. There have been some reports of racial incidents—anti-Japanese slogans scrawled on the walls, for example—but they seem to have come from workers employed by outside contractors doing construction in the plant. U.S. Mazda workers were genuinely angry and apologetic about these incidents.

In management, there is a division of labor along racial lines. The Japanese handle most of the manufacturing and technical questions, and the American managers take charge of the internal human relations, hiring, orientation, and public relations.

The dispatchees also serve as role models. Many U.S. workers comment on the dispatchees' loyalty and commitment to the company. The dispatchees often put in extra hours without pay and think nothing of suggesting that workers study materials at home. Many workers tell stories of dispatchees doing dangerous feats to get the line moving again such as riding on a moving platform through an automation area or reaching into a powered-up machine to un-jam it.

GOLD BRAID

As at NUMMI, many of the status symbols that differentiate management from hourly workers have been removed. But subtle distinctions still exist. All levels wear the same uniform of brown shirt, blue pants or skirt, and blue cap (unlike NUMMI, the uniform is required). But department managers and higher all have a gold braid around their name badges.

The uniforms are a source of considerable controversy. In the summer the nylon jumpsuits required in the painting areas are oppressively hot. In other departments the company insists that workers wear their caps at all times. Bracelets, chains, watches, rings are prohibited because they are possible safety hazards or because they might scratch the cars.[8]

Everyone eats in the same cafeteria. But many management people have sufficient flexibility on their jobs that they can get to the cafeteria a few minutes early, avoid the rush, and get the best seats. Hourly workers must keep working until the last minute, and so no matter how fast they run to the cafeteria, they still have to stand in line.

LIFE IN THE START-UP MODE

As of February 1988, the plant was still in a start-up mode. While it has a full complement of workers for the one shift it is running, the line speed is only around 40 cars per hour, as compared to the projected 65. As in all start-ups, there are quality problems and bugs to be worked out.

There are many features of life in the start-up mode that will not exist once the plant gets to full production. The line speed is slower so workers have the time to help one another out. There are frequent problems, and the company truly needs and wants worker input to solve them. The continued expansion of the workforce plus turn-over create openings for new team leaders and group leaders and plenty of opportunity for the company to reward those it wishes. There is an air of excitement among workers about being involved in something new.

But as the NUMMI experience illustrates, most of these attractive features will disappear once the plant gets up to full production. Workers will find that they have no time to help one another and that the interesting parts of the job—like problem solving—are pushed to the background. As the workforce stabilizes, promotional opportunities will be reduced to a trickle. The main task will be keeping up with a fast line every day, a challenge that gets old very quickly.

Even now problems show up. Occasionally a team makes a proposal which is ignored by management, and members feel resentful. Such resentment is frequently expressed by reduced participation in voluntary activities like pre-work exercises.

CONSIDER THE ERRORS

Mazda's disciplinary procedure begins with the standard list of offenses that bring immediate suspension or firing: illegal activities, theft, fighting, "falsifying or omitting any information on a company record," and encouraging any "illegal strike, slowdown or other interruption of work."

Next there is a list of "employee expectations" that contains rules like:

• No food, beverages, or smoking in non-designated areas.

• No reading materials in non-designated areas.

• Working hours may be varied by the company to meet its needs.

• Strict attendance required with no tardiness.

• Uniforms must be worn at all times.

The three-page list of employee expectations is summed up with:

> Mazda employees are also expected to be flexible in job assignments, to have near perfect attendance, and be responsible for the quality of all Mazda products. In short, all employees are expected to be active contributing members of the Mazda team.

Failure to live up to these employee expectations or to neglect or disrupt the performance of your job responsibilities or the responsibilities of others will be addressed through the Code of Conduct.[9]

The Code of Conduct explains how violations will be dealt with. Mazda's procedure has been used by other U.S. companies and is described in the *Harvard Business Review* as a "nonpunitive approach to discipline."[10] It is a five-step procedure:

1. Oral reminder.
2. Written reminder.
3. Second written reminder.

These first three steps are designed to gain the "worker's agreement to solve the problem" and develop "a new action plan to eliminate the gap between actual and desired performance."

Step four is a discussion with the labor relations office. This is the point from which the procedure gets its "non-punitive" reputation. After the discussion, the "disruptive" worker is given a day off *with pay* to consider the error of his ways. After the paid day off, the worker reports to the unit leader with the decision to either change his ways (with an acceptable plan for correction) or quit.

If another incident of disruptive behavior occurs, it is taken as a decision to quit and, after review of the incident, the fifth step, the worker is "self-terminated."[11]

ONE OF THE 96,500

Unlike NUMMI, which was forced by the UAW to hire mainly from the workers laid off from GM's Fremont plant, Mazda had freedom to hire whomever it wished. Considerable effort and expense went into designing and running the selection and orientation programs.[12] In full-page ads Mazda proclaimed:

> At Flat Rock, Mazda launched what may well be the most painstaking recruitment and training program in automotive history. An intensive five-stage screening process was used to select 3,500 workers from a mass of 96,500 applicants. Those hired then participated in a rigorous 10 week training course followed by off-line training with a team leader. Throughout, the new workforce was introduced to The Mazda Way of Open Management and Worker Participation.[13]

Because the selection process reveals so much about the kind of workforce Mazda desires and the kind of management Mazda uses, we describe it at some length. Both successful and unsuccessful applicants were interviewed for this account. However, most of the detail offered below is available because one of the authors, Mike Parker, went through the first four steps of the selection process. The following is based primarily on his notes.

STAGE 1: A MESSAGE FROM DEBBIE

Mazda starts hiring in 1986. I send in a letter requesting an application. I never get a response, but most people receive a standard job application form which asks for previous work history, schooling, and three references.

During the last week of March in 1987, Mazda runs an ad specifically looking for journeymen electricians or

welder repairers. I send in a copy of my resume and a photocopy of my journeyman's card.

I assume I have a fair chance of getting a job offer. Things are going pretty well for electricians in the area and I know there would not be many electricians with heavy industrial or construction experience applying for jobs that would start at two-thirds the pay of the Big Three. (I did not know that Mazda was advertising and sending recruitment teams to other areas of the country.)

I have not made up my mind whether I will take the job if it is offered. Plus side: interesting technological problems of a new plant, being part of building a new union, and I would not be on the bottom of the seniority list. Minus side: less money, long commute, concerns about how the plant would be managed and whether I would actually get to work on the technology.

Sunday, five days after I mail in the application, I receive a message on my tape machine to call Debbie from Mazda. In all my experience at Ford and Chrysler, I have never had an official company call on the weekend or evening. On the one hand, it might make more sense to call when people are more likely to be home. On the other hand, the blurring of company time and personal time gives me pause.

I call Debbie on Monday. She tells me to come to Cadillac School at 5:00 p.m. that day with two #2 pencils and a picture ID.

STAGE 2: TWO #2 PENCILS

Mazda uses Cadillac Elementary School, no longer in regular use, for its extensive selection and testing program. The other applicants and I take every other chair at long tables in a large gymnasium and have a few minutes to talk before the test starts. It seems that everyone has applied for a skilled job. (Production workers later told me they took the same tests.) Most had their applications in months ago. The only person who had applied recently was also an electrician. I figure they must be hurting for electricians so my chances are pretty good.

Three Mazda people, wearing the company uniform, administer the test. I later find out that all three are unit leaders, the lowest level of supervision. They check our picture ID's, record our Social Security numbers, and then the tests begin.

Test 1: A 15-minute Mazda Math Test checks for basic addition, subtraction, multiplication, and division skills and ability to read simple graphs.

Test 2: A Flanagan Industrial Test[14] checks for observation of "quality." There are diagrams of the correct part or object and then a number of similar ones next to it. I am supposed to circle all those which have a defect (i.e., some difference with the model). I find this test very difficult, and I probably spend too much time on the first few problems.

Test 3: Another Flanagan Industrial Test. This one

shows bunches of parts with letters indicating how they are to be put together. The object is to choose which of five diagrams looks most like the assembled item.

Test 4: A 10-minute listening test. We listen to various instructions and then write the correct answers on our answer sheets.

Test 5: A 30-minute mechanical aptitude test. The questions measure basic knowledge of gears, electricity, levers, and temperature.

The tests are run in a no-nonsense, machine gun fashion. While one test is going on, the unit leaders are placing the next set of test materials, exactly counted out, at the outside ends of the tables. When each test is over, we immediately pass our materials to the center where the piles are collected. At the same time, the new test materials are moving into place right behind. There is never a mistake; the unit leader begins instructions for the next test within a minute.

The next day there is message on my tape asking me to call Don at Mazda. There is a later message—Don giving me his home phone. I have mixed reactions again. On the one hand, I am pleased that I do not have to wait until the next day to find out what is happening. On the other hand, I feel a bit uncomfortable intruding on someone's private life with something from work which is clearly no emergency. It turns out Don is playing basketball, and his wife thinks he will be home late. Don and I cross calls a few times the next day. When we finally connect, Don apologizes. He is an electrical engineer and was out on the floor because of breakdowns.

Don tells me I passed the test and he wants me to come in for a personal interview.

STAGE 3: EVER BEEN WRITTEN UP?

While driving back to Cadillac School, I decide to be very careful at the interview. I don't want to lie, but at the same time I do not want to volunteer any more of my views on unions or industrial relations than necessary.

After filling out an application form, I go to an empty classroom with one table and three chairs in the middle. Two Mazda engineers interview me. They explain that they will be asking me questions from a typed script so that, in the interests of fairness, everyone will be given the questions the same way. They also explain that they are writing down my answers so that they and others can evaluate them.

Why did I apply at Mazda? They ask about my present job, my absence record, my tardiness record, and whether I have ever been written up. They ask about my hobbies and community activities. I mention working in a group on a job, and they ask me if I am familiar with the "team concept." I said that I know something about working in groups but don't know anything about how it works at Mazda.

Then they read some descriptions of hypothetical situations: *I am working at my job, and I notice the parts coming from the station before me have occasional defects. It does not affect my job. What do I do about it?*

They record my answer and probe a bit, then present me with a second scenario. *My job is putting heat shields on one side of the car. A woman I don't like is putting them on the other side. She misses bolts, and I have been adding them. I have tried talking to her but it doesn't work. What do I do?*

I don't like the question, and I think it shows. I figure that they must surely know that only the most disgusting apple polisher would volunteer to fink. I finally mumble something about talking to her again about taking responsibility for herself, and, unless she took her problem to the team to solve, I was not going to continue covering for her. I don't think they consider it a good answer.

We move on to a section of the interview where they read a series of statements and ask for my response. The wording here is approximate.

Mazda is aiming to achieve the same efficiency and productivity as they have in Japan.

The Mazda way is no idleness.

We discuss this a bit. At one point I am asked if I ever made a suggestion to increase productivity or efficiency. I describe some suggestions I have put in. The interviewer interrupts to explain that he did not mean a technical suggestion, but have I ever suggested a way that we could do a job with one fewer person? I think for a moment and reply that I can't recall having done so. They make a note.

Being on time and present for work is important.

What would I do if my neighbor were having problems with a Mazda car?

I honestly do not understand the question. They explain that Mazda expects its employees to stand behind the company and help out wherever there is a problem. I am beginning to realize just how strongly I feel about the separation of work and private life and how much the "Mazda way" seems to blur that distinction.

When they finish, they offer me an opportunity to ask questions. Some answers:

There is no guaranteed job security. They will try to do it "like in Japan" (presumably no layoffs), but no promises. They do not expect any layoffs because 60 percent of the product will be bought directly by Ford. (I do not understand the logic—surely Ford is not guaranteeing the cars will sell—but I do not pursue it.)

There is no seniority at the plant as yet. There is no union. The UAW participates in the orientation, but it will be up to the people to decide whether they want a union or not. Mazda has good relations with its union in Japan and has no problem with having a union here if that's what the workers want.

Teams meet for ten minutes every morning and one-half hour (on company time) on Wednesdays. Neither could give me much description of teams since they are not regular members. "We can sit in on teams and are often requested to meet with the teams."

They answer my questions for about one half hour. There is no hype. They want to make sure that I understand that skilled trades work differently at Mazda from my experiences at traditional plants.

They leave the room while I wait. Five minutes later they return and schedule my appointment for an "assessment."

STAGE 4: DINNER WITH THE PLANT MANAGER

Twenty-one of us hopefuls gather in a waiting room on the appointed Saturday afternoon. This is the first time that any of us are on the Mazda grounds. Conversations are quiet and nervous. No one knows what the assessment will be like.

All the people I talk to are applying for production jobs. They say that they had put their applications in some time last year but were called only recently for interviews. Most have numbers of friends who never even got interviews. One man, in his forties, has driven 250 miles from Norwood, Ohio. This is his third trip in the application process, and he is pleased to get this far. A uniformed Mazda person, Carl, comes in, joking about how we may not make it through the day. I ask him how far people travel to go through this application process. Carl responds that people have flown in from California and Florida for a crack at these jobs.

Finally they take us to a large room where they explain how the assessment works. We will be evaluated in groups of five or six by two Mazda assessors. Group members and assessors will be shuffled for each of four exercises. All sessions will have the same structure. At the beginning, the assessors will explain what we are to do and we can ask questions. After that, we can ask no more questions.

We go to our first assignments. Mine is called "Rewards." *Shuffle 1: Rewards*. We are told to assume that we are a functioning team. The plant manager wants to set up a rewards program, and our team has been asked to suggest a system. We are given a list of activities and told to prioritize them, suggest appropriate rewards, and decide whether these should be individual or team rewards. We should take about ten minutes to read the materials and use our work sheets and then 35 minutes to come up with our group answer.

The list of items to be rewarded includes:
• Most cooperative
• Highest productivity
• Highest team spirit
• Most work-related suggestions
• Most improved individual or team
• Best attendance
• Highest quality
• Highest score in company team sports
The list of possible rewards includes:
• Ten cent per hour raise
• $100 U.S. savings bond
• Plaque
• $500 shopping spree

• Best parking spaces for a month
• Dinner at the plant manager's house
The assessors sit back and take notes during the session. From the scratch of their pencils at certain events, I assume they are making notes about the role that each member of the group plays—surely they don't care whether we think "highest productivity" rates above or below "best attendance."

The group starts its discussion. One person volunteers to lead off, someone else offers to be recorder and write the final report. One person will keep track of time. Everybody is aware that they are being measured by their participation and is trying to play the role the examiners are looking for. It's a challenge because no one is quite sure what it is. I am trying to play the role of someone who is helpful in resolving disputes and familiar with team procedures like brainstorming.

After our team has several false starts I suggest that we all make known our individual priority lists to see where we are in general agreement. Two people make "highest productivity" their number one choice. I assume this was to impress the assessors. I suggest adding safety to the list as number one. Some group members are nervous about agreeing that the most important item was not on the original list, but nobody has a good argument against it. After some discussion we get consensus to make safety number one. I also suggest that "most improved individual or team" should rank high, but find no support. I try a second time, then drop it.

Shuffle 2: Group Assembly. The group is to act as a team to assemble an "airboat" using toy blocks (like Legos). We must use all group members and assemble the airboats as quickly as possible. The assessors show us a completed model and demonstrate how to check it for "quality." They explain that since the parts are so worn, the quality check almost always fails. Our instructions are to pass it after one check and one repair. (Now this sounds like the auto industry I know.)

For 25 minutes we devise and rehearse our assembly technique. Then they give us the rest of the parts for our time trial. It takes us four minutes and 30 seconds to assemble our units. The assessors examine them and show us a couple of "quality" problems where the constructed units are not exactly like the models. They ask us whether we want to try another model or work more on this one. We choose to improve, and we reorganize our assembly process slightly. In addition to improving our quality check, we also make sure that everyone makes sub-assemblies as well as participating in final assembly. Our time for the second trial is 45 seconds more than the first, but our quality is 100 percent.

One of the assessors senses that our team is discouraged and says that we have done it in good time. Later in the hall I hear of teams that made 100 percent quality in three-and-a-half minutes.

TEAM CONCEPT INCENTIVES Choose one of the following rewards:

DREAM VACATION — GREYHOUND

OUR MOTTO: "SHUT UP, GET BACK TO WORK, HERE, THANKS"

The Daily Schnauzer — 7,000 LAYOFFS SOON — YESTERDAY'S PAPER

SACK OF LEAVES

MATCHES

DINNER AT THE BOSS'

DOLLAR A DAY

LIVE LOBSTER

10¢ PER HOUR

BAR O' SOAP

CAN O' COKE

USELESS PLAQUE

COMPANY "STOCK" — ONE SHARE

BEST SPOT ON THE BUS TO WORK — Reserved for Handicapped and Elderly

SHOW TICKETS

TED RALL ©1988

PAT IS A GOOD WORKER, BUT...

Shuffle 3: Problems. We are a team of Mazda production employees. Four problems have come up. We are to prepare a brief outline for the team supervisor on how we think the problems should be handled.

1. The plant manager wants us to participate in a volleyball tournament because volleyball builds team spirit. Some people on our team do not like volleyball and would prefer baseball or bowling. Some even object to the use of outside time for company activities.

2. Pat (male or female carefully avoided) is "a bright, alert, and reliable worker." Pat has saved the plant thousands of dollars through suggestions and has helped our team "turn out more work than similar teams at Mazda." But Pat has a problem of regular "complaining" and being "rude and nasty" to others. The supervisor sent a letter to the team leader asking the team to deal with Pat's attitude problem and saying that "Pat must show more cooperative and flexible attitudes." The team is meeting without Pat, who is on vacation.

3. It is too hot in our part of the plant and there are three alternatives: request permission to wear shorts or go shirtless, investigate the causes of the heat, or air condi-tion the plant.

4. Lee is a good member of our team—the written story is lavish in its praise. But Lee's daughter has severe asthma, which sometimes means that Lee has to take her to the hospital. "The lateness is far in excess of what can be tolerated and the plant's production schedule does not permit Lee to make up lost time on other shifts."

We first prioritize the problems to deal with the most important ones first. Most think that the heat question is trivial, and it takes only a couple of minutes to agree that the obvious reasonable answer is to investigate the causes before making any proposal. It is an indication of just how far from reality the assessment procedure is. Trying to maintain full working speed in overheated plants is ex-cruciating. Short-term solutions—more break time, reduced line speed, fans to move the air, rotation to cooler places—are essential. I bite my tongue on this one. (This issue of deviation from the uniform would be a big issue in the plant that summer.)

The volleyball question also takes little time. Of course, we tell the plant manager, we would like to par-ticipate in his tournament, but add that some of our group would like to suggest that the next tournament be baseball or bowling.

The other questions, the group feels, are tough. Most of our time is spent on the Lee and Pat problems. The few suggestions that even remotely challenge the company are extremely tentative. My suggestion—maybe whoever decided that Lee's schedule could not be "tolerated" might be wrong and that we should inquire how this was determined—is completely ignored. The group focuses on how we might be able to give Lee some assistance. One guy volunteers his wife: "I could have my wife drive Lee's kid to the hospital." Someone else says, "Maybe Lee could hire a live-in nurse and we could raise money."

Shuffle 4: Mazda Philosophy. "Mazda wishes to be sure that new employees have no problem adjusting to work at a plant that uses new philosophies and methods." Our team is given a list of possible problem areas in the Mazda philosophy and asked to rank these in order of difficulty and suggest ways that might ease the difficulty. The list includes:

- Expect workers to make lots of suggestions
- Expect workers to do many jobs
- Trust between workers and management
- Flexible jobs and a variety of tasks
- High degree of work commitment
- No waste of material or motion.

Needless to say, no one challenges any of these. All the suggestions are the same: more training and better communication.

At the end we reassemble in the original big meeting room. This is it, we are told. Those rejected will receive a letter in the next two months. Most of those accepted will be called within the next week to make appointments for the medical exam. (The medical tests include screening for drugs.) After the physical, people will be called for a one-day "stamina, coordination, dexterity" exam where they will work with tools and materials used at Mazda. Someone asks at what point you are hired. The assessor answers that she does not know of anyone called for the stamina exam who was not hired, but it is possible.

STAGE 5: STILL WAITING

I do not receive a call, but neither do I get a rejection letter. Maybe there is still hope.

From talking to other applicants, I learn that in this final phase of the screening a mock car is set up. The applicant is given a job assignment with several specific steps: assemble the dome light, get into the car, install it, get out of the car, get back in, remove it, and disassemble it. The work varied. Sometimes it was carpet installation. Some workers recall they did this for an hour, others for four.

A GIANT GAME

The Mazda screening process is a giant game. An applicant has to invest up to five trips and sixteen hours of time to be considered for a job. The applicant is going to say and do what he or she thinks the company wants. The

company knows this. The applicant knows the company knows this. Are the interviewers and assessors, themselves newly-hired unit leaders, well enough trained in assessment and interviewing to judge who would be a good worker from this game? In mid-1987 Mazda switched to professional interviewers, but most of these had no experience on the shop floor.

From the tests and from comments made by company officials, it seems that the qualities the company was looking for were communication skills and the likelihood of developing company loyalty. The tests seemed to have a cultural bias in favor of middle-class verbal skills. Factory experience—surviving in a plant for five to twenty years—counted for little and may even have been a negative factor, implying habits that would have to be unlearned.

In any event, the results of the screening are interesting. The number of Black workers is 10 to 12 percent, low considering the number of unemployed Black auto workers in the Detroit area. Some Blacks—both unsuccessful applicants and current Mazda workers—believe that the interviewers, almost all white, reflected racial bias in their judgments. Some point out that many workers who "proved themselves" through years of experience at Ford were denied jobs at Mazda. Less than 25 percent of Mazda workers have previous experience working for Big Three companies.[15] Many have no factory experience at all. Almost half the employees are women.

ORIENTATION:
THE WILL TO PARTICIPATE

Like everything else at Mazda, the three-week "common" orientation, which all new employees attend, is executed with precision scheduling. The printed program is adhered to closely during the eight-and-a-half hour day. Actually the day is slightly longer; a ten-minute "exercise/team meeting" period is scheduled before the program officially begins.

The orientation includes welcoming remarks and procedural and administrative details. Paperwork is filled out, benefit programs explained, uniforms fitted, and safety shoes ordered. One session deals with compensation, and a UAW representative explains the relationship of the company to the union. Several sessions teach proper lifting techniques and health and safety. To ease communication and relations with the large population of Japanese dispatchees, one session is devoted to Japanese culture.

Some sessions elaborate on the Mazda philosophy. Over and over they hammer away at the idea: Where you worked before it may have been all right just to come to work and do what you are told. That is not enough at Mazda. Here part of your job is to contribute ideas to improve productivity and quality.

For example, the conclusion of the presentation on how the MMUC Manufacturing System works contains a warning: Mazda "cannot accept people who have the following characteristics." The manual lists five. The first four are the standard offenses for which one can be fired in most plants—absenteeism, fighting or property destruction, use of alcohol or drugs, disregard of company regulations and safety rules. The fifth is the clincher: "Those who don't have the will to participate in work accomplishments or *kaizen* [continuous improvement] activities."[16]

Whatever your specific job assignment, everyone is an inspector for every operation. If "a defective component is discovered coming from the previous process, the team member should press the button..."

One important message of the training program is that at Mazda the teams make important decisions. Teams design the production process and specific jobs. Partly this message is explicit and partly it is implicit in the kinds of examples and situations used in training.

Three days are spent on "interpersonal" training. Most of the examples in the manual involve the type of situation and degree of decision making power typically reserved for management. For example:

> Your department just went over the top in the United Way campaign...Jean volunteered to help you out without being assigned and did a lot of work after hours. [How do you provide recognition?]

> This morning you see next month's budget and your boss has not given you your own maintenance budget. [How do you approach your boss?][17]

While some of the problems specifically mention dealing with the boss, most are with others in your department. The manual carefully avoids specifying whether these are co-workers or subordinates. The Mazda new hires work on skills such as how to communicate problems

specifically and directly, how to give positive reinforcement, how to deal with emotional and ability problems, how to solve motivation problems, and how to "communicate the consequences for failure."

Using the slogan, "Everlasting Efforts for Everlasting Competition,"[18] the concept of kaizen is introduced. Facilitators explain that Mazda exists in a competitive world and kaizen is the key to productivity. A graph shows Mazda in comparison to other multinational auto firms. Toyota is the leader. Mazda must catch up with Toyota.

The new Mazda workers are taught how to use a stopwatch and do time and motion studies. The emphasis is on doing away with the "Evil Three M's of waste—*muda, mura,* and *muri*" (translated as waste, overburden, and unevenness). (See chapter 5.)

In order to learn to judge a "standard pace," new hires watch video tapes of work situations and rate the workers as working too fast or too slow. Then they compare their ratings to the "expert" ratings provided by the company.

New hires learn how to break down a job down into its smallest components, describe it on a "programmed work" sheet, and find ways to increase productivity. Then the jobs of the team are "balanced," and the search to remove idle time begins again. Programmed work is described in Chapter 5.

For several days the team members practice their new understanding of programmed work by assembling flashlights. They are given the parts and a detailed explanation

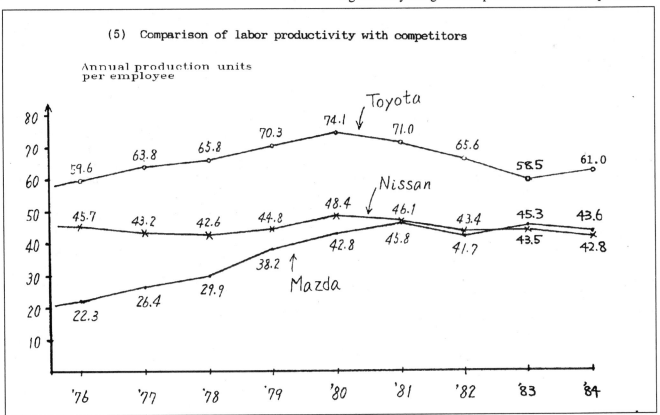

(5) Comparison of labor productivity with competitors

Productivity competition is stressed in *Mazda Kaizen Simulation Training Manual.*

of the specifications for the final product.

For example, the flashlight is packaged in a pouch with the rear end in first and wrapped twice with a rubber band. They practice breaking down the assembly operation to its smallest steps and *kaizen* the operation over and over. Using cardboard and tape they devise and build fixtures to increase productivity. Video cameras record their assembly operations so the new hires can study the tapes to find wasted motions.

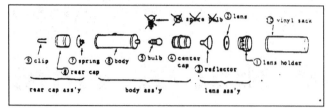

Flashlight diagram from the Mazda training manual.

REALITY HITS

The training and manuals make the point that the unit leader is "charged with making the final decision."[19] Yet the overall message is that workers will control and structure their own jobs.

One worker describes the illusions of some of the training graduates:

They think they will be meeting all the time and they can change the job or shift to another job or just stop the line if they find out that it is too hard. They don't understand that this is an auto plant and the company is going to make production.

Many new hires come out of training unprepared for what actually happens. By the time most workers actually join the teams on the lines, they find that jobs are basically defined. Most of the programmed work has been carefully specified by groups of unit leaders, team leaders, and dispatchees. The main job of the new hire is to read the programmed work sheet and follow directions exactly.

Many Mazda workers who have experience in auto plants take these orientation activities with large quantities of salt. Yet during training even they begin to look forward to a different work experience:

It would have been better if they hadn't had that orientation. They kept promising us that this place is really going to be different, that everybody was equal and all that stuff. Better they would have said it was going to be the same old shit as at GM and Ford and then people wouldn't get their hopes up.

In March 1988, the UAW and Mazda reached agreement on their first contract, which was ratified 1,492-172. The contract provided for wage parity with Ford by 1991 and a $750 signing bonus. It also included a system of "union coordinators," a "problem resolution" procedure, and job security language similar to NUMMI's.

★ ★ ★

For up-to-date information on developments at Mazda, see chapters 8 and 36.

Notes

1. Louise Kertesz, "Mazda Plant Nears Job One," *Automotive News*, June 29, 1987.

2. Paul Lienert, "Governor's Role Held Key to Mazda," *Detroit Free Press*, December 9, 1984.

3. See, for example, the remarks of UAW Vice President Odessa Komer, "The Transplants—Threat or Opportunity for U.S. Workers and Suppliers?" in *The UMTRI Research Review*, University of Michigan Transportation Research Institute, September-December 1986.

4. *Detroit Free Press*, December 17, 1987.

5. "A New Car with a UAW Label," *Solidarity,* October 1986.

6. *Manufacturing Week*, October 25, 1987.

7. *Detroit Free Press*, June 1, 1987.

8. *MMUC Newsletter*, May 22, 1987.

9. "Employee Expectations," MMUC, February 25, 1987.

10. David N. Campbell, R.L. Fleming, and Richard C. Grote, "Discipline Without Punishment--At Last," *Harvard Business Review*, July-August 1985.

11. The procedure allows for union representation at all levels. As described here, it is the procedure followed before formal recognition of the UAW in September 1987 and adoption of a local contract in 1988.

12. Louise Kertesz, "Mazda Plant Nears Job One," *Automotive News*, June 29, 1987.

13. *Detroit News*, October 16, 1987.

14. Published by Science Research Associates, a division of IBM.

15. *Detroit Free Press*, December 17, 1987.

16. Mazda Motor Manufacturing (USA) Corp., *MMUC Production System: Concept and Outline*, 1986.

17. *Interact Interpersonal Problem Solving*, Interact Performance Systems Inc., 1987.

18. MMUC Production Engineering Department, *Kaizen Simulation Manual*, p. 10.

19. MMUC, *MMUC Production System: Concept and Outline*, 1986, p. 34.

Chapter 8

Management-by-Stress: The Test of Time

Myths surround management-by-stress, from teamwork to multi-skilling and creativity. Far from a repudiation of Taylorism, management-by-stress intensifies it. Stress is critical to making the various aspects of the system function together. The negative results workers experience are due not to mistakes in implementation but to inherent features of the system. Unions are an obstacle to the functioning of the system, so mechanisms of co-optation are necessary. When they feel the power to do so, workers act to alleviate the pressures of management-by-stress.

THE GOSPEL OF MANAGEMENT-BY-STRESS has been broadcast worldwide. The business and academic press have churned out hundreds of books and articles praising the system and telling management how-to. Variously labeled as lean production, Japanese management, post-Fordism, team concept, Total Quality Management, and synchronous manufacturing, the new methods have been hailed as the answer to management's problems in every country and in every industry.

Employers are managing-by-stress in workplaces as different from the assembly line as telecommunications and health care. Under management-by-stress, the differences in workers' lives on the job—between occupation, industry, or country—grow smaller and smaller.

In this chapter, we continue to use the auto assembly line as our principal teaching tool about management-by-stress, for several reasons: 1) it has been widely studied by other researchers as well as ourselves, so we have more information to draw on; 2) management-by-stress has been in place in auto plants longer than in other industries, providing a chance to look at the system over time; 3) because it's been around longer, auto workers have had more chance to figure out how to respond to the pressures of management-by-stress; 4) workers in other industries say that neither they nor their employers have had any trouble translating the management-by-stress techniques of the assembly line to other workplaces (many chapters in this book give examples.)

The Machine That Changed The World

The single most influential work promoting the spread of management-by-stress is *The Machine that Changed the World: Based on The Massachusetts Institute of Technology 5-Million-Dollar 5-Year Study On the Future of the Automobile*. The book declares the clear superiority of the Toyota Production System, which the authors name "lean production."

Far from being neutral observers, the authors are quite open about their advocacy posture. They urge us to implement the system as quickly and completely as possible: "We think it is in everybody's interest to introduce lean production everywhere as soon as possible, ideally within this decade."[1]

Most of the "5 Million Dollars" that MIT spent was contributed by auto companies. The authors say they maintained their independence because they limited individual contributions to five percent of the total budget. But if money talks, then the study is influenced by the general views of auto managers, if not those of any particular company.

Since the publication of the book, the authors are reported to have made small fortunes as consultants to corporations.

In the pages that follow, we will cite *Machine* frequently as a source of myths about lean production.

The spread of management-by-stress has been both voluntary and forced. Many companies have adopted some or all of the techniques as their bid to survive in a competitive world. But lean production techniques are also promoted by federal and state governments, which make grants to companies for that purpose.[2] And many large corporations are requiring their suppliers to have in place programs like statistical process control training, ISO 9000 certification, Malcolm Baldrige quality award applications, group problem-solving training, and so on.

Job-hopping executives become the Johnny Appleseeds of management-by-stress. Dennis Pawley, for example, moved from early team concept efforts at GM's Fiero plant, to GM-Van Nuys in California (later shut down), to Mazda, to Otis Elevator, and most recently to Chrysler. Ford executive Marvin Runyon became head of the Nissan plant in Tennessee, then went on to become chairman of the Tennessee Valley Authority, the huge quasi-public electrical power company. In four years he cut the workforce from 35,000 to 21,000, earning the title "Carvin' Marvin." In April 1992, Runyon was appointed to head the U.S. Postal Service to apply the same methods.

As the system has spread, many of the "feel-good" elements used in the original sales pitches have been stripped away, as management concentrates on the essential core. The *Wall Street Journal* headlined, "Torrent of job cuts may partly reflect shift from paternalism to lean-and-mean policies" and "Big happy family loses." Companies such as IBM and Xerox, "long known for humane employment policies," had joined the job-shedders. As one management expert noted, the new policies were moving beyond "your classic production worker" to technical, administrative, and managerial personnel.[6]

Business Week praised the new breed of "tough CEOS" who could make the hard decisions (to slash jobs) for the "tough times."[7]

For our model of management-by-stress, we will focus on three North American auto assembly plants: NUMMI, Mazda (now officially a joint venture with Ford and Mazda and re-named AutoAlliance International—AAI), and CAMI, a GM-Suzuki joint venture in Ingersoll, Ontario.[8] Each of these three plants was an explicit attempt to use the Japanese production system in North America in a unionized context. All three continue to serve as models of lean production for corporate America.

NUMMI is particularly important because it is the oldest of the three (opened in 1984) and has had a chance to stabilize. It is hard for defenders to pass off its oppressive features as temporary or as hangovers from the past.

First we will examine some of the myths that have grown up around management-by-stress, and compare those myths to the realities as described by workers in management-by-stress workplaces. Next we will look at how the stressing technique is critical to holding the system together and keeping workers on their toes. Next we will describe management-by-stress as a system—how its parts work together. We will look at whether the negative features of management-by-stress plants are correctable mistakes or inherent to the system. We will look at the role of unions under management-by-stress, and whether, as some claim, the system needs a union to make it perform its best. And finally, we will take a critical look at reports that workers in such plants are pleased with their conditions.

CLAIMS VS. REALITY

A mythology has grown up around "lean production"; management's claims about it are accepted as an accurate description of reality. If facts come to light that contradict

---

UPS, the Brown Machine

At United Parcel Service, the Brown Machine was using management-by-stress long before the auto companies caught on.

Package car drivers (the people who deliver packages to your door) work under a manual that includes literally hundreds of precise work methods. They include:

> ...the pen is kept in the left shirt pocket (for right handers) and never left with the clipboard or placed in another pocket...

> Turn ignition switch off and remove the key with one hand; engage the emergency brake with the other.

> Release the seat belt with one hand and obtain the clipboard as you arise from the seat.

> Walk with a brisk pace (a brisk pace commands attention).[3]

The company tells drivers how fast to walk (three feet per second), how to step from their trucks (on the right foot), how to fold their money (face up), how to carry packages (under the left arm), and how to hold their keys (teeth up, third finger).[4]

Every element of the work is broken down into time allotments measured to fractions of seconds and hundredths of hours. Periodically, delivery routes are timed by someone from the industrial engineering department who rides with the driver. Each day the driver is given an allotted time for completing pickups and deliveries. A weekly report tells management how many hundredths the driver was "under" or "overallowed" each day. Drivers who consistently run under are likely to find their loads increasing. Drivers who run over face discipline.

Joe Fahey, president of Teamsters Local 912, explains the "least best" system at UPS. Suppose a manager has drivers so scared that they work off the clock, exceed speed limits, and don't request help on heavy packages.

> The result is this group of drivers exceeds the UPS standard (known as "beating the route") by a whopping two-and-a-half hours a day. Is that cause for these supervisors to kick back? No way. UPS doesn't believe in good enough. If one driver is only beating his or her route by two hours, that driver is "least best" and gets pushed to do better.[5]

the official explanations, they are treated as exceptions, or mistakes in implementation.

Both the media and most of the academic world sustain this mythology, partly because of the strong ties between business and the academic community, and partly, in the case of the media, because of anti-worker bias and ignorance.[9]

Even the name of the system is part of the mythology. The name is important because it conveys an image of what the system is and how it works. To be "lean" is to be good, healthy, and strong. Who wants to be associated with the implied alternative, "the bloated production system"? "Lean production" describes the system from a management point of view, just as "management-by-stress" describes the reality as experienced by workers.

The terminology of lean production is carefully crafted to trigger strong positive responses: teams, teamwork, job rotation, empowerment, multi-skilling, job security. But none of these concepts, if understood by their common sense meanings, is central to the lean pro-

duction system. At the same time, management uses these terms to describe features that *are* essential to the system.

All the common myths about lean production contain grains of truth, some more than others. But when examined carefully, they offer a misleading description of the system. The chart summarizes the claims and the realities as they affect the shop floor. Let's look more closely at some of these claims (see box).

TEAMS

It is the dynamic work team that emerges at the heart of the lean factory.[10]

Although the term "team concept" is widespread and the word "teams" is written into many union contracts, the system is not built around workers functioning as teams in the usual sense of the word. Usually a team means a grouping of specialists—baseball team, surgical team, project team, management team. The qualities that make a good wide-receiver in football are not the same as those of center. The neurosurgeon and the anesthesiologist cannot sub-

Lean Production

Claims	Reality
Lean: The system uses less than one-half the staffing, space, resources that "mass production" does.	Differences exaggerated, especially considering that many elements of production are simply shifted outside of plant boundaries (contracted out).
Just-In-Time, 1-2 hour stocks	Moves in this direction, although some apparent JIT actually involves shifting stocks to suppliers.
Bufferless	Workers become the buffers, at reduced or no cost to company.
Production based on teams	Teams frequently do not meet for long periods of time, little "team" functioning. Team often little more than half an administrative unit. Team rhetoric often used to mean the opposite of teamwork.
Extensive job rotation	Frequently stopped or limited by management. When it happens, normally between jobs in the same team or group.
Multi-skilling	Workers are expected to know several jobs but each is designed for the lowest possible skill content.
Flexibility	More flexibility for management to direct workers, less for workers to direct themselves.
Worker creativity	Creativity mostly limited to suggesting ways to cut labor time. Worker input lessens as jobs are standardized.
Worker empowerment	More power for management.
Job security	A. Contractual security only for a core group; depends on a two-tier system with many workers who have little job security. B. Little security, when defined as perceived ability to remain at job through lifetime. C. Atmosphere of collective insecurity (fear of plant closing) is nurtured.
Rejection of "Taylorism"	Super-Taylorism. Intensified attempts to reduce jobs to their simplest elements that can be done with minimum training, and to require all workers to do jobs in exactly the same way.
Continuous improvement (*kaizen*)	Clearly part of the operational ideology: no set job standards, etc. Focus is on improvement in labor productivity. Could be considered continuous speed-up.
Worker dignity	Dignity presumed to flow from meeting management's goals well. Practices designed to regiment, to highlight nonconformity with prescribed results, and to evoke shame.

stitute for one another. A good union leadership team includes people with expertise in bargaining, accounting, history, communication, and mobilization.

Teamwork is the way that these specialists coordinate their distinctive skills to achieve a common goal. Yet under management-by-stress, teams are never organized to allow workers to gain more specialized skills, but rather to abolish such distinctions. "Team" equals "group of interchangeable workers."

This new definition of a team is an unusual one. Perhaps it derives from "team of horses"—beasts of burden of roughly equal capabilities, yoked together to pull for a common end (determined by the person holding the whip).

At AAI, most teams do not meet as such. Rather, weekly "unit" meetings combining several teams are chaired by the supervisor, who communicates information or admonitions to workers.

At NUMMI, many teams do not meet for months at a stretch, and others meet infrequently or only for a few minutes to hear the supervisor's exhortations. By offering a free meal, supervisors try to bribe workers to meet at lunch time. At CAMI, few teams meet regularly, and monthly safety meetings by area are held only because of the union's insistence.

Often confused with production teams are small group activities (such as quality circles) that may be a subset of a team or overlap team boundaries. These are made up of volunteers. For example, NUMMI management periodically promotes Problem Solving Circles that meet weekly on overtime. Workers' attitudes toward the circles are mixed. Some take them very seriously and view them as an opportunity to solve real problems. Others view them as an easy way (especially by NUMMI standards) of picking up some overtime pay. The Problem Solving Circles often fall into disuse when production picks up.

Production teams do have important roles in lean production, however. When the team is made the responsible unit for getting the assigned work done, a powerful peer pressure is set up. If one person is absent, the system forces the other team members to take up the slack; they are then likely to take out their frustration on the absent team member.

The importance of the "team" under management-by-stress is that it is the work unit of production. By making the work unit a group of people who can be shifted around to do different tasks, management has much more flexibility than if the work were viewed as a series of individual jobs. It is not possible to remove one-eighth each of eight individual people, but it is possible to remove one-eighth of an eight-person team.

Thus even if there is no "teamwork," in the sense of cooperative work, the team is the basis for kaizen activities. And it is in these kaizen activities, described below, that the peculiar and special notion of teamwork emerges.

CREATIVITY

[Blue-collar workers] will find their jobs more challenging.[11]

Every worker is now something of an industrial engineer.[12]

Worker creativity in management-by-stress workplaces is explicitly channeled into "continuous improvement" (see the section on "Kaizen" below). Workers are indeed asked to use their brains and to contribute ideas; at CAMI, for example, management pressure to submit *teians* (suggestions) is strong (see the box). In this sense, there is a grain of truth in the claim about creativity.

NUMMI management tries to guide its Problem Solving Circles by placing boundaries on what the circles may address. Included in the untouchables list are: Company Operating Principles, Human Resources Policy and Rules, Supplier Selection, New Model Design, Sales and Marketing Policies. The message is that creativity means finding ways to meet targets established by management. The Team Member Guide for Problem Solving Circles asks,

---

CAMI's Suggestion Program

[The suggestion program] will assure the success of the plant's operation.[13]

At CAMI, a worker receives 50 cents for each *teian* (suggestion) submitted and 50 cents more if it is approved. Each worker is expected to submit five teians per month—though in the first half of 1992, less than half of workers handed in any at all.

Teams can get pizza or cash awards for teians, and individuals can accumulate points to trade for consumer items (10,000 = a CAMI car). The company president awards a monthly teian cup to the winning department, based on the number of teians turned in. Five of the top annual teian-submitters win a trip to Japan, and others get prizes ranging from $100 to $1,000.

CAMI also sponsors a yearly rally for QC (quality control) circles to compete for prizes. The winning circle goes to Japan to compete with circles from Suzuki's other plants around the world.

One CAMI manager told union researchers that the company does not measure the success of the teian program by its economic return; the only standard is the degree of worker participation, with a focus on quantity.

However, cost-saving suggestions do win prizes: in 1991 one QC circle reduced paint usage and eliminated two out of four paint-spray workers. One team leader bragged that a QC circle had altered an operation that once took two workers one hour so that it took one person only 30 or 40 minutes.

According to a Canadian Auto Workers study, CAMI workers' perceptions of the teian and QC programs have changed over time. The percentage who joined QC circles because it is a "good idea" or to "solve real problems" dropped, while the percentage who said their motivation was cash or prizes rose sharply.[14]

"What is a 'Problem' anyway?" and answers, "A Deviation from a Standard."[15]

When a plant is brand new, or just after a new model launch, usually the assembly line moves very slowly or not at all. This is a time that many workers in management-by-stress plants have spoken of fondly. Workers have plenty of time to examine their jobs and figure out how to work the bugs out of the system. Saturn worker Diane Fitzgerald, for example, says of her team's first days on the line, when they were lucky to see a few vehicles a day, "We were fighting each other for the chance to work on the job." There is time to help each other out, discuss and solve problems, and work together as a real team. This can be a genuinely rewarding experience.

But it is times like this that management seeks to eliminate. "Design for manufacture" is one of the most praised aspects of the Japanese system (see chapter 4). The goal is for engineers to design the parts and the jobs and to test them out beforehand, so that the slow start-up period on the shop floor is eliminated. According to one Mazda engineer, the goal is a seamless changeover from one model to the next (see diagram).[16]

Notice that the total production of old plus new models during changeover remains constant. This means that workers continue to work at just as fast a production

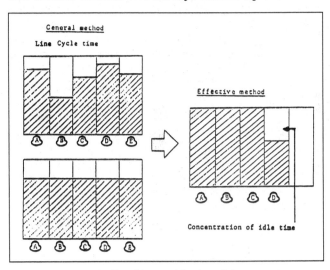

How to "balance the line," from a Mazda training manual.

pace as the new car is introduced as they did on the old car.

Further, the workers who get to participate most in those start-up activities tend to be team leaders or to be specially selected by supervisors. The NUMMI contract, for example, specifies that it is team leaders' and group leaders' job to develop each suggested standardized work. They are the first ones to staff a new line; once they have the fun of working the bugs out, regular workers are added and the line speed picks up.

Thus management's intent is to eliminate that part of the work-year that most involves worker judgment, creativity, and contributions to problem-solving.

The teian program has spurred another kind of creativity at CAMI. Since workers are paid 50 cents apiece for teians—even those that are not adopted—some workers flood the program with minor ideas. The CAW Local 88 newsletter commented on such teians as "rotating a garbage pail, removing the dead fish from an aquarium, or everyone's favorite: if it's a hazard, tape it. This has driven our fellow workers to write dozens upon dozens of the most stupid teians imaginable in an effort to milk the system."[17]

The real challenge under management-by-stress is not creativity but mental and physical survival—how to keep up with the ceaseless kaizen.

As NUMMI worker Becky Kiley put it, "Kaizening is supposed to be creative, but how many times can you sit

Team Concept Needs a Stake through the Heart

This article appeared in the January 1994 issue of The Guide, *the newsletter of UAW Local 3000 at the Flat Rock, Michigan Mazda plant.*

Some terms:

"unit" = two or more teams under a "unit leader," or foreman

"area leader" = next supervisor above a unit leader

"line balance the unit" = redistribute the unit's work

"union coordinator" = elected working steward

"downtime" = time the assembly time is stopped.

by Norm Kujawa

Article I, Section 2 of our local agreement states, "The company commits to promote an environment based on the teamwork concept in problem solving through non-confrontational practices such as mutual trust, sincerity and frankness."

The team concept is dead. Sort of.

Like the undead rising in the night, the team concept lives only in the imaginations of those whose job it is to promote such a horrific concept.

The reality is that teams exist only for purposes of attendance and overtime equalization. After that, workers are at the mercy of the managers and their "rights." Scarier still—the AutoAlliance-style team concept is being borrowed by others, including the Ford Motor Company, to the dismay of those workers.

Could all this complaining about AutoAlliance's team concept be just loud whining by a few disgruntled workers? Let's look at a recent example of AutoAlliance's team concept failure.

Part of AutoAlliance's production philosophy is doing things "just-on-time." This includes everything from the arrival of work to the work station to the delivery of parts just as the line operator runs out. Despite the built-in cost savings of operating a plant in such an efficient manner, AutoAlliance continued to have economic difficulties, caused by a struggling economy in Japan and the poor planning of a three-car model launch in 1992. Management began looking for ways to cut costs, one of these ways being their employee suggestion, or kaizen, program.

In June 1993, members of the Body Assembly Material Handling unit, unit 91 [forklift drivers, who deliver parts to the assembly line production units], began hearing rumors that their unit was going to be dispersed, or broken up. *(Mutual trust, frankness)*

Soon after the rumors started, members found out that their unit leader, team player that he was, had suggested the dispersal, for an alleged savings to the company of $800,000. His suggestion would place all forklift driver work into each production unit, and give himself a suggestion payout estimated in the five-figure range. *(Trust)*

Once it became apparent that management was serious about the break-up (this had been discussed several times over the years, but was deemed to be infeasible), the team members of unit 91 demanded to speak to management to find out why and to have some input. The answer they received was that the unit was too inefficient and costly. "Why weren't we asked for input on improvements?" asked the members. "And how were the cost savings calculated?" There was no plan written on paper for anyone to look at. *(Mutual trust)*

In July, at the request of the union bargaining committee, management allowed the members to come in early to find ways to be more efficient. These meetings were canceled after two days. *(Mutual trust, sincerity)* The area leader

there and kaizen a job after you've done it for four-and-a-half years?"[18]

KAIZEN AND TEAMWORK

> Once teams of workers design a work process, they can become the source of continuous improvement if they are given the discretion and incentives to do so.[19]

Kaizen, or continuous improvement, is a fundamental principle of lean production. Lean managers go to great pains to impress upon workers that "improving" their jobs is part of their job and their obligation.

But under lean production "improvement," like "teamwork," has a very precise and limited meaning which is different from our normal understanding of the word. The theory is spelled out in the classic work by Yasuhiro Monden, *The Toyota Production System*.[20] It is a central theme repeated over and over in lean production training materials.

The illustration on page 71 is from a Mazda training manual from the mid-1980s.[21] It shows the team how to deal with an imbalance in the amount of work each team member has to do (#1). The shaded area represents working time and the white area idle time.

The common sense notion of teamwork, and a desire for equality, would suggest arrangement #2. This, according to Mazda, is the "general method"—what most people would do. But, Mazda says, this solution is not correct. Rather than sharing the work evenly among the five mem-

---

deemed the meetings to be a "waste of time." He claimed the members had reneged on their promise of finding ways to cut jobs. But the employees' only commitment had been to improve unit efficiency. Their goal was to do it without displacing anyone from the unit.

The area leader, now in the Trim Department, met with unit 91 on August 4 and notified the members of the company's intention to disband the unit effective August 23. *(Frankness)*

Union representatives Chuck Browning and Karl Koeppen took their arguments to Bruce Bowman, the general manager of manufacturing. On August 9, Bowman canceled Body Shop's plan because their plan was not complete. *(Sincerity)*

Visibly upset, Body Shop management gathered their troops and developed a plan to disperse unit 91. They presented it to Bowman, who approved it. Once again the members of unit 91 were notified of the plan and told to pick a new work unit. The paperwork for transfers was filled out and cross-training for new forklift drivers was begun. *(More mutual trust, frankness)*

Undaunted, the union coordinators from both shifts of unit 91 developed a small booklet of problems, concerns, and costs related to the move (costs which far outweighed the projected savings). Koeppen and the A shift coordinator met with Bruce Bowman on September 2 and presented him with the information.

Bowman told them of his commitment to following the philosophy the plant was founded on *(see above)*. He said he was told by "his people" that the members of 91 wouldn't cooperate when given the opportunity. Koeppen explained that the members were committed to making the unit more efficient, but *would not do management's job* by voluntarily sacrificing any of their own. Bowman assigned an industrial engineer to look into the problem.

The Body Shop manager notified Koeppen and the UAW bargaining committee on September 15 that he would keep the unit intact if the members would help line-balance the unit after three jobs per shift were cut. The members, as they had said all along, cooperated in the line balance and began running with three less jobs shortly thereafter.

The impact of the reduction was felt immediately, as job efficiency jumped to the 95 percent level—working 57 seconds out of every minute. As the members struggled, downtime on the assembly line increased, causing constant complaints from management and adding to the job stress of the workers.

The two unit leaders from Unit 91 told their supervisors they needed more manpower to operate more efficiently. Once again management began looking at dispersing the unit rather than properly manning it. *(Mutual trust, sincerity, frankness)*

During the first week of December a senior Body Shop manager, responding to a member's question about a possible break-up, replied that as far as he was concerned, the members of unit 91 had reneged on their part of the deal and "were not trying to make the new line balance work." *(Mutual trust, sincerity, frankness)*

As the year ended, plans were being made for engineers to time-study the jobs in unit 91. Apparently management doesn't trust the judgment of their own unit leaders either. It's painfully obvious that decisions are made based on money and the opportunity to make an impression. Management was wrong about the number of jobs cut and no one wants to take responsibility for being wrong.

Hopefully, this story will have a happy ending for the members of unit 91. This isn't the only time the company's own team concept philosophy has failed. Unless management is willing to give up some of their "rights" and commit through collective bargaining to working as a team, union negotiators should drive a stake through the heart of team concept and kill it for good.

[Norm Kujawa is editor of UAW Local 3000's *The Guide* and a member of the bargaining committee.]

"Kaizen must always be tied to concrete cost reductions." From a CAMI training manual.

bers, the team should recombine the tasks so that they can do away with one worker.

The kaizen does not stop there, however. Notice that even after eliminating one worker, the correct, "effective" method does not divide the remaining tasks evenly among the remaining four. It is better to have three workers working flat-out and let worker D coast temporarily. Then Mazda can do one of two things: add tasks to worker D—perhaps from another team that has gone through the same process; or kaizen the jobs again so that D's tasks can be distributed among workers A, B, and C.

The same approach and similar "wrong" and "right" examples are repeated in two 1993 AAI (Mazda) manuals,

with explanations like: "Remember, when linebalancing it is our objective to reduce and relocate our work force."[22]

The CAMI training manual contains a similar philosophy.

CAMI makes it clear that "kaizen" does not mean improvement of just anything. The manual warns,

> Kaizen must always be tied to concrete cost reductions. For example, eliminating waste to reduce man-hours by a 0.9 person doesn't help much. Finding ways to do work with 9 persons where it previously took 10 means a genuine saving...[23]

Monden argues against mechanization that might reduce the labor effort by .9 persons, unless the remaining

Visual Management

Visual management is an idea that overlays all of lean production. It means that managers can manage best when both their orders and the results, errors, and problems (feedback) are made as obvious and visible as possible. By making these available for all to see, anyone and everyone can be responsible and held accountable for any problem.

For example, when standardized work procedures are posted near each work station, any supervisor can immediately see whether the exact process is being followed. Instead of a computer notifying a single supervisor or utility person of a problem, a flashing light and chime calls everyone's attention.

Some aspects of visual management are clearly beneficial to workers. By implementing the "4 S's," establishing a place for everything and everything in its place, the plant is kept neat and clean and missing items become obvious (see chapter 4).

But carried to its conclusion, visual management also denies privacy. Management rearranges work areas and tool shelves and opens tool cribs so that there are no spaces not visible from the aisles.

In the factory, glass walls replace opaque walls. In the office, there are very few private work spaces; everyone works in one big room. It does not matter that the system is a monument to management's mistrust of workers, that workers feel like zoo animals on display, or whether greater distractions make it harder to do certain kinds of mental work or may even pose dangers on the factory floor. Visual management improves management control.

Visual management is also part of the approach to "balancing" jobs. According to Monden:

> When the waiting time for each worker is being measured, he should stand without doing anything at all after he has finished the operations assigned to him...In this way everyone will be able to see that he has free time and there will be less resistance if he is assigned one or two more jobs.[24]

Note that Monden recognizes workers are likely to resist, and that another aspect of visual control is to expose workers to peer pressure.

.1 person ("often the watchman for the machine") can also be eliminated.[25] Reducing effort is not the issue, reducing jobs is.

If the team is successful in reducing its numbers, which worker leaves? Is he or she chosen by seniority or by volunteering, either of which would be consistent with "teamwork"? No, "the best workers should always be removed first," according to one of Monden's rules.[26] AAI advises the same thing.[27]

Why? If the work standards have been set according to the capabilities of a given team of workers, and management removes the slowest person, then the jobs will overall be slightly easier for the sturdy types who remain. On the other hand, if the hardest worker is transferred out, then the remaining workers will have to try just a little harder, to meet the standards she or he has set. Another advantage: the "best workers" will be useful in forcing up the standards in their new teams.

Rob Pelletier, then president of the union at CAMI, warned fellow members, "We must always be wary of how easy it is for management to fill up the time we save with our improvements."[28] For example, many teams at CAMI had chosen to redistribute their tasks so that one person was freed up as a "floater." The floater unpacked parts and helped other team members, and each team member got to rotate through that position. But management soon began to appropriate the floaters, moving them to other teams to cover for absences.[29]

STANDARDIZED WORK
AND THE END OF TAYLORISM

> Executives at many companies have reevaluated Taylorism and become convinced that its methods have a stultifying effect upon the worker as a thinking, creative human being...[They are] "de-Taylorizing" the workplace...[30]

The original theoreticians of the Japanese production system, such as Monden and Taichi Ohno, saw their notion of standardized work as building on the ideas of Frederick Taylor's scientific management and Henry Ford's assembly line (see chapter 4 for a description of Taylorism). Those who implemented the production system in North America were explicit that they were following in the Taylorist tradition. A Mazda manual, for example, shows how its modern Industrial Engineering approach is built on Taylor's work measurement (with standard times by stopwatch), differential wage incentives, and time study.[31]

Further, a central tenet underlying all the well-known quality programs, from Deming's to Crosby's, is that quality is achieved by removing variation from the process (see chapter 14). This in turn requires breaking jobs down to their elemental tasks, carrying out precisely defined steps as management instructs, and extremely tight process control—i.e., Taylorism.

Despite this history and these facts, in North America many advocates of lean production maintain that it represents an alternative to Taylorism.[32] In chapters 4 and 5 we argue that the standardized work at the heart of management-by-stress is best understood as an intensification of Taylorism. A system that defines waste, as AAI does, as "one hand idle while other hand performs work," is practically a caricature of Taylorism.[33]

Even where management's methods change, they clearly stay within the Taylorist framework. For example,

Standardized White-Collar Work

Reservations agents at Air Canada say that their work has become measured, standardized, and monitored, at the same time that management cuts jobs—to the detriment, they feel, of customer service. The conditions they describe will be familiar to many office workers.

Koren Millington of Canadian Auto Workers Local 2213 explains "in-line availability": "You're supposed to be on the phones x amount of hours, you're supposed to be off the phones x amount of hours. Anything above that you're answerable for, even if it involves servicing passengers.

"It's like an umbilical cord, technically. Once you plug in, you're hooked into them. They know when you plugged in, when you plug out, how long you talked on the call. They know when you go to the bathroom, how long you were off."

Once plugged in, the format of the conversation with the customer is pre-set.

"It has to be asked a certain way," explains Lydie Moore. "I've heard of people that, even though they've made the sale, just because they said the word 'or'—'Would you like me to hold the seats for you, or...?'—that was a 'deficient call.'

"That's how we're rated. Deficient calls means calls that didn't meet management's format. We're all taped."

Adds Theresa Burgess: "They have the ability to monitor every minute of your day, through the computers, through your supervisors, through your co-workers. Literally every second of your day can be accounted for and they can discipline you because you haven't used that time properly."

Dave Robertson of the CAW's Research Department explains: "If you're on an assembly line management control is immediate. At Air Canada, that control wasn't there. Because the phone would ring, you'd pick it up, and all of a sudden you'd have a private conversation with someone on the other end. And management didn't know what you were doing.

"Part of lean production is this notion of management by sight or visible management. What electronics and surveillance do at Air Canada is to make the work process visible to management and therefore controllable by management."[34]

when the Mazda plant started up, workers were trained to measure work speed against a norm established by videotapes. The new-hires were instructed, "This person is working at three-quarters speed, this one at double speed..."

Now AAI is using the more direct pit-workers-against-each-other technique called "Minimum Time Method": work is broken down into its elements, measured in hundredths of a minute. (AAI suggests that beginners not try to identify elements smaller than three seconds.) A number of workers are monitored doing the same job (say, installing a head gasket), and times are recorded for each worker for each element (five seconds to pick up and bring the gasket to the line, two seconds to position it correctly, etc.). Then AAI figures the proper time for the whole job: the total of the second fastest times for each element.[35]

Lean production aims to make each job 95 percent efficient[36]—that is, the "net times" for the individual elements add up to almost all of the time available to do the whole job. If line speed is set at 60 units per hour (one per minute), the efficient worker works 57 seconds, leaving 3 seconds as waste.

But the entire 57 seconds is taken up with physical work, leaving a paradox: despite management's claims that lean production means "working smarter," there is no time to think. Greg Drudi, union representative in charge of monitoring work standards at AAI, points out:

> Thinking time is never included in the standardized work. Different models come down the same line, and during that three seconds that you can supposedly relax, you have to read the broadcast sheet [requirements for that model] and mentally prepare for the different operations in the next job.

There are, however, important differences between Taylor's vision and management-by-stress. Taylor tended to see gathering of worker knowledge as a one-time event; management-by-stress views it as a continuing process. And management-by-stress includes methods to enable management to routinely collect the information. These include monetary rewards for suggestions; exhortations to show "responsibility" and "creativity"; control through visual management; videotaping of jobs; electronic monitoring through sensors that detect and send all line actions for computer storage and compilation in managers' offices; monitoring by special kaizen groups; rotation; peer pressure; and working supervisors.

The main argument of those who contend that lean production is different from Taylorism is the element of "volunteerism"—the idea that it is workers who time-study each other and make the suggestions themselves.

Professor Paul Adler, for example, calls the NUMMI system "democratic Taylorism," as contrasted with traditional, "despotic Taylorism." Adler recognizes that the actual work ("the technical dimension") falls clearly in the tradition of Taylorism. But, he argues, the "social dimension" is very different. The collective team discussions and creative suggestions fundamentally alter the nature of the system.[37]

But unlike traditional "despotic Taylorism," NUMMI's methods and standards are not designed to squeeze more work out of employees that management assumes are recalcitrant and irresponsible.

Instead, these methods and standards are determined by work teams themselves: workers are taught how to time their own jobs with a stopwatch, compare alternative procedures to determine the most efficient one, document the standard procedure to ensure that everyone can understand and implement it, and identify and propose improvements in that procedure. At any given time, the task of standardized work analysis might be delegated to a team leader or a team member, but everyone understands the analysis process and can participate in it.[38]

The notion that getting workers to do the time-study transforms Taylorism can be challenged on two grounds. First is the question of how much worker participation in setting work standards there really is. In general it is teams of supervisors and team leaders who write the original standardized work sheets, and it is management who selects workers to serve on the special kaizen teams later on.

In periods of normal production—that is, not a model launch—*some* workers volunteer to engage in problem-solving or kaizen activities, for no more than one-half to one hour a week. In practice, management frequently regards these activities as incidental and easily disposed of when there are production goals to be met.

Second and more important, even if workers did consistently engage in these participation activities, the decisive issue is ultimately one of control. The key to understanding how this kind of "democracy" works is that management maintains control of the parameters and goals for problem solving—the training techniques and the definition of what constitutes an "improvement." Any proposed variations must be approved by management. The final decision on using different methods belongs to management.

Thus worker suggestions and participation contribute to an *increased* management control over the work process—not more democracy.

In spring 1994, CAMI announced a campaign to get "back to the basics" of the Suzuki Production System. Union Vice President Dave Binns explained, "They're talking about 'disciplined work,' walking the exact number of steps on the chart and following the walking pattern. They've broken the pitches [work stations] down into tenths and put white marks along the side of the line to show the tenths. If your cycle time is 120 seconds, you must work 12 seconds in that space."

Perhaps these quotes from a CAMI management newsletter will indicate whether Taylorism is alive and well in North America, and who intends to control it.

> All parts and lineside furniture will be minimized and their positions painted on the floor. Process cover sheets (PCS) will hang at every station which will show the parts layout, the job sequence and the walking pattern. All Production Associates will perform the job as described...
>
> A green arrow will be painted on the floor to indicate where you will first contact the vehicle. Stick to this.

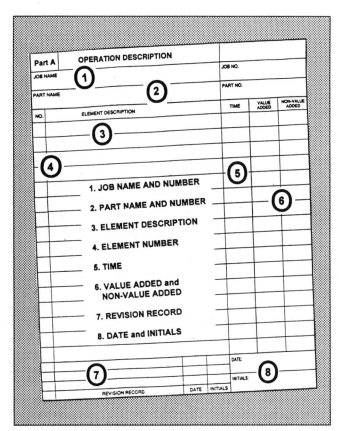

Taylorism 1990s-Style: In 1993 General Motors required workers at its Marion, Indiana parts plant to attend Standardized Operations (SOP) workshops. Kevin Kuhl, Manager of Manufacturing Engineering, explained, "The worksheets will be posted on the job so that anyone can walk up to the job and perform with a minimum of break in time."

There is one "best way" to do a job. This means the other nine are less efficient or potential safety risks. To stay competitive, we must do the job the right way...

Standardized work is coming. It will be a difficult transition for some. You have been doing a job the same way for 5 years, and somebody who doesn't do the job is going to ask you to change—tough sell...[39]

WORKER EMPOWERMENT

The workers' revolution has finally come to the shop floor. The people who work on the assembly line have taken charge and have the power to make management do their jobs right.[40]

The Parties are committed to provide workers a voice in their own destiny in decisions that affect their lives before such decisions are made.[41]

As described in the previous section, worker *participation* can actually give management more *control* over how work is done. True—this control is exercised in a more sophisticated and flexible manner than in systems where bosses simply issue direct orders. Some workers have likened the control to that of the principal over a high school student government.

In a November 1991 survey at CAMI, only one-third of the workers felt they were "actively involved in making decisions at work." Asked why they answered yes, most referred to decisions related to their immediate jobs. Only eight percent thought that the teian program or quality circles gave them any decision-making power.[42]

An indication of workers' power at NUMMI is management's instructions to the Problem-Solving Circles. They are told specifically not to address company operating principles, Human Resources policies/rules, supplier selection/price, new model design, or sales and marketing policies.

If workers may not address these areas—the ones that would actually give them some say over what happens in and to the company—what's left of workers' power? Well, the Problem Solving Circles have the power to kaizen. If "company operating principles"—i.e., leanness—are off limits, how are circles to address problems of workload or understaffing?

WORKER DIGNITY

[NUMMI is] truly committed to treating employees as their most important assets and to providing opportunities for employee growth.[43]

Lean production plants claim to impart dignity to their workers by letting them use the same parking lots and cafeterias as managers, and by eliminating time clocks. A chance for a parking space near the door is a change that workers appreciate, although their gratitude for the right to eat lunch with supervisors is questionable. The elimination of time clocks is a moot point for assembly line workers, who must be on the job when the whistle blows in any case. Actually, many prefer time clocks because they create an objective record rather than depending on the supervisor's graces. (It turns out that many plants that claim to have eliminated time clocks actually keep computer records of employees' attendance, using the special cards that open the exit and entrance gates.)

One measure of dignity on the job is the ability to determine one's own needs for sick leave and other time off, and enforce them. But this notion of dignity runs counter to the lean system, which operates with as few absentee replacements as possible. At Mazda, the union negotiated eight half-days of paid personal leave that could be taken at the worker's discretion, with only a few hours' notice. But when this right led to staffing shortages, management unilaterally announced restrictions—thumbing its nose at the union contract. (Read about the union's response to this incident in chapter 36.)

Another invasion of worker dignity is the method of focusing attention on individual foul-ups. When a worker pulls the stop cord to indicate he needs help, the *andon* system indicates the work station. There is nothing in principle wrong with this, except that the company tries to create a sense that pulling the cord represents failure and shame. At CAMI the andon system plays a nursery rhyme.

JOB ROTATION

Workers rotate through the various jobs performed by the team, increasing their skills and their understanding of the production process.[44]

Rotation has proven to be a complicated but key issue for both management and the union.

When traditional auto plants (with many classifications) switched to the team concept (with few or no classifications) in the 1980s, management motivated rotation in the language of job enrichment. Workers would find varied jobs more interesting. By experiencing all the jobs in their team, workers would understand the larger process and how the jobs fit together. This would reduce alienation. It would also improve quality, since workers would understand how even small variations in one step would affect other steps. They could recognize faults made in other steps and could help solve problems in the process as a whole.

Of course, a large part of management's motivation was to increase productivity. There would be less need for special workers who knew all the jobs in the team—relief workers or absentee replacements—since anyone could fill in where needed. No longer would anyone be able to say, "That's not my job."

Some workers liked the idea of rotation, in the hopes of gaining more skills or breaking the monotony. Others disliked it. Rotating between five boring jobs doesn't necessarily make for one interesting job. Instead rotation may force you to think just enough that you are not able to do the job by rote while lost in thought about something far away from work. Besides, if you are senior enough to have a "good" job, you may want to do it all the time, rather than a fifth of the time.

Beyond questions of individual preference about the work itself, there were the other disadvantages: more leeway for supervisor favoritism in job assignments, and job loss.

Rotation also changes the conditions for "hidden job knowledge." When a worker does the same job consistently, she may develop techniques to save time, make the job more tolerable, and create breaks in the routine. For example, the installer of the windshield wiper motor may find that if she preassembles her three parts and puts them on together, rather than tightening each one separately on the car, she can shave several seconds off the time specified on the standardized work sheet.

Without rotation, it is easier for the worker to keep these techniques to herself. But under rotation there is great peer pressure to share the information. Particularly when you have a team leader or even a supervisor acting as a relief worker, it becomes almost impossible to maintain the hidden knowledge. In the process, workers are stripped of an important bit of leeway, some personal space.

However, despite all management's claims to champion rotation and the reasons for unions to resist it, in the lean production plants we have studied, the union ends up the defender of rotation and management tries to restrict it.

It seems that whatever concern management has for workers, understanding the whole process takes second place to reducing variation in the process and raising productivity. Even though the jobs are designed to be as easily learned as possible, rotation still tends to add some variation to the process; each team member may not be equally proficient at every operation.

Thus management tries to limit rotation to the minimum required so that 1) workers learn the jobs well enough that they can be reassigned when necessary and 2) it is difficult for individuals to preserve "secret" job knowledge. Management has decided that more rotation than this is counterproductive.

This is especially true during model launch or at other times when there are quality problems. For example, a finding of the California Department of Industrial Relations describes the situation at NUMMI:

> For the 1993 passenger line start-up, NUMMI management established a policy of no rotation between jobs until employees achieved a high standard of excellence and expertise on their new "primary" job, i.e., until that task had been well-learned in terms of quantity and quality of output.[45]

Unions, on the other hand, have had to fight to keep rotation and make it a worker right rather than a management option. Many workers prefer rotation, simply because it is less monotonous. And in some plants (not lean production ones) where management has introduced a "pay-for-knowledge" system, the pay increment depends on showing proficiency on a number of jobs, so workers need to rotate. In addition, the "hidden knowledge" declines in importance, since lean production has so many other techniques for management to gain worker knowledge (supervisors working, visual management, problem-solving circles).

But one of the main reasons workers favor rotation is to minimize repetitive strain injuries. Because of the insistence on doing the job the same way every time and the lack of rest time between cycles, workers under lean production are particularly susceptible to such injuries. In 1994, one Problem-Solving Circle at NUMMI named itself "Noro Nee Bo," meaning "no rotation, aching knees and elbows."

In 1993 California OSHA cited NUMMI for a large number of "ergonomic hazards": jobs that by their design and repetitiveness could be predicted to cause injury from excessive wrist flexion, palm pounding, and static loading on back, shoulders, and elbows. The citation charged NUMMI with ignoring these dangers by implementing its no-rotation policy. According to the industrial hygienist, "Rotation is often successfully used to mitigate repetitive stress risks until engineering solutions can be implemented."[46]

Of course, rotation used this way is a two-edged sword. Workers may like rotation because their backs can take two hours of installing seats, but not eight. But the use of rotation to "solve" the problem of jobs that are just too hard also relieves the pressure on management to find a different solution—such as mechanical aids or hiring more workers.

A final note on the complicated subject of rotation: Experience has shown that rotation can provide the basis for bitter divisions among team members. What happens when a worker is injured and, under doctor's orders, is restricted from certain kinds of jobs? Typically, the union insists that the person be kept at work he can do. But this may mean removing the easiest job from the rotation—which understandably can cause resentment on the part of the remaining workers.

The situation becomes even stickier when a non-injured worker cannot do certain jobs. If two team members claim they are not strong enough to lift heavy weights,

---

MBS, RSI

To date, we know of no studies comparing repetitive strain injuries (RSI) in management-by-stress plants to those in more traditional factories. The anecdotal evidence indicates that workers become injured more quickly in the management-by-stress plants, and that more workers are injured. (They also appear to be more likely to lose their jobs.)

One reporter compared Mazda's 1988 record on such injuries to that of a Chrysler assembly plant in Michigan. Chrysler reported 54 injuries for 3,500 workers. Mazda reported 97 injuries; the workforce began with a single shift early in the year, added a second shift in May, and ended up with 2,770 workers. Thus the Mazda rate was more than twice as high—even though some Mazda workers didn't even work all year. (The UAW said there was "radical under-reporting" of injuries at all auto plants.)

At the time, Mazda said 160 people (close to six percent of the workforce) were on restricted work, some of them in a preventive program because they had symptoms that could become worse. The union president maintained that a shortage of workers had led to restrictions on rotation. A local industrial hygienist said, "It's said in the [local] medical community that there's a mini-epidemic of carpal tunnel syndrome" at Mazda.[47]

According to Michigan workers' compensation records, in 1988 Mazda's rate of serious injuries was 4.1 per 100 workers, while the rate for the Big Three was 1.2.[48]

In a 1989 organizing drive at Nissan in Tennessee, the UAW said that Nissan had nearly six times as many workers' compensation cases requiring eight days off work as Ford's glass plant in nearby Nashville. (Note, however, that the Ford plant was not an assembly plant.) Shortly before the representation election, four UAW supporters requested the company's OSHA 200 log, which lists injuries and which any employee has a legal right to see. Citing employee privacy, Nissan refused, and was fined $5,000 by the state Department of Labor.

In any case, in the auto industry, it is now probably too late to compare management-by-stress plants with "traditional" ones, since all the companies are moving to adopt lean production methods.

---

then the remaining team members may be left humping fenders all day.

Of course, management has always tried to divert workers' opposition to tough jobs into resentment toward "weaker" workers. But because management-by-stress denies people the right to select their own jobs (through classifications and seniority), it will produce greater resentment when some people get the "good" jobs by claiming inability.

MULTI-SKILLING

Lean producers employ teams of multi-skilled workers at all levels of the organization.[49]

Management-by-stress plants do spend a fair amount of time in "training" of various sorts. In the early stages of production, there is training designed to increase identification with company goals and in company procedures, mixed in with training in problem solving and group skills; these classes tend to be cut back once production is well under way. At Saturn, for example, new workers initially received at least 300-350 hours of training; as production ramped up, training was cut to 175 hours; now new hires receive only about 40 hours.

At the same time, the system quite consciously breaks down the work itself into tiny steps that are as easy as possible. "Multi-skilling" thus means training to do several deskilled jobs, or, more accurately, "multi-tasking."

Temporaries at AAI and replacement workers at CAMI can usually take over jobs with very little training (a few hours to a day). CAMI workers, asked how much training it took to learn their jobs, answered five minutes, 20 minutes, a couple of hours.[50]

Where possible the system seeks to remove discretion from the individual and place it in the machinery, with sensors or mechanical devices to check for defects or for an accumulation of production; if found, the machine automatically shuts down production. This is a combination of what its proponents call "foolproofing" and *jikoda*, or "autonomation." For example, instead of relying on an inspector down the line or even the worker at the next station to see that a part is missing, management installs a photo-eye that will shut down the line unless it "sees" the part.

Nor do workers feel that they are well trained. A union survey at Mazda, for example, reported that roughly half the workers rated the training they had received as poor or none, compared to Mazda's promises.[51]

For the skilled trades (electricians, machine repair, tool makers, die makers), the system seeks to contract out those portions of the work that require the most skill: major construction and complex or lengthy repairs. The in-plant skilled trades jobs are reduced as much as possible to predictable, standardized preventive maintenance tasks. This is an explicit part of lean production, and frequently meets with resistance from workers who seek to protect and develop their skills. The manager of NUMMI's stamping plant says:

A lot of skilled workers in the plant still believe that standardized work doesn't apply to them. Their response to standardized work is: "How can you standardize something like a maintenance function? You never know what's going to happen." But fixing things isn't maintenance—that's repair. NUMMI wants preventative systems with standardized maintenance procedures rather than fire-fighting....The general idea is to replace repairs with routine maintenance. We've just started getting the skilled trades to accept Toyota's way of doing things.[52]

See further discussion of skills and training in Chapter 35.

BUFFERLESS

There were practically no buffers between the welding shop and paint booth and between paint and final assembly. And there were no parts warehouses at all.[53]

The system is sometimes referred to as "bufferless production." But let's examine this concept carefully. Glitches are inevitable, anywhere. Could a system that really had no buffers to deal with these glitches be as productive as this system is? Lean production does remove or sharply curtail those buffers that add significant cost—a stock of work-in-progress, back-up machinery, extra workers, or spare time—but it replaces these with an alternative. The real buffers in bufferless production are the workers, who are expected to put out extra effort to maintain production *despite* the unavoidable glitches.

If the just-in-time system makes a part shipment late and the team leader has to run to get it, that's the job. If overtime is required and workers have to forego personal plans, that's the job too. Using workers as the shock absorbers of the system costs management little (except for workers compensation claims), but it can be very unhealthy for the human element.

In fact, many of the perceived advantages of just-in-time are achieved not by eliminating buffers, but by shifting or hiding them. Often, for example, the responsibility for maintaining an inventory is simply transferred (forced) onto the supplier.

Before the advent of lean production, auto workers created their own buffers by varying their work pace throughout the day. They would work faster for a little while ("up the line," somewhat ahead of their assigned work station), to get ahead and catch a minute, maybe even several minutes, to rest. Besides the attraction of breaks, many found this routine less boring than maintaining a constant pace throughout the day.[54]

Caroline Lund works on a subassembly line at NUMMI, the passenger door line. She explains the bufferless work method:

In December 1993 our cycle time was reduced from 63 seconds to 60 seconds with no change in the jobs or additional personnel. For the hardest jobs, the weatherstrip jobs, our group leader announced we were getting moving carts that would travel along with the door carrier. These carts would hold our parts—glass-runs and window moldings—and cut down on walking time back to the parts racks. They were supposed to make it possible to do the jobs in three seconds less.

But moving the parts from the rack to the cart took time. At first we were told the team leaders would stock the carts, but we soon saw that really the assembler was expected to do it.

Other workers and I protested that we didn't want the carts, even though they did make the job faster once the carts were stocked. We noted how the carts made it impossible to take advantage of down time to get a little up the line, so as to be able to keep up when two or three Prizms come in a row (Prizm weatherstrips take twice as long as Corollas), or when we get a bad part.

With the cart you can't work either up or down the line, because the cart rides on a track that starts at the beginning of your station and ends at the end of your station. So the worker has no flexibility whatsoever.

When I protested against the carts, my group leader told me: The carts are the wave of the future because they maximize standardized work. Standardized work means not only doing the job the same way in the same time, but in the same space. If someone is working up the line or down the line, that job needs to be adjusted so the worker can do it in just the space allotted.

This group leader told another worker that the cart would be good because it would keep her from working up the line to talk with another worker.

By six months after the carts were introduced, half of the operators (four out of eight) were disconnecting the carts at the start of the shift and working without them.

FLEXIBILITY: MACHINES

Lean producers...use highly flexible, increasingly automated machines to produce volumes of products of enormous variety.[55]

It is certainly true that production machinery is now designed to be more flexible than in the past, and to yield variations in products. The dies in stamping presses, for example (the heavy forms that stamp out parts from sheets of steel), can now be changed many times more quickly than in the past, so that the presses can do short runs of different products rather than dedicating entire lines to the production of a single part. This greater flexibility came about partly because of the leadership of Toyota.

It was not simply Toyota's lean production system that made the difference, however, but rather developments in technology. Some would say that such changes were not only enabled by but driven by new technology. If a company has invested in very expensive technology, it has to figure out a way not to let the machines sit idle.

Other systems of work organization also use flexible machinery; this is not unique to lean production. Automatic Guided Vehicles (AGVs), for example, heavily used in Swedish auto plants, are also a flexible technology that allows greater variety of products. But our three lean plants do not use AGVs on their assembly lines.

FLEXIBILITY: WORKERS

Under flexible manufacturing and small-batch production, where workers were required to produce a constantly changing array of products, strict work rules and narrow job classifications were no longer deemed "efficient."[56]

Perhaps the single feature most often associated with lean production is the flexible, "multi-functional" worker. The elaborate system of work rules and job classifications

"They get mean, we get lean."

that has been built up over decades is wiped away. Instead, management has full flexibility to assign workers as it sees fit. As much as possible, jobs are designed so that workers can be used interchangeably.

Such flexibility is gained because lean production does away with what the media and the companies call "outmoded work rules"—incompatible, it is presumed, with modern methods and a modern outlook. (Chrysler, for example, calls its lean contracts "Modern Operating Agreements.")

When management talks about getting rid of work rules, it means eliminating what few rights workers do have. Management wants to abolish the rules that give workers some control and some flexibility, so as to further tip the balance of power toward management. The rights, such as seniority, that workers won over the years may have made workplace functioning slightly more "inefficient" in some sense, but they did protect workers, to some degree, from management abuse of power.

1) The system of work rules, classifications, and seniority allowed workers to select the jobs that best fit their particular needs. Under lean production management eliminates what most workers consider "good jobs"—those off the line, for example—and workers' choice of jobs is replaced by management flexibility in job assignment.

2) Work rules were part of a complex balance of power on the shop floor. It was difficult for management to maintain normal operations—and virtually impossible to deal with abnormal situations—without violating one of the many work rules. Normally, workers voluntarily stretched the rules in order to get production out. Examples: a production worker would move a bin of parts even though it was technically a material handler's job; an electrician would remove a metal guard to get access to an electrical panel, without waiting for a millwright; workers would step on a moving conveyor to cross it rather than go the long way around to a safety walk.

This arrangement of convenience gave individual workers some informal bargaining power with management. Since cooperation was voluntary, if a worker felt that supervision was messing with her, she could withdraw the cooperation and become a stickler for the rules. And on a larger scale, if the union as a whole felt that management was overstepping its bounds, the union could organize a "work-to-rule" campaign on the shop floor.

For example, production workers might normally do some minimal maintenance work to keep production running, such as resetting tripped electrical circuit breakers. When management tried to raise output quotas, they could protest by refusing to reset the breakers unless specifically ordered. But once classifications are blurred so that resetting circuit breakers officially becomes part of the job, the workers have lost their means of protest.

There is no reason for unions to argue for classifications in the abstract. There are other ways of exercising shop floor power. But when workers' *power* is tied to classifications, then abolishing classifications requires a substitute way for workers to exert that power.

JOB SECURITY

> To make this system work, of course,…when the auto market slumps [management must] ensure job security…It truly is a system of reciprocal obligation.[57]

> In return for the [NUMMI] workers' contributions to productivity and quality has come a commitment to real job security.[58]

> In our plant [NUMMI], there are numerous examples of suggestions made, something like 15,000 last year, which would eliminate a particular job, replace a job with a handmade robot, for example…But people feel free and secure in making that because they don't have the threat of layoff.[59]

Job security is supposed to be the linchpin of the mutual interest understanding between union and management. Why should a worker hesitate to suggest ways to cut a job on a particular operation (that's the worker's reciprocal obligation), if no one will be laid off?

Management can certainly avoid layoffs in a fast-growing company. In fact, it was the rapidly expanding Japanese economy that made it possible for certain large companies to promise lifetime employment there. But the bubble of Japanese expansion finally burst in the 1990s, and it appears that lifetime jobs have gone with it (see chapter 28). And no company keeps expanding forever.

Thus far, the lean production plants in North American have kept their contractual pledge to avoid layoffs, even when sales have been slow.[60] This degree of job security is nothing to sneeze at, and the UAW has sought and won similar protections against layoffs at the Big Three.

Although this protection is desirable, it is also important to look at the bigger picture. One question is how far the job security reaches. In lean plants, the security of the core workforce depends on extensive contracting out and, at AAI, on maintaining a considerable number of temporary workers in the plant. These workers absorb the brunt of a downturn. You might say that the security of the core workers is achieved at the expense of the second-tier workers, who would have been part of the regular workforce, eligible for call-back by seniority, at a traditional plant.

A second question is how long a worker can last to enjoy this brand of job security.

Unions have won two different kinds of job security protections over the years: individual and collective. Contracts keep management from discriminating against individuals through seniority rights and through language that keeps management from getting rid of you because you're older, injured, or not the foreman's nephew. They protect you when management wants to reorganize the plant or put in new technology you haven't been trained on. In other words, the company can't throw you on the street just because you've become inconvenient. Over the years it is this sort of protection that has made working in auto plants and many other workplaces more or less bearable.

Unions have been less successful in winning collective job security measures that would protect against economic cycles, plant closings, market shifts, and corporate investment decisions. They would include such things as recall rights, the right to follow your work, portable pensions, a ban on plant closings, and supplemental unemployment benefits.

The collective security in the management-by-stress plants comes by giving up the *individual* protections that the union once fought so hard to establish. The NUMMI contract is explicit about this trade-off. Under "Commitments and Responsibilities," the company "recognizes its obligation to keep [employees] employed." In return, the union "recognizes the necessity of increasing productivity" and

> accepts the responsibility…to cooperate with the Company in administering, on a fair and equitable basis, standards of conduct; attendance plans and Problem Resolution…[61]

The union also promises, for the employees, that they will

> promote *KAIZEN* by continually looking for opportunities to make the Company more efficient; [and] support the team concept.

Younger workers may not be concerned, at first, about needing protections against doing jobs they can't do—but they will need those protections later on if they expect to retire from that company. Throwing out the protections that go with seniority is a short-sighted "strategy" for job security.

In addition, recent history has shown that the most important factors in management's decision to keep a workplace open include many considerations other than the submission of the workforce. In the auto industry, these include how well the plant's model is selling, the age of the plant, its geographic location, and state and local politics. A labor force that stands up for its rights will not automatically cause a plant to go belly up. UAW Local 594, which struck the Pontiac Truck and Bus plant to fight the team concept, is an example.[62]

Similarly, giving the company everything it wants in lean production plus the highest quality does not guarantee a plant will stay open.

A final note on job security: it is ironic that the atmosphere at the NUMMI plant is one of constant fear. While no one expects a short layoff, management (and some union leaders) keep the threat of a total shutdown constantly in the air, particularly if the workers do not vote right at election or contract time. And many CAMI, NUMMI, and AAI workers fear that they will not be able to last out their work lives under the tough conditions of the plant, and that if injured they will have no where else to go.[63]

STRESS AS THE SYSTEM REGULATOR

The intense discipline created by NUMMI's job design creates not only world-class performance but also a highly motivating work environment.[64]

Under traditional methods of production, management relied on sharp-eyed supervisors and the threat of punishment to make sure that workers were doing their jobs correctly and maintaining the pace set by the line. In contrast, the advocates of lean production claim that it is worker enthusiasm, dedication, and creativity that keep the lean factory running.

But if those myths about lean production are false, as we have argued above, what is the force that makes the system work?

Stress is the vital management tool, both for monitoring and for forcing all personnel in the system to keep up. The pressure felt by workers and managers alike is neither an accident nor a by-product of the system that can be eliminated.

The essence of the system is not that it turns over control to workers, but that it increases management power by using a different form of workforce control. The system does not rely on an army of managers to continuously monitor every individual employee. Nor does it rely on convincing workers that their human fulfillment and reaching management's goals are one and the same.

The key is that the *system itself* is designed so that any deviation in the process—any failure by a worker or any other part of the system—is immediately exposed and magnified. At all points in the system, the consequences of error are substantial—and sometimes those consequences are even purposely made worse.

This disciplines the whole system and allows management to focus its attention on the weak spots.

Therefore, under management-by-stress, the buffers or reserves that would traditionally shield production from minor glitches are intentionally removed. If a chain is slack it may be difficult to identify a weak or broken link. But stressing the chain instantly reveals the bad link.

Likewise, if a workplace is kept under stress at all times, problems become immediately apparent. The removal of buffers means that a stoppage in one area will quickly bring large parts of the system to a halt. Thus any problems also become immediately apparent to higher levels of management. This in turn creates added pressure from above for rapid correction.

This is management by controlling stress throughout the system.

One way to maintain the stress is to continually push past the point of comfort. Thus the term "lean" is not accurate. The principle of the system is always to strive to run on something less than lean—anorexic, perhaps—in order to "constantly improve." Like an anorexic, the system is never satisfied with itself, no matter how lean it gets. It is always striving for a better (production) figure, no matter what the cost to other parts of the body. The principle is that if the system is continually squeezed, only the strong will survive, and productivity will increase.

Does management really think this way? Undoubtedly, there are many managers who think simply in terms of efficiency or productivity. But there are many who do consciously apply stress. Here are some examples:

Consultant Masaaki Imai draws on the originator of the Toyota Production System, Taichi Ohno, to explain "how top management can deliberately make sure that kaizen is occurring."

Let's suppose that a start-up department has the requirement to make 100 cars per day. Mr. Ohno would give the

---

Tension-Productivity Correlation

Points to Remember:

1. Excessive *high tension* and extremely *low tension* correlate to *low productivity*.

2. It is the responsibility of the leader to provide an organization climate which creates an optimum *tension-productivity correlation*.

3. If an individual/organization has *low tension*, then a raising of the *tension level* would be appropriate. Herzberg refers to this as *KITA*, an acronym for *Kick In The A__* (Pants).

4. Conversely, if tension is high, it is the leader's job to reduce this tension level.

5. Some tools to accomplish *reducing tension* are counseling, additional training, lending an ear, giving recognition, allowing the person to do their own thing, etc. [Notice that reducing the workload is not a recommended tool.]

6. It is safe to assume that in our society most people have *high tension*. Therefore, a leader using leadership approaches that further *raise tension* levels creates an environment for even *lower productivity* levels. This does not take into account the personal, emotional price which drives people into the *reactive cycle*.

7. If approaches used to reduce tension do not result in *increased productivity*, a new assumption of *low tension* can more safely be made.

8. Maintaining a *high level of tension* through the *KITA approach* does maintain *acceptable productivity levels*.

9. It requires *constant time and attention* of the leader, because *productivity will fall* without that false tension being maintained.

[From General Electric.]

department the resources to make 90% of what was required. Specifically, they received 90% of the manpower required, 90% of the space, 90% of the equipment, etc. The manager would have no choice but to work overtime to meet his quota.

As time went on, the department team would find problems or obstacles that would be resolved or overcome through KAIZEN activities. No sooner would one obstacle be hurdled than another would be uncovered and addressed with KAIZEN. The hurdles could be in quality, in machine reliability, in human resources or in paper work. Regardless of type, they were overcome with KAIZEN until the department was able to put out 100% of the requirements without any overtime.

As soon as a no-overtime equilibrium was met, Mr. Ohno would com in and would again remove 10% of the resources. His way of managing came to be known as the OH! NO! system![65]

In truth, the idea of setting up the output parameters of the system so that they apply pressure backward is not particularly new. AAI gives the credit to Henry Ford himself:

> Our policy is to reduce the price, extend the operations, and improve the article. You will notice that the reduction of price comes first....Although one may calculate what a cost is, no one knows what a cost ought to be. One of the ways of discovering...is to name a price so low as to force everybody in place to the highest point of efficiency. The low price makes everybody dig for profits.
> We make more discoveries concerning manufacturing and selling under this forced method than by any method of leisurely investigation.[66]

The box on the previous page reprints a page from a course offered to managers at the non-union General Electric team concept plant in Washington, West Virginia. Note that management is quite explicit about the use of "tension" to increase productivity. And normal levels of tension are not enough—"false tension" is required (point 9).

The just-in-time system itself is an example of deliberately-created tension. Even if management does not have a true just-in-time system for delivery of supplies, once it knows the benefits of the added stress, managers can decide to *act as if* just-in-time were in effect.

For example, the NUMMI plant cannot receive components from Japan quickly enough and frequently enough to qualify as a true just-in-time system. After all, at Japanese auto plants, some deliveries are made hourly. But according to Michael Cusumano, a business historian at MIT, "NUMMI simulates some effects of just-in-time production by keeping parts away from production lines and in warehousing areas, and delivering components to assembly only as they are needed." Cusumano praises the "discipline imposed by the just-in-time pace."[67]

Management's methods for maintaining the stress can be sophisticated and pit individual workers against each other and their union. For example, AAI partially overcomes the natural resistance to job overload by offering workers voluntary days off (with no pay) when production needs are down. (If the company sends you home, on the other hand, they have to pay 80 percent.) In some depart-

ments five percent of the workforce have been able to take voluntary days off.

Union representatives discourage this practice, pointing out that if workers permit management to run the plant with fewer people temporarily, management makes its case for needing fewer people.

Besides, very soon the voluntary days disappear, as attrition reduces the workforce. But many workers, seeking some relief from the overloaded jobs and overtime, take whatever short-term relief they can get, even if it sets them up for greater stress in the future.

Stress is a control mechanism in the white-collar world too. An example is the "killer software" developed by Cypress Semiconductor Corp. If a supply is late arriving at Cypress, but no one has explained why to senior management, the software will automatically shut down all the computer systems in the purchasing department. To get the systems back into operation, the guilty party must contact the supplier, get a delivery date, and report to the chief financial officer.

The idea, as described in *Business Week*, is to "magnify the minor problem" so that it causes a major disaster. The theory is that employees will then be more alert to avoiding even minor problems. As Cypress CEO T.J. Rodgers says, "It draws everyone's attention."

Cypress also has software that automatically shuts down its inventory system, if parts sit for more than 10 days. In this case, management began with a limit of 200 days, gradually cranking down to the maximum stress level.[68]

If the central feature of the system is managing by maintaining the pressure (management-by-stress), then one of the fundamental claims about the system falls. It does not resolve the adversary relationship between labor and management. On the contrary, the adversarial relationship is intensified, because management is driven to squeeze workers and reduce autonomy. Workers, if they can, try to defend and increase their autonomy and improve their working conditions.

MANAGEMENT-BY-STRESS AS A SYSTEM

All the proponents of lean production maintain that it must be understood as a *system* of interrelated components, not just a collection of individual policies.

General Motors stressed this point in a videotape about the NUMMI system made to instruct managers in other GM plants:

> NUMMI is a unique plant, utilizing a total system concept....Remember, these principles are designed to work as a unified system....For example, adopting the stop-the-line philosophy or the JIT delivery system by themselves probably won't provide the results you're looking for. The NUMMI system is effective because everyone in the system, from Mr. Toyoda to the newly hired team member, understands the total system, believes in the total system, and is willing to follow its concepts and goals.[69]

However, there is surprisingly little agreement among

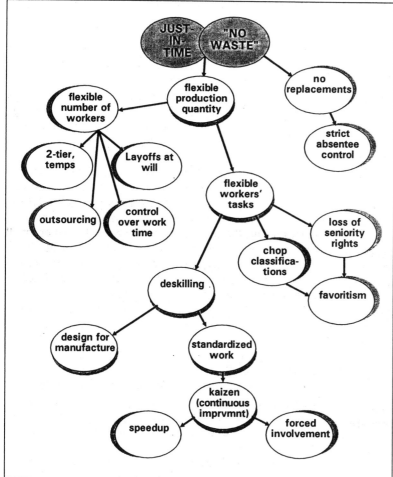

the system's advocates on just what the essential components are and how they hold together.[70]

Management-by-stress clearly is a system with a coherent logic. The strategies and policies all work together to maximize management's control, reduce variability, and increase productivity. In the real world, of course, there is always interference with logical models. In particular, as we argue in chapter 36, unions can and have forced considerable changes in the system. Nonetheless, it is important to understand the logic of the system and where it tends to go if unopposed.

The diagram shows the controlling elements of the system: just-in-time and the policy of eliminating all "waste."

1. Just-in-time. The just-in-time system is designed to run with no breathing room and no buffers: no extra stocks are kept on hand, and the finished product is shipped to customers only as needed.

2. No waste. If JIT were defined simply as "produce only in response to demand," then one way to do it would be to have plenty of extra people and machinery on hand. In times of high demand, all could work; in times of low demand, only some would. But this option is conflicts with the other central tenet of the system: elimination of all "waste."

"Waste" includes anything that does not add value to the product. It includes idle time, extra materials, inspec-

tion, repair, inefficient processes, extra space, extra tools. Combining this notion of "waste" with JIT we get...

3. No standby replacements. The "no waste" policy includes human beings; there should be no extra workers on hand to replace absentees.

4. Strict absentee control. Therefore management must ensure that everyone comes to work every day. Any absences can be filled by temporaries.

5. Flexibility in production quantity. Traditional systems were designed so that operating at a consistent, steady rate was the most efficient. Inventory would be used to smooth out the differences between steady production and fluctuating demand.

JIT, on the other hand, optimizes management's ability to vary the rate of production, to change the day's or week's quota quickly and easily. But if we reduce production while maintaining the same number of workers, we have greatly reduced labor productivity. Workers will either be working at half their normal rate or standing around with nothing to do for half the time. So the system requires...

6. Flexibility in the number of workers. This is required despite the promise of job security. Flexibility is created by...

7. A two-tier system or temporaries. Management may use temporaries for periods of more production, or have a second class of employees who are called only as needed (for example, a "support member pool"); AND/OR

8. Layoffs at will. AND/OR

9. Contracting out. Management's flexibility is increased if it doesn't have to bother with continually laying off and recalling its own workforce. And since the subcontractor's workers are usually lower-paid, this saves money.

9. Control over work time. Management must be able to assign overtime at will, so that flexible production can be achieved with flexible hours.

10. Flexibility in workers' tasks. If the production goals and therefore the number of workers are always changing, management must be able to redistribute workers' job assignments at will. The way tasks are allocated can be continually "rebalanced."

11. Chop classifications. This means that classifications that limit the kinds of tasks a worker can be assigned to must be abolished.

12. Loss of seniority rights. Without classifications, workers' seniority is much less valuable. They cannot, for example, choose a better classification and transfer by seniority.

13. Favoritism. Without seniority protections—and with greater flexibility for supervisors—favoritism be-

comes the deciding factor in who gets which jobs. The system encourages workers to apple-polish.

Favoritism does not operate simply because of evil supervisors or even their natural desire to scratch the backs of those who scratch theirs. Favoritism is built into management-by-stress: supervisors are under pressure to produce. Naturally they tend to select those people who they think make their jobs easier. Pressure plus absence of rules produces favoritism.

14. Deskilling. The need for flexibility in workers' tasks requires that each job be simplified so that anyone can learn it quickly. Jobs are often made easier to do in the sense that no training is required to do the job well—but harder to do in that more of these separate easy tasks are required in the same time frame.

15. Design for manufacture. Deskilling requires that the engineers or job planners design the product to be easily made.

16. Standardized work. Deskilling means that each job can easily be broken down into its constituent tasks, each task documented, and standardization of performance required. Workers are not allowed to change the way they do the job once it is standardized. If they have ideas, they must be checked out with the team leader and supervisor.

17. Easier to kaizen. Once jobs are documented and everyone is doing them the same way, it is easier for management—or kaizen teams, or workers themselves—to figure out ways to eliminate steps or motions, and then add new ones. This leads to eliminating workers.

18. Speed-up. Fewer workers are doing more work.

19. Forced involvement. Workers are expected to come up with ways to kaizen their jobs themselves. Often workers are asked to document their own tasks—creating a manual that management can use to teach others their jobs (workers in another plant, or even, in the event of a strike, scabs).

THE SYSTEM ITSELF OR MISTAKES IN IMPLEMENTATION?

When problems crop up in lean production plants, the system's defenders are ready with an explanation. The problems must simply be mistakes in implementation, or a failure to train properly. For example, Elmer Johnson, a former GM vice president, explains,

> We just weren't humble and modest enough to say it starts with people—getting the right people. If you have an authoritarian plant manager running each of our distant plants, you can't put in the team concepts that Toyota taught us as the way to do things now. So we didn't do it the right way.[71]

Many union members have a similar view: that the system sounds great as it's described, if only bad management weren't distorting it. This perception is encouraged by the fact that the unionized auto transplants are co-managed by Japanese and North American managers. At NUMMI, many workers blame problems on the American managers from GM who "don't understand the system."

At Mazda, on the other hand, many workers blamed the Japanese managers for not understanding American culture.

We disagree. We believe the "problems" with lean production are too basic, come up too regularly, and fit too well with what the system's advocates say about it to be dismissed as mere mistakes in execution.

Here are two examples:

When California OSHA cited NUMMI for ergonomic hazards in 1993, the hygienist noted that not only did the company fail to design jobs properly, but frequently management did not respond when workers complained or were injured:

> Serious employee injuries due to repetitive stress, as well as employee symptoms of impending stress, have increased alarmingly. Complaints of symptoms to [supervisors] frequently did not lead to adequate correction of the problem.
>
> Plant medical treatment of symptoms, including competent diagnoses of repetitive stress related injury, did not always lead to intervention to correct ergonomic hazards on the line or to measures to reduce the repetitive stress experienced by individual employees. Where modified duty or medical leave was employed, often other employees were exposed to a similar degree of risk.[72]

California OSHA also cited examples where equipment to make a job easier and safer went unused because it was slower than doing the job with muscle power alone.[73]

Reported injuries represent only the tip of the iceberg. The NUMMI local's ergonomics rep says that workers tell him "they do not come to the Medical Department with their concerns because they are being harassed by members of supervision."[74]

Is this harassment a "mistake," or a predictable consequence of the intense pressure to continuously kaizen productivity?

In April 1993 a supervisor at NUMMI issued a series of decrees at a group meeting. Here is one:

> From now on there will be no bathroom break when there is only one Team Leader off the line, because if he is on the line giving bathroom breaks, who will answer the cord pulls? I will have to and lately I have been busy running...
>
> Breaktime and Lunchtime...are to be used to refresh yourself and to go to the restroom, so don't wait until the line is running because...if only one team leader is free you won't go unless you have a doctor's verification to do so or in extreme emergencies.[75]

Can this situation be the result of a dense supervisor who fails to grasp the principles of a good system? One of the basic principles of NUMMI is no buffers. This lack of buffers forces the supervisor to protect himself by holding out the team leader for production breakdowns, which means team members cannot get a break when they need it. The only solution, from the group leader's point of view, is for workers to pressure each other to reduce absenteeism and bathroom breaks.

Bathroom breaks may not always be the issue. To relieve the pressure on themselves supervisors may use other tactics: driving out weaker producers or those who resist; making time off more difficult. The genius of lean production is that it does not dictate from above any one specific response; rather it forces those below to come up with their own coping solutions.

The fact that bathroom breaks and the systematic disregard of ergonomic hazards are an issue at NUMMI—nine years after the plant began production—reveals a great deal about whether there is worker control or dignity in the plant.

LEAN PRODUCTION AND UNIONS

> You have to assume everyone is looking for the same thing: stability, a future, the company's need to be profitable. It's hard now to say what's the role of the union, what's the role of the company. It doesn't work that way. It's a partnership. It's a total rethinking of your role.
> —UAW Regional Director Bruce Lee[76]

A managed-by-stress production system, even more than other management methods, places heavy emphasis on cooperation. Of course, a traditional workplace requires cooperation too. In any workplace, the employees have to work, and work right, in order for anything to get done. But in the old system, management had layers of supervisors to monitor worker cooperation, inspectors just in case workers weren't "cooperating" well enough, and work-in-progress buffers to minimize the effects of any non-cooperation. Now, as one response to competition, management wants to avoid the costs of such safeguards.

Another example of management's stronger need for cooperation is the switch away from multiple sourcing. Before the era of lean production, it was common to deliberately arrange for several suppliers of the same com-

ponent or service. Thus there was a back-up in case of a strike at one supplier, or some other glitch in delivery. The strategy was "just in case," and it figured the possibility of worker militancy into the equation.

Today, the strategy is "single sourcing," because of the companies' desire to be lean, to shift development and quality costs to suppliers, and to integrate supplier schedules into master schedules.[77] But the success of "single sourcing" depends on virtually eliminating disruptions caused by workers, rather than working around them.

How, then, can managers assure themselves of a cooperative workforce? According to the ideology of management-by-stress, this is not a problem. Because the system is win-win for all concerned, the system itself reinforces worker cooperation; the causes of non-cooperation are eliminated.

And best of all, these results do not depend simply on the good intentions of management. Since lean production *must* have dynamic work teams based on skilled, involved workers at its center, this is the way work *must* be organized. If managers are good managers—that is, if they understand the system's requirements—then workers will have their needs met. Thus it is lean production that both requires and produces worker dignity—not a union.

The key to this assumption is that lean production is a "fragile system," easily subject to disruption. This very fragility, the theory goes, means that management has to pay attention to worker morale, conditions, and training.[78] As a GM manager put it,

> This strategy is very sensitive and requires constant discipline. To avoid problems, total cooperation is required from everyone involved.[79]

For those who are uninterested in unions or hostile to them, this is the argument for why independent unions are not necessary.

DOES A UNION BENEFIT LEAN PRODUCTION?

So what say those who consider themselves both friends of labor *and* fans of lean production? This category would include some academics cited in this chapter, those who are starry-eyed over the productivity/quality benefits of lean production, but who want to keep workers' interests in mind. It also includes some unionists who have bought the lean production/cooperation gospel, but want their unions to survive. They have three arguments for why a union is needed under lean production.

First is that even in a mostly win-win situation, there are still adversarial issues (such as wages and benefits) that require an independent union to represent the workforce. Here they are on solid ground.

The second argument is that unions are needed "to keep management honest," to give workers more voice in those cases where management hasn't learned the new system properly or where management makes mistakes.[80]

This argument puts the union on very weak ground. The justification for unions turns on how cost-effective it is to have an organized institution like a union around to intervene in a family dispute. This violates the first principles of lean production: to get rid of all indirect labor—anything that does not add value—and to avoid setting up institutions "just-in-case" there is bad management.

By the logic of lean production, wouldn't having a union around to correct management mistakes encourage those mistakes, just as having separate quality inspectors encourages workers to make mistakes on their jobs?

The third argument, put forward by a number of union leaders, is that the system works *because* of union involvement. The AFL-CIO Executive Council says,

> The new systems of work organization require, as a first requisite, that workers be represented by free and independent labor union which they control...Trade union representation removes fear from the workplace and assures workers the protection that is essential if they are to feel free to express their views and to fully participate in workplace decisions.[81]

UAW Regional Director Bruce Lee (whose area includes NUMMI) argues, "The key to the success of every aspect of the NUMMI program is management's acceptance and respect for the workers' independent source of power—their union."[82]

NUMMI management, though, seems less clear about its respect for the union. Just six months after Lee spoke these words, NUMMI Vice President Bill Childs was informing members of their right to resign from the union ("send a registered letter") and cross its picket line. The union had taken a strike vote, and Childs circulated a memo assuring fellow "team members" that the plant would operate during a strike and asking members to inform their managers whether they would cross the line.[83]

Again, if an independent source of power *for workers* is so beneficial to *management* (the fabled win-win situation), why do companies try to keep unions out of their non-union facilities?

The UAW had great hopes that the NUMMI experience would prove what a positive partner in production the union could be, and thus temper the Japanese auto companies' resistance to unions in the United States. But no Japanese company that has opened an auto plant in North America on its own has embraced the union (despite the companies' cozy relationships with their unions back home). Indeed, the companies have fought UAW and CAW organizing drives.

Toyota—half-owner of NUMMI—is determined to keep its operations in Kentucky union-free. Bruce Lee himself noted that in Kentucky, Toyota selects young, healthy male workers who will not ask many questions, rather than welcoming a union.[84] AAI successfully resisted an organizing drive among its white collar workers. Likewise BMW and Mercedes—from the country which many laud as the model of worker-management co-determination—seem set on resisting unions at their new plants in South Carolina and Alabama.

In fact, with few exceptions, corporations of all types praise their unions' cooperation out of one side of their mouths, and slam those same unions when they try to organize non-union facilities.

Perhaps, some may argue, this resistance to unions is just an irrational carry-over of old management ideas. Surely an enlightened management would realize that the new breed of unions is a help, not a hindrance. But management looks at the bottom line, and management-by-stress operations are as least as successful at nonunion plants as they are at union ones. Nissan and the Kentucky Toyota plant have the highest productivity of any auto plants in the U.S.[85] Toyota, Honda, and Nissan all demonstrated their satisfaction with their non-union operations in the U.S. by spending hundreds of millions of dollars to expand them in the early and mid-1990s.[86] Apparently the idea that a union is essential to high productivity is wishful thinking, after all.

A UNION IS A RISK

Managers resist unions because they know that even where a union may be cooperative for the present, it cannot be counted on to stay that way. Former Labor Secretary W.J. Usery, a key figure in the original NUMMI negotiations, said after the 1991 union elections there that gave the opposition People's Caucus a temporary majority, "My concern has always been that someone would get into [union] office and knock down the system."[87]

The three plants we've been studying are all cases in point: the president of the CAMI local—self-described as having a right-wing, anti-union background—first took office determined not to let a bunch of union "hotheads" ruin the CAMI system. Before long, writes Rob Pelletier, "I became exactly what I was trying to protect CAMI from—a union hothead."[88] In 1992 the union even pulled a five-week strike. At Mazda, the original appointed union officials, models of cooperation, were soon ousted by a restive membership. At NUMMI, the workers consistently gave the People's Caucus about half their votes, and eventually elected a Caucus leader, known for his militant stance, to head contract bargaining. In 1994, they struck.

Management-by-stress translates into pressure on the union to do something about it. And as long as the union has even a smidgen of democracy, union officials are under pressure to be responsive to the members. Even leaders of the more cooperative UAW caucus at NUMMI sometimes urge members to exercise their rights.

> It is sad to say that there are still Team Members who are afraid to pull the Andon Cord. Some Team members find themselves working twice as hard as they should have to rather than pulling the Andon Cord for help. There have been situations where some team members have gotten so far behind as to have to stock up on parts during lunch just to keep up with the line.[89]

Thus management's first preference is no union at all and full management flexibility. The next preference is a tamed "enterprise union," as currently in Japan, that sees its role as a junior partner of management.[90] Not quite as good is the business union, where the union sees itself as independent of the company, but only in bargaining over wages and benefits, and essentially leaves the company a free hand on the shop floor.

But this last situation is unstable, because there is always the danger that mass dissatisfaction and democratic pressures will force the union to exercise its independence in the workplace. If a union is present, management must devote careful attention and considerable resources to maintaining the company-minded ideology, so that workers are unable or unwilling to buck the system—especially collectively. It requires that any collective thinking done by workers should be along the lines of "what's good for the company?" rather than "what's good for the workers?"

FEAR WORKS TOO

How, then, can management convince workers and union to cooperate in this way? We take up that question at length in Section III. But although management-by-stress undoubtedly works best if the workers believe in the cooperation ideology, wholehearted belief is not essential. Management-by-stress can also work even if the workers are thoroughly disillusioned.

Take the Fort Wayne, Indiana GM truck plant, for example. The union there, UAW Local 2209, did a membership survey. One question was, "Do you agree with team concept as being implemented?" Eighty-three percent said no. And to the question, "Do you feel this is a true joint-operated plot?" 90 percent said no. And yet the plant continued to turn out high-quality trucks.

So if it's not belief in teamwork that's keeping workers cooperative, what is? Often it's fear. Researcher

Don Wells points out that all the attention given to the features of lean production that might be attractive to workers leaves out the most important explanation of why workers accept the lean regime:

> Management control in both lean and non-lean workplaces is being reinforced through increasing rates of long-term unemployment and underemployment, replacement of permanent, full-time jobs by part-time and temporary jobs, cutbacks in unemployment insurance and welfare programs, as well as by an increasing number of shutdowns and runaways....Where employers credibly threaten to relocate to low-wage, high-repression labor regimes, they can...whipsaw workers into bigger concessions and deeper subordination, firm by firm, workplace by workplace.[91]

Joe Gasper, a NUMMI worker who had previously worked in the same plant when it belonged only to GM, put it this way:

> Things have changed so much from General Motors to NUMMI. I mean, the things that we wouldn't tolerate, we have to tolerate here because of the market that we have. So I think a lot of people walk on eggs, and maybe that's good. It keeps them alert. Because I watched General Motors go right down the tubes, and I'm not going to let it happen again.

His companion, Becky Kiley, echoed, "Just keep me in a job and I'll do it the way you want me to do it."[92] Perhaps most typical of NUMMI workers' sentiments was Lester Jolivet, the NUMMI union newspaper's interview-of-the-month in November 1993. Jolivet was asked:

> Q. What do you like best about NUMMI?
> A. The fact that we're working.[93]

AN INDEPENDENT UNION

Management-by-stress works only to the extent that workers actually are vulnerable to the pressures established by the system. Workers who refuse to speed up to make up for absent team members *and can defend themselves* are not vulnerable.

The system has many weapons to handle the resistance of individual workers. The stop cord/andon system immediately identifies who is not keeping up. Group leaders and team leaders can be mobilized against anyone who challenges authority. At the same time, the system strips workers of the means to defend themselves individually, by getting rid of the work rules that they could invoke as rights. In a system where management has all the authority (in the name of flexibility), supervisor favoritism in job assignments, response to injury, and leniency for special needs is a potent weapon.

This is where the union becomes so important. The system is vulnerable to collective action. And workers must depend on their collective power to have any dignity at all under the system. When workers understand their power and are willing to use it, they can win important improvements. This is why management finds an independent union an indigestible obstacle to making the system function.

And that is why we have so much to learn from the union struggles in the auto transplants, where lean produc-

Management-by-Stress, Their Version and Ours

Management's Term	Union Translation
Productivity improvement	Speed-up
Flexibility	Elimination of classifications
Temporary workers	Two-tier workforce
Just-in-time	No margin for error
Kaizen, continuous improvement	Speed-up, job loss
Attendance program	Your life belongs to the company
Multi-skilling	Deskilling
Design for manufacture	Design for deskilling
Quality	"Conformance to requirements"
Outside contracting	Job loss/two-tier workforce
Worker participation	Forced involvement
Standardized work	Deskilled work, regimentation
Recognition of merit and ability	Favoritism
Competitiveness	Worker against worker

tion has been in place the longest. Because every victory proves that the system is not all-powerful. Under lean production, unions can resist and can win important improvements for workers—but only at the expense of the system's mechanisms for regulating itself.

ARE LEAN WORKERS HAPPY WORKERS?

Workers in managed-by-stress auto plants are probably among the most media-watched and professor-studied in the world. Although the prime focus of most academics and journalists has been the plants' productivity, quality, and profit numbers, the workers too have been asked how they feel about their new jobs. Although there have been many stories of worker dissatisfaction,[94] they are probably outnumbered by glowing reports of fulfilled and happy workers.

For example, Professor Paul Adler cites the biannual surveys conducted by NUMMI management.[95] These surveys report that around 90 percent of respondents say they are proud of their work, satisfied with their jobs, and satisfied with job security.

Surveys certainly have their place; the unions at CAMI, Mazda, and Saturn have also carried them out. But results of surveys have to be treated very cautiously, since they often reflect the form of the questions, who asks, and the context. At CAMI and Mazda, these union-conducted surveys have shown far more negative results than the management-sponsored one at NUMMI or the ones conducted by team leaders at Saturn.[96]

In evaluating what lean production means for workers, our method has been not to rely over much on surveys, but instead to look at what workers *do* when they have a sense of power.

If a person says she or he is happy with their job, it can mean one—or more—of several things. It can mean I look forward to coming to work every day. It can mean I'm glad I have a job at all, and not in Oklahoma. (Many NUMMI workers had to transfer to far-away GM plants in the couple of years between the closing of the old plant and its re-opening under the NUMMI banner.) It can mean I've been working in a factory for twenty years and

this is all I know, and this is the only factory that pays these wages around here. It can mean that my particular job on the line is better than the one I had last month.

When people see no alternative to their present situation, they often respond that they are content with it. We believe a better indication of worker satisfaction with the lean system is their behavior *when they see themselves as having power*. At Mazda, as described earlier and at more length in chapter 36, the union won personal leave (PAA days) which could be taken in four- or eight-hour increments without prior permission. This gave workers a new power they hadn't had before. Before long, Mazda management was finding it impossible to run some departments on Friday afternoons. Workers had found that they could collectively "punish" poor supervisors by several using their PAA days at a time.

These workers *acted* on their desire to get out of the plant and show an abusive unit leader a lesson. But what would these same workers have told an inquiring journalist who wondered if they were happy at Mazda? Would their answers have been different before and after they used the PAA days?

As mentioned earlier, CAMI workers showed their feelings about the lean system through a five-week strike. One worker said, "We want the rules in writing. The way it is now, they just make them up as they go along."[97]

Similarly, in 1994 contract talks at NUMMI, management proposed to double the penalty for absences on Mondays and Fridays. When management feels the need to force employees to come to work, is this perhaps a sign that they are not such a high-morale workforce?

The surveys that show contentment at NUMMI are contradicted by the members' long-term support for the People's Caucus—especially since both NUMMI management and the leaders of the union's other caucus warn repeatedly that a People's Caucus victory will shut the plant down.

Finally, at both NUMMI and Mazda in 1994, the informational meetings the union held to present the newly-negotiated contracts were attended by about 500 angry workers. Almost to a person, they denounced the negotiating committees for not winning enough and for not calling a strike. Is this a sign of a happy membership?

Notes

1. James P. Womack, Daniel T. Jones, and Daniel Roos, *The Machine that Changed the World*, Rawson Associates, New York, 1990, p. 256.
For an excellent comparison of the claims of Womack, Jones, and Roos with reality at the Flat Rock, Michigan Mazda plant, see Steve Babson, "Lean or Mean: The MIT Model and Lean Production at Mazda," *Labor Studies Journal*, Vol. 18, No. 2, Summer 1993, pp. 3-24.

2. Under its Labor-Management Cooperation Program, the Federal Mediation and Conciliation Service has awarded grants since 1981 to business and labor groups that want to establish joint committees. According to *American Workplace*, newsletter of the U.S. Department of Labor Office of the American

Workplace, over 150 such committees in the private and public sectors have received FMCS grants (March 1994).

3. United Parcel Service "Methods" manual for package car drivers.

4. Robert Frank, "As UPS Tries to Deliver More to Its Customers, Labor Problems Grow," *Wall Street Journal*, May 23, 1994.

5. Joe Fahey, "Stress and the UPS Worker," *Convoy Dispatch*, June/July 1994, p. 7.

6. *Wall Street Journal* December 12, 1991.

7. *Business Week*, November 25, 1991.

8. There is one other unionized transplant in North America—Diamond Star in Illinois, originally a joint venture of Chrysler and Mitsubishi, and now owned by Mitsubishi. The major non-union transplants are owned by Honda, Nissan, Toyota, Hyundai, and Subaru-Isuzu.
We will refer to the AAI plant as "Mazda" before July 1992, when it became a joint venture, and AAI after that.

9. Following is a small and random sample: Womack, Jones, and Roos, *The Machine that Changed the World*, cited above; Barry Bluestone and Irving Bluestone *Negotiating the Future: A Labor Perspective on American Business*, New York, Basic Books, 1992; Paul S. Adler and Robert E. Cole, "Designed for Learning: A Tale of Two Auto Plants," *Sloan Management Review*, Spring 1993; John Hoerr, "The Payoff from Teamwork," *Business Week*, July 10, 1989; Bureau of Labor-Management Relations and Cooperative Programs, "Pay for Knowledge Pays Off," *Labor Relations Today*, July/August 1991, and all other publications of this agency in the U.S. Department of Labor, and its successor under the Clinton Administration, the Office of the American Workplace; Ted Blackman, "'Team Concept' involves crews in all aspects of mills," *Forest Industries*, November 1991; Thomas F. O'Boyle, "A Manufacturer Grows Efficient by Soliciting Ideas From Employees," *Wall Street Journal*, June 5, 1992; Larry Armstrong and William C. Symonds, "Beyond 'May I Help You?'" (on service industries) *Business Week* Special Issue: "The Quality Imperative," October 25, 1991.

10. Womack, Jones, and Roos, p. 99.

11. Womack, Jones and Roos, p. 14.

12. Adler and Cole, p. 92.

13. Masayuki Ikuma, president of CAMI, quoted in CAMI Report, p. 38.

14. CAW Research Group on CAMI, "The CAMI Report: Lean Production in a Unionized Auto Plant," Canadian Auto Workers, Willowdale, Ontario, September 1993, pp. 38-41. This 61-page report is an extremely thorough description of the plant, gleaned through site visits and interviews with both workers and managers. The Research Group, which included both academics and unionists, was led by David Robertson of the CAW.

15. New United Motor (T&D) *Team Member Guide: Problem Solving Circles,* Problem Solving Series #6, 1992, p.5 and p.18.

16. Shigeo Sakahara, "The Role of Manufacturing Engineering in Product Development," presentation to International Automobile Conference, Ann Arbor, Michigan, April 4, 1990.

17. CAMI Report, p. 39.

18. Transcript, "Fast Times," CBS News' *48 Hours* program, March 8, 1990.

19. Eileen Appelbaum and Rosemary Batt, *The New American Workplace: Transforming Work Systems in the United States*, ILR Press, Ithaca, New York, 1994, p. 136.

20. Monden, p. 121-122. For its application in training at Toyota, see Terje Gronning, *Human Values and "Competitiveness,"* Ph.D. Dissertation, Ritsumeikan University, 1992, p. 132.

21. *Kaizen Simulation Manual,* Production Engineering Department, Mazda Motor Manufacturing (USA) Corp., no date (est. 1986), p. 14.

22. AutoAlliance Purchase Engineering, *Kaizen and Cost Control,* November, 1993 p. 7, and *Line Balancing*, November 1993, p. 41.

23. CAMI, *For a Better Understanding of the CAMI Production System: Text 2, How to Build "A Low Cost Car,"* no date (est. 1989), p. 45.

24. Monden, p. 122.

25. Monden, p. 124.

26. Monden, p. 122.

27. AAI, *Line Balancing*, p. 9.

28. "President's Message," *Off the Line* newsletter, February 1991, CAW Local 88, p. 3.

29. CAMI Report, p. 35.

30. Bluestone and Bluestone, p. 149.

31. Mazda, Production Engineering, *Kaizen Simulation,* pp. 22-24.

32. Former Secretary of Labor Ray Marshall, for example, has called the NUMMI system the end of Taylorism. In "Work Organization, Unions, and Economic Performance," (chapter in Lawrence Mishel and Paula B. Voos, eds., *Unions and Economic Competitiveness,* M.E. Sharpe, Inc., Armonk, New York, 1992), Marshall contrasts "high performance production" with obsolete mass production: "These [high performance] systems require better educated, skilled workers who are less tolerant of monotonous, routine work and authoritarian managerial controls."
Bruce Lee, the United Auto Workers Regional Director in California, differentiates "Taylor's time-and-motion study engineers...the hated management tools who prowl traditional assembly lines with stop watches, hounding foremen and workers to quicken the pace by another one-hundredths of a second" from the situation at NUMMI, where "worker teams and groups work out the pace that maximizes production and minimizes mistakes" ("Worker Harmony Makes Nummi Work," *New York Times,* December 25, 1988).

33. AutoAlliance Purchasing Engineering, *Motion Analysis*, November 1993.

34. Canadian Auto Workers, "Working Lean" video, 1993.

35. AutoAlliance Purchase Engineering, *Line Balancing*, November 1993, p. 18.

36. The companies all seem to use 95 percent as the magic number to be achieved. See, for example, AAI, *Line Balancing*, p. 40.

37. See Paul Adler, "The Learning Bureaucracy: New United Motors Manufacturing Inc.," in B.M. Staw and L.L. Cummings, eds., *Research in Organizational Behavior*, JAI Press, 1992, for good descriptive material about NUMMI and a clear and detailed case for NUMMI as "democratic Taylorism" and a benevolent "learning bureaucracy."

38. Paul S. Adler and Robert E. Cole, "Designed for Learning: A Tale of Two Auto Plants," *Sloan Management Review*, Spring 1993, p. 90.

39. Mike Hawkins, "Standardized Work—It's Back," *News for CAMI People*.

40. Bruce Lee, "Worker Harmony Makes Nummi Work," *New York Times*, December 25, 1988.

41. NUMMI contract, 1985.

42. CAMI Report, pp. 41-42.

43. Adler and Cole, p. 86.

44. Eileen Appelbaum and Rosemary Batt, *The New American*

Workplace: Transforming Work Systems in the United States, ILR Press, Ithaca, New York, 1994, pp. 34-35.

45. California Department of Industrial Relations Division of Occupational Safety and Health (Cal/OSHA) Citation R1D4-4014 Number 2, January 6, 1993.

46. CAL/OSHA Citation 2.

47. Louise Kertesz, "Injury, Training Woes Hit New Mazda Plant," *Automotive News*, February 13, 1989, pp. 1, 52-53.

48. "Danger Rises in New Auto Jobs," *Detroit Free Press*, July 7, 1990, p. 6A. The injuries counted were only those that resulted in death, a specific loss (such as an amputated finger or reduced vision), or at least seven days missed from work. In contrast, the injury rate in non-Big 3 auto supplier plants, most of them non-union, was only 2.5 per 100. State law was changed to make these records unavailable for later years.

49. Womack, Jones, and Roos, p. 13.

50. CAMI Report, p. 10.

51. Babson, pp. 9-12.
At CAMI, management was indignant when a union report asserted that workers did not really learn new skills. It replied, "Such statements are unsubstantiated and in fact misrepresentations. The issue of skill development is an issue of expectation....more than 96 per cent [of workers surveyed] knew all or most of the jobs on their team....The survey results clearly support that people feel that they have been given the training needed to do the work. No effort was made in the study to identify what these other 'skills you need to get a better job' really are." CAMI Report, p. 60.

52. Bill Bornton, quoted in Adler, *Learning Bureaucracy*.

53. Womack, Jones, and Roos, p. 80, description of "classic lean production" at Toyota's Takaoka plant in Japan

54. When one of the authors hired in at General Motors in 1975, she was placed on a job considered very undesirable precisely because there was no opportunity to vary the work pace. The spray gun job required for applying glue to "deaders" was fixed in place and could not be moved "up the line." Though the job was not physically heavy, the union had insisted that it include an extra 20 minutes of relief because of the worker's inability to control the pace.

55. Womack, Jones, and Roos, p. 13.

56. Bluestone and Bluestone, p. 75.

57. Womack, Jones, and Roos, p. 102.

58. UAW Regional Director Bruce Lee, testifying before the Commission on the Future of Worker-Management Relations, January 27, 1994.

59. Dennis Cuneo, vice president of NUMMI, testifying before the Commission on the Future of Worker-Management Relations, January 27, 1994.

60. The NUMMI contract language is at the beginning of chapter 4. The language at CAMI and AAI is similar.

61. NUMMI contract, 1991.

62. See *Choosing Sides*, chapter 22.

63. For examples of the job closing threats or of workers' fears: at AAI see Babson, cited above; at NUMMI see Caroline Lund, "G.M.-Toyota Plant Backs Down on 10-Hour Day," *Labor Notes*, August 1993, p. 3; at CAMI see CAMI Report, p. 23.

64. Adler and Cole, p. 86.

65. Masaaki Imai, *Kaizen Communique*, Winter 1988/89.

66. Henry Ford, quoted in *Kaizen and Cost Control*, Auto-Alliance Purchase Engineering, November 1993, p. 3.

67. Michael A. Cusumano, "Manufacturing Innovation: Lessons from the Japanese Auto Industry," *Sloan Management Review*, MIT Sloan School of Management, Fall 1988.

68. T.J. Rodgers, "No Excuses Management," *Harvard Business Review*, July-August 1990; Richard Brandt, "Here Comes Attack of the Killer Software," *Business Week*, December 9, 1991. Rodgers' methods were not miracle workers, however. In 1991, profits plunged, and he moved assembly to Thailand and laid off 21 percent of his U.S. workforce. He eventually sold his microprocessor subsidiary to Fujitsu. (Richard Brandt, "Humble Pie for T.J. Rodgers," *Business Week*, November 23, 1992; "Cypress: If You Can't Beat 'Em, Sell Out," *Business Week*, May 24, 1993.)

69. General Motors Technical Liaison Office, "This Is NUMMI" Part 1, 1985.

70. For a discussion of the different definitions, see Steve Babson, ed., *Lean Work: Exploitation and Empowerment in the Global Auto Industry*, Wayne State University, Detroit, Spring 1995.

71. "GM: The Heartbeat of America," *Frontline*, 1993.

72. CAL/OSHA Citation 3, NUMMI, January 6, 1993.

73. CAL/OSHA Information Memorandum, NUMMI, January 6, 1993.

74. Joe Enos, Ergonomic Representative Report, March 1994.

75. Group Leader Agenda for Group Meeting at NUMMI (dated April 1, 1993). Management has also distributed a plant-wide leaflet warning about abuse of bathroom breaks.

76. Quoted in Michelle Levander, "Union Looks for Identity," *Detroit Free Press*, May 31, 1990.

77. Alan J. Adler, "Ford's Favored Few," *Detroit Free Press*, August 12, 1994. "Sort of the way Japanese *keiretsu* operate? 'Exactly,' said [Ford Vice President Carlos] Mazzorin...Ford now uses only one supplier of a commodity, such as tires, per model."

78. Womack, Jones, and Roos, p. 103. See also Shimada Haruo and John Paul MacDuffie, "Industrial Relations and Humanware," Working Paper, Sloan School of Management, M.I.T., 1987.

79. Tracy Webb, Material Department Manager, *OkConveyor: a News Publication for the General Motors Employees at the Oklahoma City Assembly Plant*, June 30, 1993.

80. John Paul MacDuffie, "Workers' Roles in Lean Production," presentation to Conference on Lean Production and Labor, Wayne State University, Detroit, May 20-22, 1993.

81. *The New American Workplace: A Labor Perspective*, A Report by the AFL-CIO Committee on the Evolution of Work, February 1994, p. 11.

82. Testimony before the Commission on the Future of Worker-Management Relations, January 27, 1994. The existence of the union, Lee said, makes workers feel secure enough to commit themselves to increasing productivity.

83. "Memorandum," August 2, 1994.

84. Testimony before the Commission on the Future of Worker-Management Relations, January 27, 1994.

85. Harbour and Associates report, cited in John Lippert, "An A for Efficiency," *Detroit Free Press*, June 24, 1994.

86. Norimitsu Onishi, "Breaking Ground in America: European and Asian automakers are bullish on America and its workers," *Detroit Free Press*, October 11, 1993, pp. 10F-11F.

87. Quoted in Frank Swoboda, "UAW Election No Victory for Confrontation," *Washington Post*, November 10, 1991.

88. Rob Pelletier, "How I Stopped Believing in the 'Team Concept': The Making of a Unionist at CAMI," *Labor Notes* #151, October 1991, p. 7.

89. *Local 2244 Labor News*, March 1989.

90. Under the right conditions, such as after the war in Japan, enterprise unions can be organizations that battle management. See Totsuka Hideo, "Building Japan's Corporate Society," *AMPO, Japan-Asia Quarterly Review,* Vol. 25, No. 1, p. 13.

91. Don Wells, "New Directions for Labor in a Post-Fordist World," in E. Yanarella and W. Green, eds., *Other People's Cars: Organized Labor and the Crisis of Fordism*, forthcoming.

92. "Fast Times."

93. "Auto Worker Interview," *Local 2244 Labor News*, November 1993.

94. For example: Joseph Fucini and Suzy Fucini, *Working for the Japanese*, The Free Press, 1990; Louise Kertesz, "Injury, training woes hit new Mazda plant," *Automotive News*, February 13, 1989; Neil Chethik, "The Intercultural Honeymoon Ends," *San Jose Mercury News*, February 8, 1987; Helen Fogel, "Trouble in Saturn Paradise," *Detroit News*, February 6, 1994, p. 1.

95. Paul S. Adler, "Time-and-Motion Regained," *Harvard Business Review,* January-February 1993, p. 99.

96. For the CAMI Report, union researchers spent a week at CAMI four times between March 1990 and November 1991, interviewing 100 workers, 10-15 team leaders, and 10-15 managers; they also observed and talked with workers on the shop floor. At Mazda, union coordinators distributed surveys and collected them from 85 percent of union members; see Babson, "Lean or Mean." At Saturn, team leaders (work unit counselors) conduct an annual interview with each worker.

97. Quoted in Jane Slaughter, "Workers Wage First Strike at Japanese Transplant," *Labor Notes* #164, November 1992, p. 6.

Working Smart:
A Union Guide to Participation Programs and Reengineering
Labor Notes • 7435 Michigan Ave. • Detroit, MI 48210 • (313) 842-6262

Chapter 9

Saturn: Corporation of the Future

At Saturn, partnership has reached its zenith, as union officials co-manage the factory. The theory is that self-directed teams cover their own needs for replacements, breaks, materials, hiring, repairs, and housekeeping—all by consensus. In pursuing its co-manager role, however, the union has lost sight of its representation role. Amidst uncertainty over their future, Saturn workers are pushed to sacrifice for the good of Saturn.

This is our last chance, as workers of America, to prove to the world that we are not only as good, but we are better. Our quality will be better—is better—and we're going to do it by working together. It's not gonna be us and them—we're gonna do it together. I can only see complete success down the road.

　　　　　　　　　—Saturn team member,
　　　　　　　　　from the Saturn Visitors Center video

THE SATURN CORPORATION IS THE PREMIER MODEL for labor-management partnership in the United States. Unionists and managers on the cooperation conference circuit, academics, and the U.S. Department of Labor—all cite Saturn as the most advanced example of union-management cooperation in the United States.[1] Both management and union officials from Saturn, especially UAW Local 1853 President Mike Bennett, are sought-after speakers. Saturn is overwhelmed with requests from other companies to share its secrets, and has created a subsidiary to put on its special trust-building training course for them.[2]

Saturn is held up as an example because its structure embodies jointness: management officials have a union counterpart, and the two "partners" function together. Rather than the traditional management structure with a worker participation program grafted on later, Saturn was designed as a partnership from the get-go, by a blue-ribbon union-management team. Saturn officials say this structure allows the union to get in on decisions before they are made, rather than simply reacting afterward.

There is no question that union leaders as individuals have more influence in Saturn's day-to-day decisions than in traditional factories. The question is whether workers' needs are therefore more strongly reflected in those decisions. Or does the partnership arrangement mean that

management has converted the union into a tool for greater control over the workforce?

Although we've placed the Saturn chapter in the Management-by-Stress section, the stress there is of a different type than the other workplaces examined here. Saturn is not lean in the same sense that NUMMI is. The big sources of stress at Saturn are uncertainty, a punishing work schedule (in the name of equality), peer pressure, and the knowledge that the union is not willing to back you up if you get in trouble.

In this chapter we will not be evaluating Saturn as a consumer phenomenon, Saturn's impact on the Tennessee countryside, or the fortunes of Saturn executives. All these have been written about extensively elsewhere.[3] We will look simply at Saturn's labor relations system and its effects on the UAW members who work there.

Unless otherwise noted, quotations, and much other information, come from interviews with Saturn workers in 1994 and with Mike Bennett and Bob Hoskins in April

---

Facts About Saturn

- Three integrated factories: Powertrain (engine and transmission), Body Systems (stamping and fabrication), Vehicle Systems (assembly)
- First car off the line: July 1990
- 1994 expected production: 280,000 (capacity is 322,000)
- UAW Local 1853 includes 6,700 members who work for Saturn in Spring Hill, plus about 400 members employed by contractors (cafeteria, janitorial, etc.). Plant is 100 percent union in a right-to-work state.

1993 and April 1994.

In the first part of the chapter we will describe how Saturn works, with a minimum of interpretation. We will let Saturn workers speak for themselves—often with contradictory points of view. In the last two sections, Union Functioning and Evaluating Saturn, we will give our own views.

HOW SATURN BEGAN

Saturn began when General Motors executives decided that the only way they could build a small car to compete with Japanese models was by starting from scratch. In 1982 a group of engineers and designers was pulled together at the GM Tech Center in Warren, Michigan. The brass decided early on that part of the clean-sheet-of-paper approach had to be new "people systems." Luckily, the head of the United Auto Workers' GM Department at that time was Don Ephlin, already known as a promoter of labor-management cooperation.

GM and the union set up the "Group of 99," union and management representatives from 55 plants. Subgroups traveled far and wide to research various aspects of car-making: paint, assembly, stamping, and of course, people systems. They talked to Japanese manufacturers and to Volvo, toured 49 GM plants and 60 other companies. They put in around 50,000 hours.[4]

Already, the project had an evangelistic air. Saturn's director of business systems in those days, Neil De Koker, said, "The emotions, the tears, the whatever it took to really create a team and a culture and a commitment...I get emotional now, just thinking about it."[5]

The GM Executive Committee approved the 99's proposal to make Saturn a wholly-owned subsidiary, building a completely new car, with a union contract separate from the UAW master agreement. In 1985 six people, three from each side, were assigned to write that contract. Jim Wheatley, from the UAW, said of that experience, "No one was supposed to tell us what to do. We were supposed to do the whole thing, and after we got done they could knock out what they wanted to. But otherwise, forget where we came from and who we represented...We did everything by consensus."[6]

The 28-page agreement was ratified by the UAW International Executive Board—there were as yet no Saturn

workers. President Owen Bieber called it "a degree of co-determination never before reached in U.S. collective bargaining."[7]

Recruitment began in 1988, with Saturn sending teams of recruiters throughout the U.S. All Saturn workers would be current or laid-off GM employees; none would be hired locally in Tennessee. Applicants had to pass a screening process; Saturn was looking for employees who would "step outside the call of duty," as Charter Team Member Peggy Mullins put it. Pay would be 20 percent lower than at GM, but with the opportunity to make up the difference through bonuses. New-hires at Saturn gave up their GM seniority.

Thus the first group of workers to transfer to Saturn were those who were attracted to the Saturn philosophy. Many saw in the new company a chance to move up that they would never have gotten in their old locations.

Denise Harding, daughter of a plant manager at Kodak, is a good example. She moved from a Rochester, New York GM plant in 1990. She has a degree in business administration and is a certified respiratory therapist. "I came to Saturn with a goal not to be sitting on the line the next 20 years," says Harding. "I did the point roles in my team, I interviewed for jobs four times in two-and-a-half years.

"In the old world, everything was a closed society. Seniority dictated everything. Everyone who came here at first wanted to move up."

Harding is now a full-time health and safety coordinator for Saturn's Vehicle Systems, overseeing conditions for 3,300 members and working a regular day shift (that is, non-rotating). Saturn also recommended Harding to sit on Tennessee's OSHA commission.

In 1990, the hiring pool was restricted to laid-off GM workers, and in October 1992 those at plants scheduled to close were added to that list. Thus the later arrivals were less likely to be coming because they were excited by the Saturn experiment, and more likely just to be desperate for a job.

The difference—along with the difficulties of expanding from two crews to three in 1993—has caused some friction. Peggy Mullins says, "When I got here I loved it. I came down for a change. The people that didn't have a job—they want to bring back the old ways. If I could wave my magic wand, I'd fire 'em."

The first Saturn team members, average age 36, underwent at least 300-350 hours of training. Before a single car was built the first 3,000 workers had received a million hours in class.[8]

The training, borrowed from non-union IBM and Motorola, was heavy on "Saturn awareness," team building and "people skills." It included the trust fall and team wall-climbing, described in "Building Trust," chapter 13. The goal was to break down barriers and instill the necessity of teamwork. The training also stressed taking initiative and responsibility.

Saturn Terminology

Every workplace has its own jargon, but Saturn has developed the special lingo almost to a new language.

Besides the fuzzy language of "utilizing a synergistic approach," there are many Saturn-specific terms. In particular, the words "union" and "management" are not commonly used. Instead, employees are "represented" or "non-represented," or rep and non-rep. Some others:

• Work unit: team
• WUC, work unit counselor: team leader
• Module: a grouping of teams by function or geography
• Op tech: operations technician (production worker)
• Trades tech: skilled trades worker
• OMAs, Operations Module Advisors: one rep and one non-rep employee who jointly oversee a module. The non-rep OMA receives more pay. Although in theory OMAs do not split the job, rather functioning as partners, in practice the rep OMA tends to take care of the "people issues." The non-rep OMA takes attendance, hustles up more bodies if the work unit is short that day, and oversees emergencies. The rep OMA is essentially appointed by the local union president, although officially the appointment, like others, is joint. Most rep OMAs have not had prior experience as a union representative.

HOW SATURN WORKS

Although Saturn uses some cutting edge technology and processes, the heart of the factory is a traditional, if slightly modified, assembly line. The plant's designers rejected the Swedish experiments where automatic guided vehicles give workers some control over the pacing of work, as well as the more advanced Swedish model, where teams of workers build whole cars (see chapter 30).

The Saturn "people philosophy," as included in the union contract, is, "We believe that all people want to be involved in decisions that affect them, care about their job and each other, take pride in themselves and in their contributions, and want to share in the success of their efforts."

Saturn teams are called "work units," 6-15 workers with an elected work unit counselor (WUC, pronounced "wook"). The work unit is responsible for "30 work unit functions":

1. Uses consensus decision-making
2. Is self-directed
3. Makes job assignments
4. Resolves conflicts
5. Plans work
6. Designs jobs
7. Controls scrap
8. Controls material and inventory (develops and maintains work unit inventory plan consistent with the Saturn Production System)
9. Performs equipment maintenance
10. Performs direct/indirect work [i.e., does the actual jobs]
11. Schedules communications within and outside the group
12. Keeps records
13. Makes selection decisions of new members into the work unit
14. Constantly seeks improvements in quality, cost, and work environment
15. Performs to budget (plans budget in concert with Saturn budgetary procedures and the Business Plan)
16. Is integrated horizontally with business unit resources
17. Reflects synergistic group growth
18. Determines work methods
19. Schedules relief time
20. Schedules vacations
21. Provides absentee replacements (the work unit is responsible for attendance of its own members)
22. Performs repairs (in the event a job leaves the work unit with a known or unknown nonconformance to specification, the originating work unit will be accountable for corrective action and repair)
23. Performs housekeeping
24. Maintain and performs health and safety program
25. Produces world class quality products to schedule at competitive costs
26. Assists in developing and delivering training

27. Obtains supplies

28. Seeks resources as needed

29. Schedules and holds meetings

30. Initiates initial consultative procedure for self-corrective action, with responsibility on the individual member

The WUC, who receives no extra pay, is responsible for managing daily production—quality, quantity, costs, and people. He or she attends daily meetings of the WUCs with the OMAs (see box on terminology). WUCs serve three-year terms, take the union oath of office, and can be recalled by a two-thirds vote of the unit, although this happens rarely.

The work unit chooses "point people" for various functions—housekeeping, quality, indirect materials (tools, gloves), safety, and others. These report in weekly unit meetings that discuss quality, training, and the like. Each team is responsible for fetching its own parts; there is no separate material handling department. Members get special training for this job and do it for six months or more at a time.

Bob Hoskins, who is an OMA and was narrowly defeated for president of the Saturn local in 1993, says, "The point people do their point jobs plus do their own work. It's an additional burden that, traditionally, management would have to hire somebody to do. It's a sweet set-up for GM: no supervisors, no inspectors, no line repairmen, no sweepers. No personnel department, no payroll. They're getting the team members to do it all."

No supervisors? Saturn workers say that the next level up—the OMAs—do not get involved much in the day-to-day shop-floor-level running of the plant, leaving that to the WUCs.

Team members rotate through the different team jobs, setting their own schedule for switching. "Each team has one undesirable operation," explains Don Edouard, who was recently promoted off the line.

Because filling in for absent workers is one of the 30 work unit functions, there is no pool of replacement workers. Each work unit is supposed to have enough people for each operation, plus the WUC, a materials handler, and an extra. This presumably gives the team enough members to deal with absenteeism and to give each other breaks and emergency relief. Saturn workers get two 13-minute breaks in a 10-hour day, which includes a half-hour paid lunch (compared to 60 minutes of break plus a half-hour unpaid lunch at other UAW-GM plants).

Diane Fitzgerald, who works in Vehicle Systems, tells of a day when four people were absent from her 12-person team. They kept the line running, borrowed someone from another team, and ran like that half the day. By noon the OMA had called people in from other shifts. As a reward, the team got a dinner and sweatshirts.

ROTATING THROUGH SHIFTS

Calling in people from other crews to supplement the workforce is known as "augmentation." Saturn could not run without this practice. The workforce is divided into three crews (A, B, and C), each of which rotates through two 10-hour shifts (at straight time). Saturdays are paid at straight time as well. Thus one crew's schedule would look like this:

Rotating Shifts

S	M	T	W	Th	F	S
OFF	DAY	DAY	OFF	OFF	NIGHT	NIGHT
OFF	NIGHT	NIGHT	NIGHT	NIGHT	OFF	OFF
OFF	OFF	OFF	DAY	DAY	DAY	DAY
OFF	DAY	DAY	OFF	OFF	NIGHT	NIGHT

Day shift: 6:30 am - 4:30 pm   Night shift: 5:00pm - 3:00 am
Saturn employees work three Saturdays per month.

Some Saturn workers say it's great to have five days off at a time every three weeks. But most work, voluntarily, two or more days during that time, on another crew. One International official says that management "contrives its manpower to provide the unlimited opportunity to augment. Of the three crews, you short one.

"It keeps them monetarily happy, so it is a narcotic. But the monetary narcotic can't overcome the strain of that rotation coupled with enormous overtime. I'll bet that out of 6,800 people, there aren't 200 who work a 40-hour week."

Most Saturn workers interviewed for this chapter said that rotating through different shifts is hard on the body and mind, although a few said they would not like to work a set assignment. "You don't know what day it is," was the most common complaint. At an August 1994 "town hall meeting" (the UAW Local 1853 term for a union meeting), called to discuss changing the system, workers said rotation was wearing them down.

Loberta Garron, who worked at the Framingham, Massachusetts plant before it closed, says, "Since I'm a single person, it's all right—I can come home and go to sleep. But people with families—if I had a child I just couldn't go along with the rotating shifts…Some people say it's taking seven years off your life."

Saturn workers have had the opportunity to change the system somewhat; at one point they voted not to change to a longer rotation period.

Research has shown shift work in general to have negative effects on sleep and mental agility. Dr. Timothy Roehrs of the Henry Ford Sleep Disorders Center in Detroit says rotating shifts are the worst, as the body's clock never gets a chance to right itself. "Rotating shift workers sleep the shortest and the poorest," Roehrs said. "Their job performance is poorer."[9]

Saturn has offered classes on how to cope with rotation. At one, the instructor declined to answer questions about the physiological effects of rotating shifts, saying she wanted to keep her job.

The reason workers do not have fixed shift assignments chosen by seniority, as at other auto plants, is that Saturn has rejected the notion of seniority. Saturn functions instead on the principles of equality and merit. Everyone—except several hundred union officials or appointees who are on straight days—rotates.

In September 1994 the International union called for a vote on whether to investigate a fixed shift system, and workers voted yes by a narrow margin. This vote was tricky, because the International announced in advance that if a fixed shift/seniority system was negotiated, the applicable seniority would be Saturn seniority, not GM. Many of the earlier hires, with low GM seniority, would thus have had preference over the later hires who came with 20+ years at GM.

Advocates of rotation, such as Bennett, say that introducing seniority at Saturn would undermine the equality/merit system that is one of the bedrocks of Saturn's uniqueness. Union member Don Edouard, recently appointed to Corporate Communications (a non-rotating job), explains that the "no-seniority system reduces symbolism, makes people feel equal. How would it be if I'm set on the day shift all the time just because I came here in 1989 or 1990?

"Rotation is a good way of making people share the graveyard shifts as well as the good shifts. It allows parents to say, 'At least I can to go Little League with my son every other week.'"

WORKLOAD

Saturn workers say their workload is about the same as in their previous plants. Hoskins, an OMA, says, "They keep 'em busy but it's reasonable." Fitzgerald, who has worked on time-study, says Saturn's goal (like NUMMI's) is to fill 95 percent of available time, but that in practice the workload varies from team to team. Tasks are time-studied and the results recorded—"number of seconds to take 10 steps, reach for your bolts, restock your bolts." Saturn's name for standardized work is Most Valued Method.

How would a worker deal with an overloaded job? She or he would bring it to the team, to see if all agreed that it was in fact too heavy. The team could come up with and implement its own solution, such as shifting some tasks from one job to another within the team, if the engineers say that quality will not be affected. Saturn teams seem to have more autonomy to rearrange jobs this way than do teams at such lean plants as NUMMI or CAMI.

What if the workload was too heavy overall, so that shifting work around didn't help? What could the team do about that? Workers asked this question mentioned going to ergonomics, or dealing with it as a safety question. None suggested contacting the union or even the rep OMA. "You'd have to make a business case," explains Hoskins.

Saturn is proud of the "skillets" on its assembly lines. These are wooden platforms workers stand on to move with the car, rather than having to walk alongside it as they work. The job cycle is several minutes long, compared to about a minute at NUMMI and Mazda.

Auto industry analysts are critical of Saturn for its high ratio of people to cars produced. James Harbour of Harbour Associates, a firm that does annual productivity surveys of the auto industry, says that a car Saturn's size should be at 2.77, rather than 3.77. He blames the car's hard-to-build design; the paid lunch; and "a lot of extra people."[10]

Workers got a break when Saturn dealers were overstocked in early 1994. For six weeks the plant cut the number of cars produced per day from around 1,100 to 800. Rather than laying off some workers, or sending them home early at short pay, or slowing the line (it has always run at a constant 62.5 cars per hour), the line stopped running when 800 was reached, and workers spent the rest of the day on the 30 work unit functions.

THE PARTNERSHIP STRUCTURE

Saturn is most famous for its partnership structure. Most Saturn managers have a UAW counterpart; the two supposedly function as equals. Bennett writes,

> The partnership attempts to integrate labor into the organization's long range and strategic planning and day-to-day operational decision making. Unlike most labor-management efforts, Saturn's joint committees have responsibility for strategic-level decision making, and an even more radical departure from traditional organization has taken place at the shop floor and middle management levels. Saturn's workforce has been organized into self-directed work teams responsible to a middle management organization half of whom are local UAW members. In this way the local union is in fact *co-managing* the business...
>
> Traditionally the role of a local union was to represent and organize the membership while management managed the business. The local union at Saturn is attempting to break down this dichotomy. It seeks to share responsibility for both the effective use of capital and for meeting the economic and social needs of the labor force...Instead of a division of responsibility based solely on constituency, both [labor and management] are responsible for managing people and capital.[11]

Bennett serves on Saturn's Manufacturing Advisory Council. In addition to the line partners illustrated in the diagram, various staff positions are also partnered, in sales, marketing, finance, engineering, quality, health and safety, training, organizational development, corporate communications, maintenance, and product and process development. The Local 1853 recording secretary, for instance, works in corporate communications, and the vice presidents have been partnered with the heads of business units.

Writing in 1993, Bennett explained, "The partnering involves over 375 union members including 91 module advisors, 24 crew coordinators, 51 functional coordinators with site-wide responsibility, 53 functional coordinators at the business unit level, and 155 with module support responsibilities for quality, engineering, materials, etc."[12]

Critics ask why it takes two partners to do one job. Bennett responds that because each pair of OMAs advises 100 or so production workers and the work units are essentially self-managing, the ratio of indirect labor to direct labor is actually lower than in Japanese plants.

But Hoskins, the OMA, says, "Sometimes I'm in

meetings, in humongous meetings, and I can't believe it—all these damn people there, and none of them contributing."

The partnering is the union's chance to be in on decisions before they're made. Saturn President Skip LeFauve says, "The union is in the room, not talked to about the decision afterwards. The process is inclusion, not consultation." And, of course, when the union has "ownership" of such decisions, it is more willing to defend them and make them work.[13]

HIRING

Teams are responsible for hiring their own members. A database of applicants is kept on file, and when a work unit is authorized to hire, it matches the "skill sets" it needs with an applicant. Those who pass the phone interview are invited to the plant, at Saturn's expense, with their spouses. Those who pass this interview can be hired.

Bennett says that informal lobbying goes on. A team contemplating an applicant from Van Nuys will ask other Van Nuys people already at Saturn whether the applicant is any good.

Similarly, if a worker wants to transfer to an opening on a different team, he or she applies and is interviewed by two team members, including the WUC. Seniority does not apply.

There are dozens of applicants for the desirable offline partner jobs. Again, applicants are chosen by merit. Don Edouard, for example, got his job in Corporate Communications because of his previous experience in media

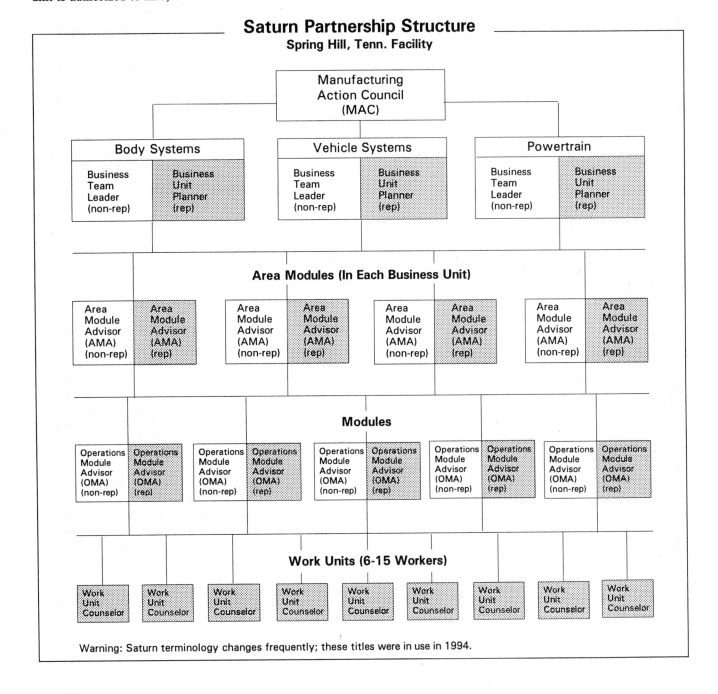

Saturn Partnership Structure
Spring Hill, Tenn. Facility

Warning: Saturn terminology changes frequently; these titles were in use in 1994.

work and his educational background.

Saturn workers say that favoritism also plays a role. Asked how he became an OMA after two years on the line, Hoskins says, "I'd like to think it was my 17 years' experience as a UAW rep, but I also knew some people." Both Mike Bennett's wife and the wife of union Vice President Joe Rypkowski have non-rotating jobs at Saturn.

The flip side of favoritism is that some union members charge they have lost appointed jobs after opposing the union leadership.[14] Bennett asked two chaplains, for example, to resign after they spoke out against rotating shifts, reminding them that they were not supposed to get involved in "politics." And the man who ran against Bennett for president in 1990, Sam Barnes, claims that company and union collaborated to get him fired. An arbitrator later ordered Barnes reinstated with full back pay, a victory he credits to the intervention of the UAW International. Other of Bennett's opponents charge that management has kicked them out of the plant for campaigning, while Bennett's Vision Team is allowed free run of the plant.[15]

QUALITY

The Saturn workforce feels strongly about quality, seeing it as their job security, and their cars have a good reputation. Saturn's customer satisfaction is second only to that of Lexus and Infiniti, both luxury cars, according to the J.D. Power survey, and defect rates are half the GM average.[16]

In 1991, the union organized a plant-wide protest over what it felt was management's inattention to quality problems.

This period, according to LeFauve, when the company was under pressure from buyers to build more cars, was a "transition from quality at any cost to quality at least cost."[17] Workers wore black armbands during a visit by GM Chair Robert Stempel. Some refused to build the car till problems were fixed, causing huge back-ups. (It should be noted that this quality protest took place during contract negotiations.)[18]

PAY

Saturn workers make about $18.50 an hour, if you include their quarterly "risk" and "reward" payments (unlike at other GM plants, COLA is also paid quarterly). The "risk" payment depends on the workforce fulfilling the goal of 92 hours of training per worker per year. Reward depends on meeting quality and output goals.

The 1991 contract called for the proportion of salary at risk to increase from 5 percent in 1992, to 20 percent in 1995.

"They told me up at SATURN that if I stuck to traditional union activity...

...I'd finish up becoming irrelevant to the changed society of the ninties!

So I looked for ways to cooperate with the management...

...went to company seminars on productivity... ...workplace reform... - the whole trip!"

"did it do the trick?"

"I became irrelevant to the workers"

D.F.

DISCIPLINE AND ATTENDANCE POLICY

A big source of friction at Saturn was the policy whereby workers could miss work without losing pay. Members say that some abused the system, making it hard on others. They demanded a fair way to deal with absenteeism, and in 1994 a much stricter absence control plan was instituted, with automatic penalties.

Many workers interviewed in April 1994 were upset, however, that the new plan "hurts the good people as well as the bad ones," so that people not considered attendance problems were getting caught in the penalty system. They complained that they had voted on one understanding and found it much more inflexible in practice.

For infractions of the rules, such as leaving early, a worker may be put in the "amber zone." The OMAs will counsel him. The next step is the "red zone," and then "D Day" (although a worker may go straight to D Day). The errant worker is sent home for three days, with pay, to think over whether he wants to continue working at Saturn. Another infraction is taken as a decision to sever the relationship.[19]

Sam Barnes estimates that Saturn has fired 250-350

people, and says that he is the first discharged Saturn worker to get his job back. This low rate could be due to the union's perspective. Denise Harding explains, "In the old days, we said you were right no matter what you did. Five percent were repeat offenders; 95 percent got no representation. Now, the union will make sure we dot the i's and cross the t's, but if you're wrong, you're wrong."

SKILLED TRADES

Saturn has three skilled classifications—die tech, mechanical tech, and electrical tech. They perform a wider variety of work—and learn wider skills—than in a traditional plant. They work Monday-Thursday or Wednesday-Saturday, rotate between day and night shifts every two weeks, and work immense amounts of overtime.

Skilled workers keep busier than at traditional plants. Rather than simply being on hand in case a machine malfunctions, they work on a project while on call. They also get more help from the op techs. Like the op techs, they cover for each other's vacations and rotate through different jobs.

RACE RELATIONS

In 1993 the Memphis-based Commission on Religion and Racism called a boycott of Saturn, charging that neither company nor union was addressing racism and discrimination in the plant. CORR pointed to a KKK calling card left in an African American worker's locker, and the firing of one worker for using the KKK as a threat against another. The Saturn workforce is 21.6 percent people of color, and some workers see this figure as a quota above which the company will not go. They point to the teams' ability to hire their own members as a mechanism for maintaining the ratio.[20]

Peggy Mullins, an African American who has been at Saturn since 1989, says teams are likely to make allowances for a white applicant who cannot read, but use the same problem as a reason not to hire a Black applicant. She says her team got upset when she and another Black worker teamed up to interview an applicant—"they felt it shouldn't have been two Blacks, but two whites would have been just fine."

Mike Bennett says that teams have sometimes had to be asked by union and management to "step up to their EEO obligations, which they have done, to their credit." But Evon Heath, an African-American worker, points out that no team is majority Black, and believes this is a conscious policy. African-Americans interviewed said they were more likely to hear remarks they considered racist than in their northern plants. "It's like they think, 'You're on our turf now,'" said Loberta Garron.

The UAW International sent down representatives from its Civil Rights Department to hold two open forums in 1993, to investigate members' concerns about race discrimination. At those lengthy meetings, according to a participant, all complaints were directed not at Saturn management but at the local union.

TRAINING

Saturn devotes many hours to training. As mentioned above, each worker must spend about five percent of his or her time (92 hours) in classes. Each team must find a way to fit this time into its schedule, by having someone fill in for the worker who is in class.

A look at the classes available reveals a mixture of soft, "people skills"; safety; Saturn-specific training (such as 4 hours on Direct Material Flow Overview); and classes which could impart transferable hard skills. Each worker designs his or her own Individual Training Plan for the year.

Classes include Robotics Operations (8 hours), Body Systems Awareness (5), Welder Training (10), Stress Management I (2), Blueprint Reading (4), CNC Mill Introduction (40), a video on Standardized Work (1), IE Point Person Orientation (8), Conflict resolution (80, Consultation Process (3), Creative Thinking (8), Decision Making (8), Design of Experiments (16), Saturn Fork Truck Safety (10), Ergonomics Awareness (1), Intro to the PC (4), Machine Shop Comprehensive (64), Robotics—Mechanical Maintenance (32), The Humor Option (8), Hydraulics for Technicians (40), President's Leader Mentoring, taught by Skip LeFauve (2), and GM/UAW History I and II (24 total).

UNION FUNCTIONING

It is difficult to write about the UAW at Saturn without focusing on Local 1853 President and Shop Chair Mike Bennett. A former local union president near Flint, Michigan, Bennett signed on to Saturn early and was groomed for his current position. His stamp is on much of the structure and functioning of the union; many speak of him as if he *were* "the union." Hoskins, who was a plant chairman in Norwood, Ohio, says the Saturn local is "totally different" from a traditional local. "In a traditional local, the president does the administration; the chairman runs the plant floor. Here you got God, and he runs it all."

As an example, in 1993 the membership voted down a $3.4 million union hall, complete with swimming pool and basketball court, that Bennett wanted to build. Bennett kept bringing it back for a vote until, on the third try, members approved the plan. For many, the votes were a referendum on Bennett's leadership, as was the September 1994 vote, sought by the International union, to look into fixed shifts.

Sam Barnes, who plans to run against Bennett in 1996, says, "You can look at that vote as people saying we want the International involved in what happens down here. Or you can say they actually wanted to look at fixed shifts. Or they could have just voted against whatever Bennett wanted. It was a big defeat for Bennett."

Terry Walton, who filed suit against Saturn for race discrimination, says, "Talking to Mike Bennett is like talking to Skip LeFauve. He is not in bed with management, he *is* management."[21]

Because of Bennett's extraordinarily prominent role—

e.g., being both president and shop chair—and a style which many characterize as dictatorial, many critics of Saturn, both within and without, have a tendency to blame problems on him rather than on the system itself (we described this same phenomenon at NUMMI and Mazda; see "The System Itself or Mistakes in Implementation?" in chapter 8). Although Bennett is certainly a chief architect of the Saturn system, we can still evaluate that system on its own merits.

Only four members of Local 1853 have the right to write grievances, the shop chair and the three vice presidents. Each of those is or was partnered with a management colleague, and according to members, is seldom seen in the plant. Writing in 1992, Bennett said that in the past six years, the union had filed only seven grievances.[22]

The union reps closest to the shop floor then, the rep OMAs, may not write grievances; any representation they give is in the context of their functioning with their non-rep partners. Bob Hoskins says that a member is much more likely to come to him than to the non-rep OMA with a problem, but that he will quickly get his partner involved, and his partner would do the same. Both OMAs are present in amber zone or red zone interviews.

Saturn's Consensus Guidelines

Saturn's union contract says that consensus will be the primary method for making decisions and resolving disagreements. This means both between union and management and within work units or the various "D-rings," or decision rings.

The contract gives these guidelines:

Resolution is achieved through the joint efforts of the parties in discovering the "best" solution.

The solution must provide a high level of acceptance for all parties.

Once agreement is reached, the parties must be totally committed to the solution.

Any of the parties may block a potential decision. However, the party blocking the decision must search for alternatives.

In the event an alternative solution is not forthcoming, the blocking party must reevaluate the position in the context of the philosophy and mission.

Voting, "trading" and compromise are not part of this process.

The joint effort is aimed at discovering the best decision/resolution within the context of Saturn's philosophy and mission while, at the same time, satisfying the stakes and equities of all major stake holders.

The process is spelled out further in the 30 Work Unit Functions:

Any member who feels the need to block is required to provide a reasonable and timely alternative solution to the problem. All members of the work unit who reach consensus must be at least 70% comfortable with the decision, *and 100% committed to its implementation.* [emphasis in original]

As described in the box, consensus decision-making is the style. "Table pounding would definitely be frowned on," says Hoskins.

Opponents of Bennett within the union have called for giving the union more of a presence on the floor by electing the OMAs and other appointees. Bennett and other supporters of the system strongly resist this notion, arguing that election

would politicize the partnership, diminishing the ability of individuals in these positions to equally balance the needs of people with the needs of the business. Popularity, not skills, knowledge, and ability, would become the dominant qualification...politicizing the process would lead to a return of the old grievance committeemen structure, an increase in adversarialism, and movement away from consensus decision making and joint problem solving.[23]

In an early 1993 referendum, members were asked whether they wanted to keep the current system (although no alternative was specified), and 71 percent voted yes.

As this book went to press, it was expected that the International union would succeed in negotiating 25 elected, full-time, company-paid, grievance-writing representatives, as would exist in any other GM plant Saturn's size.

WHAT IS THE UNION'S ROLE?

Just as important as numbers of representatives and their method of selection is how they view their responsibilities. Saturn was founded on the win-win philosophy. Therefore union officials and joint appointees often speak of decision-making as if it were possible to find a single solution for any problem that is objectively, logically the "best." (We discussed the problems with this mind-set in chapter 15.) Denise Harding: "In the old world, the union jumped in with information to win a case. The union now has to put on a different hat. We have to have facts and figures, review the data. We don't come in like a bulldog anymore. We put on our good business hat; we're not really union or management—we advocate for a good business decision.

"We throw management off-base when we come in with good business decisions. They can't just dismiss us. Making your case is more effective than table-pounding. We're smarter now. Being union doesn't mean you have to be an idiot when it comes to making business decisions."

Similarly, Bennett contrasts the Saturn method with the union's old practices: "Before, management decided on manpower and the union had to take an adversarial stance to get more. Now, really you let information make the decision."[24]

What's an example? Bennett says that early in the design process, the union advocated "mass relief" (the line stops and everyone takes a break at the same time) rather than tag relief (the line keeps running and designated workers relieve people for breaks in turn), because "mass relief requires less manpower." Bennett has also spoken proudly of the union's choice of non-union suppliers over union ones, for quality reasons.[25]

Rank and file members interviewed for this chapter clearly felt no more involved in their union than they had back home, and probably less. Views expressed ranged from "it feels like we don't have a union here" to "you only see the union at election time" to "politics as usual," referring to the battles among different slates. As in more traditional UAW plants, "the union" means "the officials"; the difference is that at Saturn they are seen as part of the management structure, as in fact they are.

If workers expect to have any say in what goes on at work, it is through their teams or through their own individual efforts to "move up," not through the union. An exception is the fairly frequent plant-wide votes that are held, for example on negotiating a fixed shift, working Sundays (this happened in 1993), or canceling team meetings (decided in late 1994, to help Saturn boost production).

In the 1993 elections, Bennett's Vision Team faced three other slates. Bennett beat Members for a Democratic Union's Bob Hoskins by 52 percent in the run-off. Hoskins claims Bennett's margin of victory was the votes of his appointees and of several hundred new-hires who had met the incumbents in their "Saturn awareness" classes. The internal political battles have been quite bitter, as have Bennett's conflicts with the UAW International.

In 1993, UAW International Vice President and head of the GM Department Steve Yokich began playing more of a role at Saturn. He sent the company a list of 10 contract clauses he wanted to renegotiate. In 1994 Yokich called for the vote on fixed shifts, and sent a team of International reps from Detroit to bargain the contract.

EVALUATING SATURN

How should trade unionists evaluate a work system or a model of labor-management relations or a combination thereof, such as Saturn? We could look at quality, productivity, and profit numbers, as management would; at the work itself—how stressful, boring, easy, or interesting it is; at job creation/job security; at strength of the union. What else? Saturn has a bank and a travel agency on site,

and a day care center nearby. There are aerobics and dance classes. There are geese on the grounds.

Let's acknowledge the desirability of the geese and the travel agency right off, and look at the other ingredients.

Quality: Excellent, according to buyer perceptions. This is what Saturn has built its image and marketing strategy around, and what workers see as their job security. Quality apparently is maintained through a good deal of inspection and repair.

Productivity: Management complains about the greater number of hours required to assemble a Saturn compared to the benchmark, the Japanese transplants. Some of the disparity could be differences in design and some could be labor productivity—which would mean that the work pace is more reasonable at Saturn.

Profits: When Saturn was born, GM had not yet adopted the cost-cutting zeal that led to so many plant closing announcements in the early 1990s. A lot of money was spent on Saturn, from the no-cost-spared research done by the Group of 99 to the elaborate landscaping to the installation of lost-foam casting in the foundry. On GM's investment of $5 billion, Saturn turned its first profit, a paltry $40 million, in 1993.

Saturn's pioneering technologies, quality achievements, and outstanding customer satisfaction clearly are secondary to GM; top management has grown increasingly impatient with the lack of profitability, and has delayed announcing whether Saturn will be expanded as planned.

Work life: Like any other workplace, Saturn is a mixture of those who welcome the opportunity for more variety or responsibility (such as point roles), those who would rather work be as hassle-free as possible, those who are sick of the Saturn rhetoric ("are you willing to change?"), and everything in-between. For the former group, there is much to like about the self-directed work teams.

Loberta Garron moved to Tennessee partly because "after 20 years at Framingham, I really thought it would be a fabulous opportunity to do it right. I like the difference. They [management] have things they want us to do, but they don't tell us how to do it. Our team can decide how we do our job and change it as a team." (Garron notes that her team, electrical check at the end of the assembly line, is considered a very good job, with a light workload.)

Of course, the involvement mode has its problems too. As Garron puts it, "You know a lot whether you want to or not.

"There are some things about GM that I really miss. I knew just what to expect from GM. You knew you got time off if you didn't get your butt in there, you didn't get paid. You *knew* this. You knew you weren't a person, you were just a number. It wasn't no big deal. You went in knowing this.

"Here, they tell you all this...Some of the things are true, some of the things they keep to. We are building a quality car. It's a new company, so you know there's

Member-to-Member Survey

In 1993 and 1994 the union conducted a survey in which WUCs interviewed team members individually. Among the results, members said that Saturn is:

	1993	1994
Great	8	7
Not perfect, but heading in the right direction	76	58
Just a job to me, I don't really have any feelings about it	6	14
Heading in the wrong direction and I am not very happy here	7	18
Such a disappointment to me that I wish I could find another job	3	3

going to be things that might not be what they really wanted. But hopefully they will eventually get to it."

Diane Fitzgerald, who likes Saturn, has been a point person and has interviewed for a partnered job. She has been her team's representative to a group that gives input on designs for future models. She says that workers themselves developed her team, Finesse, which wasn't in the original plans. They use electric torque wrenches and rubber mallets to "finesse" parts into shape, to make them aligned and flush. The work doesn't get boring, Fitzgerald says, though it does get tiring.

Fitzgerald speaks highly of the early days, before production began. Her small group worked well, with little conflict. "We hired our own people, did all our own interviewing. We were looking for certain types of people who were willing to change and willing to work with this whole process, and then of course willing to work with each other. In the smaller group of people that worked pretty well.

"We were making a lot more of our own decisions, all the decisions on the line were made by the people that were running it. There was very little conflict because we were all really goal-oriented. This is when we were building prototypes, non-production cars." She—along with everyone else—says the transition from two crews to three has been difficult—"there's a lot of ideas among 6,000 people."

There are opportunities to take initiative: Fitzgerald tells of a day when during a team meeting, a worker who was augmenting from another crew disappeared. He returned to tell the team that he had researched a problem with a fit, traced it back to its source, taken his tools, and worked on it. "He solved a really big problem for us, just on his own. And there are a lot of people who do that.

"People have the opportunity to initiate change. They can't go in and say, 'This is being changed,' but they have the opportunity to initiate it and to back it up with facts and figures."

It's a plus for Saturn workers that for many, their workload is not at the maximum, and that the plant does pay attention to ergonomics. The platforms workers stand on can be raised to adjust to individuals' heights, for example. It would be unwise to assume, however, that Saturn will escape the pressure all other GM plants are under to squeeze more out of each worker, through "synchronous manufacturing," Quality Network, SOP, and a host of other programs (see chapters 8 and 37). Given that the percentage of time spent working is already officially supposed to be 95 percent, the pressure will grow to achieve that number in practice.

Job creation/security. At this stage, Saturn has more bargaining unit jobs than a truly lean plant and probably more than other not-yet-lean GM small car plants. This is both because of the slack in the system and because of the appointed jobs. On the other hand, management can run the plant somewhat short-handed because of the huge amounts of overtime worked.

The contract says that the majority of Saturn workers will not be laid off, except due to unforeseen or catastrophic events or severe economic conditions. Workers are eligible for this level of security if they left GM to join Saturn "as part of the full initial complement" of workers, or if they are among the 80 percent with the highest Saturn seniority in their business unit.

However, Saturn workers seem to discount this promise. Indeed, the atmosphere is one of great fear for their jobs, heightened by GM's continued hemming and hawing about Saturn's future. Loberta Garron, three years till retirement: "I don't believe in job security anymore. It's just a word they throw out at you. If sales go down it's like anyplace else: something's got to happen."

Word is that the new models due for fall 1995 will require 1,200 fewer people to build, and Saturn is not saying what will happen to those people.[26]

Tops on Saturn workers' minds is the 30-years-and-out pension that other GM workers have.[27] Initially, no Saturn workers were eligible, since they had to quit GM to come to Saturn. In 1991, Bennett negotiated 30-and-out for those with over 10 years at GM. But the lower seniority workers want it as well. Some also want the contractual right to return to GM. Apparently they do not feel secure about tying their future to Saturn's.

In late 1994, even before the new contract was finalized, the union announced that some Saturn production workers would be allowed to transfer to seven GM plants in Michigan that were badly understaffed. This fit in with Saturn's plans to build the next model with fewer workers.

By that time evidence was strong that Saturn was losing its special place at GM. President Skip LeFauve, closely identified with Saturn up till then, was made GM vice president in charge of the Small Car Group, in addition to his Saturn duties. LeFauve said that cars GM produced elsewhere might be sold as Saturns. And Saturn seemed to have lost its cherished role as laboratory as well: it was clearer than ever that the NUMMI-style lean system was GM's model for transforming the rest of its factories, not the Saturn-style partnership.

UNION POWER

The UAW's vision at Saturn was union representation for members *in* decisions, rather than as a result of decisions. The reasoning was that union involvement would give workers a voice where and when it could have an effect, rather than too late. One example cited is the decision to build a station wagon, which would sell more, instead of a convertible, which would have more prestige.[28]

This degree of union power sounds good. But at Saturn the union is explicit that its role is not to represent workers' interests. Rather the union's job is "balancing the needs of the business with the needs of the people."

Now, this is different from saying "union and management will negotiate and eventually compromise on their different interests, and that process will balance the needs of the business and the needs of the people." This is what happens in a traditional, arms-length union-management relationship, if neither side has the power to overwhelm the other. At Saturn, the union has made meeting the needs of the business *its* business. This means that there are two parties looking after management's interests (or one and a half), and only half a party looking after the members' interests.

One die technician says, "The intention was good down here, but some of it they've gone overboard on. Management is for the business, the union should be for the people. There's a gray area in the middle where they can work together. Here the union doesn't just work in the gray area—it's on the management side of the gray area."

Second, this notion of balancing interests is tied to a notion of how the union exerts power. As described by Local 1853 officials, the union will show the company that it can be just as smart a maker of business decisions as any company guy. Doing that will give the union (that is, individual union officials) credibility, and that is how the union will have influence. The notion of union power through a strong, active, conscious membership is completely absent. This is the servicing model of unionism raised to a new degree.

Don Edouard, for example, says he himself has "more power than I ever dreamed of." He points to the weekly meetings of the top-level Saturn Action Council (SAC), which includes a union representative, as evidence that the corporation does not have the upper hand.

"We don't believe the union should advocate that we continue to do battle with corporate America," Edouard says. "What we would always ask is that we treat members as co-equals, and we treat them fairly and good. And this is what's happening here." What happened to the UAW's hard-won knowledge that unions have never won concessions from corporate America without doing battle?

A second question, of course, is, how much say does the union really have in running the business? It appears that the union did co-design the plant, the labor relations system, and the contract. But it is quite clear that the brass at GM are making the decisions about Saturn's future.

Throughout 1994, speculation raged about whether GM would decide to expand Saturn. Everyone seems to agree that the company cannot make a profit unless it can produce 500,000 cars a year—and current capacity, even working 20 hours a day, six days a week, is 322,000. Will the company expand the Spring Hill plant? Or will it build a car it calls a Saturn in another GM plant (Wilmington, Delaware has been mentioned)? Or will it, over the next few years, let Saturn be absorbed into the rest of the Small Car Group? Will the company listen more to the desires of the local union leadership, who want to expand at Spring Hill, or to the International union, that wants any expansion to go to a GM plant now scheduled for closure?

Certainly GM's decision will be based on the bottom line, not on the fact that the Saturn and UAW co-managers had previously planned a second assembly plant for Spring Hill.

Rank and filer Diane Fitzgerald: "Sometimes I think some of the union positions are just maybe a little bit...show. You've got these two people doing this job;

one person does the job, and the other person represents the union.

"I interviewed for a job one time where the union person would have a non-rep partner, and they asked me how would I feel about doing the same job as this non-rep person and making less money. And I thought, That says something right there."

A final point about Saturn and unionism: union leaders at Saturn clearly see themselves as special and apart from the rest of the labor movement. As Vice President Joe Rypkowski, then co-manager of Body Systems, put it, in an interview at the 1992 UAW Convention: "What we're doing is completely different."

Bennett has said that unions should concentrate on pursuing their interests at the local level. Here's an example. In 1992, GM's Lordstown, Ohio stamping plant went on strike over contracting out. GM wanted to move parts production, most of it for Saturn, to non-union shops; the local stood to lose 160 jobs.

The strike quickly shut Saturn down, along with eight other assembly plants. Bennett complained to the press that the International union should have granted those Lordstown workers who made Saturn parts an exemption, allowing them to cross the picket line. Bennett said a local union's role should be to help its own company "explore opportunities to compete. I don't support the current process [the strike]. We can't continue to remove wages from competition in the international economy."[29]

SATURN'S FUTURE

Much is new at Saturn. For most workers it is a different way of working, and there are things many like about their new plant: the ability to be more involved in what happens at work than in the traditional GM plants they left; for some, the chance to move up to more interesting and responsible jobs off the line.

When it comes to building *union* strength, however—in the sense of a conscious membership, ready and able to be mobilized collectively in their own behalf—Saturn fails. The unions at CAMI and Mazda, with no pretense of partnership, and operating under management-by-stress, are far stronger (see chapter 36).

The union, then, has helped design a system in which the individual worker gets a small amount of power, or, more accurately, involvement, in his or her day-to-day work. But the power of the union as a whole, expressed through its officials, is dedicated explicitly to "balancing the needs of the company and the workers."

It might be possible for a strong union to win a system of plant governance in which the union was in on decisions before they were made, and union officials represented members' interests, not so-called joint interests. Such a plant would still exist in a competitive world, however. Pressure on union officials to think and act like managers would be enormous (see chapter 15).

This is why, from our point of view, a union-management partnership like Saturn, that takes a particular workplace *out* of connection with union brothers and sisters, while leaving it *in* competition with other factories, is a big mistake. As described in chapter 2, in the long run, the way a particular enterprise survives is by competing with—and defeating—other firms. This competition results in the loss of decent union jobs, and the weakening or absorption of the union. The only way a union survives, on the other hand, is by banding workers together in solidarity to lessen the effects of the employers' competition.

We can see these iron laws at work at Saturn, where, unfettered by the National Agreement, the union agreed to work ten hours a day and Saturdays at straight time, in order to help the company be profitable.

Unfortunately, at this point the choices posed for Saturn workers are not great. The only options being discussed are full, "balance the needs of both" partnership,

and the traditional UAW structure in which a full-time elected official services the needs of 250 members (or doesn't). Neither option is designed to mobilize and empower the membership to challenge the company, when necessary. Saturn workers are fearful for their future, and uncertain whether their best hope lies in more intervention from the International, or in more of giving management everything it wants.

In September 1994 Loberta Garron voiced the turmoil: "There's a lot of feelings going around in Saturn right now—where are we going? If the leadership doesn't know, how are we going to know?"

There is one thing the union could learn from Saturn. The teams have shown that they can exercise responsibility. Now if the union could organize itself at that grass roots level...

Notes

1. For example, Barry Bluestone and Irving Bluestone, *Negotiating the Future: A Labor Perspective on American Business*, Basic Books, New York, 1992, p. 191-201; Saul Rubinstein, Michael, Bennett, and Thomas Kochan, "The Saturn Partnership: Co-Management and the Reinvention of the Local Union," chapter in Bruce E. Kaufman and Morris M. Kleiner, eds., *Employee Representation: Alternatives and Future Directions*, Industrial Relations Research Association, Madison, Wis., 1993, pp. 339-370; James Higgins, "Line workers really do help make decisions," *Detroit News*, May 13, 1990, p. 1D, 3D.

2. Greg Gardner, "Training Sells," *Detroit Free Press*, September 21, 1994, p. 9A.

3. For instance, Gregg Wirth, "Roger and Tennessee: Saturn Plant Is Good for GM, but Bad for the Locals," *Village Voice*, January 25, 1994, pp. 16-18; Greg Gardner, "Saturn chief wins big in shuffle," *Detroit Free Press*, October 5, 1994; Smita Madan Paul, "Owners: Saturn has life; Thousands make pilgrimage to plant," *The Tennessean*, June 26, 1994 (about Saturn's homecoming for owners).

4. Joe Sherman, *In the Rings of Saturn*, Oxford University Press, New York, 1994, pp. 77-86.

5. Sherman, p. 82.

6. Sherman, p. 84.

7. Sherman, p. 86

8. Sherman, pp. 194-197.

9. Keith Naughton, "UAW wary of rockin' around the clock at GM," *Detroit News*, July 18, 1993, pp. 4D.

10. Interview, September 28, 1994. NUMMI is at 2.52 and Chrysler's Neon at 2.72 ("An A for Efficiency," *Detroit Free Press*, June 24, 1994).

11. Rubinstein, Bennett, and Kochan, p. 339, pp. 352-53.

12. Rubinstein, Bennett, and Kochan, p. 346.

13. Rubinstein, Bennett, and Kochan, p. 354.

14. Helen Fogel, "Trouble in Paradise," *Detroit News*, February 6, 1994, and Gardner and Lippert, "Saturn's Dilemma," mention two such incidents.

15. Don Hinkle, "Challenger blasts Saturn's union head," *Columbia Daily Herald*, March 9, 1993.

16. David Woodruff, "Suddenly, Saturn's Orbit Is Getting Wobbly," *Business Week*, February 28, 1994, p. 34; John Lippert and Greg Gardner, "Saturn's Dilemma," *Detroit Free Press*, September 21, 1994, p. 9A.

17. Rubinstein, Bennett, and Kochan, p. 355.

18. Jane Slaughter, "Workers Charge Saturn with Sacrificing Quality," *Labor Notes* No. 153, December 1991, p. 6.

19. For more information on this kind of discipline system, see David N. Campbell, R.L. Fleming, and Richard C. Grote, "Discipline Without Punishment—At Last," *Harvard Business Review*, July-August 1985.

20. Mary Hollens, "Saturn May Be a New Kind of Car Company, but It's Got the Same Old Ku Klu Klan," *Labor Notes* No. 181, April 1994, p. 16, 11.

21. Don Hinkle, "Saturn suit charges racial discrimination," *Columbia Daily Herald*, May 20, 1993, p. 5.

22. Michael E. Bennett, "The Saturn Corporation: New Management-Union Partnership at the Factory of the Future," *Looking Ahead*, National Planning Association, Vol. XIII, No. 4, April 1992, p. 23.

23. Rubinstein, Bennett, and Kochan, p. 361.

24. "Working Together: Saturn and the UAW" (video), Merrimack Films, Hohokus, N.J., 1994.

25. For example, Dave Hage, "Saturn plant is GM's laboratory for testing new ways of working," *Minneapolis Star-Tribune*, October 21, 1990, p. 13A.

26. John Lippert, "UAW, GM talk about Saturn's fate," *Detroit Free Press*, January 28, 1994.

27. October 1994 Member to Member Summary Report.

28. Rubinstein, Bennett, and Kochan, p. 350.

29. Quotes from Bennett from "Labor's Days at GM," *Wall Street Journal*, September 4, 1992. After a nine-day strike, GM was forced to bring the work back to Lordstown.

Chapter 10

US West Telephone Workers: Roadkill on the Information Superhighway

Reengineering at US West meant elimination of 9,000 jobs and closure of 500 offices, with no input from the union. Decisions on who would get the new, reengineered jobs bypassed seniority. The union's response included grievances, press conferences, a possible EEOC suit, pressure on public utility commissions, and attempts to cushion the effects. But it was too little, too late.

by Madelyn Elder

ON SEPTEMBER 17, 1993, THE TELEPHONE COMPANY US West announced that it would close over 500 offices, spend upwards of $3.8 billion for "centers consolidation and process reengineering," and eliminate 9,000 jobs. US West's plan, which was not negotiated with its workers' union, the Communications Workers of America, will create 18 "megacenters" in 13 cities, replacing approximately 560 smaller centers across its 14-state western region.

Workers in the closed centers would be faced with the choice of moving, changing jobs, or being laid off. In addition, the new computerized processes planned by the company would eliminate approximately 40 percent of all job titles.

The announced consolidations were a major blow to US West's workers. Moving to a different location is not a simple matter, as US West covers thousands of miles, with very different climates and costs of living.

US West is the "Baby Bell" company for most of the western United States that was formed in 1984 out of the breakup of the old Bell System telephone (see box, next page). It combined three very different companies—Northwestern Bell, Pacific Northwest Bell, and Mountain Bell—covering most areas of Minnesota, Iowa, North & South Dakota, Nebraska, Montana, Wyoming, Colorado,

Utah, New Mexico, Arizona, Washington state, Idaho, and Oregon.

Thirteen cities do not match 14 states. Politically. When the Center Cities were chosen, all the smaller communities and rural areas were cut out, in an attempt to refocus the company and capture the lucrative business markets in the bigger cities.

It is not clear whether US West plans to maintain any presence in Montana, Wyoming, or North or South Dakota. The company has already announced the sale of several small telephone exchanges in each state. Union workers in the sold locations have few choices: move thousands of miles away from their homes or stay and take a chance on being hired by the new company, union or not.

This dilemma also confronts workers outside of the Center Cities, whose jobs will also either move or disappear. For these people, the uncertainty is double. There is no reason to trust that if they move to a strange city they will have a job two or five years later. However, in the small western towns and cities, the economy has not improved through the last decade. Overfishing, overlogging, and overgrazing have taken their toll, causing cutbacks in jobs dependent upon natural resources. Removing decent union jobs from these small fragile economies reaches beyond the families involved to all the small support businesses.

Not so coincidentally, half the cities chosen for the megacenters are in right-to-work states. The more pro-

---

Madelyn Elder is a cable-splicer for US West, and is Secretary-Treasurer of CWA Local 7901.

union areas of US West, especially the states comprising the former Pacific Northwest Bell, have already suffered massive cutbacks in working conditions and pay treatment since US West was created and the union contracts for the three very disparate regions were combined in 1989.

HOW REENGINEERING IS SUPPOSED TO WORK

The megacenters are being designed—with heavy input from outside consulting firms—to do work complete-ly differently from the way it is now done. All the jobs will be new jobs. They will be multi-tasked and dependent upon new computerized processes.

These megacenters will handle residential and small business service delivery ("mass markets"); large business, government, and long-distance carrier service delivery ("service assurance"); and engineering and design ("capacity provisioning").

Essentially, most service representatives (sales) and non-technical repair personnel will staff the mass market centers, central office technicians will staff the large business/government/carrier service assurance centers, and management engineers will staff the capacity provisioning centers.

Theoretically, when a customer orders new phone service from a megacenter, the person who takes the call will also assign all the equipment needed, do the programming to assign the service in the computer, and dispatch the installer to put in the line. In more complex services, two people will do the work. These one or two multi-tasked workers will replace up to 13 people who now do these jobs.

To accomplish this, computer screens are being redesigned to look like fast-food cash registers. If a customer wants call waiting, for example, the worker taking the order will simply point at a "call waiting" symbol on the computer screen, click the mouse, and the computer will do the rest.

The same process will theoretically happen with repair. Right now, the repair bureau takes the call and sends it to the technicians who test the line, who then dispatch it to one of several other technicians, depending on where the problem is. In the megacenter, one person is supposed to do it all. That is, if the process actually works. This still has not been proven. In September 1994 the General Manager for the Mass Markets Centers announced that the Denver Center's opening would be postponed indefinitely due to bugs in the computer processes. That holds all the other mass market centers off indefinitely as well.

US West began implementing reengineering by setting up "prototype centers." Management formed "process teams" where they decided what the new process would be. Of course, these process teams had never worked in the old jobs, and had a book understanding of how the systems worked. The first prototype centers, from the reports of activists who went and came back, were total chaos; a lot of coffee drinking and personal phone calls filled the days.

VIOLATING SENIORITY

All the jobs in the new megacenters will have new titles. Our contract says that the company must notify the union of any new job titles or changes in old ones. The union can then call for negotiations on wages and job descriptions.

After the company gave CWA the list of new job ti-

Whole Phone Industry Downsizing

Since US West's downsizing announcement, several other telephone companies such as Pacific Telesis, GTE, and NYNEX have announced similar plans, making the telephone industry the largest source of job loss in the United States in 1993-94. Why the mania to downsize at this time, when the demand for phone service is growing and the companies are all profitable?

Competition in the telecommunications industry is the driving force behind the downsizing. With new technology called "broad-band," telephone or cable tv wires will be able to carry phone, computer, television, alarm, and any other service simultaneously.

As a result, cable television and telephone companies are merging or fighting to enter each others' markets to become the winners on the future "information superhighway." US West, for example, cut the largest multimedia deal in the nation in 1993, buying 25 percent of Time-Warner Cable.

Left behind in this mad race are telephone workers, the roadkill on the information superhighway. Their work built the telephone companies, but they are being eliminated as their employers frantically cut costs to raise capital for their new ventures.

Telephone companies are also competing for each other's markets. In 1984, the U.S. government broke the Bell System into eight companies. AT&T, which had owned the huge nation-wide Bell system providing both long distance and local phone service, became a long-distance and equipment manufacturing and installation company. Local phone service was provided by seven regional "Baby Bells," such as US West, which were created out of the rest of the old AT&T. These local companies were given a monopoly of local phone service and were prohibited from competing with AT&T.

In the 1990s, however, the Baby Bells recognized that looming regulatory changes would allow competition for local calls from AT&T and other long-distance companies. They embarked on a massive campaign of cost-cutting and job-cutting to raise capital to compete with the long-distance companies.

tles, with the proposed wages and job descriptions—all drawn up with no input from the union—the union decided to wait until contract talks in August 1995 to actually negotiate on these new titles. This means the titles will have been staffed for a year before negotiations will happen, but at least the members will be able to vote on the changes.

An even bigger problem is the way the new jobs are being filled. Staffing for the new centers, many of which were not even built, began in December 1993. US West decided to staff the new jobs by "source titles" rather than by company-wide seniority, or by the normal upgrade and transfer procedure outlined in the contract. This means the company is deciding unilaterally which workers are eligible for each new job in the megacenter. For example, the new title of sales and service consultant will be filled from the source titles of service representative, maintenance administrator (tester), and credit consultant.

In January 1994, before any megacenters opened, the company began sending workers their "packets" to apply for the new megacenter jobs. In these packets were job descriptions, instructions on how to voluntarily quit the company, and applications for jobs.

The jobs were staffed through a "preferencing" process. You "preferenced" the jobs and locations you wanted. There was no way to indicate your preferences in order. If you didn't preference, it was assumed you didn't want a job in the megacenters.

It soon became evident that the general source pools had congealed to specific source titles with percentages attached to each and a 10 percent "open placement" category for those not fortunate enough to hold the source titles. As it turned out, even the open-placement category was taken by workers from source titles. The new jobs, which require flexibility and a general knowledge of how phone lines are ordered and processed, will go to service reps with low seniority over longtime employees who may have been service reps at one time, but who had taken one or more jobs since.

These lower-seniority "flexible" employees were ahead even before the game started. Everyone else was out of the loop. Approximately 350 non-source-title job-holders in Portland alone had absolutely no chance for a job in the megacenters anywhere. Seniority had nothing to do with it.

In June, during the CWA national convention, US West announced that all regular full-time service reps in center cities were guaranteed jobs, regardless of seniority. Although the union leadership was able to postpone the announcement and negotiate about 200 more jobs for other titles, US West went ahead. This caused chaos for the majority of non-service reps, many of whom had over 25 years service and were not offered work.

As the prototype centers began to be opened, vague verbal agreements were made with CWA district staff regarding how they would be staffed—by volunteers, but giving volunteers an edge, regardless of seniority, for permanent jobs in the new megacenters. This was the harbinger of things to come.

THE UNION'S RESPONSE

By the end of October 1993, the District 7 office of CWA, which covers all of US West and is located in Denver, had distributed an impact survey to all the locals. The District also researched whether or not there was a way to intervene with the Securities and Exchange Commission on the $3.8 billion writedown that US West was claiming for the cost of the consolidations and reengineering. There wasn't.

The national union did not challenge US West's right to consolidate, reengineer, and eliminate jobs. Instead, their response has been to try to develop alternatives to layoffs, such as pension enhancements, transitional leaves, longer benefits for those who leave the company, and relocating work—particularly temporary jobs—to cities where there are a lot of high-seniority workers who would then be able to fill these jobs and retire in their home

towns with no loss of benefits. As of this writing, no agreements have been made on any of these items, except for allowing retirees to receive separation pay in addition to their pensions.

At the beginning of December 1993, CWA District 7 Vice President Sue Pisha and US West agreed to form a joint Staffing Implementation Team. The local presidents in District 7 met. Assuming that reengineering could not be stopped cold, they hoped to mitigate the damage to the membership. They envisioned the Staffing Implementation Team negotiating with US West over reengineering as well as the staffing—as having some power over numbers of workers, and when implementation would occur. The District leadership, however, was unable to negotiate any power for the Staffing Implementation Team. Since US West gave no decision-making authority to the management members of the Team, it was limited to monitoring seniority lists and securing early leave dates for those who voluntarily left the payroll.

Because the December agreement was so vague and didn't address many issues, the union Team members requested that the District union sit down with US West and come up with a comprehensive signed agreement on staffing in February. The union Staffing Implementation Team members threatened to file an NLRB complaint if there wasn't a signed agreement, for the "rules" changed every other day without it. Finally, in April 1994, CWA and US West signed a letter of agreement covering the staffing process. In it, CWA agreed to all of US West's provisions. The only advantage for the members was consistency.

In Portland, activists tried in the beginning to form a membership committee to fight reengineering, but we were unsuccessful. Our members seemed to believe that they would get a job, one way or another. In fact, a company-wide attempt to restrict vacation selections in the plant department drew more protest and action from members than the consolidation announcement. Over 200 people in Denver actually staged a wildcat over vacation scheduling.

US West began a series of "brown bag" lunchtime discussions to answer employees' questions about reengineering. They published several corporate newsletters on the subject, and daily updated the internal computer news network. Most of the information was misleading, vague, or wrong. US West began to call reengineering "transformation," a vaguely New Age, feel-good term. They snowed many employees with cheerful talk and glowing terms for processes that weren't really in place. Lower-level management kept telling their crews that other crews would be the ones to be laid off, even though contractually layoffs are done by job title, regardless of skill or qualification.

The company uses pretty phrases and officers of the corporation speak about the "pain" of hard decisions. These are meaningless gestures, meant only to appease and neutralize any real protest about the downsizing. For example, they announced loudly that 200 more outside technician jobs would be added to the force, then quietly retracted the statement a few months later.

It is quite clear that the company's intention was to rid the corporation of its older workers, who are expensive in terms of wages, benefits, potential benefits, and vacation time. They plan to replace them with temporary workers, some full-time and some part-time. The company has stated this intent in its publications and letters to employees.

Meanwhile, the deadline for indicating a job preference or the desire to leave the payroll was March 6, 1994. On that day the Portland local organized a mock funeral for two corpses—good customer service and decent union jobs. Much of the membership wore black as well.

Since March 1994, the union has begun to respond in a more organized way. District 7 includes several progressive locals whose officers know that we need to fight hard to win anything. Most were stunned by the original "consolidation" announcement. There was quite a long period of disbelief, followed by a feeling of powerlessness among both the membership and the leadership.

Recently, the thirteen largest and most activist CWA locals have decided to coordinate activities separate from the District 7 CWA leadership, with each large local staying in contact with the smaller locals in their state/area. Their goal is to force US West to add more jobs in the megacenters, or offer pension enhancements to workers in locations losing jobs.

When we began to act, from the start the locals agreed to work together, and not allow the company to whipsaw any of us. The locals were also clear that the small locals were affected differently by the consolidation than the large ones. In many meetings, management tried to divide the locals, promising some benefit to the larger ones with megacenters at the expense of the smaller.

Several proposals for action came from the District 7 meeting of locals at the end of March 1994. One idea was to file an EEOC complaint or class action suit, as most jobs affected are held by women and people of color. This is the only major surplus situation at US West in which the company did not make a pension enhancement offer—and the only one that has not affected mostly technicians, who are mostly men. There is also the possibility of an age discrimination complaint, since the staffing process has also discriminated against many people with very high seniority.

The meeting also decided to begin negotiating placeholding agreements for people who are still needed at their old jobs but will be declared surplus when reengineering is complete. Under these agreements, workers will be allowed to claim non-surplus jobs such as outside technicians and clerical support (these jobs are not yet affected by the reengineering plans). Temporary workers will fill these jobs until the surplus employees can move into them.

Several locals have printed T-shirts that read "Don't Shoot Me, I'm Craft." Management's reaction was totally overblown. CWA's District leadership issued a memo asking that members not wear the T-shirts. Although this was a protected union activity, the company claimed possible threats by "union officials" against management, and the District leadership went along with the company's excuse.

We have fought many of the seniority bypasses with grievances as well as the official Staffing Implementation Team Discrepancy Forms. These forms were to be filled out and the Staffing Implementation Team was to investigate each complaint. Because the entire staffing agreement was based on numbers considerably lower than anticipated in most areas, the agreement had a negative impact on most employees outside of service representatives, because even fewer "open placement" jobs were available for other non-source-title jobholders. Whole groups of workers would be offered jobs one day, and then the jobs would be taken back the next day because of a "mistake."

We have also filed grievances charging management with doing craft work. For example, the only center for capacity provisioning (engineering and design), to be located in Denver, is planned to have a 4 to 1 ratio of managers to "occupationals," the US West term for craft workers. All the drafting, posting of records, and design work—previously done by craft—and engineering work for both outside plant and central office equipment will be done here. The company plans to replace all clericals with engineers and have the clerical work done automatically by computer.

This staffing ratio and computerization process will eliminate a majority of the union people now doing these jobs. As of this writing the grievances have not been resolved, and the union's attorney has advised against going to arbitration.

Our campaign to put pressure on US West is having some effect. In response to US West's official 90-day advance notice before layoffs on August 24, we began publicly asking customers to call us and the Oregon Public Utility Commission to complain about the long waits. We have held press conferences pointing the finger at layoffs and downsizing before new reengineered processes are in place as the reason that it takes over two weeks for repair or new service.

The media have picked up on it (they love to bash the phone company), and the company has responded by putting technicians on mandatory overtime. Where we head from here is really up to US West—they can modify their giant reengineering plans or make service worse by starting the layoffs.

HOW TO MAKE A DIFFERENCE

Many of us wonder whether we could have made a difference if only we had done something else. Because the process is not over, and because the true impact of reengineering has yet to be felt, we can only wonder. Certainly, we could have gone to the public more often in an educational campaign on phone service.

US West's decision to move nearly all work to the

larger cities and cut out the smaller cities in the Dakotas, Montana, and Wyoming is a political choice about where technology will be applied. It is just as easy to maintain a center in a small town as a large one, technically speaking.

For the public, it indicates that the historic Bell system commitment to universal service is beginning to give way to "Open Access." Poor people and rural areas will be guaranteed a "choice" of service, but not necessarily be guaranteed service itself. Historically, affordable basic residential service has been subsidized by business rates and regulated profits. Now, advanced services such as call waiting and caller ID will become more available, but the end of subsidies may make any kind of phone service unavailable to people in rural areas and the urban poor.

Several locals have published a full-page ad in local newspapers warning the public that service will decline because of reengineering and downsizing. The company is already having service problems; the number of Public Utility Commission complaints about US West service almost doubled between 1991 and 1993, probably due to previous cutbacks in technicians' jobs.

Many activists are pushing for the union nationally to intervene in state public utility regulatory bodies to link the job cutbacks to declines in service. Otherwise, most activists suspect that the public will be totally unsympathetic to the loss of thousands of phone workers' jobs. The problem is that regulatory commissions usually see layoffs as cost-cutting and therefore rate-cutting strategies—so much the better for the consumer. We need to point out that the concept of universal telephone service has gotten lost in all the debates on the "information superhighway."

It was our experience in Oregon that the Public Utility Commission believed every promise about customer service that US West made. Although not one piece of fiber optic cable has been laid, US West in Oregon received forgiveness for incredibly long waits for repair or service in the winter of 1993-94 because they promised to replace lead cable with fiber in some of the poorest areas. This has not been done, and there are no immediate plans to do so.

This intervention needs to be coordinated on a national or regional level to avoid what happened in South-western Bell. Kansas CWA locals pressured the state legislature and got a law passed prohibiting Southwestern Bell from downsizing for the next three years. Since Southwestern Bell is also in the midst of reengineering, the immediate effect for the other states in the company was a reduction in the number of CWA workers there—i.e., whipsawing.

Many questions remain because reengineering is still in process. What if the District 7 leadership had trusted the membership enough to lead a boycott of the entire reengineering program? What if we had fought them in court and on the job? What if over the years we had built a working relationship with the regulatory commissions and citizens' oversight committees? What if we had refused to participate in the prototype centers, where new processes were developed?

Whether US West's ambitious changes succeed or fail, the human tragedy of job loss, wage loss, and even worse, loss of confidence in the union's ability to effectively represent workers' interests will have a direct impact on the future of CWA and the industry's workers. It will also help to determine whether or not we organize the non-union cable companies and the non-union cellular companies, and whether everyone will have telephone service, or just the ones who can afford it.

The alternative to reengineering is humane reengineering. Let the company really have customer service as its first priority, rather than profits. Give it big tax breaks (government subsidies) for installing fiber and other new technology in low-income neighborhoods, rural areas, and other unprofitable areas. Eliminate the middle managers whose only purpose is to monitor production or make our lives miserable. Cut the salaries of all top managers and spread that money downward so that more training and hiring of young people in entry-level jobs can occur. Make telephone engineers craft jobs and train clericals for technical jobs. Give the workers the budgets and authority to change our jobs to provide better service.

The idea of one person doing a variety of tasks is great, but only if that person has control of which task will be done when, and only if no one loses jobs.

Working Smart:
A Union Guide to Participation Programs and Reengineering
Labor Notes • 7435 Michigan Ave. • Detroit, MI 48210 • (313) 842-6262

Chapter 11

Reengineering the Hospital: Patient-Focused Care

Patient-Focused Care seeks to cut costs by breaking up hospitals into stand-alone "operating units." It creates cross-trained "generic health care workers" and seeks to eliminate "non-value-added work"—any activity that cannot be billed, such as transporting. Record-keeping is centralized on the bedside computer. Workers are reorganized into care teams and departmental lines are broken down. As a result, fewer staff are needed. Although Patient-Focused Care does address real problems in how hospitals function, for health care workers it creates more problems than it solves.

by Trudy Richardson

AT FIRST BLUSH, the idea of a management program called "Patient-Focused Care" is positive; but at the same time it is annoying. Nurses and other health care workers have been asking for that kind of concern and focus for years. We find it amazing that managers do not see the irony of their having just discovered "patient-focused care" in 1994. What did they think hospitals were all about all those years?

Because the original Total Quality Management programs were designed for production industries, the initial applications to service industries were often ill-fitting. For example, U.S. and Canadian hospitals introduced guest relations programs, shared governance, and quality care programs; each of these was held out to be the answer for economic instability and worker dissatisfaction. Unfortunately, they promised more than they could deliver. One writer described these initial TQM programs as having "the shelf life of cottage cheese."

It was only a matter of time until consulting firms developed TQM programs that were "services friendly"—shaped around the realities of service production rather than goods production. Consultants are now marketing trial projects that have been designed specifically for health care worksites.

The first of these was pioneered by Booz-Allen & Hamilton Inc., an international management consulting firm operating in 75 countries and servicing more than 70 of the 100 largest companies in the world and 60 percent of the world's largest banks. We will examine their package, Patient-Focused Care, in detail.

There is controversy around whether Patient-Focused Care should be classified as a TQM program. Some argue that Patient-Focused Care is a fundamental re-engineering of health care delivery, while TQM merely tries to increase the productivity of the current system.

Although health care consultants, business academics, and health economists continue to wage a paper war over this question, for our purposes it matters little whether our employers consider Patient-Focused Care to be qualitatively different or a sophisticated and health-designed TQM program.

WHY NOW?

Why is Patient-Focused Care being introduced now? In the United States one critical reason is the dramatic increase in health care costs. And while health care costs as a percentage of spending have not risen in Canada, several provincial governments are cutting social services budgets drastically.

A second and related reason is the emergence, in the U.S., of the Diagnostic Related Groups (DRG) method of payment. Insurers decided that they would no longer make payments using the old retrospective method—the hospital itemizes all the care given, submits the bill for payment, and receives the amount from the insurance company. In-

Trudy Richardson is Education Director of the United Nurses of Alberta. This chapter is adapted from a longer pamphlet published by the UNA (see chapter 41 on Resources).

stead, depending upon the diagnosis at the time of admitting, there is a specific amount the insurer will pay, regardless of how much it costs the hospital to deliver the care.

A third factor is that as insurance companies and governments have tried to control hospital costs, occupancy rates have plummeted. What used to take a week in the hospital now requires one or two days, either because of technological advances or because insurers are demanding shorter stays. U.S. hospitals now compete with each other for patients. Having shortened the patients' length of stay, they need more patients to keep the beds filled and finances stable. Patient-Focused Care has been introduced to improve a hospital's competitive edge.

A fourth factor is the so-called nursing shortage. In the late 1980s, health care employers across North America were faced with nowhere near the nurses needed for the increasing number of jobs. Salaries of registered nurses began to improve dramatically in many areas.

In order to deal with the personnel shortage, employers began to hire consultants who quickly pointed out that not all work done by higher-paid workers had to be performed by them. Deskilling could cut staff expenditures by as much as 40 percent. Thus employers have mounted a drive to create lower-paid and lesser-skilled generic health care workers.

A final factor is the availability of new technologies that make current practices outdated. Patient-Focused Care relies heavily on computers and other technologies that replace people.

How To Recognize Patient-Focused Care

If any of the following programs are introduced into your worksite, you can be very sure that you have a Patient-Focused Care program: Creative Acting Reflecting Excellence (CARE) 2000, ADVENT Questionnaire—Hay Group, Care 2001, Continuum of Care, Coordinated Care, Differentiated Nursing Care, Dreyfus Model of Skill Acquisition, Hermann Hospital Patient Care Management Model (Houston), Holistic Care, Hospital of the Future, Hospital Re-engineering, Hospital Within a Hospital, Integrated Care, Integrated Competencies of Nurses (ICON and ICON II), Interactive Planning/Management Model (IPMM), Johns Hopkins Professional Practice Contract Model, Manthey's Primary Practice Partners in Care, New England Medical Center's Case Management Model, New Practice Models, Operational Restructuring, Operations Improvement, Organizational Re-engineering, Partners in Practice, Patient-Centered Care, Primm's Case Management Model, Quest, RN/Coworker Model, Robert Wood Johnson University Hospital Professionally Advanced Care—Team Model (ProAct TM), The Helper Model (THM), Work Flow, Worldclass Healthcare.

THE HUMPTY DUMPTY SCHOOL OF MANAGEMENT

Health care analysts have studied how the provision of health care takes place. They report a landscape of inefficiency, waste, and poor service. Hospitals, in particular, seem to perpetuate inefficient and costly organizational systems that end up providing fragmented, low-standard, and very expensive patient care.

Analysts describe the Humpty Dumpty School of Hospital Management as the delivery of services broken up into discrete tasks—admitting, nursing care, food service, housekeeping, charting and records, x-ray, laboratory, diagnostic testing, surgery, recovery—and then centralized in areas far from the patient's bed.

If it takes ten people in ten different departments to deliver these services, we must also factor in the personnel—"all the King's horses and all the King's men"—who are necessary to paste the fragmented work back together again—supervisors, auditors, controllers, managers, human resources department, accountants, clerks, directors, vice-presidents, and administrators. The administrators are the glue that holds together the people who do the real work. Most hospitals have more people gluing than people delivering services.

Some studies indicate that less that 25 percent of hospital employee time is focused on direct patient care. The other 75 percent is spent recording, ordering, transporting, preparing, communicating, coordinating, scheduling, and accounting. Patient-Focused Care literature is filled with statistical evidence that a patient admitted into a hospital for three days will normally be seen by more than 55 hospital employees, transported over 15 times to different sites, charted in hundreds of times on records that are duplicated in different activity centers, and interviewed, tested, examined, poked, and prodded by a procession of professionals, technicians, managers, and support staff who are each performing a narrowly-defined task.

One study at Florida's Lee Memorial Hospital revealed that a typical stroke patient was transported over eight miles, making 60 round trips, over five to six days. The patient was contacted by more than 105 caregivers, not including nurses and housekeepers.

A study of San Diego's Mercy Hospital documented that for every $1 worth of healing services, the patient's bill included $2 worth of bureaucratic costs. Less than 20 percent of our labor dollar goes for direct patient care—the rest is for bureaucratic "glue," including 14 percent for coordinating and scheduling, 30 percent for recording and charting, and 19 percent waiting for something to happen.

Analysts cite the number of job classifications in a hospital. For example, San Diego Mercy, a 523-bed facility, had a staff of 2,200 in 319 classifications and deployed in small specialized units. Florida's Lee Memorial Hospital had a ratio of 5.4 employees for every supervisor and 437 different classifications, with an

average of 4.8 employees in each one. Most large North American hospitals have more than 350 classifications, half of which have only one employee within them.

Are all of these discrete tasks, separate departments, and finely classified staff increasing the quantity and quality of patient care?

Nurses have long been critical of the increasing amount of time spent charting, reporting, coordinating, scheduling, transporting, cleaning, and a myriad of other tasks that take the nurse away from the bedside. The structures that have become institutionalized in hospitals mean that a lot of work has little to do with providing quality patient care.

The United Nurses of Alberta have long held that our hospitals are over-managed and under-funded for direct clinical care. We have protested the employers' and the government's attempts to control costs by understaffing clinical units, by replacing regular jobs with temporary staff, by floating nursing staff without proper orientation, by replacing registered and graduate nurses with lesser-skilled personnel, and by laying off large numbers of

skilled nurses. The union has advocated that patients need nursing care more than they need hotel-like surroundings and tropical gardens.

Nurses began to examine the Patient-Focused Care literature hoping to find a plan to reorganize the health care system so that every dollar improves the quality of patient care. The union has carefully scrutinized the details of the Patient-Focused Care model. On some issues we agree; on major points, however, we strongly oppose the model because it leads to a deteriorated quality of care.

REENGINEERING FOR PATIENT-FOCUSED CARE

FAREWELL TO THE PAST

The Patient-Focused Care model, following the principles of re-engineering, reinvents the entire production of health care services. Every member of the health care facility is asked to put aside the traditional way of thinking and acting and to adopt a new vision and a new way of doing work. No longer is there "your" work and "my" work—it is all "our" work. No longer is there allegiance to one department—loyalty is demanded to whatever increases the quality of patient care. Supervisors and managers are no longer the bosses—they are coaches, mentors, and colleagues. Outside reference groups such as unions and professional associations are less important than the internal work team. In fact, some Patient-Focused Care literature clearly denounces unions.

One hospital introducing Patient-Focused Care predicted that burying the past would be difficult for many health care workers, that old allegiances and work patterns die hard. So they staged a funeral complete with coffin, candles, and organ music. Employees were encouraged to fill out index cards with a list of past practices they thought were obstacles to high quality care. The "mourners" were asked to give up attachment to these practices and bury them, as a sign that they were walking into a whole new future. In Patient-Focused Care literature, such an exercise is said to be "self-empowering."

PROCESS IS GOD

In the Patient-Focused Care model, process is the focus. Process is god.

The first task, then, is to identify the process. Most often, participants identify a process with a department, e.g., x-ray, lab, pharmacy. The first and most difficult lesson to learn is that "the process" is not how to order and receive a lab test, how to get a patient to x-ray, how a patient goes to surgery and is brought back to the unit. Rather, the process is the entire work that is done to make a patient better. Every organizational system is predicated on restorative patient care. Every patient demands a process.

HOSPITAL ARCHITECTURE

The first re-engineering feat is to redesign the hospital architecture. Departments disappear, replaced by "service units" or "operating units" that are architecturally all but self-sufficient. Free-standing operating units are made up of 75-100 beds.

Patients in these beds are called a patient aggregation—a group of patients selected for the commonality of

their care requirements, most commonly nursing services.

Once hospital staff understand this idea, the rest of the structural redesign flows from asking: "What services do these patients need to get better?" Rather than revert into compartmentalized thinking, staff is encouraged to list all the services that should be in close proximity to the patients. Operating units, therefore, often have surgical, radiology, respiratory, x-ray, lab, pharmacy, physiotherapy, housekeeping, dietary, and administrative services located within them. Only those ancillary services which are high-volume and use very expensive equipment remain centralized for use by all.

Since cost reduction is the over-riding motive, the dramatic savings from these changes should come as no surprise. Although there is an initial financial outlay to renovate existing structures, the new Patient-Focused Care operating units actually cost 10 percent less. The operating unit design reduces total hospital space by 15-20 percent. Eighty to ninety percent of required services are located on the unit.

Basing administrative services on the unit reduces costs further, and making operating units directly responsible for buying supplies accounts for a 5-10 percent reduction in operating costs.

INFORMATION TECHNOLOGY

To reduce the amount of time spent communicating, charting, coordinating, recording, and scheduling, operating units use the most up-to-date technology. This includes bedside computer terminals. All admission, accounting, medical, nursing, lab, x-ray, and dietary records are entered into the bedside terminal, which becomes the single recording center for all information on that one patient.

Computers become an essential part of health care service. Each team room is equipped with a terminal for nurses to do shift change reports or work on patient care plans. Voice messaging and electronic mail systems are commonplace, as are pneumatic tubes, fax machines, and computer-generated forms. Automated narcotic dispensing machines (also called automated drug administration systems) are standard practice on many operating units.

TEAMS

Once the reengineering process has determined the patient aggregation, the physical layout, the specific grouping of services needed, and the technology requirements, the next question is: "Who will take care of these patients to ensure their well-being?"

The Patient-Focused Care answer is that a special team of health care providers will be assembled to assume complete control of the care provided to each patient.

Articles and books on Patient-Focused Care abound with descriptions of "self-directed work teams." Just as in TQM, work teams are central to the process of reengineering. The difference is that TQM teams are created from workers in an existing department. Patient-Focused Care

---

The Generic Health Care Worker

Universities and colleges in the U.S. and Canada are implementing new programs that produce "generic health care workers."

Other terms include Assistive Personnel, Functional Specialist, Multi-Skilled Caregiver, Multi-Skilled Technician, Multiple Competency Assistant, Nurse Enabler, Nurse Enhancer, Nurse Extender, Patient Hostess/Host, Personnel Redeployment, Practice Partnership, Skill-Enhanced Health Worker, Task Performer.

teams, on the other hand, are made up of workers drawn from numerous former departments. They might include a lab tech, an admitting clerk, an accountant, or an x-ray technician, for example.

Each hospital, using self-directed work teams, seems to use a slightly different method of construction and different terminology. For example, one hospital has teams composed of a registered nurse and a licensed practical nurse, who are called "clinical associates," a clerk or accounting employee who is called an "administrative associate," a lab or x-ray technician who is called a "technical associate," and a housekeeping or dietary person who is called a "service associate."

Within a team there may be care pairs, care dyads, or care trios. This is the clinical part of the team—registered nurses, licensed practical nurses, nurses' aides, etc. These two or three people must work closely together to ensure quality care. In some operating units, so close is the relationship among the clinical pairs or trios that the registered nurse actually hires/chooses her clinical associates. In one reported case, the clinical associates choose each other and then sign a contract that commits them to working together over a long period.

Team members are expected to be extremely loyal and interdependent. Patient-Focused Care literature contains many references to the increased employee satisfaction that teams create. A more sinister side to the glowing accounts of team compatibility and camaraderie, however, is the insistence that old ties must be severed.

Team members are encouraged to feel that their support and solidarity should rest more with the members of their team than with an "outside reference group"—meaning, of course, trade unions, staff associations, or professional organizations. Historically, workers' bargaining groups are determined solely on the basis of the job classification they fit into. Registered nurses, for instance, have been placed in a different bargaining unit from lab techs, licensed practical nurses, or housekeeping staff. In the new team model, allegiance and common purpose resides more in the team than with fellow bargaining unit personnel working on other operating units. This shift in loyalty and solidarity lines has major ramifications for unions and for collective bargaining.

MULTI-SKILLING AND CROSS-TRAINING

The single greatest cost saving of the new operating unit structure and the self-directed work teams is the reduc-

"No wonder restructuring is going nowhere. You laid off the guy in charge of eliminating jobs."

tion in staff through multi-skilling and cross-training. U.S. health care employers have moved rapidly into adopting the money-saving, multi-skilled model. So much interest is being shown that the Kellogg Foundation has funded a National Multi-skilled Health Practitioner Clearinghouse at the University of Alabama in Birmingham.[1] So big a change is multi-skilling that it threatens, with the exception of physicians, the very underpinnings of health care professions.

Some studies of multi-skilled staffing recognize that it is not a new phenomenon. In the past, rural communities had neither the patient volume nor the resources to hire specialists, so they often hired people who could perform more than one job. However, such use of multi-skilled personnel did not eat away at the foundations of regulatory legislation or professional licensing. If the job required dual licenses or dual skills, a worker simply qualified and applied for the required licenses.

Today, in large urban hospitals, more and more employers are requiring current employees to become dually or triply skilled. In some instances the hospital provides the opportunities for additional training. In other cases, the employees are left to their own devices.

The most common form of multi-skilling is to ask a staff member who is skilled in one discipline to become skilled in another, earning another license if necessary.

But if an employee was, say, a half-time x-ray technician and half-time physiotherapist, then the employers might have to pay two different rates of pay to the same individual. Assuming these complications could be sorted out, the employers would not realize tremendous savings because they would still be paying the union rates.

Thus a whole new breed of generic health care

worker is being developed. This worker would be partially trained in all health care work—yet well-skilled in none. He or she would not have to be licensed. The generic job description does not fit into any of the existing job classifications nor within any of the traditional bargaining units. This new breed of worker would be a little bit of a nurse, a little bit of a lab tech, a little bit of a physiotherapist, a little bit of a housekeeper, a little bit of a clerk, a little bit of a transporter, and a big bit tired!

The main problems in introducing this generic model are in licensing regulations that say only workers with certain training or certificates can do certain work, and the lack of education programs geared to producing such multi-skilled workers. Recently, many U.S. colleges and universities have introduced such programs.

There is no question that the advent of the generic health care worker ushers in an era of lesser-skilled, inadequately trained, inexperienced, and less-qualified health care providers. This entire process of throwing skilled workers into a pot, melting them down, and re-casting them into multi-skilled practitioners who are unlicensed and whose work is deregulated means tens of millions of dollars in health care savings and an equivalent reduction in the quality and safety of patient care.

It is clear that generic health care workers will be paid considerably less than current professional wages and benefits.

The newly reengineered hospital with its many small operating units will save some money by initially requiring that the current staff members become cross-trained.

But the employer will save much more when hiring new multi-skilled workers. One estimate is that labor costs will decrease up to 50 percent. After a year on Patient-Focused Care, one program decreased its labor costs by 30-40 percent. The literature emphasizes that staff costs in large hospitals can be reduced on the order of tens of mil-

lions of dollars after complete reengineering.

Multi-skilling poses a threat not only to workers who will be replaced by lesser-skilled personnel and to the patients who will not receive the same level of care, but to many health care professions. It is possible that in the near future we will witness the closing of schools of nursing and university nursing programs, replaced by programs that produce generic health care workers.

ROLE OF MANAGEMENT

When a care team has been put together, a clinical care manager, who may or may not be a registered nurse, is assigned. The clinical care manager is a mentor, coordinator, and coach, and all members of the care team are accountable to this leader—nurses, lab and x-ray technicians, housekeeping, administrative and accounting clerks. Presumably decision-making and authority is the responsibility of the care team. Thus the clinical care manager is depicted as less an authority figure and more of a teacher and resource.

One very important design feature in the care team is that the clinical care manager becomes the single point of entry. Doctors, administrators, or heads of centralized services can only access team members through the manager. This is a major deviation from current practices where all lab technicians are under the authority of the head of the lab; all registered nurses are under the authority of the Director of Nursing; and clerks and administrative personnel fall under the authority of the department head. In Patient-Focused Care models, care team members—regardless of their job classifications—report directly to their care team associates and the team is supported by the clinical care manager.

As a result, Patient-Focused Care almost always means the departure of management personnel.

Once the work of delivering patient care begins, the team members are accountable directly to one another and responsible to the patient. There is no longer a long chain of command and layers of management to absorb and distribute responsibility.

The care team works together and with the patient's physician to develop a total care plan that projects step by step to the discharge date. These care plans are called care paths, care protocols, critical paths, or pathways of care. They are the team's production plan.

In order to reduce the reams of charts of a typical hospital, charting by exception is the preferred method. That is, only the unexpected, the different, and the out-of-the-ordinary events are recorded. Otherwise, the care protocol records the expected and the ordinary progress.

VALUE-ADDED WORK AND VARIABILITY

One of the characteristics that Patient-Focused Care shares with TQM is the almost compulsive focus on "waste." Waste is defined as all work that does not result in economic value. The most common term to describe waste is "non-value-added work." If a patient takes a pill,

---

Consultants To Watch Out For

Few health care employers are equipped to launch a new patient care delivery system on their own. Instead, they rely on consulting firms. In many cases, employers are approached by these firms, who promise to increase the quality of services as they reduce costs.

The major consulting firms are Booz-Allen & Hamilton Inc., Llewelyn-Davies Weeks, and American Practice Management Inc. (the Curran Group).

Several U.S. foundations are providing money to hire the consultants and pilot the projects. They include the Robert Wood Johnson Foundation, the Pew Charitable Trusts, and the Kellogg Foundation.

Other consultants on Patient-Focused Care are KPMG Peat Marwick, Lewin/ICF, the American Express Health Systems Group (now called First Data Corporation), and the Institute for Health Care Improvement.

has dressings changed, or has a cast put on, this is all work that can be itemized on a bill and charged to the patient's account. Walking to the supply cupboard, transporting a patient to x-ray, pouring medicines, or walking from the nursing station to the patient's bed, on the other hand, have no economic value. You can't itemize or bill them.

Analysts have scrutinized how work gets done and computed "structural idle time"—the time in each shift where different specialized and compartmentalized workers are prepared and ready to work but have to wait because the test results are not available, the patient is not there, the medication has not been delivered or the doctor has not ordered it, the linen has not arrived, or the supply cart has not been stocked. The amount of idle time is staggering.

As much as 31 percent of hospital work is non-value-added. One study estimated that at least 50 percent of in-house time spent on patient-related activities was non-value-added work. It may be constructive work, but it isn't billable time.

Therefore, models have been developed to bring the providers to within arm's length of the patient. The services and the workers are on the unit; bedside terminals centralize and simplify the record-keeping; equipment is at hand; and medications and supplies are at the bedside. Turn-around time for lab results and pharmacy orders can be reduced 20-75 percent.

According to the literature, equally as bad as non-value-added work is variability. In the production of goods, every widget must look and feel and weigh the same as every other widget. Variability of product costs money. Therefore variability must be hunted down and eliminated.

The introduction of DRG classifications began the eradication of variation. Patient care protocols are dependent upon the DRG and the patient aggregation.

It is often difficult in reading Patient-Focused Care literature to remember that hospitals do not make widgets—they are dealing with the most variable aspect of life, people and their health care needs.

COMPENSATION AND BENEFITS

In Patient-Focused Care literature, one theme is constant—wages and benefits are based not on job classifications, years of experience, or length of employment. Wages and benefits are based solely on performance and the employer's ability to pay.

All workers are placed at a low basic rate. To earn more money, to receive more benefits, or to increase vacation time or sick leave, one must be judged by the critical care manager, co-workers, and, in some cases, by the patients and their families, to be deserving of a bonus or a merit increase. And whether there are any bonuses available at all is dependent upon whether the employer feels able and willing to provide them.

In this model seniority becomes a useless statistic. Care teams choose new associates for their teams;

seniority is not a consideration. Nor are vacations computed on the length of service. Everything is based on merit, performance, contribution, and worth as determined by the employer on a case-by-case basis—and on the employer's ability or willingness to pay.

In one dramatic instance, a hospital that was at the point of implementing a Patient-Focused Care model actually laid off its entire staff and forced them to re-apply for positions on the basis of team members' abilities to work together and on their individual commitments to Patient-Focused Care.

EXPERIENCE WITH PATIENT-FOCUSED CARE

American Practice Management—The Curran Group—is a management consulting firm based in New York with offices in San Francisco, Boston, and Chicago. The company has worked with over 100 U.S. health care facilities.

When working with hospitals, American Practice Management promises to deliver improved patient care at a reduced cost. They claim to excel at maximizing revenue from insurance companies while minimizing expense of patient care. At the forefront of American Practice Management's work with hospitals is Connie Curran, a former nurse, now National Director of Patient Care Services for American Practice Management.

American Practice Management was hired to streamline services at Boston's Carney Hospital. They called their plan "Operation Excellence," or OE. The Massachusetts Nurse's Association met with American Practice Management and listened to their plans, but initially stayed in the background. Hospital committees were formed to provide input into the action plan. Management selected nurses (those who were in favor or passive as opposed to more vocal or oppositional nurses) to sit on the committees. The Association did not endorse these committees, feeling that nurses were being asked to do American Practice Management's dirty work—the elimination of nursing jobs.

American Practice Management initially stated that ancillary jobs nurses had formerly done would no longer be assigned to them. The nurses, who had been fighting for years to remove these housekeeping duties from their jobs, were more than happy. However, they found that unlicensed helpers were being assigned more than just general housekeeping duties.

Nurses were now being asked to train helpers to read vital signs and change dressings, along the lines of licensed practical nurse work.

The Association felt the logic behind this process was simple: to save money by paying aides to do nurses' work. It was not to benefit the patient, as American Practice Management had promised. The goal was to cut the nursing staff to one or two nurses per unit—with the remaining staff being aides—and make the nurses ultimately responsible for decisions and actions of all aides in the unit.

The Nurse's Association began fighting the plan by

forming a group that talked to all the hospital's nursing units. Specific strategies and tactics were developed for each unit. All nurses agreed to refuse to delegate nursing work to aides.

The nurses wore buttons and T-shirts that said "OE"—except that OE was written as "Our Excellence" instead of Operation Excellence—thus promoting solidarity among the members.

They also contacted the press and staged pickets outside the hospital. The message: the public needs to know is "who is taking care of them at the bedside." The mere fact that a person is wearing a uniform does not make the individual qualified.

The endnote of the protest campaign was the resignation of the Vice President of Patient Services. The new vice president decided to put the project on hold.

PROS AND CONS OF PATIENT-FOCUSED CARE

There is no doubt that our present ways of providing health care things are often cumbersome, expensive, and wasteful. But do the improvements promised by Patient-Focused Care programs outweigh the deficiencies? The United Nurses of Alberta say no. While we accept that change is necessary, this form of change creates far more problems than it solves.

1. Financial Gains. By far the biggest cost saving is the lower wages that can be paid to multi-skilled generic health care workers.

2. Patient Satisfaction. Statistics indicate that the same patient who experienced a hospital stay under the old organizational structures and again under the reengineered model was much more satisfied in the new model. Patients reported that they felt known by the care team; experienced less portering and shifting; were not visited by an endless procession of unknown hospital workers; and felt they were provided with more continuity of care.

3. Quality of Care. Certainly the setting up of operating units has increased the ability of staff to provide more immediate care. But it is hard to believe that a program based on substituting lower-paid, lesser-skilled personnel for highly-skilled staff can possibly result in better quality over the long run.

4. Patient Records. Patient-Focused Care drastically reduces the amount of charting and recording that is done all over the hospital on each individual patient. The availability of administrative staff on the units, the centralization of all records on the bedside terminals, and the reinvention of charting by exception all contribute to a more accurate record-keeping system.

5. Statistical Outcomes. Patient-Focused Care programs have resulted in shorter hospital stays. In fact, insurance companies have changed their DRG numbers on the basis of new statistical information from Patient-Focused Care programs. For example, DRG #209 is Hip Replacement. The insurance companies used to pay 8.2 days of hospital care for a patient classified as #209; today they pay only 7.8 days. Hours per patient day (HPPD) of required nursing care have also decreased.

Is all success, therefore, to be measured in DRG statistics? What is not factored into these statistics is the number of readmissions with a complication; the amount of home care the family is expected to provide after discharge; and the fact that many of the reduced statistics are less a result of Patient-Focused Care and more a result of improved equipment and shortened procedures.

6. Worker Satisfaction. All of the reported worker responses are positive. Employees feel their jobs are more difficult, more challenging, and more satisfying. Job satisfaction improves, as does staff morale. By being given more power to make decisions and more direct accountability for the patient's recovery, the staff feels better about the quality of their work and the continuity of care that they provided.

On the other hand, staff were not asked such about their satisfaction with compensation methods; levels of adequate staffing; quality of care using multi-skilled, generic health care workers; absence of licensure; and the degree of increased legal liability.

One statistic quoted by supporters is that Patient-Focused Care results in a happier staff who use less sick time, less personal leave time, and fewer special leaves. This could mean that nurses who are sick feel compelled to go to work because they know they will be not replaced. It can also mean that leaves of absence for union business are frowned upon.

It is certainly too soon to believe that increased worker satisfaction is a guaranteed outcome of Patient-Focused Care programs. We should remember that early stories from reengineered, multi-skilled factories also reported happy workers who loved the new system. Once the system had been in place for a while, many felt that their new "responsibilities" translated only into additional work—without increased pay.

Notes

1. The Clearinghouse provides a newsletter on multi-skilling initiatives; book reviews of multi-skilling literature; an annotated bibliography on multi-skilled health practitioners; job descriptions of multi-skilled practitioners working in 137 participating hospitals; and information on consultants on multi-skilling. Anyone can become a member of the Clearinghouse and automatically receives their newsletter and bibliography.

Working Smart:
A Union Guide to Participation Programs and Reengineering
Labor Notes • 7435 Michigan Ave. • Detroit, MI 48210 • (313) 842-6262

Chapter 12

Why Participation Programs Endure

Participation programs show little proof of results on their stated goals. Different quality experts fight amongst each other on goals and methods. Yet the programs continue, for they do meet certain of management's needs.

ACCORDING TO THEIR SUPPORTERS, labor-management participation programs are "win-win" for everybody involved. Firms or government agencies nurture quality and produce goods and services at the lowest possible cost. Customers get what they want. As a result companies remain competitive, stay in business, and even grow. Workers have job security and owners make profits.

Better yet, we are told, this happy state of affairs is achieved through another "win-win" arrangement: management has learned that its most valuable resource is its employees. When managers grant dignity, respect, and participation, employees respond by contributing their ideas and energy.

No one can oppose quality. And with "win-win" as part of the deal, how could a union even conceive of opposing a participation program? Consultant Masaaki Imai charges that

> [unions], by obstinately opposing change, often succeeded in only depriving their members of a chance for fulfillment, a chance to improve themselves.[1]

And yet when participation programs are instituted, unions are asked to tear up contract protections that have taken years, and often intense struggle and sacrifice, to win.

If we look beneath the cheerful rhetoric of participation programs, we find a great deal of confusion—on management's side as well as the unions'. And as argued in chapter 1, the reality that emerges has little to do with quality, as we usually understand the term, or worker participation, and a lot to do with tighter management control and speed-up (management-by-stress).

In this section we will analyze participation programs.

Thanks to Ellis Boal for his help with this chapter, particularly his research related to the Dunlop Commission Report.

This chapter will present some evidence to show that they don't "work" on management's stated terms, and why management likes them anyway. Chapter 13 will examine why such programs appeal to union members and the hidden messages contained in participation training. Chapter 14 will explain the implications of management's definitions of quality, the "focus on the customer," and the "internal customer," culminating in the notion of "return on quality." Chapter 15 will look at the notion of mutual interests, labor-management "partnership," and gainsharing. Chapter 16 is a checklist of the dangers inherent in participation programs. Chapters 17 and 18 look at these programs' particular effect on minorities and women in the workplace. Chapters 19-25 are case studies of participation programs in a variety of workplaces.

DO PARTICIPATION PROGRAMS WORK?

Participation programs are a moving target. Over the past 15 years management has jumped from fad to fad: quality of work life, team concept, TQM, reengineering.

Each of these fads has been trumpeted by success stories in the press—few companies publicize their failures. Many of the success stories turn out to be self-serving, written by the consultant who shepherded the program or initiated by a company eager for the positive publicity. But it is striking how many serious academic studies find little success for these programs *on their own terms*, let alone by union standards.

One review of the research concluded:

> In a majority of empirical studies, direct participation is associated with at least a short-run improvement in one or more of the following variables: satisfaction, commitment, quality, productivity, turnover, and absenteeism.... Never-

theless, only a small proportion of participation programs can be classified as a long-term success. After a brief honeymoon, most plans peak and peter out.[2]

Here are some results from the electronics industry:

In a 1991 survey of more than 300 electronics companies, sponsored by the American Electronics Association, 73% of the companies reported having a total quality program under way; but of these, 63% had failed to improve quality defects by even as much as 10%. We believe this survey underestimates the magnitude of the failure of activity-centered programs not only in the quality-conscious electronics industry but across all businesses.[3]

In one of the most extensive studies to date, Maryann Kelley and Bennett Harrison analyzed data from over a thousand metalworking plants. They found factories with participation programs to be *less* efficient than those without. Single-plant firms with participation programs required almost 30 percent more production time per unit, and branch plants of large corporations with participation programs required over 60 percent more time per unit, than did plants without such programs.[4]

The authors of a TQM textbook, Bruce and M. Suzanne Brocka, estimate that "for every successful implementation, such as Motorola, there are 20 more disasters."[5] The Leads Corporation, self-described "leader in the field of Total Quality Management," sends out a brochure soliciting customers that declares: "Although thousands of organizations have spent millions on TQM training, 80 percent of all TQM initiatives are stalled or failing."[6]

Business journals do not hesitate to run articles bemoaning the high failure rate of participation/quality programs.[7] Increasingly, major questions have emerged from management's side in the industry press.[8] Very little of this criticism appears in the popular press, which appears to accept participation programs unquestioningly.[9] This vignette from the *New York Times* is typical:

"We had problems with quality and with customer service levels," said Tom Brock, a 25-year G.E. veteran [at G.E. Drive Systems]...Mr. Brock decided he wanted his workers to take more responsibility, to become, in the current jargon, "empowered."

[Workers received] training in communications and other skills. The Salem plant now has some 200 teams, to take on any issue employees think is important.

According to a report on G.E. Drive Systems published by the Work in America Institute, the plant has made a "quantum leap" in productivity.[10]

TQM advocate Steven Brigham summarizes business studies of TQM:

Surveys conducted by Arthur D. Little, A. T. Kearney, Ernst and Young, McKinsey and Company, and Rath and Strong...have reached similar conclusions: in more cases than not, TQM has failed to produce its promised results.[11]

Brigham falls back on what seems to be the standard explanation: these studies do not show that TQM itself is seriously flawed. Rather, "the implementation is deficient, even erroneous." According to Brigham, "The best evidence that TQM 'works' comes from a May, 1991 U.S. General Accounting Office (GAO) report that examines the impact of TQM on the performance of [20]

U.S. companies that were among the highest scoring applicants in 1988 and 1989 for the Malcolm Baldrige [National Quality] Award."

Let's examine this best evidence. The U.S. Department of Commerce, which sponsors the Baldrige Award, acknowledges that it does not seek to measure the quality of a company's products or services. The Baldrige evaluators look only at whether the company has in place certain internal organizational forms and procedures, such as ways to keep statistics on conformance to specifications. Companies are self-nominated and spend large amounts of time on paperwork and fees.

Now comes the GAO seeking to study the impact of TQM. The GAO doesn't compare TQM users to nonusers, or users' practices before and after TQM. Nor does the GAO devise its own independent measures of success. Instead, the GAO asks those applicants who scored high on the Baldrige TQM scale how they evaluate themselves on employee relations, operating procedures, customer satisfaction, and financial performance.

Is it reasonable to expect that a company that tried TQM and saw no changes would bother applying for the Baldrige Award? In effect, the GAO methodology is to ask people who think their TQM works whether they think their TQM works.[12]

Although it began with a strong bias in favor of participation programs, in its May 1994 Fact Finding Report the Commission on the Future of Worker-Management Relations (the Dunlop Commission) states:

While most of those testifying about their efforts reported their programs resulted in improved productivity, quality, or some other indicators of economic performance, the empirical studies on this issue completed to date show mixed results....

Studies that have attempted to isolate the individual effects of single programs such as quality programs or teams tend to find small or insignificant effects on performance.[13]

Still trying to make the case for participation programs, the Commission cites some studies that, it asserts, do report economic benefits, if participation is combined with other changes in management structure and policies. Unfortunately, however, the studies they cite prove no such thing. There is no way of separating out whether the participation program caused anything at all. It's as if a researcher said, "If you feed a rat celery and ice cream it gets fat; therefore celery must make rats fat." One study grouped participation programs with such policies as job rotation and whether quality inspection is assigned to production workers.[14] Another combined teamwork with such items as incentive plans and extensive screening in hiring.[15]

So for the most part all the studies do not prove very much at all. Figures like "80 percent failure" or "20 out of 21 are disasters" seem to be part of a tradition in the quality movement of made-up numbers to give the appearance of scientific precision to words like "most" or "many." How many times have we heard that "85 percent of the problem in American business today is management"—or is it 94 percent?

WHAT IS SUCCESS?

One reason the statistics are all over the place is that there is no agreement about what constitutes a program's "success" and what constitutes failure. Does a program fail when it shows no productivity increase, or when management ends it, or when people stop coming to meetings? Is a program that cuts jobs by thirty percent a success or a failure? As long as the definitions are fuzzy, the fiction of common interests can be maintained. Once success and failure are defined sharply, it becomes clear that different players, and particularly management and workers, have different interests in the game. We discuss this topic more in chapter 15.

We believe that genuine participation on the job—real say over working conditions, methods, and goals—would be great for workers. We believe it would boost quality as well—though this must remain unproven until workers win this kind of power somewhere.

We put together two facts: 1) the very weak evidence that participation programs themselves do management much good, and 2) the reality that employers are attacking workers in every aspect of economic and social life, as discussed in Section I. We believe these are strong evidence for the conclusions that:

1) Management's primary interest in participation programs is not to tap the potential of the workforce, but to figure out how to cut and squeeze the workforce.

2) The claims made for the benefits of these programs are no reason for unions to toss away past protections or give up union power.

DISPUTES AMONG THE GURUS

Another reason to be skeptical of participation programs is the fact that there are as many versions of them as there are consultants who will tell you that the problem is the other consultant.

The main quality gurus vehemently disagree about what they see as basic principles. For example, one of Philip Crosby's contributions to the quality discussion is the concept of "zero defects." One of the first and better-known consultants, Crosby runs a Quality College and is

the author of *Quality Is Free*. W. Edwards Deming, the grandfather of them all, attacked "the fallacy of zero defects":

> There is obviously something wrong when a measured characteristic barely inside a specification is declared to be conforming; outside is declared to be nonconforming. The supposition that everything is alright inside the specifications and all wrong outside does not correspond to this world.[16]

Crosby strikes back with an attack on Deming's principle of constant improvement:

> Many do not care for the goal of Zero Defects... [But] it is nothing more than exactly what we have promised our customers. "Continuous Improvement," for instance, as a program can be utilized to avoid heading for defect-free performance...If we move 10 percent nearer the target each week we will never get there...Don't deny [customers] their rights by getting tangled up in programs or efforts that delay things.[17]

Tom Peters, author of the best-selling *In Search of Excellence*, says proponents "are making ridiculous, encompassing claims for TQM. Number ninnies who were cost-control fanatics ten years ago adore the quantifiable ramifications of TQM and its cousin SPC [Statistical Process Control]."[18]

As Brocka and Brocka see it:

> The "disputes" which break out among various "disciples" of one Quality Management master versus another have lent a divisive, even faddish, look to Quality Management practice to the casual observer. This is unfortunate as [the different approaches are] probably quite similar, if not nearly identical.[19]

WHY DO THE PROGRAMS CONTINUE?

One of the precepts of participation programs is that they must be "data driven." "In God we trust. Everyone else must provide data," was a favorite Deming quip. How can it be that participation advocates see the overwhelming evidence of failure, and yet still push ahead for it with such fervor? There are at least four reasons:

1. Some say that there *is* hard evidence in favor of participation programs: Japan. These programs and their relatives, they believe, are the way the Japanese accomplished their economic miracle. So the only task is to learn how to apply these lessons in the North American context.

2. Employee participation puts a nice veneer on the other strategies managers are using—simultaneously—to

respond to the pressures of competition (union-busting, privatization, casualization, moving overseas...).

3. Whatever their outcome, the programs still serve the interests of their advocates. Consultants ride the gravy train, the human resources staff justifies its existence, a few union members get more interesting jobs as facilitators, business schools gain a whole new field.

4. Whatever the motives of the managers who bought participation programs in the early days, by the late 1980s the motivation for participation programs had become clear: to ease the introduction of the various techniques as-sociated with management-by-stress. Management's hope is that the participation program will assist in work reorganization by reducing resistance, marginalizing the union, and providing the necessary attitude adjustment.

Therefore it's not so important to management to be able to prove that a participation program itself produces measurable improvements. Rather the test is whether the program helps accomplish other goals: getting lean and reengineering the organization of work. Participation programs are important as an aid to getting the real action in place, but don't confuse them with the real action.

Notes

1. Masaaki Imai, *Kaizen: The Key to Japan's Competitive Success*, 1986, Random House, New York, p. 165.

2. David I. Levine and George Strauss, "Report 35B: Employee Participation and Involvement," project funded under grant from U.S. Department of Labor, Commission on Workforce Quality and Labor Market Efficiency, 1990, University of California, Berkeley.

3. R. H. Schaffer and H. A. Thomson, "Successful change programs begin with results," *Harvard Business Review*, Vol. 70, No. 1, Jan.-Feb. 1992, p. 81.

4. Maryellen R. Kelley and Bennett Harrison, "Unions, Technology, and Labor-Management Cooperation," in Lawrence Mishel and Paula Voos, eds., *Unions and Economic Competitiveness*, M.E. Sharpe, New York, 1991. A number of factors might explain this result. The data was "cross-sectional," comparing different plants with each other rather than looking at the effects of changes that companies made over time. That is, the authors did not look at a company before and after it started a participation program. Also, the data for the study was from 1986 and 1987; at that time participation programs in the metalworking industry had not evolved to include the lean production techniques that *do* raise productivity. Programs were still of the circle/meeting variety that actually take workers out of production.
In any case, this evidence that participation programs may actually decrease productivity has been widely ignored by those who are pro-cooperation (including the Dunlop Commission, which cited the Kelley/Harrison study but not that finding), because the study does not support the usual assumptions (or hopes) about employee involvement.
Kelley and Harrison also found that unionized plants tended to be more efficient than non-union ones. This is not an argument, from management's point of view, for unions. For management the primary issue is not productivity (time required per unit of output), but cost. In a union plant with good wages, time per unit could be low but the cost per unit still high.

5. Bruce Brocka and M. Suzanne Brocka, *Quality Management: Implementing the Best Ideas of the Masters*, Business One Irwin, Homewood, Ill., 1992.

6. "Introducing...The Leads Corporation," brochure, 1993.

7. G. Fuchsberg, "Quality programs show shoddy results," *Wall Street Journal,* May 14, 1992; Owen Harari, "Ten reasons why TQM doesn't work," *Management Review,* Vol. 82, No. 1, January, 1993.

8. Robert D. Smither, "The Return of the Authoritarian Manager," *Training*, November 1991, pp. 40-44; Patricia Mc-Glagan, "The Dark Side of Quality," *Training*, November 1991;

Albert Hyde, "Rescuing Quality Measurement from TQM," *The Bureaucrat*, Winter 1990-91, pp. 16-20; "TQM a grey area in firm's search for excellence," *European Chemical News*, April 29, 1991, p. 18; Jim Smith and Mark Oliver, "The Baldrige Boondoggle," *Machine Design*, August 6, 1992, pp. 25-29.

9. For example, John Lippert, "Wayne State prof and son give work-smarter solutions," *Detroit Free Press*, October 28, 1992, p. 3D; John Holusha, "LTV's Weld of Worker and Manager," *New York Times*, August 2, 1994; Barbara Presley Noble, "Retooling the 'People Skills' of Corporate America," *New York Times*, May 22, 1994, p. 8.

10. Noble, cited above.

11. S.E. Brigham, "TQM: lessons we can learn from industry," *Change*, Vol. 25, No. 3, p. 42. Brigham is director of the Continuous Quality Improvement Project at the American Association for Higher Education.

12. U.S. General Accounting Office, "Management Practices: U.S. Companies Improve Performance Through Quality Efforts," GAO/NSIAD-91-190, May 1991.

13. P. 45.

14. The commission cites John Paul MacDuffie and John F. Krafcik, "Integrating Technology and Resources for High Performance Manufacturing: Evidence from the International Auto Industry," in Thomas Kochan and Michael Useem, eds., *Transforming Organizations*, Oxford University Press, 1992.

15. Casey Ichniowski, Kathryn Shaw, and Giovanna Prennushi, "The Effects of Human Resource Management on Productivity," unpublished paper, Carnegie Mellon University, June 1994. The authors' statistical analysis designed to test the independent effects of different elements actually shows "high participation" associated with a loss of productivity. We discuss the authors' logic in connecting participation to high performance work systems in chapter 15.

16. W. Edwards Deming, *Out of the Crisis*, Massachusetts Institute of Technology, Cambridge, p. 141.

17. Philip Crosby, *Quality Update*, Vol. 8, No. 5, Nov.-Dec. 1989, p. 38.

18. Tom Peters, "TQM is yet another trend that ignores business problems," *Baltimore Sun*, September 9, 1991.

19. Brocka and Brocka, p. 6.

Working Smart:
A Union Guide to Participation Programs and Reengineering
Labor Notes • 7435 Michigan Ave. • Detroit, MI 48210 • (313) 842-6262

The Appeals and Hidden Messages of Participation

Participation programs appeal to workers because they are designed to meet certain needs: to make a contribution, to learn new skills, to be part of a group. But training contains hidden messages: that "we are all in this together," and that there is an objective, conflict-free way to look at workplace problems.

Here, we don't have management and we don't have labor. We have teams. And we have what you call consensus. Everything's a group decision. In the last seven months, I've only had a few days off here and there. But this is where I want to be. This is living heaven.

—Alton Smith, die technician,
member of UAW Local 1853, Saturn[1]

What makes participation programs attractive to union members? There are two parts to the answer, and they have shifted some over the years.

In the early years, the union members who went for QWL tended to enjoy the act of participating itself. QWL programs were designed to be fun and interesting; members could learn a lot, including about human interactions.

As the 1980s progressed, however, management's offensive for "competitiveness" became more aggressive. Workers were bombarded with constant reminders of the difficulty of survival in the (often global) competitive environment. Team concept, TQM, and reengineering were argued as necessary to beat the competition. So workers had another motivation for joining in with participation programs: saving their jobs. Today, in the 1990s, this motivation for getting on board is undoubtedly primary.

However, the intrinsic appeals of participation programs are still touted and still there. Consultants and management still work hard to "manufacture consent." In this chapter, we will discuss how participation programs are designed to appeal to workers' needs.

WHY PARTICIPATION FEELS GOOD

Feeling good is no accident. The explicit aim of participation programs is to have the participant identify with the program itself because the process fulfills a number of worker desires. With this kind of motivation, the ends are not as important as the means; the outcome is not as important as the group process.

This is different from the kind of motivation that usually gets us to do things. Most union members, for example, go on strike to improve their contract, not because they enjoy standing on a picket line. But in participation training, it matters less whether the group works on placement of fans or work rule changes or quality improvements than whether everyone in the group participates and takes pride in what the group is doing. Thus the training draws heavily from sociology and psychology. It draws on a number of important needs for both process and outcome:

1. Participation builds on workers' natural desire to identify with the product or service they produce and to do a good job. Now workers are not only asked to think about the quality of "their" product, they are invited to take responsibility for it.

2. Participation promises a better-run workplace, without the stupid inefficiencies that make everyone's work more difficult—or just make them feel stupid. Many workers welcome the chance to show that they could run the place better than management.

3. Participation expands workers' opportunity to make a contribution. They can deal not only with their own jobs but also with those around them. In circle meetings, members are encouraged and rewarded for observations and proposals covering the entire operation.

4. Participation provides new skills. The organizational, management, statistical, problem-solving and even personal skills give people a sense of being more in control of their lives. Entire areas such as statistics or accounting are demystified. Many workers have not previously received training in chairing a meeting or making a brief presenta-

tion. Now, for the first time, they learn these skills and begin to envision themselves in a leadership role.

5. Participation promises to end needless conflict with supervisors. The program is supposed to end harassment and change the supervisor into someone who actually helps deal with problems on the job.

6. Participation offers respect to the individual. The entire process is built on the idea that each person's ideas are important. In "brainstorming," everyone contributes and no one's ideas are rejected out of hand or even criticized directly. Around the circle, everyone from top management to the janitor is equal and on a first-name basis.

7. Participation provides a group identity. Meeting together regularly to solve problems naturally builds cohesiveness. The special procedures and jargon further build that identity. And the program consciously nurtures it. Often the first thing a circle does is to decide on a special name. Groups often develop their own symbols or

The Hierarchy of Needs

The theories of psychologist Abraham Maslow are often presented in participation training.[2]

Maslow ranks human needs. The first level involves immediate physical survival—food, clothing, and shelter. In the workplace context, the first need would be the wage itself. The next level, safety, would include job security and a pension. The third level, belonging, is being accepted by a group. The desire to excel in some area is an example of the ego-status level. At the top is the need for personal fulfillment.

The idea is that once human beings' basic needs are satisfied—the needs we share with animals—we can move on to meeting higher ones.

slogans and order circle jackets or caps.

In addition to these appeals, there is the more immediate one of time off the job. If your job is tiresome enough, anything—even donating blood—seems like a reprieve. And some workers see the chance to move up to permanent time off the job, by becoming facilitators.

Participation fills needs that are very legitimate. There is more than enough in everyday experience to make people feel bad about themselves and about the world. Work is one of the major contributors. Anything that promises to make people feel better about their work and better about themselves in relation to work is bound to win avid supporters.

HIDDEN MESSAGES OF PARTICIPATION TRAINING

Participation programs are sold as beneficial to both unions and management. Consultants carefully nurture their image as a friend to both sides (although, in the new era, we aren't supposed to think in terms of "sides" anymore). The presence of an outside consultant acceptable to both union and management suggests impartiality.

Yet despite this carefully cultivated image, participation training is far from neutral. The training is designed to meet management's needs. This is not surprising. After all, the companies butter the bread, and consultants are smart enough to recognize the butter side.

Because of its apparent simplicity, most participants do not recognize that participation training is a highly sophisticated form of attitude and behavior modification. Precisely because of its "win-win" image, the program can more easily penetrate natural defenses. It is therefore a powerful tool for challenging and shifting our traditional assumptions about the way the world works.

We'll first look quickly at what goes on in participation training, and then examine the hidden messages.

Participation training is expensive: consultants charge hundreds of dollars per hour, not to mention the cost of time lost from work during the classes. Most consultants do not claim expertise about the particular workplace. Rather, they are there to teach a process.

Following are some examples of the topics covered in participation training. Certain techniques such as brainstorming, fishboning, and problem-solving are common to almost all programs. Most of the ideas have been around for a long time in industrial psychology or management theory.

SEVEN STEPS TO PROBLEM SOLVING

One of the most powerful tools taught in participation training is a methodical approach to problem solving. Group members learn the advantage of this approach over a scatter-shot attack. Here is one version:

1. Identify the problem. Get the group to agree on just which problem it is trying to solve. Be explicit, write it down.

2. List all possible causes. Try to make the list in-

clude all possibilities.

3. Choose the most likely causes.

4. Consider all possible solutions. Get as many as possible. Encourage creative, seemingly wild solutions. There are no limitations at this point.

5. Choose best possible solution.

6. Implement the solution.

7. Evaluate the results.

BRAINSTORMING

Brainstorming is not just "hard thinking." It is a specific method for soliciting ideas.

The facilitator goes around the circle taking ideas one at a time; all ideas are accepted, and far-out ideas are encouraged. All suggestions are written on a flipchart so that everyone knows his or her idea was heard. Ideas are not criticized or even discussed at this time. This is the time to go for quantity and a broad scope. A good brainstorm results in many flipchart sheets taped to the walls for everyone to examine.

"Quick, jump on my back, Gingerbread Man," said the fox. "If we stay together we can make it across the stream!"

THE FISHBONE

A technique for finding and organizing possible causes of problems is the Fishbone or Ishikawa Diagram

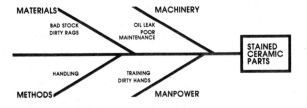

(developed by Professor Kaoru Ishikawa of the University of Tokyo in 1950). The idea is first to list the general causes of the problem. In factories, these are usually categorized as "the 4 M's" (manpower, materials, methods, and machines). The general causes are then subdivided, and further subdivided, until all possible causes are listed and their position in the flow is stated.

STATISTICAL TRAINING

After all possible causes are identified, the next logical step is to determine which one actually causes the most problems. Here is where statistical training is useful. Most start by teaching graphing in order to visualize trends and

distributions. Particularly popular is Pareto analysis (named after an Italian mathematician), which uses bar graphs with the data shown in order by size. This shows the most likely problem-causers.

Here is an example used in one training group whose assignment was to reduce keypunch errors. To identify the possible causes, they drew Pareto diagrams relating keypunch errors to two different factors—operator and type of keypunch machine.

The first Pareto diagram indicated that the errors seemed to come pretty evenly from all the different types of machines. The second diagram indicated that most of the errors were made by one or two people. This led the group to look at possible reasons that Cathy and Andy were making errors. Happily, the problem turned out to be insufficient lighting in their work areas. When the lighting improved, Cathy's and Andy's errors decreased.

Once the causes of problems and their possible solutions are identified, the next step is to determine which, if any, of the proposed solutions should be pursued.

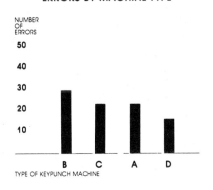

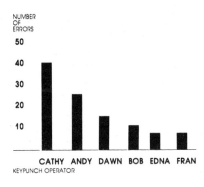

COST/BENEFIT ANALYSIS

The idea behind cost/benefit analysis is to add up all the ways in which a proposed solution will provide benefits and all its possible costs. The ratio of costs to benefits can then be calculated. The lower the cost/benefit ratio, the more desirable a proposal is.

For example, a General Motors training manual[3] gave this hypothetical case: "A group is considering one solution which involves the installation of an additional machine. The machine itself would cost $1,000." The problem gives the costs and benefits for the first year as follows.

New Machine Cost/Benefit Analysis

Costs

Machine	$1000
Rewiring and installation	500
Lost production during change	500
Retraining operators	250
	$2250

Benefits

Reduce rejects by 10%	$ 750
Reduce production time	500
Reduce shipping delays	250
	$1500

Clearly, from this analysis, the costs would exceed the benefits for the first year. But by the second year, total benefits would more than pay for the new machine.

ORGANIZATIONAL AND SOCIAL SKILLS

These include: how to organize a meeting, prepare an oral presentation, improve your memory, listen to others, draw others out, encourage participation, and deal with conflict.

TRY IT YOURSELF

You can best understand the power and impact of these training techniques by trying them yourself. If possible, get a number of people together to try out the exercises in this section. This is an excellent first step for a union group beginning to investigate a participation program. The instructions that follow are shortened versions of the regular exercises. If you can spend longer on each exercise, then do so.

1. Ask everyone to pair off with someone they do not know well. For five minutes one person should interview the other to prepare a one-minute introduction of that person. Then the roles should reverse for five minutes. When the group reassembles, everyone introduces his or her partner to the whole group.

2. Divide into small groups of 6 to 10. Use a method, such as counting off, that will put people with people they don't know. The following activities take place within these small groups.

Have each group member introduce him or herself. They should tell where they were born, how many brothers and sisters they have, and whether they are older or younger.

Then have each person take a minute to describe his or her first paying job and how he or she felt about it. Start this exercise with the person born farthest away and continue around the group clockwise. (If time permits, do some additional questions in the same way, but start with a different person for each one. Have them tell which was their most difficult subject in high school and how they got through it. Have each person tell the name of their favorite TV show and what they like best about it. Ask them to name their favorite spectator sport and participant sport.)

3. Ask group members to consider this problem individually and write down their answers:

Lost At Sea[4]

You are adrift on a private yacht in the South Pacific. After a fire the yacht is now sinking. Your location is unclear, but your best estimate is that you are approximately 1,000 miles from the nearest land. You have a rubber life raft large enough for everyone in the group, and oars, pocket items, and the 15 items listed below. Your task is to rank the items below in terms of their importance to your survival.

___ sextant	___ shaving mirror
___ 5 gallon can of water	___ mosquito netting
___ 1 case C rations	___ maps of Pacific Ocean
___ flotation cushion	___ 2 gal can gas oil mix
___ transistor radio	___ shark repellent
___ 20 sq ft opaque plastic	___ 1 qt 160 proof rum
___ 15 ft nylon rope	___ 2 boxes chocolate bars
___ fishing kit	

Each group discusses the problem and arrives at a consensus ranking. After 20 minutes, they report their recommendations. Spend some time discussing the different answers. Finally, the leader should present the "expert" answers:

If you are a thousand miles from the nearest land, you are not likely to save the group by rowing. Therefore items like the sextant or maps should be low in the list. Starvation is not an immediate problem, but dehydration, including water and the opaque plastic, are a high priority. Food, particularly protein and alcohol, causes extra water usage so the fishing kit, rum, and other food items go low on the list.

Making sure you can be seen by a search party should be the top priority. The shaving mirror would reflect sunlight, and the flotation cushion soaked with the oil-gas mixture, set on fire, and towed with the rope would serve as a signaling device.

Most groups don't automatically use the Seven Problem Solving Steps discussed earlier. Groups that do will start by trying to agree what the problem is (is the main task to row to safety, or to survive while waiting to be rescued?). They will usually come to better and quicker answers.

4. Have the group discuss what it learned about the process of group problem solving from this exercise. What roles did individual group members play? Look for roles like the "dominator," the "facilitator," the "cynic." How did the original individual answers compare with the group answers? A group process usually results in better answers. This is called "synergy."

Even these abbreviated exercises should demonstrate how attractive these training techniques are. You learn some useful skills. You learn about the other people. You get to talk about yourself. It is clear why many people believe that participation programs have opened up a new world to them and why they enjoy it.

Behind the fun and games, however, a closer look at participation training techniques shows that they teach much more than they claim.

LEARNING TO THINK
THE COMPANY WAY

Participation training goes beyond problem-solving techniques. The training is designed to change the way group members think—about their work, about themselves, about their relationship to management and their union.

Look at the exercise on the next page, that examines the cost/benefit analysis we looked at earlier.

Cost/benefit analysis can be a valuable tool—if it is clear by whose standards the costs and benefits are being measured. The unstated assumption is that costs and benefits are measured in terms of savings to management, and not in terms of workers' needs like job security or learning new skills. But one of the assumptions of participation training is that there is only one set of interests. So when a trainer teaches cost/benefit analysis, he or she can do so only by ignoring any possible conflicts.

Participation training depends heavily on the psychological theory of "behavior modification": if you can get people to act on the basis of certain assumptions, even if they do not initially agree with the ideas, over a period of time they will move closer to accepting those assumptions. It is part of a process psychologists call "reduction of cognitive dissonance." Participation training is designed to get people to act on the idea that "we and management are all in the same boat." This notion is in conflict with many union members' previous experience: "management is only out for itself." The purpose of the training is to get group members committed to the new idea and to alter or drop their previous opinion.

Much of participation training seems elementary and trivial. This is not because the program designers think this is the only way workers can understand it. Participation training is like the illusions of the best magicians: the audience is led to believe that it has seen every step along the way.

The training is purposely designed *not* to directly challenge the fundamental beliefs of unionism, such as solidarity, or that management's bottom line is profits and not people. Instead, the training tries to tip-toe past or outflank these ideas and establish new outposts in the mind. These new sentiments are then constantly reinforced with the good feelings, the sense of accomplishment, and the new group identity, as well as the perks of participation (the hour off the job, the trips).

POOR LIGHTING
IS USUALLY THE ANSWER

In participation training, the solutions to the sample problems presented are never disadvantageous to workers. No jobs are eliminated, no one has to work harder. For example, recall the group that discovered by using Pareto bar graphs that most of the keypunch mistakes could be traced to two workers. The group then investigated and found out that the problem was poor lighting.

A similar exercise, used in a General Motors training manual and elsewhere, is called "The Assembly Problem."[5] Team A is not quite meeting the company-set targets for production or quality. The participation trainees are given a floor plan and some data showing better quality figures during the summer months and for teams nearer windows. Again, the solution turns out to be higher wattage. Everybody wins and everybody is happy. Meanwhile, the trainees have gone along with the notion that they should measure and compare the productivity of their fellow workers.

This example illuminates another problem with participation training: the real questions are kept in the dark. Who set the production targets in the first place? Are they fair? Is this the kind of issue the group wants to work on, or would they rather work on job satisfaction? The

---

The Assembly Problem

Jim, Bob, and Susan work together on Assembly Team A. In their area are two other assembly teams doing exactly the same detailed work. Each team can choose its own method of operation. Jim, Bob, and Susan rotate positions every hour or so. They began this procedure in May. Team C rotates, too. Team B doesn't.

Jean Smith became the new supervisor of all three teams in November. She reviewed the records of past production and rejects. She also timed all operations and made check lists for November. She feels there is a problem with Team A, but can't put her finger on it. There is no pattern to their rejects. And an inspection of their materials and tools failed to show a problem. Yet they fail to meet the targets of 93 percent production and 4.5 percent rejects.

You have been asked to identify and solve the problem.

facilitator guides the group toward certain answers. In this case, the leader's manual suggests that the proper way of defining the problem is "how to achieve 93% production and 4.5% rejects for Team A."

But the exercise is cleverly constructed so that it usually isn't necessary for the trainer to intervene. Even in all-union workshops where the group has declared their intent to be "people-oriented, not productivity-oriented," most

---

Exercise

Whose Cost and Whose Benefit?

Objective: To demonstrate how cost/benefit training is slanted toward management thinking.
Time: 30-40 minutes
Materials: A sheet for each participant as follows:

The REMLUX Powder Line

Your quality circle has been studying the problem of rejects on the REMLUX powder line. Ten people work the line, which normally runs only on the day shift.

Normal production is about 100 pounds per hour (about 4,000 lbs. per week or 200,000 lbs. per year). On the average about 10 percent of the production is rejected by Quality Control.

The REMLUX line usually runs 50 weeks per year and is down two weeks for cleaning and maintenance.

The company estimates that each pound of rejected REMLUX costs $5.00, breaking down as follows:

> $2.00 energy costs
> $2.00 production labor
> $1.00 raw materials

The circle discovers that almost all of the rejected material is caused by inaccuracies in a single old mixing station which is operated by one person full-time.

The circle comes up with a solution:

A completely automated mixing station that will produce virtually defect-free powder can be purchased for $100,000 and can be expected to last five years. Installation will cost about $100,000. Downtime for installation will be one week. Two maintenance people will have to go to school for two weeks to learn how to set up and repair the machine.

Do a cost-benefit analysis of this solution. List all of the costs and all of the benefits, figured on a *yearly* basis. The company figures its hourly labor costs at $20 including benefits.

Cost/Benefit Analysis

Costs		Benefits	
_____	$_____	_____	$_____
_____	$_____	_____	$_____
_____	$_____	_____	$_____
_____	$_____	_____	$_____
_____	$_____	_____	$_____

Participants should work on the problem in groups. After they have had time to fill in their sheets, ask them to volunteer their answers, and fill them in on a flipchart or overhead projector. You are likely to get answers similar to these:

Costs		Benefits	
new machine	$20,000	no need for operator	$41,600
installation	20,000	eliminate rejects	100,000
schooling	3,200		
lost profit during downtime	??		

Notice that, by the logic of the analysis, "no need for operator" is listed as a benefit. This is likely to send up a red flag. But there are other, less obvious points to bring out. Schooling is listed as a cost. Why should training be considered a cost rather than a benefit to the workers who will increase their skills? "Installation" may be a cost to management, but if the union insists that the work be done by plant workers, it could be a benefit, in the form of more jobs, to the union's skilled members.

Look closely at the $100,000 saved because the new machine eliminates rejects. The company says that two-fifths of this savings is in labor—about $40,000. Therefore another job will be lost on top of the machine operator's. In addition, if the machine really works as perfectly as it's supposed to, management can eliminate an inspector too.

members will define the problem in this example as productivity and quality.

In the real world, of course, the problem isn't always poor lighting. In fact it usually isn't. Suppose that in the keypunch error case, Cathy was just not quite as accurate as the others. Family problems prevented her from getting sleep, she had arthritis, she was having trouble with the supervisor, or she just was not as coordinated as the others. What would the group do then? Again, the psychological process comes into play. If the group has gone this far in trying to solve the keypunch error problem, then it is committed. It will try to settle the problem, perhaps by peer pressure on Cathy to improve. Even if the group does nothing, it is more likely to passively accept management's attempts to deal with "the Cathy problem."

Participation training uses examples with neutral solutions to legitimize an approach that is, in fact, thoroughly pro-management—that some workers should cooperate with management to determine which workers are not measuring up to company standards. How long will unionism survive among the keypunch operators with workers fingering each other or using peer pressure to enforce management's arbitrary rules?

The emphasis on statistics and gathering data tends to encourage workers to delve into areas traditionally carefully watched by unions. For example, unions have long understood the danger of company time-studies—that they mean speed-up, not easier work. Most union contracts include limitations on the company's right to (or method of) time-study. Yet one of the results of participation programs is that workers end up doing a time-study on themselves.

At Ford's Dearborn, Michigan, assembly plant, a group of electricians was justifiably proud of an electronics repair facility they had initiated. In order to demonstrate how much money they saved the company, the electricians kept extremely accurate records showing exactly how much time was spent on each repair—the very kind of record-keeping the union had successfully fought in the recent past. (After this was pointed out, the electricians kept their records in more general terms.)

NO MORE WE/THEY

The "we-they" concept is really the fundamental idea in trade unionism. Solidarity means *we* stick together against *them*. Participation training doesn't attack the notion of union solidarity head on. But one of its main purposes is to establish new group identities to replace old ones.

One of the eleven foundations of quality circles, as described by Sud Ingle, a leading consultant, is:

Reduction of the "we" and "they" mentality...Since everyone (labor and management) is encouraged to participate in problem solving, the feeling develops that the

"You know, I kind of suspected it from the beginning."

employees are all in it together...[6]

U.S. Secretary of Labor Robert Reich has a similar idea. To evaluate a company he uses what he calls

The "pronoun test." I ask front-line workers a few general questions about the company. If the answers I get back describe the company in terms like "they" or "them," I know it's one kind of company. If the answers include words such as "we" or "us," I know it's another kind.[7]

The Lost at Sea exercise builds this group identity. Virtually every training program uses a "survival" problem of this type: plane crash in the desert, survival after accident on the moon, Antarctic exploration, lost in the woods. In their imagery, these survival problems contain hidden assumptions:

• We are all in the same boat.

• Our very survival is at stake—it's a question of life or death.

• We can only survive if we stick together—no one can be selfish.

• Everyone is equal and has an equal voice in determining strategy.

• Discipline is necessary, including self-discipline.

• Anyone who tries to divide us threatens our survival.

Note how these assumptions mirror what management has been telling workers about the need for cooperation: our workplace may not survive if we don't pull together, everyone will have to sacrifice, our employees' ideas are essential and valued.

When the group members act on those assumptions to solve the exercise—and this can be fun—the assumptions are reinforced.

If a trainer simply wanted to teach problem-solving skills, he or she wouldn't have to choose exercises with a "we're all in this together" philosophy. Suppose that the

Lost at Sea problem were stated differently:

> There are two kinds of people in the boat: Blue people and Green people. Only the Greens can row. The Blues have guns. The only search helicopter is controlled by Blues. It has room for the Blues plus a few Greens. It will rescue the people in the boat if the boat can be quickly rowed a considerable distance to a calm area and if the number of people in the boat is reduced to the number the helicopter can hold. There are 15 items...

Imagine how different the group process would be with this story. And these assumptions are a far closer parallel to the situation in most workplaces than the Lost at Sea story. This revised exercise could also be fun and

---

Facilitator Manipulation

This exercise was used to train facilitators in the GTE/Communications Workers of America Quality Improvement Process.

Throughout the training, the facilitator-trainees are reminded how important it is to appear "neutral" and "unbiased."

The trainee reads about a task force that is looking at the problem of periodic under- and over-utilization of the Word Processing Department. One task force member, Tony Jenks, has a suggestion. The trainee chooses from three possible responses to Tony (A, B, or C).

> Tony Jenks strongly insists that the answer is to decentralize—buy four more word processors, for a total of eight, and give each department its own. Most of the participants think this is a great idea, although it is *not* a viable solution because of cost. You should:
>
> A. Briefly interrupt the conference and advise that the idea may have merit, but based on cost alone it is prohibitive.
>
> B. Do nothing. The participants will ultimately sense that this solution is too costly.
>
> C. Challenge Tony directly by saying. "Do you realize that this solution will not only be very costly, but it will create as many problems as it will solve?"

Make your own choice before looking below for GTE's "best" answer.

> A. Wise decision. Another legitimate time to interrupt or get directly involved in the conference is when the participants are wasting valuable time on a solution that is not do-able or one that is against policy. (ADD 3 POINTS)
>
> B. This is wishful thinking, especially when Tony Jenks has the "platform." He may go on forever! Option B is not a good decision. (ADD 1 POINT)
>
> C. Not a bad move, but it will probably be less effective than option A above. You may encourage Tony to debate you on the point and that will really throw the conference off track. (ADD 2 POINTS)

• Who decided that Tony Jenks' suggestion was too costly?

• What happened to trusting the participants to come to the correct conclusion?

• What happened to "neutral" and "unbiased"?

---

interesting and teach problem-solving skills. But it would require a different set of assumptions. It would bring up for discussion a point that participation trainers would prefer to leave untouched.

ACCEPTING THE LIMITS

Another assumption of participation training is the acceptance of the group and its limitations. When the group discusses problems to solve, one of the first questions is whether a particular problem is appropriate for the group. We discuss how this works at NUMMI in chapter 8.

Say one member of a hospital quality circle says she wants the group to work on how the hospital can shift away from high-tech machines that duplicate other facilities in the area, and toward primary care like prenatal and well-baby care. She believes this would improve the quality of health in the neighborhood.

A well-trained facilitator will intervene. He or she will ask whether this problem is really within the scope of the circle force. Weren't they convened to look at issues such as equalization of staffing, vacation scheduling, and implementation of multi-skilling? Mission decisions are really the job of the hospital board....

The facilitator encourages the task force to deal with problems whose solutions are within easy reach so that the group can experience success. That is why training concentrates so heavily on group identity. If group identity is strong enough and someone suggests a problem that isn't "appropriate" for the group, the pressure will be to drop the problem, not the group.

BUILDING TRUST

Participation training sometimes includes exercises to build trust and break down barriers between management and workers; we've called this approach "labor relations in a hot tub." Here, for example, are a few exercises used at GM's Saturn plant when it was new. All employees had transferred from GM plants around the country, and Saturn management wanted to build teamwork, using a course called EXEL.[8]

Jumping off the pole. Employees climb a 47-foot pole, wearing a safety harness. At the top, they must rotate all the way around, standing on a small disc. Then, as teammates yell, "You can do it!", they must jump off the pole and ring a bell.

The purpose, according to Charter Team Member Al Burris, was to learn to let go. When new team members were brought on, early hires like himself had to learn to let go of some of their former functions.

Tony Kemplin, a former UAW official, says, "There I was, forty feet up, and four people holding a rope are keeping me from breaking my neck. Two assembly line technicians, an engineer, and a finance guy.

"That's when it really hits you what Saturn means when they talk about partnership."[9]

The wall. The wall is higher than the pole. Three

employees hitched together climb it, grabbing onto pegs. No one can get too far ahead, and if one falls, they all fall. The lesson? Teamwork.

The trust fall. The employee falls backward off an eight-foot-high ledge, into the arms of teammates. Al Burris describes what happens next: "Once you falls backwards, some of them takes you and rocks you from side to side, and sings you a little old song. What they call the *Baby Rock*, for two or three minutes. Ease your mind. Ease you down real slow."[10]

Techniques like these are used in many kinds of programs, from Outward Bound to therapy. The question is when, and with whom, these kinds of exercises are appropriate. You probably can trust your boss not to let go of the rope. But when bosses are at work, they have roles to play and jobs to do. Can you trust the boss not to close your plant and move it Mexico? Can you trust the boss to protect you if a higher boss thinks you are a troublemaker for standing up for your rights?

In other workplaces, instead of sharing a dangerous physical experience, participants may be asked to reveal deep personal values and attitudes. Imagine being asked to do the following exercise with your boss and co-workers:

> Read the following story and then, as a group, rank the characters in the order in which you like or admire them.[11]
>
> A ship sank in a storm. A girl, a sailor, and an old man reached an island. The girl was certain that her fiance and his best friend were on another island within sight. She begged the sailor to take her to the other island. The sailor agreed on condition that she sleep with him.
>
> The girl agonized and asked the old man for advice. He told her to look into her own heart. She finally agreed to sleep with the sailor, after which he repaired the boat and took her to the island.
>
> The girl found her fiance and ran into his arms. After a while she told him what had happened. In a rage he pushed her away, saying he did not want to see her again.
>
> The best friend put his arm around the girl and said,

"I'll try to patch it up, but meanwhile I'll take care of you."

This kind of exercise can be revealing and enjoyable, if you like that kind of thing. But shouldn't we have the right to choose with whom we will talk about such issues?

HIGHER NEEDS ARE MANAGEMENT NEEDS

Maslow's "hierarchy of needs" (the pyramid described earlier in this chapter) can be used to put unions in their place—low in the hierarchy. And since the supposed aim is to get "members of the organization" to operate in the higher levels of the hierarchy, the message is that unions are not very relevant, despite all the partnership rhetoric to the contrary.

Under the participation philosophy, Maslow's argument translates: the need for a secure job and a decent wage (unions' traditional goals) are not very "evolved." An admirable person will be striving for the higher needs of recognition and achievement. Luckily, these can be found in a participation program.

Compare this notion to President Bill Clinton's advice in March 1994: "When I address audiences of young people, I tell them they will probably change jobs seven or eight times in a lifetime."[12] To be prepared, Clinton says, they will need training, training, and more training.[13]

Safety and security are out; "self-actualization" is in.

When participation programs succeed in shifting loyalties and breaking down the ideas of union solidarity, the reason is that they do fulfill some needs. They fill a vacuum. When a union challenges participation but has no alternative of its own, it risks reinforcing the very message of participation training—that satisfaction comes from the new group identity and that the union stands in the way of satisfying work. The void participation programs fill is real. But there is no reasons that unions cannot fill it.

Notes

1. Ad in *The Plaindealer* (a union newspaper in Wichita, Kansas), Vol. 73, No. 10, July 1991.

2. A.H. Maslow, editor, *New Knowledge in Human Values*, Harper & Row, 1959.

3. *Leader Manual*, GM Education and Training, Publication SIF-334, 1984.

4. Abridged version of exercise used in PPG Industries, Circleville, Ohio training program, based on 1975 Annual Handbook for Group Facilitators.

5. *Leader Manual*, GM Education and Training, Publication SIF-334, 1984.

6. Sud Ingle, *Quality Circle Master Guide*, Prentice Hall, 1982, p. 5.

7. Robert B. Reich, "'Pronoun Test'" Measures Company's Performance"(*Washington Post* Commentary), *Detroit Free Press,* September 1, 1993.

8. Joe Sherman, *In the Rings of Saturn*, New York, Oxford

University Press, 1994, pp. 210-213.

9. Advertisement, *Scientific American*, October 1990.

10. Sherman, p. 212.

11. Abridged version of exercise used at GM Hydra-matic Division/UAW Family Awareness Training during the 1980s. The "family" referred to is the Hydra-matic employees.

12. Remarks by President Bill Clinton at the G-7 Jobs Conference, Detroit, Michigan, March 14, 1994.

13. This philosophy was spelled out by Peter T. Kilborn, "Job Security Hinges on Skills, Not on an Employer for Life," *New York Times*, March 12, 1994. According to Kilborn, "[Labor Secretary] Reich believes that once people have the right skills the demand for those skills will appear" ("Action Defies Theory, Labor Secretary Learns," *New York Times*, July 15, 1993).

Working Smart:
A Union Guide to Participation Programs and Reengineering

Labor Notes • 7435 Michigan Ave. • Detroit, MI 48210 • (313) 842-6262

Chapter 14

Taking Quality Programs Apart

Though "quality" sounds like a win-win proposition, management's definition of quality results in fewer jobs and a tightening of the screws. Rather than improving quality to the real customer, workers are taught to serve the "internal customer." Management uses programs such as ISO 9000 and the Malcolm Baldrige Award an an excuse to reorganize the workplace. Management now says openly that the goal is not quality per se, but the "return on quality."

MANAGEMENT'S DRIVE FOR A PARTICIPATION PROGRAM often begins with the following propositions:

The buying public is highly conscious of quality. Only a quality product will sell. Only a quality product will make profits. Therefore only a quality product will maintain jobs.

Training for participation programs emphasizes "win-win" solutions. Surely, we are taught, quality is win-win. Management makes profits, workers keep jobs, the customer is happy. Add to this the fact that workers take pride and satisfaction from doing quality work, and there seems to be every reason that workers and their unions should join wholeheartedly in company quality efforts.

But it is precisely because quality ranks with baseball, hot dogs, and apple pie that management has been able to change the definition of quality to something quite different from the common sense meaning.

QUALITY = WASTE REDUCTION

The everyday definition of quality is found in the dictionary: "a degree or level of excellence."[1] When consumers speak of quality, they mean that the product will last, that it will perform the use for which it was intended, that it will look good, or a combination of these.

But consider a very different use of the term "quality," implicit in the following exercise. It is modelled on those used in participation training.

There is poor quality on the widget line. Normal production is about 200,000 widgets per year. But about 10 percent (or 20,000) have to be rejected because their holes do not line up properly.

The company estimates that each rejected widget costs

$4.00, of which the cost of raw materials equals $1.00. (This totals $80,000 per year in scrap, of which $20,000 is the cost of raw materials.)

In the training exercise, a team of workers attacks the problem of the defective widgets and figures out how to make all the holes line up, through some clever means that involves no cost to the company. What are the results? The workers are proud, they have achieved "zero defects," the company saves money, quality goes up.

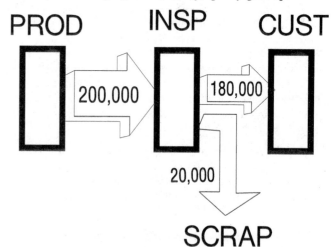

But let's look more closely at what's happened. Quality? There is no increase in quality for the consumer. The consumer never had to put up with defective widgets in the past. Inspectors caught them and they were scrapped. The quality of widget the consumer sees is the same as before.[2]

The company, however, has saved $80,000 ($4 x

20,000) because it no longer has to produce the 20,000 widgets previously scrapped. Of this, $20,000 is the savings in raw materials.

Quality defined as reduction of waste usually means job loss.

Where does the other $60,000 come from? Previously the company had to produce 200,000 widgets to get 180,000 good ones. Now it needs to produce only 180,000. The $60,000 savings comes from not having to pay anyone to produce the extra 20,000 widgets. The savings to the company is a reduction in paid worktime. Perhaps the company reduces the number of people on the widget job from ten to nine. Thus the "quality" improvement is really a productivity improvement. Management may also save from reducing or eliminating inspectors and those who handle the scrap.

QUALITY = CUSTOMER SATISFACTION?

This is not to say that unions should favor wasted time or the production of faulty goods. But if we recognize that the waste-reduction sort of "quality" achievement comes in part at the expense of workers, that is a first step to a union strategy for dealing with such worker suggestions. See chapter 34 for some ideas on how unions can promote quality themselves, in a way that maintains or increases jobs.

After all, the common sense meaning of "quality" would involve improving value for the customer. Often

---

Quality = Productivity

Sometimes management stops beating around the bush about quality/productivity almost immediately. At the JFK Airport mail facility, the Postal Service initiated a new program called "Index on Quality (IQ) Rating." But here is how management explained the Quality Index was to be established:

> Each unit (work area, crew, team) will select an output of their own and establish a performance level for that output. This goal should represent a near perfect performance.
>
> Along with a maximum performance level, a minimum performance level will be established. Normally this level will be reasonably close to the maximum goal.
>
> These goals are strictly for the purpose of employee participation and establishing a quality rating, in order to measure progress, for the facility...
>
> The goal should reflect the quality of the operation and not be limited to productivity alone.
>
> The quality performance level goal cannot alter the process in a manner that would have a negative impact on productivity unless overall facility productivity gains can be demonstrated or the ability to dispatch a better final product can be guaranteed.[3]

---

this kind of quality improvement can be achieved only by adding jobs. For example, reducing the number of defective parts shipped may require increasing the number of inspections. Adding an extra operation to improve a product (like an additional row of stitching around buttonholes) or providing greater service to the customer (like immediate and thorough investigation of complaints) usually require more labor.

Quality that is passed on to consumers can create jobs.

One problem is that the term "customer" adds to the confusion, as we discuss below.

QUALITY = CONFORMANCE TO REQUIREMENTS

Management's definition of quality is an attempt to direct efforts toward the waste reduction view and away from concern for the value to the consumer. Most training in quality control begins by having workers discuss the meaning of the word "quality." The instructor then explains why the common sense definition is not workable. How do you measure excellence or superiority? Isn't one person's view bound to be different from another's?

The solution, we are told, is to define quality as "conformance to requirements" or "conformance to specifications."

One of the leading proponents of this view is Philip Crosby, former vice president and director of quality for ITT. General Motors owns part of Crosby's Quality College in Florida. Companies as diverse as Ore-Ida, Union Carbide, and the Big Three have adopted Crosby's methods and materials.

It is easy to see why Crosby is so popular with management. First, his prescriptions are comfortable for the bureaucrat. Many other quality specialists, such as W. Edwards Deming, place the blame for poor quality on management and call for a management shake-up. Not Crosby. According to his manual, management need only carefully execute each of his 14 steps and quality will be the result. Second, according to Crosby, "quality is free," to use the title of his book.[4] Actually, it is better than free. Whatever minor costs a quality program entails are far outweighed by the expense of doing things wrong, including scrap and rework.

In theory "conformance to requirements" works this way. Only the customer can know his or her exact requirements for a new washing machine. The factory must meet the washer buyer's requirements. To do this it must make these requirements its own, and pass them on to its parts suppliers, who in turn must pass them on to their suppliers. If everybody conforms to the specifications set by the next stage, in the end the customer will have what he or she wants.

In the abstract it sounds plausible, but the appliance industry does not work this way, and neither do very many others. Washing machines are not built to order. Instead, the manufacturers do research to try to guess which features combined at which prices are most likely to sell three to five years from now. They then design those washers, and the factories build them. Management also decides on market and pricing strategies and targets specific consumers.

Thus, when quality is defined as "conformance to requirements," those requirements are the ones dictated by management's chosen design. "Conformance to requirements" means "do what management has decided and do it the way management has decided." Discretion for the worker is erased. "Quality" becomes the justification for the rigid system of standardized work discussed in chapter 5.

"Conformance to requirements" means do it exactly the way management wants it.

Thus when quality consultants talk about "getting control of the process," they do not mean mastering a tool or a manufacturing procedure. They mean that management must have complete control over what happens in the workplace. One of the characters in Crosby's book, *Quality Is Free*, describes an incident to make one of Crosby's major points:

> We were running behind in the machine shop, and we took some parts we had been making for years and put the raw materials plus the paperwork in a box and sent it out to a very good machine shop [i.e., to a subcontractor].
>
> You know what? They couldn't make them. If you did it just like the print it didn't compute. No way. All kinds of little variations were involved. And none of them were written down. We found that we had several very proud craftspeople in our shops who know how to shave a little here and there in order to make the product come out usable in spite of faulty specifications.

At this point the unsuspecting reader might assume the narrator will praise the craftspeople who didn't just do what they were told; instead they did what was necessary to satisfy the customer. He might be concerned about why the print specifications were off, but surely a bright spot was those craftspeople. Perhaps they will be given a quality award for their efforts. But the narrator goes on:

> Do you know how horrible that was? The company management didn't control the place anymore. They were at the mercy of the Mr. Fixits in the shop...[5]

Horrible? The consumer was getting quality and the workers had some protection against contracting out. The horror was the lack of management control. From management's point of view, it would have been better for the craftspeople to produce the parts to the specifications that didn't work, so that management could discover that its specifications were wrong—and maintain control.

QUALITY = REDUCTION IN VARIATION

This concept of quality is similar to "conformance to requirements," but different enough to cause major disputes among the quality gurus (see chapter 12 on one disagreement between Crosby and Deming).

The idea is simple enough. If a product is out of specification, the reason is that one or more of its components, or the process that put them together, varied from *its* specification. Even if the variation of each particular element was within permissible limits, it is possible that by chance the variations all combined to magnify the error, rather than canceling each other out.

The answer, then, is simple. Start with inputs (raw materials) that are as free from variation as possible. Keep the processes they are subjected to as nonvarying as possible. Check processes for sources of variation and work

---

Exercise:

What Is Quality?

Objective: To establish the common sense understanding of quality. Should be done before discussing management's definition of quality as "conformance to specifications."

Time: 20 minutes

Materials: Quality Worksheet as below, with room for participants to write their answers.

Quality Worksheet

1. What would you consider "quality" in a breakfast cereal?
2. What would you consider a "quality" interaction with a directory assistance operator?
3. What would you consider "quality" in a new car you are considering buying?
4. In buying a car, would you sometimes turn down higher quality because it costs more? Give an example.
5. A relative's Social Security check does not arrive. You call the agency. What would you consider quality service?
6. Describe the customer for whom you try to do quality work.

Ask volunteers to give their answers and discuss them briefly. Tell them that you will be coming back to their definitions of quality later.

After the discussion of management's view of quality as conformance to requirements, contrast the answers given by participants with management's definition.

TOTAL QUALITY MANAGEMENT

This cartoon depicting "continuous improvement" under TQM was used by a company called Alliance Group Ltd. in New Zealand. It was accompanied by these words: "We realize that we are in a race without a finish line. As we improve, so does our competition. Five years ago we would have found that disheartening. Today we find it invigorating..."

to reduce or eliminate them. If variation is introduced because a machine shaft wobbles, fix it. And be sure the work itself is always done in exactly the same way each time.

This approach to quality is the basis for Statistical Process Control. SPC theory recognizes that there will always be some variation; the idea is to monitor it, and to understand which variation is built into the process and will be there until the process itself is changed (common cause), and which variation happens because of special circumstances (special cause).

Reducing variation can be a powerful quality tool. And it makes a lot of sense when you're talking about ball bearings for motor shafts. But quality programs often turn a good concept into an absolute. Thus a Quality Alert seminar promises to explain

Why "service design" must proceed on the basis that discretion (or variation) is the enemy of order, standardization, and quality. (For example, McDonald's raw hamburger meat patties are carefully prepacked and premeasured, which leaves neither the franchise nor employees any discretion as to the size, quality or raw material consistency.)[6]

Since they don't vary, McDonald's hamburgers are top of the line. Under this definition of quality, it is inappropriate to ask what these unvarying burgers actually taste like.

Reduction of variation is not always an appropriate measure of quality, especially when there are human beings involved. In chapter 25 we discuss what it means to

apply this concept to education. Indeed, in general in the service sector there is a constant tension between standardization, so that customers can have reasonable expectations, and adapting the service to fit individual needs. See the box on Standardized White Collar Work in chapter 8.

Reducing variation makes sense for machines, not people.

For example, insurance companies have imposed on hospitals the concept of Diagnostic-Related Groups. The companies pay only what they have determined is appropriate for each particular diagnosis, no matter the patient's actual length of stay or what procedures are actually performed. In other words, patients are to be treated more like ball bearings—expected to react exactly the same to being "processed"—and less like individuals. The result is that even highly skilled workers—doctors—are allowed to use less of their own judgment.

Reduction of variance usually has a cost. We can readily measure the cost of sharpening a tool or realigning a machine more frequently. But the human costs are harder to measure. What is the cost to a worker's body when Dr. Deming insists that a process be done exactly the same way each time—the right hand always holds at the same angle and the left hand always twists in the same way? Repetitive strain injuries, for example, appears to be greater in auto plants that use these "standardized work techniques" to reduce variation (see chapter 8).

Reducing variation means reducing the use of judgment in daily work. To maximize exact repeatability, jobs would best be done by robots.[7]

QUALITY = JOB SECURITY?

Up to now we have used hypothetical examples to illustrate the significance of the two definitions of quality. The real life story of General Motors' two-seater Fiero demonstrates the importance of these distinctions.

Doing high-quality work does not guarantee your job.

One day in February 1985, Plant Manager Dennis Pawley and UAW Shop Chairman Bob Farley hosted a free lunch for the Fiero plant's 2,400 workers. They were celebrating what was then the highest weekly quality rating in GM's history—138 out of 145.[8] The car included many technological innovations, including a plastic body bolted to a "bird cage"-type metal frame. Many of the production methods for the car broke new ground in the auto industry.

The plant was an early team concept experiment: the union had agreed to cut classifications, allowed supervisors to work on the line, and reduced the number of grievances to a trickle. Through 1985 the plant was one of GM's featured models for other team concept plants.

Quality = Science?

Quality programs are presented as though they incorporate a body of known facts and procedures. Quality, we are told, is a science, and it is taught in the same way as "cells have a wall and a nucleus" and "Force = Mass × Acceleration."

This notion is reinforced by the use of such tools of quality as Statistical Process Control and Pareto charts.

Being thrown into such programs can be an overwhelming experience for those who have not previously been exposed to these methods. Math and its related tools are poorly taught in American school systems.

But these techniques are tools, not principles. The old saying goes, "If the only tool you have is a hammer, everything starts to look like a nail."

For example, workers often learn the "80/20 rule." The idea is simple. If there are many different causes of a problem, they will not be distributed equally. Instead, most likely they will be distributed "geometrically": 80 percent of the problems are produced by 20 percent of the causes.

Armed with this tidbit of science, it is only a step to activities such as we discussed in chapter 13, where workers draw Pareto graphs to show which of their co-workers are causing the most problems.

But sales of the Fiero plunged from nearly 100,000 in 1983, its first full year, to under 50,000 three years later. In March 1988, GM announced it was discontinuing the model and closing the plant.

Why were the Fiero workers out of a job? It couldn't have been poor quality. The high audit figures showed that workers were producing in "conformance to requirements"—they built the car exactly as they were told. "We did everything they asked us to do to improve quality and productivity and to cut costs," said one UAW official. "And we still couldn't keep the plant open."[9]

So why did the Fiero die? GM claims that the main reason was a shift in customer preferences, away from two-seaters. Another reason was the well-publicized recalls because of engine fires and a high failure rate of engine connecting rods; the entire 1984 model year was recalled. (The problems, according to GM, were the owners' or their mechanics' fault: operating temperatures were set too high or hoses and wiring were connected improperly.[10])

But most analysts believe that the car was misdesigned from the beginning. While it was marketed as a sports car, it was underpowered. In 1983 the *Detroit Free Press* reported that "car enthusiasts appeared to be disappointed in the sluggish performance of the new Fiero two-seat sports car (it is equipped with a rather mundane X-car engine)."[11]

The choice of an X-car (Chevrolet Citation) engine to power the Fiero was part of GM management's overall business plan. According to a Massachusetts Institute of Technology auto industry expert, by doing so GM avoided the costs of developing a new powertrain for the Fiero. "What they are doing there is an extremely important part of GM's long-range strategy," said [Martin] Anderson. "GM is looking at its high-volume componentry and using it to build low-volume cars in new ways."[12]

In other words, GM was more concerned with using a particular engine that it wanted to produce in high volume than it was with choosing an engine suitable for the Fiero's special niche.

Workers had no control over the design of the car, the choice of engine, how to market the car, or GM's high-volume components strategy. Workers had no control over the design of connecting rods or the placement of the hoses that GM claimed were being disconnected by customers or mechanics. Workers may have made suggestions through the teams about how to meet management's design with less scrap or fewer workers. But it was always up to management to decide. The workers just continued to produce in "conformance to requirements" set by management.

Yet workers believed that management had made them a promise. As one put it:

> We built the best quality in the corporation for four years. Why are we being laid off? All we've heard since we came to this plant, is that if you build good quality you won't get laid off.[13]

Unfortunately, Fiero is only one of many examples

where quality has not protected jobs.

For example, Zenith, known for its top-caliber televisions, shut down plants in Missouri and Illinois and moved to Mexico. American Home Products, makers of Advil and Anacin, moved from Indiana to Puerto Rico. In these cases, management's desire for a quality product with a tested workforce was not as strong as its desire for cheap labor. In any case, with modern methods and equipment, low-wage workers in developing countries are producing products of equal quality to those made in the USA (see chapter 29).

QUALITY = SERVING THE INTERNAL CUSTOMER

In the 1980s, both production and service companies began to use the idea of the "internal customer." A document for the General Motors Production System, for example, explained: "While the ultimate customer is the purchaser of the product, each production process along the line is the 'customer' of the preceding process and must be treated as such."[14]

If your department in the washing machine factory subassembles timers, then your "customer" is the department that installs the timers in the washers. If you are a hospital orderly, the "customer" you must please is the Radiology Department to which you're wheeling the patient for X-rays. If you are a service representative at the phone company, your internal customer is the worker to whom you hand John Q. Public's order for call-waiting. In order for that internal customer to do quality work, you must do quality work—that is, fill out the order form in conformance to specifications.

Internal Customers Slow To Learn

In March 1994 the newsletter of the Inspire/TQM program for West Virginia state employees did a survey. Workers were asked, "As an organization we all have customers, people who receive our work and services. Who are your customers?"

Apparently the program facilitators did not get the answer they wanted. In the May newsletter, they reprimanded their fellow employees:

Respondents identified their customers as the citizens of West Virginia who received their services. *We are all customers of each other.* People, both inside and outside the Department, who require information or services are our customers, whether they are clients, patients, immediate coworkers, colleagues, or providers or vendors.

The newsletter editors also noted, perhaps with regret, that some state employees had objected to using the term "customer" for the people who received their services, feeling that "client" or "patient" would be more appropriate.

While this idea contains a grain of truth, it denies the fundamental structure of the corporation. No appliance manufacturer, for example, is a big free enterprise marketplace where every machine operator or assembler works out the best combination of product, service, and cost with his or her internal suppliers and customers. Nor do departments work this way. A corporation is a top-down economic system with overall planning. Someone decides what products will be offered for sale. The product is designed as a whole, and specific operations are assigned to specific departments.

Similarly in a hospital, the orderly is not free to sell his service—patient delivery—at a cost negotiated between him and the Radiology Department. His work is scheduled from above according to the requirements of the doctors' orders.

Workers can fine-tune management's plan and make it more efficient and profitable. But this effort has nothing to do with behaving like "suppliers" or "customers." It also has nothing to do with whether they are meeting the desires of the ultimate customer, the buyer (or patient).

Notice that the internal customer notion also negates any role for the union. Workers' tasks and schedules are set by management—but modified by the union, which negotiates break times, job classifications, and the like. Under the supposed free market of the internal customer concept, these would all be negotiable by individual customers and vendors.

According to one quality newsletter, the L.L. Bean company, which many customers swear by, lost in the 1988 Baldrige Award finals because "the entire focus was on end-customer satisfaction." "The basic philosophy of total quality management—that everybody in the company has a customer—is a concept we hadn't really grasped," explained Catharine Hartnett of L.L. Bean. Afterwards, workers were encouraged to adopt the internal customer mentality.[15]

QUALITY = REORGANIZATION

Management often gives quality as the reason for a major reorganization of work. Management's case is stronger when it says, "We have no choice—our major customer is requiring that all suppliers go through the Baldrige Application," or

"The contract specifies that we be ISO 9000-certified."

ISO 9000

The ISO (International Organization for Standardization) is a worldwide federation of national standards bodies, based in Geneva. The U.S. is represented by the non-government organization American National Standards Institute (ANSI). By establishing international standards for threads on nuts and bolts, the ISO makes it possible to buy a bolt manufactured in one factory and have it thread into a nut manufactured in another factory in another country.

In 1987 the ISO adopted the 9000 series of International Standards for Quality Management.[16] The standards can have country variations and different names. Thus in the U.S. they may be called Q90 standards. ISO 9000 gets organizational support in the U.S. from ANSI and the American Society for Quality Control (ASQC).

A quality program can mean work reorganization.

Contrary to a widespread misunderstanding, ISO 9000 certification is not legally required for most business in the European Common Market. ISO 9000 is one of the options for meeting certain safety requirements. Where the standards get their teeth is that many companies and governmental units may include ISO 9000 compliance in their specifications. The Food and Drug Administration, for example, is incorporating ISO 9000 specifications as part of its own regulations.

As their name suggests, the ISO 9000 standards cover ways of *managing* quality. The standards do not test the product produced or the service provided to see whether they're any good. Rather, conforming to ISO 9000 standards means that the firm has an internal quality system in place, that it documents its quality procedures, and that employees observe those procedures.

The general form of the quality procedure is included in the standards. The idea is to provide a common set of

standards so that two-party contracts can easily be written with a common set of assumptions, and to provide for reliable recordkeeping so that it is not necessary for a company either to regularly visit its supplier or to inspect what it purchases in order to assure quality.

ISO 9000 provides for certifying three levels of quality assurance:

Final inspection and test (ISO 9003)

Production and installation (ISO 9002)

All aspects from design through production, through installation and service (ISO 9001).

A company that wants ISO certification establishes and reviews its own procedures, writes up a quality manual, and then calls an accredited registrar in for an examination. The registrar issues registration after any deficiencies have been corrected. Regular surveillance audits to maintain certification are required twice per year, and a complete assessment is required every three years. Certification can cost from $5,000 to $25,000.

It is important to understand how vague the standards are. Here are some *complete* sections of ISO 9003:

Inspection, measuring and test equipment:

The supplier shall calibrate and maintain inspection, measuring and test equipment to demonstrate the conformance of product to requirement. (4.6)

Handling, storage, packing, and delivery:

The supplier shall arrange for the protection of the quality of the product and its identification after final inspection and test. Where contractually specified, this protection

shall be extended to include delivery to destination. (4.9)

Training:

Personnel performing final inspection and tests shall have appropriate experience and/or training. (4.11)

What ISO 9000 is really about is establishing fixed and documented procedures, and then having other procedures in place to make sure that the first procedures are followed and records are kept:

Inspection and testing:

The supplier shall carry out all final inspection and testing in accordance with the documented procedures and maintain appropriate records to complete the evidence of conformance of product to specified requirements. The final inspection shall include a verification of acceptable results of other necessary inspection and tests performed previously for the purpose of verifying requirements. (4.5)

Not only do the ISO standards ignore the quality of the actual goods or services, they do not even say much about the quality of the procedures. All that is required is to state the procedure and then keep records to show that it has been done. It can be efficient or inefficient, state-of-the-art or from the horse-and-buggy period. It can measure to the nearest inch or the nearest .0001 millimeter. As Patricia Kopp, standards administrator of the ASQC, puts it:

There is no one right way to do ISO 9000. Industries are free to find their own way. They can view it as a creative opportunity rather than an additional burden.[17]

The vagueness of the requirements shifts the technical issues to the registrars. Since the criteria are vague, the best way for a company to assure it will get certified is to hire a consultant who has experience with ISO 9000, or perhaps even some links to a registrar. And if management knows what workplace changes it wants to make—say getting rid of classifications—it is easy to find a consultant who will weave these changes into a "quality program" that is supposedly designed to gain ISO 9000 certification.

There have been complaints. A U.S. Commerce Department official warns:

Since the onset of the ISO 9000 "craze," a large number of registrars has surfaced in the United States many of whom have no credentials or proof that they are competent to perform quality systems audits to acceptable standards.[18]

But tightening the accreditation of registrars and auditors, which is currently happening, means the system will be dominated by whatever is fashionable at the time in the quality establishment that controls the institutions that certify the registrars.

Quality is not a science, though its proponents like to pretend it is. At the root of any quality program are value

"I thought I'd introduce a little democracy to this department. Bring me your suggestions and I'll vote on them."

judgements about what is and is not important. There are deep philosophical debates in the quality field about the fact that ISO 9000 is not "customer driven." Its defenders rely on the market to make the connection with the customer.

The general guidelines contained in ISO 9004 reveal much about the underlying philosophy of ISO 9000. It starts with the needs of the company:

In order to be successful, a company must offer products or services that
a) meet a well defined need, use, or purpose
b) satisfy customers' expectations
c) comply with applicable standards and specifications
d) comply with statutory (and other) requirements of society
e) are made available at competitive prices
f) are provided at a cost which will yield a profit. (9004.0.1)

Notice that a concern for profits is built into the standards. There is no similar concern for good working conditions or satisfied workers. Where are the workers? Here they are:

...the company should organize itself in such a way that the technical, administrative, and human factors affecting the quality of its products and services shall be under control. (9004.0.2)

Workers are among the "factors" that need to be under control.

An effective quality management system should be designed to satisfy customer needs and expectations while serving to protect the company's interests. A well structured quality system is a valuable management resource in the optimization and control of quality in relation to risk, cost and benefit considerations.(9004.0.4.5)

In other words, quality should exist at the intersection of customer needs and the company's need to make a profit. In this world view, the corporation has the right to a good profit and the customer has the right to a product as specified. But workers have no rights at all.

And that is why it makes sense, under the ISO vision of quality, to organize production so that workers are interchangeable and disposable. As Dave Erdman, Director of Quality at DuPont Electronics, says:

> If someone came in and wiped out your work crew, in theory, you should be able to bring in a new one off the street without missing a beat.[19]

ISO 9000's emphasis on documenting procedures is particularly dangerous. We discuss that danger in chapter 16; see the box "Management Learns the Jobs."

MALCOLM BALDRIGE AWARD

The Malcolm Baldrige National Quality Award for U.S. corporations is modeled on the famous Deming Award given in Japan. It is administered by the U.S. Commerce Department but is financed through fees and private contributions. Applying for the Baldrige requires substantial effort, money, and paperwork. Yet hundreds of corporations have applied. In 1990 over 180,000 copies of the Awards Guide were circulated.

One reason for applying is that the Award can be of great advertising value to corporations (witness Cadillac's campaign).

But since a maximum of six awards is given per year, most companies pursue it for a different reason. The examination process for the Award gives the company an additional reason for any shake-up that goes with the introduction of a quality program. The application process gives management an opportunity to set target dates, a sense of urgency, an atmosphere of competition, and the chance to build a cheerleading team spirit to go after the trophy. It also provides a standardized form that large corporations can use to evaluate suppliers. Motorola, for example, requires its suppliers to show their Baldrige applications or the equivalent. Pursuit of the Award is a central part of the strategic plans of large companies like Consolidated Freight.

The examination process represents the current business consensus about quality in the U.S. It covers documentation procedures as ISO 9000 does, but also other areas, particularly the methods used for handling feedback from customers. The main categories and the items within each are broad enough to encompass virtually all of the popular quality programs. The Board of Examiners (approximately 250) are "quality experts" chosen from business, professional, government, and educational institutions.

Again, as in ISO 9000 certification, the Board does not take a *Consumer Reports* approach that samples products and compares them to those of other manufacturers. For the most part, the Board is examining the company's internal procedures. For example, the "Quality and Operational Results" category focuses on internal measures of reliability, accuracy, and timeliness, as well as cycle times, waste reduction, and "use of manpower."

Only half the points in the "Customer Focus and Satisfaction" category represent measures of actual customer responses, and, again, these use the company's internal records.

Thus the Award measures the internal procedures of the company against a supposed standard of quality management. The process awards no quality points to a company for paying prevailing wages, restricting outsourcing, having procedures to avoid favoritism, providing services to its workers and the community, or taking extra effort to preserve the environment.[20] Indeed, the 1992 small business winner, Granite Rock in Watsonville, California, has made many attempts to bypass provisions of its contracts with the Teamsters Union. Granite Rock has sued one local, moved work to secret non-union subsidiaries, and tried to shift blame for safety problems to hourly workers.

At the same time, many of the issues that the Award promotes should be subjects of collective bargaining. Job assignments, reward systems, and training are all areas likely to be altered in the attempt to win the Award.

Managers in some companies see the Baldrige competition as the road to redemption. A number of states have established "mini-Baldriges." There is a proposal to create a Baldrige award in higher education.

But there is also some management backlash. In a survey of managers in the auto industry, the Baldrige award ranked lowest as a measure of quality. Fully 60 percent felt it was not a meaningful assessment of product quality.[21] *Business Week* suggested that the Wallace Co.'s winning pursuit of the 1990 Baldrige caused it to lay off a quarter of its workforce and declare bankruptcy.[22] Other business writers have called the Baldrige a "boondoggle."[23]

There is some suspicion that the Award depends on connections and publicity among the professional quality establishment. Former Award judges become highly paid consultants to applicants.[24] It appears that the Commerce Department may have a secret political test for the Award. In 1991 Westinghouse Idaho Nuclear Power Co. was the judges' selection, but their choice was blocked by the Department.

Companies often use the Baldrige criteria even without undergoing the application process. For example, the Field Container Company had what was widely recognized as a successful quality effort.

> The company asked the University of Chicago's graduate school of business to do a mock Malcolm Baldrige quality review in 1993. Field came out with a score about in the middle range of companies which actually do apply for the award. The most startling comment made by the "review" team was that there was actually too much empowerment and teamwork on the floor and not enough direction from management.
>
> As a result the company is now putting a member of management on each of the process teams to help focus the teams on company-wide goals and projects.[25]

Ironically, many of the top quality gurus don't think much of the Award, although in some cases their criticisms come from opposite directions. Philip Crosby:

As a quality practitioner who for the past 40 years has had the real-life responsibility for installing quality management in organizations, I recognize that the Baldrige criteria have trivialized the quality crusade, perhaps beyond help. One day this do-it-yourself kit may be recognized as the cause of a permanent decline in product and service quality management in the United States.[26]

W. Edwards Deming:

The Baldrige Award does not codify principles of management of quality. It contains nothing about management of quality. The award is focused purely on results....

[A Baldrige defender] makes a common mistake in the misuse of figures. Anyone could write down six or eight companies that are doing famously well in spite of management practices that would throw other companies in the ditch. They do well under bad management by plain luck. To copy them or try to learn from them without theory would lead into disaster.[27]

The popularity of the Award is now declining. Only 90 companies completed applications in 1992.

QUALITY MUST = PROFITS

The business community, and management in general, are as susceptible to fads as is the world of fashion. Just as fashion writers hail this fall's fluid, gentle lines and disparage the boxy silhouettes they applauded last year, so do executives—and consultants—greet each new vogue as if it were received wisdom on stone tablets—until they move on to the next phase. The humane, caring, people-person manager becomes the prophet of lean-and-mean, without batting an eyelash.

Thus it is with quality. By 1994, the quality mania that swept the corporate world in the 1980s and reached the public sector in the 1990s was being strongly questioned. The new buzzword was "return on quality." As the editors of *Business Week* put it, "Quality improvements can only be justified if they eventually lead to the coin of the corporate realm—higher profits."[28]

The covers were off the previous decade of pious exhortations to focus on the customer. Business was being reminded what they were about: not winning quality awards, not having better defect numbers than the competition, not even rating high on a Customer Satisfaction Index, but Profits.

We will borrow extensively from a *Business Week* cover story titled "Making Quality Pay,"[29] to portray the "return on quality," or ROQ, movement, because Business Week has always been on the cutting edge of the latest management fads.

The magazine notes that, contrary to expectations, quality has not always meant higher profits. It cites the bankrupt Wallace Co., mentioned above, as an example.

Therefore, when it comes to quality, the bottom line must be...the bottom line. Says consultant and professor Roland Rust, "one of ROQ's chief apostles," "If we're not going to make money off of it, we're not going to do it." Curt Reimann, director of the Baldrige Award, says, "There's been an insufficient focus on the aspect of quality improvements that will make the largest contribu-

tion to overall financial performance."

Under the ROQ philosophy, "Everything from the installation of new technology to methods of improving billing accuracy is held up against an array of financial yardsticks, such as potential sales gains and return on capital." AT&T, for example, requires proponents of any proposed quality initiative to demonstrate that it will yield a 30 percent drop in defects—and a 10 percent return on investment.

To be sure, there are customer-friendly aspects to the ROQ movement. In addition to talking about money, there is also a thread of concern for discovering what really matters to consumers, rather than compiling abstract quality numbers.

A hotel chain found that its guests really wanted irons in their rooms. It installed the irons (and no longer needed the service people who ferried irons from room to room on request). A maker of scientific equipment began packing its cables in plastic bags rather than styrofoam popcorn, saving on clean-up time and therefore clients' money.

On the other hand, *Business Week* praises Zebra Technologies, maker of high-quality bar-code printers, as an ROQ stand-out. Zebra wins points for coming out with a less expensive, no-frills version of the same printer—but designing it to be impossible to upgrade. That way, the new model wouldn't compete with the expensive one; "margins on the new printer match those from Zebra's

---

Quality = Political Hammer

The following is excerpted from a speech by Representative Newt Gingrich of Georgia at the 1992 Republican National Convention:

The second contrast is between the Republican commitment to Edwards Deming's concept of profound knowledge and the quality revolution which his teaching has created. And on the other hand, the Democrats' commitment to their big city machines with unionized work rules. Deming taught the Japanese to focus on building quality with continuous improvement focused on the customer. If Deming's teaching was applied to education, health, defense, and other government systems, we would cut costs by at least 20 percent and double the quality of service. Yet the Democrats can't adopt the Deming quality revolution. Their unions simply won't let them.

In the January *Reader's Digest* article we learned that New York City has a contract with a janitor who gets paid $57,000 a year to mop a public school three times a year. That's right, not three times a week, not three times a month, not three times a quarter. Once every four months that $57,000 janitor has to mop the floor. Of course, he has to mop the cafeteria once a week. However, they serve 25 meals a week in the cafeteria and the principal said, I have children who study around the filth.

The truth is, you can't deliver quality and you can't deliver continuous improvement for the citizen when you have a unionized government bureaucracy.[30]

original line."

Business Week points out that a healthier economy and rising sales in the mid-1990s may have made some companies more nonchalant about quality. U.S. companies that compete with Japanese firms have gotten a break because of higher prices for imports, caused by the expensive yen. Companies' focus on quality is likely to fade in and out, depending on their view of what the market will bear.

Our guess is that the Return on Quality movement will prove longer-lasting, if not under that name, than the 1980s' mad dash for quality. Quality, after all, can come and go, but profits are always the bottom line.

Notes

1. *Oxford American Dictionary*, 1980.

2. This is simplified. Under some conditions producing to tighter tolerances might in fact produce slightly greater benefit to the customers, and under other conditions might produce slightly less.

3. Management leaflet, 1991.

4. Philip B. Crosby, *Quality Is Free: The Art of Making Quality Certain,* Mentor paperback edition, New York, 1980.

5. Crosby, p. 40.

6. Brochure for seminar put on by Quality Alert Institute, December 11-13, 1991, Troy, MI, at Institute for Quality and Productivity, Eli Broad Graduate School of Management, Michigan State University.

7. See Janice Klein, "The Human Costs of Manufacturing Reform," *Harvard Business Review*, Vol. 67, No. 2, March-April 1989, pp. 60-66.

8. Helen Fogel, "Blueprint for Saturn: Union, Company Work in Harmony at Fiero Factory," *Detroit Free Press*, February 17, 1985.

9. John Lippert and Paul Lienert, "How Pontiac's Fiero Met Its End," *Detroit Free Press*, March 20, 1988.

10. John Lippert, "GM Recalls All of Its '84 Fieros," *Detroit Free Press*, November 26, 1987.

11. James Risen, "Assembly-Line Innovations," *Detroit Free Press*, September 18, 1983.

12. Quoted in Risen.

13. John Lippert, "GM To Idle Fiero Plant, Kill Model," *Detroit Free Press*, March 2, 1988.

14. R.M. Donnelly, "GMPS Report #1" to General Motors Operating Group Vice Presidents, June 18, 1987.

15. *Total Quality Newsletter*, Lakewood Publications, Minneapolis, sample issue, 1991.

16. All information about ISO standards, unless otherwise noted, comes from ISO 9000: *International Standards for Quality Management*, 2nd edition, ISO Central Secretariat, Geneva, 1992.

17. Quoted in Gary Spizzen, "The ISO 9000 Standards: Creating a Level Field for International Quality," *National Productivity Review*, Summer 1992, p. 334.

18. Sara E. Hagigh, "Obtaining EC Product Approvals after 1992: What American Manufacturers Need to Know," *Business America,* February 24, 1992, p. 30.

19. Quoted in *Total Quality Newsletter*, April 1992, p. 3.

20. Twenty out of 1,000 points are allocated to "Public Responsibility." This is explained as "how the company promotes quality awareness" and encourages employee leadership with external groups, and how the company includes business ethics, environmental protection, and waste management in its quality policies and practices. Even this tiny reference to "environment" is not about how much damage is done, but the internal procedures for handling environmental questions.

21. *Ward's Auto World*, April 1991

22. Mark Ivey, "The Ecstasy and the Agony," *Business Week*, October 21, 1991, p. 40.

23. Jim Smith and Mark Oliver, "The Baldrige Boondoggle," *Machine Design*, August 6, 1992.

24. *Detroit Free Press*, December 14, 1990.

25. Paul Froiland, "Quality in a Box," *Training,* February 1994, Vol. 31, No. 2, p. 66.

26. Philip Crosby in "Debate: Does the Baldrige Award Really Work?" *Harvard Business Review*, Vol. 70, January-February, 1992, p. 127.

27. W. Edwards Deming in "Does the Baldrige Award Really Work?" p. 134.

28. "Quality: From Buzzword to Payoff," *Business Week*, August 8, 1994, p. 80.

29. Unless otherwise noted, information following is from David Griesing, "Making Quality Pay: How Companies are Rethinking the Management Buzzword of the 1980s," *Business Week,* August 8, 1994, pp. 54-59.

30. Transcript ID 861115, Tuesday, August 18, 1992.

Chapter 15

Mutual Interests and Partnership

Advocates of participation say that employers and unions have more in common than in conflict. But a comparison of employers' goals and unions' goals shows that the areas of conflict are larger than any temporarily overlapping interests. The notion of "win-win" avoids the question of who wins how much. Mutual gains bargaining encourages bargainers to reach an agreement no matter what; to consider the interests of the bargainers themselves; to focus on the local situation rather than a pattern or principle; and to pretend that power is not an issue at the table. In joint committees, the employer has far more resources than does the union: a hierarchical structure, access to experts, power of implementation, the consensus process. Gainsharing plans pit workers against each other, for ever-diminishing rewards.

THE IDEA THAT WORKERS and management have mutual interests is the theoretical underpinning of participation programs, joint programs, and partnership. In this chapter we put this idea under a microscope, and then look at how it is applied in practice. In particular we will look at joint committees, partnership, mutual gains bargaining, and gainsharing.

The argument for mutual interests goes something like this:

> Perhaps the adversary relationship between labor and management made sense some 50 years ago. But the situation has changed.
>
> New technology requires a higher level of skill, working together, and communication. The high levels of competition, particularly from abroad, and customers' demands for higher quality require that we all work closely together. In the last generation we may have been able to pass along the cost of poor quality and inefficiency to the customer, but those days are over. These days, we have more in common in than we have in conflict.

In the public sector the argument flows along similar lines:

> The days when the government could keep expanding and printing money are over. The taxpayer revolt combined with the scrutiny that modern media can give to public operations means that waste and inefficiency are no longer tolerated. We can't afford not to work together to rebuild trust in government operations.

Frequently this notion is expressed by a familiar diagram:

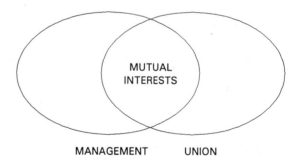

A particularly dangerous variant is the one with three circles: union, management, and "the people."

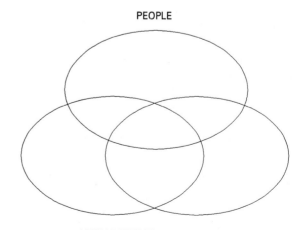

The idea is that the shaded area of mutual interests provides a foundation for working together without resentments, since both sides can feel that they are making gains. The solutions reached on this basis are "win-win."

Much of the argument for participation programs is based on the idea that unions and management have overriding mutual interests that can serve as reference points for decision making. The old style of adversarial bargaining is inappropriate. The main task is to "problem solve." The parties start from the overall principle of mutual interests, gather the facts in some objective manner, use a neutral facilitator and experts to help them see the truth, and then deduce (problem solve) the objectively best solution for the problem. See chapter 9 on Saturn for an example of this approach.

Consultants Edward Cohen-Rosenthal and Cynthia Burton are leading pro-union promoters of the mutual interests method. They insist that the method is based not on interpersonal relationships or trust but rather

> A hard-nosed version of cooperation. It may involve cooperating with people you don't trust—or even like.

Managers and union leaders do it because it is in their inter-

ests. The starting point for cooperation is mutual respect and common interest. Unions are there to promote worker's interests—not to fight management. The managers' role is to promote shareholders' interests—not to engage in ideological combat with unions. You can have mutual gain.[1]

CONFLICT IS PRIMARY

Our approach is different. It is based on the experience that the *conflict* of long-term interests between companies and their workers is both fundamental and primary. Some mutual interests do exist, but most are based on changing circumstances, and they are outweighed by the conflict. This is not a question of the good will of the parties, but of bottom-line interests and roles. It is the job of management to maximize profits for the company, and a "good" management (from the stockholder point of view) does this by any means necessary. It is the union's job to secure a better life for workers. Look at the Goals vs. Means exercise for a graphic representation of this simple (and time-honored) idea.

That said, let's back up for a moment and discuss the common interests of management and workers that do

---

Exercise
Goals Vs. Means

Time: 20-30 minutes
Equipment: overhead projector or flipchart; different colored markers
Materials: handout for participants like grid below (blank)
Objectives: The purpose of this exercise is to help participants see 1) the difference between management's long-term goals and the means or methods management uses to reach those goals, 2) the difference between management's goals and the union's goals, 3) the difference between the union's goals and the union's means, 4) where all these do and don't overlap.

This exercise is intended for use with private employers. It can be adapted for public employers, though that relationship is more complicated.

Description for instructor: On the projector or flipchart, draw a simple grid like the handout. First, ask what management's goals are. (Explain that "management" means top management, not supervisors.) People are bound to say "profits." Often other goals such as "increase market share" or "quality" are mentioned. If so, ask whether these are the end goals, or a means to reach the end goal. For example, sometimes management tries to increase profits by increasing market share. Other times, they decide to carve out a small but lucrative niche in the market. High quality may be a means to profits, but so may mediocre quality at a low cost. Write any "means" that are mentioned in the means square.

Power or control are frequently suggested as goals of management. This sometimes generates intense debate. If the group is divided, list it in both "goals" and "means."

Next, ask for management's means.

Participants should generate a long and sometimes contradictory list. For example, sometimes companies try to increase profits by increasing market share. Other times, they decide to carve out a small but lucrative niche in the market. High quality may be a means to profits, but so may mediocre quality at a low cost. Similarly with labor relations: at times when there is a labor shortage, management may need to pay high wages to attract skilled workers; high wages could be a means to the goal of profits. More often, cutting wages as low as possible is the chosen tactic.

The point is that management has a wide range of means to choose from, and will choose based on the prevailing management fad, the situation in the economy (such as exchange rates, recession), and other factors. Management is not committed to quality or even productivity for their own sakes, but according to whether and how much they will help the company to be profitable.

Next, ask for a list of the union's goals. This will turn out to be a much longer list than management's. Don't forget the larger, societal goals that unions fight for, such as unemployment insurance, women's rights, national health care. Is "quality" a union goal? Why or why not? Is it a means? You may have an interesting discussion if some par-

"Our workplace cooperation philosophy can easily be applied to other areas of conflict."

exist. After all, there must be an area of mutual interest in any voluntary relationship. Presumably, the only reason they continue the relationship is that there is something in it for each of them. So management hires workers, and they come to work, because their interests do intersect—workers' interest in making a decent living, and management's interest in making a profit.

There are more. Both employer and employee have an interest in the building not burning down. It is in neither's interest to be on strike all the time. Probably both the union and the company do better with shorter, well-organized bargaining meetings than with rambling wastes of time.

As the exercise shows, there are some policies that *could* be in the interest of both management and union. Management might decide to operate with high capital investment and high wages for workforce stability. But at some future date managers may very well decide that a more profitable strategy is to operate at very low wages, and absorb the costs of high turnover.

Similarly, improving quality could seem to unite the two sides. Say the company insists that to get

ticipants say that the union should have only one bottom line goal (like job security).

Next, look at the union's means.

Try to get as broad a list as possible, including tactics that are not commonly used nowadays and tactics that don't often work. For example, during the 1980s many unions made contract concessions as a means to win the goal of job security.

Finally, ask participants to look at where the two lists—management's and union's—overlap.

Do the goals overlap at all? Do the means? Under what circumstances? Can the union count on management to keep using the same means indefinitely? What could cause management to switch tactics?

Participants should see that when the answers for union and management are the same, the overlap involves means, not goals.

A Typical Grid:

	Management	Union
Goals	Profits Control or Power?	Good wages Benefits Safe work Equality on the job Fairness (no favoritism More jobs Job security Healthy work Interesting work Control over work life Control over management decisions Civil rights Women's rights National health care Social justice Clean up environment

Means	Quality
	Productivity
	Reputation as a craft producer
	Low wages/benefits
	Outsourcing
	Contracting Out
	Low prices
	High prices
	Advertising
	Speed-up
	Union-busting
	Lock-outs
	Hard bargaining
	Whipsawing
	Lobbying
	Deregulation
	Election of friendly politicians
	NAFTA
	TQM
	Eliminate classifications
	Reengineering
	Training for employees
	Good personnel policies or
	  high wages to reduce turnover
	Cheap raw materials
		Collective bargaining
		Strikes
		Grievance procedure
		Legislation
		Demonstrations
		Labor law reform
		Organize the unorganized
		TQM
		Concessions
		Solidarity
		Do high-quality work
		Cooperation with management
		Increase productivity
		Work harder
		Whipsawing
		Training
		Union education
		Seniority
		Committees
		  (women's, civil rights, etc.)
		Lobbying
		Elections
		Ally with community

MANAGEMENT SEMINARS INC.

THE 3 Cs of Cooperation
1) COOPT
2) CONFUSE
3) CRUSH

R⌐M

"It's what we call a win, win, win situation!"

quality, it must keep the same worker on the same job every day, though workers would prefer to rotate (see chapter 8). Union officials agree, feeling that high quality will ensure job security—a win-win situation. But as worker after worker has testified, management's attention to quality can very soon revert to the usual push for quantity. When that happens, will the union be able to get rotation back?

When any tactic on the two lists of means overlaps, it is likely to be a temporary phenomenon, dependent on changeable conditions, and not because there is a harmony of overall aims.

The conclusions we draw: 1) When the union thinks it's in a situation where it can use the same means as management to reach their separate goals, it had better check out exactly what temporary conditions seem to make this true. 2) The union should never give up its ability to use its own means—say a strike—to pursue its own separate goals.

This is especially true in the arena of changing work methods and work relations. Since management has the upper hand, once it gets what it wants, the promises, the sweeteners, and the idea of a trade-off seem to disappear. See chapter 21 for an example involving the Postal Service and the Mail Handlers Union. In 1993 the UAW spent months negotiating a Modern Operating Agreement with Ford Dearborn Assembly Plant. In order to be cooperative so that the new model launch would run well, the union agreed that the company could start up under the new work rules even while they hammered out the details

of the contract. But once production was running smoothly, the company had second thoughts about a number of provisions, including full training, job rotation, and team leader selection, and lost interest in further bargaining.

We suggest three reasons why the mutual interest approach is not helpful for unions.

1. AVOIDS THE REAL ISSUE

In chapter 13, we noted that the sample problems used in participation training courses always have clear solutions that hurt no one. "Improve the lighting," for example, conveniently turns out to be the way to help workers do a better job. Similarly, when consultants train unions in the notion of "win-win," one form or another of the orange problem is popular. This problem is used to teach the distinction between "positions" and "interests," discussed later on.

We have a box of oranges. John, Bob, Tom, Steve, and Joe each demands to have all of them. To the extent that one gets more oranges, the others get less. But do not despair. If we look beneath the boys' demands to get the oranges (the "position") and discover the real interest of each person, we see that there *can* be a win-win solution.

It turns out that each one wants a different part of the orange for a different purpose. John wants them for a juggling act and then will be through with them. Bob wants orange juice, Tom wants the seeds, Steve needs the peel to flavor some cookies he's baking, and Joe wants the pulp.[2]

Glory be. It is possible for everyone to get *all* they wanted from *all* the oranges just by understanding and working from their true interests, rather than hardened positions. And, of course, by communicating honestly.

Both the lighting problem and the orange problem are convenient for the win-win argument because they are written to contain a clear optimal solution for all parties concerned. But most win-win situations are not like that at all. The question is not just whether each party comes out ahead, but *how much* each party gains—how the pie is divided, in other words.

In most of the real issues that confront unions and management, there are no solutions that are optimal for everybody at the same time, even if they are "win-win." Consider this example:

> Two people work together to move some furniture. One owns the truck and the other does most of the lifting. They get paid $100. What is the win-win solution for dividing the money?

No matter how the money is divided, as long as each gets more than zero we could call this a win-win arrangement. Neither would get the money if they did not work together.[3] Both are ahead ("win-win"). True but trivial. The truck owner could argue that she should get $90 and the muscle-guy $10. The second person could argue the reverse. "Win-win" does not equal "fair." The win-win notion doesn't help us answer the question of how to divide the money.

A union analogy: clerical workers agree to word-process more pages per day, in exchange for a wage increase. It's win-win for workers and employer—but who decides how big a wage increase?

Nor would "expanding the pie" by itself solve the question. We still need to determine how the extra pie is to be divided.

2. BOILS DOWN TO MONEY OR POWER

Proponents of "win-win" bargaining like to distinguish between "distributive" and "integrative" issues. Distributive issues are ones, like wages, that involve how to distribute a fixed pie. They are the issues where is still a place for the adversary relationship. Integrative issues, on the other hand, provide the opportunity for both sides to gain something.

Cohen-Rosenthal and Burton, for example, suggest that absenteeism, job security, flexibility, classifications, productivity, benefit cost containment, and overtime are all areas that may have integrative solutions.[4]

But most workplace questions—including those that sound win-win—translate into money or power. And on money and power, interests are not mutual—rarely is there a solution optimal for management and labor.

• Flexibility. As described in chapter 8, flexibility means more choice for managers and less for workers, and these days it almost always means loss of jobs.

• Quality. In chapter 14 we illustrated the possible costs to workers of management-defined quality programs.

• Making the company "competitive." See chapter 2 for a discussion of how competition is opposed to workers' interests.

• Training for better skills. In chapter 35 we discuss

how management often refuses to give workers advanced training because it increases their marketability and thus their power.

• High wages for workers, so they can afford to buy the products they make. We describe in chapter 2 why companies are not concerned about their own employees' buying power; they've found other markets.

• Health and safety. Workers' interest in a safe job is absolute. Managers may have a humanitarian interest in preventing injuries, and they certainly don't like the costs of workers' compensation and sick leave. But management also weighs the expense of working safely and the need to get production out.

• Employee Assistance Programs. Workers with problems get help; management retains experienced workers. Win-win? Such programs may make sense for management when there is a labor shortage or when the workers in question are hard to replace. But when new workers are a dime a dozen...

• An attendance bonus. Management gets better attendance; many workers get extra money. Is this win-win? Although the bonus may look like extra money, in any contract there is a total money package. Any money devoted to a special bonus is subtracted from what could have been a lump sum or wage increase for all. So the effect may actually be a wage *cut* for those whose attendance is less than stellar. And if the bonus is awarded by group, it's a set-up for peer pressure.

We could go on. Dig a little deeper into any contract clause or agreement that's claimed to be win-win, and you're likely to find a sharp conflict.

3. REALITY CHECK

Cohen-Rosenthal and Burton refer to a model that puts labor relations on a continuum with four categories.

| Confron-tation | Armed Truce | Working Harmony | Union-Mgt Cooperation |

The first, confrontation, is not explained but presumably means management is taking direct action against the union.

The authors then cite several characteristics for each of the other three categories, the first being "management's attitude":

> Armed Truce: A feeling on the part of management that unions and collective bargaining are at best necessary evils in modern industrial society.
>
> Working Harmony: A genuine acceptance of collective bargaining on management's part based on the conviction that the union is an asset as well as a liability in running the business
>
> Union-management Cooperation: A conviction on the part of management that the union as an institution is both willing and able to organize cooperative activity among employees to achieve lower costs and increased efficiency.[5]

Fair enough. Now just what is "management's attitude" toward unions today? Not what they say, but what

they do. If you want to find out, try organizing the non-union sectors of a partly-unionized company. Toyota, the United Auto Workers' partner at NUMMI, for example, is resisting the union at its factory in Kentucky. See also the box in chapter 1 titled "War Zone," for a current example of "management's attitude."

PARTNERSHIP

It used to be that when labor-management cooperation took a highly organized form it was called "jointness." In principle, the employer agreed to bring in the union as an equal partner in all kinds of activities and policy areas it had previously declared to be management's sole prerogatives. Thus the union and management had equal say on bodies in charge of quality, absenteeism, safety training, ergonomics, and the like. See, for example, the chart on "QWL/EI Structure" in chapter 16.[6]

"Partnership" goes beyond jointness. No longer are the mutual interests for specific defined purposes. Partnership suggests *fundamental* mutual interests covering the whole operation of the company or agency. Thus in the federal sector, the unions will be partners in "reinventing the agency and creating a high performance organization,"[7] which means union leaders and management will reorganize the agency to increase productivity. What this means in practice is described in chapter 19.

Most workers do not take pronouncements of *worker*-management partnership seriously. It does not jibe with the increased stress, speed-up, and insecurity they are experiencing on the job. If anything, though, they do take seriously the idea of partnership between the *union* and management. They think of "the union" as the union leadership. Therefore partnership, with its elaborate structures and innumerable leadership meetings, feeds the feeling that union officials are in bed with management. If the two circles in the mutual interest diagram are smushed further together, they ultimately become one. If the circles overlap so much, do we really need a union?

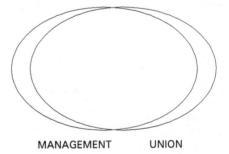

MANAGEMENT   UNION

Cohen-Rosenthal and Burton give two examples of what they consider the highest form of mutual interests behavior: the partnerships of UAW Local

1853 and Saturn, and the Shell-Sarnia plant in Ontario with the Energy and Chemical Workers Union.

The Saturn plant has become the best-known model of "partnership." But many union members there are beginning to feel that they have no union at all, as we discuss in chapter 9.

The Shell-Sarnia plant also has problems. One steward said the union has begun to feel "on shaky ground, with no way to protect people." Shell management used the plant as a model to set up a new, non-union plant. Labor researcher Don Wells concludes, "Overall, Shell managers have learned more from the Sarnia project about keeping unions out than the ECWU has learned about getting unions into such plants."[8]

The Communications Workers and AT&T have what the Dunlop Commission called an "integrated partnership" in their joint "Workplace of the Future" program. AT&T describes it as a "framework for change which includes unions as joint partners in planning and implementing change based on mutual respect and mutual gain."[9] At the Dunlop Commission hearings, though, CWA organizers testified that AT&T was backing its non-union NCR division in fighting a CWA organizing drive. Indeed, the parent company was moving high-tech work out of its unionized sectors and into NCR.[10] See chapter 24.

Xerox and the Amalgamated Clothing and Textile Workers Union (ACTWU) have had a longstanding cooperative relationship. In the 1970s the company went into crisis, plunging from a market share of 80 percent to 40. The union gave substantial concessions and participated in one participation plan after another, including study teams, a no-layoff guarantee in 1984, a Business Area Work Group structure, and a top-down Total Quality Management Program.[11] Union leaders there have been known to refuse speaking invitations unless their company counterparts are invited too.

But despite all the cooperation, in 1993 the *New York Times* headlined, "A Profitable Xerox Plans to Cut Staff by 10,000." Although the cuts amounted to 10 percent of the workforce and business experts warned they might damage employee morale, Wall Street responded with a big jump in stock prices. Apparently the public announcement caught the union leadership by surprise.[12] The company has also decided to assign the bulk of its internal computer operations to the notoriously anti-union contractor EDS.

Under certain circumstances unions may gain something from partnership. In the federal sector, one of the conditions of partnership is that management will bargain over issues it previously declared off limits to the union (although as yet management does not seem to have lived up to this part of the deal). ACTWU and Levi Strauss announced in 1994 that in exchange for a partnership arrangement in the company's union plants, management will remain neutral when the union tries to organize the non-union ones.

Perhaps many unions would jump at this deal. But they should first consider carefully: in becoming a "partner," in throwing in its lot so completely with the company, is the union trading away its right to actually *represent* its members on the shop floor, in exchange for the right to collect dues from a larger number of members? Is the union trading off quality of representation for a greater quantity under contract?

At Levi Strauss's Harlingen, Texas plant, workers have been reorganized into teams that work under incentives. The goal is to cut the time to make a garment from 10 days to less than a week. The first result was a drop in wages for many workers. The Economic Policy Institute, in a study of the apparel industry, found that "working in modules—or teams—is more stressful on average" than the old system. ACTWU's president agreed, adding "but we are trying to preserve jobs."

The partnership agreement, however, offers no job guarantees. Meanwhile, on the union side, the percentage of membership at the Harlingen plant rose from 50 percent to 65 percent in six months. A company vice president explained the neutrality agreement: "A [joint] steering committee...will decide in which plants to proceed with the redesign effort. Should the committee choose to go into a non-union facility, then both sides, in a non-adversarial manner, will give information to employees concerning union membership. At that point it will be totally up to the employees to decide."[13]

This example illustrates that for unions, partnership is junior partnership. Here's how one advocate of cooperation describes the situation:

> In the great majority of the cases unions have little choice but to cooperate...Union leaders as advocates for the general welfare and benefit of employees must become tomorrows human resources management experts and must understand far better the running of a profitable business. As advocates and experts, union leaders have the opportunity to improve the lives of their members and simultaneously show the full potential for deriving necessary added value via the improved management and utilization of its human resources.[14]

Guilt and Shame

The foundation for partnership, we're told, is that management has finally realized workers are not just there for the money; they are interested and motivated. They don't need supervision constantly watching them. But some of the literature reveals very different assumptions.

For example, one of the studies the Dunlop Commission uses to support its case argues that firms should

> develop an environment of positive peer pressure by instilling a sense of guilt and shame in workers...Workers who do not respond to shame must be "weeded out" or "converted"...Practices like quality circles and work teams may be just as important for their cultural effects on team spirit and for the opportunities they create for workers to monitor each other as they are for the specific work tasks that take place in teams.[15]

We suggest that when you have no other choice, cooperation is not really cooperation at all, but bowing down to power. If you can't beat them join them. In this view, the future for labor leaders is to serve as an extension of the company personnel department—to make sure that company policies have a human face.

MUTUAL GAINS BARGAINING

"Mutual Gains Bargaining," sometimes called "Mutual Interest Bargaining" or "Principled Bargaining," contains some useful ideas for unionists, but often actually undermines a union's ability to bargain in its own behalf.

The best place for information on mutual gains bargaining is the basic books on the subject. *Getting to Yes: Negotiating Agreement Without Giving In*, by Roger Fisher and William Ury, came out of the Harvard Negotiation Project.[16] The book and its sequels make for pleasant reading with interesting examples. Much of what they present is good applied common sense. Negotiating a contract requires some special skills. It is possible to understand the issues, know how to motivate, mobilize, and lead the membership, and still feel lost when you get to the bargaining table. So the information in these books can be useful to union bargainers. That is the good news.

Mutual Gains Bargaining (MGB) teaches a number of techniques that can help two parties reach agreement in a range of relationships: union-management, parent-child, supplier-customer, and others. Many of these are the familiar skills taught in team training: active listening skills, or repeating in your own words what the other person has said (also called "mirroring"); describing problems in terms of how they affect you rather than ascribing intent to the other person (use "I" statements instead of "you" statements); brainstorming; problem-solving techniques.

At the same time, mutual gains bargaining also includes techniques that experienced negotiators can use to manipulate situations. These include how to show concern for the other negotiator's standing and provide face-saving language. The literature discusses how to use and counter tactics such as "lock-in" (say, purposely painting yourself in a corner by making a public commitment), and good cop/bad cop.

The basic elements of MGB are:

1. Separate the people issues from the substance issues.

Address both. Recognize that people have deeply held emotions and values and therefore different ways of perceiving things. Try to understand the way that the other sees the situation. Build a long-term relationship and a foundation of mutual trust in the sense of being able to count on each other's word. Use techniques that increase communication rather than stop it.

For example, beginning with certain stock phrases reduces defensiveness and allows more attention to the issues:

Please correct me if I'm wrong...

Could I ask you a few questions to see if my facts are right?

What is the principle behind your action? (What interest is your position intended to satisfy?)

Let me see if I understand what you are saying.

2. Bargain over interests, not over positions.

A "position" usually takes the form of a specific demand. For example, a *position* would be the demand for two additional holidays. But underlying that specific demand would be a more general *interest*: the members want more time off.

The company's position would be firmly against the extra holidays. Its interest is to maintain the number of days production is running. There is no possibility of reaching a common ground on these two counterposed positions.

However, if the focus is on the two parties' *interests*, it may be possible to find a solution that gives everyone additional time off while maintaining the total number of days of production. For example, workers could get two additional vacation days, that they would take at different times of the year, the plant would stay open, and the needed replacements could be hired.

The idea is to treat negotiations as a joint problem-solving activity. Specifying all the interests that a solution has to satisfy becomes a problem-solving activity in which both sides can participate.

In discussing interests, "peel the layers off the onion," ask the "five why's," and somehow get to and work with the root interests.

3. Invent options for mutual gain.

Brainstorm a list of possibilities that might satisfy some or all of the interests of either party. You might find solutions that give both sides everything they want. Identify shared interests and look for a way to build on them. Which different interests dovetail, like items that are low cost to you and high value to them? Jack Spratt and his wife did not have to argue about dinner.

4. Use objective criteria.

Agree on the standards to use in measuring. For example, if the question is wages, agree on the method of gathering data on comparable wages in other companies.

The more you bring standards of fairness, efficiency, or scientific merit to bear on your particular problem, the more likely you are to produce a final package that is wise and fair.[17]

Given that so much of the participation/partnership literature builds on the assumption that an overall dominant common interest does exist, it is refreshing to find in mutual gains bargaining the idea that interests might actually be in conflict, and that it is still possible to bargain under those conditions.

BATNA

One of the most valuable ideas of mutual gains bargaining is that each party has a BATNA (Best Alternative to Negotiated Agreement). To negotiate successfully, you have to know what you will do if you *don't* succeed at the

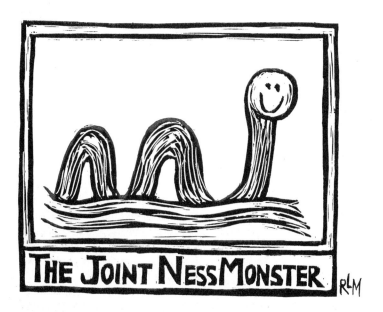

THE JOINT NESS MONSTER

Widely believed to be a dinosaur from an earlier era, "Nessy" sightings have occurred in the 1890s, 1920s, 1930s, and 1990s.

table. That is the real alternative you must measure against any possible negotiated settlement. And for obvious reasons, you must try to understand the BATNA of the other side.

> Keep your BATNA in your pocket. When you're under heavy attack and feel panicky, you can pat your pocket and say to yourself, "I'm okay if it doesn't go okay."[18]

This point cannot be overemphasized. There are always alternatives to a negotiated settlement. There is no reason that a negotiated alternative, or one negotiated at this time, is necessarily your best approach.

The BATNA concept suggests that an important aspect of negotiations is not what goes on at the table but what happens outside. You can help yourself by strengthening your BATNA and/or by weakening that of the other party.

> A good BATNA usually does not already exist; it needs to be developed. If your BATNA is not very strong, you should take steps to improve it.[19]

For example, if management knows that your members are not prepared to strike and will be resentful if you call one, then you probably don't have a good BATNA. You will have to accept a very small settlement in the contract. But if you and management both believe that the membership is aching for a strike, that you will win the strike, and your standing will rise in the membership, then the bargaining situation is very different.

On the other hand, management's BATNA may be a strike, believing that this is its chance to bust the union. Or, recognizing the risks of a strike, your BATNA might be a well-organized internal campaign. And so on.

The BATNA concept applies not just to the whole contract; it can also be used on smaller items. Suppose

management has added new tasks to a number of jobs and the union wants some negotiated language to clarify the issue. The alternatives for the union are not simply negotiated agreement versus the way things were. The union can consider a number of BATNAs—group grievances, work-to-rule, or T-shirt protests. There are lots of possibilities.

This view of negotiations fits very much into the notion of strategic planning that we encourage (see *A Troublemakers Handbook*, the *Strategy Guide*, and chapter 31). The BATNA concept implies that in thinking about negotiations, your attention should focus first on what you can do to strengthen your BATNA and de-fang management's.

THE BAD NEWS ABOUT MUTUAL GAINS BARGAINING

Embedded within the general ideas of mutual gains bargaining are concepts that undermine the union.

1. In principle, MGB training would not have to imply that a mutual interest must exist. Two parties with very different interests can bargain in the trade-off style, so that each party gains something, even if there is no common interest in any one area. With this understanding, MGB can be a useful tool. But in practice, the thrust of MGB is to assume that significant mutual interests do exist; the task is to identify them.

For example, training exercises freely interchange the bargaining parties, from spouses, to parents and children, suppliers/customers, nations, individuals and bosses, unions and management. This helps feed the implicit notion that a common overriding interest exists for everyone ("let's start with the assumption that we are committed to each other"). That's a reasonable starting point when talking about spouses and family and maybe even when talking about suppliers and customers. But it can never be the starting point in labor-management negotiations.

2. MGB heavily biases toward reaching an agreement—any agreement, even if it is not in your interests. We have already mentioned how easy it is for trainers and facilitators to forget the BATNA part of preparing for negotiations. MGB training usually recommends that the parties use a facilitator. Trainers and facilitators have a vested interest in concluding an agreement. Failed negotiations do not look good on a facilitator's resume.

When the principle becomes "come to an agreement," then other principles are submerged. Having an agreement becomes so important in and of itself that the union can lose perspective on what the stakes really are.

The dynamic of the mutual gains bargaining process itself also pushes artificially toward reaching an agreement. MGB can be time-consuming, with interest identification exercises, brainstorming, option charting, and so on.

Since most negotiations take place against the backdrop of time constraints, using so much time for the MGB process itself places a lot of pressure on the negotiators to make the final decision quickly. It is good to keep in mind the advice in the MGB basics (even though it is often ignored in practice):

> A good negotiator rarely makes an important decision on the spot. The psychological pressure to give in is too great. A little time and distance help separate the people from the problem.[20]

3. MGB methods contribute to separating union bargainers off from the membership. This is already a big problem for many unions: leaders lose touch with the members or see themselves as servicing the members rather than leading and organizing them.

This kind of thinking is reinforced when the bargainers are trained to think in terms of "interests," because it is easy to slip into thinking in terms of the interests of the negotiators themselves, rather than the interests of those they represent. For example, in one study of MGB, union bargainers thought of the membership as a "second table"—another group with which the leadership had to bargain the same issue.[21]

On top of this, MGB encourages negotiators on both sides to think about their common interests as negotiators. In training, bargainers are encouraged to understand that the people on the other side of the table are human, that they have a need to save face. While this concern itself is reasonable, it is dangerous to give it much weight. And the MGB training is designed to magnify this mutual identification (see the box).

Perhaps the subtle pressure to shift the union bargainers' loyalty to "the process" and to the "negotiations community" can be seen in the Federal Mediation and Conciliation Service's (FMCS) definition of consensus: Each understands the other's view and "Whether or not I prefer this decision, I support it because it was arrived at in a fair and open manner."[22]

Because of this emphasis on the togetherness of the bargainers, MGB also tends to exacerbate the problems most union negotiators have with the "confidentiality" issue. Some degree of confidentiality is needed, to allow for the possibility of frank discussion without concern that a slip of the tongue or a partial proposal will prove embarrassing. But what confidentiality often means in practice is that union bargainers are disconnected from their base, while upper management is able to stay on top of the bargaining.

4. It turns out that most "interests" behind the "positions" themselves have underlying interests.

Let's say we start with the position:

> The union asks for an 8-hour limit on mandatory overtime. (All other overtime would be voluntary.)

The interest behind this:

> The membership would like a reduction in mandatory overtime.

The interest behind this:

> Members would like to be able to spend more time with their families or other personal activities.

The interest behind this:

> Members feel they should work to live, not live to work.

And so on.

If you continue digging beneath interests (for both labor and management), you will end up with conclusions like those in the Goals vs. Means exercise earlier in this chapter. Namely, ultimately management's interests tend to reduce to more profits. Workers' interest is a better life.

5. This brings us to the question of power. The outcome of negotiations is not determined by the process the bargainers use or by the genius of the negotiators. It is determined by how much power each side has.

But MGB advocates suggest that MGB is an alternative to using power, threats, and intimidation in bargaining. FMCS training reminds us that "power is not used in Interest-Based Bargaining."[23] To deny that power exists when one side is clearly more powerful should be seen simply as an attempt to maintain power relations as they are.

Power determines the framework for the negotiations.

The MGB Training Package

The hidden message of many MGB training programs is that everything the union does revolves around negotiations. One sure give-away is when the training downplays or loses the BATNA concept, which provides the critical external reality check for the internal negotiations process. Federal Mediation and Conciliation Service training materials ignore the BATNA concept, and most training programs zip by it if they mention it at all.

If negotiations per se are the center of the union-management relationship, then there are two kinds of "success." Short-term success is measured by whether you reach a formal agreement. Long-term success is determined by whether the relationship between the negotiating parties is improved. If negotiations are the key, it is only one step to seeing the relationship between the negotiators (union leadership and company personnel department) as the most important concern, rather than the relationship between workers and corporate policy.

Most MGB training covers the full gamut of the kinds of participation training we discussed in chapter 13, with all the subtle appeals and dangers. FMCS's Interest-Based Bargaining training, for example, includes a "lost at sea" exercise, and its partnership training uses joint "values clarification," with a modern version of the "girl-sailor-friend" exercise.

It should come as no surprise when management or a facilitator proposes MGB training as a five-day experience off-site at a nice out-of-town hotel with a golf course and other amenities, so that both sides can get a better understanding of each other as human beings.

But power is fluid. Much of the company's power derives from its legal authority over the basic financial decisions. Most of the union's power depends on its solidarity, ability to mobilize in concert, and take actions that prevent management from carrying out its will. If the bargaining arrangement itself weakens the union, by separating off the leaders from the members, then the balance of power has changed. That is why it is so important that union leaders approach all aspects of the negotiations process, including confidentiality, from the point of view of maintaining the solidarity of the union.

6. To disallow bargaining over a fixed "position" can put the union at a disadvantage. Positional bargaining is what unions have used to maintain an industry-wide pattern. Interest bargaining, on the other hand, emphasizes that each situation is unique, and therefore tends to break down pattern bargaining and industry standards. Its focus on local and immediate interests helps set the union up for whipsawing.

This is nothing inherently wrong with taking a position—also known as taking a stand. A position put forward by a union in negotiations may embody the experience of the trade union movement and its collective goals. To the extent that MGB makes illegitimate or strips the union of these two references, the union becomes more dependent on analyzing the details of the immediate circumstance from scratch. This in turn makes the union more dependent on so-called experts and consultants. And it turns out that neutral experts and consultants do not exist.

RESOURCES FOR JOINTNESS

There is no reason for unions to oppose "joint" union-management activities in principle. Unions should seize any opportunity to have more say over more of the aspects of work life than they do now. Ideally, workers through their union would have say over the quality of the product or service they produce and the methods, tools, and process of work, as well as health and safety and wages and benefits.

Proponents of jointness claim that joint committees give unions such a say. But how real that power is depends on two things: 1) how decision making is organized; 2) how union members and leaders view their joint activities.

Number 2 is the most important. The union will do best if leaders and members understand that any mutual interest with the employer is temporary, and if the union is prepared to act independently—adversarially—at any time.

Some areas allow for more mutual interest than others. At one end there is minimum mutual interest: e.g., a joint committee to reduce the number of jobs in the shop. At the other end might be the United Fund drive. Even there, the union needs to be clear that management has an agenda of its own.

Even supposedly technical questions usually reflect a management vs. a worker interest: for example, how many parts per million sulfuric acid is acceptable in the air

around a battery room? Which means that even so-called technical questions are really a form of bargaining.

Virtually all participation programs create new structures for decision making. These include joint committees of management and union representatives, both to deal with specific tasks and to oversee the program.

The most common demand that unions make about the operation of a joint committee is that at least half the members be from the union. Management and consultants give these committees more thought. For example, instead of a rectangular table with two sides, union on one side and company on the other, as in collective bargaining, seating may be at round tables with union and company intermixed. Instead of decision making through a two-sided negotiation process, with each side having the right to caucus, some form of problem-solving procedure and consensus resolution is used.

An important exercise for any union involved in joint activity is to consider what influence or power the com-

Mutual Gains at Unisys

The Labor-Management Council for Economic Renewal of Southeast Michigan reports on a mutual gains bargaining success story.[24]

The issue: "Team leader filled by management selection. In the union's eyes these bargaining unit members were too close to management, and too likely to overstep their bounds and act like supervision. Tensions between the leaders and shop floor workers led to two serious group grievances in 1993."

The group used mutual gains techniques, generated lists of interests, brainstormed options. One was proposed by the plant chair based on his visit to Mazda: that team leaders be elected.

Instead, "after intensive discussion it was agreed to use an innovative option that gave management as well as hourly employees a role in the decision."

The name of the position was changed to coordinator, rather than leader. Coordinators would be picked by consensus of the departments in which they worked, including area supervision and all hourly workers. If no agreement was reached, then the coordinators' responsibilities would be spread through the department.

The report does not say whether the union had a BATNA.

In effect, the mutual interests approach led to the union agreeing that the team leader was responsible both to management and to workers. In chapter 36, we discuss how two other locals took a different stand: that the team leader's first responsibility was to help and defend members, and if there was a conflict with management, leaders should know which side they were on. In other words, these locals took the position that the definition of the team leader's job was not a win-win situation, and fought for their own definition.

pany brings to the joint committee and what power or influence the union brings.

An examination of these lists reveals certain important patterns.

1. Management personnel are united.

Management is organized in a clear hierarchical fashion with power and authority derived from the level above.

That doesn't mean that management people will always be united in their functioning on a joint committee. To be effective, management will have to allow its members to disagree on various issues, maybe play good cop/bad cop. And, as every worker knows, there is a great deal of factionalism and backbiting among different sections of management. But on important issues, every management person will carry out the roles assigned by senior management, toward a common goal.

Compare this style to union functioning. Union power is more dispersed and, fortunately, subject to democracy.

Exercise

Resources for Jointness

Objective: To compare the different resources of management and union in joint programs.

Time: 30 minutes

On a flipchart, write "Resources for Jointness" at the top and make two columns, headed "Union" and "Management." First ask participants to put on the hat of a union representative on a joint committee. What resources or power can your management bring to bear on the joint program? You are likely to get a list like the following:

　　Knowledge about where management is going
　　Information on trends in the industry
　　Access to other companies
　　Money for research, organization, staff time
　　Speaks with one voice
　　Assigned people must participate
　　Ultimate power to approve
　　Has alternative methods to accomplish goals
　　Usually controls the agenda
　　Controls interpretation and implementation of committee decisions
　　Hires the consultants

Then ask what resources the union has. Typical responses are:

　　Trust and confidence of the membership
　　Knowledge about what is really happening in the workplace
　　Members know how to run the workplace and how to improve its functioning
　　Power to withhold labor and stop or slow production

Discussion: Whose resources are greater? Why? What conditions might cause the balance of resources to change? Important point: the joint program is designed to switch the *union's* resources—at least the first three mentioned above—to management's side.

There may be political factions within a union, divisions around work lines (skilled vs. production vs. office) or by department. In some workplaces more than one union represents the workers.

In addition, most unions do not think of a participation program as a place where union lines of authority might operate. Members are more likely to function as individuals.

For management, the unifying mechanism—"do what you're told"—is always in place to be used when top management needs it. On the union side, is there a mechanism to insure unity of functioning? If so, how does it get put into action?

2. Management has deep pockets.

Management hires the consultant and determines how much staff time will go into the participation program. It can research which version of participation program will best fit its needs. It is willing to invest big bucks in perks in the hope of influencing participants to management's way of thinking.

3. Management can influence the committees toward pre-planned "solutions."

Management knows that employees are more likely to "buy in" to a change if they believe they've thought of it themselves. In chapter 37, Al Benchich describes how his Quality Network group discovered that management not only had a solution in mind—the engineer had already designed a machine to implement it, waiting in a storeroom. Throughout the group's discussions, this engineer tried to steer the union members in the "logical" direction. Similarly, Larry Adams, in chapter 21, describes how a mail handlers' circle "came up with" an idea that cut certain jobs by half.

4. Management controls the implementation.

Once the joint committee makes a decision—say to buy a new machine—it's up to management to actually carry it out. There is lots of leeway to interpret what the decision meant: "The committee said that the machine would be installed by our own people, but we didn't have the proper equipment..." Or management can stall on implementing a decision—much as it does with implementing contract gains.

5. "Consensus" works in management's favor.

While consensus has its place, management and consultants tend to make it into a principle of joint operation. This should be a signal that the supposedly neutral and friendly atmosphere of joint operations is actually a stacked deck.

The usual meaning of consensus is that, as on a jury, all participants must agree with the proposed decision. The idea is that if doubts and disagreements are discussed thoroughly enough, and if everyone subjects their hesitations to enough scrutiny, a resolution can be reached that will satisfy everyone. But in practice, this takes too long—after all, the joint committee may only meet for an hour a week.

Therefore pure consensus is often modified to enable a group to actually reach a decision. For example, participants may not have to agree with a decision, but just be able to "live with it." At Saturn, members must be "70 percent comfortable" with consensus decisions (for more on Saturn's consensus procedures, see chapter 9).

Imagine how this might work: your circle, at management's request, has come up with an idea that will remove one person from your team. You don't like the idea, but everyone else has said it's okay with them. The leader, looking at his watch, asks you, "Well, Bob, are you at least 70 percent okay with this?" You think, "What's 70 percent okay? I won't feel like I have to go to confession. I won't toss and turn all night. I don't like it, but I can stand it..." Consensus is achieved.

Consensus is often described as "union veto power." But in practice, it is much harder than it sounds for union representatives on joint committees to use this power.

For one thing, the joint committee meets with the expectation that it will reach a decision—that it will not dissolve because consensus cannot be reached. Therefore the pressure is on to reach consensus, by hook or by crook.

Then, when there is a clear majority in one direction, peer pressure creates a sense of a group position. It then becomes very hard for an individual or a few people to stand against this sense of violating the group. The consensus norm itself creates the pressure that it is both desirable and important for everyone in the group to agree. This means that for one person to block consensus is at the very least asking a lot of the group, and possibly threatening its existence. Your commitment to the minority position has to be greater than your commitment to the group itself. In some workplaces, including Saturn, the "blocking party" must come up his or her own alternative.

Second, those who control implementation are more powerful under consensus decision making because the agreement that was reached may be more vague. This leaves more room for interpretation during implementation.

6. The program shifts union resources to management's side.

One of the main goals of participation programs is to transfer the members' knowledge of how jobs are done to management. Programs are designed to give management direct access to this information, in work teams, problem-solving groups, and suggestion plans, as well as procedures to get workers to document their jobs. The function of the joint committee is to get union leaders' cooperation in making the transfer of knowledge.

In addition, the program seeks to replace loyalty to the union with loyalty to management goals. Thus, two of

the important resources the union brings to the joint program are turned into their opposite—management resources.

In the Strategies section we suggest how to overcome the imbalance of power in jointness activities. But what unions should be concerned about most is that unless the union consciously moves in a different direction, jointness activities tend to promote the corporate agenda of competitiveness.

GAINSHARING

Piecework is giving workers whips so they can beat themselves. (old union saying)

Gainsharing is giving workers whips so they can beat each other. (labor educator observation)

Gainsharing is another one of those concepts that has an attractive sound. Its very name suggests that everybody wins and that it is all about fairness—i.e., that gains will be shared. Despite (or perhaps because of) the high sounding connotations, unions would be wise to avoid most gainsharing plans.

PROFIT SHARING

For management, the disadvantage of profit sharing is that many factors contribute to profitability which are beyond the control of most employees: management decisions within the company, general economic conditions, the actions of competitors, the price of raw materials, and so on. Because there is not necessarily a one-to-one connection between any action by an employee and short-term profits, it is unlikely that profit sharing will be an effective motivator in the long run.

For many unionists the issue is one of fairness. Why shouldn't workers reap part of the rewards when the company does well? But historically, unions have rejected profit-sharing. Walter Reuther of the UAW, for instance, argued that workers were subject to peaks and valleys of economic cycles and that profit sharing only exaggerated the effect of both highs and lows on workers' lives. The union's job was to flatten out the effects of the business cycle on union members. So the union chose to go for the conceptual opposite of gainsharing: in the profitable periods it would demand funding for programs that would help people through the valleys. The UAW fought for programs like a guaranteed annual wage, supplemental unemployment benefits, and extended medical benefits during layoffs.

The history of the business cycle since then has shown the wisdom of this idea. Since the union can't guarantee a strong economy and that the company will always be profitable, the union's responsibility is to advance working people over the long haul.

TRADITIONAL GAINSHARING

The main features are:

1) Direct connection between work and bonus. Gains are measured and rewards are divided in such a way as to make a clear connection between the rewards and specific employee actions. Events and decisions over which the employees have no control (such as economic conditions, management decisions) are separated out, and employees can see that they have direct control over the size of their bonus.

2) Promotion of team work rather than individual work. Rewards are based on the results of a group's activity, such as a department.

Most programs come up with a formula that rewards an increase of productivity (or a reduction in "controllable" costs) for an economic unit (factory, department).

There are two basic kinds of gainsharing programs.

1. *Single Factor.* Total amount of reward is based on a single factor. Money is divided up according to each worker's contribution (e.g., hours worked, or gross wages for the period). One example is a program in the Social Security Administration's Field Operations that began in 1988. Fifty percent of any savings above .5 percent of the pervious year's budget could be distributed to both management and bargaining unit employees. The site manager got a specified bonus and distributed the remainder as she/he saw fit.

2. *Multifactor.* Several different kinds of activities are rewarded. These are the most common today. First, the company creates a reward pie. Then, that money is paid out if workers are successful in certain specified areas. These formulas can get very complicated.

Examples:

Consolidated Freight (1989-90)

This trucking company proposed a reward pie consisting of the savings made in "employee-controllable costs" to move freight. But only gains above CF's normal levels of improvement (historically 1.1 percent annually) would be shared. This pie would then be distributed if there were

improvement in each of five areas:

Safety	10%
Maintenance	10%
On-time delivery	10%
Claims (damage, losses)	15%
Customer Satisfaction	20%

If there were improvements in all five areas, employees would divide up 65 percent of the reward pie. Management would get no less than 35 percent.

Bethlehem Steel (1988):

Each of five factors is tagged with a percentage. Each person's reward is calculated by multiplying this percentage times the number of hours worked, times a specified standard hourly wage rate (the same for everybody). A reward of a maximum of 15 percent of your annual wage (roughly) could be achieved if improvements in all five areas reached specified goals.

Man-hours per prime tons shipped	.3.0%
Hourly employees per 1000 prime tons shipped	.3.0%
Yield (reflects scrap production)	.2.5%
Claims (reflects quality, customer complaints)	.2.5%
Operating expense per shipped ton (reflects power consumption etc.)	.4.0%

CONSTANT IMPROVEMENT, OR THE ROLLING BASE

The key to understanding the generosity of any plan is the method for calculating the base. All of them have a rolling base.

Compare the rolling base to a piece rate situation. If the piece rate formula rewarded a worker for making more than 100 units per hour, it would not seem fair to raise the figure to 110 the following month. Yet this is exactly what most gainsharing plans do.

No modern management is willing to allow a workforce to maintain a comfortable, relatively constant, rate of work. The name of the game is to reward kaizen, or constant improvement. In gainsharing this translates into some form of moving baseline for rewards.

For example, at Consolidated Freight the formula was based on "controllable cost savings." Assuming they did everything right, the workers were to get 65 percent of the savings, the company 35 percent. But part of the fine print was that workers were not entitled to the "historic 1.1 percent" increase in savings that management had been getting over a period of years. So the 1.1 percent increase came off the top. You can see the result in the first year of the graph.

But the biggest kicker is the moving baseline in the formula. Each year's bonuses were based on improvements over the previous year.

The gray area on the graph represents the total savings workers would generate over the five-year period, just from their activities in the first year. The dark area is what workers themselves would take home as gainsharing over the same five-year period. This is not a good deal. Even if you take into account interest rates, assume that the savings will show diminishing returns, and assume the total savings are only as much as line A, it's still not a "fair share" for the employees.

DEFINING THE REWARD FACTORS

The individual reward factors can themselves get very complicated and may produce unexpected results. Take for example safety. We all want to reward safety, and there it is, a factor in most plans. But what really happens under those conditions? There are three ways for workers to get their safety bonus in this situation.

One way, of course, is to actually improve safety. But that may be hard to do, as safety conditions are likely in management's control. Another way to improve safety is not to work too fast. But then the safety bonus tends to compete with the productivity bonus.

A third way to improve the safety statistics is just to cut down the number of accidents reported. The peer pressure: "Oh, come on, that's just a little cut. You know it'll heal up by itself. You don't need to go to medical, do you?" Or "you didn't really need to take off so many days for that bad back."

This kind of pressure is likely when workers feel they can't do much about safety. Especially once the accident has already happened.

Bethlehem Steel slipped in a ringer. Note that there are rewards for reduction of both man-hours per ton and persons per ton. What's the difference? This is a clear invitation for members to reduce crew size in favor of overtime.

Especially if a gainsharing plan pays off by depart-

CF Gain Sharing

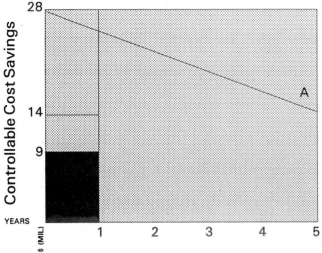

Assume there are 18,000 workers. Suppose that in the gainsharing plan's first year, they reduce costs by 2.2%, or about $28 million total.
Results: CF takes its historic 1.1% off the top ($14 million). Then CF takes its 35% "share" of the rest ($4.9 million). CF gets $18.9 million in one year, and $130.9 million over five years—just for the cost-cutting the workers did in year one. Workers divide among themselves $9.1 million the first year (65% of $14 million). This works out to about $500 apiece. They get nothing over the next four years for these cost cuts.

ment, it tends to pit workers against workers, or the worker against the union, as the union is seen as the defender of outmoded practices and precedent.

In addition, gainsharing programs tend to involve union and management in unnecessary technical questions. These issues don't affect the running of the enterprise, but they require that both sides spend an enormous amount of time just servicing the plan. The formulas and calculations become incredibly complicated. Huge debates arise over the percentage assigned to production units versus customer complaints versus job loss. What happens, for instance, when the proposal is to have the truck drivers do certain maintenance checks on the road? Would that be billed as maintenance cost or operator costs?

These questions have very little to do with the amount of money workers achieve in the long run. They tend to have a differential result in terms of who gets what, when. They are a giant waste of time, both from management's and the union's point of view (a mutual interest!). Union officers are forced to develop expertise in order to have some reasonable say in the plan, and are distracted from paying attention to their own business.

WHERE DO GAINS COME FROM?

Typically, gainsharing is "front-loaded" so that the first year will bring quite substantial rewards. People will be excited; there will be an outpouring of ideas that workers have accumulated over a period of time but were never particularly willing to share with the company, or the company was never willing to listen to. The program seems to pay. It appears to be win-win. The company is careful that no jobs disappear, so there are no apparent problems.

By the second year members are used to a big paycheck, and counting on it. But they don't have quite the same reservoir of ideas, they've already given them. This is when members start getting into the gray areas— trying to change a contract item, perhaps, or putting pressure on co-workers. This is the point where the employer does well with the gainsharing program, when people begin to break down the rules they didn't want to break down in the first year because they were trying to protect the contract.

By the third year people don't have much more to give, and the gainsharing program starts to collapse.

But the biggest problem with gainsharing is that it disguises where the gains are coming from.

Where do savings come from? Someone may come up with a brilliant idea to help the trucking company save gasoline. But usually the savings are job cuts. So gainsharing essentially means that workers as a group take money out of their right pocket, and put it in their left pocket. Most may not see it that way, because the plan is designed so that one worker's advantage comes at the expense of another, in other departments, in other places down the line.

In chapter 34 we suggest some ways that unions can respond to gainsharing.

Notes

1. Edward Cohen-Rosenthal and Cynthia Burton, *Mutual Gains: A Guide to Union-Management Cooperation*, ILR Press, Ithaca, New York, 1993. p.4 Cohen-Rosenthal and Burton are very even-handed in their approach. For example: "The threat of a strike or a lockout can help the parties come to compromise... The right of management to say no to unreasonable demands or to resist intimidation is also important." (p. 9) They warn about union-busters posing as consultants and also suggest avoiding consultants who can see only the union perspective. (p. 180)

2. This is a paraphrase of a version used in Federal Mediation and Conciliation Service training in 1994: "Interest Based Bargaining," San Antonio Field Office.

3. A more sophisticated analysis would introduce the element of "opportunity costs" and market value. If the muscular worker could make $12 an hour on another job, the moving job won't be a winner for him unless he makes more than $48 for a four-hour job. But even adding this complication, a range of settlements would be possible and the question of how to choose among them remains.

4. Cohen-Rosenthal and Burton, p. 61.

5. Cohen-Rosenthal and Burton, pp. 11-12. The quotes and original categorization come from Frederick Harbison and John R. Coleman, *Goals and Strategy in Collective Bargaining*, Harper, New York, 1951.

6. See also Elly Leary and Marybeth Menaker, *Jointness at GM: Company Unionism in the 21st Century*, New Directions Region 9A, Woonsocket, R.I., 1993.

7. National Partnership Council, *Partnership Handbook*, July 1994

8. Donald Wells, "Are Strong Unions Compatible with the New Model of Human Resource Management?" *Relations Industrielles/Industrial Relations*, Vol. 48, No. 1, 1993, p. 63.

9. Commission on the Future of Worker-Management Relations, *Fact Finding Report*, May 1994, p. 41.

10. Andrew Rivers, "How One Company Is Using a Modern 'Company Union' to Keep Out the CWA," *Labor Notes* No. 177, December 1993, p. 11.

11. See Joel Cutcher-Gershenfeld, "The Impact on Economic Performance of Transformational Workplace Relations," *Industrial and Labor Relations Review,* Vol. 44, No. 2, January 1991, p. 244.

12. John Holusha, "A Profitable Xerox Plans to Cut Staff by 10,000," *New York Times,* December 9, 1993.

13. All information from Louis Uchitelle, "A New Labor Design at Levi Strauss," *New York Times*, October 13, 1994; and press release, "Levi Strauss & Co. and Amalgamated Clothing and Textile Workers Union Ratify Ground-Breaking Partnership Agreement," October 13, 1994.

14. William N. Cooke, *Labor-Management Cooperation: New Partnerships or Going in Circles*, W.E. Upjohn Institute, Kalamazoo, Michigan, 1990.

15. Casey Ichniowski, Kathryn Shaw, Giovanna Prennushi, "The Effects of Human Resource Management Practices on Productivity," unpublished paper, Carnegie Mellon University, June 1994, p. 5. The paper borrows concepts on this point from Eugene Kandel and Edward P. Lazear, "Peer Pressure and Partnerships," *Journal of Political Economy*, Vol. 100, No. 4, August 1992, pp. 801-817.

16. Roger Fisher and William Ury, *Getting To Yes: Negotiating Agreement Without Giving In*, Penguin Books, New York, 1983. See also two sequels: Roger Fisher and Scott Brown, *Getting Together*, Penguin, New York, 1989, and William Ury, *Getting Past No*, Bantam, New York, 1993.

17. Fisher and Ury, p. 86.

18. Ury, p. 23.

19. Ury, p. 22.

20. Fisher and Ury, p. 129.

21. Raymond A. Friedman, *Front Stage, Back Stage: The Dramatic Structure of Labor Negotiations*, MIT Press, Cambridge, Mass., 1994, p. 187.

22. FMCS, "Interest-Based Bargaining," p. 47.

23. FMCS, p. 51.

24. All quotes from "Contract Bargaining and Mutual Gains Techniques," meeting summary, September 13, 1994.

Chapter 16

Assessing the Dangers: A Checklist

The dangers of participation programs for unions are summarized, from changes in work itself to challenges to the strength of the union.

THE PREVIOUS CHAPTERS IN THIS SECTION have gone into depth about the many problems unions can expect to face from participation programs. This chapter will outline the dangers to workers and unions briefly, with references to more information in other chapters. In particular, see chapter 32, Pitfalls of Protective Involvement.

❑ **1. Work itself is made worse.**

As explained in previous chapters, participation programs ease the way for the introduction of various lean or management-by-stress techniques. Despite the promises that you'll be working smarter, not harder, jobs are likely to be combined, sped up, and more tightly controlled.

❑ **2. Job loss is designed in.**

As described in chapter 14, quality programs that focus on eliminating "waste" usually cut jobs. And the term "lean production" is no accident; it means no "bloated" employment rolls. Contracting out is a central component of lean production.

Sometimes the job loss is hidden; see the discussion of attrition in chapter 32. But some par-

ticipation programs are quite explicit about the goal of wiping out jobs. Management will say that job cuts are a way to improve service to the customer, say by cutting red tape. Or management tries to add a sweetener to the job losses: union members will get to reengineer the work themselves.[1]

At Bethlehem Steel's Indiana plant, for example, the

"Won't keep you a minute, Schmidt — just like you to participate in the following decisions."

gainsharing program provides financial incentives for workers to cut "man-hours per prime ton and hourly employees per 1,000 prime tons." At Boston City Hospital, management introduced TQM in 1991 with the goal of cutting 900 out of 2,400 jobs. The National Partnership Council of federal employee unions with the government agreed to wave good-bye to a quarter of a million federal jobs through attrition.

❑ **3. Job control is transferred to management.**

One of the chief goals of participation programs is to transfer workers' job knowledge to management. This enables management a much tighter control of the workplace. In the philosophy of quality programs, it is not enough for workers to make the product well; management must know exactly how they do it.

If you can figure out a way to do something in less time, keep your secret within the team! This is your time, you've earned it!

—Rob Pelletier, former president of Canadian Auto Workers Local 88 at CAMI

When workers are induced to document each step of their day, they are essentially writing a work practices manual for management. Supervisors can then compare one worker's methods with another, and enforce the "best practice." Once it has become established that everyone must follow the best practice, supervisors can decide when to enforce the rules and when not to, whom to crack down on and whom to let slide.

In principle, of course, documenting a work process as the first step to improving it makes a lot of sense, all else being equal. But in the workplace all else is never

equal—especially power. One of the few sources of power an individual worker or her union has is the knowledge that workers have accumulated about how to do the job right. The fact that this knowledge is usually rather different from management's official procedures manual is what makes "working-to-rule" an effective tactic. If workers write an accurate manual, they've lost this tactic. And when they expose all their short-cuts to management, they are opening themselves to speed-up.

❑ **4. Workers are easier to replace.**

When they document their hidden knowledge, workers may be writing a "scab manual." Sometimes this goal of participation programs is expressed openly. For example, a DuPont manual for implementing the ISO 9000 standards explains: "The unwritten standard for the ISO audit is that if all personnel were suddenly replaced, the new people could continue making the product or providing the service as before."[2]

❑ **5. New technology is more easily introduced.**

One of the conditions for introducing some kinds of new technology is that jobs be exactly specified and standardized. If a machine is to take the place of a person, the machine designer must know the exact operations it will perform; it helps if the worker to be replaced has cooperated in getting these right.

The other condition for introducing new technology is a cooperative workforce, especially in the debugging stage. Participation programs are ideally suited for creating both of these conditions.

Of course, new technology is not necessarily bad, but when it is used to replace workers, deskill them, monitor them, or force them to keep to a machine's pace, the union may want to investigate how the introduction of technology is connected to the participation program.

❑ **6. Reliance on experts is reinforced.**

Workers and managers intent on "finally doing it

Management Learns the Jobs, Then Locks Workers Out

At the Ravenswood Aluminum Corp. (RAC) in West Virginia, management set up Quality Realignment Teams. Charlie MacDowell, grievance committee chair of United Steel Workers Local 5668, said, "Each worker was asked how he did his job and what it consisted of, what improvements he could make, any suggestions that he had for doing his job, or shortcuts." Some workers filled out the sheets.

Soon management was using the information for speed-up. The casting furnace, for example, ran with four crews on four shifts. Management went to the crew with the lowest productivity and told them they had to use the methods documented by the crew with the highest productivity. The next step was to discipline the crew if their productivity didn't measure up.

In addition, says MacDowell, "some of these good ol' boy foremen would go to the rolling mill crews and say 'let me do this, let me do that,' and they practiced. Any time you get a chance to sit down and watch somebody else do your job, most people, they're going to do it."

Management also identified where supervisors' skills were weak, such as overhead crane operation, and promoted those workers to supervisors. This was a year or more before the contract expired.

When that day came, management was ready. In November 1990, it locked the workers out, hired a thousand scabs, got an injunction limiting pickets to six, and resumed production.

The lockout lasted 20 months, but because of an intensive corporate campaign and much solidarity from other unions, RAC workers eventually returned to work with a contract. Unfortunately, the new contract eliminated many work rules and combined jobs.[3]

right" look to pre-packaged programs for guidance. Novices at the participation game, they may tend to rely on experts who act as if they have all the answers. The consultant lays out what kind of data should be collected, how meetings should run, the rules for decision-making. Figures such as Deming's "management is responsible for 94 percent of the problems in the workplace" are thrown out as if they came from God on high. The rules of the particular program may not be questioned, because "this is how it's done" (perhaps citing a successful competitor who's used this program).

❑ **7. Union leaders are swamped.**

When union leaders try to oversee a participation program responsibly in addition to all their other duties, one or both is likely to suffer. If management is devoting staff full-time to the program, they have all day to sit in meetings and "consense" endlessly—time union leaders do not have. Management may also want to take union leaders on off-site jaunts that take them away from the workplace. See chapter 20 for an example of an Employee Involvement program that threatened to engulf a local officer.

❑ **8. Union leaders are distracted from the real issues.**

This can be a matter of not seeing the forest for the trees. Perhaps the union is so caught up in the question of whether to go for a participation program that it fails to

---

Exercise

Misdirection

Objective: To demonstrate the simplicity of misdirection.

Time: 10-15 minutes

The workshop leader gives the following instructions:

> We want to do a simple experiment about observation.
>
> Get out a piece of paper and look at it.
>
> When I tell you to start I want you to look around the room for 15 seconds and pay special attention to the color of items. Pay particular attention to those that are brown.

After 15 seconds, the leader says,

> Now look only at your paper and write down as many objects as you can that are blue.

Ask if people feel that this was a cheap trick. Admit that it is a cheap trick, but one that is used quite commonly. Discuss examples of misdirection in sports, in magic.

Discuss possible instances of misdirection in participation programs. Examples:

Stewards are sensitized to look for circles altering terms of the contract and don't see other problems, like job loss.

Members demand equal numbers of management and workers on joint committees; they fail to see other problems, like management's greater resources.

---

react to the steady leakage of jobs to Mexico. Or perhaps the whole workforce gets caught up in a campaign to win the Baldrige Award, and lets large chunks of the contract fall by the wayside.

The forest/trees problem can also occur within the participation program. Say the company proposes that workers cooperate in a reengineering plan to cut jobs by 30 percent. In order to share the pain, though, management offers to trim its own ranks as well, by 20 percent. Union leaders bargain hard, and get the company to agree to cut managers by 30 percent as well.

The union is proud that its leaders have won "equality of sacrifice"—and the company treasurer is laughing all the way to the bank. The union has been misdirected into thinking that both sides are sacrificing equally. In fact, the company is almost as glad to get rid of low-level supervisors as it is of union members.

See the section on gainsharing in chapter 15 for another example of misdirection.

❑ **9. Grievance procedure is weakened.**

In the ideology of participation programs, grievances are considered a bad thing; they signify disagreement and conflict. Union leaders as well as managers and consultants often point to a decline in grievances as the measure of a program's success.

But what is wrong with using the grievance procedure to solve problems? A high grievance load does not necessarily indicate that there are more problems in the workplace, or less justice, than a low grievance load does. The filing of many grievances only indicates that the stewards are addressing the problems.

The grievance procedure is usually far from perfect: it may seem to take forever, it may be expensive, the worker may taken out of the process and kept in the dark. As part of the union's strategic plan, these problems need to be fixed. But the grievance procedure provides some rules, assistance, and representation for the worker, to combat the enormously lopsided power when the conflict is simply worker against manager. Management obviously prefers the latter for problem solving.

❑ **10. Union is bypassed.**

Management can choose which structure—the union or the participation programs—looks or is effective. Stewards frequently tell of struggling unsuccessfully for years to get a water fountain installed, only to find that the quality team has gotten a fountain on their first try. This trick not only demoralizes the steward, it also teaches the members where they should go if they want results.

An Administrative Law Judge pointed out long ago:

> It is evident that if employees can get quick responses from management to issues raised in quality circles, they will naturally channel their work-related concerns to the quality circles, rather than through the resources provided them in the collective bargaining agreement.[4]

In addition, when management installs a participation program, say TQM, the union suffers by comparison. TQM is "in." TQM gets the new meeting rooms, the conferences, the travel. If the company channels goodies through TQM, its participants get the successes and the gratitude. The union is left with the dirty jobs and the company's hard side.

❑ **11. Traditional union skills and behaviors are devalued.**

Part of the participation message is that the old ways of doing things, and by extension the old people doing them, are no longer relevant. In a participation program, democracy (majority rules) is out and elaborate procedures to reach consensus are in. The language of unionism is replaced by the jargon of the flavor of the month program ("change agents," "the 5 S's," "associates"). At Saturn, for example, the words "union" and "management" are avoided, in favor of "represented" and "non-represented."

The participation program becomes the avenue for those who want to make their mark on the world, rather than the traditional route of running for union office.

❑ **12. Potential union leaders are lost.**

Members who are attracted to participation programs are often dedicated union members with initiative and drive. Unions must continually attract such potential leaders, competing directly with management, which seeks to lure these same people to its own ranks. Here the participation program can be a gold mine for management. It provides a convenient way to encourage and observe management skills among workers. Of course, the perks management can offer are another way to "turn" potential union leaders.

❑ **13. Current union leaders are lost.**

These programs also take a toll on current union leaders. On the one hand they can be swamped or confused; on the other hand, there is a carrot. Union officials at some high-profile companies have become well-known travelers and speakers on the benefits of cooperation. A few have even become high-paid consultants. And there is always the possibility of moving into management. Joel Smith, for example, was a UAW International Rep who helped set up the first NUMMI contract. He was then hired by McDonnell Douglas to bring the team concept to the aerospace industry.

Usually, when union leaders get their heads turned it's not a question of bribery. Everyone likes to be appreciated. Everyone has buttons that can be pushed. Participation programs work hard to find the buttons. As

---

Turf War[5]

by Ernie Hite

As a newly elected district committeeperson [steward] for the maintenance group at a GM component parts plant, I made monitoring the joint committees in my area a top priority.

A few months prior to my election, one joint committee had advocated combining skilled trade classifications and changing the overtime equalization agreements in the maintenance group, in a misguided attempt to make us more "competitive." A groundswell of rank and file opposition convinced the bargaining committee to reject this suggestion.

I arranged for my alternate, Dawn, to attend joint meetings while I addressed members' problems. At her first meeting, Dawn suggested that some nominees for union "clipboard" appointments come from the group that they were charged with assisting. She met stiff resistance.

A union appointee told Dawn that the next joint committee meeting had been canceled. Suspicious, Dawn went by the meeting room and discovered the meeting being held without her.

She confronted the appointees and demanded a schedule of all the joint meetings in our district. They refused. Dawn and I constructed a complete list of joint meetings in our district with information from the Superintendent of Maintenance and a sympathetic appointee.

Support for us in our district was high, but we needed to broaden it to keep appointees and the Shop Committee on the side of the rank and file. The direct approach—bringing up the issue at the general membership meeting—was risky, since appointees make up a large percentage of those meetings.

So I first introduced the issue at the local's skilled trades members meeting. With the earlier attempt by a joint committee to change their work rules still fresh in their minds, the skilled trades members voted unanimously to request that all joint meetings be attended by an elected alternate committeeperson. This resolution was reported out at the general membership meeting and won a majority vote.

No resolution passed by the membership is ever a solution by itself. It must be enforced with action. Dawn continued to attend meetings and voice her opinions. The General Superintendent of Maintenance told Dawn she couldn't talk at meetings anymore. She approached the Shop Committee. They asked the second-shift maintenance alternate committeeperson to attend the meetings with her.

It wasn't long before the situation came to a head. During a presentation to propose a new maintenance program, an appointee stated that the union had no voice in the matter. The Shop Committee was livid. They called a meeting with the appointees where they told them their place in the structure. No appointee was removed, however.

Since the showdown, the appointees have been more cooperative. Management continues to push their agenda, often with the support of at least some appointees. Dawn has been able to block the worst of the proposals, and she provides a voice for the rank and file.

experts on brainwashing know, people who believe they have no buttons to be pushed are the ones most easily sucked in.

❑ 14. Union is divided.

Having two competing structures in the workplace—the union and the participation program—is a set-up for disaster. Sometimes the two structures war over turf (see box).

Sometimes workers are pitted against each other. For example, in one training program workers are taught tools for "charting clerical errors" and establishing a "matrix for counting performance."[6] What does the union do when one of these tools indicates that most of the quality problem is a particular worker? How do you build solidarity in that department?

The divisions become worse when the participation program outgrows the union structure. See the chart for an example from the auto industry, where jointness is oldest and the most advanced.

At worst, the membership is divided into two camps, the "dinosaurs" and the "sucks." If union reps try to enforce union principles in circle meetings, they raise the hackles of participants who have bought into the program. If they don't, the union is discredited among members who oppose the program.

In addition, the finger-pointing in team meetings or the increased opportunity for management favoritism may worsen racial or sex divisions (see chapters 17 and 18). The push for "multi-skilling"—knowing all the jobs in

your team—may cause resentment of injured or less strong workers.

The worst scenario occurs when union leaders pretend that the promises of the participation program have come true, and the membership knows better. The result is confusion, outrage, or cynicism.

❑ 15. Anti-union ideology of competition is promoted.

Since the motivating factor behind most participation programs is to beat the competition, when a union joins in, it is implicitly giving the union stamp of approval to the notion that workers should be in competition with other workers.

❑ 16. Union vision is co-opted.

Many participation programs seem to adopt the union vision of better jobs: they promise more interesting work, better working conditions, and job security. Suddenly management becomes the deliverer of the union vision! Where is the union's role?

❑ 17. Union vision becomes illegitimate.

In many workplaces, management talks about a quality product (as defined by management) as if that is the only goal of human endeavor. (Profits are conveniently forgotten in these pep talks.) If quality "requires" robotization, so be it. If quality requires standardized work, and standardized work increases repetitive strain injuries, that is the price we have to pay. It is easy to forget, under the barrage of propaganda for quality, that a decent quality of working life is just as reasonable a right to pursue. See chapter 3 on a union vision of work.

Notes

1. See Kenneth Noble, "Paying Workers Extra To Be Their Own Efficiency Experts," *New York Times*, August 28, 1988; Thomas F. O'Boyle, "A Manufacturer Grows Efficient by Soliciting Ideas from Employees," *Wall Street Journal*, June 5, 1992.

2. Du Pont and Co., "ISO 9000 is Here! The Answers to Your Questions," Du Pont Quality Management and Technology Center, 1991.

3. Jane Slaughter and Camille Colatosti, "How Two Companies Wrote 'Scab Manuals,'" *Labor Notes* No. 156, March 1992, p. 10.

4. *Defense Logistics Agency, Defense Depot Tracy*, FLRA Case No. 9-CA-20241 (1983) (Summary Affirmance of ALJ), p. 17.

5. This article first appeared in *The Voice of New Directions*, the newsletter of the New Directions Movement in the United Auto Workers, March 1994.

6. Kaset International Training Materials, *Information Guide* (Instructor's manual), 1992, I-4-20.

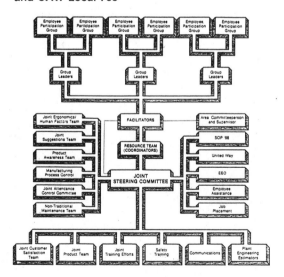

QWL/EI Structure GM Hydra-matic Willow Run and UAW Local 735

Jointness at a GM Plant

According to a 1988 Department of Labor study, the 18 joint programs identified in the chart employed about 200 hourly workers, full time, and 53 salaried personnel.

Working Smart:
A Union Guide to Participation Programs and Reengineering
Labor Notes • 7435 Michigan Ave. • Detroit, MI 48210 • (313) 842-6262

Chapter 17

Workers of Color: On the Team?

With teamwork training or diversity training, companies can appear to be a step ahead of unions in addressing the concerns of workers of color. But in practice, team concept can be harmful. With no work rules, "flexibility" can mean management favoritism/discrimination. Team meetings can be forums for criticism of co-workers or scapegoating, leading to racial divisions. When team concept weakens the union, it weakens the most effective vehicle for fighting discrimination.

by Mary Hollens

MANY UNION MEMBERS and leaders are aware of team concept's back door attempt to undermine contract language that protects wages, jobs, and benefits. But team concept's specific impact on workers of color is rarely, if ever, addressed. Seldom do unions link an aggressive, on-going, up-front fight to eliminate racism to their efforts to confront the team concept. And yet team concept can undermine gains made on the shop floor on issues of on-the-job bias.

It has been demonstrated over time that workers of color cannot rely on the good wishes of management for workplace fairness. Management has historically been dragged kicking and screaming through the courts—repeatedly—to gain their compliance with even the most basic of workers' rights.

And then along comes team concept, which plays on a universal need by all people to be heard and listened to. For workers of color this can be doubly attractive, as in this country as a whole, and in many workplaces, the views of workers of color are rarely sought, prized, or given credence.

Workers of color who were tokens in their workplaces may find that they are now being cast in a new role: that of team members, where we are all part of the group. But workers of color who have never been taken off the employment bench and given full participation may

Mary Hollens is Outreach Coordinator on the staff of Labor Notes. She is the author of The African American Worker *and* The Changing Face: Latino Workers in the United States.

find that what team concept promises and what it delivers are quite different.

IS MANAGEMENT SINCERE?

As we approach the year 2000, the issue of race, equality, and equity is a volatile dynamic in both communities and workplaces. Is management sincere in its stated desire to treat every employee with respect and dignity?

In 1990 companies were at the White House door begging for—and getting—changes in the proposed Civil Rights Act, to make it harder for employees to sue them for discrimination. Now many corporations are instituting multi-million dollar in-house "workplace diversity" programs. Why the change?

Any agent of organizational change will tell you that it is easier to facilitate a change if people participate in the change and believe those instituting the changes have their best interests at heart.

These techniques are reflected in the move for "appreciating diversity" and "diversity training." Companies realize that the workforce is changing. They read the research that says more and more people of color are entering the workforce. They are vying for those workers' loyalty. In addition, projected changes in population provide a clear signal to companies that their staffs should reflect to some extent their customer base.

Many young workers of the future will come from growing people of color populations. But will corporate diversity extend beyond the rank and file into real changes in decision-making and equality in the corporation? The statistics do not bear out the idea that corporations will allow people of color or women to break the glass ceiling in the workplace. The consultants who set up these diversity programs—sometimes even for unions—are not workers but corporations who have a distinctly management perspective.

WHY UNIONS SHOULD BE CONCERNED

Too often management is steps ahead of unions in visibly addressing the concerns of people of color. With the "race card" in its hand, management can set up programs, hold meetings with "lots of lights," bring in the experts to address the needs of workers of color—but in reality change very little. What *has* changed is that management has scored high visibility points over a union which may have done little on issues of race.

Some companies have linked "diversity" programs to team concept. Team concept can fill up the places the union leaves empty. Sandy talks about a case in point. She works as a technician at a large telephone company.

"I hate to say it, but teams brought a new way of looking at things for union members. I was tired of not being taken seriously by my union. I was tired of the old boy crap...and non-support for issues of women and people of color. Someone paints racist graffiti in the washroom—does the union ever address it? No.

"But the company addresses it through a team concept meeting or diversity meeting. Who do you think is making an impression with the workers? Not the union.

"Our workplace is racially diverse but our top union leadership is all white male. The company pointed this out subtly to the union members through programs that stressed, 'Our management looks like and reflects many cultural viewpoints.' And it did.

"I realized that the company had a poor record on affirmative action, but they put a stop to a lot of what the men call the 'crybaby' issues—like not calling women 'girls'—and they put out a lot of information around the entire office and plant about no tolerance for sexual harassment.

"People were flocking to these company seminars and workshops and the union was shut out. I mean they shut themselves out.

"The teams started to become mini-companies where people would refer problems back to company programs and not the union. The teams started to eat together and hang out together, and this further cuts you off from other union members.

"If you don't go to union meetings anyway, you start to get a lot of your information from teams and

company-related perspectives."

Sandy's point is well taken. If the person who is supplying information to workers on the floor or in the office has bought into these programs, what is the result for the union?

The process Sandy describes shows how management can use team concept to better its reputation around race or sex discrimination—while keeping its actual employment practices unexamined and unchanged.

PROTECTIONS WEAKENED

Team concept can also exacerbate discrimination and/or racism, as the examples below demonstrate.

Union seniority rights and job classifications, defined through strong contract language, have had contradictory impacts on workers of color. In some unions, strict adherence to seniority rights has diminished discrimination which denied workers of color promotions and wage increases. In these cases, when team concept weakens or eliminates specific language such as the right to transfer to a different classification by seniority, workers of color find they are once again dependent on the goodwill of ill-defined company policy. "Flexibility"—a hallmark of team concept—is another word for "discretion." Where, how, and if African Americans and other workers of color will work is left to the discretion of management.

Team concept can also include "merit raises," meaning that workers are rewarded on the basis, i.e., merit, of their work performance. But who decides what job performance merits a raise, and under what conditions? Again, this is left to management discretion, which for workers of color rarely means equity.

In many other industries, however, seniority rules and job classifications have protected white workers but excluded people of color, particularly African-Americans, from skilled jobs. In such cases, team concept ideas can look attractive to workers of color and aid management's goal of breaking down historic job classifications.

Another complaint about racial harassment on the job.

This is the type of problem we can't ignore.

The only solution is to air it publicly

There!

CAROL ✱ SIMPSON / CALM 1-92

HOW WE GAVE OUR CLASSIFICATIONS AWAY

Clark, a member of the Graphic Communications International Union, tells what happened in his shop:

"Management really worked our union over. It was our fault, leadership and membership together.

"In our print shop we all got along pretty well, new guys and the old-timers. We were pretty well balanced as a union racially: Black, white, Latinos, and Asians. When teams were first introduced in the shop, everyone was prepared to fight it, we thought. One of the first things they started in on was classifications.

"Our shop is modernized and high-tech, but not everyone works on every piece of equipment and we still maintain many of the original classifications in the print shop. Some of the Black and Latino guys had bid for jobs on different shifts in order to work with the computerized machinery.

"They also requested training on the new printing technologies from the union, but some members thought this would bust classifications. The minority workers wanted this training, and they reached a stalemate with the union over receiving training and seniority rights.

"The union had done a lot of work on talking about how teams would harm the union and the shop. But when they put it to a vote, it passed. The company guys along with the minority vote was enough to vote the team concept in.

"The union leadership was really pissed. I went around and talked to some of the brothers who had voted for teams, and this is what they told me: 'You only want to keep team concept out so that you can keep progressing while holding the rest of us back. It was clear from the moment that you failed to support unionized training for all of the shop members.'

"I asked them how long did they think our jobs would last with teams. The response: 'The only job you were concerned about lasting eight months ago was the high-dollar-end classifications for you and your buddies. Now we're all in the same boat together.'"

JOBS

What type of jobs is team concept likely to bring to workers of color? The outlook is not good for high-paying, safe jobs. Workers of color are already segregated into the lowest-wage sectors and frozen out of many skilled positions. They also suffer a higher rate of occupational illness and injury than other workers. Will team concept—which combines jobs, eliminates many classifications, and requires more worker flexibility—result in more jobs? Will it mean higher paying jobs? Most importantly, will it enhance job security?

An evolved team concept job is one that offers more work for less money, with eventual unemployment. Management flexibility through team concept has already led to widespread job loss and cutbacks. For African American workers, who have one of the highest unemployment rates in the U.S. and a longer period of unemploy-ment when they lose their jobs, team concept will erode small workplace gains by institutionalizing job loss.

"Teams had a very real effect on me as an African American," says Dennis Jones, a Teamster with 12 years at a recently closed Pepsi bottling plant in Detroit. "We had worker participation from the start. We had slogans, 'The Company Is You' signs, and the orientations to the team way.

"The company told us everything was fine and participation would just be icing on the cake to keep us competitive. Our plant had the highest productivity in the region.

"The things that team concept required initially were simple. The company said that to maintain productivity they needed more flexibility in personnel choices. No classifications would be lost or changed. They requested that summer people and part-timers could be brought in to supplement personnel if all full-time unionized staff had refused the work, and only for that shift, time, and day. So we knew we were covered on the company bringing in somebody to replace Joe Blow on the 11-7 on Friday and then keep replacing him every Friday.

"We never had a lot of people who were refusing work or who didn't want overtime, so it was easy to go along with. The thing is, the company chose who these summer people and part-timers would be. This was the first crack in our classifications. If they needed an additional person in maintenance, production, or technology, they'd send one of these people in.

"But what no one realized: these people who worked maybe twenty hours in a month were rotating into every department, learning every job, as well as noting any work-saving cuts we had adopted, and reporting back to management.

"The union had never had a handle on the part-timers and summer people, and as union members started to ask questions [the company] quickly began to phase out jobs.

"When our plant closed, people who had 30 years with the company were passed over to work in the new plant the company was building down the road. They were passed over for some of these same part-time and summer people, who in this case were just people picked by the company to learn our jobs, steal our job knowledge, and assess how soon and how many of us they could lay off.

"For us, the African Americans, the older workers, and women, we found out the hard way. Out of our whole facility, only four white males were hired in at the new plant. The company built a new bottling plant less than ten minutes away from the old plant, brought in workers from the suburbs—and this from the company that we were all in this together with."

There is no other arena where we will proceed without defined and written agreements. A loan, purchase of a house or car, or even charging a pair of sneakers—all are covered by written contractual agreements. If these agreements are important enough to warrant such protection, why are we willing to give away strong contractual language that protects jobs?

UNITED WE BARGAIN

DIVIDED WE BEG

KONOPACKI ©1993
HUCK/KONOPACKI LABOR CARTOONS

SCAPEGOATING

Since unions are made up of people who live in our society, they reflect both the pluses and minuses of that society. The plus for unions: they stress total worker solidarity and working for the good of all workers. The negative: they reflect, just as the company does, the attitudes and socialization that come from living in a society that is racist.

Teams provide an open forum for worker evaluation and criticism of other workers. What may once have been uttered in a joking manner among two co-workers is now a matter of open knowledge to management and the entire team. This sharing process is by design, not by accident.

Criticism among team members can result in a witch hunt. It can easily lead to scapegoating, and from there to racially defining workers and work habits.

This management technique can be used to put the words and aims of management into the mouths of workers. Unfortunately, the anger generated by these practices is most often directed at other workers.

Team concept tends to break down positive relationships between workers. Where team concept has been effective in doing this, what is left in its place? Competing against another union member—someone who now represents an obstruction to their merit raise or their team concept perks.

'Isn't it about time some of these people around here did a little more work?'

David, a Detroit UAW member, describes the problem. "The teams create unreal appearances. You have people who get into a management role, but they are not managers.

"We had two people who had the race thing going on pretty badly from day one in the plant. They ended up on the same team. The one who was team leader went out of his way to lean on this guy. After what seemed too long to me, the union came in and talked to these guys. But it placed the team leader on the side of the management and the union in the middle as the bad guy for not taking the 'right' side.

"Because whoever one group liked and associated with the most made the other person the bad guy. So whichever side the union took, they were in the middle.

"Teams are supposed to keep hands off union matters and contract issues, but what happens on this touchy-feely stuff? That's not strictly union business, is it? How I feel about someone—is that union business? No. Believe me, what goes on in those teams will mean something when you're trying to put together an election slate that wants to do something positive in the plant for the union.

"We have two of the most popular people in the plant sandbagging everything that could help our local because if one supports something the other one will automatically put it down.

"These people have a lot a friends. Maybe the stakes aren't that high now, but management sure has its foot in the door to start a lot of trouble for this local, just because somebody said something that should never had been discussed in a work setting in the first place."

RACIAL TENSIONS

In an atmosphere of competition, old racial rivalries are often reawakened or encouraged. As the economy worsens, to what length will workers without solidarity go to keep their jobs?

The wave of Japan-bashing in 1992 is an example of how economic hardship can lead to racism and harassment of people of color who have no connection to the problem at hand. Some Japanese Americans now fear for their lives, because it is easier to blame a racial minority than to search out and then accept the real reasons for economic collapse.

When racism against one group becomes acceptable, it is easy for other forms of racism to grow as well. This is why racism escalates quite easily into divisions along racial lines, at a time when unions cannot afford to have their ranks broken by lack of worker solidarity.

Racism allows the company a ready-made weapon which every worker knows how to use and is available at no monetary cost to the company. Management would rather that workers fight each other over race than concentrate on the steady flow of jobs out the shop floor doors.

This use of racism can end permanently any sense of worker solidarity, because it is rare the person who will forgive and forget racial harassment after the current tide of bashing of people of color has ended and the crowd has moved on to the next victim.

Tyler B., a member of AFSCME, works in an office that has recently been organized along team concept lines. Her department has a team leader. Tyler describes her experiences.

"When the teams were set up we no longer reported directly to a manager. We were to work on a team and decide how we could best accomplish our work. Before teams came into our office we had some problems with racism, but as a union member I had some protection because the union would back up my complaint and investigate on their own, and this forced management to make changes they wouldn't have.

"With teams, now I am isolated from the union. My team leader subjects me to subtle forms of racial harassment. Now the other team members are telling me to keep it quiet and let's just get the work done.

"In one of our team meetings her treatment of me was brought up. I would not have initiated this type of discussion in a team setting, but someone else did. Now I was being confronted by two team members and the team leader. I also felt that management enforced and encouraged her behavior.

"By the time I talked to a union steward, the team leader felt the union was trying to stand in the way of her advancement.

"The team concept passes right over regular supervision channels—after all, this wasn't a manager and a union member, it was two union members. Management just sort of stepped aside and let the union intervene.

"Team concept passes over the union because this was a 'team problem,' and pressure was placed on me to keep it that way. The team shut itself off from people who normally might have projected some sort of insight into the problem, even though they only worked two desks away.

"I know that the teams have affected how the company and the unions deal with these issues. It has been all negative for me."

To win on the shop floor, in the office, barn, or unit, solidarity is essential. When your workforce is divided along racial interests as opposed to union interests, you have laid the groundwork that management would have had to pay millions to a union-busting firm to accomplish.

Workplace discrimination requires a group effort to overcome. Any individual may initiate an attack against discrimination, but it is the group that must support that attack. Team concept starts the process of dismantling the most effective group for supporting an end to discrimination: the union.

Working Smart:
A Union Guide to Participation Programs and Reengineering
Labor Notes • 7435 Michigan Ave. • Detroit, MI 48210 • (313) 842-6262

Chapter 18

Women and Participation Programs

Participation programs and management-by-stress can affect women workers differently than men. Management can use such programs to divide the workforce. Low pay, low seniority, and lack of work autonomy may make the promises of participation particularly attractive to women. Management may try to use women's traditional skills, such as consensus-building, for its own purposes. The push for "constant improvement" means electronic monitoring of many women's jobs. The focus on "return on quality" puts workers who are in customer contact on the front lines.

by Mary Hollens

IN THIS CHAPTER WOMEN WORKERS TALK about their experiences dealing with participation programs and with management-by-stress.

This two-pronged management offensive affects women in a variety of ways. On the one hand is the sheer work overload. Women still face the multiple demands of homes, families, and communities. Over and over women talk about increased workload (job enlargement), speed-up, and their inability to continue working at the pace the new workplace demands. Over the last twenty years the average U.S. worker has increased the annual amount of time spent on the job by 163 hours.[1]

The workplace superwoman is alive—if not well.

In addition, cooperation has increased the difficulty and the stress of telling the employer no, on any level. Employers realize the financial vulnerability of women workers and willingly exploit it.

On the other hand, after years of workplace sexism and discrimination, for many women participation programs appear to be the white light at the end of the tunnel. Women are not listened to nor are given fair monetary compensation for their work. What participation programs can provide with their meetings, emphasis on process, individual opinion, and recognition feeds into our society's methodology of socializing women.

Mary Hollens is the Outreach Director for Labor Notes and author of The African American Worker *and* The Changing Face: Latino Workers in the United States.

There is no question that the work women and men do and the rewards they receive continue to be substantially different. There is, on the other hand, considerable disagreement about the reasons why this is the case. The explanations may generally be divided into two broad categories, one emphasizing differences in voluntary decisions of individual workers, the other focusing on differences in the treatment women and men receive in the labor market.[2]

Can team concept affect the lives of women workers differently than their male counterparts? For most women the answer is yes.

WOMEN ON THE FRONT LINES

Participation programs use the woman worker's desire to have more control over her job. Lack of work autonomy is particularly prevalent in the low-wage, lower-level positions and service occupations women tend to occupy, and is characteristic of much part-time, temporary, and contingent work. A typical participation program pitch appeals to women with the tantalizing hope: You will decide how to work. You will organize and control your own work.

Studies show that women who report having a heavy workload and limited job control are at three times greater risk for coronary heart disease than women who have heavy workloads combined with control over their work.[3] Women are more likely to have high-strain jobs that are low status, involving routinized, bureaucratized, or heavily commercialized work.

With this fact in mind, it's pretty easy to see how the promise of greater job autonomy is of particular relevance for many women. Because women have been oppressed so long on the job, they want recognition, and participation, in the short term, offers that.

Just as men do, women bring their socialized roles to the workplace, and these management seeks to exploit. Many of women's traditional skills are ones that participation programs seek to use, such as relative ease in working in groups and toward consensus, and—a major focus of many quality programs—serious attention to details.

It's not that management is particularly fond of women: that's reflected by their inaction on issues that would benefit women workers. What management does like is the perspective and skills that women offer.

In many industries—from communications to health care, hotels, and insurance—women are on the front lines of contact with the customer. Consequently, women workers are often pivotal to insuring customer satisfaction.

Employers are shifting away from a focus on "the process" to a focus on "return on quality" (ROQ). As *Business Week* remarks, "Quality that means little to the customer usually doesn't produce a pay-off in improved sales, profit or market share."[4] Therefore, women's importance in convincing customers that they are getting quality will increase management pressure on women to cooperate.

In order to see "constant improvement," particularly in customer contact, electronic monitoring is increasing in many industries where women work. Customer service, 911 operators, service reps, telephone operators, clerical workers—all labor where the calls and follow-up never end. The pursuit of "quality" has meant electronic monitoring of everything from phone calls to copier use, e-mail to computer files. This electronic eavesdropping and even video observation increase the stress load, but rarely is it a contractual issue for unions outside the communications industry.

Management uses women's very real financial vulnerability to induce cooperation. Lack of a union, lack of seniority, and lack of pay equity are concrete reasons why many women feel powerless and unable to withstand management's offer to become a "team player." Further, the lack of pay equity leaves women open to the idea of profit sharing, pay incentives, and wage increases linked to productivity.

Participation programs seek to add an additional layer of responsibilities, without any increase in wages. Kathy Schreier, administrator of the Education Fund for

AFSCME District 37 in New York City, says, "Quite often employers are interested in giving more skills and responsibilities to workers, but no new money."[5]

One key element of management by-stress or lean production is for each firm to downsize, to function with only a small core workforce, and to contract out as much work as possible, usually to non-union workplaces. The workplaces that were heavily "womaned" have been consolidated, trimmed, part-timed, or outsourced.

Participation programs teach women via training workshops how to handle the stress. What is often missing from women's work environment is something that can come only from a union perspective: a strategy that addresses not how to make overworking tolerable, but rather putting a stop to overwork, with contract language that addresses speed-up.

TRADITIONAL ROLES

Jan, a UAW member who works as an electrician, a non-traditional job in the skilled trades, says that team concept plays into already defined roles for men and women on the job. "In my plant," she says, "women are placed in traditional jobs even within team concept. Men evaluate jobs; women are assigned to clean-up committees. In teams it's normally the men who evaluate jobs for modification."

"Management is very clear," Jan explains. "They know workers know how to cut jobs and save their own. They know that the temptation is there for workers to use that information for their own personal gain. With teams comes favoritism and nepotism. Management has so much riding on job reduction it has gotten worse, much worse for women.

"They want workers to do what management is unable to do because of the union and the contract: cut jobs while keeping management's hands clean.

"Most men who are in charge of job modification will look elsewhere for job cuts, and that leads directly to the jobs that women work."

In addition, teams no longer get their job assignments from a salaried person but from another worker. "If I have a problem with his assignment," says Jan, "—and it

usually is a man assigned as team leader—I can't grieve my team leader."

One possible appeal of participation programs for women in non-traditional work is that the facilitator and broad-based clerical-type jobs connected with them are often appointed ones; they can move women out of production and into a more comfortable, "clean" job. For women who have been beating their heads against the brick wall of sexism on the job, such an assignment can seem like a promotion.

Helen Bamford of Communications Workers Local 7901 in Portland has been a full-time co-facilitator of quality programs at US West for six years, with a management counterpart. Helen says: "Participation programs seek to push the notion we are one big team working together with equal status.

"The whole QWL process is driven and run by men. Most teams are run by men and it has just gradually changed over the last two years.

"I've noticed that when women give advice or make recommendations they are not as quickly accepted as when similar advice is given by a man. As a female facilitator I'm seen as not as effective as a man.

"Teams can provide a woman with an opportunity to get her foot in the door, but whether what she says will be implemented is another story."

Stories From the Inside

Working Woman magazine's column on "Career Strategies" instructs managers on how to give women more work: "It's a fact of today's downsized corporate life: At some point managers will need to ask an employee to take on more work without raising her pay." The secret to making this talk go smoothly, say authors Stephen M. Pollan and Mark Levine, "is to make the employee see what's in it for her."

Pollan and Levine provide scripted, color-coded scenarios for breaking the news. Their suggestions:

Since the alternative may be unemployment, you can present the increased workload as good news. Point out that while others are losing their jobs, she's making herself more valuable to the company.

If she's already a prized employee, see if you can reward her increased productivity through other means—a better title or larger office, training in new skills, more vacation time.

Of course, Pollan and Levine also have a message for the "non-essential" worker: "You should just get across the point that this is a take-it-or-leave-it deal."[6]

Spot the Changes?

The computer operator on the right works in a management-by-stress workplace. Can you spot the four changes from her previous working conditions?

1. Diminished union rights. 2. Bigger workload. 3. Smaller pay-check poking out of her pocket. 4. Less job security (closer to the door).

TRAINING AS A WEAPON

Participation programs often come with training programs attached. Management and unions alike say that training is essential in the new work environment. Yet Jan sees "this issue of training used as a weapon against women all the time." For women who don't "cooperate" she says, it can take many grievances to get requested or mandated training.

"Women have always had to rely on men to train them—men who for the most part did not want women on the job. So some women were never trained properly, and there are gaps in their knowledge that disqualify them from moving on. In other cases, women trained them-selves—and that causes resentment because you *can* do the job."

Jan gives an example of how management shapes training. "Sometimes management will select a woman to receive training. This will divide the group, because now you have a woman who's in no position to turn down train-ing and kiss her job good-bye. Then she has to face the day-to-day resentment of the men, who don't see it as a tactic of management but as a 'women's lib' thing. Then the rest of the women think there is a real opportunity for them, which makes them fall right into management's hands.

In 1991 the Government Accounting Office studied what happened to people trained under the Job Training Partnership Act. In over half the areas studied, only nine percent of women received training for occupations paying over $7 an hour.[7]

This is particularly significant because women (like people of color) are already underrepresented in higher-paying unionized skilled trades jobs. These are the jobs that provide skills more easily transferred to other settings.

SENIORITY VS. COOPERATION

Jan points out another way cooperation programs can create a double bind for women in a mostly-male workplace. In many plants, women are at the bottom of the seniority list. Management seeks to break down seniority rights to achieve a flexible workforce, but it also forces women who feel they cannot win by seniority to seek cooperation as a way to advance.

But because of job combination and speed-up, the jobs women might have hoped to advance into no longer exist. Jan explains: "Many women who just might have been inching toward some seniority find that with teams their job no longer exists because it's now combined through flexibility."

The newly created "flexible" jobs are likely to be specific to that particular workplace rather than preparing the worker for the breadth of the industry. This means that women now moving into these jobs are denied the sort of training that would give them a marketable skill.

BECOME A TARGET

"Teams really do pit workers against each other," says Jan. "The message is, if you are malleable and cooperate, that equals a smooth ride for you. Management makes the point, keep your mouth shut around team concept and you'll get everything you want, right up until the plant door closes. When management is under intense pressure to downsize, speaking up can make you a target of harassment, and the harassment that women experience is quite different from what happens to men.

"This leaves many women in skilled trades unwilling to speak up about inequities because they don't want any more negative attention focused on them than they receive already."

Because of the backlash against women who speak out against workplace inequity, many women who realize they are not equal members on the "team" are afraid to speak out. Others who feel that they have made the transition to respected worker, not merely "woman worker," don't want to jeopardize this (mostly illusionary) position by saying anything to support women who are perceived by men as whining about problems on the job.

Since women don't have the workplace pull to push or bargain many of their issues through, the teams create a world where women who are more assertive may be less likely to talk about problems other women face with teams.

PLEASE THE CUSTOMER

Pam, who works in customer services for a multi-national hotel chain, was surprised by how her co-workers, 98 percent of whom are women, accepted merit raises: "Since this program began two years ago, not one person has suggested that we do something about the fact that even though we meet the productivity goals, very few of us ever receive a full merit raise. This is because the system is tied into so many subjective factors that have nothing to do with job performance.

"Reaching productivity is tied to an incentive payment program, so everyone bought into it because management set relatively low production figures which everyone felt they could meet. Then management announced that those who did not meet those goals were out."

This has led to a situation where overtime pay is used to replace raises. If more work cannot be jammed into the increasingly *passe* eight-hour day, then women workers—like men—are encouraged to work overtime. Not much encouragement is needed in light of women's low wages.

"With raises so low," Pam says, "overtime becomes a real issue. But when you have children you have to constantly choose to work, rest, or take time away from your kids. With participation you literally feel guilty for staying home on your day off.

"What really bothers me is how fast people get sucked into these programs. We have people literally fighting each other over who gets to meet the CEO when he comes down for a walk through the departments.

"The bosses know exactly the real position of women in this company. They keep a ready workforce of contingent workers in our office working right alongside us." This use of contingent workers to keep organized and unorganized workers in line is a fact of work life today.

Pam brings up another problem presumably related to management's desire to "please the customer": "Women in the service industry don't talk about how you have to have the right look to get ahead." Pam gives an example, a contest that was open to employees from around the country. The employee who got the most positive responses from customers, via phone calls or letters, won.

The winner was an African-American woman from Detroit—but then management attempted to change the prize and didn't want to put her picture in the national publication.

"Now here's a woman who'd received many personal letters from customers saying how much she'd helped them," says Pam. "She even helped some woman customer who'd become disoriented and called our office by mistake. So you can see management is not truly interested in customer service, quality, and dedicated employees.

"The company wants people who look right, and that can be anything from the right color to the right size. Team concept puts increased pressure on women to 'look good' at work in a very traditional female way.

"Our managers often tell us they want people who can 'walk the walk and talk the talk.' But the talk and the walk both make me sick."

Pam believes that management manipulates workers through "trust and openness." "If sales are down," she says, "they will let you look at any financial information they have and let you decide what *you're* going to do to improve the situation. Work longer hours, defer raises, whatever. Once they have you cooperating, every union principle goes out the window.

"Team concept does get people involved in their work, but it's all the wrong aspects. People spend nearly 75 percent of their time evaluating managers and their performance problems, for management. They do this on their own time.

"The teams don't get it: management is not going to hire anyone spectacularly different from this guy they want workers to participate in 'firing.'" Pam believes this is a warm-up exercise: "They do it to build you up to the point where they'll start team evaluations and you won't think twice about shipping somebody out of here."

Finally, Pam points out that women are socialized to "naturally" take on more and more work without complaint—housework, children, job. Pam remarks, "I think it is just understood that we'll do the extra work without any extra compensation. Women are used to taking on increases and shifting things around." This fits in nicely with team concept.

DOING MANAGEMENT'S WORK

Colleen works at a major metropolitan newspaper. Her union successfully filed a grievance to get out of a participation program because members were not being compensated for the work they were doing.

"We were doing everything from developing budgets, attending committee meetings on customer satisfaction, employee relations, and safety, all without compensation," Colleen explains. "Some of these meetings were two hours long and held every week or every other week—and you still had to do your real job.

"I think that women tend to be more nurturing in many offices and with teams we tended to pull together more to get the job done. But the downside was that many women set themselves up as unofficial leaders, taking on the role of management and attempting to discipline other team members."

Management also shifts a lot of dirty work onto the teams. One is job assignments, another is scheduling. Before, management scheduled and that was that. "Now," Colleen remarks, "you have to fight it out among the team, and there are hard feelings because many women with childcare concerns feel they should have priority.

"Our schedules have changed as a result of the team concept. Many of us had to come to work at 8:00 a.m. instead of 9:00 a.m. because of 'business demands' and rotate on weekends for five-week stretches.

"We found that with teams there was a lot of downsizing. When the job cuts come it's always the departments or units that are heavy with women workers that seem to go first. The billing department was combined, which is nearly all women.

"As a result of the downsizing, jobs were combined and every employee had to reapply for their job."

Colleen's experience is that "essentially all team concept does is put you on a long leash, which management holds. As long as you are going in the direction they want you to, it's fine, but if you venture off into other areas, the leash is jerked."

ARE WOMEN MORE PATIENT?

Kathy is a public service worker for a utility company. She is a union officer in a local with a 700-person clerical unit, where only 50 of the workers are men, and a 2,200-member production unit, where there are only 150 women. The labor-management participation teams at this company started out with creature comfort tasks such as putting in a water cooler or painting the bathrooms.

Kathy believes that teams have divided the local. She says, "We have people who think it is the greatest thing, and other union members see the downside. I think that many women are more willing to be involved because they are patient and willing to wait for a positive outcome. This waiting hurts the union, because the company can approach so many workers directly to do things that by-pass the union and 'step on the contract,' and this has weakened our bargaining position."

'WE ARE ALL WORKERS'

Women hear that we have achieved workplace equity and our situation is now no different from men's because "we are all workers." This assertion that workplace equity has arrived, together with the assault on affirmative action programs, has left many women unwilling to speak out about workplace problems and participation.

Affirmative action programs and laws that address discrimination in the workplace are often viewed as functioning only to address the needs of people of color, specifically African Americans. But white women workers have also been beneficiaries of these programs, and to a lesser extent other women workers of color. With the backlash against affirmative action, what's left? Management wants women to fall in with the idea that participation equals workplace fairness. It does not.

The participation mechanism declines to acknowledge that the average working woman has been continually placed at the back of the economic wagon. Gaining the right to participate on a team doesn't address that fact, much less alter it.

When participation programs weaken unions and contract language, they weaken the mechanism that could tie the needs of women for real workplace participation to stronger affirmative action policies in the workplace.

LOOK WHO'S TALKING

Management seeks the cooperation of union leaders to push its programs. "Partnerships work well within union settings when top levels of the unions are involved," writes Jill Casner-Lotto of the Work of America Institute.

But in most unions women are not involved at the top levels. So their perspective on participation programs doesn't seem to be filtering up or down the union hierarchy.

Pam, the hotel worker, for instance, feels that the lack of respect shown to women by society spills over onto the way women are treated in participation programs. "Our own union is pushing this team program," she says, "and if there were more men here I don't think they would make the same requests of us or even bring the contracts to us that they do."

It is hard to believe that teams would accept "business necessity" clauses that dictate people work weekends and start work earlier if more women were an integral part of union leadership.

Over the past 25 years, women workers have fought to end job segregation and discrimination in hiring, training, and promotion. Some unions now include these issues in their bargaining demands. But the struggle for women's full representation continues. If unions are not addressing the issues that women have organized for—such as childcare, pay equity, and ending sexual harassment and discrimination—some may see participation programs as an alternative means of making progress.

Unions cannot afford such a development. As Sharon, a CWA member at Bell South, put it, "Team concept can't break down sexism at the workplace, but it can make it worse—by giving everyone written approval to pretend that it doesn't exist because 'we're all on the same team.'"

Notes

1. Juliet Schor, *The Overworked American: The Unexpected Decline of Leisure*, Basic Books, 1991.

2. Francine D. Blau and Marianne A. Ferber, "Occupations and Earnings of Women Workers," chapter in *Working Women: Past, Present, Future*, Industrial Relations Research Association, Washington, D.C., 1987, p. 46.

3. U.S. Office of Technology Assessment, 1985.

4. "Making Quality Pay," *Business Week*, August 8, 1994.

5. Kalima Rose, "Women and Job Training: A New Agenda," *Equal Means*, Fall 1993, p. 8.

6. "Finding the Right Words: Adding Work Without Adding Pay," October 1994, p. 73.

7. Rose, p. 7.

Working Smart:
A Union Guide to Participation Programs and Reengineering
Labor Notes • 7435 Michigan Ave. • Detroit, MI 48210 • (313) 842-6262

Chapter 19

Public Employees: What Happens When Governments Adopt Quality?

Public workers are natural targets for quality programs, since no one is satisfied with government services. But quality programs have been aimed at cost-cutting and contracting out rather than improving quality, both in state and federal government and in schools. Some locals have developed guidelines, such as work reduction for those participating, sunset language on projects, and elected representatives. The most important is making both the overall program and its details subject to collective bargaining.

by Dan La Botz

AMERICANS HAVE A LONG TRADITION OF MAKING JOKES about public employees. Remember Ralph Cramden and Ed Norton from "The Honeymooners"? Ralph was a bus driver and Norton was a sewer worker—goofy guys. Or Cliff Claven, the letter carrier on "Cheers": in one episode the bunch at the bar remind Cliff of the time he burned a bag of mail; in another Cliff talks about reading his customers' mail. In yet another he distributes magazines to the regulars while he has a beer. Cliff, who regularly recites the postal oath "nor sleet, nor snow," is portrayed as an irresponsible and incompetent (though lovable) public employee.

Television sitcoms make jokes out of the same stuff that fills the editorial pages in newspapers. Pundits regularly attack public workers as incompetent, lazy, wasteful, and unfortunately pretty much non-firable, because of union, equal employment, and civil service protections.

The roots of this antagonism to public employees may seem to lie in the public consciousness. Who isn't critical of politicians and government bureaucrats—usually for good reason. The government takes our tax money and

Dan La Botz is the author of A Troublemaker's Handbook. *He has worked for a number of public employee unions, including AFSCME and the American Federation of Teachers. He wishes to thank Dianne Feeley for her valuable contributions to this chapter.*

provides inadequate services. Most people have little contact with the politicians who make the laws so they take out their frustrations on the public employees who are right there. When we stand in a long, slow line at the post office, we blame the clerk rather than the politician. The public worker is attacked for practices the worker had no hand in creating and in many cases opposed and resisted.

But this common tendency to criticize the public worker is not simply the public's natural reaction. Over the last fifteen years, conservatives have launched a systematic attack on social services and public employees. Conservative think tanks, Republicans and Democrats (in Canada Conservatives and Liberals) argued that business should be the model for government, that government had to downsize and get lean. Government was too big, too fat, and so, presumably, were its employees. Public employees were portrayed as hogs eating out of the public trough (an image originally applied to politicians).

Of course, this attack on government and public employees was motivated by business's self-interest. Business wanted to reduce taxes, which were cutting into profits; to gut regulations that added to the cost of doing business, such as OSHA and the EPA; and to enter areas previously monopolized by government. There were companies that wanted to provide janitorial services in public buildings, and others prepared to take over entire public school districts. All these business interests found expression in an ideology dressed up as "economy and efficiency" in government.

Right-wing pundits argue that government is just a business like any other and should be subject to the same economic laws of supply and demand, competition and profitability. The argument is that business methods would allow public enterprises to provide better services at less cost. When the politicians brought business methods to government, they brought along Total Quality Management (TQM).

Not surprisingly, when governments act like business they tend to reduce public services, cut the workforce, attack benefits, and resist wage increases. The result has generally been poorer service and a deterioration of public workers' jobs.

THE REAL PROBLEMS OF GOVERNMENT

Public employees knew better than most of us what was really going on: the problem of inefficient government was its byzantine bureaucracy. Government bureaucracy—both military and civilian—was often an accumulation of different legislation and regulations resulting from various policies and programs adopted over the years. The result was layers upon layers of bureaucrats and managers administering tomes of complicated and sometimes contradictory rules and regulations.

Conscientious public employees committed to serving the public often tried to by-pass top-heavy management and cut through the rolls of red tape. Lower-level managers and workers knew they had a public to serve. Teachers' and social workers' unions, in particular, had made alliances with parents and welfare clients since the 1960s or earlier. Through the agency, the union, or informally, workers and clients attempted to improve services.

But public employee unions often found it hard to fight the bureaucracy and the politicians. Historically, public employees unions, especially federal workers unions, were weak. Some public employees had no right to organize unions, many had no right to strike, and most had severe restrictions on their collective bargaining rights.

So when TQM appeared, it held out the promise that public employees could by-pass the bureaucracy, cut the red tape, and better serve the public. Given the historic weakness of public employee unions, TQM seemed to provide a new vehicle for worker organization and negotiation.

Unfortunately, most of the promises would turn out to be false.

Quality programs first appeared in the public sector in the United States in the 1980s. However, they didn't really catch hold until the 1990s, when the U.S. government and many state and local governments developed quality programs as a way to cut costs, reorganize the workforce, and—in many cases—challenge the union. Federal, state, county, and municipal governments, universities and school boards all adopted the new quality slogans. Offi-

cials talked about "total quality schools," created "total quality hospitals," and established quality circles among toll takers and tree trimmers.

TQM has clearly been driven by the government's fiscal crisis, not by a genuine desire on the part of its initiators in management to improve services. It was a way to cut costs, not to "empower" public workers. Politicians have reduced the workforce and introduced TQM to compensate. The great danger is that unions are expected to share responsibility for cutting the budget.

As in the private sector, TQM has frequently been accompanied by contracting out, usually to non-union employers. The criterion for contracting out seems to be simply cost cutting, not maintaining or improving services. And in many cases, contracting out does not mean lower costs, although it does lower wages. United Auto Workers Local 6000 (representing 22,000 state employees) prepared a two-year study on contracts in the state of Michigan, and discovered problems and deficiencies in 40 percent of the cases. These included no-bid contracts and cost overruns, and a case where the state spent $145,000 for contract technicians to do work that state employees could have done for $59,000.

WHY IS THERE A PUBLIC SECTOR?

Traditionally the American people have viewed the public sector as serving a number of essential functions. At least in theory, the welfare of the community and its essential services were too important to allow the profit motive to be the driving force.

Public schools, for example, were not created to be profitable or cost effective, but because Americans believed that free, universal education was essential to citizenship in a democratic republic. Many Americans saw public education as the basis for equality of opportunity.

Similarly with other public sector work. Rather than hiring mercenaries, we have a citizen army. Public hospitals and clinics were intended to ensure the nation's basic health care. The various public welfare systems—social security, workers' compensation, unemployment insurance, aid to families with dependent children, general assistance, public housing programs—were to help people who needed special support.

Obviously, when a country has a portion of people who are ill-fed, ill-housed, and illiterate, it's not just those particular individuals who suffer, but the quality of life of the entire nation. Public services were designed to meet social needs—not the demands of the marketplace.

Many others areas of the public sector—national parks, public transit, sanitation, and fire protection—were also predicated upon the idea of serving the common good. It was assumed that if it was impossible to make some services pay for themselves—a subway system, for example—then their operation would be subsidized out of general funds.

Of course, today private firms *are* trying to muscle in on areas that we once thought were too important to be left to them (see box).

Because of the nature of the work, the economics of the public sector are different from those of business. As Tim Nesbitt of the Oregon Public Employees Union explains, "It's not like in the market with a product. You won't suddenly find that there's no more demand for your product and you have to shut down. It's not the same threat."

HOW STATE GOVERNMENTS CAME TO LOVE TQM

The Reagan and Bush administrations transferred greater financial responsibility for social programs onto state and local governments. Since 1978, Washington has reduced its financial aid to states and cities by 10 percent (after adjusting for inflation). By eliminating general revenue sharing, the federal government reduced its commitment to education, health care, penal systems, and grants to low-income people.

As the Reagan-Bush administrations cut taxes for the wealthy, the shaky economy meant public services were more necessary than ever. But the money wasn't there. During the 1980s non-military public spending fell to 25 percent of the level sustained during the 1950s and 1960s.[1]

In fiscal 1990 40 percent of state governments cut their budgets, laying off workers and contracting out services. In some cases the state governments sought the unions' help to continue providing services with less money and fewer workers. Many TQM programs developed out of those efforts.

MASSACHUSETTS—FROM MIRACLE TO MIRAGE

Massachusetts is a good example of a state where fiscal crisis drove the reorganization of the workforce. Two key industries in the state—high-tech industry and military research—both saw downturns. But Governor William Weld, a Republican and former Reagan appointee, blamed the problem on "tax and spend" policies of the state's "liberal" traditions. He privatized some public services and launched a massive assault on public employees.

"Our state was one of the first to hit rock bottom economically," explains Sandy Felder. Felder, a former social worker in the Department of Mental Health, is president and executive director of Service Employees International Union (SEIU) Local 509, representing 9,500 human service and education workers. Mostly professional employees, the local is 70 percent women and 20 percent people of color.

"Governor Weld," says Felder, "used all the 'reinventing government' rhetoric. He talked about 'worker participation' and TQM."

The Massachusetts Department of Mental Retardation serves severely and profoundly mentally retarded clients who live in the community, either at home or in group homes. Case workers or coordinators who serve these clients have an average caseload of about 40 patients.

Governor Weld's new commissioner of mental retarda-

Quality, Not Layoffs!

The following article is from the *Tech Guild News* of AFSCME Local 375 in New York City (January 1994). It illustrates the pressures leading public worker unions to want to try TQM.

We are now, and will remain, eager to work in a spirit of cooperation with the Giuliani Administration. But as we feared, he and his appointees are now hinting at major layoffs and outspoken in stating that private or "non-profit" corporations are to be preferred to civil service employees.

It might shock the mayor to learn that public workers *agree* that government is often badly managed. We see it every day. We *also* know what can be done to improve it, if given a chance.

Instead, downsizing and privatization have become a kind of religion.

To The True Believers in the managerial class, it isn't necessary to analyze whether the public can be better served by a contractor or new agency, or by better use of the existing workforce. They *know*, as an article faith, that it should be privatized. And, not surprisingly, it is the True Believers who "inherit the earth" when the "forces of darkness" (public workers) are swept away.

The City Council voted 39-10 in December 1993 to hand over plumbing and fire-suppression inspections provided by the Buildings Department to a newly created non-profit "Buildings Services Corporation."

Pointing to last fall's arrest of 26 plumbing inspectors, Acting Building Commissioner Stewart O'Brien said chronic understaffing created a huge backlog and guaranteed that frustrated builders would offer bribes to expedite their paperwork.

When I and others asked the City Council why they didn't just add inspectors, we got only an embarrassed silence.

"The new publicly sponsored agency would require a complete bureaucracy...that would duplicate existing operations...a more costly patronage mill," wrote Al Engel in *The Watchdog*, publication of the Civil Service Merit Council.

Sure enough, the president of the new Building Services Corporation is to be none other than....Stewart O'Brien! In the privileged world of the Privateers, you *can* become captain of the rescue vessel after you steer your own ship onto the rocks.

In other words, your job could be next. At the very moment in history when National Health Care could finally provide a revenue stream to pay for uninsured poor people, Giuliani proposes selling off four or more municipal hospitals. WNYC could be on the block. At DOT, DGS and elsewhere, engineering and architectural work could go to consultants instead of the in-house design staff.

Total Quality Management is one promising approach to doing more in hard times. But it means a true partnership with employees, and a willingness to make cuts in upper management, not just layoffs at the bottom.

—Louis G. Albano, President

tion wanted a quality council, with Local 509 involved. "We looked forward to it," explained Felder, "because our workers wanted to make their work better. But we would only participate under certain conditions."

Local 509 agreed to the project for one particular job title: service coordinator. This involved some 400 workers (in 20 different area offices) who were community social workers. The union deliberately picked a narrow title because they didn't want SEIU members' decisions to impact another union's members.

(SEIU would have been willing to join in a TQM program with other unions. But AFSCME did not want to participate because it had been burned: a previous program had brainstormed the idea of privatizing housekeeping services, and nearly 2,000 AFSCME members lost their jobs.)

So SEIU brought the following conditions to the negotiating table:

- No layoffs or demotions through TQM.
- Training of labor and management on work time.
- Retraining if existing work became no longer necessary.
- Revenue sharing if the program saved money, for training or upgrading skills.
- Release time or work reduction to participate in the program. (This last was important given that the worker representative could come back from TQM to find the same cases waiting on her desk as when she left.)
- Workers elect their representatives.
- Any proposals for changes in conditions of employment or productivity would be subject to the collective bargaining process.

While the union was in the middle of negotiations over the program, the commissioner had his managers hand-select five workers to sit on a TQM committee. They were part of a team of 17 (the rest being managers, private providers, and consumer representatives). Nonetheless, the union leadership decided they would try to work with the committee that management had unilaterally appointed. They approached the five workers to discuss the pros and cons of TQM. This made the commissioner furious, and he broke off negotiations.

The five workers recognized that the focus groups were management-dominated committees. They organized themselves to exert their rights. They reported that the commissioner openly criticized the union at meetings. Three resigned; but the commissioner continued on, hand-selecting other workers.

In clear violation of state collective bargaining law, the committee conducted a survey of all service coordinators. In this survey, questions about privatization of certain job functions, productivity, and other illegal subjects were asked for worker opinion. The unity of the workers was shown when only 40 out of 400 were returned. And on the 40 returned, the answers were consistent with the union's position.

The commissioner filed "prohibited practice" charges against the union for allegedly interfering with his ability to talk to his employees. He claimed that the union was coercing the workers.

SEIU responded by filing charges at the State Labor Relations Commission, over the agency's creation of an employer-dominated joint committee. At this writing, the charges were still pending.

According to Felder, "What could have been a positive process where service coordinators would have improved the quality of their services to their clients through worker participation has turned into a tainted process that has created distrust and confusion."

OREGON: GAINSHARING

The SEIU's experience in the Oregon Department of Transportation illustrates the problems unions may run into with gainsharing. While ultimately the Department and the Oregon Public Employees Union, SEIU Local 503, reached an amicable settlement of their differences, the union had to fight to protect its rights.

Management first presented its plan as simply a team-based approach to work and a way to develop measurements of performance. But it soon became apparent that management wanted performance-based pay. "Gainsharing systems provide extra compensation for meeting or exceeding production goals," explains Tim Nesbitt, OPEU assistant executive director.

Nesbitt explained the process through which the union belatedly learned: "It was only after promises were made and workers had been through trial periods of six months or so, and expected to get paid, that management approached the union saying, 'We need to bargain over this now because it's getting into the area of compensation.'"

Management said it was willing to bargain, but would only pay the bonuses it had already promised to workers *if* the union accepted gainsharing.

New York: Union Checklist

In 1992 New York state began introducing Quality Through Participation (QtP) in six agencies. By 1994 eleven agencies were involved.

The Civil Service Employees Association (CSEA-AFSCME) developed a checklist of points for locals to bargain. They included:

Sunset language: All quality projects should end with the current collective bargaining agreement. In this way, the parties can determine the future of any individual QtP project.

Measurement of results: CSEA members must be involved in developing project measures so that issues important to the union are measured.

A joint project review process: This could include a form that indicates whether the project involves out-of-title work, a mandatory subject of negotiations, or a contractual issue.

Documentation of projects: A record of projects should be kept, to be used during subsequent contract negotiations.

OPEU had a number of concerns—from the creation of the teams, which were designed to function without first-level supervisors, to the method of computing payment. As Nesbitt explained the process of speed-up: "People understood very well that you can be stuck on a ratcheting escalator where you work harder to earn your bonus, and then the basis for bonuses is recomputed to a higher level. Then you work harder... We were not able to get management to agree that they wouldn't continually readjust the standards."

The union was also concerned that there were no job security provisions in management's proposal. The members voted overwhelmingly to reject it.

At that point OPEU filed an unfair labor practice charge, arguing that management had unilaterally established a new wage payment program. As Nesbitt explains, this put OPEU "in a no-win position with some of our members who expected to be paid."

"We took the position," says Nesbitt, "that it was an unfair labor practice to condition bargaining." The remedy the union sought was that the employer pay the bonuses already promised.

Eventually there was a settlement for the full amount of bonuses for two periods, the length of the pilot pro-

gram. Then the program was terminated. Management didn't like it because it turned out to be too costly. In a sense, the workers in the pilot program got the best of both worlds: substantial bonuses without having their production standards ratcheted up. As Nesbitt remarked, "The checks we finally got for people were significant, $3,000-4,000 for people earning $20,000 a year.

"It was important to go through the educational experience and to have the debate among the members. Because if management comes to you with money in hand you can't just say no to it. You have to deal with the proposal and go through the membership on the decision."

OPEU does not reject the establishment of teams or gainsharing out of hand. "Instead," says Nesbitt, "we've come up with principles we feel can work. With the public sector under a lot of pressure to reinvent itself, and with money for wage increases hard to come by, we're not willing to shut the door on these programs if they are done right. It's important to educate the members about the pros and cons."

OPEU's policy on pay for performance and gainsharing includes:

• Any such system must be based on group performance and not individual performance.

• Any financial reward must be supplemental to the existing compensation plan, including step increases and cost of living increases, and not used in lieu of competitive equitable wage rates.

Any Union Members Present?

Even after the Total Quality Partnership was begun, it appears that federal government managers were still practicing and preaching an adversarial stance toward unions. In May 1994 a doctor with the National Institute for Occupational Safety and Health (NIOSH), himself a supervisor, attended a workshop on Labor and Employee Relations, given by the Human Resources Management Office (HRMO). Afterwards, he wrote to the head of the Centers for Disease Control to complain about the attitudes displayed there:

Dear Dr. Satcher,

...I was very concerned at the way the facilitators encouraged an adversarial relationship to the AFGE Unions throughout the training session. I am especially disheartened because on one hand, we are being told there is a new spirit of cooperation between management and the Unions, yet at the same time, this course focused on ways for managers to steer around Union involvement in the day-to-day operations of work, and to treat Union members, especially Union officials, with suspicion.

[The HRMO facilitators] prefaced their discussions by asking (in lowered voices) if there were only supervisors and managers present in the room, and them remarked that they could then be up-front about discussing the Unions because no members were there...

Several times during the day-long workshop, [the facilitators] both made comments that the Unions were just trying to be obstructionists and keep management from dealing directly with employees... One made other disparaging remarks about the Unions, such as stating the Union was just a big business itself, with its own VISA card, health care plan, and was marketing itself to employees just to make it more powerful...

Instead of stressing open communication, we were told by her not to use E-mail or to avoid writing things down when dealing with employees because there would be a paper trail, and thus, it would be more difficult for the Labor Relations Office to suggest that there was "no intent" if there was a Union dispute...

We have been told we are moving away from an adversarial relationship between employees and management, yet the message was clearly in the other direction...

Bruce Bernard, MD, MPH
Supervisory Medical Officer
Hazard Evaluations and Technical Assistance Branch

• The measurement of group performance must be based on objective verifiable criteria bargained with, and agreed to, by the union.

• Financial rewards must be bargained with, and agreed to, by the union as part of the contract in regular contract bargaining.

• Job security must be guaranteed for all participants.

FEDERAL EMPLOYEES: FROM TQM TO TQP AND REINVENTION

The culmination of a decade of federal government experiments in quality programs was the Clinton administration's call to "Reinvent Government." Vice President Al Gore took the lead in outlining an overhaul.

The Gore Commission conducted its National Performance Review of the government and in September 1993 issued a report called "From Red Tape to Results: Creating a Government That Works Better and Costs Less." The report suggested junking the 10,000-page federal Personnel Manual and creating a new, more "flexible" management system.

The report rejected adversarial labor-management relations and called for alternative forms of dispute resolution. The centerpiece of the proposal was the creation throughout government of "labor-management partnerships."

Shortly thereafter, on October 1, 1993, President Clinton issued Executive Order 12871, "Labor-Management Partnerships." The order established the National Partnership Council, made up of seven executives from government departments and four union leaders. The National Partnership Council was arguably the biggest union-management cooperation program in the country.

To cement the partnership, the presidents of three federal unions agreed to the elimination of 252,000 jobs.

While the administration said the elimination of jobs would occur through attrition, buy-outs, and targeting middle-management positions, not by a reduction-in-force, a RIF soon occurred in the Office of Personnel Management. Many agencies immediately began "hiding" their targeted management personnel by changing their titles to non-supervisory ones, with no reduction in duties, grade, or pay. Those managers had rights to bump union employees.[2]

The new working arrangement is called Total Quality Partnership (TQP). Federal managers have begun creating TQP agreements, starting at the highest levels of departments and agencies. These are expected to "cascade" down until they eventually reach the grass roots. At the time of this writing, only a few partnership agreements had been negotiated, so it is difficult to assess their effect on the rank and file.

But clearly the National Partnership Council isn't a partnership of equals. The gut issues—union security clauses, agency shop, service fees, contracting out, pay, employment security, benefits, and retirement—will be dealt with as the council's "recommendations," to be worked out in the legislative arena. Congress began to voice its intent to resist the recommendations before the ink had dried.[3]

The Executive Order instructed federal managers that they would now have to bargain over what were known as "permissive subjects"—"the right to determine numbers, types, and grades of employees assigned to a work project or tour of duty; and the technology, methods, and means of performing work." Under the order these "previously permissive subjects"—which were almost never bargained over in the past—were "now mandatory."

Because the union officially has a voice in TQP, some union leaders and activists see TQP as an improvement over previous top-down TQM programs. With federal unions having such limited bargaining rights, any chance to bargain over working conditions that were previously off-limits is welcome.

However, the Executive Order has no enforcement provisions. In the spring of 1994, officers of the American Federation of Government Employees (AFGE), the largest non-postal federal union, were complaining that they had as yet seen no bargaining on permissive subjects. Second, if the parties do negotiate over the permissive areas, the primary criterion to evaluate proposals is "to make Government capable of delivering the highest quality services to the American people." This is standard TQM ideology that places all the emphasis on the "customer," while ignoring the worker.[4]

AFGE produced a ten-minute video for local union leaders titled "Full Partnership," in which President John Sturdivant declares that the partnership program is an "historic opportunity" to move the union from the "traditional workplace" to the "workplace of the future.170

In the video, Butch Henry, president of Local 2302 at Fort Knox, Kentucky, explains how partnership worked there:

> Although management's philosophies in reducing the budget had always been directly related to reducing our employees, they offered our local the ultimate challenge. If we could develop a process that would achieve the ultimate dollar savings—without violating a law, rule, or regulation—they'd agree to our plan. In effect, all the permissive subjects were negotiable.
>
> We reduced our payroll budget by 16 percent in 14 months. That's four percent more than is going to be required [by the administration] over the next five years.

Henry stresses that no employee was laid off or downgraded. But the fact remains that the union not only put its stamp of approval on job cuts, the union helped implement the cuts and then bragged about them.

Since Sturdivant cites Local 2302 as a model, it appears that TQP will be a tool to reduce the workforce. That's a lot of partners without jobs.

Several AFGE vice presidents maintain that TQP is simply another management tool for speed-up, weakening the union, and downsizing the workforce.

"I think it really started with Ronald Reagan's Grace Commission," says Terry Rogers of Minneapolis. "It was made up of top corporate industrialists, and it recommended streamlining government, eliminating all sorts of programs. They proposed slashing every program that they could and contracting out what was left."

In what respect are the Reagan and Clinton programs different? In Rogers' view, "The lines were clearer with Ronald Reagan. He fired all the air traffic controllers. He set the tone for corporate America to attack working people and the labor unions that represent them. So the lines were clear. This administration has blurred the lines." As Rogers sees it, Clinton is carrying out many of Reagan's policies, only now in the name of partnership and participation.

Garret Anglin of Vancouver, Washington, vice president of AFGE's 11th District and candidate for president against John Sturdivant in 1994, cites his experience with Total Quality Initiative (TQI) in 1992. One area of controversy, according to Anglin, was work schedules. Many agencies, especially the Department of Defense, had been reluctant to allow flexible scheduling, but after litigation the union was able to secure some flexible scheduling in its contract. Management then tried to use TQI work groups to reverse these schedules. Anglin commented, "What they couldn't win legitimately at the table they were trying to take away through the TQI process."

Anglin takes note of the private sector models that the federal government and AFGE studied in arriving at their partnership. "Only one, Saturn," says Anglin, "did not involve layoffs of significant numbers of employees. At Xerox and IBM and AT&T and the Baby Bells, they are decimating the worker ranks of their employees."

WHY HAVE THE UNIONS ACCEPTED PARTNERSHIP?

Why have federal unions accepted partnership? One has to look at the last fifteen years to appreciate

"Okay, we move the White House to Mexico...the Congress to Indonesia...the Supreme Court to Nigeria..."

their situation.

First, Ronald Reagan's 1981 firing of some 11,000 members of the Professional Air Traffic Controllers (PATCO) intimidated the federal unions.

Second, under Reagan and Bush, many social welfare programs were terminated or shrunk. Some workers were lost through attrition, others were fired. Federal workers found they were doing more work with fewer co-workers.

Third, throughout the 1980s, politicians, corporations, and the media maintained a constant barrage of propaganda suggesting that there were too many public employees, that they were incompetent, and that they were too highly paid for unneeded services.

Fourth, public employee unions and especially federal workers have never enjoyed all of the fundamental union rights (the right to strike, the right to bargain collectively over wages, hours, and benefits).

Fifth, because of these constraints, unions have become quite dependent on the Democratic Party in Congress to solve the problems they have been unable to solve through collective bargaining.

All of these factors have weakened the unions. They spent the Reagan-Bush years dealing with a hostile federal government and budget cuts. So they welcomed the Clinton administration and the *idea* of participation and partnership. This was true for the national leadership of the unions as well as many local leaders and rank and file.

Peter Grossi, AFGE vice president for New England, points to another way the new Total Quality Partnership is attractive: "I think that as workers the federal workforce has very low self-esteem. TQP provides people an opportunity to get rid of their frustration, and believe that someone in a responsible position is willing to listen to them."

Pick your brains to pick your pockets.

Asked if he thought the participatory process was real, Grossi explained, "It's real in that they're having meetings. But beyond that it's illusory. To the degree that substantive ideas or solutions might be secured from such schemes, those solutions being presented with the best of intentions are going to come back to haunt people. I call it, pick your brains to pick your pockets, and end up throwing you out the door."

ONE LOCAL'S APPROACH

One experiment with Total Quality Improvement was at a Social Security Administration Program Service Center in Philadelphia. (Philadelphia was an unusual situation in that it was allowed to continue as a local experiment while AFGE's SSA Councils negotiated nationally.)

Warren Davis is vice president for grievances and equal employment opportunity of AFGE Local 2006 at the Center. About one thousand people work there reviewing and resolving claims.

Davis explains that over a decade of inadequate staffing in SSA has resulted in large caseloads. About one-

third of the workforce has been cut, mostly through attrition. The only reason employees have not fallen more behind is that much of the work has been computerized.

Another problem is the complexity and redundancy of the system. "We have different levels of authorizers and support people," Davis explains. Particular issues of law (evidentiary requirements, relationships of spouses and children) are handled by claims authorizers. Benefit authorizers handle the payment portion, correcting the payment record. Then there's an accounting process where payees for beneficiaries are accountable for their spending. Each operation has its own set of procedures. "It's a jerry-built system that has accumulated so much process over the years," Davis notes.

"So I suppose that [Regional Director] Larry Massanari figured that the best thing to do was to attack these processes, instead of trying to figure out how to wrest more work out of the employees. They were at the point where they had no choice but to try to introduce some sort of process adjustment rather than attitude adjustment in the employees—though there's certainly the intention to have an attitude adjustment through TQI too." ("Attacking the processes" also goes by the term "reengineering," discussed in chapter 1.)

Davis worked on negotiating the TQI agreement for his local. He and his fellow negotiators used the Labor Notes books as guides. "We went very slowly and deliberately and had a lot of safeguards built in, taking the examples of language from Labor Notes' book on team concept," says Davis. "It's been a little over two years now; we've finally got five teams in place and they're just beginning to do their work."

Local 2006 and management worked out a Memorandum of Understanding (MOU) on a Quality Council with three top management representatives and three top officials of the union.

"There have been some disagreements about interpretation of the MOU," says Davis, "even though the people on the Quality Council were essentially the ones who negotiated it. If a team comes up with a recommendation for a change, we retained our right to bargain on impact and implementation of that change. The MOU also says that the proposal will come back to the Quality Council for review.

"But now management is saying that it's simply a rubber stamp review. We're saying, no, the proposal shouldn't go anywhere unless the Quality Council signs off on it. We say there must be full review, full consultation, and nothing comes out of the Quality Council for bargaining unless the full Quality Council has consensus on it."

When the time came to train the TQI teams, Local 2006 found that management tried to hand-pick people. Since the union is an open shop where workers are not required to join the union or even pay an agency fee, Local 2006 worked to prepare the entire workforce for a full year before they negotiated the MOU. Their union newsletter reprinted articles from *Labor Notes* and Labor

Notes books, and raised the level of discussion.

"Nevertheless," says Davis, "there are those who think TQI might be a good thing, and those are the people who management targets to get on the teams. They will tell management where the system can be improved, even at the risk of their own speed-up. So we've had a bit of a struggle trying to select people. We think we have the right to choose people for those teams."

The union developed its own plan to deal with TQI training. Davis explains, "We said in our negotiations that since this was a voluntary program, we wanted every employee to have some idea of what they were getting into before they volunteered. We didn't just want them volunteering blindly. So we wanted a one-day orientation to TQI."

The union got management to outline TQI and explain how workflows are analyzed. After hearing management's conception, the union pointed out the dangers through the newsletter. Davis summarizes the results, "Generally the workforce is highly skeptical; our education effort worked well. Of course, we had the advantage that management was seen as totally corrupt, of no use to the employees and trying to beat them up."

QUALITY SCHOOLS

While Total Quality Management has not yet been adopted by most school districts, many are experimenting with pilot programs. Because most TQM projects in primary and secondary schools are new, unions, teachers, staff, parents, and students have not yet had much time to react. Nevertheless, TQM is clearly a growing trend in education.

TQM, privatization experiments, and contracting out of janitorial and transportation services spring from the same impulse, the notion that the corporation is the model for everything in American society, even the education of our children. We will examine here the TQM experience of the Chicago Public Schools, one of the nation's largest school districts.

After going bankrupt in 1979, the Chicago schools were run by a School Finance Authority, which oversaw the deterioration of the physical plant, stagnation of teaches' salaries, increases in class size, falling student test scores, and parental disappointment. When the Chicago Teachers Union struck for two weeks in 1987, they forced the state legislature to act.

In July 1989 the Illinois Legislature passed the Chicago School Reform Law, creating Local School Councils (LSCs) made up of parent, teacher, and community representatives. The six parents, two teachers, two community members, the principal, and student (if a high school) have three powers: to hire a principal; to adopt a School Improvement Plan (SIP); to approve the final budget and allocate discretionary funds to meet the goals of the SIP.

As a gesture to the unions, the law also created a Professional Personnel Advisory Committee (PPAC)

elected by teachers and certified personnel to advise the principal and the LSC on curriculum, staff development, the SIP, and the budget. It is, however, only an advisory committee with no power over budget or personnel.

The creation of the LSCs was a fundamental change that weakened the power of the Chicago School Board's large bureaucracy. It shook up the school system. Many teachers, parents, students, and community members saw the LSCs as an opportunity to create democratic institutions that could reform the schools. However, the LSCs were taking on the difficult task of reform with no money.

At the same time, Chicago's corporations also took an interest in the schools. The Kellogg Graduate School of Management at Northwestern University initiated one corporate-inspired program. In 1992, Kellog began a Total Quality Schools (TQS) program to train Chicago principals, teachers, and LSC members. None involved in the Kellogg program had a background in education. The leader of the program was Stuart Greenbaum, director of Kellogg's Banking Research Center. All the rest were professors of business management.[5] Schools were invited to send three representatives to a five-day seminar at a cost of $1,000 each to learn the basics of TQS.

Kellogg courted school principals and LSC members, including teachers. However, the management professors made no attempt to work through the Chicago Teachers Union; in fact, Kellogg attempted to work around the union.

At first Kellogg targeted Chicago's Lovett and Prescott Elementary Schools for its Continuous Improvement •

Process (CIP). That meant getting the schools involved with various community organizations, social service agencies, and state education programs. There was little real reorganization of the school.

But Kellogg saw the program as the opening wedge for greater business involvement:

> Corporate resources may be a key to the rapid and low cost diffusion of our learning from the first two schools. We have identified several people who work in Chicago corporations and who are qualified to help implement the CIP.[6]

In 1993 Kellogg expanded its program to include 23 other schools. A *Chicago Tribune* story about TQS at the Perkins Bass School in the Englewood neighborhood captured the spirit of this experiment:

> What's at stake is whether the kind of management reforms that in the 1980s turned around flawed manufacturing processes and management systems at corporations such as Motorola Inc., Xerox Corp. and Ford Motor Co. can help turn around Chicago's 600 public schools.
>
> After all, reason the Kellogg experts, many of those schools are like poorly run factories. And, like those factories they are using outmoded processes and management techniques to turn out one flawed product after another—in this case poorly educated children unable to function in a global economy that is unrelenting in its demand for skilled, literate workers.[7]

Kellogg assigned a team of consultants made up of a corporate executive, a management faculty member, and a business graduate student. A sign over the principal's office proclaimed Perkins Bass to be a "Total Quality School, J.L. Kellogg." School bulletin boards were covered with portraits of W. Edwards Deming.

The school faced problems involving drugs, weapons, and theft, so much of the TQS team's time was spent in identifying defects in the school's security system.

TQS in the Chicago schools appears to have been less concerned with reorganizing the workplace than with getting principals, teachers, and the LSCs to take responsibility for running schools with inadequate budgets. Asked by a Kellogg graduate student, "What does a total quality school mean to you?" a student pointed to the water dripping into plastic buckets and responded: "It means fixing the leak in the roof."[8] Thus TQS in Chicago meant attempting to do more with less, to teach in deteriorating buildings with inadequate supplies and too many students per class.

Yet the teachers union has generally favored TQM programs. A resolution of the Illinois Federation of Teachers 1992 convention stated:

> We need to work on both substantially improving the schools we have while at the same time working to create a new model. What General Motors and the United Auto Workers are doing with cars is very similar. In developing the new Saturn model, UAW and GM are mounting a great effort to create a car that can successfully compete using a new manufacturing process—one that does not resemble the old factory.[9]

When Superintendent Argie K. Johnson organized a public discussion, Rodney Estvan, a teacher and parent activist, responded with a paper strongly criticizing TQS:

> To develop self-analysis the Chicago Public Schools must abandon the philosophy of TQM. Children are not products: their educations cannot be repaired like faulty cars rolling off production lines. We must look to far more humanistic models of education, and there are many.

Estvan argued that school reform was not possible as long as the schools remained in a state of perpetual economic crisis.

> One of the central ideas of TQM is that for workers to produce a quality product they must have the collaboration of the management in procuring quality materials to work with. In the Chicago Public Schools the principal or the LSC is often powerless to provide quality materials because of the permanent fiscal crisis.[10]

Rather than using TQM as the basis of school reform, Estvan argued that the district should work to create more small schools, given research indicating that students do better in schools with enrollment less than 350.

While the Chicago schools continue to experiment with TQM, business is now demanding other experiments with corporate-run schools. Some parents and teachers fear that the Chicago School Board will attempt to turn over several public schools to corporate managers, as an experiment in privatizing education.

Notes

1. John Miller, "The Speculative Bubble Bursts,", *Dollars & Sense*, June 1991, pp. 6-9.

2. Garret Anglin, "Federal Sector Partnerships: Boon or Boondoggle?" *Labor Notes* No. 186, September 1994, p. 10.

3. Anglin.

4. Warren Fretwell, "Downsized Federal Workforce Faces 'Total Quality Partnership' Scam," *Labor Notes* No. 180, March 1994, p. 14.

5. The Kellogg faculty members involved in the TQS program were Professors of Management Strategy; Managerial Economics; Strategy and Organizations; Financial Institutions; Marketing; Accounting and Information Systems; Ethics and Decision in Management; Dispute Resolution and Organizations; and Operations Research. From the invitation to the Kellogg TQS program, November 1992.

6. Kellogg Graduate School of Management, "Total Quality Schools," a report, 1993.

7. Ronald E. Yates, "School gets a quality education," *Chicago Tribune*, March 7, 1993, Business Section.

8. Yates.

9. Illinois Federation of Teachers 1992 Convention proceedings.

10. Rodney D. Estvan, "Rational Expectations: A Contribution to the Discussion of School Improvement," June 6, 1994.

Working Smart:
A Union Guide to Participation Programs and Reengineering
Labor Notes • 7435 Michigan Ave. • Detroit, MI 48210 • (313) 842-6262

Chapter 20

Letter Carriers vs. E-I

The author experienced E-I as both a facilitator and a local union president. Over the years, he saw the program changed from above to give management more and more of a free hand. His local pulled out of E-I and organized other locals to do so, taking their opposition to the union's national convention.

by Jon Gaunce

IN 1981 CONTRACT NEGOTIATIONS between postal unions and the Postal Service had broken down. This nearly led to a nationwide strike when Postmaster General William Bolger refused to come to the bargaining table, insisting that the postal unions must negotiate separately. He refused to recognize the Joint Bargaining Committee of the National Association of Letter Carriers (NALC) and the American Postal Workers Union (APWU). It took outside intervention to force Bolger to the bargaining table, where a national agreement was finally hammered out.

In March 1982, less than seven months after the bitter negotiations, Bolger approached the NALC with his idea of a "better way of doing business." In October 1982, NALC agreed to participate, and the NALC/USPS Employee Involvement Process was born.

The E-I Process has a National Joint Steering Committee, five Regional Joint Steering Committees, and Local Joint Steering Committees (LJSC's), each with an equal number of union and management representatives. Initially, volunteer workteams in each work location had from four to twelve members, and all craft participants had to be union members.

Each Local Joint Steering Committee has at least one pair of full-time facilitators, one from the union and one from management. By 1990 the total number of facilitators employed in the process was over 700. Both union and management facilitators have their salaries paid by the Postal Service.

Union facilitators are appointed by the Regional Business Agents and approved by the National President. Originally, the criteria for choosing them were that they be local leaders and knowledgeable about the contract.

Later, however, the job became more of a political appointment.

While union facilitators are allowed to hold an officer position within local NALC branches, they are not permitted to provide representation in the grievance procedure. Apparently both sides viewed this as a conflict of interest.

By January 1984, E-I reached us at the Van Nuys, California sectional center. I recall quite a bit of skepticism from union representatives who were concerned that workteams might work on contractual items. We were assured in no uncertain terms that workteams were allowed to work on anything *except* items that dealt with national or local agreements or productivity.

SELLING THE PROCESS

I was chosen as the union facilitator. My job found me, along with my management "partner," on the road quite a bit, "selling the Process" to letter carriers. We also spent 16 hours in a classroom setting, teaching workteam members about E-I and communication skills. Periodically, we would report back to the Steering Committee on our progress.

As a facilitator, I received almost daily offers to go into management. A management official on the steering committee said that if I would "change sides" I would be appointed as the management facilitator. Many union facilitators have in fact gone into management. Over the past ten years, local unions have lost many of their experienced leaders.

After about a year, I resigned as facilitator to become a full-time local branch president. I was placed on two Local Joint Steering Committees, and found that E-I was taking 8 to 16 hours a week away from other responsibilities.

Jon Gaunce is president of Tri-Valley Branch 2902 of the National Association of Letter Carriers, in Chatsworth, California. In 1994 he ran for president of the NALC.

Union members on workteams would present issues important to letter carriers, such as reducing stress and conflict on the workroom floor, improved service to our customers, and items that would improve our quality of work life. But management seemed content to keep the status quo. Workteams were spending countless hours on projects, only to see their ideas rejected by their postmasters. Many times, management arbitrarily canceled workteam meetings.

As a result of management stonewalling, growing frustrations, and lack of credibility, veteran rank and file letter carriers lost interest in E-I and refused to participate. They were replaced, in many cases, by newer letter carriers, some still on their 90-day probationary period.

Management tried to exploit this situation in weekly workteam meetings. Employees were told that problems faced by the Postal Service were because of the union and "inflexible work rules." Union representatives on workteams in many cases were painted as "the bad guy." Management tried to turn letter carriers against shop stewards for being "inflexible" and not being "team players."

After approximately three years in E-I, the rules were suddenly changed by the National Joint Steering Committee. The requirement for a steward to be on each team was dropped as more and more stewards refused to participate. We were also told, despite earlier guarantees, that workteams *could* work on contractual items and productivity. Now we had some workteams discussing contractual or productivity items without a union representative present!

Union leaders, including myself, who protested such changes were castigated and accused of "not believing in E-I" or being "dinosaurs." These accusations came not only from management, but from national union officers as well.

Letter carriers complained that what they said during workteam meetings was used against them later by management. Because of problems we were experiencing, the LJSCs' role became to fix workteams that weren't working and to sell the idea to new ones.

PRODUCTIVITY

During this period, we began to hear stories of other workteams across the country working on projects that dealt with productivity and work rules. One workteam came up with a way to reward letter carriers for speeding up and for not calling in sick. Based on a point system, the faster they went, the more points they got. If they called in sick, or did not make their newly-established productivity goals, they lost points. The one who received the most points in a three-month period would receive a cash prize of $100.

Letter carriers were supposed to sign applications to participate in this "Self-Management Plan." One expectation cited on the application was that participants "would keep their goals consistent with those of management."

These incentive plans did nothing more than pit worker against worker. A letter carrier who called in sick, had an accident, or used overtime was criticized by fellow workers for ruining their perfect record. As a result, some letter carriers worked when they were ill, began skipping their lunch and break periods, and refused to report on-the-job injuries.

In Massachusetts, we discovered, union and management representatives from one LJSC even sent out a newsletter calling themselves "The United States Postal Union"!

For years, NALC had withstood management's attempts to weaken work rules. New gimmicks or attempts to speed up letter carriers had always been met with a strong negative response. Management knew they could not get what they wanted by fighting us. Their purpose for launching E-I was to get a foot in the door. Many items we had won years before, and had fought to keep, were suddenly being given away by workteams.

I wrote about this situation in our July 1989 local newsletter (see the box).

PULL-OUT

By early 1989, the membership of our branch was disillusioned. For many, E-I was nothing more than a wolf in sheep's clothing. We began independent research on team concept programs. It is interesting to note here that NALC does not publish anything about the other side of E-I. Even as a facilitator and steering committee member for over five years, I never received any training or information on possible dangers of these programs. Much of what we found was published by Labor Notes.

After extensive research, we decided we had more to lose by staying in E-I than anything we could possibly gain. E-I had become a serious credibility issue, as we could no longer tell the membership it was working when everyone knew it wasn't. We voted at our July 1989 membership meeting to completely disengage from E-I. At the time of our vote, we had 18 active workteams on line.

For the next several months, we received political threats and were accused of being "disloyal" by some of our national officers. Prior to withdrawing from E-I, our branch was permitted to do our own Step III grievances and many of our own arbitrations. We were told that if we got out of E-I we would lose this privilege. Immediately after the vote to get out, this threat was carried out.

After withdrawing from E-I, our National Business Agent told us we should get back in, just to "burn" management for all those hours spent on workteam meetings!

Political threats and reprisals only made our resolve stronger. Armed with first-hand knowledge, we began sending our message to other NALC branches across the country.

Our branch advertised a thick informational packet about the dangerous side of E-I in NALC's national publication, *The Postal Record* (each local branch has the right to submit a monthly article to the *Record*). We received more than 200 requests for the information we offered.

Then, together with three other branches, we sponsored a forum called "The Other Side of E-I" at our 1990 national convention, featuring a speaker from Labor Notes. The crowd was standing-room-only. We videotaped the talk and distributed the video as well.

At the convention, we supported a resolution to establish guidelines for E-I workteams. The guidelines would have kept workteams from trying to control sick leave usage, speed up carriers, or adopt incentive programs that pitted worker against worker. They would have had teams concentrate on better service, job safety, and working conditions, and required a steward to be present at any meeting where decisions were made.

The resolution drew strong opposition from national officers and E-I facilitators. One delegate said the guidelines were nothing more than "censorship." After much debate, they were defeated, with about 35 percent voting for them.

One resolution did pass, disqualifying those who have applied for management positions from being facilitators.

NATIONAL OPPOSITION

Growing out of organizing at the convention and the communication that had gone on beforehand, a Rank and File Coalition was formed by representatives from all across the country, many of whom were drawn together because of similar concerns about E-I. The Coalition decided to extend communication and continue meeting at future national NALC gatherings.

We had come a long way. Only two years before, there was virtually no opposition to E-I at the national convention.

In early 1992, a motion was made at a Committee of Presidents meeting (the twice-yearly national gathering of local presidents). It supported a national membership

---

A Modern-Day Trojan Horse

Greek mythology tells us of a ten-year war between the Greeks and a city named Troy that lasted from 1193 to 1184 B.C. Accounts of the war are found in the Greek epic *The Iliad*, written by Homer.

For ten years the vastly outnumbered citizens of Troy fought off the Greeks. For ten tears the Greeks were unable to get within the city's walls. Despite overwhelming numbers and resources, the Greeks were unable to defeat the people of Troy, who refused to compromise their principles.

Then a strange thing happened. One morning when the people of Troy awoke they found a huge wooden horse at the main gate of their city. Much to their surprise, the Greek armies had disappeared overnight.

The people of Troy decided amongst themselves that this giant horse was a gift from the Greeks and that it was a symbol of peace. Leaders of the city ignored advice and brought the wooden beast into the city. Others went throughout the city proclaiming peace and victory. The people laid down their now seemingly useless weapons and started to celebrate.

That night, while the citizens of Troy lay drunk and sleeping, the Greek soldiers, who had been hiding inside the horse, opened the gates to the city from the inside for the rest of the Greek army, who had returned under the cover of darkness. They had been waiting in ships just over the horizon. Troy was destroyed within hours. Legend tells us that only two people out of the entire city survived.

What the Greeks could not accomplish through ten years of battle, they accomplished in a matter of hours with treachery and false promises of peace.

There are some amongst the NALC who are travelling across this land proclaiming peace, when there is no peace. There are those who are telling us to lay down our weapons because our enemies have left a beautiful gift of peace (Employee Involvement) at our gate.

Management has been attacking Letter Carriers and our union for a hundred years. Have they changed any? The answer is an unequivocal NO!

We have done battle with management for many years and we have been victorious. Why would we want to weaken our position?

Some tell us that the company is in danger. But the truth of the matter is that the harder we work in making a profit for the company, the more supervisors they hire to make us work harder. Recent reports show that the Postal Service added another 80,000 managers between 1971 and 1987. Does this sound like they are worried about the company or the budget?

Postal Service management is not our friend. Friends don't treat each other the way Letter Carriers are being treated. Management does not want peace. They are only trying to do what they have not been able to do after years of battle—destroy the NALC! Already some of our people have fallen into a drunken stupor after tasting of this strange new elixir, thinking that our enemies have left us. But they have not left us, they are only waiting on the horizon hoping that we will make that fatal mistake.

referendum on pulling out of E-I. The motion lost—but it was close to require a division of the house.

In addition to our membership, our branch newsletter now goes out to about 300 people and other branches across the country, some of whom are in the other postal unions. There is now a solid core of people in NALC who oppose E-I. Many branches have withdrawn completely. Others refused to participate from the very beginning. Other branches remain in E-I; some of them are happy with the process, but most say it is stagnant and all but dead in their cities.

In 1991, in what they called a "last ditch effort" to save E-I, management switched to the "unit concept." They eliminated workteams, which were made up of volunteers, and now, unless the branch has withdrawn from E-I, the entire workforce must participate, right on the workroom floor. This means that non-union members participate as well. (By law, the Postal Service is an open shop.)

The past ten years have not been kind to letter carriers. Today, for the first time, letter carriers with low seniority are worried about layoffs. Management continues to ignore our input, while pushing automation that is increasing our workload by making routes longer. This is all but destroying service to our customers. In many cases, working conditions are worse than before. Stress and violence have increased on our workroom floors. Oppressive managers continue to be promoted and encouraged by their superiors. Management has forced "transitional employees" on us and can now hire part-time, temporary workers with much lower wages and reduced benefits.

E-I is also causing a rift between the two largest post-

al unions, NALC and APWU. APWU has refused to participate in E-I. This rift has led to both unions issuing public statements criticizing each other. By 1994, the situation had deteriorated to the point that the two unions did not bargain jointly for the national agreement.

What Postmaster General Bolger had tried and failed to do in 1981 had come to pass.

Management never lost sight of its long-term goal of busting our union and creating a company union. Over the past twelve years postal management has poured millions of dollars into E-I. If they are successful in destroying NALC, their investment will pay off handsomely.

In a speech given in 1982, Senior Assistant Postmaster General Carl Ulsaker stated that E-I would benefit unions because, "As the number of grievances diminishes the union officials can devote an increased amount of time to serving all members instead of mostly the complainers." For years, trade unionists have fought this management philosophy with the response: "An injury to one is an injury to all." Yet, at a 1987 NALC educational conference, our National Business Agent (now a national officer) told the audience, "Ninety five percent of the grievances are filed by five percent of the members," and "The union needs to spend more time on the majority of our members." Sound familiar?

In an interview in the September 25, 1989 issue of the *Federal Times*, David Hyde, president of the National Postmasters Association, exposed management's hidden agenda for E-I. Hyde said, "If an office properly uses the program, you don't have a need for unions."

Working Smart:
A Union Guide to Participation Programs and Reengineering
Labor Notes • 7435 Michigan Ave. • Detroit, MI 48210 • (313) 842-6262

Chapter 21

Mail Handlers Resist QWL

A large local successfully fights a QWL program, at the same time watching the "jointness" concept spread throughout the union's national agreement. Meanwhile, management tires of QWL, preferring more unilateral means of increasing productivity.

by Larry Adams

QWL FIRST ENTERED OUR NATIONAL AGREE-MENT IN 1981, when a Joint Committee to Improve the Quality of Work Life was established at the national level. In order to sell the local presidents on the idea, they were allowed to enter or withdraw participation at will. Fewer than half the 37 Mail Handler locals chose to participate; Local 300 was one of them. We have 19 branches within our local; at any one time, probably no more than six participated.

Participation was probably low because many local presidents were apprehensive about the political impact of a competing apparatus. And some local presidents objected on principle. But there was no coordination among presidents who elected to go in and those who elected to stay out.

In fact, except for one issue of the Mail Handler magazine in 1992, the issue of QWL has never been addressed systematically by the union. The program was simply delivered to the union as a whole in national contract negotiations. It has not been brought to a head, with a pointed discussion over what QWL means. That debate has arisen from below.

Thus, locals were left on their own. In our local, the previous president's position was that if Administrative Vice Presidents (AVPs) of branches wanted to participate, they could. But there was never any policy guidance on dangers or on what the union should want to get out of QWL.

Larry Adams is president of the largest local in the Mail Handlers Union, Local 300. With approximately 6,000 members, it covers New York City and parts of Connecticut, New York State, and New Jersey. Adams became president in 1990.

HOW THE CIRCLES WORKED

QWL circles were made up of volunteers from work areas; they met weekly for one hour. The meetings were run by full-time facilitators, appointed by the local president in conjunction with the AVPs. The pay policy for facilitators was "no loss, no gain"; in other words, they would make the same pay as if they were working. Appointed coordinators oversaw the facilitators. Management, of course, had its own facilitators and coordinators.

On the Postal Service's pay scale, mail handlers are Levels 4 and 5. The Northeast Regional Coordinator of QWL for the Mail Handlers got paid at Level 18. So he had a major stake in keeping QWL alive.

'CREATURE COMFORTS' PHASE

My home branch, the New Jersey International and Bulk Mail Center (NJI&BMC), was the showcase pilot site for QWL. Management talked as if the budget were unlimited; they said they wanted to provide "creature comforts" to improve morale.

The first thing they did, to impress everyone, was to spend $10,000 for an Astroturf picnic area in the parking lot. It took up a number of prime parking spaces, and it was outside the barbed wire fence that circles the facility, outside the guard shack manned by armed postal police. Therefore employees could only get to it before or after work or at lunch. It was adjacent not only to the exhaust fumes of arriving and departing automobiles but also to the drainage moat surrounding the facility that is populated by rats.

The allure of the picnic area quickly wore off. The employees complained so much that the picnic area was moved out of the parking lot—they preferred their parking spaces.

Frequently, in this period of securing creature comforts, things that both the Mail Handlers and the American Postal Workers Union (APWU—the clerks, maintenance, and motor vehicle operators union) had fought for years suddenly became available through the QWL circles. One example was stress mats—foam rubber mats for standing on the concrete floor.

Another example: since at least 1984 our National Agreement has called for a committee to address the feasibility of childcare facilities. And that project has never gone beyond the committee level. But in 1990 in Brooklyn, childcare in a planned new facility was promoted through the QWL apparatus.

By providing an alternative mechanism to the union, management hoped to undermine members' confidence in their local. In addition, QWL had an effect on internal union politics. The QWL apparatus became an immediate pipeline for information from the national office to the base. In election campaigns, the QWL apparatus became a mailing list, a mechanism to reach into locals that, in the Mail Handlers, are rather autonomous.

For example, when Joe Amma was in charge of QWL from the national office, and then ran for National President, the QWL apparatus became his campaign apparatus within Local 300. (Joe Amma later switched sides and became a Labor Relations Specialist for the Postal Service.)

PHASE TWO: PRODUCTIVITY

As the members pursued projects they perceived to be in their interests, a backlog of circle projects developed. But when the attention turned to productivity enhancement, those projects were implemented.

The clearest example was the circle that received a "Best of Best" award. Their idea was to palletize and shrink-wrap the mail of one particular large-volume mailer. The immediate impact was to reduce the eight jobs in the incoming container dock by half. The circles were literally planning themselves out of work.

Now, palletizing and shrink-wrapping was not a brand new idea that just sprang from the eight guys in the dock. Shrink-wrapping was not something the Postal Service was unaware of. But the company might have had more difficulty introducing the change if they had to sell it as their own idea. QWL facilitated the introduction of certain procedures, by giving the workers the sense that they had come up with the plan.

It may not seem harmful for workers to buy in to these productivity improvements, since postal workers with more than six years of seniority are protected from lay-offs. But the postal workforce shrank by 95,000 people from 1989 to 1994, and Postmaster General Marvin Runyon has plans to shrink it more. By offering an early retirement deal in 1992, he got rid of 47,000 workers and managers in his first six months in office.

Management was shocked by the unexpected number of craft workers who left. Overtime bills went through the sky because there were not enough people on board to process the growing volume of mail. The Postal Service had an answer: hire temporary, lower-paid workers.

Within a year, management had hired more craft workers than had retired—but at considerably lower wages. The APWU and NALC (Letter Carriers) contracts both allow management to do this, through a new category of temporary workers—"transitional employees," with lower wages and fewer benefits. And in 1992 the Mail Handlers increased the allowable percentage of casual workers from 10 percent to 18 percent. The period of time a casual could work was increased from two 90-day periods to two 359-day periods.

This push to get out more work at less pay went along with a shift in the stated goals of QWL. Both management and union officials began to emphasize more and more that the goal of QWL was to make the Postal Service "competitive"; improving worker morale and life on the job became secondary. Increasingly, they emphasized the need to make the service competitive against Federal Express, UPS, and other private sector mail companies.

They had pulled the covers off: the purpose of the whole ten years prior had been to ideologically prepare the workers and union leaders for buying the agenda of the Postal Service as their own.

Thus QWL's second phase implied the trickle-down theory: if you make the company successful, then in the sweet by-and-by, the company will pass down crumbs from their table to the workers.

However, extra crumbs are hardly mentioned anymore; instead our supposed benefit is just being able to keep our jobs. And when it came to the real business of contract negotiations in 1990 and 1993, management did not let anything trickle down. In fact, when the joint bargaining committee of the APWU and the Letter Carriers took their compensation package to arbitration, the arbitrator ruled that although downsizing and automation would increase productivity and profitability, he would grant only a minimal pay increase because postal workers enjoy a "wage premium" over the private sector.

TQM

In 1991, at our JFK Airport branch, management announced they were initiating Total Quality Management. The union was not consulted, but management was gracious enough to invite the branch union reps to a meeting to hear the consultant describe what was going to change. This consultant got his experience at IBM, which is well known for its anti-union attitude.

One of our reps asked, "How does this relate to QWL?" The consultant brushed him aside: "We're not doing that anymore." His recommendation to management was to eliminate QWL. That would eliminate any potential for union participation—since QWL is supposedly a joint program.

FOR INCOMPETENCE AND MISMANAGEMENT ABOVE AND BEYOND THE CALL OF DUTY, **POSTAL SERVICE MANAGERS** ARE AWARDED NEARLY $20 MILLION IN BONUSES!

FOR INCREASED PRODUCTIVITY AND HARD WORK, **POSTAL WORKERS** ARE AWARDED...

©1991 HUCK/KONOPACKI LABOR CARTOONS

JOINTNESS SPREADS

While in the 1981 National Agreement the concept of jointness was pretty much confined to Article 31, Section 31.4, which set up QWL, by 1990, the concept of jointness had spread into our compensation package.

QWL laid the groundwork for SET—"Striving for Excellence Together." SET is a pay incentive program based on improving the Customer Satisfaction Index, competing against other districts on this Index, and increasing the ratio of Postal Service revenues to total paid hours.

Now, how can mail handlers increase postal revenues? The SET literature says we can "promote Postal services to current and potential customers." I suppose that means we could encourage our friends to buy stamps and use Express Mail. But what we *are* supposed to affect is total paid hours. This means, according to the Service, "improve attendance; discourage abuse of paid leave; and encourage cooperation with mechanization and automation."

The idea is to discourage us from using our leave time, and to make it in our interests for the Postal Service to cut jobs.

This 1990 contract was the same contract, by the

way, that included a wage freeze and substituted one-time lump sum payments for percentage wage increases. That concession was sold to our national negotiators on the basis of jointness. The Service argued, "We can't compete, you've got to understand the economic climate. You'll be doing your part to save the Service." The agreement was reached through a mediator, and the talks were approached as "win-win." The parties applied QWL concepts to the actual contract negotiation process. As a result we ended up with a national agreement that was more joint than ever before. By 1993, top step Level 4 mail handlers earned less than top step Level 3 custodians in the APWU.

The Joint Education and Training Fund is another example of the concept of jointness spreading into other aspects of the agreement. JETF is money put up by the Postal Service for training programs aimed at lower level managers and union functionaries, to be undertaken together. For example, there have been classes on contract interpretation and on Article 12, which deals with reassignment, excessing, and reductions in force.

In other words, this joint fund promotes the idea that union and management have no separate and distinct interests in how the contract is applied; we're both just bureaucrats whose job it is to administer what's set down on paper. There's no sense of the contract as the product of a struggle between two opposing sides.

CHANGE THE RULES

When it has become necessary to safeguard the interests of the QWL program—of "the process," as management calls it—they have changed the rules. While originally QWL was sold as "voluntary in, voluntary out," at the discretion of the local president, in 1991 and 1992 both management and pro-QWL union officials tried to impose the theory that QWL is somehow a contractual right, and that regional and national intervention of the Joint Steering Committees would be necessary before a local would be allowed to withdraw. As the trend among Mail Handler locals turned against QWL, and more people started asking questions, both management and the national union leadership made it more difficult to get out. As you approached the goal line, they moved the goal posts.

THE PULL-OUT

The struggle over QWL in our local came to a head in July 1991. In local newsletters and other forums, the local officers constantly tried to highlight the contradiction between management's daily practice and what they espoused for one hour a week in the QWL circles. Managers would play QWL for an hour, and then come back out and be the same domineering, militaristic managers that they had always been.

In the wake of the 1990 national agreements, with the concessions suffered by mail handlers and other postal workers, a majority of the local union Council voted to withdraw the local from all QWL participation.

The fall-out was that QWL loyalists, including the Regional Joint Coordinator with his unlimited access to Postal Service funds and resources, launched propaganda attacks on our local leadership. These included appeals for intervention from the national office and attacks on the local leadership for denying a "contractual right and benefit" to the members. Some QWL loyalists in branch leadership positions tried to make individual deals with the Postal Service, to continue the process.

These individuals who functioned within the apparatus were desperate to keep it, for two reasons:

1) They had bought into the whole notion of jointness.

2) They had a personal, material stake in keeping their easier facilitator jobs rather than the difficult, alienating manual labor that mail handlers perform. In the case of the regional coordinator, he also had a considerable pay increase.

Finally, after much pressure on our part, in January 1992 National President Glenn Berrien recognized our decision to withdraw as valid. But Berrien sent a letter to every member of Local 300, attacking the local leadership for "dictatorship," and again alluding to denying the members a benefit. (This was part of his losing campaign for

re-election later in the year.)

Berrien called us dictators even though the anti-QWL forces in our local's Council had proposed a local-wide referendum on whether or not to allow QWL anywhere within Local 300 (This was part of his campaign for re-election later in the year.) This was our proposal for a democratic solution to the debate within the Council that raged from July 1991 to January 1992. We specified *anywhere* in the local, and that the whole membership should vote, because we were apprehensive about branches being whipsawed against each other. We could foresee management favoring those who supported QWL and victimizing those who opposed it. If QWL got past the first vote, we proposed, then it would be determined branch by branch whether each one wanted to participate. But the pro-QWL forces didn't want a local-wide referendum, and at that meeting they carried the vote.

In July 1992, Berrien and the management co-chair of the National Joint Steering Committee wrote to the Regional Postmasters offering their services in helping the company cut costs. "We both realize the financial challenges the United States Postal Service faces..." they said. "We feel the Quality of Work Life Process can be used as a positive influence in helping to generate strategies in keeping our prices competitive." They sent this memo to the Mid-Hudson General Mail Facility, which is in Local 300's jurisdiction, even though Local 300 had completely withdrawn from QWL a year previously.

RESULTS

The fight against QWL in Local 300 has sharpened the politics of recognizing the differences between us and them, union and management. It has consolidated the political forces within our local to more clearly identify what our interests are in contrast to those of the employer. More and more people learned through the experience how in fact QWL is a management-directed process of subverting the union.

Overall, the fight has been good for our local. For example, our JFK branch has been more consolidated as a result of the struggles around QWL. When management there tried to introduce a program called IQ, the members saw it for what it was and rejected it. They notified me immediately, and the letter of apology from management states: "There have been no completed forms returned by anyone of any craft. Due to the total lack of response, use of these forms has already been discontinued."

DONE ITS WORK

By 1994 QWL had become a stepchild of the Postal Service. With the wave of retirements and restructuring, managers were more concerned about securing their own positions than about QWL. They have concentrated instead on developing Performance Clusters, the mechanism for implementing TQM. These are managerial circle meetings to address "customer satisfaction, employee commitment, and revenue enhancement." Employee organizations, which means both the unions and supervisors' associations, are periodically invited to participate.

Instead of using QWL circles to extract information from workers, we're seeing more frequent use of employee opinion surveys and focus groups. For example, in the wake of the shootings at the Dearborn, Michigan post office in 1993, Runyon initiated "focus groups" on workplace violence across the country. His main focus was how hard it is for management to get rid of "problem people." He used the focus groups to push the view that problem people should be more easily removed—i.e., an attack on due process—and to target veterans. One of their solutions was to more closely scrutinize applications. But in fact it is work-related stress and authoritarian managers that have provoked the outbursts.

For Mail Handlers, then, management's focus is no longer on QWL per se, now that QWL has done its dirty work. This means that many union QWL facilitators are now crying and begging and grasping at the ankles of the Postal Service as management walks away, pleading, "Please come back and play in the sandbox."

However, in May 1994 the national Joint QWL Steering Committee issued a new statement of purpose. They said, "QWL is not a euphemism for productivity, but because this process unlocks motivation, commitment and creativity when properly managed by the local joint steering committees, organizational effectiveness, including productivity, will improve."

Management has moved on from one alphabet soup to the next, and mail handlers are still confronted with the task of defining and distinguishing our interests from theirs.

Working Smart:
A Union Guide to Participation Programs and Reengineering
Labor Notes • 7435 Michigan Ave. • Detroit, MI 48210 • (313) 842-6262

Chapter 22

Total Quality Management In Health Care: Wonder Drug or Snake Oil?

Despite the "quality" label, TQM is wielded mainly as a cost-cutting measure, with the foremost goal being the elimination of jobs. TQM can also lead to divisiveness when hospitals implement "self-scheduling" or peer performance appraisals. TQM does not address the real problems of the health care systems in either Canada, which this chapter mainly addresses, or the United States.

by John Price

HEALTH CARE FACILITIES joined the Total Quality movement just as its defects were becoming more obvious. Does this mean that health care unions can dismiss the TQM fixation as the latest "flavor of the month"? Hardly. Some administrators and consultants want Total Quality Management to become the new benchmark for quality assurance in hospitals. In Canada they are lobbying hard to require all facilities to implement TQM in order to be accredited and to qualify for funding from provincial governments.

TQM is the prescription that will help cure Canada's supposedly-ailing health care system, according to its promoters. Philip Hassen, president of St. Joseph's Health Centre in London, Ontario and author of the recent book *Rx for Hospitals*, says TQM promises to maximize "human skills, creativity and resourcefulness, customer satisfaction, employee involvement, effective and efficient use of resources, continuous improvement of all processes large or small, and the consistent achievement of high standards of service and productivity."[1] Administrators

across Canada are buying Hassen's prescription.

"We're talking about emulating the market system," said Carol Clemenhagen, Canadian Hospital Association president, at the opening session of the Association's 1993 convention. "There should be competition." TQM now looms as the vehicle of choice for bringing the market into Canada's single-payer health system.

Is TQM the wonder drug that some claim, or is it a new brand of snake oil with some nasty side effects for health care workers and for the health care system as a whole?

QUALITY CONCERNS OR COST CUTTING?

No one can argue with quality. But there is more to TQM than meets the eye. Behind the quality label is a sophisticated, comprehensive system based on production techniques used in the private sector.

TQM programs appeal to health care workers' desire for some real control over their work. The emphasis on the importance of human resources, examining processes instead of individuals, comparing why some hospitals or regions perform excessive numbers of caesareans—these are developments that can and should be welcomed. But TQM seems to have more to do with cutting costs and jobs than with improving the quality of health care.

Hassen, Canada's foremost TQM advocate, believes

John Price teaches labour studies at Capilano College and is an advisor to the Trade Union Research Bureau in Vancouver, British Columbia. Much of the information here was compiled as part of a project on TQM undertaken for the Hospital Employees Union (HEU), the union for health care support staff in British Columbia. Price would like to thank the HEU and its staff, particularly Anne Burger, for their insights and advice.

costs are the main threat to Canada's government-supported health system, and that runaway health care costs may actually threaten Canada's ability to compete in world markets. TQM, he states, will help recover the "30 percent of [hospital] resources lost to waste and inefficiencies."[2]

By exaggerating health care costs and targeting inefficiencies, Hassen and other TQM advocates in Canada and the United States conveniently sidestep key aspects of health care economics.

WHY ARE HEALTH CARE COSTS RISING?

Rising costs are used as the reason for TQM programs in both U.S. and Canadian hospitals and nursing homes. Will TQM in fact stop the escalating costs? Not likely.

Labor costs are a significant factor in hospital budgets, but they are not the reason for escalating health care expenses in the U.S. or Canada. Many other factors are at work.

In the United States advocates for health care reform have estimated that billions of dollars could be saved by eliminating the heavy burden of administrative costs caused by the irrational medical insurance system.[3] Another problem is the uncontrolled rising costs of pharmaceuticals and the duplication of expensive new technologies.

In U.S. private and nonprofit hospitals, outrageously high executive salaries and perks often push up expenses, while public hospitals are being hit with enormous unreimbursed costs incurred by treating uninsured patients and those who are forced to use hospital emergency rooms because they do not have private doctors.

Revenues in the United States are being squeezed by government cuts in Medicare and Medicaid payments and by local government budget-balancing, which often drains public hospitals of cash. Meanwhile, insurance companies and HMOs are trying to save money by insisting on discounts, by cutting length of in-patient hospital stays, and by requiring that more procedures be done on an out-patient basis.

In comparison with the United States, Canada's health care system is more efficient and more just. Canada has a "single-payer" system, where health care is mainly financed by tax revenues and administered by the government. Patients are free to use the doctor of their choice.

But the Canadian system faces some of the same pressures on costs as the United States. For example, at St. Paul's Hospital in Vancouver drug costs have been the single largest factor responsible for budget increases over the past two years. And the Canadian system is seriously threatened by the federal government's policy, in the name of deficit reduction, of reducing transfer payments to the provinces to cover health care costs.

TQM advocates refuse to address such issues. Instead they promote TQM as the solution to money problems, using manufacturing as the model. *Rx for Hospitals* lauds Ford Motor Co. because it has "half as many employees

today as it did in 1978, yet is producing almost the same number of cars."[4]

In other words, a major thrust of TQM is cost containment by eliminating jobs. The more honest quality gurus acknowledge it. "You are headed for downsizing and layoffs anyway. Why not have a proper plan?" Connie Curran, a quality consultant with APM Consultants, told a Manitoba conference.[5]

This is not to say that workers and unions should be unconcerned about waste and inefficiencies. But let's not mix up apples and oranges. TQM should not masquerade as a quality movement when it is not about quality. TQM is not about improving patient care or helping workers better their skills to prepare for changes in the health care industry. It is a cost containment strategy with a strong anti-labor bias.

The basic element of TQM is the organization of project teams to study a work process with the objective of continuously improving it. On the surface such a proposal may appear sound, but when put in the context of diminishing resources, continuous improvement can become a means of speeding up the work process, to the detriment

---

Irrational Change Should be Opposed

Quality advocates stress that change is inevitable and necessary. In a sense this is true. But how things change is subject to human decisions; it is not the result of some immutable force. TQM can be irrational in itself or, in failing to identify major problems, it may perpetuate existing inefficiencies.

For example, Local 1199 in New York City reported in March 1994 that one-third of hospital beds in the U.S. are empty on an average night, partially because the average length of stay has fallen since 1985 from an average of five days to four. Yet 35 million people often have no access to those empty beds because they cannot afford health care insurance.

Some hospitals are developing off-site primary care centers to cut costs and provide poor neighborhoods with more preventive care.

Such cost-cutting moves could actually lead to a more sensible approach to medical care, but for hospital workers they are a potential disaster. Hospitals are merging and restructuring—and cutting and changing the jobs of hospital workers.

According to Local 1199, over half the U.S. hospitals with over 500 beds are planning to lay off workers. This is not only a waste of a valuable health care resource, it flies in the face of a progressive health policy that recognizes social factors, including having a job and a decent income, as an essential element in preventive medicine. In so far as TQM avoids such issues, it can only end up as a tool for downsizing.

of the caregiver and the patient.

This is particularly true when waste is defined as reducing "unnecessary" labor time. What might appear to be unnecessary from an efficiency perspective—for example, a nurse or aide taking a few minutes to stretch—may be essential if the worker just finished lifting heavy patients. And how does one measure the smile on a patient's face for the extra time taken to chat?

Under TQM, workers are often asked to undertake task analysis to study how to do their jobs better, but the purpose of such projects is seldom to enrich their work or develop their skills. It is usually to discover how to reduce the number of people necessary for a procedure, how to get workers to take on more tasks, or how to devolve the work onto lower-paid workers.

PARTNERSHIP OR UNDERMINING THE UNION?

TQM programs often call for a new partnership between management and labor and for the empowerment of staff. But while management may talk about partnerships and empowerment, in fact they refuse to "walk the talk."

In a number of cases, TQM programs have bypassed unions entirely and tried to create divisions between workers and their unions, by recruiting volunteers to sit on committees that are often dealing with contract issues.

At Queen Alexandra Hospital in Victoria, B.C., for example, the administration created four quality task forces, recruited employees to sit on the committees, and began deliberations without even consulting the three health care unions on site.

At the Greater Victoria Hospital Society, management began to implement a similar program that would have seriously affected the collective agreement. They did this without consulting the unions or employees. They then asked the three unions to accept one position each on a steering committee made up of 17 people. When the Hospital Employees Union objected to such arbitrary action and refused to sit on the committee, the administration abandoned the program.

There are different dangers when employees or union representatives become involved in the hiring or firing process. As part of the shared governance program at Mt.

St. Joseph's Hospital in Vancouver, union representatives were placed on the hiring committee for the new director of personnel. The intent, of course, was to make it difficult for the union to fight against the policies of a personnel director that it had helped hire!

TQM appeals to administrators because it offloads many responsibilities onto line staff. As such, decisions appear to be made by workers. A key component in this is the formation of teams. In some cases, the teams are temporary multi-disciplinary groups assigned to complete a special project, but the long-term goal of most programs is the creation of "self-directed work groups."

Obviously there is nothing wrong with teams and work groups in and of themselves. The nursing team, for example, has always been part of the care delivery system. But teams take on a specific role under TQM: to set up a competitive ethic among workers by taking advantage of workers' legitimate desires for recognition, and then manipulating group dynamics.

This process can begin by introducing self-evaluations. Self-evaluation can be the first step toward workers taking on peer performance appraisals. For example, under the shared governance program at a hospital in Campbell River, B.C., nursing team members were asked to evaluate their peers, confidentially. Questions included: "Seldom complains? Adapts easily where patient acuity and workload increases? Performs mundane duties cheerfully?" Clearly, such questions reflect management's conception of the model employee: a cheerful, unquestioning workhorse.

Another assignment often given teams is to develop their own work schedules. Many workers and unions embrace this idea, but at St. Joseph's in London, Ontario, teams not only self-scheduled but undertook a "no sick leave replacement program." In other words, if a team member is out sick, other team members must cover the work. The result: many workers come to work when they should be staying at home.

Peer pressure is often activated through the use of incentive programs. Prizes are awarded for teams with the best attendance record or for having submitted the most suggestions for improving operations. At the extreme, the incentive programs develop into a sophisticated bonus scheme, a form of pay-for-performance. In many cases,

TQM programs openly call for a performance-based wage system.

Most people would agree that delivering health care is different from making cars. Yet this rather reasonable perspective is construed as obstructionism under TQM. At Caritas Health Centre in Edmonton, workers are told they must change: "If we are committed to Caritas, our mission and values, these excuses are no longer acceptable." Included in the list of 50 no-longer-acceptable excuses are "there's not enough staff" and "the union will scream."[6]

Taken to their logical extreme, TQM programs can assume the qualities of a cult, where absolute conformance is expected and dissent is construed as deviance. One quality expert put it bluntly: "Adopting the quality vision is in some respects like a religious conversion. It is a religion in which mistakes and negativism are unacceptable."[7]

Unions and union activists can easily become targets if this type of TQM tyranny takes hold in the workplace. Health care unions will have to innovate, go beyond traditional collective bargaining strategies, articulate their own quality vision, and bring this vision right down into the workplace.

Notes

1. Philip Hassen, *Rx for Hospitals: New Hope for Medicare in the Nineties*, Stoddart, Toronto, 1993, p. 2.

2. Hassen, p. 3.

3. For a comparative study on why universal health care in Canada is more cost-effective than the U.S. system, see D.A. Redelmeier and V.R. Fuchs, "Hospital Expenditures in the United States and Canada," *The New England Journal of Medicine*, Vol. 328, No. 11, March 18, 1993, p. 772.

4. Hassen, p. 9.

5. Quoted by Frances Russell, "Health Care Reform Means Fewer Jobs," *Winnipeg Free Press*.

6. As cited in United Nurses of Alberta, *Total Quality Management Programs*, June 1993, p. 113.

7. Robert F. Casalou, "Total Quality Management in Health Care," *Hospital and Health Services Administration*, Foundation of the American College of Health Care Executives, 1991.

Working Smart:
A Union Guide to Participation Programs and Reengineering
Labor Notes • 7435 Michigan Ave. • Detroit, MI 48210 • (313) 842-6262

Chapter 23

TQM in the Home Care Industry

In a not-for-profit home care agency, visiting nurses and non-union business office staff joined together to boycott management's TQM efforts. The management-dominated TQM task forces had recommended use of less-trained workers and hiring of non-union nurses.

by Stephanie Pearson Breaux

NO WORKERS WOULD WELCOME improvements in quality more than health care workers. But at the Visiting Nurse Association of Chicago, Total Quality Management task forces recommended increases in contracting out and assignment of work to less-skilled workers, rather than improvements in patient care. TQM meant a generous increase in management positions and a great deal of money spent.

Both unionized registered nurses, members of Service Employees International Union Local 73, and the non-union business office staff, which was in the process of organizing, resisted TQM. You could call the strategy "passive aggression": after an initial honeymoon phase, workers simply refused to participate in the TQM task forces. Although a TQM department still exists, TQM is now dead for all practical purposes.

The VNA is a not-for-profit home care agency in existence for over a hundred years. With a caseload of 1,800 cases per month, it is the largest in the Chicago area, and the only home care agency in Illinois with a union contract for nurses and other professional staff. Providing professional home care services to the insured and underinsured alike, regardless of their ability to pay, has been the philosophy and mission of the VNA. Crusade of Mercy and other philanthropic organizations contribute large sums.

Home care is the delivery of services to homebound patients, under the direction of a physician. Skilled nursing is the primary service, but home care may include physical, occupational, speech, or respiratory therapy, as well as social worker services. Home care workers also include home health aides, much like nursing assistants in hospitals, who provide personal care to patients under the direction of a registered nurse.

A visiting nurse evaluates the physical and psycho-social needs of homebound patients. She may take a history and make physical assessments, carry out skilled procedures, and educate patients and their caregivers about medications, special diets, and complications of illnesses. The nurse reports the patient's status to the physician, makes recommendations for care, and gives information to everyone involved with the patient's treatment plan. Maintaining patients in their homes and helping families to cope with the illness is the focus of home care.

The VNA business office staff schedules patients, keeps records, and does billing. It includes computer programmers, secretaries, and accounting specialists.

At the VNA there are 65 business office staff, 60 full-time nurses (members of SEIU Local 73), three full-time social workers (Local 73), 10 fee-for-visit social workers, 20 fee-for-visit nurses, 35 home health aides, and 10 licensed practical nurses. Management numbers about 40, including supervisors.

TQM IN A TIME OF RECESSION

VNA management instituted Total Quality Management in 1991, a time of economic recession, when the health needs of the indigent were increasing and the home care industry expanding. With the escalating cost of health care, hospitals are discharging patients earlier, and the demand for home care is increasing.

Management introduced TQM shortly after an unsuc-

Stephanie Pearson Breaux is chief steward for SEIU Local 73 at the Visiting Nurse Association and a registered nurse.

cessful campaign to decer-
tify Local 73. The busi-
ness office staff was in
the beginning stages of organizing, and the timing
of TQM triggered the
suspicions of union mem-
bers.

For one thing,
management did not ap-
proach the union prior to
beginning TQM, nor did
they include the union in
their ongoing evalua-
tions. In addition, for the
past six years VNA
management had been
strongly anti-union, a
stance which required
costly litigation and used
hours of staff time—af-
fecting the agency's business operations.

Management's initial
presentation said that
TQM would improve

with hiring consultants
and strongly urged
employees to sign up for
the voluntary TQM task
forces. Task forces were
appointed on Client Rela-
tions, Retention, Com-
munications,
Recruitment, Orientation,
Education, Policies and
Procedures, Quality
Management, and Sys-
tems.

VNA's work is
decentralized: the
majority of the union
members work in the
community, which in-
cludes both Chicago and
the suburbs. Holding task
force meetings at only
one office in the city of
Chicago was not con-
ducive to participation.
In addition, nurses have
productivity standards to

working conditions. Management talked about an appreciation for staff loyalty and their willingness to embark on a
new enterprise called participatory management.
Employees were told they would become self-actualized,
self-managed, and self-empowered. With management and
staff working together as a team, the goals of TQM were
to improve business operations and upgrade services to
our clients.

Historically, the VNA philosophy and practice has
been to educate the patient and the family in the prescribed
treatment programs in order to reduce the number of
skilled nursing visits made to the home. This was both
cost effective and quality care.

However, in the last six years, management had been
requesting the nurses to *maximize* the visits approved by
Medicare and the insurance companies. This was a means
to increase revenue for VNA, although skilled nursing
visits might not be required for the duration of the approved visits.

Now, with TQM, management said that competitors
in the home care industry had compelled the VNA to look
at strategies to reduce the cost of each skilled nursing
visit. TQM, they said, was designed to improve and
streamline home care for the benefit of our patients and
the hospitals and insurance companies we contract with!
The latest proposal in this "improvement and streamlining" is a "telepatient" program: nurses would check on
patients by phone rather than in person.

Management distributed several questionnaires requesting employees' input, to evaluate the systems and
departments at VNA. A small percentage were returned
and tabulated. Management then aggressively proceeded

meet, and patient assessment and education are time con-
suming. Nurses did not see participation on task forces as
a priority. However, business office staff were prime
recruits, and they were solicited to join the task forces.

Employees were excused from their business duties to
attend the TQM meetings, which lasted from one to four
hours. Each task force elected a chairperson, and objectives were formulated with strong influence from management representatives. Putting in time outside of working
hours was not uncommon.

To start the program, a management consultant
presented a communications workshop for all departments.
He defined his role as independent observer, arbitrator between staff and management, and facilitator to improve
communications among staff. Staff were encouraged to express their feelings about supervision and their style of
management. The consultant discussed methods of communication and means to resolve disputes one-to-one.

STAFF RESPONSE

The initial responses to TQM varied among the staff.
Many recognized TQM as a means to prevent them from
organizing a union by immersing them in time-consuming
committees. Some believed management would display
goodwill to the staff as long as they did not try to organize. Others felt obligated to participate in the task
forces to reduce management's suspicion of their union efforts.

Organizing and running TQM committees was itself
time-consuming, and so created many new jobs for administrative and management support personnel, not for

rank and file members. The TQM program generated a Total Quality Management Department, with an appointed Vice President directly responsible to the Chief Executive Officer. Coordinator positions were created in all departments. In the hospice program, for example, the following positions exist: Medical Director, Hospice Director, Clinical Supervisor, Hospice Coordinator, Volunteer Coordinator, and Business Coordinator. Yet bargaining unit positions go unfilled, and fee-for-visit nurses staff the hospice program.

The recently created position of Social Service Coordinator is another manifestation of TQM philosophy: initially, this coordinator had only one other social worker to "coordinate." And new positions for social workers are advertised as fee-for-visit positions. This policy aims at further reducing the number of staff eligible for the bargaining unit.

Management had its own separate training program, called a forum, which met off-site. Satellite presentations were given on college campuses, with the content not revealed to the staff. Management and consultants attended retreats together without inviting union representatives. The cost of consultants and management training was astronomical in relationship to the agency's cash flow problems. In addition, the direction of energies toward TQM resulted in a slow response to resolving business operation problems.

TASK FORCE RESULTS

Let's look at the work and results of some of the TQM task forces:

The Orientation and Continuing Education Task Force conducted a survey on new employees' orientation needs. Out of 205 surveys distributed, 63 were returned. However, the task force proceeded to develop action plans. A sub-group was formed to develop ideas for an employee handbook. It made a strong recommendation to orient staff to the TQM program. Training videos and team-building exercises are now part of the orientation of new employees, who are informed of how VNA and the TQM process benefit them. But after the orientation sessions, there is no further follow-up on TQM for new employees.

This task force recommended hiring new nurses on a fee-for-visit status. That is, the nurse receives a flat fee per visit rather than being on salary, with benefits. About 20 nurses are now working fee-for-visit, usually part-time, and they are not in the bargaining unit. Consequently, the

salaried nurses are functioning as case managers, and fear that their numbers will be dwarfed by the non-union fee-for-visit nurses.

For fee-for-visit nurses, who cost management less, the pressure is to make as many visits as possible, while full-time salaried nurses are able to devote the necessary time to patient education and care. Fee-for-visit nurses often hold full-time jobs in another facility, and pick up VNA home care work as extra. Management encourages nurses and social workers to accept fee-for-visit positions at the time of their employment interviews.

The Quality Management Task Force consists of program directors, supervisors, contract professional service persons, and one staff nurse. One of its major decisions was for VNA to hire its own home health aides.

This indicates that management has plans to de-skill nursing, by substituting aides for the more highly skilled licensed practical nurses. Neither the home health aides nor the LPNs are protected by the union. Management is increasing the scope of aides' duties and responsibilities. They may now apply medicinal creams and ointments to wounds, for example, when longstanding policy did not permit this.

Increasingly, management is recommending home health aide services to patients, and obtaining physician approval. Maximizing visit frequencies is the focus, and supervisors encourage this practice.

The Policies and Procedures Task Force reviewed and revised policies such as sick leave, vacation, dress code, tuition reimbursement, use of radios, and short-term disability benefits. Initially, this task force proceeded to interpret selected policies such as sick time and vacation, issuing their own interpretations that were not necessarily in line with the contract.

The business staff are afraid that management will move to eliminate some benefits, as this task force looked at the feasibility and cost of health care programs. Management frequently reminds staff of the high cost of health care benefits.

The Systems Task Force was involved in training staff for upgraded data entry positions, which put business staff on guard for the potential elimination of some positions. "Improving" job operations and streamlining departments were ongoing TQM goals.

Management verbally reassured the business staff that seniority would be a priority when it considered applications for promotions or position changes caused by departmental consolidation. But when senior business office staff have applied for newly created positions, management has hired new employees for these positions instead. Many senior business office staff have been terminated without just cause, or their positions have been eliminated.

The Retention and Recruitment Task Force was not able to influence nurses to stay at VNA. The attrition rate is high. During their three months' probation, nurses are inundated with paperwork, procedures, and TQM philosophy that conflicts with the reality of actual time consumed in and out of the workplace. It is impossible to complete both our visits and the required documentation within our scheduled 7.5 hours.

Management has a history of denying that nurses resign due to supervisory and organizational deficiencies. With TQM, assembly line nursing has evolved. High productivity expectations, emphasis on number of visits performed, and increased responsibilities without adequate support have caused nurses to seek employment elsewhere. However, nurses who resigned from VNA are now returning to the agency because experience with non-union home care agencies and hospitals has awakened them to the benefits of a union environment.

Local 73's goal is to organize all the nonprofessional staff, including the home health aides. The organizing drive for the business office staff is ongoing. We are up against Seyfarth Shaw, the notorious union-busting law firm, which guides and directs VNA management in anti-union strategies. VNA insists it has a cash flow problem, while spending money on TQM consultants and Seyfarth Shaw to help preserve the top-heavy administration.

THE END OF TQM

TQM task forces no longer meet at the VNA. Each task force disbanded as a result of non-participation by employees who became disillusioned with the process, or the union members who declined to sign up.

At union meetings, the stewards told the membership the dangers of TQM. Articles about TQM were mailed or passed out to the members. After the consultant presented the initial communications workshop, the stewards met with members to assess and evaluate it. The conclusion was that management was using TQM to union-bust and dissuade staff from joining Local 73.

The union membership voted not to sign up for the TQM task forces. Phone calls to members who did not attend the union meetings were made asking them not to sign up. However, it was decided that a few key union members would sign up for the committees, to obtain information and minutes of the meetings.

Filing unfair labor practice charges against VNA was considered as an option, but voted down by the members because we believed we could be more effective in eliminating TQM with collective action.

The members who did participate brought information to the meetings to educate the members. The participating union members on the committees were vocal and often voted down recommendations by the management-dominated committees. Their example encouraged others to become more vocal at these meetings and to challenge the issues presented.

Both union and non-union employees at the VNA experienced the results of these meetings. The Policies and Procedures Task Force instituted a policy change regarding absenteeism. Non-union staff would have their sick time allowed at the discretion of the supervisor. Employees were angered by this policy, and several sought union advice. Many employees not covered by the union contract agreed to stop attending meetings, offering excuses to the supervisors. Supervisors were unable to enlist support for the TQM committees.

Some staff recognized the danger of TQM when a business office employee involved in the Communications Task Force was fired. During the task force sessions, this worker had vocalized the problems with communication among departments that affected efficiency. She had made recommendations for improvements. Shortly after she made a presentation to the staff on "active listening skills," this person was fired. Management may have identified her as a leader and suspected that she was organizing for the union—which she was.

The demise of TQM was a gradual process occurring over two years. Collective action by union members and the business office staff, by agreeing not to participate on the committees, was the key strategy.

Having a few key union members join the TQM committees permitted the union to receive accurate information about the content of the meetings. Informing the membership about this content was vital in maintaining solidarity with our decision not to participate.

TQM now exists in name only, with a vice president of operations who collects a large salary but does not hold meetings with employees. VNA management informed the employees at an all-agency meeting that the TQM committees were no longer necessary, and that money allotted for TQM would be diverted to other needs in the agency.

The failure of TQM at the VNA of Chicago is due to the perseverance and solidarity of the working men and women who are committed to providing quality home care to the people of the Chicago area.

Working Smart:
A Union Guide to Participation Programs and Reengineering
Labor Notes • 7435 Michigan Ave. • Detroit, MI 48210 • (313) 842-6262

Chapter 24

AT&T and CWA in the Workplace of the Future

Although the AT&T/CWA partnership is held up as a model, in practice the multi-tiered "Workplace of the Future" program is management-dominated. AT&T continues to announce massive layoffs without consulting the union—and then asks the union to help implement the cuts. The union's hope is to develop its independent strengths.

[According to the advocates of labor-management cooperation, there are certain star companies and unions that have mastered the process, creating a win-win situation and providing a model for other workplaces. The list is familiar to participation junkies: Saturn, Xerox, Florida Power & Light, Corning Glass, NUMMI, sometimes Ford or Cadillac.

One of these stars is the Workplace of the Future program of AT&T and the Communications Workers of America. The Clinton Administration showcased AT&T at its July 1993 Conference on the Future of the American Workplace. The May 1994 Fact-Finding Report of the Commission on the Future of Worker-Management Relations (the Dunlop Commission) called Workplace of the Future an example of an "integrated partnership."

Eileen Appelbaum and Rosemary Batt, authors of *The New American Workplace: Transforming Work Systems in the United States,* list AT&T as a company that is experimenting with "American team production," which "leads to a real redistribution of power and authority in the workplace." The contract, they say, "clearly provides for...substantial union influence in strategic business decisions, particularly as they affect employment levels and skill requirements."

Government and academics like the Workplace of the Future. What about CWA members? Here Laura Unger provides a participant's view.]

by Laura Unger

IN MARCH 1993 A MEETING WAS HELD in a large ballroom in the suburbs of northern New Jersey. Over a thousand AT&T managers and local and national leaders of the Communications Workers of America came together to jump-start the Workplace of the Future.

While listening to speeches by the leadership of AT&T and CWA's President Morton Bahr, lower management and local union leaders struggled to understand the meaning of working within this program, which had been negotiated as part of the 1992 contract. As lunch was served, Secretary of Labor Robert Reich anointed this program of labor/management "collaboration" the best hope

for the future of rebuilding the American economy in the new global economy.

Though he certainly didn't intend it, that word—"collaboration"—just served to increase the discomfort of the local union leaders in the room. We had been through nine years of post-divestiture AT&T, with the loss of over 100,000 bargaining unit jobs, union-busting at NCR and other subsidiaries, and constant attacks on our contract. Few were ready to accept the idea that AT&T had any intention of meaningfully working with the union to improve our jobs and give us a better chance at employment security.

One local president involved in a plant closing in Chicago called it the "the illusion of inclusion." Unfortunately, but not unexpectedly, that turned out to be a good description of what has happened so far.

The contract language of Workplace of the Future calls for several different levels. The first is "Workplace

---

Laura Unger is president of CWA Local 1150 in New York City and a representative on a Workplace of the Future Business Unit Planning Council. She was a member of the CWA Bargaining Team with AT&T in 1992, and is an elected member of the 1995 Bargaining Team.

Models." These are any joint bargaining unit/management teams like quality teams, process management teams, committees around general office policy, etc. The bargaining unit people on these teams are picked exclusively by the union. The formation, function, and goals of the teams must be mutually agreed on by local management and the local union.

Since AT&T workers do everything from clerical work, operator assistance, and sales to computer manufacture and repair, construction and maintenance of the long-distance network, and high-level testing using sophisticated software, and since we work in groups as small as two or three or in offices of hundreds, the nature of these committees will vary tremendously.

The next level is "Business Unit Planning Councils." AT&T is divided into a large number of business units that market and provide different services or are focused toward different groups of customers. Each is supposedly responsible for its own costs, revenues, and profits, but in reality all answer to a higher authority—the corporate strategy and business needs of AT&T as a whole.

These Planning Councils are made up of a fairly high level of AT&T management from the business unit, and union leadership picked from among local officers and union staff. Their function is to oversee the formation of the Workplace Models and begin to participate in long-term planning with the various business units.

This is the level that is supposed to give the union some input into the direction of the business, job design, and reengineering. It also makes decisions on all joint training programs for Workplace of the Future that are used in the local committees. (Rutgers University in New Jersey has been contracted to develop that training.)

The next level is the Constructive Relationship Council, which is made up of a higher level of management and union leadership and must approve any trials coming out of the local committees that would impact on the contract.

The highest level is the Human Resources Board, whose function is "to review key Human Resources issues worldwide and provide input to the Executive Committee of AT&T."

AFTER A YEAR

Over a year has passed since that meeting in New Jersey. Very little has developed in terms of "Workplace Models." Mainly what has taken place on a local level has been a struggle to transform pre-existing teams that the company had set up unilaterally into the Workplace of the Future bargained-for models. These teams had dealt almost exclusively with company-directed quality efforts and "processes," and the bargaining unit people on them were generally hand-picked by management.

For example, workers involved in selling private telephone circuits had participated in groups called "Branch Councils" to suggest how to improve sales promo-

HUCK/KONOPACKI LABOR CARTOONS

KONOPACKI ©1993

LABOR'S
TRADITIONAL
ADVERSARIAL
STANCE IS
OUTMODED
DON'T YOU
THINK?

point. Planning Councils have been set up in many different business units. Meetings are generally infrequent and often canceled as high-level managers balance them with other priorities. Company organizational changes replace the players just as members are beginning to get to know each other. AT&T, constantly in a budget-cutting mode, is always willing to cancel face-to-face meetings in favor of ineffectual "conference calls."

Hours are being spent developing something called "Ideal Futures," which is supposed to be a perfect end-state that the union and company agree they are working toward. The "Ideal Future" is supposed to give us a common goal that takes into account the separate interests of the workers, the union, the company and its shareholders, and the customers.

If anything, they portray a vision of loyal employees, labor peace, "delighted customers," and "empowered" employees who "share the pain and gain" of the company's ups and downs—but stop far short of guaranteeing job security. Job security, we are told, is "unrealistic."

tions. Technicians had been invited to contribute ideas to improve the servicing of the network.

AT&T's "Process Management" and other quality programs are very entrenched, and local managers are often not willing to find a way to integrate any union control into this structure. Despite instructions from the Planning Councils, local management has been very reluctant to turn these committees over to conform even minimally to the Workplace of the Future language. At a most basic level that would mean letting the union pick the people, which might mean removing people previously assigned.

Some local union leaders are also resisting this process. For some it is because they are politically against all joint activities and have chosen to just stay out of them. (Unfortunately, in many of these cases the company-dominated committees have continued to function.) In other cases, local leaders have been unwilling to confront either the management about reforming the committees or the members who will have to be removed. In many cases, overextended local leaders just can't keep up with all committees that have been set up without their knowledge.

Part of the delay in setting up local Workplace Models is that locals are waiting for the Planning Councils to finish developing the education package that will be used to train committee members. This is generally a correct decision, since most locals do not have education programs in place to prepare their members to participate effectively on behalf of the union.

The Planning Councils have also not come close to meeting last year's shining speeches. If anything, this is where the "illusion of inclusion" has been exactly to the

'IDEAL FUTURE' INCLUDES LAYOFFS

While Planning Councils talk about this "Ideal Future," the present is very much upon us. Simultaneous to discussions going on in the Planning Councils, in almost every business unit massive layoffs were announced without any discussion with the union or, in many cases, any advance warning. In February 1994 AT&T announced nearly 15,000 layoffs with no prior notice to the union.

In announcing the layoffs the company was quick to point out the "special payments," up to 104 weeks, that laid-off employees get. What they failed to mention is that those payments are negotiated benefits in the union contract and are no "special" gift from the company.

The union's response to the layoff announcement was to "wonder" if their time spent on Workplace of the Future had been wasted. Unfortunately, after some initial expression of "shock and disgust," the union has chosen to continue participating in these committees. "Inclusion" in most cases has meant that the union was asked--after the announcement—to sit on joint committees to talk about how the layoffs would be accomplished or how work would be redesigned based on a smaller workforce. This has happened over and over again during the last year.

So where are we? "Workplace of the Future" has not met anyone's expectations. It certainly has not taken even a small step in "transforming the workplace" on a local level. Workers are still not participating in any decision making on issues of substance to their interests, nor are they making any real improvements in work flow or quality from the point of view of the company.

On a higher level, the union's hopes that they would have input into decisions before layoffs are announced have not been fulfilled at all. Other issues the union hoped would be discussed, like outside contracting and moving bargaining unit work to management, have been touched on at meetings, but nothing has yet been accomplished.

Union people have been put on various high-level company task forces, but with little effect. There are generally one or two union people on large teams of managers, some of whom have been working on these issues for years. The union members are thrown onto these task forces with little guidance about what the union wants to accomplish, or even how to develop a union agenda on reengineering. They are given no technical training to help them understand the issues, terms, and systems the company is discussing.

It's too easy for individuals assigned to these committees to get disoriented and lose their grasp of their role as union representatives, and too easy for the company to make decisions and announce "union input" without that input being real.

On the other hand, some of our worst fears about Workplace of the Future winning the hearts and minds of the members and weakening the union have also not been realized. Partly this is because the process is moving so slowly it has not had much effect on anything.

In locals where some workplace committees have been set up, the union's selection of committee members has increased the union presence in the workplace and given the union increased access to the workers on company time. This is generally uneven, and locals that have been stronger in the past are the ones who use this to their advantage. The training program developed by Rutgers has a fairly good section on the history, function, and organization of unions, and that has been a good educational tool for the members (and management) where it has been trialed.

Finally, the workforce is generally so angry and cynical because of the attacks of the last few years that even those who are disillusioned with the union are not likely to see Workplace of the Future or any AT&T program as a potential savior.

INDEPENDENT UNION STRENGTH

Workplace of the Future at AT&T arose out of the union's frustration over its inability to fight the layoffs and other attacks on our jobs. Some of that inability arose out of conditions that were beyond our control—certain aspects of the technology, deregulation, and increased competition. Some came out of internal weaknesses in the union. Those are exactly the same weaknesses that will make us less able to use Workplace of the Future as a weapon to benefit the union and the members.

The lack of education of the members and many of the local officers, the lack of a real strategy around job design, new technology, and job protection, the disunity among different parts of the country as some places grow and others are losing jobs, the disunity about regulatory strategy, the apathy and general lack of militancy among a good part of the AT&T workforce—these are conditions that have undermined our ability to fight in traditional ways and will also contribute to a failure to achieve real power through this new process.

What incentive does the company have to give us power at the workplace? Some improved quality? Even more labor peace? Less disgruntled employees providing better customer service? Will the company really give the union power in exchange for these meager rewards? I think not.

The only hope for this program is to strengthen the language so it requires union input and participation before decisions are made about new technology, job design, and reengineering.

But mainly, the way to save our union and members' jobs is for the union to simultaneously work on developing its *independent* strengths—increasing union education for the members, developing independent political action and an independent strategy towards regulation, mobilizing around on-the-job issues, and building coalitions around worker and consumer issues surrounding the "information superhighway"...the list goes on and on.

The company's greatest weapon with Workplace of the Future is that the union at all levels is spending so much of its time and energy on it that very little else gets done. Even basic grievance handling is falling to the wayside as staff spends more and more time on Workplace of the Future committees.

It would be a mistake not to participate in Workplace of the Future now that it has been bargained. However, it will be a hype and a sham if the union is not strong enough and clear enough in its goals to turn it into a tool to fight for its members. Our main task has to be working within the union to build that strength and define those goals.

Working Smart:
A Union Guide to Participation Programs and Reengineering
Labor Notes • 7435 Michigan Ave. • Detroit, MI 48210 • (313) 842-6262

Chapter 25

TQM and Higher Education

Total Quality Management applies manufacturing concepts to higher education. Administrators push TQM even though there is no agreement on "who is the customer" of education. The stress on reducing variability, valuing the quantifiable, the internal customer, and cutting jobs results in less autonomy for faculty and staff and more control for the administration.

AT FIRST GLANCE, it may seem difficult to imagine how Total Quality Management could be applied in universities and colleges.

But university administrators—like their counterparts in management elsewhere—think differently. "Can a university be run more like a business? You bet it can," says John Curry, chief financial officer at UCLA. "Most universities can do a significant job of cutting costs through the same reengineering of processes and work that have characterized the best for-profit corporations."[1]

TQM is now at the center of the strategic debate on the future of education. Academic consultants and administrators have written dozens of books and articles explaining how to use TQM in higher education. Entire issues of the journals *Higher Education, Change, Educational Leadership,* and *Educational Record* promote TQM.

Corporations have jumped into the fray, seeing TQM as a way to advance their own agendas. Six major corporations are sponsoring annual gatherings of academic and business leaders to promote TQM in higher education. IBM gives grants to universities to use and teach TQM. As a public service, Polaroid donates staff to train educational institutions in the use of TQM.

Why should corporations be interested in evangelizing for TQM outside their own walls? For one thing, TQM often creates "true believers," who want to go out and spread the message to others. Some corporate executives undoubtedly think they are doing community service in bringing TQM to campus to solve the crisis in education.

It is also in corporations' interests that the next flock of university graduates be well-trained in the corporate

mentality. Witness the barrage of newspaper and magazine editorials urging that education better prepare students to fit into the new world competitive order.

TQM advocates usually begin by pointing to the pressures on higher education. Technology is driving a sustained information explosion. The globalization of the economy requires increased knowledge and understanding of world-wide developments in virtually every field.

The public expects education to solve, or at least to compensate for, every social problem. If workers do not have good jobs, then the problem must be their training. If young people are into drugs, sex, violence, racism, or selfishness, then the cause—and the solution—must lie in the education system.

Costs are escalating while budgets are slashed. Teachers are being forced to research and teach in areas out of their main fields. Over the years many colleges have constructed huge bureaucratic fiefdoms which serve only themselves. And even if not the majority, there are plenty of examples of lack of direction, corruption, poor teaching, lack of concern for students, and needless bureaucratic rules.

All of this makes the case for *some* sort of overhaul of the system.

WHAT IS TQM IN EDUCATION?

However, the substance of the TQM movement sweeping through higher education is hard to pin down. TQM can range from a new name to freshen up the same old policies, to a full-scale education reform program, to a reorganization of the institution. A TQM program may contain many positive elements or it may be the cover for an all-out attack on faculty unions and other institutions of faculty influence.

Initial TQM experiments concentrated on administration and plant services, carefully avoiding teaching and re-

This article is based on a longer one titled "Beware! TQM Is Coming to Your Campus," Thought and Action: The NEA Higher Education Journal, *Volume X, Number 1, Spring 1994. Thanks to Harry Brighouse, Dianne Feeley, Steve Hinds, Dave McCullough, and Tony Smith for useful comments on this draft.*

search. Reports of TQM successes are widely cited: Oregon State University's physical plant TQM team reduced the average time of remodeling jobs by 29 percent (estimated savings: $219,539). The printing/mailing team implemented six solutions to cut pre-press time (estimated savings $16,224).[2] (Notice the precision of these estimates.) The University of Wisconsin reduced the time for graduate school processing of admissions applications from 26 days to 3.[3] Fox Valley Technical College claims "high measurable returns" in morale, cost control, learning, and community support.[4] Perhaps of greater impact, it has also created a Quality Academy—a source of considerable prestige and income.

TQM advocates acknowledge "that TQM [has] much in common with good-sense management techniques."[5] And many of the TQM success stories seem to be just that: TQM provided the opportunity for management to hear or use common sense. If all TQM means is that "we want to improve quality using good sense," then there is no argument here. But then the definition of quality—which means what we see as the goal of education—becomes the core of the discussion.

The problem is that there is no agreed-upon definition of quality in education. Therefore the TQM prescriptions for teaching and research vary widely and often contradict each other: from increasing cross-disciplinary studies to more rigidly compartmentalized curricula; from abolishing grades and any form of examination (inspection) to organizing the curriculum around nationally developed standardized tests.

Debates over the purpose of education, how learning happens, questions of assessment and accountability raged before TQM. TQM cannot be faulted for failing to resolve these issues. But we need to ask what the implications of TQM are in this context. Does TQM tilt the debate in a particular direction?

TQM THEMES

FOCUS ON THE CUSTOMER

All TQM programs insist that the focus of activities must be on the customer. As one consultant on TQM in higher education warns:

> Customer focus is the cornerstone of Total Quality. It's the customer who decides what quality is and then judges how well you are doing in relation to their standards. An organization that does not take the time to build a sound and complete knowledge base of what their customer needs are can't begin to build a solid foundation for a quality system.[6]

But determining who the customer is turns out to be more difficult than it appears. In higher education, the question always generates intense debate: Is the customer the students? Their parents? The taxpayers, the academic community, businesses who will hire the graduates, graduate schools, the local community, the national public interest, the international public interest, truth, knowledge, justice?

If the customer is the student, are customer needs what the student *thinks* she needs when she applies to college, what she wants while she is in college, or what the student will discover in later life was beneficial? Or should her needs be determined by others who already know these things? Are we talking about what the student needs for her envisioned career, the skills she will need to support herself, or what she needs to be a good citizen? Do government and literature courses help a person become a better engineer?

The list of questions grows. The definition of "the customer" is really the pre-TQM questions: *What are the goals of education? What are the purposes of educational institutions?*

In theory, TQM cannot happen without defining the customer. You can't gather data on "how we are doing" if you don't know how to weight conflicting evaluations by

© 1993, UCS   CALM 6-93

"I think computers are helpful too, but I don't think they should have named one teacher of the year."

students, colleagues, future employers, and alumni. You can't decide how much time should be allocated to the competing demands of teaching, research, advising students, community service, or keeping up in the field.

Some TQM advocates resolve this problem by asserting that the student is the customer but someone else must determine what the student needs. Others argue that the model can be simplified by assuming that employers are the critical customers of higher education; luckily, the interests of other customers will turn out to be the same in the long run.[7]

Even where it is not explicit that future employers are the primary customer the idea often comes through clearly. Carol Tyler, a consultant for the well-known Fox Valley Technical College Academy for Quality Education, says that what "may be the most significant thing we have done [is provide a] guarantee to employers that all graduating students will have mastered these [five clusters of TQM] competencies in the program"[8]

In practice, despite TQM's own requirement for clarity on this question, TQM programs tend to side-step it. Some issue a vague mission statement including everybody as a customer. The consultant cited above—who warned about the importance of identifying customer needs—goes on to provide the (positive) example that a college of engineering has identified and prioritized its customers as follows:

Primary Customers
1. Students
   Undergraduate
   Graduate
   Outreach
2. Employers
   Industry
   Government
   Military
Secondary Customers
3. Parents
4. Legislators
5. Society
6. Research Agencies
7. Taxpayers

By including everyone, the college fudges the question.

Another way to avoid the question is the device of the "internal customer." Under the internal customer paradigm, participants are told to look at the institution as a series of processes. Understand that the person (or process) who receives the results of your activities is your customer.

TQM theorists suggest that this conception greatly simplifies and focuses quality activity. The last operation in the process meets the needs of its (external) customer, and thereby establishes what it needs from its supplier, of which it is the customer. And so on back through the process. Every step is both a supplier and a customer. Put another way, if each step works to serve its immediate customer, then all steps will be working toward serving the external customer.

The analysis is very much in the tradition of a conservative approach to economics. By each unit taking care of its own business without interference, the "invisible hand" of the process takes care of the big picture. Similarly, the sum total of all the activities will tend to force the individual components to do the proper job.

In an academic setting, we can flow-chart the process of a student's education. As one TQM consultant explains, if you are a 10th grade math teacher, then your customer is the 11th grade math teacher.[9] (Every teacher who has had students with the formal prerequisite courses but without the content can appreciate the important element of truth here.)

Some processes—say in manufacturing—may diagram in such a neat, unambiguous, linear fashion. But the real world of education does not work that way. Try to construct a flow-chart for a four-year college, with a diverse student body and faculty, that does not require the student to fully commit to a profession when she enters.

For a moment, though, accept that the learning process can be reduced to a neat flow-chart and that the internal customers are correctly identified. A moment's consideration indicates how the model clouds the real decision makers. The customer focus of the 10th grade teacher is relatively clear—but only if we have correctly determined the requirements of the (unknown) customer at the end of the chain. We also have to determine the requirements for the student raw material that enters in the beginning of the process (e.g., prerequisites for high school math). Further, someone has to determine whether trigonometry should be covered in 10th grade or in 12th.

Thus for the teacher, the internal customer concept "solves" the problem of what to teach by assuming that some-

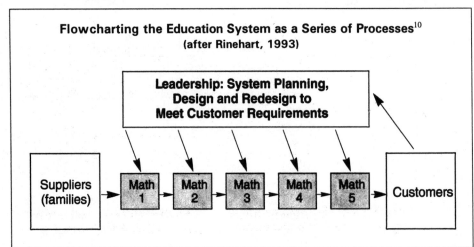

Flowcharting the Education System as a Series of Processes[10]
(after Rinehart, 1993)

Leadership: System Planning, Design and Redesign to Meet Customer Requirements

Suppliers (families) → Math 1 → Math 2 → Math 3 → Math 4 → Math 5 → Customers one else makes all the key decisions: what are the goals of education, which students are admitted to the process, and how are the "customer requirements" for each step to be defined. Someone has to decide the sticky questions of who the ultimate customers are and their relative importance, and translate their needs into specifications that mark the steps in the process.

This conception helps make sense of the TQM puzzle. Yes, faculty and staff are supposed to take more control over their work. But only within a more tightly controlled, defined space.

The flexibility in the system, then, is not flexibility for faculty or staff to experiment. It is flexibility for the administration, freed from restrictions imposed by unions, traditions, or faculty governance, to move the pieces around to bring them into alignment with the big goals.

To be sure, under TQM the administration opens communication and gets advice from faculty, staff, students, the community, business, and others. But in the final analysis, the administration sets the goals and determines the resources.

The fact that the administration controls the essential goals of education is nothing new. But the history of teacher unions is to struggle against this control, believing that teachers have knowledge, values, and insights that administrators lack. These insights come not only from teachers' training but from their on-going direct contact with students. TQM adds an ideological and organizational bias toward stronger administration control over what goes on in the university.

This is a question of both power and educational philosophy.

TQM presentations frequently include two arrow diagrams illustrating the relationship of the overall objectives of the institution (large arrow) and the objectives of the individual components or departments (small arrows). TQM claims to bring the small arrows into alignment with the overall goals.

The Power Question: since working conditions are bound to be greatly affected by "realigning" the individual and departmental activities, do the staff and faculty have any control over the fundamental goals with which they are to be aligned?

Consider this widely reprinted parable from *Once Upon a Campus: Stories about Quality Concepts in Higher Education*.[11] It illustrates how TQM methods can seem to give participants some control over—or at least "input" into—the solution of certain problems. But it also illustrates how this input is restricted to the small questions, while the larger ones remain unasked. The author is explaining one TQM method: getting at the root cause of a problem through asking repeated "why's."

In this case the student, Jimmy, failed. Why? He was exhausted from studying. Why? His school workload was overwhelming. Why? The part-time teachers who had taught the prerequisite courses did not cover the material required in Jimmy's recent courses. Why? Because they did not have contact with the other professors. Why? The department did not do orientation for part-timers, and there was little communication between part-timers and full-timers.

At this point, the teachers are admitted to the process, to solve the Jimmy problem. The implied solution is to make sure that part-timers understand what they need to teach and that they have better communication with the regular faculty. But the fact of part-timers is taken for granted. The parable does not question why the teaching is done by part-time rather than full-time faculty and pursue the solution along that logical path.

The Philosophical Question: Does it serve education to create institutions where all parts are aligned? Or does good education require the give and take of independent directions and goals?

The only way that the TQM model can serve the multiple "customers" of education without breaking down is by viewing the world as a place without any fundamental conflicts of interest. This view goes beyond simply finding a "win-win" solution. It suggests that education can be organized in such a way that the best solution for each customer separately turns out to be the same. Thus we can serve all the different customers at once.

But we would suggest that the "who is the customer of education" debate cannot and will not be resolved, because institutions of education exist within a society of fundamental and deep social conflicts. The needs of employers *do* conflict with those of taxpayers, for example. These struggles are reflected back into every aspect of education. But there is no place in the TQM model to acknowledge this conflict.

REDUCE TO QUANTIFIABLE UNITS

Another central theme of TQM is that it must be data-driven or use "management by fact."[12] In particular, there

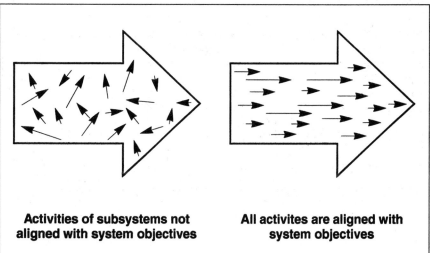

Activities of subsystems not aligned with system objectives

All activites are aligned with system objectives

is a strong orientation toward measurements and evaluations that can be expressed numerically. The classic tools of TQM include statistical process control charts, Pareto charts, histograms, and scattergrams. TQM's goals are vague, but the tools provide the illusion of precision. Thus the statistical tools tend to define how TQM is used—rather than the goals of change determining how the tools are used.

The emphasis on measurement defines the world of important things as those which can be easily quantified. This leads to a distortion and routinization of academic work.[13] TQM tends to bias the educational debate towards standardized tests, multiple choice, and other forms of easily quantified measurements. Fields that are not so easily quantified, such as writing, may get reduced resources—although the inability to write seems to be one of graduates' biggest problems.

Universities already exhibit a strong contradiction between their proclaimed goal of fostering students' critical reasoning abilities, and their usual practice of transmitting certain accepted ideologies regarding the nature of the economy, certain views of history, and the like. The drive to quantification makes it even harder for teachers to encourage critical thinking. Even the problem-solving methods of TQM become rigid formulas. "Learning how to learn" becomes a synonym for learning how to follow directions.

TQM also biases the debate against important roles for teachers that are not so easily measured, including motivation, counseling, and role modeling. Similarly, a data-driven approach to research is biased toward that which produces large short-term results, is of more immediate use to business, or can attract large grants.

REDUCE VARIATION

The most prominent person associated with the TQM approach is W. Edwards Deming, who is revered in Japan for his contribution to rebuilding industry there after World War II. One of Deming's contributions to manufacturing quality was to reject the idea that if parts came into the process with variations, the process would adapt to make them work. This is "tampering," according to Deming, and only adds to the deviation from specifications that will result. In TQM, quality means standardizing each step of the process and insisting that the raw materials come in at spec. This is done by applying the TQM method to parts production as well.

If all the raw materials are standardized and all parts are made exactly the same, the final assembly will also show less variation. If a process is changed, it must be done only in a controlled way with the baseline established, the change recorded, and the results analyzed—and only with permission from management.

Reduction of variation is clearly desirable when we are talking about the surface of a roll of sheet steel (although if achieving that smooth surface requires a more stressful job, we would need to deal with the costs to the worker). But is uniformity either the goal or the best

process in education? Uniformity might help administrators do their jobs. It simplifies the operation and makes it easier for administrators to stay in control of the system. Should these be the considerations that drive education?

The standardization logic of TQM implies that "quality teaching" is to present the same material in the same way each time or to adjust it only under controlled circumstances with approval from whoever sets the overall specifications.

The power aspect of this conception is that it implies the reduction of individual judgment in daily work. Judgment thus tends to be limited to making recommendations to those responsible for the bigger system.

The no-variation concept is biased against a learning atmosphere where variation thrives and in particular where unpopular ideas are protected. The TQM definition some use—"doing it right the first time"—is an indication of the standardization mentality that is completely antithetical to a learning atmosphere.

Although reducing variation is central to TQM theory, many TQM advocates, including Deming's followers, make an exception for education: they call for "understanding" rather than reducing variation. Other consultants in the education field simply transfer the methods from industry. Polaroid's training for educators emphasizes that "Variation is the Enemy!!"[14]

Programmed learning materials, with computer control of the path from one bit of learning to the next, are heavily promoted by training corporations and some educators. While this approach may be useful for some individuals in dealing with some topics, TQM's focus on standardization and measurability make a case for programmed learning as a universal method.

JOB LOSS

In manufacturing, TQM lays the basis for more use of part-timers, temporary workers, and contracting out because it breaks down jobs to their smallest units and sets standard procedures for doing the job.

The same methods are easily transferred to education. From an exact repeatability point of view, teaching would best be done by robots, computerized lessons, or videotapes of professional actors following a carefully crafted script.

Arizona State University Professor Paul Privateer, for example, who is a leading advocate of new technologies and forms of education, argues that it is inefficient for three different professors to lecture to three classes of students. Privateer would like to see the three profs collaborate to produce a lecture that students could tap into via computer at their convenience.

"Rather than paying three salaries for twice-a-week performances, is there a more efficient way of doing that?" asks Privateer. "Obviously, yes. [The instructors] could work much more as active mentors of applied information rather than presenters."[15] Indeed, some TQM advocates see the use of telecourses ("distance learning

THE POWERS THAT BE

technologies") as a central strategy.[16]

Another approach to cost-cutting is Responsibility Center Budgeting. A Cornell University dean explains how it works: "We share all the financial information with the faculty. When you say, "With some percentage that we save by you not filling that open position, we will make "X" available to you, maybe in terms of higher salaries for those who are left,' it is striking to find out how many can get away with five people instead of six."[17]

TRANSFER OF CONTROL

TQM allows the administration to increase its control over all aspects of the university, both through organizational forms and through ideology.

The very vagueness of TQM makes it all the more attractive to those in charge. They can "cherry-pick" the policies and educational philosophies that fit their agendas, confident that they can find a defense from one or another quality guru or from the thousands of consultants who have created their own brands of TQM. Or they can claim they have synthesized and adapted the best in-house. As a result there are wild and contradictory extremes in TQM approaches.

The aspects of TQM philosophy that are closest to unions' are among the first to be discarded. Few programs eradicate what Deming calls "deadly diseases": performance evaluations, merit ratings, and annual reviews. And most administrators of TQM programs consciously do the opposite of Deming's admonition to "drive out fear" (number 8 of Deming's famous 14 Points). Deming pointed out, "It is worthy of note that the 80 American Nobel Prize winners all had tenure, security. They were answerable only to themselves."[18] Through short-term contracts and part-timing ("flexibility"), fear is precisely the atmosphere that administrators have created.

But TQM advocates embrace those of Deming's points that conveniently fit administrators' agendas. Deming's injunction to "maintain constancy of purpose" becomes the rationale for chopping the weaker sections of the university community, thus creating an atmosphere of fear and insecurity for the workforce. This is a vision of continuous intense competition to survive. "Agile institutions"—the newest buzzword—focus on their "core businesses" and contract for everything else on an as-needed basis.

One administrator urges:

Administrators and boards at many institutions will need to perform triage on their institutions' programs. Weak programs will need to be eliminated in order to redirect resources to strengthen middle-quality programs (to protect them from distant but higher-quality competitors) and/or enhance already strong programs (which might be exported via distance technologies...).[19]

One problem with this approach is the question of how to measure the "strength" of a program. Clearly, these measures will quickly drift to the quantifiable and powerful factors: how much grant money or contracts a department can pull in. Does anyone think that an institution faced with resource problems will eliminate a business school TQM program, no matter how shoddy, that draws in paying customers from local corporations before it cuts back the general humanities program?

Secondly, this whole notion puts academic programs in competition with each other for survival. It will undermine the interaction and cooperation between disciplines that both educators and TQM advocates are supposed to value highly.

A UNION STRATEGY FOR TQM

Besides the general advice we give to all unions in chapter 33, a strategy toward TQM for campus unions should include the following elements:

1. Propose a union agenda to address the problems that exist, including the hard issues like budget cuts.

2. Recognize that the conflicting aims in higher education reflect conflicts of interest in the society as a whole and therefore cannot be neatly resolved on a single campus. Policies will therefore reflect power, bargaining, compromise, coalitions, and overlapping interests, rather than logical progression from principles.

3. Insist on being in on determining the big goals in any quality program. These will determine the standards at the lower level and therefore directly affect working conditions.

4. Approach TQM as a collective bargaining situation.

5. Champion the cause of students, faculty, staff, and teaching assistants as partners in the education process. To use the TQM jargon: students should be regarded as the customers of higher education. But students are more than passive consumers—they are also active participants in the process of learning.

Often politicians and administrators encourage the view that faculty and students are adversaries for scarce resources. Too often the union gets cast in the role of defender of special privilege. This is one reason for faculty unions to look for every opportunity to work in coalition with student and community groups.

Putting together coalitions like this can be tricky. Just as with coalitions of multiple unions in the same workplace, or different groupings within unions (gender, minorities, seniority, departments), the different and sometimes conflicting interests of each group must be addressed. When job security for faculty depends almost entirely on research and publishing, for example, spending time with students drops to the bottom of the list; the workload on teaching assistants increases.

Similarly, faculty may not understand the pressures on students to take large course loads and get out quickly;

costs are higher and they face far worse job prospects than the faculty themselves did when they graduated. Combine these pressures with the need for many students to work part-time or full-time, and it is not surprising that some students seem to care only about grades and not about learning. Under these circumstances, the separate self-interests of both faculty and students could lead to a downgrading of the curriculum.

The truth is that coalitions between progressive faculty and students have been more likely to occur around larger movements and goals—union organizing drives in the 1930s, civil rights, anti-war activities, environmental issues—than around campus issues. The university is built (at least in theory) around ideas, after all, and students have the chance to absorb new ideas, adopt them passionately, and act on them, sometimes quite apart from their immediate interests simply as students. While such activism is at a low ebb nowadays—and many teachers who remember their own student days are discouraged—it is when students do take up larger ideas outside themselves—and push their teachers into action—that coalitions around campus problems become most possible.

In the meantime, in building a campus-wide coalition a faculty union might consider arguing for alternate promotion tracks for faculty who want to concentrate on teaching, or at least for less reliance on publications for tenure. Enforceable limits on class size would benefit faculty, teaching assistants, and students. And teachers should hold organized discussions of students' and teachers' expectations of themselves and each other at the beginning of each course.

6. Insist at the same time that the union's interest in improving teachers' and other employees' lives is also legitimate on its own terms and does not have to be justified solely in terms of service to the "customers." If the "system" we seek to improve is society, one way to improve it is by improving the working conditions of all workers. Unionized workers lead the way by moving standards upward.

7. Look behind the rhetoric and select those parts of TQM that make sense; reject the others. Do not accept any particular consultant as the authoritative interpreter of TQM, or the notion that TQM must be a particular package. If management can pick and choose from the TQM smorgasbord, so can the union.

For example, the trend to use temporary and vulnerable part-time instructors undermines educational continuity and the learning community that is integral to the learning experience. Fighting to expand the number of faculty with full rights and benefits is a quality issue. If the students are the customers, then the faculty and staff in contact with the students are in the best position to evaluate and respond to customer feedback.

Be prepared to use the writings of TQM gurus to buttress the union position. In particular pay attention to the writings of Deming and his followers on education, as they often contradict the practice of most TQM programs.[20]

Because many different reforms are now presented under the TQM initials, it is often possible to find a program labeled TQM that fits your educational philosophy. The Polaroid Corp.'s project to introduce TQM into education may treat variation as the enemy, but it is also possible to find "TQM" reforms based around variation in learning.[21]

8. Clarify which issues will be pursued through the union and which through traditional academic governance bodies.

George Keller, University of Pennsylvania Higher Education Division Chair, says, "TQM is like a penny a child has swallowed. It too will someday pass."[22] But even while passing through, the implications of TQM for higher education staff and faculty may be enormous if TQM changes work rules, methods of teaching, and workloads as well as the general direction of the institution. Even if TQM proves to be a total failure in terms of its stated goals, the damage from its passing through may not be reversible. Unions representing faculty and staff need their own agenda for quality, not "business-like" ways to run education.

Notes

1. Ron Gales, "Can Colleges Be Reengineered?" *Across the Board*, March 1994, pp. 16-22.

2. E. Coate, "The Introduction of Total Quality Management at Oregon State University," *Higher Education*, Volume 25, No.3, pp. 303-320.

3. Joanne Nagy et al., "Case Study Number Three: Madison, How TQM Helped Change an Admissions Process," *Change*, Vol. 25, No. 3, 1993, p. 40.

4. T. Marchese, "TQM reaches the academy," *AAHE Bulletin*, November 1991, p. 8; S.J. Spinbauer, *A Quality System for Education*, ASQC Quality Press, Milwaukee, 1992.

5. David Entin, "Case Study Number One: Boston, Less Than Meets the Eye," *Change*, Vol. 25, No. 3, 1993, pp. 28-31.

6. Cathy Hageman, *Malcolm Baldrige-type Assessment in Higher Education,* video tape produced by Engineering Professional Development College of Engineering, University of Wisconsin-Madison, 1993.

7. G. Rinehart, *Quality Education: Applying the Philosophy of Dr. W. Edwards Deming*, ASQC Quality Press, Milwaukee, 1993, pp. 58-60.

8. Presentation, "Total Quality Management in Education" Workshop, Niagara County Community College, April 2, 1993.

9. A. Hyman and C. Lawrence, "Total Quality Awareness for Education" (Revision 4), a Project Bridge Program sponsored by Polaroid Corporation and presentation to Massachusetts Teacher Association Leadership Conference, August 11, 1993.

10. After Rinehart, p. 58.

11. Daniel Seymour, *Once Upon a Campus: Stories about Quality Concepts in Higher Education*, Avalon Press, Palm Springs, 1993. See also Barbara McKenna, "TQM Coming Soon

to a Campus Near You," *On Campus*, American Federation of Teachers, October 1993, p. 10.

12. See Ted Marchese, "TQM: A Time for Ideas," *Change*, Vol. 25, No. 3, May/June 1993, p. 12; Robert Cornesky, Sam McCool, Larry Byrnes, Robert Weber, *Implementing Total Quality Management in Higher Education*, Magna Publications, 1992, p. 55.

13. H. Allen, "Measuring Academic Work in an Era of Consumerism: Trends in Faculty Accountability and Productivity," paper presented at NEA Higher Education Conference, April 1992.

14. Hyman and Lawrence, p. 43.

15. Gales, p. 22.

16. G. Godby, "Beyond TQM: Competition and Cooperation Create the Agile Organization," *Educational Record*, Vol. 74, No. 2, 1993, pp. 37-42.

17. Gales, p. 21.

18. W.E. Deming, *Out of the Crisis*, Massachusetts Institute of Technology Center for Advanced Engineering, 1986.

19. Godby, p. 41.

20. See for example, Ron Brandt, "On Deming and School Quality: A Conversation with Enid Brown," *Educational Leadership*, Vol. 50, No. 3. November 1992, pp. 28-31.

21. J. Cleveland and P. Plastrik, "Learning, Learning Organizations, and TQM," *Total Quality Management--Implications for Higher Education*, College and University Personnel Association, 1994.

22. Society for College and University Planning, "SCUP-28 Conference Highlights," *E-Mail News*, Vol. 8, No. 5, 1993.

Working Smart:
A Union Guide to Participation Programs and Reengineering
Labor Notes • 7435 Michigan Ave. • Detroit, MI 48210 • (313) 842-6262

Chapter 26

Legal Status of Participation Programs

Under current law, participation programs are illegal without union approval. Unions have the right to "just say no." A union can ask the NLRB to disestablish a unilaterally-imposed program. Within a program, unions may insist on the "collective bargaining model," with each side functioning in its own interests.

by Ellis Boal

SECTION 8(a)(2)[1] OF THE NATIONAL LABOR RELATIONS ACT gives unions considerable power in dealing with employee participation programs. It declares that a company cannot dominate a labor organization. National Labor Relations Board cases brought by unions against participation programs—*Electromation*,[2] *DuPont*,[3] and others—show that 8(a)(2) is very usable.

NLRA Section 8(a)(5)[4] is equally important. It says a company must bargain in good faith once a union is recognized.

For a variety of reasons unions have brought few 8(a)(2) cases against participation programs. Even so, employer organizations are working to reinterpret or amend these laws in the courts and Congress.

As this book goes to press Congress has not acted. This chapter reflects the law as of 1994. If the law is subsequently changed, write to Labor Notes for an update. Even if it is changed, employer conduct committed while the old law was in effect will still be judged under the old law.[5]

Copies of the cases, laws, and regulations noted here are available at any law library. For a more extensive treatment than what follows, see chapter 41.

ILLEGAL WITHOUT UNION APPROVAL

The bottom line is that under the current law virtually all real-life participation programs are illegal without

Ellis Boal is a lawyer in Detroit. He wrote Labor Notes' brief in Electromation *and its submission to the Commission on the Future of Worker-Management Relations.*

union approval, and some may be illegal even if the union consents to them. A program set up unilaterally by the employer will be struck down by the NLRB, if the union challenges it.

Because the National Labor Relations Act itself is so clear, the NLRB and the Supreme Court have been clear in their rulings. Following is a summary of the legal principles.

Finally, although legalities are important, any union's strategy toward a participation program is advanced immeasurably by an organizing approach: an educated, mobilized, and informed workforce.

DOMINATION AND ASSISTANCE

1. Under section 8(a)(2), an employer may not dominate or assist a team, circle, task force, any participation group that is a labor organization, or any other entity that is a "labor organization."[6]

2. The difference between domination and assistance is a matter of degree. The significance of the distinction is that in the first case the NLRB will order the dominated entity itself to be disbanded ("disestablished"), and in the second it will issue only a cease-and-desist order to the company to stop assisting.[7]

3. Unlawful domination can take many forms. The presence of one or more of the following can mean domination: controlling the membership of the participation group,[8] paying for members' time in participation groups,[9] providing meeting space and materials,[10] requiring supervisory personnel to be present in participation group meetings,[11] controlling the group's agenda,[12] controlling the facilitator or training,[13] giving extra perks to

the labor-side members,[14] requiring a consensus decision-making procedure thus giving supervisor members of the group a veto,[15] and having no formal structure, dues, or officers.[16]

The NLRB has not specifically ruled on the legality of groups which prohibit labor-side caucuses or distribution of group information to the rank and file, but presumably groups that prohibited these actions would also be held to be dominated.

4. Unlawful assistance can also take many forms. Examples: having company officers vote on a contract proposal,[17] providing clerical support,[18] and permitting a superintendent to be a union officer.[19] (The most commonly litigated example, recognition of a union without objective evidence a majority of the workers support it, does not usually arise in participation cases.[20])

5. An employer that provides meeting space and pays for the time of stewards or shop committee members to negotiate or process grievances does not thereby unlawfully assist that committee, if the space and payments are provided by a collective bargaining contract negotiated at arm's length.[21]

'LABOR ORGANIZATION'

6. It is only a "labor organization" that the employer is forbidden to dominate or assist. A labor organization is defined in section 2(5)[22] as any body 1) in which "employees participate" and 2) whose purpose at least in part is to "deal" with the employer about wages and/or working conditions.[23]

7. A union is therefore a labor organization, and employers may not dominate unions (including NLRB-certified unions[24]). Participation groups can also be "labor organizations" susceptible to illegal domination.[25]

8. "Dealing" does not necessarily have to involve "bargaining." A participation group can be a labor organization dealing with management even though it has no contracts and/or does not try to bargain contracts.[26] It is a labor organization if its purpose is to deal with employers even if it has never actually done so.[27]

9. "Working conditions" cover a broad range. They can include matters that are not in the contract or are non-grievable.[28] Thus work standards and work rules,[29] work hours,[30] work schedules,[31] work loads,[32] and work as-signments[33] are considered working conditions. If the participation group also gets involved in management prerogatives not related to working conditions (such as product design, advertising, or investment), it is still a labor organization if it exists "in part" to deal about working conditions.[34]

10. A participation group can be a labor organization even if it has supervisors in it.[35]

11. The NLRB has to date left open the question whether it is a necessary part of the definition of a labor organization that a participation group's members subjectively interact with or "represent" the workforce.[36]

12. A "brainstorming session," where workers spin out ideas but do not necessarily expect or get any management response,[37] is not a labor organization.

13. A "work crew," where workers simply do their work together, is not a labor organization.[38] Though the NLRB has not considered such a case, if a work crew had periodic meetings where working conditions were discussed, it would presumably become a labor organization on those occasions.

14. A body, such as a shop committee, civil rights committee, or bargaining committee, which is a subcommittee of a recognized union is not a labor organization. It is not a separate entity.[39]

15. A two-sided joint committee engaged in ongoing collective bargaining or grievance handling is not a labor organization.[40] Rather it is an ongoing coupling or meeting of two distinct sides, each with their own constituency. In a joint committee the labor-side members either are a labor organization or are a subcommittee of a labor organization.[41]

BAD FAITH BARGAINING

16. It is bad faith bargaining under section 8(a)(5) for a company to set up a participation program against a union's wishes. A recognized union has the absolute legal right to "just say no" to company proposals for a participation program.[42]

17. The union may demand the names of any officers or stewards who have applied for management positions.[43] The union can amend its constitution to bar from office anyone who has applied.[44]

DANGERS FOR THE UNION

18. The union is the exclusive representative of the workers in its unit.[45] If a union allowed participation groups to function autonomously without union monitoring or a union presence in each group, a group might emerge as an illicit dual power on the floor.[46] A group untethered to the union could assume a separate obligation to represent members fairly.[47] It could itself be charged as a dominated labor organization,[48] and the union could be charged for failure to represent for allowing the group to exist.[49]

MEMBERSHIP ACTION

19. Concerted worker agitation for or against a participation program, and agitation within a participation group for better conditions, is protected activity.[50] Provided members continue to obey direct orders, they may not be fired for organizing, educating other members, and speaking their minds to others. Efforts to press for better product quality through the team, however, are not protected.[51]

20. The employer may not use a participation program to interrogate an employee in the absence of a requested steward.[52]

21. Workers who participate in participation groups as management-appointed leaders or facilitators may find themselves legally ruled to be supervisors without union protection.[53] Elected leaders have been held to be on a different footing.[54]

22. When management wants a quality program, members might strive for quality by working to rule—concertedly and rigidly following management's explicit rules. There are no NLRB decisions specifically on discipline for working to rule. But working to rule is legitimate so long as workers can point to specific rules they are following, and there is no refusal to obey direct orders. However, use of similar tactics (partial strikes, intermittent strikes, refusals to work scheduled overtime, slowdowns) to achieve tactical advantage (such as during contract negotiations) are unprotected.[55]

CONDUCT CODE

23. A union might consider adopting an "honor code" or "code of conduct" to educate members involved in teams. The idea is that a member should never do or say anything that could get a fellow member in trouble or out of work. Without education, an unthinking member giving the employer an assist might do this. Ideally, everyone complies with a code either through feelings of solidarity or through peer pressure.

In extreme cases union codes might be enforced with union discipline. "Conduct unbecoming a union member" is a time-honored charge in the bylaws of practically every union, traditionally used against strikebreakers. Members who cooperate with management in teams against the whole membership's interest are just as bad.[56]

Discipline, after a union trial with due process,[57] legally can range from counselling to ostracism, barring from attending meetings or holding office, suspension, expulsion, and court-enforceable fines.

Codes of conduct should be handled carefully if they are to be enforced by more than counselling or ostracism. The legal rules are intricate, and vary according to the type of conduct of the offending member, the type of sanction ordered by the trial committee, and changing policies of the NLRB. Generally, the NLRB and courts are more interested in individual rights than collective rights in these situations.

NLRB PROCEDURE

24. Workers and/or unions suspicious of participation programs as company-dominated set-ups on the shop floor

Union Had Right To Say No

The contract between Deerfield Plastics and United Electrical Workers Local 274 expired in 1991. The company then proposed an Employee Involvement program and refused to bargain on anything else until that was settled first.

The local filed an NLRB charge, saying that EI was not a mandatory issue of bargaining—the company could not force the union to bargain about it.

While the charge was still pending, the UE decided to agree to a program in negotiations, but under its own terms:

• the union could select the employee members on the teams

• only 15 named topics could be discussed—all of them production and quality issues

• any changes in working conditions would be voted on by the membership.

Later, the NLRB endorsed the union's position by requiring the employer to post a notice in the plant: that EI is a subject that can only be bargained with the union's permission, and the company could not declare an impasse over that subject.

Back on the shop floor, the union was not idle. "The company wanted big changes in one department," says UE International Rep David Cohen, "and they tried to form an EI committee on that subject. The union allowed volunteers, and the only two who volunteered were two guys who were pretty close to the company.

"So the company rammed through all these changes that they wanted. When these two guys brought it back for a vote in that department, the people unanimously voted it down. These two guys were under so much pressure that even they voted against it.

"So we had destroyed the committees in the plant anyhow."

[The UE now circulates an Organizer's Bulletin describing what the union won in this fight, to help other locals beat back similar plans. It is available from UE Local 274, 80 School St., Greenfield, MA 01301.]

may challenge them at their local NLRB office by simply filing a charge giving the date of the conduct and outlining the facts in a few sentences. A lawyer is not necessary and anyone can file.[58] There is no filing fee. The statute of limitations for filing and serving is six months from the date the employer did the illegal act.[59] The six months begins when the final decision is made and communicated.[60] The time limit can sometimes be extended beyond six months, if the violation "continues" into the six-month period.[61]

COLLECTIVE BARGAINING MODEL

25. Though the NLRB has not yet directly ruled on this point, in a case where the facts showed a participation group dealt with working conditions, the Board would likely hold that legally, the group must conduct itself as a two-sided bargaining session.

Thus in cases where participation groups dealt with the employer on working conditions, the NLRB General

Counsel has held that a union is privileged to appoint only union members to a participation group.[62] This is because ordinarily in negotiations the composition of the labor side is an internal union matter with which the employer may not interfere.[63]

Labor Notes calls this the "collective bargaining model" of participation.

In this model, there is a union presence in each participation group. The labor-side members of each team have and exercise the right to caucus separately. Their decisions are subject to leadership consultation and/or membership ratification. As in any other bargaining, if the two sides cannot compromise, the matter can be grieved to an outside arbitrator. Or, if there is a right to strike during the contract over grievances,[64] or if the contract has expired, after impasse the union side of the team can assert or exercise the right to strike.

Notes

1. NLRA Section 8(a)(2), 29 USC 158(a)(2).

2. *Electromation Inc*, 309 NLRB # 163, 142 LRRM 1001 (1992), aff'd ___ F2d ___, 147 LRRM ___ (CA7, 1994).

3. *E I DuPont de Nemours & Co*, 311 NLRB # 88, 143 LRRM 1121, 1123 (1993).

4. NLRA Section 8(a)(5), 29 USC 158(a)(5).

5. *Landgraf* v *USI Film Products*, ___ US ___, 114 S Ct 1483 (1994); *Rivers* v *Roadway Express Inc*, ___ US ___, 114 S Ct 1510 (1994).

6. NLRA Section 8(a)(2), 29 USC 158(a)(2).

7. *NLRB* v *UMW District 50*, 355 US 453, 458-59, 78 S Ct 386 (1957).

8. *Electromation Inc*, 309 NLRB # 163, 142 LRRM 1001 (1992), aff'd ___ F2d ___, 147 LRRM ___ (CA7, 1994); *F M Transport*, 306 NLRB # 156, 139 LRRM 1389 (1992); *Spiegel Trucking Co*, 225 NLRB 178, 179, 92 LRRM 1604, 1606 (1976).

9. *Rensselaer Polytechnic Institute*, 219 NlRB # 85, 89 LRRM 1879 (1975); *Spiegel Trucking Co*, 225 NLRB 178, 179, 92 LRRM 1604, 1606 (1976).

10. *Spiegel Trucking Co*, 225 NLRB 178, 179, 92 LRRM 1604, 1606 (1976).

11. *Ryder Distribution Resources*, 311 NLRB # 81, 143 LRRM 1225 (1993); *Spiegel Trucking Co*, 225 NLRB 178, 179, 92 LRRM 1604, 1606 (1976).

12. *Research Federal Credit Union*, 310 NLRB # 13, 142 LRRM 1250 (1993).

13. *Ryder Distribution Resources*, 311 NLRB # 81, 143 LRRM 1225 (1993).

14. *Ryder Distribution Resources*, 311 NLRB # 81, 143 LRRM 1225 (1993);

15. *E I DuPont de Nemours & Co*, 311 NLRB # 88, 143 LRRM 1121, 1123 (1993).

16. *Spiegel Trucking Co*, 225 NLRB 178, 179, 92 LRRM 1604, 1606 (1976).

17. *Upper Great Lakes Pilots Inc*, 311 NLRB # 21, 144 LRRM 1060 (1993).

18. *Upper Great Lakes Pilots Inc*, 311 NLRB # 21, 144 LRRM 1060 (1993).

19. *NLRB* v *General Steel Erectors*, 933 F2d 568, 137 LRRM 2466 (CA7, 1991).

20. *Garment Workers (Bernhard-Altmann Texas Corp)* v *NLRB*, 366 US 731, 81 S Ct 1603, 48 LRRM 2251 (1961).

21. *BASF Wyandotte*, 274 NLRB # 147, 119 LRRM 1035 (1985), aff'd 798 F2d 849, 123 LRRM 2320 (CADC, 1986).

22. NLRA Section 2(5), 29 USC 152(5).

23. NLRA Section 2(5), 29 USC 152(5).

24. *Homemaker Shops Inc*, 261 NLRB # 50, 110 LRRM 1082 (1982), enf denied on other grounds, 724 F2d 535, 115 LRRM 2321 (CA6, 1984).

25. *Titanium Metals Corp* Cases ## 31-CA-16000, 31 CB 6773, 125 LRRM 1375 (GC Advice Memo, 1987); *US Postal Service*, Case # 19-CA-16909(P), 118 LRRM 1654 (GC Advice memo, 1985); *Local 235 UAW*, 313 NLRB # 18 (1993) (summary affirmance of ALJ); *E I DuPont de Nemours & Co*, 311 NLRB # 88, 143 LRRM 1121, 1123 (1993); *Cabot Carbon Co*, 117 NLRB 1633, 1640, 1644, 40 LRRM 1058 (1957), aff'd sub nom *NLRB* v *Cabot Carbon Co*, 360 US 203, 79 S Ct 1015 (1959); *James H Matthews & Co* v *NLRB* 156 F2d 706, 707 (CA3, 1946); cf *Sears Roebuck & Co*, 274 NLRB 230, 243-44, 118 LRRM 1329 (1985) (summary affirmance of ALJ).

26. *NLRB* v *Cabot Carbon Co*, 360 US 203, 79 S Ct 1015 (1959); *E I DuPont de Nemours & Co*, 311 NLRB # 88, ___, 143 LRRM 1121, 1123 (1993).

27. OLMS Interpretative Manual 030.610-12.

28. *NLRB* v *Jacobs Mfg Co*, 196 F2d 680, 30 LRRM 2098 (CA2, 1952); *Titanium Metals Corp* Cases ## 31-CA-16000, 31 CB 6773, 125 LRRM 1375 (GC Advice Memo, 1987); *US Postal Service*, Case # 19-CA-16909(P), 118 LRRM 1654 (GC Advice memo, 1985); *Local 235 UAW*, 313 NLRB # 18 (1993) (summary affirmance of ALJ); *E I DuPont de Nemours & Co*,

311 NLRB # 88, 143 LRRM 1121, 1123 (1993); *Cabot Carbon Co*, 117 NLRB 1633, 1640, 1644, 40 LRRM 1058 (1957), aff'd sub nom *NLRB v Cabot Carbon Co*, 360 US 203, 79 S Ct 1015 (1959).

29. *Miller Brewing Co*, 166 NLRB # 90, 65 LRRM 1649 (1967), enf'd 408 F2d 12, 70 LRRM 2907 (CA9, 1969).

30. *Meat Cutters v Jewel Tea Co*, 381 US 676, 85 S Ct 1596, 59 LRRM 2376 (1965).

31. *Inter-City Advertising Co Inc*, 61 NLRB 1377, 16 LRRM 153 (1945), enforcement denied on other grounds, 154 F2d 244, 17 LRRM 916 (CA4, 1946).

32. *Beacon Piece Dyeing & Finishing Co*, 121 NLRB # 113, 42 LRRM 1489 (1958).

33. *Charmer Industries Inc*, 250 NLRB 293, 104 LRRM 1368 (1980).

34. NLRA Section 2(5), 29 USC 152(5).

35. *Masters, Mates & Pilots (Chicago Calumet Stevedoring Co)*, 144 NLRB 1172, 54 LRRM 1209 (1963), supplemented, 146 NLRB 116, 55 LRRM 1265 (1964), enf'd 351 F2d 771, 59 LRRM 2566 (CADC, 1965).

36. *Electromation Inc*, 309 NLRB # 163, 142 LRRM 1001, 1006 n 20, 1008 (1992), aff'd ___ F2d ___, 147 LRRM ___ (CA7, 1994); *E I DuPont de Nemours & Co*, 311 NLRB # 88, 143 LRRM 1121, 1123 n 7, 1126 n 17 (1993).

37. *E I DuPont de Nemours & Co*, 311 NLRB # 88, 143 LRRM 1121, 1123-24, 1126 (1993).

38. *General Foods Corp*, 231 NLRB # 122, 96 LRRM 1204 (1977).

39. OLMS Interpretive Manual 030.603, 634. Cf *General Shoe Corp*, 122 NLRB # 192, 43 LRRM 1350 (1959); *Warner v McLean Trucking Co*, 136 LRRM 2633 (SD Ohio, 1991).

40. OLMS Interpretive Manual 030.625.

41. OLMS Interpretive Manual 030.603, 625, 634. Cf *General Shoe Corp*, 122 NLRB # 192, 43 LRRM 1350 (1959); *Warner v McLean Trucking Co*, 136 LRRM 2633 (SD Ohio, 1991).

42. *E I DuPont de Nemours & Co*, 311 NLRB # 88, 143 LRRM 1121 (1993); *E I DuPont de Nemours & Co*, Case 4 CA 16801, JD 208 89 (1/30/90) (summary affirmance of ALJ); *Jafco*, 284 NLRB # 139, 126 LRRM 1038 (1987); *Oak-Cliff-Golman Baking Co*, 207 NLRB 1063, 85 LRRM 1035 (1974), enf'd 505 F2d 1302, 90 LRRM 2615 (CA5, 1974), cert denied 423 US 826 (1975); *Defense Logistics Agency, Defense Depot Tracy* and *Laborers Local 1276*, FLRA Case No 9 CA 20241 (1983).

43. *NLRB v US Postal Service*, 841 F2d 141, 145, 127 LRRM 2807 (CA6, 1988).

44. *Martin v Letter Carriers Branch 419*, 965 F2d 63, 140 LRRM 2442 (CA6, 1992).

45. *Emporium Capwell Co v Western Addition Community Organization*, 420 US 50, 95 S Ct 977 (1975).

46. *Cabot Carbon Co*, 117 NLRB # 211, 40 LRRM 1058 (1957), aff'd 360 US 203, 79 S Ct 1015 (1959).

47. *Steelworkers v Rawson*, 495 US 362, ___, 110 S Ct 1904, 1911 (1990); *Electrical Workers v Hechler*, 481 US 851, 860, 107 S Ct 2161 (1987); *Sams v Food & Commercial Workers*, 866 F2d 1380, 130 LRRM 2805 (CA11, 1990); *Warner v McLean Trucking Co*, 136 LRRM 2633 (SD Ohio, 1991); *General Shoe Corp*, 122 NLRB # 192, 43 LRRM 1350 (1959).

48. *Cabot Carbon Co*, 117 NLRB # 211, 40 LRRM 1058 (1957), aff'd 360 US 203, 79 S Ct 1015 (1959).

49. *NLRB v Magnavox Co of Tennessee*, 415 US 322, 94 S Ct 1099 (1974); *Ford Motor Company (Rouge Complex)*, 233 NLRB # 102, 96 LRRM 1513 (1977); *Ford Motor Co*, 221 NLRB # 99, 90 LRRM 1731 (1975), enf'd, 547 F2d 418, 93 LRRM 2570 (CA3, 1976); *Boilermakers Local 202*, 300 NLRB # 4, 135 LRRM 1142 (1990); *Branch 6000 Letter Carriers v NLRB*, 595 F2d 808, 100 LRRM 2346 (CADC, 1979); *Walker v Teamsters Local 71*, 714 F Supp 178, 191, 131 LRRM 3185 (WDNC, 1989), aff'd in part and rev'd in part 930 F2d 376, 137 LRRM 2059 (CA4, 1991), cert denied 112 S Ct 636, 637 (1991); *Service Station Operators (Ulrich Oil Co)*, 215 NLRB # 154, 88 LRRM 1152 (1974).

50. *Hancor Inc*, 278 NLRB 208, 121 LRRM 1311 (1986).

51. *Harrah's Lake Tahoe Resort Casino*, 307 NLRB # 29, 140 LRRM 1036 (1992).

52. *NLRB v J Weingarten Inc*, 420 US 251, 95 S Ct 959 (1975).

53. *Health Care & Retirement Corp of America v NLRB*, ___ US ___, 114 S Ct 1778, 146 LRRM 2321 (1994) (licensed practical nurses); *J C Brock Corp*, 314 NLRB # 34, 146 LRRM 1193 (1994) (line coordinators).

54. *Anamag*, 284 NLRB # 72, 125 LRRM 1287 (1987).

55. *Elk Lumber Co*, 91 NLRB 333, 26 LRRM 1493 (1950) (slowdown); *Valley City Furniture Co*, 110 NLRB 1589, 35 LRRM 1265 (1954), enf'd 230 F2d 947, 37 LRRM 2740 (CA6, 1956) (refusal to work overtime); *Honolulu Rapid Transit Co*, 110 NLRB 1806, 35 LRRM 1305 (1954) (weekend strikes); *Pacific Telephone & Telegraph Co*, 107 NLRB 1547, 33 LRRM 1433 (1954) (pattern of intermittent strikes).

56. Cf *NLRB v Allis-Chalmers Co*, 388 US 175, 87 S Ct 2001 (1967); *Scofield v NLRB*, 394 US 423, 89 S Ct 1154 (1969); *Meat Cutters Local 593 (S & M Grocers)*, 237 NLRB # 181, 99 LRRM 1123 (1978); *Boilermakers (Kaiser Cement Corp)*, 312 NLRB # 48, 144 LRRM 1121 (1993).

57. LMRDA Section 101(a)(5); 29 USC 401(a)(5).

58. *Vee Cee Provisions Inc*, 256 NLRB #125, 107 LRRM 1416 (1981), enf'd 688 F2d 827, 111 LRRM 2833 (CA3, 1982).

59. NLRA Section 10(b), 29 USC 160(b).

60. *Teamsters Local 42 v NLRB*, 825 F2d 608, 615, 126 LRRM 2046 (CA1, 1987); *E I DuPont de Nemours & Co*, 311 NLRB # 88, 143 LRRM 1121 (1993).

61. *Teamsters Local 293 (R L Lipton Distributing Co)*, 311 NLRB # 58, 143 LRRM 1237 (1993).

62. *Titanium Metals Corp*, Cases 31-CA-16000, 31-CB-6773, 125 LRRM 1375 (GC Adv Mem, 3/31/87); *US Postal Service*, Case 19-CA-16909(P), 118 LRRM 1654 (GC Adv Mem, 1/22/85). Cf *Letter Carriers Branch 6000*, 232 NLRB # 52, 96 LRRM 1271 n 1 (1977), aff'd *Letter Carriers Branch 6000 v NLRB*, 595 F2d 808, 100 LRRM 2346 (CADC, 1979).

63. *General Electric Co v NLRB*, 412 F2d 512, 71 LRRM 2418 (CA2, 1969).

64. *NLRB v Lion Oil Co*, 352 US 282, 77 S Ct 330 (1957).

Working Smart:
A Union Guide to Participation Programs and Reengineering
Labor Notes • 7435 Michigan Ave. • Detroit, MI 48210 • (313) 842-6262

Chapter 27

Postal Workers: We Reject All Company Unions

The American Postal Workers Union has consistently rejected Employee Involvement programs, from the national level down. When the union filed charges, the NLRB got the Postal Service to agree to stop using EI to bypass the union and deal directly with employees. The Postal Service was using such programs as early as the 1920s to avoid the union.

by Greg Poferl

OF THE FOUR MAJOR POSTAL UNIONS, only the American Postal Workers Union has rejected the U.S. Postal Service's Employee Involvement (EI) program. APWU represents clerks, maintenance workers, and motor vehicle operators.

In early 1992, the APWU won a major victory in its ongoing fight against USPS labor law violations committed through its Employee Involvement/Quality of Work Life program. In a National Labor Relations Board settlement agreement, the USPS agreed to post notices throughout the country advising employees that management would stop using EI/QWL committees to bypass the union or deal directly with APWU unit employees. Management would no longer bargain with EI/QWL committees over terms and conditions of employment of APWU unit employees.

The settlement resolved issues raised in the NLRB's 90-page complaint alleging that the Postal Service's EI/QWL program violated the law. That complaint consolidated more than 50 charges in over 25 locations, from Ithaca, New York to Los Angeles.

In the complaint, the NLRB charged that the EI committees were management-"dominated and assisted" labor organizations, and therefore illegal. They had discussed mandatory subjects of bargaining that affected APWU members without the union's input.

The Labor Board said management had made unilateral changes in working conditions arising from dis-

Greg Poferl is a National Business Agent in the Support Services Division of the APWU, based in Minneapolis.

cussions in EI meetings. For example, the NLRB said, USPS worked through the EI teams to establish attendance and smoking rules, sick leave and safety policies, and starting times.

In Ithaca, the first local where the NLRB filed a charge, President Mike Oates said, "In our case, they forced an APWU member to attend an EI meeting. They gave him a direct order."[1] The Ithaca EI team discussed discipline for failure to wear picture ID's; express mail delivery procedures; hours of work; employee awards for not using sick leave; and changing start times. Other issues discussed by EI committees in the complaining locations included allocation of parking spaces, work flow and assignments, placement of water fountains, painting of break rooms, smoking areas, incentive awards, use of phones, changed job descriptions, use of particular machinery, and attempts at resolving grievances.

The NLRB found that the EI committees had received franking privileges, use of phones for long distance calls, typewriters, and payment of wages to employees while attending meetings. All of this employer "aid and assistance" was withheld from the APWU.

Management agreed to provide the APWU with minutes of the EI/QWL meetings that went on with the other unions on-site. The APWU argued that it needed this information to enforce its right not to be affected by the EI program. An arbitrator upheld this right as well.[2]

APWU President Moe Biller, who led the APWU's fight against EI, said settlement of the NLRB complaint is a "victory in our ongoing struggle against company unions, which the USPS attempts to disguise as EI/QWL

committees. The NLRB has again upheld APWU's position that the USPS has used the EI/QWL program as a vehicle for union avoidance..."

AFTER TEN YEARS...

Since 1983, the Postal Service has spent untold millions on outside consultants to develop EI programs, allegedly to improve operations and service. Yet, after ten years with some 6,000 EI/QWL committees in place, EI is a flop.

The Postal Service continues to ballyhoo these phony programs. Where they fail or meet worker resistance, the programs are repackaged and recycled under the "new and improved" heading in hope that a few of them will take root. A partial list follows:

- focus groups
- employee advisory councils
- quality process groups
- employee opinion strategies
- quality of life programs
- "commitment to employees" programs

- employee satisfaction committees
- employee of the month competitions
- employee opinion survey groups
- quality first teams
- quality clerk positions
- leadership team performance clusters
- lunch with the boss
- tiger teams

WHAT IS MANAGEMENT REALLY UP TO?

The Postal Service stubbornly holds to the popular private sector propaganda that EI programs and other gimmicks promoting "quality" are a prerequisite for any company to remain competitive in the global economy. But the real story behind management's focus on "quality" is different. We experience it first hand.

Recently, I had the opportunity to work on a labor-management task force to improve operations at the Mail Equipment Shops. Our goal was to eliminate once and for all any need to subcontract.

For several meetings we listened attentively to management's concerns regarding operational needs, productivity, and outsourcing. But when the union offered concrete proposals to increase efficiency by implementing alternative work schedules and reducing supervisory positions, management was stunned. It quickly became apparent they only wanted to focus on their agenda.

Recent developments at the Postal Data Centers and Supply Centers show yet another side of management's idea of "cooperation." Management has been using blatant union-avoidance tactics such as "lunch-with-the-boss" and work floor strategy sessions to improve morale, quality, and productivity. These activities have not gone unchallenged by the APWU locals; however, despite the 1992 NLRB settlement, postal supervisors continue to ignore their legal and contractual obligations.

OLD TRICKS

Management's "union avoidance" committees hark back to the early 1920s. The 1945 book, *History of the National Federation of Post Office Clerks,* discusses the 1921 "New Era" of postal unionism:

The new Postmaster General, Will Hays, announced that he had in mind the creation of a Welfare Department through which employees could canalize [channel] their grievances and suggestions for a better Postal Service and better working conditions. An as yet unselected "big man" would be asked to head the welfare service.

Experienced trade unionists are always inclined to look askance at any of these "welfare" concessions as merely backfires set by so-called "liberal" or paternalistic types of employers to head off or destroy real independent unionism. By granting pseudo-recognitions or "employee representation plans," actual and bona fide union recognition is avoided as "unnecessary." In fact, unionism is dismissed as "old fashioned and obsolete."

These "welfare councils" in private industry usually labor mightily to provide extra water coolers, ice, free soap and towel service, better furniture in the restrooms, more lights or larger spittoons or any other "reasonable" requests which the employee may make.

Better wages, shorter hours, union recognition or a closed shop, however, are met with a show of injured feelings as clearly demonstrating the gross ingratitude and insatiable unreasonableness of the workers or the fact that radical snakes are loose in the Garden of Eden.

AS APWU SEES IT

Notwithstanding the APWU's rock-solid stand against EI and other bogus programs trumpeting workplace har-

mony, our union does have a traditional commitment to cooperation with management which flows directly from our collective bargaining agreement.

We have negotiated national as well as local and regional labor-management meetings, which have existed since we've had collective bargaining. These can best be defined as "arms-length" meetings of the two parties to deal with issues of mutual concern, including ones that are not grieveable. These meetings have discussed safety and health, ergonomics, alternative work schedules and flextime, training, staffing, and technology and mechanization issues. They are carried out in the spirit of collective bargaining.

At last, in this memorandum, the foundation for real cooperation—Union involvement—has been established. The Postal Service makes an unprecedented statement recognizing the role of the union as the employees' representative:

"The Postal Service will work through the national, regional and local union leadership, rather than directly with employees on issues which affect working conditions and will seek ways of improving customer service, increasing revenue, and reducing costs [emphasis added]. Management also recognizes the value of union input and a cooperative approach on issues that will affect working conditions and postal policies and affirms the intent of the parties to jointly discuss such issues prior to development of such plans and policies."

No one should get the idea that this commitment to work through the union means that employees' input will be excluded in the listed areas. The opposite is true. Broadbased, rank-and-file employee involvement in all areas of their work lives is encouraged—but *through their union— APWU...*

The fact is that the union *is* the employees—it is *their self-created and freely-chosen representative. The law flatly prohibits management from creating a representative body for employees.* Cooperation is easy enough when management's and employees' interests coincide, but that is not always the case...

Our labor history, especially the tumultuous beginnings of the American Postal Workers Union in the Great Postal Strike of 1970, has taught us that solidarity is our strength. Any employer program that could in any way weaken postal worker solidarity must be stamped out.

APWU has aggressively fought the Postal Service's multiform EI programs, but we have come to realize this is only a part of the struggle. Postal workers want and deserve a strong voice at their places of work. Through "Union Involvement," the APWU must continue to build *real* workplace democracy, which is, after all, one of the labor movement's greatest challenges in the 1990s.

Notes

1. Mark Kodama, "Employee Program Violates Labor Law, Board Charges," *Federal Times,* July 8, 1991, p. 13.

2. Roman Lewis, "Employee Participation Programs: A critical look at their development," paper written in Masters in Labor Law program, Georgetown University Law Center, Washington, D.C., 1994, pp. 42-46.

Working Smart:
A Union Guide to Participation Programs and Reengineering
Labor Notes • 7435 Michigan Ave. • Detroit, MI 48210 • (313) 842-6262

Chapter 28

The Japanese Model Falters

Corporate executives and academics alike tout the Toyota production and management system as the model of the future. Employers in Canada and the United States have been rushing to implement teamwork, just-in-time, Total Quality Management, or other schemes based on the Toyota system. Recent developments in Japan, however, pose serious questions whether the Toyota model is sustainable.

In this chapter, John Price and Watanabe Ben take us behind the scenes of Japan's workplaces and document the recent sweeping changes in work and labor-management relations and the upheavals that have accompanied them.

by John Price and Watanabe Ben[1]

LEAN PRODUCTION STRESSED OUT

The production system that made Japan the world's leading manufacturer and is setting the pace in workplaces around the world has faltered at home. Criticized by unions and battered by the recession, the Toyota system, often referred to as lean production or management-by-stress, is undergoing serious change.

Two of the underpinnings considered fundamental to the lean system in Japan—rising wages and lifetime employment—are also being battered, as employers seek ways to cut costs in face of the strongest recession to hit Japan since the 1970s oil crisis.

Advocates of lean production in North America, however, have been so enamored with spreading the gospel that they have ignored the tensions within the system. They have been blinded to the far-reaching changes that are causing much society-wide discussion and soul-searching in Japan.

Thus it came as a shock to some when Nissan announced that its high-tech plant in Zama would close in spring 1995 and that Nissan would reduce its workforce by 5,000.

That decision barely made the business pages in North America. But it created a furor in Japan, as analysts specu-

John Price is a labor researcher and educator in Vancouver, British Columbia, who lived in Japan for four years. He teaches at Capilano College and is an advisor to the Trade Union Research Bureau. He has a Ph.D. in Japanese history. Watanabe Ben is the retired president of the Tokyo South District of the National Union of General Workers. He lived in Detroit for two years, speaking widely in the U.S. and Canada.

lated whether Japan's auto industry, the symbolic masthead in Japan's successful quest for industrial preeminence, had finally reached a turning point.

Other equally important changes have received little fanfare in North America:

• The Japan Auto Workers (JAW), the national federation of company-based auto workers unions, issued a policy statement in 1992 criticizing the industry for excessive competition and taking advantage of employees.[2] Coming from the normally cooperative JAW, this was a milestone.

• Shioji Ichiro, who had collaborated with management at Nissan to break an independent union there in 1953, was forced by management to resign from his posts as president of the replacement union and of the JAW. Although Shioji had been indispensable to management's control of the workforce, apparently he was not cooperative enough. Shioji, who was featured in a PBS Frontline special, "We Are Driven," revealed that one of the reasons he fell from grace was for encouraging American Nissan employees to join the UAW.[3]

• And, in a small but symbolically dramatic turnabout, Toyota has introduced buffers into its new assembly plants, Tahara No. 4 in Aichi and the Kyushu plant in southern Japan. Under the traditional Toyota system, such buffers were considered waste and a violation of the just-in-time system.

Are the North American gurus of lean production selling a pig-in-a-poke? In their rush to embrace the Toyota system, are employers in North America in fact adopting a system that has already proved itself outmoded in Japan?

FACADE OF LABOR-MANAGEMENT HARMONY FALLS

The JAW policy statement tore away the facade of employer benevolence and labor-management harmony invoked by advocates of Japanese-style management, and described a workplace environment in which workers are exploited.

"Employees are exhausted," stated the JAW." The workers had to do 350 hours of overtime per year, which has continued for several years...Under the pretext of sharing a common destiny, which is pleasing to the ear, companies do seem to have been too demanding of their workers."[4] Less than five percent of auto workers in Japan would recommend that their children work in the industry, a JAW survey of its members revealed.[5]

The union's advisor, noted industrial relations scholar Shimada Haruo, was even more direct: "Competition for the sake of competition has dominated, and everything was sacrificed, including wages, working hours, profit, subcontractors, dealers, the lives of Japanese workers, and employment opportunities for workers abroad."[6]

"Trade unions cooperated in this desperate competition for a share. Working hard, they lost their vision about for whom and what growth should be achieved," concluded Shimada.

These revelations from the wellspring of lean production vindicate the criticisms of writers such as Kamata Satoshi who, nearly twenty years ago, first exposed the pitfalls of the Toyota system in his book, *Japan in the Passing Lane*.[7]

When it was first released in 1992, the JAW statement seemed to come out of the blue. In fact, however, it was the culmination of a decade of controversy in the auto industry.

In the late 1970s, for example, Nissan and its union had agreed to jointly promote a sustained program of *kaizen* (continuous improvement) called "P3" (participation, productivity, and progress).[8] Nissan management, however, insisted on using the movement to speed up production through its waste elimination program (*muri, muda*, and *mura*), and the subsequent speed-up contributed to the death of a Nissan employee in 1981. This, and the company's attempt to use the P3 movement to bypass the union, led to work stoppages. The Nissan union finally decided at its 1982 convention to boycott P3. A dispute over where to locate Nissan's overseas car plant led to the final rupture between Shioji Ichiro and Nissan management and Shioji's subsequent departure from the union.

ALTERING THE LEAN SYSTEM

Labor shortages and long work hours finally precipitated some major innovations in the auto industry in the late 1980s.

Auto workers in Japan have been obliged to put in huge amounts of overtime because the system was designed to operate with few workers.

Furthermore, few people wanted to work for Toyota or Nissan—the tough working conditions had become legendary throughout society. The younger generation was not as willing as their parents had been to submit to ceaseless, unremitting toil.

Japanese researcher Nomura Masami estimates that the turnover rate among new recruits to the auto industry was about 25 percent a year. Half, he estimated, retired in less than five years.[9]

Because of the labor shortage, the auto companies were obliged to make some changes. Even MITI, the government's powerful Ministry of International Trade and Industry, was obliged to launch a campaign for shorter hours, in response to pressure from foreign competitors of Japanese companies, who saw the long work-year as an unfair advantage.

Surprisingly, changes in lean production began at Toyota, not Nissan. Toyota had been known for its autocratic approach—it was Toyota's way or no way. But times changed. Toyota moved quickly to clear out the dead wood in its personnel departments and embarked on the consultative route with its union. Management and the union established two joint committees in 1989 to study reducing annual work hours and to introduce worker-

---

Why the Crisis in the Auto Industry?

As domestic sales accelerated in Japan in 1989, automakers competed ferociously to increase their share of that market. One method was to constantly introduce new models. Between 1986 and 1991, the number of new models increased from 106 to 152. Yet domestic sales peaked at 7.8 million units in 1990 and have been declining ever since.

Nissan posted operating losses for two years in a row. Even Toyota fell into the red. The domestic sales slump may have precipitated the current crunch, but the problems go much deeper.

In the past, problems in domestic demand were offset through increased exports, but that solution is no longer viable. Overseas market share is in some cases declining, and the rise in the value of the yen has limited the automakers' ability to compete.[10] Furthermore, U.S. and other manufacturers have become increasingly competitive and are regaining some of the market share they lost to Japanese companies in the 1970s and 1980s.

Many people in Japan, including the JAW, blame "excessive competition." Introducing new models so fast and furiously—a practice hailed by fans of lean production as an excellent use of the system's flexibility[11]—costs huge amounts of money. This means less money left for profits—or workers. In addition, frequent model changes are hard on workers because of the more frequent opportunities for management to "rebalance" their jobs and thus speed them up.

friendly changes on the assembly line. Other automakers followed suit.

The change in direction had tangible if not earthshaking results. Toyota, for example, has attempted to flatten its management structure. In 1989 the company asked all directors, managers, and supervisors to "turn in" their titles. Only two-thirds were reappointed to the same positions. The middle managers who were left could be more easily transferred to new jobs.

To further put middle managers in their place, Toyota initiated changes in language protocol. It had been customary for employees to call supervisors by their title—"Kato kacho," for example, meaning "Supervisor Kato." Now Toyota decided that everyone should be called Mr. or Ms. (*san* in Japanese). Supervisor Kato is now simply Kato-san, or Mr. Kato.[12]

With the agreement of its union, Toyota also tried innovations in work policies. In the non-assembly line sectors it has experimented with flex-time, and engineers have even been allowed to set their own hours. Productivity pay is being reduced or eliminated and instead merit pay, based on supervisors' evaluations, is becoming a

Participation Without Power

Many Western commentators have portrayed the Toyota system as a new "post-Fordist" model of production that has dispensed with the traditional norms of assembly line work. Worker participation in quality circles has supposedly erased the division between planning (by managers) and doing (by workers).

Workers at Toyota or Suzuki Motors, for example, meet to discuss production problems and are given some training in the use of analytical tools such as Pareto charts, fishbone diagrams, and so forth. To the extent this occurs, there is indeed a diminution in the strictly operative role assigned workers in traditional auto plants.

But there are important limitations to worker participation in quality circles that are related to their origins and role. Statistical quality control as a distinct movement in Japan began in the late 1940s. But quality circles began only in the 1960s, after the main elements of the Toyota system, including just-in-time, kaizen (continuous improvement), and so forth, had already been developed under the direction of Ohno Taichi.[14] In other words, quality circles came after the system was already in place.

Nor were quality circles a spontaneous manifestation of worker enthusiasm for production matters. Kamii Yoshihiko, a noted Japanese scholar, states bluntly: "The quality circle movement is a management-based system of personnel and production control. Generally it is initiated by management and supervisory personnel are the organizers."[15] Indeed, at Toyota, and also at Suzuki, quality circles initially faltered because workers were unenthusiastic. Only after circle activities had been integrated into the performance evaluation system that determines wages did workers conform to management expectations.

Top Down

In his study of Nissan and Toyota, Michael Cusumano suggests that "stereotypes of decision making in Japanese firms as being 'from the bottom up,' that is, with initiatives rising upward from the lower ranks of the company, rather than 'top down,' need review."[16]

The father of Japanese quality control, Ishikawa Kaoru (inventor of the fishbone diagram widely used in quality training), recognized that quality circles were subject to management goals and directives: "Unless policies are determined, no goal can be established. These policies must be determined by top management."[17]

Nomura Masami, an expert on Toyota, says that the image of workers and managers working together to continuously kaizen the workplace is mistaken.[18] Nomura suggests that getting workers involved in quality circles is just a form of "human relations activity," and not a serious institution to reform the workplace.

Most quality circle activities are directed at costs, efficiency, control procedures, maintenance, and quality. Safety issues are also discussed. At times, workers do use these circles to propose changes that improve working conditions. But on the whole, quality circles are a forum for limited or token worker participation or else a vehicle for management to extend its values onto the production line.

Even some enterprise unions have recognized this problem. The electrical workers union (Denki Roren), for example, stated in a 1976 policy paper that the quality movement had "problems and limits where it tended to become a means for controlling workers according to company goals."[19] Indicating that the quality movement was far from "joint," the paper stated, "What we aim for in workplace participation is the transformation of a unilateral management system into a joint labor-management approach, which is inevitable."

Most unions in Japan did not challenge the quality movement and even those that did, such as the electrical workers, failed to have any significant impact.

Job Content

How many times have North American workers been told that under the Japanese system, job rotation and teamwork have supposedly eliminated the boring and repetitive jobs associated with the assembly line? In fact, cycle times

larger component of the base wage. This will bring Toyota more in line with the wage system at other automakers.

The most significant development, however, was the automakers' decision to build new, worker-friendly plants that would be ergonomically sound as well as efficient. In the past two years, Nissan, Toyota, and Mazda have all built new factories.[13]

The largest new plant is Nissan's Kyushu facility; it can turn out 600,000 cars a year. The plant is fully air-conditioned and cars on the assembly line can be height-adjusted to allow employees to work in a relatively comfortable position. Furthermore, buffers—heresy under the traditional system—have been introduced on sub-assembly lines. Some stock is allowed to accumulate at the end of each sub-assembly process. Such buffers would have been considered "waste" in the past and been the target for elimination through kaizen.

Toyota has followed suit with similar reforms at its expanded Tahara plant and its new Kyushu facility. Today, Toyota is re-appraising its concept of waste elimination and considers that there may indeed be a form of "necessary waste," in order to improve working conditions.

---

for job routines (the elapsed time before repeating an operation) are in the one-to-three minute range. Generally speaking, the shorter the cycle time, the more repetitious the work. This type of work is one of the hallmarks of Fordist work methods, and the Toyota system does not change this, as any visitor to an auto plant in Japan can attest.

In addition, quality guru Ishikawa stressed the importance of standardization (discussed in chapter 5), another hallmark of traditional Taylorism. "The key to success," he suggests, "is to standardize aggressively those things which are understandable and to let a subordinate handle them."[20]

Job descriptions are not institutionalized and workers are expected to rotate jobs within their groups. This measure is often portrayed as multi-skilling, but the narrow content of the jobs means that, for the most part, there is little elevation in workers' skills.

Control Systems

North American workers often view their Japanese counterparts as zealous workers, always ready to sacrifice for the good of the company. Mazda managers, sent to the U.S. to open a plant in Michigan, were amazed that American production workers took vacations the summer immediately after a model change. In Japan, many if not most workers would have "voluntarily" given up their vacation at that time. It's worth asking, however, how voluntary such conduct really is. Japanese employers have developed sophisticated methods for controlling workers.

Large Japanese employers promised lifetime jobs in exchange for a very explicit quid pro quo: workers would participate in kaizen. They could make suggestions that cut work because they had no fear of losing their own jobs.

The wage structure has also been an important management tool for inducing worker conformity. While it is often asserted that wages in Japan are based on seniority, this is not strictly speaking the case. It is true that wages go up the longer one stays with a company. But wages do not increase evenly. Once or twice a year, supervisors conduct a performance evaluation for each worker that plays a large part in determining wage increases.

Of course, this type of "merit" system has also been used in North America, but it was expressly opposed by unions because it breeds favoritism and discrimination. In Japan, the performance-based pay system became institutionalized in the 1950s.

Quality expert Karatsu Hajime puts it bluntly: "In the firm, there is the saying that subordinates listen only to the person who conducts the evaluation to establish bonus payments. That is exactly the way it works."

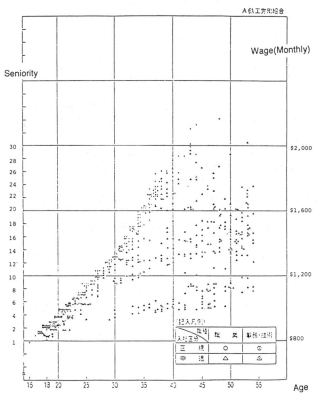

図6-1　賃金実態表（基本給表）

Actual Range of Basic Wage (a Subcontractor of Toyota)

Source: *Auto Industry and Workers*, Nohara Hikaru and Fujita Eishi, eds.

Perhaps the most significant development at Kyushu was the plan to operate on a continuous two-shift basis (days and afternoons), eliminating night shift and also the mid-afternoon break during which day shift workers had often been compelled to do substantial overtime. And after forty years of discrimination, Toyota has finally begun to hire women for the assembly line.

At Kyushu, Toyota has also revised its famous suggestion system. In the past, visitors to Toyota facilities were always told how workers had contributed thousands of suggestions each for savings of millions of dollars. What visitors were not told, however, was that workers had quotas for suggestions which, if unfulfilled, resulted in lower wages and fewer chances at promotion. At Toyota's new facility the suggestions quota has been abolished.

Also, "voluntary" after-work social activities—a hallmark of Toyota control at its traditional plants—have been eliminated and the Kyushu facility hopes to allow workers to have more of a private life away from the factory.

Turnover at Toyota's Tahara plant has dropped. The big question is why. Toyota points to the changes it has made, but a much more important reason may be the recession. Industrial instability and growing unemployment make it even more difficult for workers to change jobs than it had been in the past.

The recession and projected slow growth may jeopardize the reforms currently under way. If unemployment should increase and if profits continue to be squeezed, the automakers may feel they have no choice but to kill the reforms and squeeze workers harder.

CLOSURES AND JOB CUTS

Coming on top of the reform-type changes were big cuts in jobs and hours. Nissan's February 1993 announcement that it would close its plant in Zama landed like a bombshell, and sparked an ongoing public debate about the future of the auto industry and other industrial sectors in Japan.

The reason for the furor was simple. The Zama plant had been the Nissan flagship, and was fairly advanced technologically. Body assembly, for example, was done completely by robots. Even the trim line, where parts such as seats, dashboards, and so forth are attached (and the hardest part of assembly to automate) was high tech, with robots and workers toiling side by side. If this plant was to close, what was next?

Next was not long in coming. Between February and June all the automakers cut temporary workers, who had been used to make up for shortages of permanent employees. Following the dismissal of this flexible workforce, automakers then cut overtime. And then went regular work. A visit to Nissan's Murayama plant in spring 1994 revealed that workers were on a four-day week that week, to reduce costs.

On the one hand, the cut in hours was a welcome development and had been a union demand. But because the cut was done without negotiation and planning, it brought to light other serious problems. Union surveys indicate that even with overtime, which has equalled up to 20-25 percent of the yearly salary, auto workers' wages do not cover household expenses, especially for those raising a family.[21] The cuts in overtime sparked a wage crisis. Mazda workers, for example, demanded to transfer from the new Hofu plant to the old plant where there was still some overtime. Toyota had to offer loans to some employees, using future summer bonuses as collateral.

The wage crisis was further aggravated as employers attempted to limit wage increases in the 1994 annual negotiations. Toyota asked but the union refused the option of cutting bonuses. Nissan was able to get a slight cut in the winter bonus.

SPRING OFFENSIVE FALTERS IN RECESSION'S WAKE

"Judging from the objective we set of winning at least a 3.2 percent wage increase, I have to say that I am extremely dissatisfied with the results [of this year's Shunto]," announced Yamagishi Akira, chairman of Rengo, Japan's largest trade union federation, at a hastily called news conference in March 1994.[22] Shunto is the annual round of collective bargaining, carried out in all industries in the spring.

Yamagishi's statement came after Japan's largest unions accepted the lowest increases since annual bargaining began in 1955. The steel unions accepted 1.56 percent, the electrical unions 3.05 percent, and the auto unions 3.02 percent.[23]

The results were worse than they first appear, because the percentage increase includes the cost of covering incremental increases that workers receive as they move up the performance-based wage grid. For example, a steelworker with 17 years seniority will receive only about $10 a month increase in base pay. Most of this small raise, $35 a month, will come through increases dependent on the supervisor's evaluation.

The low returns came on the heels of reports that wage bonuses in 1993 declined for the first time since 1975.[24] The bonuses (usually paid in summer and winter,

---

Revolt of the Middle Managers

In 1993 and 1994, Japanese society was shocked by the news that middle managers were forming their own unions. When companies began downsizing during the recession, middle managers, with no union protection, were targeted. Some responded by joining unions, and the Labor Commission ruled that they had the legal right to do so.

Most managers did not want to join Rengo, because Rengo's unions had always pressured upper management to get rid of middle managers. So they joined independent unions such as the National Union of General Workers.

and worth about two or three months' salary each installment, or about 30 percent of a worker's total income) declined by .3 percent.

Western managers have long envied the bonus system, assuming that it could be easily adjusted if sales or profits should decline. But such was not the case in Japan. The bonus system had become institutionalized; often home mortgage payments have a balloon payment built in to correspond with bonus income. Furthermore, bonuses are subject to annual negotiations with unions. Thus the .3 percent decrease last year, while small, is nevertheless significant from a Japanese perspective.

Weak results in the Shunto prompted some unions to call for a general reassessment of its effectiveness. The employers federation Nikkeiren, on the other hand, was pleased with Shunto 1994. Nagano Ken, chair of the federation, stated, "I think we got them [the unions] to understand that our ability to pay was limited because of the extreme downturn in enterprise profitability."[25] According to Nagano, the unions had to choose between jobs or wages; by accepting modest wage increases unions were helping to protect jobs. Does this sound familiar to North American workers?

A closer examination of the situation reveals, however, that instead of trading off wages for jobs, workers were getting neither.

SLIMMING DOWN

"Surimuka." "Reesutora." Japan's business press is filled with these terms. They are the Japanese pronunciation of the word "slim" and a short version of the term "restructuring." Whatever the language, the meaning is the same for workers—job loss.

The promise of lifetime employment is rapidly fading even for the few who had come to expect it. Executives have stated openly that they will re-examine the lifetime employment system.

Shin Nittetsu (New Japan Steel) announced in March 1994 that it would shed 7,000 of its 27,000 employees over the next three years (4,000 office and 3,000 production).[26] The recession had left the five major steel producers with losses of roughly $3 billion to March 1994. The cuts were to be carried out mainly through restricting new hires, attrition, transfers, and early retirements. However, layoffs seemed inevitable, because the company was already paying $600 million per year to subsidize the wages of workers it had transferred to other companies. The new dimension to this downsizing, however, was that the corporation was aggressively going after white collar workers for the first time.

This appeared to be a growing trend. According to the Labor Ministry, employment in February 1994 increased by 160,000 compared to February 1993. But supervisory posts decreased by a similar amount.[27]

Other manufacturers were aggressively downsizing as well. Of firms surveyed, the average reduction planned was 11.8 percent of the workforce.

Job Cuts Planned at Major Corporations in Japan (1993-94)

Firm	Cuts	Current Workforce	Percentage to be cut
Toshiba	10,000	95,000	10.5
Nissan	6,000	48,000	12.5
Mazda	4,500	30,000	15.0
Nippon Steel	3,000	52,000	5.8
Sanyo	3,000	30,000	10.0

Source: Nomura Research Institute, *Quarterly Economic Review*, Vol. 21, No. 1, February 1994.

Even without a formal change in policy, management has found many ways to rid itself of unwanted workers. Nissan, for example, said that workers from the closed

---

The "Bubble Economy" and the Recession

A serious recession began in Japan in late 1990 and is still continuing. It is the largest and longest recession in two decades or more of high economic growth.

This recession hit most major industries, including automobiles and electronics. Domestic demand sagged and the yen's high value made exports more difficult.

Since the oil crisis of 1973, big business in Japan had concentrated, very successfully, on developing exports. Japan's increasing share of world trade, however, provoked a backlash in other countries. Some imposed quotas on Japanese imports, such as the "voluntary restraints" on autos in Canada and the U.S. In order to reduce trade friction, Japanese auto producers began to build assembly plants in other countries.

Overseas expansion accelerated after 1985. At that time, the advanced industrialized countries (known as the G-7) exerted further pressure on Japanese exports by forcing the yen to become more expensive. In the past decade, the yen has appreciated by nearly 250 percent. A modest lunch that cost about US$4 in 1985 cost $10 in 1994. A car that previously cost $10,000 became $25,000 if purchased in U.S. dollars. In other words, exchange rates have been used to make Japanese-made goods more expensive.

In the late 1980s the Japanese government attempted to counter the effects of the rising yen by stimulating domestic spending. However, this gave rise to the "bubble economy" in which speculation on stocks and land went rampant. The bubble burst in late 1990, however, and led to recession. Despite signs the recession was easing somewhat in 1994, the structural imbalances in Japan's economy showed no signs of easy resolution.

Zama plant would be transferred to the remote Kyushu plant, 800 miles away. But how many workers will not be able to make the move?

In 1992, Hitachi and Japan Victor closed their VCR plants and proposed to transfer the excess workforce. Each union agreed with the company's plan to transfer workers to different plants.

Other auto and electronics firms followed, introducing many types of workforce reductions one after another: *kata tataki* ("tapping on the shoulder"—a not-too-subtle suggestion that a worker should leave for the good of the company), voluntary (virtually forced) retirement for older workers, transfer from a production line to a sales department, demotion to dead-end bench warmer jobs.

For example, Pioneer Electric moved workers who were over 45 to a basement. In a room with no window, they were given no work for more than two months. Over a period of weeks, the lighting was gradually dimmed. Finally, most of them quit.

The supposed trade-off of wages for job security, in other words, simply isn't happening.

The job reductions at large enterprises have led to a slight increase in unemployment. The rate increased in February 1994 by .2 percent, to stand at 2.9 percent on a seasonally adjusted basis.

In the context of the world recession that saw unemployment jump to over ten percent even in countries such as Sweden, Japan's unemployment rate remains low. It is the legacy of the high growth period and workers' struggles for job security in the 1950s and 1960s. Japan's employers do not resort to layoffs as quickly as do employers in North America, and even when job cuts do occur, they are usually carried out through transfers or attrition.

But Japan's low unemployment rates may be somewhat understated because of different methods of defining and calculating unemployment statistics. Furthermore, government subsidies to designated industries help to reduce unemployment. In 1993 the government was subsidizing 171,000 enterprises and four million workers as part of its adjustment policies for industries in economic trouble.[28]

However, the fundamental reason for Japan's low unemployment rate is that small and medium-size businesses act as a buffer in times of recession, absorbing workers laid off or transferred from large enterprises.

Less than 12 percent of the Japanese workforce is employed by companies with 300 or more employees. Large companies such as Sanyo or Toyota contract out as much work as possible, leaving only a core workforce. The contracting companies in turn contract out to still smaller companies, who may also ship work out. Workers in the subcontractors work longer hours for lower pay and benefits and, at the lower levels of subcontracting, are not unionized. In many cases older and part-time workers, often women or immigrants, make up the peripheral workforce.

When hard times hit, these disposable workers are laid off and "permanent" workers in the large companies can be transferred to supplier companies.

Take Toyota as an example. Much of the work that goes into its vehicles is done by perhaps as many as 10,000 companies that act as subcontractors. Workers in the second-tier suppliers earn about 85 percent as much as Toyota workers. The third-tier suppliers—the ones the second-tier companies contract to—make only 70 percent. And workers in the fourth tier—many of them part-time women workers—make only 25 percent as much. This pattern means that Toyota employs only about 50,000 blue collar workers in Japan. General Motors builds about the same number of cars in the U.S. as Toyota does in Japan, but GM employs 247,000 hourly workers.

Of course, in attempting to compete with Japan, auto producers in Canada and the United States are moving to expand the tiered system here.

At times, large employers directly employ part-time or temporary workers, but as Japan's economy enters an era of instability, this flexible workforce is being squeezed.

For example, hospitals run by the national government told all workers on temporary contracts not to come to work on March 31, 1994, the last day of the fiscal year.[29] The forced day off obliged the National Children's Hospital to limit operations to emergency cases only.

This move was in preparation for the dismissal of 1,862 temporary workers in 243 health care facilities across the country over the next two years. There were 14,000 workers on temporary contracts at the facilities, about 20 percent of the staff. Four hundred municipal councils passed motions opposing the Ministry's plans to cut temporary staff. In the past, national medical facilities have tried to reduce discrepancies in wages and working conditions between permanent and temporary staff, but the Ministry's recent move would clearly make this more difficult.

Foreign Workers in Japan

The government says there are 297,000 undocumented foreign workers in Japan. But supporters of undocumented workers put the number far higher, over 600,000.

Lured by high wages, many male workers from Asia and the Middle East are employed in the construction industry. Contractors or brokers often bring Asian women to Japan under false pretenses. In many cases, women are promised jobs in restaurants or as domestics, only to be forced into the sex trade. Women at the Women's Space in Kanagawa have organized to provide protection and shelter for immigrant women fleeing exploitation.

Unscrupulous contractors use the workers' illegal status to blackmail them. Many are without health or social benefits.

In 1990, the first foreign workers' union was formed in Japan.

WORKING HOURS

Keizai taikoku, seikatsu shokoku is a phrase one hears with increasing frequency in Japan. It means Japan's economy is powerful but its people remain poor. Improvements in the quality of life have not been commensurate with economic progress. On this point there is, theoretically, a consensus.

Despite this consensus, minimal progress is being made to improve the quality of life. After carrying their industries to worldwide success, Japanese workers search in vain for the rewards that economists say come with increased GNP, productivity, and sales.

Japan has the longest working hours of any industrialized country (see the table). The problem is compounded by the tremendous amount of time spent commuting. Japan's concentrated development along the east coast, the result of insufficient urban planning among other things, has meant that most people cannot afford to live anywhere near their work. The problem was further aggravated by speculation in land, particularly in the urban areas, making property far too expensive for most

people to afford.

For example, one of the authors lives in a 70-square-meter condominium in central Tokyo. Its cost when he bought it in 1970: 7.8 million yen, or $22,000. Its price in 1990: $1 million.

What this means is that many people do not get home from work until late in the evening, leaving little time for physical let alone spiritual recovery.

International Comparison of Annual Work Hours, 1991

	Regular Hours	Over-time	Total Annual Work Hours	Annual Vacation Days
Japan	1,876	204	2,080	9
United States	1,756	187	1,943	19
England	1,739	163	1,902	24
Germany	1,499	83	1,582	29

Source: *Rodo Hakusho* [Annual White Paper on Labor], Ministry of Labor, Tokyo, 1993, p. 68.
Note: These figures do not include unreported overtime, which in Japan's case would increase its totals substantially.

The Japanese government and unions have each called for a shorter work week, but despite goal-setting (1,800 hours per year by 1992) and exhortation, little progress has been made. Part of the reason is that the lean production system relies on overtime to adapt to fluctuating demand. Overtime rates cost the company only 25 or 30 percent more than straight time (compared to time-and-a-half or double-time in other countries).

The performance-based wage system also contributes to the problem. With wage increases and promotions based on supervisors' ratings, workers compete against each other to gain a favorable evaluation. One way is by working overtime or foregoing vacations, a sign of devotion to the company.

Workers in small and medium-sized businesses are hardest hit. Workers in enterprises with under 30 employees work on average 2,431 hours per year, or an extra day per week.[30]

The long hours, high expectations, and constant treadmill of "continuous improvement" have given birth to the *karoshi* syndrome, or "death from overwork." In some cases, workers compensation boards have recognized karoshi as a legitimate work-related phenomenon, in which medical problems such as strokes are directly tied to working conditions.

According to a survey conducted by Karoshi Dial 110, a citizens volunteer group, some 1,500 cases of alleged karoshi were reported as of June 1990.

For the time being, the recession has cut work hours in some large enterprises, but this does not mean there has been any fundamental resolution of the problem.

Statistics published by the Prime Minister's office indicate that monthly overtime is less than 30 hours per worker. In reality many white collar workers do almost 100 hours overtime, approximately one hour in the morning and four hours in the evening.

Why this extreme discrepancy in overtime statistics? These office workers believe that if they request payment for all their overtime work, their managers will not recommend them for promotion. Many employers tell their employees not to ask for more than 30 hours of paid overtime per month. One rarely hears of unions filing complaints about this practice. This means that there may

be more than 700 "phantom" or unpaid annual overtime hours per worker that never appear in the statistics.

WAGES, DEMOGRAPHICS, AND FAMILY INCOME

Wage increases have been steadily declining in prosperous Japan. Recent increases in family incomes can mainly be attributed to the increasing number of women working for wages. However, two fundamental structural problems will put a squeeze on family incomes over the next period.

First, because of the ongoing appreciation of the yen, Japan's wage levels are among the highest in the world. Employers are already using this as an argument to lower wages.

Japan's changing demographics are perhaps even more important and help explain the country's relatively low unemployment rates. During the period of rapid growth in the 1960s and 1970s, the expanding economy absorbed the expanding population. However, the birth rate has been dropping; by 1989 women were having on average 1.57 children, the lowest birth rate in Japan's history. This has contributed to the chronic labor shortages in certain sectors of the economy and the import of workers from developing countries.

The declining birth rate has also meant that the proportion of older workers and retirees is rapidly rising. This will have two consequences.

The number of retirees drawing pensions will rise and, because the number of workers contributing to the national pension plan will decline, the pension fund will go bankrupt. Employees currently pay 7.25 percent of their wages for pension coverage, which is matched by employers. Japan's National Pension Council has estimated that employee contributions would have to rise to 17 percent (matched by employers) to keep the fund solvent.[31] Even then, workers would only be able to draw on pensions after age 65, as opposed to the current age of 60. This proposal has met substantial opposition from unions and community groups.

Caring for the aging population will create further problems, particularly for women. Eighty-four percent of married women have had to look after bedridden elderly parents, and 80 percent of senior citizens living alone are women. The relatively few social services for the elderly mean that families are mainly responsible for helping the aged and, given the division of labor within the family, women will be particularly hard hit. In other words, women may be forced to abandon paid work in order to keep up with the unpaid labor involved in caring for the aging family. Or, conversely, they will be forced to work longer and harder than ever before. Either way, the stress on the family will increase.

The Japanese government allots a lower percentage of its national income to social security infrastructure than any other industrialized country. This has meant that housing, community and recreational facilities, health care, and even education are often under-funded. This weakness has strong repercussions on the quality of life in Japan.

Solidarity Links

The Asian Pacific Workers Solidarity Links—Japan Committee (APWSL-Japan) is an organization of grassroots union activists in Japan. The committee is part of a growing network of solidarity throughout the Asia Pacific region. In 1993 APWSL-Japan sent three delegates to an international conference sponsored by a sister organization, Australia Asia Worker Links.

APWSL-Japan publishes an English-language newsletter with up-to-date labor news from Japan, as well as a Japanese-language newsletter. To subscribe to the newsletter, see chapter 41.

Owning a home a reasonable distance from work, for example, is impossible for most young people.

WOMEN DEMAND JUSTICE

Though their numbers are still small, a growing number of Japanese people are calling for a major shift in national direction. They want humanization of work and life. "It is no exaggeration to say that the issue of women and work is central to finding that alternative," says Shibayama Emiko, an instructor at Nagoya Women's College and prominent essayist on women's issues.[32]

Women in Japan are making some progress in their fight for equality, but that progress remains woefully small given Japan's status as an economic superpower. In this era of globalization, women's status within Japan is no longer just a domestic issue but has international repercussions, says Shibayama.

Thus women's issues have increasingly come to the fore within Japan. The defeat of the conservative Liberal-Democratic government in 1992 and the establishment of a coalition government including the Social-Democratic Party of Japan helped loosen the bonds and propel women in increasing numbers into prominent positions. In 1993, for example, Takako Doi, the former leader of the Socialist Party, was the first woman ever to be nominated as the Speaker of the House. And for the first time, a woman has been appointed to the Supreme Court. Women have increased their roles in government at both the local and national levels.

Furthermore, the range of issues women are addressing has broadened. For example, when a woman writer won her suit for wrongful dismissal against a harassing boss, the publicity generated by the case made many more people aware of sexual harassment.[33] The Ministry of Labor released a video on sexual harassment and the Tokyo Lawyers Association published a legal guide.[34] Two hundred people turned out to a Tokyo play, "Midnight on D Drive: Sexual Harassment," commemorating the publication of the legal guide. These small developments reflect important shifts in Japanese society.

Women are marrying later and divorce rates are on the rise. According to a 1993 white paper, women's average age at marriage was 26, the highest since World War II.[35] The percentage of respondents opposing divorce dropped by nearly 16 percent over the past decade.

Propelling women's concerns to the social forefront has been the increasing role women are playing in the economy, despite tremendous social barriers to such participation. Nearly 20 million women hold jobs today, compared to only 11 million in 1975. Women currently hold 40 percent of all jobs in Japan.

Yet of all the industrialized countries, more women in Japan are obliged to give up their jobs in order to give birth or raise young children. When women marry or become pregnant, they receive *kata tataki* from their supervisor, who politely informs them that they would be well-advised to retire. While this practice is beginning to change, it is far from over.

Furthermore, over 30 percent of women's jobs (5.9 out of 19 million) are part-time (defined as working less than 35 hours per week). On top of this figure must be added the large number of contingent workers (those on temporary contracts, working out of personnel agencies, and so forth) who are also excluded from many of the benefits that regular full-time workers enjoy even though they work more than 35 hours per week. In total, over half of working women in Japan may be what are considered "non-regular" employees.

Wages for women in Japan are also the lowest among industrialized countries. This is due not only to overt discrimination, but also to structural discrimination: part-time work pays less, women work for smaller corporations where wages are lower, and women are streamed into low-paying clerical jobs. In 1988 Japanese women were at 50.7 percent of men's pay (average monthly cash earnings per regular worker, in firms with 30 or more regular workers). Compare this to U.S.

John Z. Gelsavage

women at 70.2 percent (median weekly earnings of full-time workers).[36]

And to top it all off, women in Japan have an even tougher row to hoe at home: according to one government report, Japanese working men spend on average as little as eight minutes a day on domestic chores.

STREAMING

Perhaps one of the biggest obstacles for working women is the streaming of women into low-paid jobs. It is estimated that nearly 40 percent hold clerical jobs. Most are excluded from the fast-track job placement and promotional system. This discrimination adds to the pressure for women to quit work when they marry or become pregnant. Why stick with a dead-end job?

The situation persists despite the passage in 1985 of the Equal Employment Opportunity Law. Most progressive groups in Japan criticized it at the time as being inadequate. After nearly a decade little had changed and the Japan Institute of Labor, a government-funded research body, stated, "The lack of penalties for violations makes it difficult for the weakly-worded Law to have any practical effect."[37]

A 1989 Ministry of Labor report said that 75.1 percent of companies surveyed reported that they had no women at all in managerial positions.[38] Of those that did have women managers, nearly two-thirds said women were less than one percent of their managers.

The recession has hit women harder than men. The unemployment rate for women in February 1994 was 3.2 percent, an increase of .3 percent over a year earlier. This is the highest unemployment rate for women since the government began its survey in 1953. Women in the 24-34 age bracket faced 5.0 percent unemployment, a jump of over 1.1 percent compared to February 1993.

In some sectors, however, the situation is changing. In certain parts of the service industry, including department stores, some companies are providing better jobs for women as well as more flexible working conditions. Recently, a publishing company opened a day care center at a train station in Kawasaki.[39] In a country where most people commute by train, having a day care center at the

History of Enterprise Unions

Enterprise unions in Japan today are found in such large corporations as Toyota and Toshiba. Such unions have become, for the most part, an extension of managerial control in the workplace. Often, enterprise unions came into being in the 1948-60 period in the course of intense labor disputes. They were created either through purging an adversarial union or through the establishment of a breakaway union (some would call them rat unions), as at Nissan.[40]

This period was the height of the Cold War. The United States continued to exercise considerable influence over Japan's internal life during this period. U.S. government and labor officials played an important role that allowed enterprise unions to triumph in Japan.[41] In the broad sense, then, enterprise unions were very much the creation of the international labor movement.

Enterprise unions in Japan basically accepted the employers' agenda, ceded almost exclusive managerial rights over the workplace, tended to reject job action as a pressure tactic, and limited their role almost exclusively to consultation over wages and work hours. Moreover, such unions accepted the employers' "production first and foremost" philosophy and actively worked to suppress opposition in the ranks of their members.

A representative example is the Federation of Toshiba Unions. In the early postwar years, this union was very much an adversarial-style union. After it lost a major battle with Toshiba in 1949, however, it took on the features of enterprise unionism described above.[42] Yamamoto Kiyoshi, a professor at Tokyo University, has documented how the union became completely integrated with Toshiba management.[43]

When faced with a resurgence of adversarialism in the late 1960s, the company and union responded by forming a company-wide underground organization called the Ohgi Caucus. This caucus, which included top management representatives as well as union leaders, constantly surveyed Toshiba employees for signs of "troublemakers." When such troublemakers were identified, the Ohgi Caucus conspired with Toshiba management to force these employees to accept the status quo or resign.

Another example of the Toshiba experience with enterprise unionism was the Toshiba-Ampex dispute that began in 1982.[44] Toshiba attempted to close this plant, a joint venture with Ampex of the United States. When the workers resisted the closure, the Ohgi Caucus and the union intervened to stifle the protest. Those workers who continued to fight the closure were forced to leave the union. They subsequently affiliated with a more democratic union and eventually won a landmark settlement against Toshiba.[45]

Many enterprise unions exist in Japan, particularly in major corporations such as Nissan, Toyota, Sanyo, Panasonic, Toshiba, and elsewhere. They have been accused of being "company unions" and in many respects they are. However, they retain a formal independence because Japan's labor law prohibits employer interference in internal union affairs. Actual practice often makes a mockery of such regulations.

Even enterprise unions will resort to strike action when members are demanding change and further union inaction would jeopardize the union's role. As Japan's economy falters, enterprise unions are coming under increasing pressure to defend their members' interests.

station is extremely convenient.

In a number of cases, women who have protested layoffs have found union support lacking. At Nippon Telegraph and Telephone, for example, a number of women formed a counter-union after they accused their union (Zendentsu) of collaborating with the company in compelling women to take "voluntary" retirement. NTT had announced it would reduce its workforce from 260,000 to 200,000 over the next three years.[46]

ENTERPRISE UNIONS UNDER PRESSURE

The contradiction between corporations' competitive success and workers' problems in quality of life, combined with the specter of growing unemployment and lower wages, have put new pressures on Japan's unions. At the same time, it becomes harder for them to respond, as membership figures decline. Japan's union density dropped to 24.4 percent in 1992.

National Trade Union Organizations (1993)

Name	Membership	Largest Affiliates
Japan Trade Union Confederation (Rengo)	7,819,000	Prefectural & Municipal Workers (1 million) Automobile Workers (782,000) Electrical Workers (751,000) Construction Workers (567,000) Textile Workers (549,000)
National Confederation of Trade Unions (Zenroren)	856,000	Prefectural & Municipal Workers (300,000) Teachers Union (210,000) National Public Service (180,000) Health Care Workers (175,000)
National Trade Union Council (Zenrokyo)	300,000	Railway Workers
Unaffiliated Federations	2,818,000	N.A.
Unaffiliated Locals	1,126,000	N.A.

Source: Japan Institute of Labor, *Japan Labor Bulletin*, Vol. 33, No. 3, March 1994.

As Japan's major labor central, Rengo plays a predominant role in establishing labor's goals and agenda for action. It has faced substantial difficulties in realizing the limited goals it has set. The weak Shunto in 1994 is one example. It had previously set the objective of an 1,800-hour work-year by 1992. This goal was not met and Rengo has now set 1996 as the target.[47]

Rengo has also set the goal of building its membership to 10 million by 1997. This will require the recruitment of nearly 500,000 new members each year for the next four years. But for each of the past two years Rengo has organized only a little over 100,000 new members. To reach its target Rengo has called for the establishment of a new labor movement center for workers in small and medium-sized businesses.

There are some signs that Japan's enterprise unions are beginning to emerge from their cocoon of company dependency. The JAW's hard-hitting criticism of the auto industry was one such sign. During the 1994 spring offensive, the electrical workers union took a strike vote for the first time in many years. And certain Rengo leaders are calling for more militancy. But Rengo's ability to deliver remains problematic. As a union center it does not control the agendas of its affiliates.

The future of Japan's union movement to confront and overcome the challenges ahead may well depend on Rengo's willingness to open up its ranks and create an atmosphere where debate and confrontation can take place.

Notes

1. We use the Japanese custom of placing surnames first.

2. Confederation of Japan Automobile Workers' Unions, "Japanese Automobile Industry in the Future: Towards Coexistence with the World, Consumers and Employees," Tokyo, 1992. Hereafter referred to as JAW Policy Statement.

3. Interview with I. Shioji, April 9, 1994, Saitama, Japan.

4. Excerpts from JAW Policy Statement, pp. 1-5.

5. Poll results are reproduced in Nomura Masami, "The End of 'Toyotism'? Recent Trends in a Japanese Automobile Company," presented at the Lean Workplace Conference, Port Elgin, Ontario, Sept. 30-Oct. 3, 1993, Figure 7.

6. Shimada Haruo, "Expectations of the Advisor," Chapter 5 in the JAW Policy Statement, p. 33.

7. Kamata Satoshi, *Japan in the Passing Lane*, Pantheon, New York, 1982.

8. This account of the Nissan situation is based on Kamii Yoshihiko's account, contained in Totsuka Hideo and Hyodo Tsutomu, eds., *Roshi Kankei no Tenkan to Sentaku* [Transition and Choice in Industrial Relations], Nihon Hyoron Sha, Tokyo, 1991, pp. 78-88; an unpublished paper by Watanabe Ben, "Difference in Union Leadership between Toyota and Nissan"; and an interview with Shioji Ichiro, April 9, 1994.

9. Nomura Masami, "The End of 'Toyotism'?," p. 15.

10. Because of the appreciation of the yen, Japan's unit labor costs are increasing faster than any other country in the world. See Edwin Dean, "Trends in Costs, Productivity and International Competitiveness in Manufacturing, 1979-92," a paper presented at the International Productivity Symposium VI, Vancouver, June 1994, p. 13.

11. See, for example, James P. Womack, Daniel T. Jones, and Daniel Roos, *The Machine that Changed the World*, Rawson Associates, New York, 1990, pp. 118-127. "Between 1982 and 1990 [Japanese firms] nearly doubled their product portfolios from 47 to 84 models." (p. 119)

12. Nomura Masami, "End of 'Toyotism'?," p. 4.

13. This account is based on Nomura, "End of 'Toyotism'?" and Christian Berggren, "Toward Normalization? Japanese Competi-

tive Position and Employment Practices after the Heisei Boom," a paper presented to the Industrial Relations Research Association, Boston, January 3-5, 1994.

14. John Price, "Lean Production in Japan: Historical Perspectives," in Steve Babson, ed., *Lean Work: Empowerment and Exploitation in the Global Auto Industry*, Wayne State University Press, Detroit, Spring 1995.

15. Kamii Yoshihiko, "Minkan Daikigyo no Rodo Mondai" [Labor Issues in Large, Private Enterprises] in H. Totsuka and S. Tokunaga, *Gendai Nihon no Rodo Mondai* [Labor Issues in Contemporary Japan], Mineruba Shobo, Tokyo, 1993, p. 78.

16. Michael Cusumano, *The Japanese Automobile Industry*, Council on East Asian Studies—Harvard, Cambridge, 1985, p. 379.

17. Ishikawa Kaoru, *Nihon teki Hinshitsu Kanri* [Japanese Quality Control], Nikka Giren Shuppan Sha, Tokyo, 1988 edition, p. 77.

18. Nomura Masami, *Toyotizumu* [Toyotism], Mineruba Shobo, Tokyo, 1993, p. 126.

19. As cited by Yoshihiko Kamii, "Labor Issues in Large Private Enterprises," p. 86.

20. Ishikawa Kaoru, *Japanese Quality Control*, p. 90.

21. The Toyota union estimates that wages for workers in the 30-35 age group do not cover expenditures at present. See Nomura, "End of 'Toyotism'?," Figure 5.

22. *Shukan Rodo Nyusu* [Weekly Labor News], March 28, 1994, p. 1.

23. *Shukan Rodo Nyusu*, p. 3.

24. Japan Institute of Labor, *Japan Labor Bulletin*, Vol. 33, No. 2, February 1994, p. 3.

25. *Shukan Rodo Nyusu*, March 28, 1994, p. 1.

26. *Asahi Shimbun*, April 1, 1994.

27. *Asahi Shimbun*, April 1, 1994.

28. Japan Institute of Labor, *Japan Labor Bulletin*, Vol. 32, No. 11, November, 1993, p. 5.

29. *Japan Times*, April 1, 1994, p. 2.

30. As reported in *Asahi Shimbun*, April 1, 1994.

31. As reported in the Mitsubishi Economic Research Institute *Monthly Circular*, April 1994.

32. Emiko Shibayama, "Josei Rodosha" [Women Workers] in H. Totsuka and S. Tokunaga, eds., *Gendai Nihon no Rodo Mondai* [Labor Issues in Contemporary Japan], p. 193.

33. *Asia Labor Update*, Asia Monitor Resource Centre, Hong Kong.

34. *Asahi Shimbun*, April 3, 1994, p. 12.

35. Japan Institute of Labor, *Japan Labor Bulletin*, Vol. 33, No. 3, March 1994, p. 1.

36. *U.S. and Japan in Figures*, Japan External Trade Organization, Tokyo, 1991, chart 25.

37. Japan Institute of Labor, *Japan Labor Bulletin*, Vol. 33, No. 3, March 1994, p. 5.

38. As cited by Masuda Reiko, "Nice Try, but...," *Look Japan*, Vol. 35, No. 414, September 1990, p. 6.

39. *The Daily Yomiuri*, April 2, 1994, p. 3.

40. The story of the defeat of the militant 1953 strike at Nissan is told in the video "We Are Driven." See chapter 41.

41. To examine the compromised and often tortuous role of some U.S. labor officials in Japan, see John Price, "Valery Burati and the Formation of Sohyo during the U.S. Occupation of Japan," *Pacific Affairs*, Vol. 64, No. 2, Summer, 1991, pp. 208-225.

42. For an account of the 1949 dispute, see Joe B. Moore, "The Toshiba Dispute of 1949: The 'Rationalization' of Labour Relations," *Labour, Capital and Society*, Vol. 23, No. 1, April 1990, pp. 134-159.

43. Kiyoshi Yamamoto, "The Japanese-Style Industrial Relations and an 'Informal' Employee Organization: A Case Study of the Ohgi-kai at T Electric," University of Tokyo, Institute of Social Sciences, Occasional Papers in Labor Problem and Social Policy, December 1990.

44. Tsuzuku Ken, "A Message to American Workers: The Japanese Management Style as a Means of Controlling Workers," (unpublished manuscript, available upon request). Tsuzuku Ken was one of the leaders of the Toshiba-Ampex struggle and plant occupation. He toured Canada in the fall of 1991, where he spoke about the Toshiba-Ampex fight and demonstrated a high-tech radiation detector that the union had developed in conjunction with anti-nuclear groups in Japan and was producing inside the occupied plant.

45. While the Toshiba-Ampex struggle was going on, newspapers in Japan reported that Seino Tadashi, Toshiba's managing director in charge of labor affairs, and Sohno Hiromi, chairman of the Toshiba union, were enjoying themselves on a company-paid outing to a subcontractor in northern Japan. They played golf together, attended a banquet in their honor and then spent the night with teenage prostitutes provided by the subcontractor. Both Seino and Sohno were subsequently forced to resign their positions. *Mainichi Newspaper*, evening edition, October 7, 1989, as cited in Tsuzuku Ken's paper, "A Message to American Workers."

46. Hugh Williamson, "Seku Hara," *Asia Labor Monitor*, Issue 11, April 1993, p. 3.

47. Japan Institute of Labor, *Japan Labor Bulletin*, Vol. 32, No. 12, December 1993, p. 2.

Chapter 29

The Team in Mexico

Corporations are introducing the same forms of work organization in Mexico that they are in the rest of North America. In Mexico, this process is called "modernization," and it is heavily promoted by U.S. corporations, the Mexican government, and unions that subscribe to "new-unionism." Therefore the argument that workers in the U.S. can outcompete Mexican workers by adopting the "high performance model" is false. Case studies of Volkswagen and TELMEX, the Mexican telephone company, bear this out.

by Dan La Botz

Multinational corporations and the U.S. government have argued that in the world-wide scramble for survival, U.S. workers can save their jobs and their standard of living by accepting new forms of cooperative work organization. According to this argument, U.S. and Western European workers will work in highly productive teams in technologically advanced, high-skill, high-wage jobs, while workers in Latin America, Asia, Africa, and Eastern Europe do the grunt work of the world. If American workers embrace cooperation, they tell us, we will be among the world's chosen people.

The reality is much more complicated.

MULTINATIONAL CORPORATIONS AND WORLD PRODUCTION

Around the world, governments and corporations are adopting similar technologies and all are experimenting with new forms of work organization. Precisely because corporations are multinational and are engaged in world production, they tend to introduce the same technologies and similar forms of work organization almost everywhere.

In their drive to create a system of world production, the multinationals have been helped by the World Bank and the International Monetary Fund (IMF). These institutions have pushed countries around the globe to open their borders to the multinationals' factories, technologies, and management methods. Under pressure from the World Bank and IMF, many nations have sold off their formerly

nationalized industries to private investors—often multinational corporations—and dropped barriers to investment and trade.[1] Consequently, today the same corporations, the same technologies, and the same forms of work organization can be found from Texas to Taiwan, from Sweden to Singapore.

This includes the countries of Latin America and Asia, as well as the former Communist countries of Eastern Europe. To take just one example: Ricardo Semler has instituted a team concept program at his mechanical engineering firm, Semco, based in Sao Paulo, Brazil. According to *Business Latin America:*

> By 1985 Mr. Semler had reduced the company's 11 hierarchical job categories to three and had given the lowest-level employees major decision-making powers. These workers now have input into such decisions as setting production targets and inventory levels as well as determining new plant locations. Workers also are allowed to decide upon and coordinate their work hours with peers.
>
> Going even further, Semco does not hire or promote people until they have been interviewed, evaluated and accepted by all their future subordinates. Dress codes, punch clocks, name tags, titles, storeroom padlocks, audits on petty cash and the frisking of workers have also been abolished.

The company's sales and profits have risen enormously, and Semler has written a book on the new management titled *Virando a Propria Mesa* (Turning the Tables) which is being published in 14 languages.[2] Leaving aside *Business Latin America's* breathless wonder at this "workplace democracy" (just imagine, no more frisking at work!), the article shows just how pervasive team concept has become.

Perhaps it is not surprising to find the new management methods in Sao Paulo, one of Latin America's largest industrial centers. But now even Cuba has quality circles. Cuba does not allow unions which are independent

Dan La Botz is the author of The Crisis of Mexican Labor; Mask of Democracy: Labor Suppression in Mexico Today; *and the Labor Notes book* A Troublemaker's Handbook.

of the government or strikes, but it does allow "Japanese-style quality control circles" in more than a dozen enterprises overseen by the Ministry of Basic Industry.[3]

The point is this: if U.S. managers are adopting and U.S. workers are accepting cooperative methods such as team concept, we are not alone. Management is attempting to impose these same methods everywhere, whatever the nation, culture, or language. Mexico provides an excellent example.

THE MEXICAN ECONOMY—HISTORICAL BACKGROUND

To understand the enormous changes taking place in Mexico today, it's necessary to understand the history of Mexico's relationship to the United States and the nature of its unions.

U.S. corporations have played a very large—often a dominant—role in the Mexican economy since the nineteenth century. Standard Oil, for example, controlled oil production, and ASARCO dominated metal mining. The Mexican people found U.S. corporate control of their economy unacceptable. The Mexican Revolution of 1910-1920 was in part a reaction against U.S. control of the Mexican economy. In 1938 Mexico nationalized the oil industry, taking over plants owned by Standard Oil and Royal Dutch Shell. For most Mexicans, the nationalization of the foreign-owned oil fields and refineries was a great victory for the Mexican Revolution and for the Mexican nation.

At about the same time there was also a great labor upheaval. While the CIO was on the rise in the United States in the 1930s, the Confederation of Mexican Workers (CTM) and other Mexican unions were organizing workers in basic industries throughout the country.

The combination of nationalized industry and union organization strengthened the Mexican workers and weakened, at least briefly, the grip of foreign management in some industries. During the 1930s and early 1940s when foreign companies resisted union organizing drives, the Mexican government sometimes threatened to nationalize them. Faced with such a threat, the corporations relented and recognized the union.[4]

However, between the 1930s and 1970s Mexico did nationalize many industries, among them steel, electrical manufacture, utilities, airlines, railroads, and telephone.

Mexico's nationalist model of economic development thus led to a mixed economy with four major sectors: 1) Mexican state corporations; 2) U.S. multinationals such as ASARCO, Ford, and General Motors; 3) large Mexican-owned firms such as the Garza-Sada family's beer, glass, and steel factories; and 4) some 300,000 plants owned by smaller Mexican firms. The Mexican state played an important role in the economy because of its control over the key industries.

The state also played a dominant role in the labor movement. By 1948 Mexico's unions had been completely taken over by the ruling Institutional Revolutionary Party (PRI). The PRI used the police, the army, and even gangsters to put party loyalists into leading positions in the unions.[5] The PRI wanted control over the unions to keep wages low, in order to keep attracting foreign investment (though they preferred not to let foreign investors have majority ownership).

The result of this combination of nationalized industry and a one-party state that controlled the unions was a situation something like that in Eastern Europe before 1990. In Mexico some employers, the unions, the labor relations boards, and the government at all levels were all dominated by the same party. The state-controlled unions negotiated contracts that provided some protections on working conditions and wages, but most workers had virtually no voice in their unions.[6]

Despite nationalization of some industries and foreign investment, Mexico remained an economically backward and relatively poor country. So, with labor now under strict control, in the 1940s Mexico adopted an economic policy known as "import substitution." This meant that Mexico would try to industrialize by manufacturing for itself products that it had previously imported. While this program worked for some light industries, it was much less successful for heavy industry, and it clearly failed in crucial sectors such as the machine tool industry.

The Mexican government wanted to speed up the process of industrialization, so beginning in the 1970s it pumped huge quantities of oil to pay for it. Vast oil reserves made it possible for Mexico to borrow tremendous sums, mainly from U.S. banks—a total of $100 billion. The loans paid for the construction of new steel mills and nuclear plants, as well as new schools and social services. But when the price of oil fell from $28 to less than $14 a barrel, Mexico faced ruin.

In August 1982 Mexico found itself unable to pay the interest on its debts. At that point the U.S. banks that were Mexico's creditors, the International Monetary Fund (IMF), and the World Bank all intervened to force Mexico to reorganize its economy.

FORCED REORGANIZATION OF THE ECONOMY

Under pressure from the banks and the IMF, the PRI scrapped the import substitution model of industrialization, and adopted instead the idea that Mexico should exploit its "natural advantage" of low wages, and concentrate on manufacturing for export.

The new plan was called "modernization." It included:
- privatization of government-owned industries
- ending barriers to foreign investment and ownership
- promotion of the maquiladoras
- elimination of government subsidies for transportation and basic food products
- "flexibility" in the workplace.

Modernization was carried out by Presidents Miguel de la Madrid and Carlos Salinas. They sold off 1,100 nationalized industries—everything from telephone to basic food products to government services—to private investors, often foreigners or multinational corporations. Mexico ended subsidies for basic food products, dropped tariffs and quotas, joined the General Agreement on Tariffs and Trade (GATT), and negotiated the North American Free Trade Agreement (NAFTA).

As planned, this program attracted much more foreign investment. For example, when Mexico sold its government-owned telephone company to private investors, Southwestern Bell became one of the stockholders.

THE MAQUILADORAS

The maquiladora program was a big part of "modernization." It had been created in 1965. Foreign companies were permitted to establish assembly plants along the U.S.-Mexico border, producing parts or products only for export. They usually built an assembly plant on the Mexican side and warehouse facilities on the U.S. side. U.S. corporations such as General Motors, Hewlett-Packard, and Zenith predominated, but eventually Japanese companies like Hitachi and Korean companies like Gold Star also set up plants.

The maquiladoras were exempt from many Mexican taxes and enjoyed preferential treatment under U.S. tax laws. The maquiladora program expanded rapidly after the currency devaluation in 1982 cut Mexican wages in half. In the 1970s, wages for all workers in Mexico were one-fourth those of U.S. workers; by the 1990s they had dropped to one-tenth.

Mexican maquiladora workers were predominantly women, about 80 percent in the 1960s and 1970s, about 65 percent in the 1980s and 1990s. Most of these women workers were young, between 14 and 30, and had moved from villages and towns in the interior of Mexico.

By 1992 there were 2,000 maquiladora plants in Mexico employing 500,000 workers.

The rapid growth of population around the border towns' new maquiladora zones led to the growth of vast *colonias*, poor neighborhoods where maquiladora workers lived in shacks and small concrete block houses, often without water, sewage, or electricity.

At first most of the maquiladora plants were engaged only in assembly and packing. For example, Mexican workers assembled components into circuit boards for radios, televisions, stereos, and computers, which were then reshipped to manufacturing plants in the United States.

As the maquiladoras proved themselves successful, companies tended to introduce ever more expensive and advanced technology into the plants. Soon some ma-

GE Workers, North and South, Get Pizza

At Labor Notes' Cross-Border Organizing School in May 1994, General Electric workers from the U.S. met Mexican GE workers from Ciudad Juarez. David Johnson, an international representative for the United Electrical Workers (UE), tells what happened when they talked:

"Like many companies these days, GE has new production systems and quality circles in a number of plants. They're called 'Work-Out'—GE's idea of labor-management cooperation.

"Work-Out has also been imposed at Compania Armadura, S.A. (CASA), the GE motor plant in Ciudad Juarez. In fact, they call it Work-Out—they don't even bother to translate it into Spanish. They bring workers together to talk about jointness and togetherness and boundarylessness and all the b.s. that the company espouses.

"When workers from the two sides of the border got together, they talked about Work-Out. They talked about the company eliminating supervision, and putting together workteams, and speed-up and what that's meant. Despite the differences in the wage levels, a lot of the production questions are incredibly similar, so there's an immediate identification.

"Mexican workers were saying, 'When we pass our production goals the company throws us a party and gives us all pizzas.'

"Which also happens in the U.S. plants. So there was a whole discussion about the use of pizza vs. wage increases.

"When our brothers and sisters returned to their plants in the U.S. and talked to their members about what happened, there was a visceral identification that really helped the level of support among our own ranks."

quiladora workers were using the most advanced technologies in the world.[7]

At the same time, during the 1970s and 1980s, multinational corporations were beginning to create systems of world production, producing components in various countries and assembling them in others for final sale in yet others. For U.S., Japanese, and some German and Korean corporations, Mexico became strategically important because of its proximity to the huge U.S. market, and because of its low wages and state-controlled unions, which meant labor peace.

Thus with the help of the Mexican government, multinational corporations are importing into Mexico both the most modern technologies and new forms of work organization.[8]

GOVERNMENT PUSHES 'FLEXIBILITY'

In Mexico, these new forms of work organization are known as "flexibility" (flexibilidad). The introduction of flexibility was by no means peaceful. Flexibility was achieved only after a concerted assault on workers in which the Mexican government used the police and army to attack unions, occupy workplaces, close factories, and fire tens of thousands of workers. When the dust cleared, one era of industrial relations had ended and another era had begun.

While Mexico's unions were controlled by the ruling party, these unions and their contracts did offer some protections for workers. Many contracts contained detailed job descriptions, specific job titles, and seniority. These contracts were seen as an obstacle to the "modernization" of Mexico. The first task then was to break the unions.

From his first days in office, Carlos Salinas attacked his own party's unions. Throughout the 1980s and early 1990s the government repeatedly attacked union officials, broke unions, and eliminated or gutted contracts. Salinas arrested the leaders of the Petroleum Workers Union and replaced them with more pliant officials. He sent the army to occupy the Cananea copper mine in Sonora, intimidating the Mining and Metal Workers union. The occupation was a preemptive strike, to prevent the copper workers from organizing a protest over the privatization of the historic mine. While the union survived, its labor contract was rewritten for flexibility.

Privatization and plant closings were essential to modernization. Many older plants, such as the Fundidora de Monterrey steel mill, were simply closed down. As many as 400,000 Mexican workers lost their jobs in this process. Other nationalized industries were sold off to private investors, who in many cases refused to accept the existing unions and contracts. In some cases the union was completely eliminated. Where the union survived, as at PEMEX, the employers demanded new flexible contracts.

In this way, the Mexican state acted as a bulldozer, clearing the old labor relations away so that the new system of flexible industrial relations could be established.[9]

Alejandro Covarrubias, a Mexican researcher, found that "the Mexican state had led the transition to 'flexibility,'" and the multinationals and other very large enterprises had played the key role.[10]

Of course, flexibility is not limited to the multinationals. One study tells how at a Mexican-owned ceramics company, management fired two hundred workers with the highest seniority and replaced them with younger workers and flexible labor relations.[11]

The combination of world production, advanced technology, and maquiladoras means that Mexico is becoming fully involved in the most modern methods of work organization.

TECHNOLOGY AND WORK ORGANIZATION IN MEXICO

Harley Shaiken, a professor at the University of California, conducted a study of the auto, computer, and consumer electronics industries in Mexico in the late 1980s. He found that the U.S. automaker he studied "utilized the most advanced technology and represented the highest level of investment. In addition, the plant employs new forms of work organization which are often associated with Japanese companies."[12] (Shaiken does not identify the factory in his study, but it is clearly Ford's Escort assembly plant in Hermosillo, which is patterned after a Mazda plant in Japan.)

Ford Hermosillo used all the techniques associated with modern management: contracting out, few job classifications, no separate skilled trades, job rotation, and nearly complete flexibility, meaning management had the right to deploy the personnel as it saw fit. Management also encouraged peer discipline, so that workers persuaded each other to overcome absenteeism and suggested punishment if workers failed to improve.

The grievance procedure was extremely informal, and the union was virtually non-existent on the shop floor. The local, affiliated with the CTM, was almost worthless in improving workers' conditions.[13]

Moreover, Shaiken found that "the plant's novel work organization, which partially integrates skilled and production work, could prove to be a prototype for changes throughout the company's global operations."[14] That is, team concept experiments in Mexico could set the pace for the United States.

Both quality and production quantity in these plants were as good as that anywhere else, in many cases better. Meanwhile, workers in U.S. auto plants made $30 per hour in total compensation, while workers in Mexico made $2. The difference in wage costs in one plant alone could save a company up to $100 million per year, Shaiken explained.[15]

Flexibility is now being introduced throughout the Mexican auto industry. After a series of very bitter strikes, involving mass firings and violent confrontations between management and workers, and even one murder, management was on its way to making Mexican auto workers part of the team—whether they liked it or not.[16]

But flexibility is by no means limited to the auto industry. One study of 100 multinational manufacturing and assembly plants in two maquiladora zones, Ciudad Juarez and Chihuahua, found that many managers were successfully using "continuous improvement technologies." Other studies have reported similar findings.[17]

One article, titled "Maquiladoras: Where Quality Is a Way of Life," describes plants such as the Shure Brothers' Juarez facility. This plant cut its manufacturing steps from 349 to 96, and production time from 32 days to two. Mattel's MABAMEX facility in Tijuana uses just-in-time, and hourly workers supposedly control the speed of the assembly line.[18]

Since multinational corporations have been the driving force behind "flexibility," these methods will spread as multinationals invade more and more of the Mexican economy. Mexican firms have entered into 60 important joint ventures in the last three years, mostly with U.S. corporations but also with Canadian, European, and Asian companies.[19] NAFTA is expected to increase the number and size of joint ventures. In such partnerships, U.S. capital tends to impose its methods on its Mexican partners.

At the same time, of course, Mexico is an enormous country with tens of thousands of medium-sized and small firms and with a huge underground economy. Many of the smaller firms use outdated technologies and have not introduced flexibility. Many employers in these sectors compensate for their antiquated equipment and old-style labor relations by paying lower wages or demanding longer hours than the large Mexican and multinational firms.

THE BOTTOM LINE

A combination of international bankers, multinational corporations, and the Mexican state have determined to impose "flexibility" on the Mexican worker. The international financial organizations decided on the new industrial order, and the Mexican state, sometimes violently, imposed it. This combination of economic blackmail and crude violence was sanctified by NAFTA, which offered political guarantees to the multinationals.

The argument, then, that U.S. workers can win the international competition for jobs and economic survival by adopting advanced technology and cooperative methods—the "high performance model"—that argument simply fails. Since multinationals everywhere are introducing these same technologies and same forms of work organization, the reality is a forced intensification of competition among workers in different countries.

As the rules are now set by the powers-that-be, we

will not see some nations prospering by going high tech and others flourishing by doing the grunt work. Rather, the multinationals' strategy is leading in all countries toward small islands of relatively advanced technologies, surrounded by a sea of smaller subcontractors, many unemployed workers, and the very poor. While parts of both the U.S. and Mexico are rapidly being brought into the 21st century, other parts of both countries are falling back into the 19th century's darkest days of tenement sweatshops and the desperate armies of the unemployed.

The way to resist this corporate vision of the future is international union solidarity. See Labor Notes' publications on cross-border organizing strategies for some first steps.

CASE STUDY #1: VOLKSWAGEN

At Volkswagen, a multinational corporation and the Mexican government cooperated to break the strike of a militant union and rewrite the collective bargaining agreement for "flexibility."[20]

Volkswagen built a large assembly plant at Puebla, south of Mexico City, in 1964. Throughout the 1980s, while the rest of the Mexican auto industry was in a slump, the VW Puebla plant produced more cars than any other in Mexico.

The VW plant was first organized by the Confederation of Mexican Workers (CTM), one of Mexico's "official unions" controlled by the ruling party, in 1964. The VW workers were known for their militancy; between 1974 and 1987 they carried out eight strikes, over both economic and contractual issues. They formed the Independent Union of VW Workers in 1972.

Because of their militancy and their independence, the Puebla VW workers were at the center of efforts to form a national auto workers union in Mexico. (Since the founding of the auto industry in Mexico in the 1920s there has been no national union of auto workers—only separate unions for each individual plant.) This attempt to create a national union was opposed by both the auto companies and the Mexican government.

Through the 1980s, VW introduced many aspects of "flexibility" into the contract. The company was permitted to subcontract service and maintenance work. In many cases, workers could be moved from job to job, with little or no distinction between production and inspection or production and maintenance. Yet, at the same time, the contract had relatively good wages and benefits and still offered many traditional contract protections.

SHOWDOWN

The company was unhappy with this situation, and decided to make the 1992 negotiations a showdown. International developments strengthened VW's hand: the negotiations took place in the shadow of the NAFTA talks. The VW Puebla negotiations became a test of Mexico's willingness to meet the demands of multinational corporations.

Under pressure from VW, the union's general secretary, Gaspar Bueno, met secretly with company officials and signed a contract that included a 5 percent productivity increase and complete flexibility. When workers found out, they began work stoppages and finally struck. VW got the city to send in police with shotguns to attempt to break the strike.

Bueno's leadership in the union was challenged by Jesus Valencia, head of an opposition group that represented a majority of the workers. An assembly of 8,000 striking members unanimously voted to remove Bueno from office.

VW claimed it was unable to reach an agreement because the union was divided. The company filed a demand with the Federal Arbitration and Conciliation Commission to terminate the contract. Five thousand VW workers traveled to Mexico City to protest. The Commission found in favor of the company, citing an "intra-union dispute," and declared the strike illegal. VW proceeded to fire all 14,289 workers. They no longer had any right to jobs at VW.

NEW CONTRACT

Just weeks later, the Secretary of Labor got the union, the employer, and the Commission to reach an agreement. This new flexible contract allowed management to arbitrarily assign jobs and work schedules and to hire an unlimited number of temporaries. Workers were made "fully responsible for the manufacturing, quality, register and control of materials and continued improvement. They must clean and take care of all equipment and work areas." All seniority was lost. Salary was to be determined by management according to the worker's "knowledge, ability, experience, aptitude, efficiency and work attitude." All training would occur after work hours with no pay.

Gaspar Bueno, who had signed the original productivity agreement, remained the head of the union. Bueno changed the union's by-laws to make the workers' general assembly no longer the final decision-making body. Instead, any changes or ratifications would be made by the executive committee plus one representative from each of the eight plant divisions. Shop floor stewards were eliminated.

The company agreed to rehire the workers, but, when they began to return to their jobs, VW refused to take back 2,000 whom it identified as union dissidents.

By September 1992, Volkswagen, with the help of the Mexican government, had broken the back of the militant VW Puebla union and imposed a "flexible" agreement. At the same time, the government had also weakened attempts to build a national union of auto workers. The Mexican government had shown multinational corporations that if NAFTA were passed, Mexico could be relied upon to protect their interests.

CASE STUDY #2: TELMEX

Achieving a flexible contract and a cooperative union at the Mexican phone company, TELMEX, was a big success for the forces of "modernization." The bonus was a whole new pro-cooperation union federation.

In the past, Mexico had waged a long struggle against foreign domination of its telephone industry, which had been owned by the Swedish Ericsson Co. and U.S. ITT. The Mexican government had gradually nationalized TELMEX, finally gaining majority control in 1972. When President Salinas decided to sell TELMEX in 1989, he reversed 50 years of government policy.[21]

During the 1950s and 1960s, the Mexican Telephone Workers Union (STRM) was controlled by union bureaucrats, or *charros*, loyal to the government. But during the turbulent 1970s, rank and file opposition forces grew in the union. In April 1976 a strike by women operators led to the ousting of the old *charros* and the election of a more militant and democratic leadership headed by Francisco Hernandez Juarez. Between 1976 and 1987 the STRM carried out five strikes at TELMEX, mostly for higher wages. On each occasion the government sent federal troops to seize and occupy the telephone facilities and force the strikers back to work.[22]

In the 1980s, TELMEX was key to the plans of the ruling party, the PRI, for the party saw telecommunications as central to the integration of a modern Mexico with the U.S. and world economy. Telecommunications linked not only the telephones and faxes but also the computers of international banking and manufacturing networks. Presidential candidate Salinas asserted in October 1987, "Telecommunications will become the cornerstone of the program to modernize Mexico's economy."[23]

NO LEMON

Unlike some nationalized industries, TELMEX was not an economic failure by any means. TELMEX sales in the 1980s exceeded $1 billion annually. In 1988 TELMEX earned more than $200 million and its net profit was over 20 percent. But because the state used TELMEX's profits for its general operating expenses, sufficient funds had not been set aside for modernization, a process that would require billions of dollars. The PRI leaders saw no way to pay for the modernization of TELMEX except foreign investment. They were, moreover, increasingly convinced in principle of the need to privatize.

When the PRI leaders began to think about selling the national industries, they were aware that their strongest opponents would be the unions. Privatization would threaten both the union officials' status and privileges and the workers' wages and conditions. In the case of TELMEX, the government would have to deal with a militant and fairly democratic union.

Candidate Salinas had wooed STRM President Hernandez Juarez, a political independent, with promises of making him an important figure in the coming period. When Hernandez Juarez supported Salinas in the 1988 election, it was a significant shift in the union's policy, a move away from limited political independence, to incorporation into the new administration. For its support the union was given two seats in the Mexican Congress.

By early 1989 Salinas was vaguely suggesting that TELMEX should be privatized. The STRM at first resisted this idea, as well as attempts to modify the contract.

NEW UNIONISM

In privatizating most of the state-owned industries, Salinas used the state's economic, political, and military power to suppress the opposition. In aviation and mining, the state announced its privatizing plans, the workers struck, the enterprise declared bankruptcy, the workers were terminated, and the military moved in to keep order. But in the case of TELMEX, the state decided on a policy of cooptation: they would transform TELMEX into a model enterprise and the STRM into a model of "new-unionism" (neo-sindicalismo).

At some point in early 1989, Salinas and Hernandez Juarez seemed to have arrived at a deal. The STRM would not oppose privatization, and would accept a flexible contract. In exchange, TELMEX would not lay off employees, and Salinas would promote Hernandez Juarez as the leader of a new union federation.

In April 1989 the STRM leaders signed a "Cooperation Agreement." Job classifications were reduced. Workers could be assigned to different steps of the production process and transferred to different departments and jobs, and the company could hire temporaries as needed. Fifty-seven departmental agreements were replaced with a single pay scale. There would be a reduction in force through early retirements, voluntary resignations, and termination of temporaries.

MODERNIZATION + PRIVATIZATION

Salinas moved indirectly toward privatization. He concentrated the discussion on the need to modernize TELMEX, which he linked to the modernization of Mexico, to

social justice, and to political reform. He laid out a challenge to TELMEX: to expand the telephone network by 12 percent, installing 4.5 million new lines; to increase the residential penetration rate from 26 to 38 percent; to expand rural service to all villages of more than 500; to extend a digital network to more than 250,000 large users. The cost: $10 billion over five years. Both economically and technically, these goals were beyond TELMEX's capacity.

Two days later, the Minister of Communications and Transport, accompanied by Hernandez Juarez, announced the decision to privatize TELMEX. Hernandez Juarez, who had once opposed privatization, now supported it.

TELMEX was sold to a consortium made up of a Mexican private group, Southwestern Bell, and France Cable et Radio. The STRM got 4.4 percent of the non-voting shares. The government and the union advertised that telephone workers were now "co-owners."

Not only had the PRI accomplished its goal of privatizing TELMEX with a flexible labor agreement. It had also gotten Hernandez Juarez to play the role of leader of "new-unionism" in Mexico.

Salinas had come into power as a technocrat. He wanted a political alternative to the Confederation of Mexican Workers (CTM) controlled by Fidel Velazquez, who was resisting his economic program. Although the PRI still had control over the CTM, Salinas wanted a less bureaucratic, younger, and more flexible type of unionism that would accept and even help to promote privatization and flexibility. The CTM is considered a dinosaur on these issues: too slow, taking on traditional wage and benefit issues, and unwilling to accept sweeping changes.

With the encouragement of Salinas, Hernandez Juarez led the STRM to join with the Electrical Workers Union, the pilots union, and three smaller unions to form a new labor federation called FESEBES—with Hernandez Juarez as its secretary general. Salinas granted registration to FESEBES after Hernandez Juarez helped negotiate a new contract at Volkswagen.

PRIVATE TELMEX

How did TELMEX fare under new ownership?

For the workers, life changed dramatically. With the new flexible agreement they could be moved from one location to another and from one job to another, even to other cities. Such transfers could be particularly hard on the mainly female operators, many of whom were mothers and sometimes single heads of households. Sometimes job transfers were used to punish union activists. Many wage levels were reduced to a smaller number, frequently to the disadvantage of the employees. A number of former union jobs became "confidential," i.e., non-union, positions. The new digital equipment increased productivity and the workforce was reduced through attrition. At the same time, as part of the agreement to avoid lay-offs, the company sent tens of thousands of workers for training in new technologies.[24]

For the public, prices went up. In December 1990,

the new private company announced two rate increases for private customers, totalling over 20 percent. Free phone calls were reduced from 150 to 67 per month. Long distance rates were raised 36.5 percent. Installation costs remained high at $338 for residential and $580 for business phones. Mexico's phone service had become the most expensive in the world.[25]

For TELMEX stockholders, life has been rosy. Widely promoted in the U.S. by brokers and mutual funds, TELMEX became the most important stock traded on the Mexican stock market, and rose in value, at least until the Chiapas rebellion in January 1994.

Once again, Mexican and foreign businessmen were in charge of the telephone business.

Notes

1. Peter Koorner et al, *The IMF and the Debt Crisis: A Guide to the Third World's Dilemma*, Zed Books, London, 1986; and Cheryl Payer, *The Debt Trap: The IMF and the Third World*, Monthly Review Press, New York, 1974.

2. Michael Kepp, "Cellular activity: Democracy plays a growing role in the Brazilian workplace," *Business Latin America*, November 22, 1993, p. 6.

3. Andrew Zimblast, *Journal of Latin American Studies*, Vol. 24, May 1992, p. 415. Zimblast, a leading authority on the Cuban economy who is rather sympathetic to the Communist government, refers to these circles as "democratic management practices."

4. This point is made by Harry Levenstein, *Labor Organizations in the United States and Mexico: A History of Their Relations*, Greenwood Publishing Company, Westport, Conn., 1971.

5. Dan La Botz, *The Crisis of Mexican Labor*, Praeger, New York, 1988.

6. Dan La Botz, *Mask of Democracy: Labor Suppression in Mexico Today*, South End Press, Boston, 1992.

7. "America's New Industrial Belt: Northern Mexico," Business Section, *New York Times*, March 21, 1993.

8. Sidney Weinbtraub, *Transforming the Mexican Economy: The Salinas Sexenio*, National Planning Association, Washington, D.C., 1990.

9. Dan La Botz, *Mask of Democracy*. See the accounts of the steel industry, Cananea copper workers, and petroleum workers. Also see Alejandro Covarrubias V., *La flexibilidad laboral en Sonora*, El Colegio de Sonora/Fundacion Friedrich Ebert, Hermosillo, Sonora, 1992.

10. Covarrubias, pp. 183-91.

11. Carmen Montero, *Proceso de trabajo y relaciones laborales en la industria de la loza y la ceramica en Mexico*, Friedrich Ebert Stiftung, Mexico, 1992, p. 165.

12. Harley Shaiken, *Mexico in the Global Economy: High Technology and Work Organization in Export Industries*, Center for U.S.-Mexican Studies, San Diego, 1990, pp. x-xi and 3. For a summary of this study see: Harley Shaiken, "Advanced Manufacturing in Mexico: A New International Division of Labor," *Latin American Research Review*, Volume 29, No. 2, 1994, pp. 39-72.

13. Shaiken, pp. 45-71.

14. Shaiken, p. xi.

15. Shaiken, p. 9.

16. Dan La Botz, *Mask*. See my discussion of the Ford Cuautit-lan strike. See also Arnulfo Arteaga, *Proceso de Trabajo y Relaciones Laborales en la Industria Automotriz en Mexico*, Casa Abierta al Tiempo/UAM Iztapalapa/Fundacion Friedrich Ebert, Mexico, 1992.

17. The study mentioned is Steven Rone Wilson, "Continuous Improvement and the New Competition: The Case of U.S., European, and Japanese Firms in the Mexican Maquiladora Industry," Ph.D. Diss., University of Tennessee, 1992. See also: Jane Herring Stanford, "Measuring the Implementation of Employee Involvement in the Maquiladora Industry: A Matched-Pairs Analysis of United States Parent Companies and their Mexican Subsidiaries," Ph.D. Diss., University of North Texas, 1992; James E. Boyce and Manab Thakur, "Participative management in Mexico: the growing maquiladora industry is providing a seed bed in Mexico for less traditional, more innovative management styles," *Business Mexico*, Vol. 5, June 1988, pp. 38-39.

18. Martha H. Peak, "Maquiladoras: Where Quality is a Way of Life," *Management Review*, Vol. 82, March 1993, pp. 19-23.

19. Jeffrey Ryser, "Joint venture mania in Mexico," *Global Finance*, Vol. 7, June 1993, pp. 68-70.

20. I have relied heavily on Graciela Bensusan and Carlos Garcia, "Las relaciones laborales en Volkswagen de Mexico," *La Jornada*, special section "La Jornada Laboral," August 27, 1992 (the article was originally published in December 1990). For the account of the strike I rely on Oscar Alzaga, "El conflicto de VW," *Trabajo y Democracia Hoy*, No. 9, Ano 2, September/October 1992, pp. 4-8. See also three articles by Anthony de Palma, "Painful Lessons for Mexican Labor," *New York Times*, November 13, 1993; "Mexico's Unions, Frail Now, Face Trade Pact Blows," *New York Times*, December 14, 1993; "An Auto Sea Change in Mexico," *New York Times*, November 16, 1993.

21. I rely heavily on: Won-Ho Kim, "The Mexican Regime's Political Strategy in Implementing Economic Reform in Comparative Perspective: A Case Study of the Privatization of the Telephone Industry," Ph. D. Diss., University of Texas at Austin, December 1992.

22. Rodolfo Rojas Zea, ed., *Tres huelgas de telefonistas*, Editorial Uno, S.A., Mexico, D.F., 1980. See also: Dan La Botz, *Mask of Democracy*, South End Press, Boston, 1992, pp. 126-30.

23. Kim, p. 114, citing *El Financiero*, October 15, 1987.

24. Interview with maintenance technician and STRM member Rosario Ortiz in Mexico City, December 18, 1990.

25. Kim, pp. 158-163.

Working Smart:
A Union Guide to Participation Programs and Reengineering
Labor Notes • 7435 Michigan Ave. • Detroit, MI 48210 • (313) 842-6262

Chapter 30

The Swedish Model

To attract reluctant workers to their factories, Swedish employers tried to build worker-friendly plants. At one Volvo plant, a team of workers built a whole car. The pressure of the assembly line was replaced, however, by peer pressure. And when unemployment rose in the 1990s, Volvo closed the "humanized" plant, and adopted lean production methods instead. A less-known truck plant, meanwhile, also adopted the group style of work. In this case, however, a strong union meant that workers kept their knowledge of production to themselves. Management found that the less they poked into the "black box" of workers' job knowledge, the better the plant ran.

by Lars Henriksson

"BORED PEOPLE BUILD BAD CARS. That's why we're doing away with the assembly line." That's how SAAB, the Swedish car producer, advertised in the U.S. in the 1970s. In 1990 German car buyers too could read large ads saying: "Ford invented the assembly line. Volvo abolished it. For natural reasons."

Although these ads would certainly not have been possible in Sweden, they seem to have made a lasting impression on how the Swedish car industry is perceived internationally. Some progressive academics who have not been completely bewitched by the Japanese model refer to the "Swedish model" as the other option. The Swedish way of building cars is supposed to be the humane—yet productive—alternative.

But just like the Swedish model of the economy (a welfare state, high standard of living, relative equality, cooperation between labor and capital), the Swedish model of work organization is also surrounded by myths. There are lessons to be learned from the Swedish experience for all who are trying to come up with a counter-strategy to management's present offensive.

WE ARE PEOPLE, NOT MACHINES

The Swedish experiments with work organization come out of a particular history. In 1969, Swedish society was shaken by wildcat strikes in the mines in the far north of the country. (This was at about the same time as the famous GM Lordstown wildcats and others in the U.S.)

These strikes showed in a flash that Sweden was far from the perfect classless society that the official representatives of state, politics, and labor claimed. The strike was followed by others, and a wave of radicalization swept the country.

The miners struck for higher wages, but behind the strike was a much deeper discontent. They revolted against an increasingly authoritarian management, more sophisticated time-study systems, and a general management offensive designed to increase productivity through tighter control and supervision.

The core of the discontent was expressed in a slogan that has lived in the hearts of many of us ever since: "We are humans, not machines!"

This workers' revolt led to much debate and many projects on management-worker relations and the organization of work. For example, the so-called "Volvo Report" made in 1975 by SAF, the employers' organization, mentions the wildcat strikes at Volvo as a major reason to change the organization of the labor process. At about the same time, Pehr Gyllenhammar, for 20 years the emperor of Volvo, wrote a book that condemned the assembly line as inhumane.

Group organization soon became the buzzword, the antidote to worker alienation. This was true not only in auto but in most industries. Even the self-managing group was a popular concept, appealing to the spontaneous feeling among workers that we don't need anybody giving us orders all the time.

After the Swedish government tightened up on immigration policies in 1967, management had even more reason to make the factories appealing. Previously, the

Lars Henriksson is a union representative at the Volvo plant in Gothenburg, Sweden.

auto industry had recruited immigrants in large numbers. But with the supply of immigrants cut down, the companies faced a labor shortage.

In the boom years of the 1980s it was often hard for the carmakers even to get the lines running in the mornings. The extreme turnover and absenteeism were constant issues of discussion. The employment expectancy of a newly-hired worker at Volvo was about six months. After this time, most of the workers, who were very young, would look around for a "real" job or go back to school.

All this, plus the fact that both SAAB and Volvo made enormous profits and saw no end to their expansion, led each company, in the mid-1980s, to build a new plant entirely designed for group organization. There were no assembly lines, and the groups would each build one-fourth, one-half, or even an entire car.

Both plants were located at the sites of newly closed shipyards, Volvo's in Uddevalla on the west coast and SAAB's in Malmo in the south. Both were heavily subsidized by the government.

Thus the Swedish model of work organization was management's answer to a rebellion among workers. At first this rebellion consisted of a conscious, collective union movement involving strikes, and later, a more unconscious, individual movement, the "blue collar blues," where people, due to the ease of getting another job, voted with their feet and fled the assembly line.

This new model contained concessions to workers' demands for more humane jobs. It began as an attempt to control the discontent and to overcome it, *but it was also an attempt to increase productivity*.

The companies were looking for a new way to increase productivity because the increasingly complex process of auto manufacturing no longer responded as well to the old Taylorist techniques. The increasing variety of cars, with different markets and options, meant that every car coming down the line required a different set of tasks. It was harder for management to "balance the line" so that each worker's time was filled up on every car. A new method of getting workers to work 60 seconds out of every minute needed to be found.

In addition, the companies were eager to get rid of white-collar, non-value-added labor. Thus the move to have blue-collar workers take over more of the white-collar work—in the name of "humanization" and "more responsibility."

Finally, with such high turnover, it was impossible to achieve high quality—except by using hordes of repair workers. Management needed to attract a workforce that planned to stay long enough to learn the jobs well.

THE SWEDISH MODEL— A BALANCE SHEET

What, then, are the lessons of these decades of experimenting with work organization, and even building whole new plants with the goal of humanizing factory labor?

Like everything else, such a balance sheet has two sides: that of the employers and that of workers. In Sweden, the employers have demonstrated their conclusions in a very brutal way: both SAAB and Volvo have closed down their "humanized" car plants. When the economic crisis hit Sweden, the bosses no longer had any need to make their working conditions attractive. Although it was never said out loud, in a society with 10% unemployment, the need to compete for labor is greatly reduced.

Labor's balance sheet is more complicated. Like the employers, we too have an interest in producing good quality products in a reasonably rational way—though our definitions of these terms differ a lot from those of the bosses. Quality is only interesting to them if it increases the profitability of the company; it has nothing to do with filling a need in a better way. Likewise, a system that hurts and wears people out, physically and mentally, is not "rational" to us. Workers have demands and needs that are completely contrary to the demands of the employers. We have a lot more to demand from the way production is arranged than the bosses do.

KALMAR— THE CHANGE THAT WASN'T

Every Swedish company with any self-respect had some sort of program for self-managing groups in the 1970s and 1980s. I will limit myself, however, to Volvo's car plants in Kalmar and Uddevalla, partly because they are the most widely known examples of the Swedish model, partly because the car industry has such great similarities worldwide, and partly because I myself work at Volvo and have learned a few things about these plants over the years.

Opened in 1974, Volvo's car assembly plant in Kalmar, a small city on the southeastern coast of Sweden with comparatively high unemployment, was the jewel in the crown. It was built to be a prototype of what the bosses called "new plants."

The traditional line was abolished. Automatic Guided Vehicles (AGVs) transported the car bodies to the different stations, where work was done in long cycles (12-20 minutes). Group organization was the key word. The plant was even physically divided into smaller units. The purpose was to give people a group identity. (And, not to forget, to prevent protests and strikes from spreading from one part of the plant to another and closing the whole plant down...)

In 1977, less than four years after the plant opened, the Swedish auto industry was hit by a severe crisis. At Kalmar this led to a wave of "rationalizations." MOST, a new time-study system specially designed to be used on long-cycle jobs like those at Kalmar, was introduced. This made it easier for the company to appropriate the short cuts the workers had devised. The effect was a substantial speed-up. The time to assemble a car was reduced by 1.5 worker-hours. The average degree of utilization of work-

ing time rose to 95 percent, as compared to 80 percent at Volvo's main plant at Gothenburg with a traditional assembly line.

As time went by, most of the features that distinguished Kalmar from traditional plants—buffers that were controlled by the workers, parallel assembly—were abolished. The plant became more and more like any other assembly plant, with the AGVs transformed into a very expensive conveyor belt.

The result was, of course, the return of all the traditional problems of the assembly line: work injuries, high levels of absenteeism, and high turnover.

UDDEVALLA—WORKERS' PARADISE?

The Uddevalla plant is more complicated to evaluate, primarily because it existed for only five years. Of those years, at most one or two were at normal production. Moreover, workers from the plant give very different pictures of it.

Unlike Kalmar, Uddevalla was consciously built to make it impossible for the line system to reappear. The plant consisted of six parallel shops, with eight teams of 8-10 workers in each shop. Each team built a whole car, and each team ordered the bodies to the work area themselves. Their parts arrived on AGVs in kits from a special materials shop. In order to improve ergonomics, the cars were built in big fixtures that made it possible to turn the bodies 360 degrees.

The teams had no foremen or supervisors. They elected their own team leader who was the main contact with the head of the shop.

The plant was built with the involvement of work sociologists and the union, and the official version talked of "re-skilling" car workers. They even talked of car workers at different levels of skill as "apprentices," "journeymen," and "masters," to indicate that car assembly would once again be a skilled craft.

Building cars without an assembly line was no new or unique feature invented by Volvo. Before 1914 all cars were built that way, and cars like Lamborghini and Ferrari still are.

But in 1914 Henry Ford discovered that it was possible to reduce the time needed to assemble a car by 90 percent if the process was organized on an assembly line. This transformed cars from a luxury industry to the industry most associated with the concept of mass production.

The assembly line has since been the main tool used by the bosses *to make people work harder than they want to*. When it comes to forcing people to work, the line has an almost magical capability. When you work on a line you have only two options: to take on the job that comes to you or to refuse it—that is, either complete submission or revolt. And even though revolts occur now and then, both on the individual and the collective level, in the long run, the general rule for the line worker is submission.

In the Uddevalla plant the teams themselves decided when to start building a new car; the technical system did not force them. But since Volvo, as opposed to Lamborghini or Ferrari, is engaged in mass production, they had to keep up the work pace in order to keep up the profits.

The method chosen in Uddevalla to take the place of the assembly line was peer pressure.

To begin with, the wage system was designed to create pressure both between the teams and within them. In each shop there was a substantial bonus which was dependent on the quantity produced. If one team failed to meet the required number of cars per week, all teams lost their bonus. This caused tension and pressure between workers without management having to interfere.

Another stress-creating measure was that management put the responsibility of meeting production goals on the team leaders. They transferred this pressure onto their co-workers, especially those who, for some reason, could not keep up the pace needed to produce the required quantity.

The great attention directed towards the plant from the media and from researchers also affected the atmosphere. It helped create a pioneer spirit that made some people feel special, and also the feeling that the plant was threatened by "traditionalists," inside and outside the company. This made it important to stick together and "show 'em we can make it." Critical workers were told, even by co-workers, not to speak to journalists visiting the plant.

The system caused pressure from the very beginning and was probably the main cause of the substantial turnover during the first year. But as long as the plant was regarded as being in its start-up period, it was bearable to most people. When management's demands rose, however, after the summer of 1992, the pressure increased sharply. Kaizen consultants were brought into the plant, and worker-hours needed to build a car dropped.

The way Uddevalla was built no doubt made it possible for people to do the manual labor necessary in mass production in a more humane way than the assembly line. The plant's most important achievement, perhaps, was to show that it was possible to build cars in a more humane way.

But even if the Uddevalla system was considered superior to line work by most of those who tried both (not all, though!), it showed that it was also possible to create the same pressure and high work intensity as in a traditional plant.

Had the plant been allowed to continue, it quite likely would have reproduced many of the problems it was designed to solve.

But in the fall of 1992, Volvo decided to close both Kalmar and Uddevalla. The official reason was over-capacity. Both plants were small, and neither was a complete plant. They were just assembly plants, with no stamping, welding, or paint shops. Production was moved to Volvo's main, large plant in Gothenburg.

But the whole scenario in Sweden had changed. With unemployment soaring to a 10 percent level for the first time since the 1930s, and social cutbacks that, among other things, lowered sick benefits, the old problems of turnover and absenteeism were taken care of without the employers having to do anything at all.

Suddenly it was no competitive advantage for a plant to be more humane. Workers had to stay put even at jobs they disliked. At Volvo's traditional plant, all projects concerning alternative ways of building cars were stopped. The assembly line was triumphing again.

BACK TO BUSINESS AGAIN

The shift away from the Swedish model has been taking place at all levels of Swedish society, and the workplace is no exception. As unemployment rose many of the bosses felt relieved. They no longer had to pretend interest in the well-being of workers. Instead, they could devote all their interest to what they were there for in the first place: profit.

First at SAAB and then at Volvo, the bosses were all too willing to learn the language of lean production. Massive rationalizations took place. The management-by-stress bible, *The Machine that Changed the World*, appeared on the desks of managers at all levels. Many of the props of management-by-stress, like kaizen and andon systems, were brought in. "Teams" (at the beginning they even used the English word!) replaced the old "groups." Individual wage systems, where the foreman decides a part of the workers's wage, were imposed.

Too often, this development took place in cooperation with the unions. For example, the closure of the Volvo plants was done with the approval of the joint committee of the blue-collar unions. The Kalmar local even voted for the closing of its own plant! All was justified in the name of competitiveness and in order to save jobs.

Sweden is rapidly becoming a "normal" country. Does this mean that the 20 years spent discussing the humanizing of the workplace were just a parenthesis? A luxury problem created by lack of workers? The bosses' answer would most definitely be yes. (It's important to note, though, that many of the changes introduced in the 1970s and 1980s are still in effect and even expanding, just as most parts of the Swedish welfare state still exist, though threatened. A society is not changed overnight.)

Having some control and influence over our daily work, or having a job that is more than just a necessary evil you want to get away from as soon as possible, or having a job that is less monotonous than the assembly line—for workers these goals are not luxury items. They are as much a worker's right as health and safety rules, union rights, the right to be treated as a human being, or other things that employers see only as obstacles to competitiveness.

The employers are right about this. Every demand from our side *is* an obstacle to competitiveness, or maximizing corporate profits, to put it in plain English. But this fact has not stopped unions from demanding decent wages and working conditions earlier in our history, and it should not stop us now either.

THE TEAM CHALLENGE

Today management worldwide often presents the changes they want to carry through in the workplace in terms of job enrichment, teamwork, or high performance.

It would be a completely wrong answer to this challenge to say: "We don't want to do anything else besides just tighten those four nuts and two bolts the rest of our lives. Anything else would be lining up with management and treason to the cause of the working class."

First, this answer is stupid. It is not by chance that skilled workers are mostly better off than unskilled. The more you know, the more valuable you are on the market—and, at least potentially, the more powerful you are.

Second, and more important, unions are very likely to lose the battle of hearts and minds to the employers unless they can offer something more interesting than just a life of tightening nuts and bolts. Unions should not let management portray *us* as the last defenders of Taylorism.

A TALE OF TWO PLANTS

As mentioned, Uddevalla and Kalmar were far from the only places in Sweden where new ways of organizing work were introduced. But they were definitely the ones boosted the most by both the company and the media. In Sweden most people have heard of Volvo's car plant in Uddevalla. But very few have heard of the truck plant in Umea in the north of Sweden.

In this plant, just as in Uddevalla, workers are organized in groups that are responsible for the whole process. There are no foremen and no inspectors. The workers order material and arrange delivery of the complete product (truck cabs).

The difference between the plants is who is in charge. Of course, the bosses are in charge at both places.

But at Uddevalla, one of the preconditions of lean production was fulfilled. Everything was visible to management. The shop manager knew exactly when and how everything was done. There was no place to hide. The freedom of the groups to make decisions existed only as long as their decisions corresponded to the wishes of management.

At both plants, the hours needed to produce one unit have constantly been reduced. At Uddevalla, this meant increasing pressure on the workers and more production for the company.

At Umea, the new group-based organization meant the opposite. Because of their increased knowledge and control of the production process, the workers could, at least for periods of time, turn the process into something like a "black box" for management. Management soon found that this black box worked better the less they tried to poke into it. By refusing total management control and by keeping knowledge to themselves, the workers used the new forms of work organization to improve their working conditions rather than to increase the work pace.

The difference between the two plants lies in the respective balance of strength between the workers and the company.

At Uddevalla, the group system was introduced when the plant was built; there was no history of workers' col-lectivity. From the first to the last day, despite all that was said about workers' independence, management kept tight control. The union was involved from above. It was even built in to the plant: the workers inherited the former union leaders from the closed-down shipyard! The union did not respond on the shop floor to the company's demands; the company was free to impose its will. Many of the workers strongly identified with the plant. Therefore most short cuts by the workers did not, as in a traditional plant, remain the property of the workers in the shape of small breaks, social life, etc., but were appropriated by the company through the constant drive to meet quotas. Which is exactly the core of kaizen.

At Umea, there was and is a strong and militant union, both on the shop floor and in the leadership. The workers have managed, through old-fashioned unionism, to use the new forms of work organization to increase their own autonomy and independence.

Of course, this situation is not stable—as in any workplace, there is always a tug of war between the conflicting interests of the employer and the employees. Especially at model change time, the company tries, and sometimes succeeds, to speed up production and regain control. But the fact remains: the workers and their union have used the company's own scheme—the group-based organization of work and group autonomy—not only to improve their working conditions but also to increase their independence. They have taken the company's ideas and developed them in a workers' direction.

MAIN LESSON

The comparison between these two plants contains many of the lessons to be learned from the Swedish experience. The main lesson is that the important thing is not how management has organized the workplace. It is instead the strength of the union and the consciousness of the membership. When these exist, the workers can take on management's challenge in a way that can be described as "taking the cheese from the mousetrap without getting caught." How far this tactic can be carried out depends on the concrete conditions in the workplace, its history and traditions, and, in the final analysis, the balance of forces between the company and the union.

The key word here is autonomy. In considering which tactics to employ, we need first to ask ourselves: How do we want the workplace arranged to increase our independence from the company and the solidarity within the membership?

Our strategy should be to fight to keep as much knowledge to ourselves as possible and make the production process as hidden from the bosses as possible. This is the antithesis of management-by-stress, because it is focused on workers' control.

Working Smart:
A Union Guide to Participation Programs and Reengineering
Labor Notes • 7435 Michigan Ave. • Detroit, MI 48210 • (313) 842-6262

Chapter 31

Choosing a Strategy

There are no "instant mashed potatoes" answers to participation programs. A union response to such a program must be part of an overall strategic plan and mobilize the members. The five possible stances toward a participation program are ignoring it, total acceptance, protective involvement, mobilized involvement, and active opposition.

THE WRONG STARTING POINT

IN THIS SECTION we discuss union strategies for dealing with participation programs. We want to stress as strongly as we can: **the starting point in your thinking should not be management's latest program.**

All too often management suddenly confronts a union with a proposal for a participation program, and the union feels compelled to make a quick answer. Some unions think the best they can do is damage control. Others focus on the new program itself—maybe do some research on the particular consultant involved or scrutinize the terminology.

Unfortunately, unions that proceed this way are off on the wrong foot. In fact, they've shot themselves in the foot—they have allowed management to set the agenda and define the terrain.

Your management did not adopt a particular participation program—let's call it Quality Action Committee for Putting us On Top (QuACPOT)—because QuACPOT was universally acknowledged to be the best in the field. If your managers have anything on the ball, they developed an overall strategic plan for the organization, determined what they wanted to achieve in the next several years, and identified what they felt they needed to achieve those goals. They then went to the participation program cafeteria and picked out the policies that best fit their strategic plan, and called it QuACPOT.

The only chance a union has to respond successfully to the participation program is to do its own strategic planning. This starts with 1) understanding what is behind management's actions, 2) recognizing that management is not always monolithic, aware of its own best interests, or competent, and 3) estimating future management actions. But it goes on to factor in the economic and political environment, health of the union, trends in the industry, nature of the workforce in the industry, resources for support, and so on. In *A Union Strategy Guide for Labor-*

Management Participation Programs, the pamphlet which is the companion to this book, we describe a process that a union can use to develop its own strategic plan, and, flowing from that, a plan to deal with a participation program.

Only when the union has analyzed its total situation and planned a *general* union strategy can it make any sense of the possible options for dealing with participation programs.

SHOULD WE PARTICIPATE?

If you've read Section III, you're aware of the many dangers that participation programs pose for unions. In the next chapter, we talk about the pitfalls of certain strategies for involvement. Taken as a whole, these dangers may make a good case for a union refusing to participate at all—the "say no" option.

But life is not that simple. The program may have appealing aspects, protection against some of the dangers may seem to be provided, significant sections of the union may want to get involved or at least give it a try. Often management will try to run its program with or without the union's involvement (see chapter 37, for example). In these cases, "say no" may not be the best alternative. See section 6 of the *Strategy Guide* for more thoughts on making this decision. Often unions conclude that their participation in some form is simply the best of a set of bad alternatives.

No strategy is risk-free. In the real world, everything is risky and everything is interrelated. Compensating for one problem will likely cause others. The key is to prepare to take risks, know what you are dealing with, and try to shift the problems into areas you can handle.

INSTANT MASHED POTATOES

Late-night TV tempts us with ads for quick cheap fixes: knives that can cut anything, easy strategies for making a fortune, phone calls that can solve any problem. They're appealing, and so are simple recipes for a union response to participation programs. Life would be so much easier if we could just buy and apply a package of five collective bargaining demands that would keep the union from harm. Labor Notes staffer Mary Hollens calls such formulas "instant mashed potatoes."

There are good reasons that unionists are attracted to the instant mashed potatoes approach. The pressure on union leaders to get quick results is enormous.

In contrast, strategies—like ours—that begin with analyzing the over-all situation, starting a local-wide education program, and challenging management on many fronts may seem just too difficult, if not impossible.

Unfortunately, a quickie prefabricated plan is not likely to get the results you seek. A participation program never happens in isolation; it is going on at the same time as many other management initiatives. For that reason, there are no short cuts. Unions cannot expect to solve the participation problem in isolation from their other problems.

(Of course, it is often necessary for the union to respond immediately to management's announcement of a new program. You may need to get out a quick leaflet to the membership to let them know the union is on top of the situation, or to make a demand that will buy the union some time.)

Another problem in choosing a strategy is that many union leaders are looking for one they can carry out by themselves. They hope to discover some "magic bullet" contract language they can bargain, for example. The state of the labor movement is such that many leaders are accustomed to a "do-it-yourself" approach, without a lot of activity on the part of the rank and file. This is sometimes called the "servicing model" of unionism. A far-reaching and ambitious strategy that trains and mobilizes the membership may seem irrelevant when union meeting attendance is down to the die-hards and most members feel beaten down.

But like it or not, a strategy that relies solely on the officers is not likely to work when it comes to participation programs. Such programs make their appeal to rank and file members, often on an individual basis. Therefore the union's strategies must address the rank and file as well. The most brilliant contract language in the world is not worth much if rank and filers are ignoring it and joining in with management's program, each with his or her own individual goal.

Participation programs exploit workers' healthy desire to be involved at work; the union is not likely to win members' hearts and minds without an involvement strategy of its own.

TELL THE WHOLE STORY

We caution against a common practice in the labor movement: calling necessity a virtue and defeat a victory.

Unions are on the defensive these days; management's superior power can cause almost any union to get stuck with a bad contract or a bad participation program. But because unions are political institutions, it is always tempting for leaders to put a positive face on agreements. When the agreement in reality is a bad one, or as usually happens, a mixed one, claiming a pure victory promotes a distorted version of the union's goals, confuses members, and makes them cynical.

Say the union has been forced to sign an agreement that strips away work rules, commits the union to helping management cut the workforce, but includes some language about "union-management partnership." Which is wiser:

Union leaders say, "We lost this round. We fought, but the balance of forces was against us. Now it's up to all of us to make the best we can out of the situation. Here's our plan for taking over the team meetings..." OR

Union leaders say, "We have entered a new era of union influence in this company. In this competitive global economy, management recognizes that they need us. Our partnership will help us reach our goals more effectively than ever."

Rare is the member who is fooled by this sort of

To Participate or Not? (Short Form)

I. a. The employers have the upper hand.

b. Participation programs are designed to weaken unions.

c. Therefore unions have to choose their strategies toward such programs carefully.

II. a. Refusing to participate is a valid position.

b. Most of what is promised by participation programs, including teamwork, empowerment, participation in "management's rights" issues, are possible through the union or by allowing workers more control over their jobs.

c. Where a union can do it, saying no is usually (but not always) the best choice.

d. But these days few unions are truly in a position to say no.

e. Even where it can say no, the union has to do more; it still must win the hearts and minds battle and must organize and mobilize the members.

III. a. Choosing strategic involvement is also a valid position.

b. But to succeed at this strategy means not fostering illusions about what the employer wants or the nature of the program.

c. Involvement turns out to be more difficult than first appears. Too often "involvement" means the union gets some nice words in exchange for endorsing the employer's program. (As someone put it: "a management program, jointly delivered.")

d. It is one thing to participate in a program. It is quite another to embrace it as your own.

"The lions have the day off. We're throwing you to the productivity analysts instead."

rhetoric. Members can understand the ambiguity of complex situations. Unions seldom win everything. By facing this fact directly we are better able to prepare for the problems down the road.

For example, chapter 37 describes the approach of a Quality Network group in one transmission plant. Management wanted the group to help them cut jobs and speed up the work. The members approached the problem with a collective bargaining mind-set and did a good job of derailing management's plan. But their victory had its potential problems. It is possible that management could take the productivity improvements the group made to a sister transmission plant, and hold them over those workers' heads. In other words, they could whipsaw. Problems like this need to be discussed out front.

Of course, it's not just the members who need to understand the negatives. When leaders keep repeating that an agreement is a victory, they tend to convince themselves. As a result, they fail to prepare for the dangers in the new situation and may even end up defending their "success" long after it has created big problems for the union.

FIVE STANCES

Unions' responses to participation programs fall into five general categories:
1. Ignoring (or passive opposition)
2. Total Acceptance
3. Protective Involvement
4. Mobilized Involvement
5. Active Opposition

When management first began participation programs years ago, it was fairly common for unions to ignore or passively oppose them. This "strategy" didn't and doesn't work. Unions have learned the hard way that these programs will not benefit workers without a great deal of hard work from the union. Nor do the programs usually die of their own weight. Instead, specific programs may

do their damage, become discredited, and fade away—and then be reincarnated with new names and new twists.

"Total acceptance" means just that—the union essentially puts itself behind a management-initiated participation program. Union leaders may genuinely believe the program is in the best interests of the membership, that a Quality of Work Life program, for instance, will improve working conditions *and* product quality. Sometimes the union joins in an arrangement where it takes full responsibility for a joint program, under the banner of "partnership." Examples are the National Partnership Council adopted by federal employee unions or the massive jointness structures in the auto industry.

At the level of language only, there are certain similarities between "partnership" and "mobilized involvement." Advocates of both approaches say the union should take an active role in the program. But in practice, partnership and mobilized involvement are altogether different. Mobilized involvement actually shares a common outlook and activities with "active opposition." The emphasis in both is on unified and mobilized union members and leaders. These are the basis for the campaigns in the *Strategy Guide*.

Active opposition usually requires some serious membership education. Chapters 20, 21, 23, 26, 27, and 40 give examples of unions that opposed participation programs successfully. See also chapter 5 of *A Troublemaker's Handbook* for some winning oppositional tactics.

In the next chapter we discuss the pitfalls of "protective involvement," probably the most common union response to participation programs. In chapter 33, we go into detail about "mobilized involvement," which includes the collective bargaining model. Chapter 34 discusses a union approach to some of the substantive issues that may arise out of or along with participation programs. Chapter 35 gives advice on how to confront the question of training. Chapter 36 uses three locals as case studies of how unions have responded to lean production, or management-by-stress. Chapter 37 describes how one quality group used the collective bargaining model. Chapter 38 portrays a local that has gone to great lengths to maintain its independence in the program, including eight hours of "solidarity schooling" for each member. In chapter 39, the local used education and organizing around the participation program to rebuild the local overall. In chapter 40, the union organized a successful boycott of a quality program. See also Section IV for advice on legal strategies.

In chapters 13-16 and 32 you will find exercises you can use in your membership education plan. Many of these were developed in the Labor Notes Team Concept Schools and the many other workshops that Labor Notes has held. For more on the Team Concept Schools, see chapter 41.

Working Smart:
A Union Guide to Participation Programs and Reengineering
Labor Notes • 7435 Michigan Ave. • Detroit, MI 48210 • (313) 842-6262

Chapter 32

Pitfalls of Protective Involvement

The protections unions commonly negotiate don't really protect them from the risks of participation programs. Keeping collective bargaining subjects off limits backfires on the union. Job losses caused by the program can be disguised through attrition. Making the program voluntary can serve to divide the union. Stewards cannot keep on top of all the groups they have the right to look in on. Even union-appointed facilitators are subject to heavy management influence.

UNIONS' MOST COMMON REACTION to participation programs has been "protective involvement."[1] This means accepting management's initiative on the participation program in exchange for an understanding that the legitimate interests of the union will be protected. A list of rules is drawn up to protect those interests.

This approach, and even the list of rules, has been remarkably stable over the past 15 years, even while the participation programs themselves have changed substantially. In 1978 Irving Bluestone, the UAW vice president who was one of the early union backers of QWL, declared that seven fundamental conditions were necessary for union participation.[2]

The list evolved slightly, and in 1982 the Communications Workers (CWA) and AT&T came up with a joint Statement of Principles (order changed):

1. Collective bargaining and the grievance procedure are off limits for QWL; worker participation is a *separate* process.

2. The effort is *joint*, the union is involved as an equal partner from planning through implementation.

3. No one can be laid off or downgraded as a result of ideas which come from the participation process.

4. It is *voluntary* for the union, the company and each individual worker.

5. The goals of the process include *human satisfaction* and *efficiency*.

These are the principles, according to Glenn Watts, then CWA president, that separate the good programs from the union-busting ones, so they "can be used as a kind of litmus test. If employers accept these principles in writing, we have a good basis from which to move forward."[3]

Two other rules are also often included in such lists:

6. Stewards can attend any meeting in their jurisdiction.

7. Facilitators must be acceptable to the union.

There's nothing wrong with these guidelines, as far as they go. The problem is that they seem to protect the union and give it some power over the program, when in reality they do little. If a union relies on rules such as these to form its strategy, it will be misled by a false sense of security. The list above didn't help the CWA much. (See chapters 10 and 24. The telephone industry was the largest source of job loss in the United States in 1993-94, and CWA leaders characterize the QWL program at AT&T as a "trap" and a "failure.")[4]

Let's examine each of these guidelines to understand where the problems are:

False Security Guideline #1. Drawing a line between collective bargaining and the participation program.

Since participation programs began, many unions have believed that their best protection was to make sure the programs didn't encroach on collective bargaining or the grievance procedure. Circles were expressly prohibited from discussing grievances or contractual issues. This is one of the most common clauses in union agreements about participation.

The impulse to protect collective bargaining is certainly healthy. But when unions create a wall to protect collective bargaining, they paradoxically end up harming the union more than helping it. The old maxim that walls keep in as well as keep out applies here.

Many unionists covered by the National Labor Relations Act (NLRA) have the mistaken impression that there

Mandatory vs. Permissive

The National Labor Relations Act does make an important distinction between *mandatory* and *permissive* subjects of bargaining. The law *requires* management (and the union) to negotiate about "wages, hours, and other terms and conditions of employment." These, by themselves, cover a lot of territory. But beyond these issues, the law *allows* unions and management to negotiate about any subject and make any agreement as long as the agreement itself is not illegal.

Thus it is possible for the parties to negotiate what products or services the company should produce, what equipment and processes should be used, and even executive salaries. However, since these are permissive subjects, the union cannot insist that the company bargain over them, nor can it take negotiations to impasse or strike over these issues.

Over the years the mandatory category has broadened considerably, as unions advanced into areas previously thought untouchable. For example, the NLRB and the courts once viewed pensions and contracting out as permissive, but now call them mandatory. In addition, in practice unions have learned to bargain effectively over permissive issues, even though technically the union cannot strike or close down bargaining over them. After all, most bargaining covers a package of issues. For example, the UAW has managed to raise pensions and benefits for previously retired workers—a clearly non-mandatory subject.

Sometimes bargainers will cite a "management rights" clause in the contract as the reason certain issues cannot be addressed in bargaining. But such clauses do not flow from divine rights or legal rights. They are nothing more than a part of the contract.

A Service Employees contract contains a typical clause:

All management functions and responsibilities *which the Hospital has not expressly modified or restricted by a specific provision of the Agreement are retained and vested exclusively in the Hospital.* (emphasis added)

Without limiting the generality of the foregoing, the Hospital reserves to itself the right to establish and administer Policies and Procedures relating to [a long list ranging from patient care to education and training, job descriptions, classifications, qualifications, and the size and composition of the work force].[5]

The union can take anything away from management's rights simply by negotiating it as part of the contract. In fact, the Service Employees negotiated a pathbreaking training program in spite of the clause above (see chapter 35). Even while a contract is in force, any so-called management rights item can be negotiated and changed if the company chooses or is pushed to do so. And if a company allows an issue to be discussed in a quality team but not in a collective bargaining session or in a meeting between a supervisor and a steward, that is only management's choice, not required by the law.

The laws for public employees are different, varying from state to state. See chapter 19 for the new rules on what federal employee unions can bring to the table.

are issues open to their union in participation programs that cannot legally be taken up in collective bargaining. They hope the participation program will allow the union to break new ground or get "two bites on the apple." Often unions point to the possibility of getting into areas they think are off-limits because of a "management's rights" clause in the contract.

In fact, any issue that can come to a quality circle or a problem-solving task force can also be discussed in a formal union-management collective bargaining session (see the box).

In practice, the supposedly firm collective bargaining line is very often violated. The list of topics actually discussed in participation groups overlaps greatly with bargaining demands. A 1984 study found that 50 percent of the programs listed in a Labor Department resource guide explicitly dealt with mandatory bargaining subjects. An additional 26 percent apparently dealt with such subjects, even though they had guidelines stating they were excluded.[6] One review of all studies of participation and work redesign carried out since the 1970s found that "despite their name, quality circles frequently deal with subjects other than quality, for example, work flow, productivity, safety, and employee welfare."[7]

Many union leaders try to draw the line between what is specifically covered in the contract—the union's turf—and everything else—the participation program's turf. The problem with this approach is that it is exactly what management wants—to marginalize the union. The union is defining its turf as the narrowest possible conception of unionism—the contract itself. In reality, the union's reach is much broader—or should be.

The union represents its members through letters of understanding between contracts, health and safety procedures, the grievance procedure, and enforcement of past practices. Union methods include not only formal negotiations by elected representatives but also group pressure on supervisors, work stoppages, work-to-rules, and other semi-organized methods of worker influence. Any issue can be handled through one of these union channels in addition to or instead of the contract (unless the union has waived further bargaining via a "zipper" clause).

When the union draws the collective bargaining line, it is saying, in effect, that it won't try to expand its territory. Union leaders seem to be reinforcing the media view: "The union may be appropriate for dealing with old issues, but the new issues such as technology and how work is organized require new institutions—management's institutions." If these are separate, non-union issues, then the logical conclusion is that they need separate, non-union structures, with different people to handle them. The result: a boom in parallel structures.

Nothing helps make management's case that the union is a dinosaur, appropriate only to yesterday's battles and irrelevant to restructuring for the 21st century more, than for the union to make the same case.

False Security Guideline #2. The effort is joint, the union is involved as an equal partner from planning through implementation.

We dealt with the dangers of partnership and jointness in chapter 15. In chapter 33 we suggest some strategies for dealing with joint programs.

False Security Guideline #3. No one can be laid off or downgraded as a result of ideas which come from the participation process.

This guideline is almost universal. Sometimes it's stated more strongly: no jobs will be lost as a result of suggestions that come from the program.

In practice the agreement means little. Management does not need to be so crude as to say, "Great idea, Higgins, we'll lay off Jones and Smith tomorrow!" Attrition is usually quite sufficient to eliminate any jobs that become unnecessary because of a quality circle's suggestion.

And if attrition is not working fast enough to downsize the workforce, management can nudge it along. Tolerance for absenteeism, medical restrictions, or injuries can decrease; buy-outs can be offered; work can be made harder.

False Security Guideline #4. The program is voluntary for the union, the company, and each individual worker.

While it seems to protect individual rights, this guideline can divide the membership. When only some members participate, management can provide its favored few with extra perks. Often the two sides become polarized. The non-participants consider the circle members "company sucks," and the circle members call the outsiders "dinosaurs" or "professional complainers." By sponsoring the idea that the program is an individual question, the union seems to endorse both positions. Management, of course, has no objection to dividing the union.

Exercise

What's Possible in Collective Bargaining?

Objectives: To establish the potential breadth of collective bargaining; to clarify the concepts of *permissive* and *mandatory*.

Time: 15-30 minutes

This exercise is for unions covered by the National Labor Relations Act. The issues may be slightly different for workers in other countries, government employees, and those covered under the Railway Labor Act.

1. The leader asks the group: "What kind of issues do you think people *do* talk about or *should* talk about in their teams (or quality circles, or TQM meetings)?"

The leader writes the responses on a flipchart in two columns, mandatory subjects of bargaining on one side, permissive subjects on the other. These are not labeled, however. Do not explain the basis for your choosing between columns at this point. If a topic is ambiguous, say so, post it in one column, and draw an arrow to the opposite column.

If someone comments that they think a particular topic is inappropriate for discussion in a team, put a mark near it and say you will come back to it later.

Typical responses might be:

Ventilation	Reducing scrap
Absentee replacement	Scheduling machine maintenance
⟷	Work assignments
⟷	Holiday party
Health and safety	Errors on forms
Dress code	Vending machines
VDT screen glare	Flex-time
	Mismanagement
	Sand in the paint
⟷	Obnoxious supervisor

2. The leader asks the group for suggestions on how the columns might be labeled. Post all suggestions. You may hear bargaining/non-bargaining, union/management.

3. Usually someone will suggest the mandatory/permissive distinction. In drawing it out, you may have to ask what the phrase "wages, hours, and conditions of work" refers to. What happens to other issues?

4. Make sure everyone understands the mandatory/permissive distinction:

• Mandatory/permissive distinction applies only to bargaining to impasse. It does not prevent bargaining over permissive subjects.

• Management's rights clauses are contractual provisions. They do not need to be there and have only as much meaning as the parties give them. Nothing in law prevents the company and the union from bargaining over virtually anything.

• Most permissive subjects usually involve elements of mandatory subjects in their solution. For instance, a company can unilaterally decide to close down a part of its business but it must bargain about the effects of its decision.

• The boundaries between mandatory and permissive are not fixed. (At one time profit-sharing plans were ruled permissive.)

• Unions have found ways to put the full weight of the union behind permissive subjects (for example, demanding a union seat on the Chrysler Board of Directors).

In addition, if the program participants are chosen simply through volunteering, the union has no control over who they are or what they do. The pitfalls of this type of voluntarism are obvious.

Finally, the notion that participation is voluntary has sometimes been used in a different way than it was intended. In some cases, when a union leadership or the majority of a local have wanted to pull the local out of a program, defenders of the program have argued that participation is a member's "right." Neither the union nor management have the authority, under this viewpoint, to take that "right" away from individuals who voluntarily choose to participate.

The bottom line, of course, is this: Do individuals or groups have the right to divide the union in dealing with management? Do individuals have the right to cut their own deals with management, in an area where the union is trying to act as a united whole?

What's Wrong with Attrition?

[The following is excerpted from the July 1991 edition of *The Orange Empire News*, newsletter of CWA Local 9510.]

by Mike Drake

For those of us employed by General Telephone, the latest news is force reductions over the next four years. The body count will be 11,300. Management says, "The reductions will occur over several years and as in the past, most likely will come from attrition and retirements."

It might sound good on paper, i.e., many think attrition is an orderly form of workforce reduction by not replacing those departing, thereby avoiding layoffs. WRONG! According to my dictionary, the definition of attrition goes like this:

1. The act of wearing or grinding down by friction. [Example: sucking the union into ongoing negotiations to modify what was negotiated so that on a day-to-day basis the rules were changed after the game started.]

2. The act of weakening or exhausting by constant harassment or abuse. [This happens when: workers are uprooted by consolidations and "technological change" to new work locations, adding anywhere from 1-3 hours to the working day due to commute time; changing work rules in order to meet "service requirements," under the euphemism "needs of the service"; telling us all the time that we're lucky to have jobs and to count our blessings.]

3. Gradual reductions of personnel as a result of resignation, retirement or death. [This means that if they don't kill us, they get us to quit in order to preserve our health and sanity.]

The word stem is from the Latin *attritio-at-terere*, "to rub against." Well, it sure rubs me the wrong way, and by rights it should be rubbing you the wrong way.

False Security Guideline #5. The goals of the process include both human satisfaction and efficiency.

Who could oppose a program that enriches work life and boosts efficiency at the same time? The problem is that, all the win-win rhetoric to the contrary, the normal situation in the workplace is that *there is a conflict* between competition, productivity, and efficiency on the one side and satisfaction and good jobs on the other. Doing more work with fewer people and more unemployed does not expand human satisfaction.

The union view should be that our priority is human satisfaction, even at the expense of productivity. We discussed this in chapters 2 and 3. A key to the battle for members' hearts and minds is the idea that union demands for good jobs are legitimate *even if they are not as efficient*.

At best, this guideline feeds into the false belief that there is no conflict between management's goals and unions', and therefore the union can safely line up behind productivity drives.

False Security Guideline #6. Stewards can attend any meeting in their jurisdiction.

This guideline gives the illusion that the union can keep a watchful eye on the program. In reality, it is usually not possible for a steward to keep on top of a participation program, which may include a number of different problem-solving groups and meetings, in addition to his or her other duties. More likely, the steward is called in after a group is well on its way with some project, and someone—probably not a group member—hears about it and gets worried.

If the steward believes the project is harmful—say it will eliminate a job—he or she may try to stop it. It's not likely that the group members will feel grateful to the union for reminding them of their responsibilities as union members. They may be embarrassed, and most likely, they will get angry, feeling that the union stepped in with no knowledge of their history or intentions, to rain on their parade.

On the other hand, if the steward does try to participate in all the task force meetings, so that her input is there from the beginning, she will neglect her grievance handling and representation duties—and possibly antagonize the members who are skeptical of the program.

False Security Guideline #7. Facilitators must be acceptable to the union.

In some programs the facilitators are selected jointly, with veto power for the union. In other programs the union may get to choose half or even all the facilitators. With the union appearing to take responsibility for the facilitators' actions, other union members are put at ease. But experience has shown that this safeguard doesn't begin to ensure that facilitators carry out union objectives. They face powerful pressures:

1. The training of facilitators is heavily weighted toward management thinking. See the box on Facilitator Manipulation in chapter 13 for an example.

2. The facilitators' new working conditions may put

"WE SAID WE'D BE HAPPY TO CONDUCT NEGOTIATIONS...
WE NEVER SAID ANYTHING ABOUT REACHING AN AGREEMENT."

them in close and constant contact with their management "counterparts," carrying out similar tasks, in a program structured around the company agenda. You are what you eat; if you are carrying out management plans all day, you start to think like a manager.

3. If these persuasions aren't enough, there are perks such as out-of-town trips and company credit cards to win loyalty. Management can make the facilitator's job hard or easy, depending on their assessment of whether she is a team player.

4. The facilitators may have few union resources to draw on. Usually, they are not part of an elected union team—the executive board or bargaining committee. They are isolated from those who are carrying out traditional union functions. They may find themselves in the position of choosing between past union practices and the desires of a particular circle, with little guidance.

5. In some programs, it is not clear whether the union has the right to remove a facilitator. This weakens the sense of responsibility to the union. Often, the only threat to the facilitator's job is the cancellation of the program. This gives the facilitator a strong interest in defending the program no matter what. See chapter 21 for an example of facilitators organizing to keep a defeated program going.

Notes

1. Adrienne Eaton and Paula Voos, "The Ability of Unions to Adapt to Innovative Workplace Arrangements," *American Economic Review*, Vol. 79, No. 2, pp. 172-176.

2. Irving Bluestone, "Human Dignity is What It's All About," *Viewpoint, an IUD Quarterly*, Vol. 8, No. 3, 1978, p. 23.

3. *Workplace Democracy*, Summer 1982.

4. Jim Irvine, speech at Workplace of the Future Conference, March 8, 1993. Reprinted in *A Report on the Workplace of the Future Conference*, AT&T and CWA, 1993, p. 7. CWA leaders' conclusion was to replace QWL with "partnership."

5. "Union Contract: Cape Cod Hospital and Hospital Workers Union Local 767 SEIU, 10/1/92 — 9/30/95," p. 99.

6. Donna Sockell, "The Legality of Employee-Participation Programs in Unionized Firms," *Industrial and Labor Relations Review*, July 1984.

7. David I. Levine and Laura D'Andrea Tyson, "Participation, Productivity, and the Firm's Environment," chapter in Alan S. Blinder, ed., *Paying for Productivity*, Brookings Institution, Washington, D.C., 1990, p. 189.

Working Smart:
A Union Guide to Participation Programs and Reengineering
Labor Notes • 7435 Michigan Ave. • Detroit, MI 48210 • (313) 842-6262

Chapter 33

Mobilized Involvement

The union should use a collective bargaining approach not only to bargain a structure and rules for the participation program, but also in every circle or team meeting that takes place. This includes the right to caucus. The structure should be simple and give the union maximum independence and flexibility, but in particular it should aid in mobilizing members. Have participants take the union oath of office; trust them; and set up regular communication between participants and the regular union structure. Avoid the jointness mind-set or perks, and be prepared to pull out if necessary.

SOMETIMES WE REFER TO THIS STRATEGY simply as the "collective bargaining model" for participation programs. The idea is to organize and conduct union member involvement in every level of participation programs as if they were an extension of collective bargaining. The union members in the program think in terms of we/they, not jointness. Every union member regards her/himself as part of the union collective in dealing with management.

Note, however, a big difference from the usual practice of collective bargaining today: this strategy cannot be carried out just by a small bargaining team. A big chunk of the membership must be mobilized and involved, or it won't work.

In this model, the union side has its own agenda, its own proposals, and its own way of resolving differences

UNION CAUCUS

Don Stone

among its members. It chooses which of members' ideas will be put forward to management. To reinforce the collective bargaining style, the union members sit on the opposite side of the table from management, even in team meetings and quality circles.

Further, the union side should view the issues discussed with management in quality meetings or the like as no different from issues talked about in contract bargaining. If no resolution can be reached in the meeting, the union has every right and responsibility to pursue it through other means, including, where appropriate, contract bargaining, job action, grievance, or strike. This position also best protects the union's legal position (see chapter 26). It means that the union has not given the program its blanket approval, and any element of it, such as a quality group, can exist only as long as the union wishes to be part of it.

Two reasons we call this strategy mobilized involvement: "involvement" to emphasize that the union is actively applying this approach *within* a participation program. The union has not simply used collective bargaining to negotiate the rules of the program; it also uses the collective bargaining approach at every level and on every significant issue within the program.

Secondly, "mobilized" to indicate that the main question isn't structure and rules (although these are important). Rather, whether the union succeeds or fails in the program depends on whether significant numbers of members thoroughly understand the union goals and strategies. These members act on their own and in small groups as well as in large collectives to implement the union strategy.

A "mobilized involvement" strategy is the hardest strategy of all for a local union to carry out successfully, harder even than active opposition. This is because it requires an *on-going* high level of consciousness and activity from both officers and rank and file. It requires members to understand not only the principles of unionism but also the language and techniques of rapidly changing, faddish participation programs. And it often pits union members against consultants who have been trained in "attitude change" and manipulation.

Maintaining mobilized involvement means that members must be educated and organized to respond on their own to the daily challenges of the participation program. This section includes several case studies of unions that have applied this approach.

The mobilized involvement strategy consists of:

1. Fix the union.

2. Organize membership education about participation programs.

3. Build a union presence in the teams or circles.

4. Bargain a structure for the program that allows members to mobilize.

5. Adopt an independent, collective bargaining approach to jointness activities.

6. Determine the key issue about the participation program or the workplace changes that go with it, and build a campaign around it.

1. FIX THE UNION

If your union is as flabby as most are today, this will take some doing. It means getting the *whole* union in shape, officers and rank and file. It means re-establishing the notion that the union is alive and well in the workplace—"the union" is not just a set of officers off to the side. Fixing the union could include:

• starting a regular newsletter (or making the existing one more interesting)

• getting members involved in their own grievances, investigating, writing, following up. Make sure members know the status of everyone's grievances. Make them group grievances when possible.

• putting out department leaflets when the need arises

• in workplaces where each steward represents hundreds of people, electing or appointing large numbers of unofficial stewards

• revitalizing committees; make it possible for more members to be involved

• making the union meetings interesting.

We recommend one of the many publications on internal organizing. See chapter 41.

2. ORGANIZE MEMBERSHIP EDUCATION

Use this book. In particular, use the exercises in chapters 13-16 and 32. And see the *Strategy Guide*, section 8. Education is more than bringing in some experts and holding classes. It is about finding and developing expertise among the members. It means involving the natural leaders and interested members in thinking through the union's campaign.

A key point to get across: any mutual interests or win-win solutions that may be developed in the participation program represent a limited and probably short-term overlap, not a fusion of the employer's and the union's fundamental goals. These remain in conflict.

3. UNION PRESENCE IN THE TEAMS OR CIRCLES

See the *Strategy Guide*, sections 10 and 11, and chapters 19, 23, 30, 36, 37, 38, and 39 of this book.

4. A STRUCTURE AND RULES THAT ALLOW MEMBERS TO MOBILIZE

It would be ideal to bargain a structure and rules for the program that reflect the collective bargaining approach throughout. See, for example, the structure developed by Andy Banks and Jack Metzgar in *Participating in Management*,[1] summarized in the *Strategy Guide*. But if you cannot win such a structure, have a fallback position that at least deals with the major points. For some suggested demands, see section 13 of the *Strategy Guide*, or *Negotiating New Work Systems* (chapter 41).

In this section we suggest a union-friendly way to structure a program, paying special attention to points that can encourage or discourage membership mobilization. In point 5 we give advice on how the union should function within the participation program.

The idea is to structure the program so that participating members can think of themselves as union representatives, rather than just as individuals, and so that they can easily organize themselves within the program.

a. *Keep the structure as simple as possible.* Avoid creating an unwieldy bureaucracy with many functionaries who become committed to the program as an end in itself. While adding numbers of union appointees may seem to strengthen the union, if they are placed in positions where their jobs and perks depend on the program, the union will have created its own fifth column.

In addition, creating a participation bureaucracy will shift the responsibility and initiative away from the membership, to a few officials acting *for* the membership. The appeal of these programs is that workers finally get the opportunity to be involved. So the union must create an opportunity for members to be involved too, the union way.

As much as possible, whatever assets the union gets for participation purposes should be spread out among the members, including part-time and temporary assignments, union-oriented educationals, and cross-union contacts.

b. *Limit the purview of the program to areas the union knows something about and can keep on top of.* Know your own limits. It is better to leave contracting out to the company than to agree to a joint committee, if union leaders do not have time to take it seriously.

c. *Keep the structure tied to the contract.* Make sure there is a sunset clause for all committees and other structures so that none have an existence independent of or beyond the contract.

d. In all teams or participation groups, *union members must have the right to call a time-out and caucus among themselves or with a union resource*. They should also have the right for union-only planning time before the joint meeting. If the company refuses to grant the union this pre-planning time—which management-side participants certainly have and use—it is clearly evidence of bad faith. The union must then decide whether to pull out altogether or to make it possible for participants to meet and caucus on their own time.

e. *Develop a clear understanding of how the union will handle the overlap between traditional collective bargaining arrangements (say bargaining committee meetings with management) and joint program meetings*. For example, general discussion about classifications might be appropriate but any working out of specifics belongs to the official bargaining bodies.

f. *Be cautious about problem-solving procedures that work against union unity*. In joint meetings it's fine to brainstorm initial lists of possibilities. But pruning the list, formulating solutions, and resolving differences should be done by the union side meeting separately and then approaching management as a unified group. What you don't want is an atmosphere of the good old boys and girls sitting around working out their internal differences.

Of course, when you get into your union caucus, the union side is not limited by the initial brainstormed list. You may come up with completely different ideas when management is not in the room.

g. *Reject any structure or training that makes facilitators responsible to both management and the union*. The union must have the exclusive right to select its facilitators. It must be clear from the beginning that they are representing union interests in the program, not the interests of "the process" or of some vague notion of jointness. Some locals have the facilitators take the union oath of office.

Because of the heavy pressures on facilitators discussed in chapters 13 and 16, the union should have procedures worked out *in advance* for appointment or election and *removal*. Facilitators must be considered part of the union leadership and union structure. They should get traditional union training in the contract, grievance procedure, and union history.

They should meet regularly with an appropriate union body, such as the executive board or bargaining committee.

The union should also work out a position regarding the facilitators' special status. How do overtime rules, bumping rules, promotion rules, and wage rates apply to facilitators? Should facilitators be prohibited from running for union office because their job provides an unfair advantage? Or would such a rule work against the need for facilitators to think of themselves as part of the union leadership? Would it tend to keep union activists from becoming facilitators? Answers to these questions will vary from local to local, but they must be worked out in advance.

In any case, the facilitators' job should not be so attractive that it "spoils" them. The "no loss, no gain" position may be the best for most locals.

h. *Beware of "neutral" consultants*. While many consultants claim to be able to take both labor and management interests to heart, most consultants are trained and have experience in a pro-business atmosphere. Of those who have a labor background, many became consultants in order to opt out of the labor movement. It is management who pays the high consultant fees, and he who pays the piper calls the tune.

Consultants are invested in the program itself. Their pay comes from keeping the program going, no matter what.

If consultants are necessary, then the best approach is

The Union Is in the Procedure

Quality groups at the University of Wisconsin-Whitewater use a list of seven problem-solving steps. The facilitator must sign off as the group completes each step. The first sign-off sheet includes the item, "Have you contacted the union?"

Steve Barnes of AFSCME Local 1131, the Wisconsin State Employees Union, says, "Whoever forms a circle anywhere on campus has to confirm that they contacted us. A union rep has to be there."

Neutral Consultants: When the Chips are Down

Allied Industrial Workers Local 837 believed that the consultant guiding the Illinois A.E. Staley plant through a joint business improvement process was pro-union. They remember Charlie Krone, the California-based consultant, assuring them, "It must be for the betterment of both parties or I'm out of here."

But the situation in the sugar processing plant changed. Management switched tactics, and made contract proposals that, the union says, would have destroyed the grievance procedure, cut pay, and undermined seniority. The relationship in the plant turned into a mighty struggle, leading ultimately to an eight-month work-to-rule campaign and then a lock-out in June 1993.

As part of their battle, local union leaders wrote a letter to Charlie Krone reminding him of his assurances to the union. They asked that he withdraw his services from the Decatur plant because continued involvement would be seen as endorsement of management's anti-union activities.

Krone responded by thanking the union president for "sharing with me your feelings...." but said, "our contract prevents us from stoppage of our services."[2]

for the union and the company each to have its own. Most unions insist on their own experts on pensions or health and safety for collective bargaining situations. The same logic should apply to joint programs.

If you are stuck with a single consultant, take the selection very seriously. The professional expert mystique can do a lot of damage at critical times. Never accept as a "neutral" consultant one who comes with the program the company is proposing. Be sure the union has the unilateral right to terminate the consultant, with binding guarantees that the company will not continue to use the consultant for other work.

Start with a background check. Has the consultant worked for a non-union or union-busting company on participation programs? If yes, what does this say about their understanding of power in the workplace? Question prospective consultants on their understanding of the history of the labor movement, as well as their understanding of what it's like to work in your kind of workplace. Finally, ask for some clear understanding of the conditions under which the consultant would recommend stopping the program.

Of course, having a consultant should never stop the union from developing its own sources of expertise from within the membership, within the union, or outside.

i. *Resist blanket confidentiality agreements*. The effect of such secrecy agreements is to put a barrier between leaders and members. When the members are not allowed to know what the leaders are discussing, the influence of those leaders on the joint committee is undermined.

Union leaders should insist that responsible openness is the union mode of functioning, that the entire membership has a right to know what is going on in the participation program, and that confidentiality can be proposed and considered only in specific cases.

j. *Insist on adequate notice of when meetings will be held and of what management wants to put on the agenda*. The union, of course, has an equal right to set the agenda.

5. WORKING INSIDE THE PARTICIPATION PROGRAM: THE COLLECTIVE BARGAINING APPROACH

The structural approach outlined above is fine, but a successful mobilization depends in part on how union leaders and members actually behave in the various joint committees. The jointness structure can look fine on paper, but the devil is in the details. The union's primary job in the program is to build the union's ability to survive and thrive in the long haul.

Say the contract calls for a joint steering committee for a quality program and specifies four union officers and four managers. The first step is to look over chapters 12-18 and do the Resources for Jointness exercise in chapter 15. Analyze the union's strengths and weaknesses under the jointness conditions. This will provide clues for steps to take.

a. *Treat all union participants as representatives of the union*. Have them take the union oath of office. Members who have a healthy skepticism about the program should be encouraged to take assignments. The work they do in the program will affect their co-workers. They should go back to those co-workers regularly for advice and instructions.

b. *Remove any artificial limits on what can be discussed by these union representatives*. That is, don't tell them that any collective bargaining matter is off-limits. Obviously, no team can change conditions in the contract or discuss pending grievances. But union leaders should make clear that they trust members to discuss any issues with the company, and to make any recommendations for contract changes, or for grievances that need to be filed, through the regular union channels.

These rank and file union representatives can press the union's overall agenda in the program. For example, if the union has decided that computer training is essential for members' job security, use quality meetings or team meetings to press management for that training. A circle can decide to research information the union needs to make the case for a contract change or to back up a health and safety grievance. Ideas can be generated in the teams or circles, and the full agreement worked out through regular collective bargaining channels.

At the same time, the union must make it clear to management that the participation groups cannot be used to undermine those traditional bargaining channels. Management may not refuse a steward's request for a fan and then grant the request when a participation group makes it. Some unions have countered this management tactic by making it clear that what the company refuses to discuss or grant through bargaining, it may not discuss or grant through the participation program.

The back and forth between traditional channels and the participation program could work this way: say a worker files a grievance over unsafe conditions. The relevant team can also discuss those conditions and make proposals for how to make them safer. But the grievance should not be withdrawn while the group is discussing the question.

c. *Assign an organizer for the union side, to oversee the union's involvement*. This might be a key union officer, or perhaps one of the program facilitators, working with an officer. This person should make sure that union participants on any top-level committee are briefed in advance on key issues that are arising in the program. Where there are disputes she or he should bring participants together to resolve them.

This person should know and have access to external resources, say from labor educators or from the international union. Most important, the job of the organizer is to see that the union prepares, presents, and presses its own agenda in the program.

d. *Set up regular communication between participants in teams or circles and the union structure*. "Team stewards" could meet regularly with the union leadership, the organizer, or an oversight committee.

e. *Take the initiative*, or be "proactive," to use the current terminology. View joint meetings as the place to press the union's agenda, not simply to respond to management initiatives.

f. *Insist on the right to delegate activities of any joint leadership committee, and then do it.* Delegating creates more leaders and makes it possible to deal with a broader range of issues.

g. *Put on a union orientation to the participation program*, completely separate from any company training. In this training, you should "inoculate" members against the company messages they will receive. It's a good idea even to use some of the exercises the company is likely to use, such as "Lost in the Desert" for team-building (see chapter 13). Members are less likely to be brainwashed by the interesting and fun—sometimes even emotional—aspects of company training, if they've experienced a version of it beforehand.

Once you've picked apart the hidden messages, members can laugh when the company repeats the union's predictions. By clearing away the fluff, members will be in a better position to evaluate the substance and the hidden agendas.

h. *Find resources for the union, to lessen dependence on management's experts.* These could include other unions, labor studies programs, and your own members. You may be surprised how many people already have expertise in computers or accounting, for instance, or would be willing to take courses—if only they were asked.

The members' eyes and ears are the most valuable data collection instruments in the workplace, a resource the company tries very hard to coopt. The union needs to find a way to capture these members' talents.

i. *Approach off-site joint meetings or investigative*

Use Trips Wisely

Although management sets up out-of-town junkets for bonding purposes, union members can learn valuable information on such trips if they take the initiative.

Here's an example: when NUMMI installed a new plastic process, the company insisted on being able to hire people off the street, claiming that the new jobs required expertise. But bargaining representatives insisted on visiting a union plastics plant. By carefully choosing whom they talked to, they established that the skills required could be learned quickly by present bargaining unit members. As a result, all the new jobs were opened to transfers.

In another case, a company kept pressing a Machinists local leadership to visit another plant that had the team concept. The union leaders finally agreed, but arranged for a meeting with a Labor Notes speaker in the same city. The meeting provided members with points to look out for and made their guided tour of the plant much more interesting.

---

trips carefully. On the one hand, they can look like junkets: officers playing golf while not around to help members deal with problems. Management also uses such trips as a sort of bonding experience, to get union leaders into liking the way management does things.

At the very least, when taking such joint trips union leaders should go out of their way to avoid even the hint that they are in bed with management. Avoid first class travel, hotels, and restaurants. Allowing the company to cover such costs is a subtle method of buying leaders' participation and is rightfully suspect by the membership.

Insist that any activities done with management stick to the purpose of the trip. If you want to play or be entertained, find unionists from the local area to do it with.

j. *Arrange activities that bring members in contact with members of other unions in the company/industry/area*, especially unions that are trying a mobilized approach.

k. *Maintain the union's willingness and ability to get out of the program.* However hard the union is willing to work to try to bend a participation program to its own ends, it still must be prepared to get out. If the union is not capable of withdrawing from the program in a unified and organized way, with the support of most of the leaders, members, and facilitators, then the leadership is in a weak position to deal with management *in* the program.

If management believes that significant sections of the union are dependent on the program for patronage jobs or for a parallel political structure within the union, it may not take seriously the union's stated willingness to pull out.

6. BUILD A CAMPAIGN

Choose a particular issue that arises from the participation program and build a campaign around it. The campaign could range from a fight to save a particular work rule to a full-fledged corporate campaign. But it must be about something that directly affects members' lives. We have chosen some examples in chapter 34.

Finally. In all your work in the program, adopt unionism—not jointness, not competitiveness—as your underlying philosophy.

Notes

1. Andy Banks and Jack Metzgar, *Participating in Management, Labor Research Review* No. 14, Fall 1989.

2. Correspondence between AIW Local 837 and Charles Krone Associates, March 5, 1992 and March 29, 1992.

Working Smart:
A Union Guide to Participation Programs and Reengineering
Labor Notes • 7435 Michigan Ave. • Detroit, MI 48210 • (313) 842-6262

Chapter 34

Mobilization Issues

Participation programs produce a host of issues to build a membership involvement campaign around. These include quality (union-defined), fighting stress, job documentation, work rules, contracting out, ergonomics, preserving skills, and gainsharing. Both model and fallback demands, along with campaign arguments and tactics, are presented for these issues.

WHAT WE HAVE DISCUSSED in the Strategies Section up to now—bargaining a decent structure, finding ways for the members to be involved, getting on top of the program—are all necessary and important. But to tap the full power of the members, the key is building a union campaign around a specific issue.

Structural issues and "union power" feel abstract and distant unless it is clear why they are needed and how individual participation can make a difference. When members feel that union power and a union vision are directly linked to their health, their job security, possibilities for advancement, dignity on the job, or fairness, they will find the interest, time, and energy that are needed to maintain a strong union.

Selecting the issue or issues to campaign around is not easy. The choice should flow directly from the union's long-range strategic planning that we keep harping on. The union's particular slant on the issues must take into account the economic and political environment, management's strategy, the union's strengths and weaknesses. Some issues will be damage control and others will be about long-term direction; it's important to know the difference.

Following are some issues that often come up for unions dealing with participation programs. Besides the ones covered here, see Training, chapter 35, and Surviving Lean Production, chapter 36. The latter tells how three locals dealt with a full-blown lean production system.

A UNION APPROACH TO QUALITY

In chapter 14 we described the different meanings of the word "quality." When management builds its plan for reorganizing the workplace around the concept of quality, the union had better have its own concept of quality well defined and widely shared in the membership.

Your management may be losing interest in quality now that the fad cycle has moved on to reengineering and the bottom line. But it may still make sense for the union to develop its own campaign for quality. Some suggestions:

1) *Make quality for the real customer (not any so-called internal customers) the focus of the union's quality campaign.* In chapter 14 we explained that usually campaigns against "waste" are simply repackaged productivity or speed-up drives. Focusing on the "internal customer" is a mystification of the work process and simply another way of implementing "conformance to specifications." The union should try to shift the focus of every "quality" effort onto quality for the end customer.

Often *this* kind of quality improvement can best be achieved by adding jobs. For example, an airline reservationist, a phone service representative, or an information operator could ask additional questions to make sure the service matches the customer's needs. In factories, tighter tolerances or greater assurance against defective parts may require more inspections or more thorough ones. Assigning workers to follow up with customers can create new jobs.

Of course, not every improvement in consumer quality creates jobs. Sometimes a simpler technique or a different application of technology can increase quality to the consumer but also reduce the labor required. But however it falls, unions should be the champions of quality to the customer; most of the time this will mean more and better jobs.

2) *Bargain over the savings that result from "waste" reduction.* The union cannot, of course, favor wasted time or the production of faulty goods. But since reducing waste often does cut jobs, and sometimes makes existing jobs worse, it is perfectly reasonable for the union to demand that workers benefit from (or at least not pay for) waste-reduction suggestions, through the creation of new jobs or shorter worktime. (See the section on gainsharing below.)

Of course, carrying out this perspective requires that the members be well educated about what "cutting waste" results in, as discussed in chapter 14. Members must make the commitment to bring their waste-reduction ideas to the attention of the union rather than management. One way to keep on top of this question is to require that any suggestion coming out of a quality circle include a "jobs impact statement" (analogous to an environmental impact statement). Each circle is required to research, as part of its mission, how its suggestion will affect not only the number but the livability of jobs in the workplace.

Requiring a "jobs impact statement" will not end all job-cutting suggestions. But it will help members in circles keep the jobs issue in focus and give the union ammunition in bargaining over the results.

3) *Learn from the gurus. Use the contradictions.* In chapters 12, 14, and 25 we pointed to the sharp contradictions among the quality gurus. We suggested that when management claims to be combining the best features of the available quality programs, what it has done is simply pick and choose those gurus and those parts of quality programs that best fit its particular strategic plan. By the same token, they tend to leave out those recommendations that could be most valuable to the union. The union should point out management's contradictions and do its own picking and choosing.

Make no mistake: all of the name-brand quality gurus operate in a business culture and have a fundamentally pro-management perspective. This was true even of W. Edwards Deming, who delighted in denouncing management inefficiency and stuck pins in many of management's favorite bywords, like "competition." Because of this, many unionists have latched on to Deming as the best of the lot.

Despite Deming's sharp words, however, major corporations sponsored his seminars and continue to use his advice in their reorganization plans. A careful reading of Deming's work shows he has no real place in his system for unions. He has no reflex hatred for unions—as long as they are on his program—but the idea of workers' rights or distinct worker interests have no essential part in his scheme.[1] Deming's idea of the role of unions is that of the

Quality Lingo

The union should choose members to develop as its own experts on quality. By understanding what it is all about, these experts can help the union avoid being snowed by the jargon and technical aspects of quality programs, and sort out what is genuinely valuable. Here is a mini-lesson on some quality concepts that are relevant to this section (including an argument for why inspection is needed):

Variation, according to such experts as W. Edwards Deming, is the enemy of quality.

If you measure very accurately the weight of a one-ounce bag of potato chips, you find that most bags weigh a little more or a little less than one ounce. Any manufacturing, service, distribution, or packing process produces some variation.

This variation can result from two kinds of causes. The first is *common causes*, which are built into the system and appear as random but stable variation around an average value. For example, because of its design the speed on a grinding machine varies by five percent. This causes a variation of plus-or-minus one-thousandth of an inch in the final size of the bearing the machine is making.

Special causes produce non-random changes or cause the average to shift. In our example, if the operator changed the cutting speed, that would be a special cause of variation.

In quality theory, it does no good for the operator to try to compensate for a common cause variation or to do anything to try to reduce it. In fact, such initiative will likely make things worse. Deming condemns it as "tampering." According to the theory, only management can reduce common cause variation, because such a reduction can be accomplished only by changing the system.

It is this distinction between common causes and special causes that gives rise to Deming's famous assertion that 93 percent of the problems of business are the responsibility of management and 7 percent the worker's.[2] Deming is not anti-management. On the contrary, he believes that management does control and should control the system. His well-known criticisms of managers center around how well they exercise their control.

Control Limits

Management sometimes allows two different quality concepts to get confused. One concept is the control limits in Statistical Process Control; the other is the customer's specifications (or the specifications that management has set). Many people think that the Upper Control Limits and Lower Control Limits (those lines on the SPC chart between which all of the plottings are expected to fall in a process that's "under control") have some direct relationship to the customer's specifications. They don't. The lines represent a statistical calculation about the capability of the process or machine. The upper and lower control limits are the boundaries of the common cause variation.

There is nothing to prevent management from setting specifications for acceptable results that are *tighter than* the machine's current control limits. If such tighter specs are set, inspectors can sort out the bad products. Alternatively, management could improve the machine so as to reduce the common cause variation.

The concept applies to any process. We could measure the number of typographical errors, the amount of time it

enterprise unions in Japan.

Still, there are elements in Deming's works that unions can use. For example, Point 8 of his 14 points is "drive out fear." Deming was clear on this: "no one can put in his best performance unless he feels secure."[3] And yet creating an atmosphere of fear and insecurity is one of management's most common tactics for winning work rule changes and union concessions. General Motors, for example, sponsors Deming seminars for its executives and union leaders. General Motors also sponsored the national spectacle that pitted its Willow Run plant in Michigan against its Arlington, Texas plant, while its stockholders applauded, so that all employees would get the message: cooperate or die.

Unions can use Deming's arguments to demand job security arrangements and to remove rules that threaten the workforce (like disciplinary action for "poor job performance").

Similarly, other of Deming's points directly contradict the advice of other gurus and the typical practice of management. Point 10, Deming's call to eliminate slogans and exhortations for quality, can be used against the phony-baloney quality campaigns. Under point 11, Deming opposes numerical quotas for workers. And in point 12, Deming insists on "removing barriers that rob people of pride of workmanship."[4]

The union can also point out the obvious contradictions as a way of debunking the notion that the particular guru management has chosen is the font of all wisdom. For example, in his classic text *What is Total Quality Control?*, Karou Ishikawa (of the famous Ishikawa fishbone diagram) argues that the principle of voluntarism must be respected. People have their own wills, Ishikawa has noticed, and will be more creative if they participate voluntarily. "Our basic principle is that there can be no coercion from above." Yet a few pages later, Ishikawa insists, "If there are six persons in one workplace, all six of them must participate in QC circle activities."[5]

4) *Defend inspection*. Quality programs have given inspection a bad rap. Such slogans as "You can't inspect in

---

takes to process a service request, or the amount of static in a telephone line. We would find upper and lower control limits of the type of variation that just seems to go with the territory.

Again, if management wanted to set and try to enforce tighter specifications, it would have two choices. In the case of typing errors, say the average common cause variation is one error per page, even after computer spell-checking. If management wants to reduce errors, it can 1) assign someone to proofread the finished copy, or 2) buy a software program with a more sophisticated spell-check program (one that can tell you meant "from" when you typed "form"). But, according to the theory, what will not work is to exhort, demand, or plead with the typist to try harder.

Management chooses by estimating the costs for each approach. If all that really mattered was a "fit" or "no-fit" condition—say of a ball bearing—then there would be no difference to the customer between the two alternatives—"inspecting in" quality or producing to tighter specifications. But if, even within the "fit" category, it would be better for the part to be as near-perfect as possible, then the latter method may provide higher quality to the customer. In either case, inspection would still be required to more closely approach zero defects.

Process Under Control

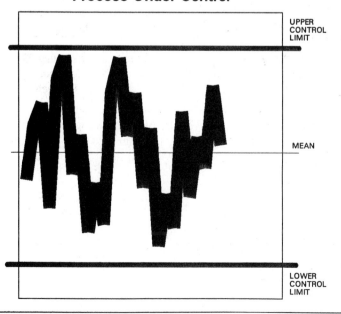

Process Out of Control

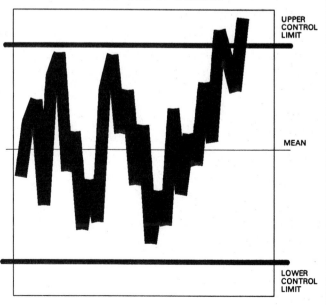

quality" and "Do it right the first time" are taken to mean that a good quality process does not require inspection. Or, to put it another way, that having to inspect the product or service means the manufacturing process is not as good as it should be.

In fact, inspection is not eliminated by any plan that really intends to improve quality. Often inspection is shifted to an earlier stage of the process, to make sure that the individual elements and the process itself are not introducing error. But since variation always exists and it is always possible for "special causes" to have an effect, it is still necessary to use some form of inspection.

Sometimes inspection can be shifted to technology, say a machine that weighs and checks the level of every bottle of dishwashing liquid. But often inspection is simply added on to the jobs of workers who are "adding value" to the process. A worker may be required to check the work of the previous worker in the process, for example. There is no reason in principle why inspection cannot be kept as a separate job, and the amount of inspection increased to produce a higher quality product or service. The union should not allow inspection to be added to a job unless other work is removed.

Final inspection—inspection of the finished product— is also still valid, even when all the parts of the process have been subjected to rigorous quality control. The final product or service is more than the sum of its parts, and can only be tested as a unit. Checking a car for water leaks in a heavy rain requires a final test. "Building in quality" along the way may minimize the number of failures, but the only way to catch the failures is with some form of final test or inspection.

5) *Look for jobs in management's quality plan.* Frequently management's plan for quality contains elements that the union can use to push for job creation within the bargaining unit. For example, after the initial attempts to get "lean," management frequently begins to talk about "robustness" or Taguchi methods. A robust system is one that is less sensitive to variation or disturbances and can still deliver the product or service on time, to specification. In one sense this is a retreat from just-in-time or lean production principles and back to "just-in case." But it is a planned retreat, often based on extensive testing to see how the outcome responds to variation in inputs.

Where are the jobs? In the first place such experimentation requires staffing. The union should try to create new classifications within the bargaining unit for this kind of work. Second, there is usually more than one way to make a process "robust." Management will overlook good alternatives in its desire to keep the job count down.

6) *Emphasize quality conditions for the human component.*

Management recognizes that quality requires good conditions for the production equipment. Compare the way management typically treats machines to the way it treats human beings. The hotter it gets in your plant, the more likely that the machine control cabinets are air-conditioned. And they certainly have ventilation and are likely to be filtered so that the equipment is not exposed to the dirt in the air. (If you want to know what you're breathing, take a look at the filters that protect the equipment in your plant.) If a machine requires a liquid coolant to function, management sees that the coolant is available whenever the machine needs it, and if for some reason the coolant is not available, the machine automatically shuts down. (Think about the human analogy. Can you take a break every time you're thirsty?)

Likewise, people cannot do high-quality work—use good judgment, for example—if the body is sick or the mind is elsewhere. This implies that to champion quality, unions must directly challenge a basic tenet of management-by-stress. They must demand a flexible policy on absenteeism, including absences to care for sick family members. If employees are to take pride in their work and feel motivated to do a good job, they need more flexibility, not less. This means having a big enough cadre of replacement workers to cover for the inevitable absenteeism. Workers need the right to take a certain amount of time off when they need it without having to grovel or fear retribution. (Chapter 36 describes the personal absence rights won by Mazda workers.) Unions should strictly enforce the provisions of the Family and Medical Leave Act, which in some cases gives workers more right to time off (though without pay) than their union contract will.

Unions should not permit management to have it both ways about absenteeism. On the one hand, management claims that absenteeism somehow contributes to poor quality. On the other hand, it is management that presses to make workers as interchangeable as possible, so that it shouldn't matter who is doing the job from one day to another.

If absenteeism is a problem, insist that management deal with the source of the problem and not the manifestations (remember the 5 why's). Disciplining people who are absent or late is like kicking the machine that produces bad parts. It may temporarily jar the machine into working again, but the improvement is likely temporary. Press for programs that deal with the causes: difficulties with child care, transportation problems, too much required overtime, stress built in to the job, uninteresting jobs, and overbearing supervision.

7) *Use your leverage when management demands a specific quality program.* Frequently management will come to the union and say, "Our big customer will drop us unless we have XYZ quality program in place." Sometimes the requirement is ISO 9000 certification, sometimes an application for the Baldrige award. Sometimes the demand is a specific set of SPC procedures.

The union needs to discover what the customer is actually asking for and where management is using a customer as a cover for something it wants to do anyway. When the program is in fact required by a major customer, it is hard to mobilize opposition to it.

On the other hand, the fact that XYZ is a customer requirement can give the union leverage. Management may settle for little more than the name and a shell of a plan, and let the union shape the content.

Similarly, unions should also see the opportunities in management's efforts to win the Baldrige or gain ISO 9000 certification. No company will win the Baldrige Award while it is dealing with a work-to-rule, informational picketing, or the union's refusal to participate in documentation or suggestion plans. The emphasis on quality may make the company more vulnerable to an external "corporate campaign."

FIGHT STRESS

That constant stress does damage to physical as well as mental health is well documented. Just recognizing that external factors cause stress is a good first step to reducing it. One important cause of stress at work is heavy responsibility without enough authority or resources (such as time) to do the job. In section II we explained how this set-up is the engine of management-by-stress. Management organizes all kinds of pressures to keep people working under these conditions, including peer pressure, guilt, and shame, as well as appeals to ego.

One technique for resisting speed-up and stress is the Over-Assignment Form (see the box). The form puts management on notice that for eight hours' pay management gets eight hours of work; what doesn't get done is up to management to decide. It also serves to maintain records for grievance documentation or contract campaigns.

JOB DOCUMENTATION

When workers write down for management how they do each step of their jobs, this documentation helps management shift work to other shops or other countries, automate, and even write a "scab manual" (see chapter 16). Although the trend is for management to gain more control through more knowledge of what goes on in the workplace, workers are stronger if they keep as much of this knowledge to themselves as they can (read about the Umea plant in chapter 30). This is the old-fashioned means of worker control of the shop floor.

Educate members in the importance of keeping their job knowledge to themselves. Stewards might want to give informal instruction in how to fill out the documentation sheets to impart as little information as possible. See the story of Maggie the sewer in *Participating in Management* as an example of a worker determined to hold onto her skill.[6]

There are situations where good job documentation is necessary for safety reasons or for ability to do the job correctly. In these situations, the union can reasonably require protections, such as an enforceable guarantee, separate from and extending past the contract, that management will hire no scabs. Any documentation should not be a one-way transfer of skills. Workers should have the opportunity to learn new skills associated with

The Over-Assignment Form

"An ongoing problem we have with downsizing," says Laura Sager, program director of the Clerical-Technical Union at Michigan State University, "is that the people on the bottom rungs are still expected to cope with an escalating amount of work. As one of our members put it, 'I get a you-must-have-this-done hot item hourly.' They're working for 52 professors, all of whom have egos...There are no real limits.

"We tell our members, 'You can only do as much as you can do. It is your supervisor's responsibility to prioritize your work. You tell the supervisor, "I'm going to do everything I can to get the work done, but I need you to prioritize; here's the list."'

"This generally drives the supervisor nuts. They don't have a clue how to prioritize. They don't want to know, they just want it done.

"Using the form makes it clear on paper what is being expected. It's good for people who have a hard time being assertive. And it can open up the need for union intervention if the supervisor responds inappropriately."

Over-Assignment Form

If you've become mired down in uncompleted tasks due to over-assignment, you should ask your supervisor to prioritize your tasks. Make two copies. Keep one for yourself and give the other to your steward.

Date: _____
Office/Location: _____
Supervisor: _____
RE: Over-assignment

I have numerous tasks requiring my time and attention. If time does not allow for completion of all tasks, I will continue with these tasks unless instructed otherwise by you. I would appreciate your assistance in prioritizing these tasks.

Tasks (Estimated Current Priority)	Supervisor Priority
1. _____	
2. _____	
3. _____	
4. _____	
5. _____	
6. _____	
7. _____	
8. _____	
9. _____	
10. _____	

Employee signature _____

Supervisor: Check here and initial if you are authorizing overtime ❑ Initials_____

Employee: Check here if the supervisor did not respond ❑

documentation (writing, desktop publishing, computer use).

WORK RULES

Work rules are a main subject of attack under any type of work reorganization plan. The union should look carefully at work rules and decide which ones to strengthen, which ones to concede, and which new ones to fight for. Use the ideas in chapter 5 to make sure everyone understands that work rules are not "union rigidity"; they are *rights* at work. Making the analogy to the Bill of Rights is useful.[7]

Work rules can be defended only if the members care about them and are vigilant. Stewards might do a pledge campaign around enforcement, gathering cards from those who will "pledge always to take my full break" or "never to work alone." Beyond the argument that work rules save jobs or health, enforcement lets management know that workers can't be pushed around.

Finally, don't forget: a just-in-time system actually gives the union a new (or at least sharper) weapon. Just-in-time magnifies the power of a work-to-rule.

Here's an example of a union campaign over work rules, from United Parcel Service:

The day after the Teamsters signed the 1994 contract, UPS announced a quality improvement for customers: the company would now accept packages weighing up to 150 pounds. The previous weight limit had been 70 pounds. Looking out for members' backs, the International union demanded bargaining over the issue. When UPS would not budge, the union violated a judge's injunction and went on strike. They won a letter of understanding that workers may call for help *from a bargaining unit member* to lift any package weighing over 70 pounds.

Of course, management's pressure on individual workers to forego this rule (that is, the right) is unrelenting: use a dolly; you don't have to carry it far; you always did it before; a supervisor will help you; get the customer to help you unload; what are you—a wimp?

Two locals initiated a Save Our Backs campaign, encouraging members to enforce the letter of the agreement—to always, always call for help. The International union

and Teamsters for a Democratic Union did the same. The union pointed out that once you start letting the rule go by, there is no past practice to fall back on. If the driver gives in, he is endangering not only his back but jobs.

CONTRACTING OUT

Fighting subcontracting is something that members can do, which makes this a very good issue for a mobilization campaign. Members can collect information about where the work is going and what conditions are like in those shops (pay, benefits, union or not, working conditions).

Members can relate contracting out to a quality campaign. Services or products from a contractor should be inspected extra carefully for quality problems, and workers should not hesitate to reject inferior goods.

Warning: trying to resist contracting out can be a tricky business. Some unions have bargained joint committees to look at contracting in, or contract provisions that provide for bringing back work that can be done "competitively." This approach can put the union in the position of rewriting work rules or making other concessions in order to compete with cheaper suppliers and contractors.

Management usually claims that it must contract out to save money. Don't accept management's definition of costs. While the trend toward contracting out is part of management's desire to become more flexible, there is also a backlash of concern about losing the advantages of doing work in-house. In-house work is more available and may be more readily adjusted for quality. The union should push these arguments.

ERGONOMICS AND SAFETY

The demand for more standardized work, less resting time, and increased production is a recipe for repetitive strain injuries. The union can demand:

1) a union-appointed ergonomics representative, including the necessary worker-friendly training.

2) very specific language giving the union the right to challenge workload. The aim here is to reduce management's flexibility to change the amount of work required

at will, and to get very specific about what the limits are. In chapter 36 we describe how the union at Mazda enforces "no more than three sunroofs out of five." See the section "Establish a mechanism to challenge production standards" in that chapter for more suggestions.

One problem with most contract language around workload is that the member keeps working under the new conditions imposed by management until the dispute is resolved. And management uses the fact that she *did* do the extra work as proof that she *can* and should continue to do the work. The union should aim for language that says management may not add new work without resolving any potential dispute beforehand.

On safety, consider demanding that workers never work alone but always with someone to watch their backs in any non-standard situation.

SKILLED WORK

Skill gives workers bargaining leverage. In these days when there are long lines for every decent-paying job that opens up, it is only to the degree that workers possess special skills that management cannot threaten to replace them with scabs or move away. When NUMMI workers struck for only a couple of hours in August 1994, applicants started lining up at the gates.

1. Skill resides in more than just those jobs that are designated as skilled. One of the reasons many initial attempts to introduce technology flounder is management's failure to understand the skill involved in so many ordinary jobs, from telephone receptionist to warehouse worker. Ultimately, as management gathers this knowledge, the technology succeeds. Speeding the process of extracting this special knowledge is one of the goals of quality programs. As discussed above under Documentation, unions should minimize the transfer of this knowledge to management, and use it to bargain.

2. Pay attention to classifications, or "lines of demarcation." Examine them, redraw them to match the current technology, and be prepared to defend them.

In the manufacturing skilled trades, for example, workers need to understand the basics of other trades in order to communicate and work together. An electrician working on a computerized numerical control milling machine needs to understand something about mechanical power transmission (the machine repairer's job), and the machine repairer must understand the basics of electronic controls.

But "cross-training" in this sense—which the union should support—is not the same as "cross-working," which is management's program for flexibility and breaking down classifications. Knowing the basics of another trade does not mean that one has the experience and detailed knowledge required to perform a job correctly and safely. You work together with other trades, understand their work, but do not do their work. The same principles apply in other skilled jobs.

3. Maintaining and advancing skills is inextricably linked to training. For a union campaign around training, see chapter 35.

GAINSHARING

We discussed the problems with gainsharing in chapter 15. The idea sounds equitable and is often popular, but it undermines the union and is bad economics too. Our recommendations are:

1. Where you can avoid a gainsharing plan, do so. Such plans tend to embroil the union in a lot of red tape and calculations and usually make more enemies among union members than friends.

2. If you can't avoid gainsharing, have it cover the biggest unit possible. When the UAW began demanding a three percent annual wage increase back in the 1950s, the union based its claim on the increase in productivity in U.S. industry as a whole.

If you can't get industry-wide gainsharing, go for corporation-wide. Resist strongly plant-wide, departmental, or individual calculation systems, which inevitably end up pitting worker against worker.

3. Tie the pay-out to total productivity (total output divided by number of workers) rather than to profits. Basing your paycheck on corporate profits nudges you toward support of such policies as closing less profitable plants. Productivity is only slightly less dangerous in this way, but at least productivity can be improved through investment rather than speed-up. Here we are clearly dealing with a lesser evil situation.

4. Try to get the rewards in a form that will increase the union's strength and members' ability to weather bad times. Have the pay-out put into a low-interest loan fund, a sabbatical program, or a reduced work week at no loss of pay.

5. Expose the anti-worker economics of a rolling base gainsharing plan (see chapter 15).

6. Use the gainsharing concept to put forward a formula for dealing with worker suggestions that cut jobs. Here is one that takes off from the widget factory example at the beginning of chapter 14.

The union points out that the savings from "waste reduction" come partly from reduced labor time, i.e., it's at the expense of the workers. Therefore the union proposes a fair gainsharing arrangement: the company keeps any savings that *do not* come from reduced labor, and the workers get the benefit of reduced labor time through improved jobs.

Say workers discover a way to solve a waste problem that costs $60,000 per year. Analysis shows that this saving breaks down as follows:

Eliminating one job $40,000
Energy $10,000
Raw materials $10,000

Let the company do what it wishes with the $20,000 saved on energy and raw materials. But make the company create a new job, equivalent to or better than the one that is lost. The new jobs could come from new projects, contracting in work, or added inspection to improve quality.

Alternately, the $40,000 could go into a fund to hire new workers, making possible a shorter work week at no loss in pay, or flextime, which would be less expensive. That would be "win-win," wouldn't it?

ORGANIZE THE UNORGANIZED

Why might a local union struggling over a participation program or management-by-stress make a priority of helping other workers build a union?

Organizing the unorganized is part of the long-term strategic planning that the whole union movement should be doing. Unionism cannot survive in a sea of unorganized workplaces. We won't belabor this point, because everyone knows it; yet most often locals themselves do little about it. See the story of UAW Local 3000 at Mazda (AAI) in chapter 36 for an example of a local that sees its own fate tied to bettering the conditions of the plant's low-wage suppliers.

Apart from any immediate benefit, there is the long-range view. A stronger labor movement overall gives each local union more power to deal with its own employer. It helps stanch the hemorrhaging. It helps change the feel of what's possible and what's not.

Finally, getting the local's members involved in organizing new members creates a sense of movement that can't be matched. When members make house calls to explain to potential new members why they should form a union, they remember why the union is so important to them. It rekindles union feelings long dormant. Any organizing drive taken on by a local union should involve as many rank and filers as possible.

Notes

1. Deming was a firm believer that there was a win-win solution for virtually any question. Therefore "optimization for everyone concerned" should be the basis of all negotiations. "Optimization is voided if one party goes into the negotiation with the avowed aim to defend his rights, or he makes a game of it or if he sets out with demands and stands firm on them with a time limit for assent." *The New Economics for Industry, Government, Education*, Massachusetts Institute of Technology, Center for Advanced Engineering Study, Cambridge, 1993, p. 100.

2. W. Edwards Deming, *Out of the Crisis*, Massachusetts Institute of Technology, Center for Advanced Engineering Study, Cambridge, 1986, p. 315. At other times Deming has given different, but similarly precise, figures. His 84/15 ratio is often quoted. See Mary Walton, *The Deming Management Method*, Putnam, New York, 1986, p. 94.

3. *Out of the Crisis*, p. 59.

4. *Out of the Crisis*, pp. 65-77.

5. Karou Ishikawa, *What is Total Quality Control?*, Prentice Hall, New York, 1985. From David I. Levine, "The Quality Movement," unpublished paper, 1992.

6. Andy Banks and Jack Metzgar, "Who Will Control Shopfloor Knowledge?" *Participating in Management, Labor Research Review* No. 14, pp. 16-19.

7. See chapter 8 of *Choosing Sides* for a detailed explanation and defense of work rules.

Chapter 35

Training Is Never Neutral

Rapid change in the workplace requires increased attention to training programs. Much current training is designed to further managment's agenda and does not necessarily produce better-skilled workers. A union agenda for training recognizes the separate interests. It includes training connected to work and to workers' experience, training available by seniority, training that captures new work for the bargaining unit (such as with new technology), broad training for marketable skills rather than company-specific training, basic skills upgrading, and career ladders into the higher-skilled jobs. It avoids over-reliance on "experts." Five case studies demonstrate these principles.

by Mike Parker and Nancy Jackson

THE FAMILIAR REFRAIN: if we don't want to cut wages to compete with workers in Mexico and Asia, then we must have a highly-skilled, highly-productive, high-wage workforce. Training is what we need to get us there.

These days, work-based training is a part of virtually every labor contract and occupies center stage in joint union-management programs. What better example of mutual interest or a win-win situation for both management and workers than better training and higher skills?

At first glance, union involvement in training looks simple: negotiate a training program that specifies who gets trained and how much is spent; then hand the program over to training specialists to decide the technical issues and the details of implementation.

Unfortunately, the result of this approach can be a long-run disaster for the union. Training turns out to be at least as complicated and filled with critical decisions as any other task that unions face.

Like technology, training is often equated with progress, with enhancement of the working life of individuals. But also like technology, training can work for us or against us, depending on how it is done and who

Mike Parker has designed and taught training courses in electronics and computers for skilled workers. Nancy Jackson is the former Co-Managing Director, for the Canadian Auto Workers, of the Automotive Parts Sectoral Training Council in Toronto, and currently is Associate Professor of Education at Mc-Gill University in Montreal.
Besides those who contributed the case studies here, we would like to thank for their useful comments on this chapter Charley Richardson, David Robertson, Gary Saganski, Jane Slaughter, and Hal Stack.

is in charge.

In the past, the employer has largely been in charge of training, and unions have had little interest or involvement except in apprenticeships. Today, we let that situation continue at our peril.

The objective of this chapter is to contribute to the development of a union approach to work-based training. Some useful resources are listed at the end. Two particularly useful books are *Training for What?*, which contains materials from the Canadian labor movement, and *Worker-Centered Learning: A Guide to Workplace Literacy*, from the AFL-CIO Human Resources Development Institute.

But even these books must not be taken as recipes. New technologies, work reorganization, the employers' offensive against unions, and government policies have all been changing too rapidly to depend on a recipe-style book. Instead, an effective union presence in training means a lot of work: a willingness to experiment and to use the experience of the rank and file.

Another warning: good slogans such as "worker-centered education" and "union-approved" can be used to promote very different types of training programs. "Worker-centered" should mean defining things from a worker's point of view, like saying "speed-up" instead of "efficiency," and learning cooperatively in a way that promotes solidarity. For example, the various COSH groups (committees on occupational safety and health) do training that emphasizes the union procedures for dealing with safety problems, while most commercial safety training programs teach people to act as individuals or through company channels.

However, the terms "worker-centered" or "learner-centered" can also disguise an isolating approach to learning that may erode worker solidarity. These same slogans may translate to sitting in front of a computer terminal with a training package chosen by management. The words "adult education" can turn out to be a code for a "dumbing-down" approach—paternalistic, condescending, alienating, and ineffective. Learning to spot these troubles before it's too late is part of what this chapter is about.

A JOBS-DRIVEN APPROACH

Training itself is not the goal. More training is not the key to more jobs or more good jobs. Training is not the fundamental solution to what ails the economy. Our focus should not be on training for training's sake, but on securing more good jobs and enabling people to move from the poorer jobs to the better ones.

Unless the focus is kept on creating more good jobs, training can become part of the problem: it can be used to hasten the process of replacing people through technology and work reorganization.

Unfortunately, the main reason for the current wave of attention to training is that politicians and corporate officials can use training slogans to make economic problems sound manageable—if you accept their assumptions. If the problem is defined as "workers lacking skills," then individuals can be blamed for not seeking out training (this is the conservative approach). Alternatively, the government can respond with a training program and look like it is doing something (the liberal approach).

Both conservatives and liberals, in this case, talk as if the problem were lack of supply—there aren't enough high-skilled workers. In reality, the problem is lack of demand—employers are not necessarily looking for high-skill workers. So in either case, focusing on training as the "solution" to our economic ills diverts attention from the more basic and difficult challenge: changing government and corporate policy to make good jobs a priority.

"Training" versus "Education"

Some people object to the word training and suggest that we should use the term "learning" or "education." "Training" is what one does to dogs and pigeons—teach them to respond in fixed ways to certain specified conditions. "Learning," on the other hand, is about being able to analyze complex situations and make judgments.

The distinction is an important one: most corporate training programs fall into the first category. Such programs often begin with a "task analysis" to break down complex work skills into the smallest possible individual activities. Workers then go through independent modules for each of these independent tasks.

While the distinction between training and education is crucial, we have used the word "training" because it is still the popular language of the workplace.

There is no point in training people for jobs that will not exist. Yet big bucks are spent on programs to train and retrain workers for occupations that are rapidly declining, like spot welding, or for careers that are already over-supplied, like cosmetology, or to learn obsolete word-processing programs.

U.S. Secretary of Labor Robert Reich strongly promotes the idea that a highly-trained workforce will attract substantial investment from abroad, thus countering the trend to move overseas in pursuit of cheaper labor.[1] But despite a few exceptions—Lionel model trains moved from Mexico back to Michigan looking for skilled workers, automotive design studios locate in California—there is ample evidence that U.S. corporations feel they can safely move to low-wage areas and train the workforce they need. A 90 percent lower wage rate can look very attractive in exchange for a small dose of training. As Harley Shaiken has shown, auto companies moving to Mexico have certainly had this experience.[2] In addition, other countries like Taiwan and South Korea are developing specialized infrastructures for niches in high-technology enterprise.

The evidence shows that even where the so-called high-wage/high-skill option is available, companies tend not to choose it unless unions or government block the low-wage/low-skill strategy.[3]

TRAINING AND UNION PRIORITIES

Training is about far more than technical issues. It shapes not only what we do and how we do it, but also how we think about our work, how we relate to our co-workers and bosses, and what opportunities we have for future work and training.

While training cannot be a substitute for jobs, it is a critical part of any plan to protect jobs and the union over the long run. Training can be the bridge that allows workers to move to better jobs or just maintain their current ones.

Training can influence:

• The level of individual security. Workers with current, portable skills have more. On the other hand, training for narrow, task- or firm-specific skills can make workers more vulnerable in times of change. Narrowing of workers' skills makes it easier for the employer to contract out or to replace strikers.

• The sense of confidence and power that workers feel. This comes partly from knowing that they have marketable skills and partly from a sense of mastery. This in turn creates a workforce more willing to stand up to management and assert its rights.

• The base and size of the union. Whether particular jobs are in the bargaining unit is partly determined by training programs.

A common scenario: a computerized printing system is introduced in an office. Several jobs are lost. Management claims (accurately) that no one in the office has the skills to service or adjust the new equipment. The contract

says that the equipment may not be used until a bargaining unit person is trained. But management says that if the union insists on enforcing this right, the company will lose important contracts, thus threatening its future.

The union agrees to let the work be contracted out or to let non-bargaining unit personnel take it over. There is talk that this arrangement is temporary and that there will be training programs. But these assurances don't turn out to mean much, as the new arrangements become institutionalized.

• The power of the union in years to come. Power is determined by a combination of numbers, cohesiveness, and a shared understanding of the members' position in the workforce. Training affects all of these.

Because training touches on all these issues, it is not neutral terrain. Both the content of training and how it is done open up a hornet's nest of questions of power and privilege. Some critical issues:

• Who controls access to training and what are the criteria? Does the boss decide, or are there clear contractual rules?

• Whose job ladders will be enhanced and whose put on dead-end roads by training programs or access criteria? For example, will younger workers with more education be able to bypass more senior workers? The new emphasis on "school-to-work" training can be used to undermine both union apprenticeship programs and the union's demand for company-provided training.

• What aspects of the contract will be affected by training in the short term? in the long term? For example, how are seniority or mobility rights affected? Are new technical skills being developed so future work stays in the bargaining unit?

• Does the training create a situation where one group of workers challenges the traditional work of others (e.g., production workers doing maintenance; clerical workers doing printing work)?

• Do the access criteria (e.g., math ability) conflict with other union priorities (e.g., seniority)?

• If women or other designated groups are "pre-selected" for training through equity or affirmative action policies, what positive and negative impacts will that have on the workplace? On the union?

• What forms of work organization does the training

promote? For example, is cross-training designed to break down classifications and give management "flexibility"?

• How broad or narrow will the learning be? Will workers learn about the purposes and impacts of new processes and equipment, or just how to use them? Will they be better prepared for decision-making?

• Where and when will instruction take place? Who will face barriers (transportation, accessibility, scheduling, childcare)? Who will face psychological or educational ones (bad schooling experience, difficulties in reading)?

• Who will do the instruction and why? External experts? Peers? What messages will be given by this choice?

• Will individuals be intimidated or encouraged? Is the training designed to produce success?

• What kind of learning experience will it be? Will it be a social or an individual process? Will it be competitive or cooperative? Will it encourage understanding and solidarity with other workers, or will it promote peer pressure?

The crux of the matter is that training is never neutral. It is a battlefield for a broader struggle over knowledge and control of work. That is why working people need a voice and an agenda of our own.

Myths About Training

1. More training is necessary because we are moving to a high tech future.

Almost every projection on future jobs—including those done by the federal government—points to the following six occupations as having the fastest growth over the coming years: secretaries and stenographers, janitors, cashiers and tellers, office clerks, waiters, and truck drivers. The government studies concluded that most of these future jobs can be filled by people now unemployed or those needing little training.

2. Highly-trained high-technology jobs mean higher wages.

Many high tech industries—like computer chips, computer processing, and auto production—have moved to low-wage countries like South Korea or Taiwan. Within Ontario, there are many high-tech companies with relatively low wages. Higher wages are not just technologically determined but depend on unionization and social and political factors.

3. A more highly trained workforce will mean jobs in Canada.

It is not true that more training is the key to jobs in Canada. The reason for Canada's particular economic structure is complex and simply increasing training will not change our economic structure. Training is not the critical factor explaining our economic dependency on resources, assembly, and U.S. technology.

4. A lack of training has hindered the development of the Canadian economy.

The problem has not been inadequate skills but the under-utilization of existing skills: workers with skills being laid off; workers forced to work part-time because no full-time jobs exist; educated workers doing menial jobs because there are no openings in their fields.

5. Good planning for specific skill shortages is a priority.

Detailed planning for the future is not possible in a changing, unplanned economy. The alternative is to provide broad skills training so that workers (and companies) will have the flexibility to adapt their abilities to specific uses as the need arises.

6. Training is not a controversial issue.

Aside from the question of how much training should be done, there are fundamental disagreements about who is to benefit from the training, and about the kind of workplace and society the training is meant to reinforce.

Labour's agenda is for training that equips workers to have more control over their jobs and their work lives; builds on workers' existing capabilities; prepares workers for what they want and need to know now and in the future; puts workers in a better position to shape that future and that starts eliminating job discrimination based on gender, race or ethnicity.

The employers' training agenda is to make workers willing and able cogs in the corporate machine.

7. Training is a good thing.

Not all training is good. It can be harmful. Just as the educational system has made many workers doubt their abilities and competence, bad training can weaken self-confidence, scare people away from opportunities they could pursue, reinforce stereotypes and past discrimination, and undermine critical
abilities and initiative.

This is why the labour movement wants the ability to shape training so it meets the needs of workers.

8. Multi-skilling will provide greater job security.

There is no evidence for this. Jobs are vulnerable as long as employers have the unrestricted right to close workplaces and relocate work. Since multi-skilling often undermines traditional trades, it may even weaken job security. Traditional trades are portable whereas employer-designed multi-skilled work is usually not portable. Multi-skilling can make workers more dependent on the whim of the current employer.

[From the Ontario Federation of Labour Policy Statement, 1989[4]]

POOR TRAINING IS NO ACCIDENT

Employers and politicians engage in much public wailing and gnashing of teeth about how poorly trained North American workers are, especially when compared to our Japanese or German counterparts. But a poorly-trained workforce is the logical product of the economic and power relations that underlie our whole approach to training.

ECONOMICS

Training is not considered an investment, as new capital equipment is. Instead, training is treated as a cost item, and it can be an extremely expensive one, in two ways.

First is the cost of the training itself, including instruction, materials, and lost time. And if the employer wants a "flexible" workforce, with each worker capable of doing a number of jobs, then training costs are multiplied.

Secondly, if a worker gains marketable skills, she might leave to get a better job elsewhere. Then the original employer is faced with the added expense of having to find and train a replacement. Or instead of leaving, the newly-trained worker might use her increased market value to bargain for higher wages. Either way, the lesson is clear to all employers: why invest in training your workforce, especially in generally desirable or marketable skills, when training may just increase the probability of problems? It may cost less to recruit workers who have been trained elsewhere than to invest in your own workforce.

So the cycle of "poaching" goes on. This approach to a training system may be very inefficient on a social scale, but for the individual employer, the rational economic choice is to play the game as long as everyone else does.

The upshot is that there are strong economic incentives to limit training and to distort the training that exists. Some employers have tried to redesign jobs so they can use standardized, interchangeable, and low-level skills. Others have opted for a just-in-time approach to training: give it only when the worker actually requires it for a specific task. A related approach differentiates the "need-to-know" material from the "nice-to-know." It is not unusual to hear comments like:

> He just needs to know when to turn that valve from the meters—not about the chemistry of metallurgy.

> She doesn't need to know how to program a Programmable Logic Controller, only how to trouble-shoot inputs and outputs when something doesn't work.

> We only need 50 percent of what an electrician knows.

Other firms try to reduce training costs by shifting job-specific training to the public schools. It is cheaper to force out older workers and hire younger ones trained in newer techniques at the public's expense. Or they may shift their resources to recruitment—spending more on looking for workers who already have the right skills. This escalates the "poaching" problem.

Even where employers understand the inefficiencies of these approaches, their solutions may not benefit workers. Some may try to make it very costly for workers to switch jobs. Hence they fight against universal health care and portability of pensions so that any worker switching jobs has a lot to lose.

Thus each firm's "rational" economic behavior to improve its own bottom line ends up being costly not just for individuals, but for society as a whole.

MANAGEMENT RIGHTS

Another reason training seems to fail is that it is made secondary to management rights. That is, management wants to "own" the work and wants workers to be instruments. This kind of premise leads to a very restricted view of the role of workers on the job and to an even more restrictive philosophy of learning.

A recent report from the U.S. National Council on Vocational Education criticizes a number of common but faulty assumptions in training programs. Among these are:

> Learners are best seen as empty vessels to be filled up with knowledge.

> The process of learning is essentially strengthening the bonds between stimuli and response.[5]

These ideas may be old, but they are still alive and widely in use, in part because they serve the management rights approach. As discussed elsewhere in this book, despite the propaganda about working together and smarter, a chief objective of management in workplace reorganization schemes is tighter control over the work process as part of achieving tighter control over costs. For management, training must contribute to tighter control.

Management can get away with outdated approaches to training because that's what workers have been taught to expect. Indeed, many workers expect that education means "experts" feeding them correct knowledge. To counter these notions of what learning is, unions must be prepared to battle over both the content and the operation of training. Beyond technical training, workers have a right to understand the context of their job, the larger process of which their job is a part, the trends in their industry and the economy.

This kind of information not only makes jobs more interesting, it also makes training more effective. However, winning broader training creates another problem for the union. If management remains in control of the big picture, education on trends in the industry will turn into eduction for why workers must join in the fight for competitiveness. David Robertson of the Canadian Auto Workers calls this "training for cultural integration."[6] The United Auto Workers/General Motors Paid Education Leave program is a good example of a forum for this sort of management propaganda.

POWER

A final reason that the current approach to training lets us down is that management has a conflict of interest over seeing union workers highly trained: their skills are a major factor in the power equation at work. For one thing, as mentioned above, when skilled workers can say "take this job and shove it," they are less likely to put up with guff in their current job. For another, the more highly skilled the union workforce, the harder it is to replace them with scabs during a strike. Management takes every opportunity to move skilled work out of the bargaining unit, either to management staff or to outside contractors.

Good training should keep the skilled jobs within the bargaining unit. Better training still should enable the union to challenge for work currently outside the unionized sectors.

A UNION AGENDA FOR TRAINING

It should be clear by now that unions cannot simply sign on to or trim the edges of employer training programs. Unions need their own agenda and their own plan.

During the 1980s, a vigorous discussion about workplace training generated a 1989 policy statement from the Ontario Federation of Labour.[7] This document provides guidelines for good training in different contexts: for employed workers, for displaced workers, for new entrants, for apprenticeships. Some of these recommendations have generated considerable debate within the labor movement, and many have been adapted to meet different circumstances. But they remain an excellent place to start thinking about a union agenda. The general guidelines for all types of training are reprinted here.

Guidelines For Good Training
[Excerpts from the Ontario Federation of Labour Policy Statement, 1989][8]

1. Skills training must be developmental. Every training program must teach skills in a way that goes beyond a particular job and leaves the trainee better able to take on different tasks in the future. This must be the case whether the program lasts two hours or two years.

2. Skills training programs must be open to all, not just the youngest or fittest. Special efforts must be made to use training as a vehicle for equality for women, visible minorities and others who have been discriminated against in the educational system and the workplace.

3. Skills training must be designed to raise the level of skill of the entire workforce, not just selected occupations or selected areas.

4. Skills training must flow from a worker-based identification of skill needs and not be restricted to narrowly-defined job performance factors identified by employers or consultants.

5. Skills training must support the development of good job design and technology that enhance the skills of workers.

6. Skills training must equip the trainee to be better able to have more control over his/her work.

7. Skills training must incorporate the practices of good adult education. It must start with what trainees know and want to know. It must respect abilities people bring to the training. It must use active learning techniques that make trainees' questions central. It must encourage questioning, discussion and participation.

8. Skills training must incorporate information that helps the trainee work safely, learn about individual and col-

lective rights and be better equipped to put one's knowledge and experience into action.

These principles might appear to be common sense, and indeed they should be. They emphasize putting workers' understanding at the center of both work and learning. They demand that instruction be built on workers' existing abilities as well as address new needs. They insist on learning that is in the long-term interests of workers. Unfortunately, when we look around at programs available today, these principles are hard to find. It is not a pretty sight.

Some examples of what these principles might look like in operation are the four cases discussed at the end of this chapter. But first, here are some recommendations for unions who are beginning to develop their own agenda in training. They focus on establishing a strong presence in the decision-making process and recognizing the breadth of issues to speak up about.

1. Recognize that training is about changing workplace relations and power. On virtually all questions there are two sides—union and management—each with its own interests and agendas. A successful joint program must begin by all participants recognizing this and building it into the structure and operation of the program. See case #1 below for more specifics.

Union influence cannot exist simply at the top policy levels of the program but must extend into the design, writing of training materials, delivery, and day-to-day administration.

2. Avoid these common pitfalls:

• viewing training as an objective science, where certain "experts" have the correct answers

• seeing training as an opportunity for the union leadership to hand out patronage

• using training as "bread and circuses" for the membership to distract from concessionary contracts or downsizing

• treating control over training as a bargaining item to give the company in exchange for "something important."

3. Make union control real. As we have seen in

many joint programs and apprenticeship programs, a union slot, official concurrence, or equal numbers in committees is not sufficient. If the union people know little about the area themselves or are just "serving time," then the only thing accomplished will be putting a union label on the company's program. If they have no union agenda and have adopted the company initiative, the same thing happens. See the discussion of "resources for jointness" in Chapter 16. In particular, the union must locate independent training resources, course designs, and subject matter experts. Other unions and labor studies centers are good sources.

Union control increases in importance because good training is a long-term process. These days, when the management fad is reorganization, executives put in charge of training frequently are young hotshots on their way up. They may be involved in training only temporarily and looking for fast returns. Often direction and long-term stability depend on the union.

4. Make sure content and teaching methods are relevant to learners' experience[9] (see the box).

5. Reject fragmented or pseudo-scientific approaches to learning. The sure signs are an emphasis on "establishing competencies," "performing task analysis," and defining job-specific skills. "Hands on," for example, can describe a legitimate and powerful approach to applying theory and creating the rules. But in corporate training programs, "hands on" usually means learning to follow

---

Training and Real-World Experience

Training can be the mechanism to help workers bridge the gap between the skills of yesterday and the technologies of tomorrow. But this can be true only if:

1) There is a social will to build that bridge by designing an appropriate curriculum, making the necessary training readily accessible, and providing income support during training.

2) The training is designed and presented with a clear sense of and respect for existing skills and knowledge.

3) The training is designed and presented in ways that will help people to gain more control over their lives than they give up by accepting change.

For example, Computer-Aided Manufacturing (CAM) software is used to write programs for computer-controlled machinery, without the user having to learn complex computer languages. Much of the software has been designed with engineers rather than machinists in mind. The language, the commands, and the thought processes that are built into the software reflect those of the engineer rather than the machinist.

Even still, despite the weaknesses of the software, appropriate training could bridge the gap between the software and the workforce. Instead, the available training tends to make the problem worse. Training by vendors, with its assumptions about who it should be teaching, often starts, in essence, by telling shop floor workers how stupid they are. They set the stage by saying that the software is so simple that high school students learn it easily and then they proceed to build on the kinds of experiences high school students have had while ignoring the experience of veteran workers.

Consider a class in CAM which included both high school students raised on computer games and skilled machinists who had no computer experience. The instructor, wanting to get "hands on" right away, started by telling the participants to "pick up your mouse and click through the first three menus in the program."

Now think about this. Highly skilled, experienced machinists, confident in their own arena, were left wondering why there were small rodents running around and especially why they had to pick them up. They were trying to imagine what kind of behavior clicking was and whether they could do it alone or needed a partner. And they were confused about why they were being asked to order lunch when they had just had coffee and donuts.

And then the machinists realized that the high school kids in the room knew exactly what to do. Feeling stupid, the machinists learned very little that day.

An alternative approach to training is easy to imagine. It would start from the assumption that the people that should be doing programming are the machinists, and that therefore the language of training begins with the language of the shop. It would respect and build on the skills that the machinists already possess. (The high school students who excelled at computerese didn't know the first thing about machining a piece of metal.) It would recognize that many machinists don't know how to operate a computer and provide the necessary basics, using analogies to the complex machines they already operate. And finally, it would be designed to help the machinists gain control and feel control over the programming function.

The success of this approach is the problem with this approach, for management. People who are trained this way go back to their workplaces and make demands of management—demands for control, demands for new skilled work in the bargaining unit, and demands for more training. They are not scared off by technical jargon that used to make them feel insecure.

The struggle over training can never be reduced to a struggle for "more." The nature of training, and how it relates to the processes of production, is a crucial piece of the battle to take control over, and define, our futures.

—Charley Richardson, Technology and Work Program, University of Massachusetts at Lowell

recipes as directed.

6. Don't separate training from work. The most important learning often takes place outside the classroom, but work has to be consciously organized to allow this to happen.

Too often, classroom training is not connected to the trainee's current work assignment. The training never becomes integrated into the worker's experience and months later is virtually forgotten. So work assignments should be coordinated with classroom work. In particular, the union needs to make sure that workers get on-the-job training with new technology and get assigned to working with the vendors or contractors who are installing or servicing it.

Of course, getting control over job assignments may require breaking new ground.

Finally, workers need non-production time in the work environment to think, to problem-solve, and to test ideas. They need access to manuals, computers, new equipment, experienced people, and experts.

7. Tie job advancement to clear requirements for training, while keeping in mind union priorities around both seniority and equity. In filling the higher-skilled jobs, current workers must have preference for training over hiring already-skilled workers off the street. See Case #2 below for one example.

Another example is the Career Ladder Program initiated by Service Employees International Union 767. This program at Cape Cod Hospital makes it possible to move up to a wide range of jobs in the hospital, including both mid-range jobs (medical technicians, supply coordinators) and top grades (electricians, dieticians, social workers). All 200 job classifications have clear requirements, and the contract provides that the most senior qualified applicant will get the job. The program provides for four different kinds of training: on-the-job, formal traineeships, in-house courses, and courses outside the hospital.[10]

In manufacturing, insist that virtually all of new skilled trades be hired from the ranks of production workers. The only exceptions should be to bring into the bargaining unit specific missing skills. This would preserve skilled jobs as separate classifications, strengthen job ladders for production workers, and force the company to take training seriously.

Hiring from within is possible because the company's claim to need new skilled workers immediately rarely holds up. Company plans for new equipment are made months or years in advance; people hired off the street may take considerable time to learn the procedures of the new workplace. While it may take a long time for a production worker to be fully skilled, many parts of the skilled job can be done with initial training; most two-person jobs work well with one experienced and one inexperienced.

Requiring that skilled jobs be filled from within can make some contribution to overcoming past discrimination based on gender and racism, since the production workforce will tend to have a greater proportion of women and minorities than the "skilled pool from the street."

A good example comes from the electronics industry in Canada, where the union has negotiated the creation of internal "trainee" positions; workers can apply for these strictly on the basis of seniority. This eliminates the barriers often posed by additional qualifications, such as experience in specific prerequisite jobs, from which women or other groups have historically been excluded. This approach has met with some success in workplaces where women and men, or white workers and workers of color, have roughly equal years of service but in separate job ghettos.[11]

8. Offer training by seniority, on the principle that people know themselves best and few would take a job they didn't think they could learn. Then when a job becomes open, the highest seniority person who has taken the training should get it.

Under these circumstances, some lower seniority people may move ahead faster than higher seniority ones. This pattern of advancement can help us in special cases, such as in reaching equity goals.

9. Support a variety of training methods. Programs must be designed so that people can move in different ways and at different rates.

There are good arguments for the traditional union demand that training be on company time; we should continue to press this point. At the same time, to keep work in the bargaining unit, we need some flexibility here, because companies have no trouble finding applicants who have been trained on their own time.

For example, if a programmer job requires some years of college courses and the union cannot win this training on company time, it may be better that the union win whatever partial support it can for the training than to allow the programmer jobs to be defined outside the bargaining unit.

10. Support union-run literacy and basic education courses in the workplace. These courses are not about imparting missing technical skills to learners so they can follow instructions better at work. They are tools to enable working people to overcome the silence often imposed on them and to take more control of their lives at work and in their community. A good example of such a program is described in Case #5.

11. Define bargaining unit jobs in terms of their function instead of their current tasks, and make sure all training programs do the same. The training programs to watch out for are those that define relevant work and skills in ways that prevent union workers from laying claim to work generated by new technologies.

For example, there are courses in Programmable Logic Controllers that say it's the electrician's job to trouble-shoot inputs and outputs, but not to do any programming. Or a desktop publishing course may define the clerical worker's job as no more than entering information into layouts pre-defined by others. This kind of training enforces boundaries we are trying to erase.

JOB TRAINING   JOB RE-TRAINING

Other examples:

a) An inspector's job may be defined as "using a micrometer to measure" finished parts. But if management buys a computerized Coordinate Measuring Machine, it could claim that operating this machine is a different job, and assign it to someone outside the bargaining unit. If, on the other hand, the inspector's job is defined in terms of function, say, "responsibility for determining as-produced dimensions," then the union can make the case for the inspector keeping the job, becoming the CMM operator, and getting the necessary training.

b) A clerical worker whose job is defined as "typing" or "filing" has already lost her claim to much new work, since typewriters and filing cabinets are on their way out. However, if the job is defined as "preparation of materials for printing or viewing" or "storage and retrieval of information," then the job includes desktop publishing and computerized databases.

c) For an electrician, "installing and maintaining control wiring" is a job task. "Responsibility for all equipment for communications between machines and controls" is a function that not only covers the traditional wiring jobs but also fiber optics and wireless communications. The 1993 GM-UAW contract specifically lists energy management systems, tool cutting paths, and fiber optics as areas where work functions will not be shifted away from skilled workers.[12]

If the union wins an enforceable commitment that certain job functions belong to the bargaining unit, then negotiating proper training is easier, because it now is also in management's interests to see that the workers are correctly trained.

12. Insist on long-term or intensive training where necessary. Few people can pick up programming competency in a computer language, for example, in one week of training or a few in-house classes. Many new skills may require ten hours a week for a year, or even a year or two of full-time training. Extensive training needs to be built into contracts.

This implies some modification of traditional union positions. Partly to eliminate favoritism and partly from the democratic impulse, a traditional union position has been to press for training across the board: everyone within a job title gets it. But specialized intensive training is so costly that, faced with this union policy, employers often choose not to give training to anyone (say, by contracting out instead).

The union's first priority has to be keeping the work in the bargaining unit (or bringing new work in). If specialized training is required, the union needs to insure that the opportunity for it is available fairly. For example, the union could insist that a new classification be created for the specialized job, and people could move into that classification by normal contractual means.

This approach may open up jobs that had not previously been considered part of the bargaining unit. With college courses, clerical workers could take over accounting functions, production workers could become paint specialists.

13. Press for bargaining unit members as instructors or peer trainers.

One reason is simply the issue of jobs. "Trainer" is one of the categories of jobs created by new technology and reorganization. Why shouldn't current workers get to move into these jobs?

But a more important reason flows from the conception of training. In the management-promoted view (training is simply the delivery of a body of knowledge selected by experts), experienced professionals clearly have the advantage.[13] But if effective teaching is making information available so that the learners can connect it to their own frameworks, then peer trainers become a vital part of the training approach. They understand the real problems and environment faced by the learners, as well as the social and technical history of the workplace. They can supply the links between theory, the new information, and the experiential framework of the trainee. (See case #4 below.)

Further, since peer trainers are in the workplace, they can help with continuing on-the-job learning.

Finally, the classroom is never a neutral place. Trainers who believe the union is irrelevant communicate that view in examples, approaches to problems, and informal discussion. Peer trainers who identify with the union create an environment where union views are heard and respected.

14. Select training providers carefully. Should the training be done by an in-house training department or should all or part be done by outside firms, consultants, or institutions? The illusion that training is an objective scientific procedure is very strong and tends to give an outside consultant enormous influence over the shape of the training program.

Private business consultants and training organizations should be assumed to have a management perspective toward training unless they demonstrate otherwise. The odds for unions' finding suitable training partners is slightly better in public adult education institutions like community colleges.

15. Monitor how training in one area affects other jobs. For example, introducing Computer Aided Design (CAD) not only affects how drawings are made but also how machines are set up, how production is run, and how clerical operations are conducted.

16. Demand increased training for every new machine purchased, possibly based on the dollar value of the machine or on some other measure, such as computer memory size or on the value added in production.

17. Demand contractual restrictions or penalties on the use of vendors and outside contractors. Every time a vendor (whether manufacturer or third party) is called into the workplace, or work is shipped out, or someone outside the bargaining unit does anything that could be bargaining unit work, this occurrence should be treated as official recognition that the bargaining unit has gotten insufficient training. The formula might be something like "one week of training per vendor-representative day; two days of training per plant engineer intervention."

18. Gain some control over what tools and equipment are used. A jobs-driven approach to training means the union fights for workers' ability to do the job, once trained. When management fails to provide adequate tools, machinery, or software, it creates an excuse for contracting out. If workers can't do the jobs, training loses its connection to work and becomes ineffective.

19. Press for a career ladder into the higher-level, non-bargaining unit jobs. In the auto industry, for example, this would mean demanding a formal route into plant engineering through the skilled trades, just the same as a route into skilled trades from production work. Such a career ladder means there must be a way for workers to get the formal training required.

As part of the same strategy, we should increase efforts to organize such higher-level jobs, and fight to keep them in-house. Again, the importance of this is visible in auto, where the total number of plant engineers is growing, but increasingly through the use of outside contractors. The lack of in-plant engineers often leads to outsourcing major jobs, even where otherwise the plant is fully capable.

20. Organize the technical workers who work as service people for manufacturers and vendors. Real technical training of in-house workers will happen only when management chooses not to depend on outside contracting for skilled work. So reducing the "low-cost provider" option should be part of our agenda, even though the difficulties (especially "professional consciousness") can hardly be exaggerated. Along the way, creating common union bonds between plant workers and the workers for outside contractors increases the possibilities for learning from, and supporting, each other.

Case Studies From the Front Lines

Following are examples of union-promoted training programs developed in some relationship to employers. They're not perfect; all reflect the relative power of the unions and management. But they contain imaginative approaches and ideas that other unions can use. The issues include dealing with a joint program; reinforcing the training/job advancement connection; dealing with economic pressures; use of peer instructors; and teaching literacy.

CASE #1. APSTC: INDEPENDENT UNION AGENDA IN COOPERATIVE PROGRAM

The Auto Parts Certificate is a training program for

production workers in which the union has maintained its own independent agenda while agreeing to work with management to develop and deliver the program. Maintaining this balance is a complex process, demanding time and attention at every level of decision making.

The certificate is an Ontario-based program of the Automotive Parts Sectoral Training Council (APSTC), a cooperative venture between the Canadian Auto Workers (CAW) and the Automotive Parts Manufacturers' Association. It is a 120-hour upgrading program for currently employed production workers, delivered during working hours at the rate of one week per year over a three-year period. It is designed to be universally available to production workers in participating firms, on a voluntary basis, through community colleges in southern Ontario.

The program focuses on three content areas: industry awareness, technology preparation, and workplace communications.

In all these areas, the aim is to promote critical awareness, to give equal voice to a labor point of view on technology, work organization, and quality, and to develop the confidence in learning that will open doors to further education both inside and outside of the workplace. The end point of the training will be a certificate recognized by employers throughout the industry.

The Canadian Auto Workers went into this venture with some clear bottom lines. They got agreement on the program framework, including the basic content areas, as a condition for getting involved in the creation of the APSTC. They also insisted on a clear bi-partite operating structure to ensure that the different interests of labor and management would be represented.

These early decisions laid a solid foundation for a working relationship that takes seriously the political character of training activities. What's important about the APSTC case is the way it asserts legitimacy for an independent labor perspective at every level of the training process.

APPROACHING COOPERATION

When it comes to partnership, labor could take a lesson from a joke often heard around the women's movement a decade ago: "When two people get married, they become one person: him." Working relationships at the APSTC were designed to avoid this style of "jointness" and to build instead an organization explicitly committed to equalizing gains from training for workers and management.

This goal is reflected most explicitly in the Training Council's Statement of Goals and Objectives. Its aim is to "develop the productive capacity of individuals as well as of the industry as a whole." For employers, the Council promises to develop "skilled learners capable of continuous learning on the job"; for individuals it promises to contribute toward "improved employment security and mobility in the sector" and to serve as "a ladder to further learning."

MONEY, STRUCTURE, AND INDEPENDENCE

Money always comes with strings attached, and training money is no exception. In Canada in 1991, federal and provincial governments were putting public dollars on offer throughout the private sector as part of committing the "industry partners" (labor and management) to certain kinds of action: to more "jointness" in labor/management relations; to accepting more responsibility for labor adjustment activities (usually meaning layoffs and closures) in their own industry; to planning for and spending more of their own resources on training; to participating in the shift of training activity out of public sector institutions into the private sector; to acceptance of a new federal policy of redirecting money from the unemployment insurance fund to training for employed workers.

The Canadian Auto Workers could not accept this agenda, and responded by agreeing to a limited mandate in the creation of the Council. They agreed to work with employers initially to develop and deliver a training program for currently employed production workers. If that was successful, they would examine broader activities. They agreed to a program model that would be delivered in partnership with, rather than in place of, the public system of community colleges, using college faculty from the full-time bargaining unit to teach alongside peer trainers from the workplace. And when the federal government tried to bluff them into taking politically unacceptable funding through the unemployment insurance scheme, they said they were prepared to walk away, and meant it.

The independent position of the union is protected through a bi-partite structure from top to bottom of the Training Council. The Board has equal numbers of voting members from labor and management and a staff headed by two co-managing directors. Committees, consultants, and curriculum are all assembled with care to preserve this balanced perspective. Virtually all decision-making to date has been achieved by consensus through a process of candid, no-nonsense debate.

POLITICS OF PARTICIPATION

The principles of universal access and voluntary participation are essential to the Certificate program. They mean that management can't choose only their friends to get training (nor can the local union, for that matter). The decision to participate in the program must be a joint one in the workplace; the program must be freely advertised to all employees in hourly production jobs who are interested, but participation cannot be required. Each firm can send a maximum of five workers each week (classes of 20 participants from four to six firms), so volunteers are scheduled by a local workplace joint committee, giving priority to equity goals as well as seniority. Of course these policies are only as good as their practice in local workplaces, and over time the situation will need to be monitored to see how well these principles of access and equity are being achieved.

ADULT EDUCATION FOR ADULTS

The Auto Parts Certificate program attempts to dissolve the distinction between education and training for production workers. It rejects common industrial training approaches and attempts a progressive, holistic approach that integrates technical, social, and general learning. It emphasizes peer instructors, incorporates the prior knowledge and skill of the learners, and uses a collective learning process free of formal assessment or evaluation. It attempts to accommodate different levels of education and different learning styles, and strives to build a discrimination- and harassment-free learning environment.

The curriculum includes three areas agreed to in the formation of the APSTC: general industry awareness, technology preparation, and workplace communications. The strategy is for each training activity to operate on several levels at once. For example, brainstorming might be used to explore students' experience of the technical or social impacts of a new manufacturing technology (e.g., computerized inventory). Next, key skills related to that technology might be introduced using a hands-on exercise (e.g., operating a simple spreadsheet on the computer). Then the product of that exercise (a printed spreadsheet) could be used to explore why management chose a certain technology or job design. In this way there is integration not only among topics and methods but integration of skills application with knowledge acquisition.

Peer trainers and an extensive Train-the-Trainer program are the key to success of training so deeply embedded in workplace knowledge. All classes are taught by two instructors, either two production workers recruited from the auto parts sector, or one production worker and a full-time community college instructor, also specifically screened and trained by the APSTC in the same Train-the-Trainer program as the peer instructors. Empathy and mutual respect between learners and trainers of all different backgrounds is a key to program success.

In fact, "respect" is the Council's catch-word to capture a range of program goals—a word that both labor and management can agree on. Under this banner, the program strives to provide learning that is useful to workers' lives as employees and union members, as workers and citizens, and that respects their right to participate in decisions that affect all aspects of their lives.[14]

Respect in the classroom includes starting with the knowledge and experience of learners and accommodating different levels and ways of learning in the group. These principles are meant to enhance individual comfort, confidence, and motivation in learning. What workers already know is treated as a relevant and appropriate starting point for whatever they might need or want to learn. That is, they are respected as "knowers" and even "teachers" in some areas as well as "learners."

Curriculum design takes for granted that people will participate in training not only for a variety of reasons, but with equally varied learning styles, academic skills and education backgrounds. They are provided opportunities to enter the process in different ways and at different starting points, each equally respected: printed words and numbers; pictures, diagrams and charts; paired, small-group and plenary discussion; watching, listening and speaking; asking, answering and reporting; experimenting, drawing constructing and demonstrating. No learning outcome depends primarily on trainee skill or comfort with any single learning method; no method becomes an insurmountable barrier to learning.[15]

These basic principles of respect include a discrimination- and harassment-free classroom. Care is taken, in the classroom and in Trainer Training, to explore how social differences and inequities—gender, race, class, sexual orientation—affect teaching and learning as well as everyday dynamics in the workplace. Training activities include practicing techniques for counteracting these problems and creating environments where everyone feels welcome.

—Nancy Jackson

For more information: Lynn Brophy, Co-Managing Director, Automotive Parts Sectoral Training Council, Ste. #203 - 140 Renfrew Drive, Markham, Ontario L3R 6B3

CASE #2. AFSCME/ILLINOIS: TRAINING FOR NEW CAREER PATHS

Many employer training programs only train for the next job on what may be a dead-end track. A challenge for union-supported training is to provide opportunities to make major changes in career paths, to use training to fulfill lifelong dreams. The Illinois American Federation of State County and Municipal Employees (AFSCME) Council 31 has negotiated an innovative workforce development program in the public sector which could also serve as a model for the private sector.

The Upward Mobility Program (UMP) combines career counseling, educational plans, pre-paid tuition and fees, and priority promotional opportunities for 45,000 State of Illinois employees covered under the master agreement.

During a one-on-one worksite session with an independent career counselor, each employee chooses a target job classification within state government. Targets for the training program are those which employees do not normally move into through the internal promotion system. Target jobs can be in fiscal management, human services, or technical/office work. Some jobs require degrees or licensing, and UMP covers the appropriate training. Through the program one office worker moved into a professional position as a state agency Program Representative. Another earned a bachelor's degree in social work to become a case worker. A couple, both hospital dietary workers studied computers, one becoming a data processing specialist and the other a programmer/analyst.

Employees can choose any one of the target jobs; it need not be related to their current field; nor do they need any qualifying level of education or experience.

UMP develops an education plan for each target job. About half require a specific college degree. Previous degrees and work experience are recognized. Education plans for the others are tied to exams written for UMP which are divided into the relevant knowledge areas. Employees need take college course work only for those sections of the exam which they could not pass. Employees in the program may receive up to half their course time off work each semester. Employees pay for their own books and contribute their personal benefit time when they must be away from work longer than their UMP time provides.

One of the most important features of the Upward Mobility Program is that it offers a priority for promotion to the targeted job. Once employees have completed the necessary testing and education, they receive a certificate that makes them eligible to be placed on a priority promotion list. The most senior on the list is given preference for the next available vacancy in that job (after factors such as shift preference of those currently in the title, or recall of those currently holding the job title, are taken into account).

Nearly one-third of those who have received a certificate for their job classification have been promoted. This has proven key in motivating employees to take on the often arduous task of returning to school, sometimes traveling considerable distances, coping with additional childcare problems, bearing additional costs, and dealing with the stress involved in such an endeavor.

Since AFSCME Council 31 first negotiated the UMP in 1989 as part of their master agreement with the State of Illinois, over a thousand employees have received promotions to their target jobs. With a budget of $3-$3.5 million ($2 million or more goes for tuition), nearly 44 percent of eligible employees have met with a career counselor. The response has been especially strong among women and minorities. Over two-thirds of the current participants are women and over one-third are people of color. The 1994-1997 agreement expanded the program to include displaced state workers, so that employees who complete the program are able to promote from layoff status.

The report of the Illinois Commission on the Future of Public Service praised the State and AFSCME because they have "recognized and invested in ongoing career development among many entry level employees and middle managers through the Upward Mobility Program." UMP is providing the State of Illinois with appreciative, motivated and highly qualified employees. Most important is the sense of opportunity in the workforce. As one participant wrote, "One of the strengths of the Upward Mobility Program is that it gives you the flexibility to try for jobs your talents qualify you to perform, without getting blocked into a bureaucratic pigeonhole."

—Kathy Wood, AFSCME UMP Coordinator

For more information: Upward Mobility Program, AFSCME Council 31, PO Box 2328, Springfield IL 62705. (217) 788-2800.

CASE #3. WISCONSIN REGIONAL TRAINING PARTNERSHIP

The Wisconsin Regional Training Partnership is designed to remove the two most common barriers to skill upgrading. First, companies often adjust to intensified competition with short-term, low-wage strategies that undermine development of a highly skilled and committed workforce. Highly qualified workers are unlikely to contribute much to upgrading skill levels and technology without having confidence that the benefits will be shared.

Second, many companies are reluctant to invest in a highly and broadly skilled workforce because other firms may reap much of the returns by hiring away their trained workers. Since every firm has the same incentive, each of them tries to limit its training to narrow, task-specific skills. Small and midsize companies are especially prone to restricting their training activities to informal on-the-job training.

Business and labor leaders formed the Wisconsin Regional Training Partnership in late 1992 to promote workplace transformation and family-supporting jobs. The WRTP has 23 charter member companies concentrated in the Milwaukee metropolitan area's durable goods sector. Workers are represented mainly by the Machinists, United Auto Workers, United Electrical Workers, Paper Workers, and Steelworkers. The WRTP's Executive Council is composed of an equal number of management and labor representatives and a smaller number from the public sector. The executive council developed policies in the following areas, and member companies and unions commit to adopting these recommendations in the context of their own bargaining agreements, past practices, and specific conditions.

Incumbent Worker Training: Joint steering committees create on-site skills centers for confidential assessment, counseling, and training services provided by local technical colleges. Peer advisors promote the programs to fellow workers, and increasingly participate in tutoring, training, and curriculum development. The model is being transferred to multi-worksite skills centers for clusters of small businesses.

Future Workforce Programs: The WRTP has developed an employment-linked training program for unemployed workers and a youth apprenticeship program for high school students. In the adult model, private industry councils fund intensive programs in machining or other occupational areas at local technical colleges or qualified community organizations. Companies guarantee jobs to participants who successfully complete the program.

In the school-to-work model, high school students receive workplace training and related classroom instruction during their junior and senior years. Graduates qualify for production jobs and gain advanced standing in technical college programs. Both the incumbent and future workforce programs will conform to industry standards.

Training Standards: The State of Wisconsin has designated the WRTP as its representative to develop and implement voluntary skills standards. The WRTP is working with area technical colleges to create a progression of training certificates for: 1) basic skills that all workers need to perform entry-level jobs, learn new skills, and advance their careers; 2) applied skills that all workers need in a "high performance" workplace, such as process control and team-building; and 3) technical skills that all workers need to use new technologies, such as parts programming and data editing in machining occupations. These certificates should enable workers to participate in more technical aspects of the design and manufacturing process, gain new jobs and higher wages, qualify for apprenticeship programs in the trades, and achieve advanced standing in a variety of related technical college programs.

Public Resources for Industry: As the advisory board of the state of Wisconsin's regional program to aid manufacturing, the WRTP is identifying small and medium-size companies to participate in a needs assessment and technical assistance process. The WRTP is working with management and unions to develop agreements on employment security and sourcing decisions as a condition for providing technical assistance to suppliers. Public resources would be devoted to small businesses that are complying with training commitments incorporated in supplier certification standards. Collective bargaining, supplier certification, and public resources should be combined to drive upgrading of industry for everyone's benefit.

Resource Center: The WRTP is working with public sector partners to establish a resource center to provide technical assistance and improve access to these model programs and resources.

The WRTP demonstrates how a wide variety of state and federal policies and resources can be used for the benefit of working people. Most of these programs were not created with any intention of benefitting unions and workers. In fact, national policies to create youth apprenticeships and training standards could be used to exclude current workers from promotions and pay increases, while state programs to aid manufacturing could facilitate the movement of jobs from high-wage to low-wage companies. But that is all the more reason for unions to put forward their own strategies and direction.

—Eric Parker, Research Associate

For more information: Wisconsin Regional Training Partnership, c/o Milwaukee Area Technical College, 700 West State Street, Milwaukee WI 53233. (414) 297-6867

CASE #4. UAW/ROUGE STEEL: PEER TRAINERS

Peer trainers became a central part of an extensive skilled trades retraining program operated by UAW Local 600 and Rouge Steel Company, working with Henry Ford Community College.

The role evolved as a result of special circumstances in the project. From the beginning the plan was to use Rouge Steel skilled tradespeople as peer instructors who

would eventually lead all instruction in the project. In the earliest phases, the conception of the peer instructor was minimal and vague, ranging from "script readers" of prepared lectures to lab assistants.

The original approach to developing the electrical/electronics curriculum was quite traditional. The electronic skills upgrading classes were to start at the beginning of basic electronics theory, using appropriate lab experiments to illustrate the theory. The modules would build on this base, finally reaching the level of application.

This plan was terminated. Experienced faculty found the behavioral, block-by-block learning modules ineffective. Experienced skilled tradespeople felt insulted by the way elementary material was presented in the blank slate approach. It also became clear that the peers had much more to offer than serving as warm versions of videotaped presentations.

Four critical elements came together. 1) The union/management/ community college guiding body was willing to learn from its problems with the traditional approach and to experiment and revise its plans. 2) The training program began to adopt an adult education model with many elements of a worker-centered approach. 3) Some of the peer trainers in the program demonstrated considerable initiative and knowledge.

As a result, the peer trainers were involved almost from the beginning in the design and delivery of the electrical curriculum.

Great portions of the traditional approach to teaching electronics were discarded. The problem was that it assumed that experienced electricians knew nothing from their experience and that they should throw away the knowledge framework they had developed and used over the years.

Instead, the training began with the assumption that the tradespeople themselves largely knew what they needed and wanted to learn—both specific and general, factual and theoretical—and that the most effective training would build from those interests. The training for each content area made the information and theory available; each tradesperson could dig in where he or she chose.

Wherever possible the training started with and built from situations faced in the plants. Theory was used to answer real questions, instead of hypothetical questions being used to test knowledge of abstract theory. When a participant came to class with a question developed on the job, it wasn't treated as a distraction from a lesson plan; instead it might become the focus of the class attention for several days, with participants gathering relevant information at their worksites.

The peers were essential at the early stages of designing this course because they were in the best position to identify the equipment, the context, and the problems to be used. Similarly, the peers had a lot to offer as classroom instructors. They could understand problems brought into class from the plant and pose examples known to other participants.

At the same time, this training method places much higher demands on even experienced instructors: a command of a large body of knowledge as well as real world experience, since the class could take the discussion in many directions. Some of the tradespeople in the class will be more knowledgeable than the instructor in several areas, and the instructor needs to be able to encourage participation and use this as a resource rather than being threatened by it.

Adjusting to these methods was personally difficult for some experienced instructors used to traditional classrooms. Peer instructors faced these difficulties plus a lack of teaching experience and in-depth knowledge in some areas. They were also on "front street" with the people with whom they would continue to work closely for years.

To address these problems, special training for the peer instructors included the following:

1. Peers participated in a general orientation and discussion about the aims and methods of the program.

2. Peers were involved in conceptualizing parts of the course, developing equipment for the course, trying out exercises, reviewing, and critiquing curriculum.

3. Initial classes were taught by experienced instructors selected by the college. Peer trainers first took the course and assisted small groups during the exercises.

4. As they developed confidence in teaching and their ability to deal with the content, the peers took over more and more of the courses.

In addition various support activities were set up.

1. The peer instructors regularly met to discuss among themselves and with the college instructor any problems with subject matter or handling of classroom situations.

2. Special classes in teaching skills were designed and provided.

3. Peers were encouraged and supported in getting outside training (vendor or community college) in areas that would be helpful to the curriculum.

4. Special classes were set up on some technical subjects. For example, a math course designed to fill in knowledge gaps and take the peers through the basics of calculus was started.

5. All involved worked to create a supportive atmosphere where there was no shame in an instructor not knowing everything and where a good answer was, "I don't know but I'll find out and get back to you tomorrow."

Training began in 1990. About 200 skilled workers went through Electrical Module I. Most people involved considered the training program a clear success. In the fall of 1991 the program was suspended pending resolution of some general contract disputes between the union and the company, and it has not been restarted.[16]

—Mike Parker

For more information: Office of Corporate Training, Henry Ford Community College, 5101 Evergreen, Dearborn MI 48128. (313) 845-9656

CASE #5. BASIC EDUCATION AND SKILLS DEVELOPMENT

BEST (Basic Education and Skills Development) is a worker literacy program of the Ontario Federation of Labour. It has over 100 sites in operation, in mines, hospitals, factories, hotels, breweries, nursing homes, municipalities, and even universities throughout Ontario. It is labor-run and supported financially by governments, unions, and employers.

The BEST program develops better skills in reading, writing, and math, but in the context of the broader union struggle to empower working people. Its philosophy comes from labor's conception of the broader goals of social unionism: to empower working people to take control of their lives individually and collectively; to be better able to speak with their own voices; to be better able to make those voices heard; to question, criticize, evaluate, and act as full citizens with a broad social vision in a democratic society.

BEST is taught right in the workplace, where workers can learn in an atmosphere that they know and in which they feel competent. It is offered at all hours of the day and night, depending on the needs of the group. Co-workers from the same workplace do the instructing, with training and support from regional program coordinators. Usually half the class time is on working hours and half on the employee's time.

The BEST program uses small group learning. There is no standard curriculum. Instead, each group does a collective self-assessment of participants' needs and interests to set the direction for their class. Small groups provide a place to practice the skills useful for collective action: discussion, questioning, listening, analysis, goal setting, assessment of progress, and evaluation of the process. Every aspect of the program is designed to facilitate growth in the collective ability of working people to shape the world in which we live.

—Jim Turk and Jean Unda

For more information: BEST Training Officer, Ontario Federation of Labour, 15 Gervais Drive, Ste. 202, Toronto, Ontario M3C 1Y8.

Resources

Rosemary Batt and Paul Osterman, *A National Policy for Workplace Training: Lessons from State and Local Experiments*, Economic Policy Institute, Washington, D.C., 1993.

Sue E. Berryman, "Summary of the Cognitive Science Research and its Implications for Education—Designing Effective Learning Environments," *Solutions,* National Council on Vocational Education, Washington, D.C., 1990-91.

Sheryl Greenwood Gowen, *The Politics of Workplace Literacy: A Case Study*, Teachers College Press, New York, 1992.

Nancy Jackson, "Working Knowledge: The Politics of Skills

Training," *Our Times*, May 1989, pp. 18-21.

Nancy Jackson, ed., *Training for What? Labour Perspectives on Skill Training,* Our Schools/Our Selves Education Foundation, 1992. (1698 Gerrard Street East, Toronto, Ontario M4L 2B2)

Lisa M. Lynch, *Strategies for Workplace Training: Lessons from Abroad*, Economic Policy Institute, Washington, D.C., 1993.

Jane Mace and Martin Yarnit, eds., *Time Off to Learn: Paid Educational Leave and Low-Paid Workers*, Methuen and Co., New York, 1987.

Daniel Marschall, "Unions and Work-Based Learning: The Rediscovery of Apprenticeship," *ILR Report*, Vol. 28, No. 1, Fall 1990.

Ontario Federation of Labour Policy Paper, "Education and Training," adopted 1989. The entire text is available from the Ontario Federation of Labour, 15 Gervais Drive, Toronto, Ontario M3C 1Y8. It is also reprinted in *Training for What?*

Gary Saganski, "A Worker-Centered Approach to Education and Training," in Steve Babson, ed., *Lean Work: Exploitation and Empowerment in the Global Auto Industry*, Wayne State University, Detroit, Spring 1995.

Anthony R. Sarmiento and Ann Kay, *Worker Centered Learning: A Guide to Workplace Literacy*, AFL-CIO Human Resources Development Institute, Washington, D.C., 1990.

Jim Turk and Jean Unda, "So We Can Make Our Voices Heard: The Ontario Federation of Labour's BEST Project on Worker Literacy," in Maurice Taylor, Glenda Lewe, and James Draper, eds., *Basic Skills for the Workplace,* Culture Concepts, Toronto, 1991.

Notes

1. See Robert Reich, *The Work of Nations: Preparing Ourselves for 21st-Century Capitalism*, A.A. Knopf, New York, 1991.

2. Harley Shaiken, "Lean Production in a Mexican Context," in Steve Babson, ed., *Lean Work: Exploitation and Empowerment in the Global Auto Industry*, Wayne State University Press, Detroit, Spring 1995; Harley Shaiken and Stephen Herzenberg, *Automation and Global Production: Automobile Engine Production in Mexico, the United States and Canada*, Monograph Series, 26, Center for U.S. Mexican Studies, University of California, San Diego, 1987.

3. See Lawrence Mishel and Ruy A. Teixeira, *The Myth of the Coming Labor Shortage: Jobs, Skills, and Incomes of America's Workforce 2000*, Economic Policy Institute, Washington, D.C., 1991.

4. Addendum to "Education and Training," a policy adopted at Ontario Federation of Labour Convention, November 1989.

5. Sue E. Berryman, "Summary of the Cognitive Science Research and its Implications for Education—Designing Effective Learning Environments," *Solutions,* National Council on Vocational Education, 1990-91.

6. David Robertson, "Workplace Restructuring and the CAW Response," paper presented at Canadian Sociology and Anthropology Association, 25th Annual Meeting, May 1990, Victoria, B.C. Also Robertson's articles in *Training for What?* (see Resources, above).

7. Contained in the appendix of Jackson, *Training For What?*

8. "Education and Training," a policy adopted at Ontario Federation of Labor Convention, November 1989.

9. See Anthony R. Sarmiento and Ann Kay, *Worker-Centered Learning: A Union Guide to Workplace Literacy,* AFL-CIO Human Resources Development Institute, 1990, for examples of this approach in workplace literacy programs.

10. See contract with Hospital Workers Union Local 767 SEIU, Hyannis, Massachusetts and *Career Ladder Program,* Service Employees International Union, no date.

11. See Karen Hadley, "Working Lean and Mean: A Gendered Experience of Restructuring in an Electronics Manufacturing Plant," Ontario Institute for Studies in Education, Toronto, 1994.

12. See UAW *Skill,* Spring 1994, for a discussion of this concept.

13. In general the idea of peer training is not highly regarded among training professionals. Self-interest may motivate some, who find it more lucrative when companies leave the job of training to the "professionals" rather than the amateurs. The claim is that this kind of training is haphazard, that bad work habits are perpetuated, and most of all, the training does not build management's control of the work process.
Some programs use peer trainers to save money, or to get the union leadership to buy in (new appointments to be made), but the role of the peer trainer is simply to deliver a script designed and written by the experts.
Even where peer training is defended, it is called "structured peer training" and frequently takes the form of a checklist of prescribed activities. (Bob Filiczak, "Frick Teaches Frack," *Training,* June 1993, Vol. 30, No. 6, pp. 30-34.)
On the other hand, some promoters of participation programs claim that use of peer trainers is one of the characteristics of successful union involvement in training. (Jerome Rosow and Robert Zager, *Training—The Competitive Edge,* Josey Bass, San Francisco, 1988.)

14. See Jeffry Piker, "Auto Parts Certificate: An Innovative Approach to Training," Automotive Parts Sectoral Training Council, Toronto, 1994, p. 7.

15. Piker, pp. 7-8.

16. See Mike Parker and Gary Saganski, "Technology Training: Transferring Control to the Learner," *Proceedings of International Federation of Automatic Control Symposium on Automated Systems Based on Human Skill and Intelligence*, Pergammon Press, London, 1993. Also Gary Saganski, "A Worker-Centered Approach to Education and Training," in Steve Babson, ed., *Lean Work: Exploitation and Empowerment in the Global Auto Industry*, Wayne State University, Detroit, Spring 1995.

Working Smart:
A Union Guide to Participation Programs and Reengineering
Labor Notes • 7435 Michigan Ave. • Detroit, MI 48210 • (313) 842-6262

Chapter 36

Surviving Lean Production

Using traditional adversarial tactics, unions have modified lean production to make it more survivable for workers. Changes include electing team leaders, establishing ways to challenge work overload, requiring replacements for absentees, enforcing the right to rotate jobs, using seniority for job openings, and organizing the subcontractors. In doing so, they have challenged some of the bedrock assumptions of management-by-stress.

ALTHOUGH ALMOST EVERY INDUSTRY is trying to implement some form of lean production, or management-by-stress, the auto industry has been at it the longest. Therefore local unions in the auto industry have had the most time to figure out what to do with it.

At the Japanese-managed transplants in North America, auto workers and their unions have managed to impose their own modifications on the system. It's still management-by-stress, but their experiences illustrate that the system is not all-powerful.

As in chapter 8, we will examine NUMMI, Mazda (AutoAlliance International), and CAMI to see what lessons other workers facing management-by-stress can learn. Union members facing the introduction of management-by-stress techniques may want to use the achievements of these locals of the United Auto Workers and the Canadian Auto Workers as a checklist for union positions and contract language to consider.

The histories of union-management relations in the three plants are quite different. All three locals began with the union open to a cooperative approach. At CAMI, experience with the system moved the officers to become more militant and more adversarial. The local had the strong backing of the national Canadian Auto Workers.

At Mazda a group of rank and filers ran on a militant platform in the first election and won several key positions. These officers also received active support from their regional UAW office.

At NUMMI, leadership of Local 2244 has been hotly contested almost since the plant opened, between a frankly pro-cooperation group, the Administration Caucus (backed by regional and International officials), and a more militant group, the People's Caucus. Therefore NUMMI has seen fewer modifications to the system than have CAMI and Mazda.

HOW THE UNIONS MODIFIED MANAGEMENT-BY-STRESS

• Establish working stewards

The UAW insisted on one of the most important modifications to the management-by-stress system before the plants even opened, in the initial contracts with NUMMI and Mazda. This was working stewards, called "union coordinators." In the Big Three, this tradition had died decades earlier. The closest union rep to the shop floor was the full-time, company-paid "chief steward" or "committeeperson," representing 250 people. Perhaps because NUMMI would initially agree only to a smaller number of committeepersons than at the Big Three, the UAW insisted on some form of shop floor representation.

Thus each two "groups" or "units" of workers elects a union coordinator. A group consists of two to six teams under one supervisor (called "group leader" at NUMMI or "unit leader" at Mazda), so each coordinator represents 30-60 workers. They work full-time on regular jobs and assist co-workers with problems during breaks or lunchtime. They receive two hours' extra pay per week. Contractually, any potential grievances must be dealt with by the coordinator and the supervisor first, before entering step one of the grievance procedure, which involves the committeeperson.

At NUMMI, the coordinators are not particularly well organized by the local union to play any particular role and thus have not fulfilled their potential: to be the union leaders' eyes and ears on the shop floor, to organize team members to act collectively on their own behalf, to be the workers' first line of defense. (As of mid-1994, union leaders were making plans to change this.) At Mazda/AAI, however, the local has put resources into educating the coordinators through special classes. Their level of activism varies, but as a group they have been very effective in contract campaigns, strike votes, and other mass action issues (see below).

The existence of the coordinators is an important ideological break with management-by-stress, because it implies that workers and managers do have different interests on the shop floor.

• Change the function of teams

The role of teams is contested terrain. Unevenly, but in a significant number of teams, workers have transformed them from management-manipulated groups for applying peer pressure, to teams of workers who stick together to defend each other.

Teams do not actually have an essential function in the system. In fact, from time to time management stops calling team meetings altogether and then resurrects them again. At the same time, the team structures and ideology do exist, and at times workers use the teams to articulate demands and pressure management. The following article written by David Binns in the union newsletter at CAMI gives an example:

CHANGING THE DEFINITION OF TEAMWORK

What does teamwork mean to you?

To the members of Final 4, YOE Assembly, it means solidarity.

It was unfortunate that, on May 21 at 7:00 a.m., the team collectively had no alternative but to exercise their rights under the Occupational Health and Safety Act and enact a work refusal. [Ontario's law permits workers to refuse unsafe work, and Local 88 had recently passed out wallet cards instructing members how to use this right.]

These workers knew that too many of their fellows were afflicted by Repetitive Strain Injuries with no relief manpower. The facts acknowledge this—12 RSIs this model year (5 current) and two cases requiring Workers Compensation claims.

Ergonomic concern job elements had not been removed from the team and a Priority I tool arm identified by Ergonomics in early April had not been supplied.

There were several circumstances which also contributed to the severity of their concern that day:

—the model mix was not balanced;

—station #65 had been identified as a "hard on the

Different from Japan

Even before the local unions at our three plants got hold of it, management-by-stress in a union plant in North America was not exactly the same as in the home plants in Japan. We'll note these differences here because there are signs that, if it could, North American managements would like to introduce more of the practices used in Japan. In 1994, for example, CAMI began a campaign to get "Back to the Basics" of the Suzuki Production System.

Some of the differences described below were introduced by management to make the system more acceptable to North American workers. Others were consciously imposed by the unions here. Others existed just because of cultural and historical differences.

But some policies failed to survive the journey across the Pacific, at least initially, simply because management did not dare to introduce them. Management understood the power of the unions, how deeply certain traditions were embedded, and how costly the attempt to change those traditions might be. Even the non-union transplants had to go easy in many areas for fear of stirring up a union drive.

1. Workers' varying backgrounds. In Japan, until very recently, the auto companies recruited only male high school graduates for their production lines. Single workers are encouraged to live in dormitory-style company housing, and married ones may buy company-owned housing as well. A worker starts at, say, Mazda, and stays there his whole working life, with no chance to experience any other work culture than Mazda's. This gives the company the chance to mold its workers and exert greater control.

In contrast, at Mazda's Michigan plant, workers had a variety of previous work experience before hiring in there, they were of different ages, and they lived in a wide radius in all directions around the plant. At NUMMI, the company had little control over choice of its initial workforce, because the UAW insisted that the company recruit from among the workers who had been laid off by GM at the same plant. The workforce was therefore older and union-wise.

In addition, plant populations in North America tend to be diverse ethnically and to include both men and women, in contrast to the monoculture which characterizes Japanese plants. Attempts by corporations to avoid this diversity may be met with legal penalties. Honda, for example, was fined for discrimination against African-Americans in hiring.[1]

Also unlike Japan, in North America many workers are single parents and do not have an extended family readily available to help out in emergencies. In Japan, it is more feasible for companies to expect workers to be at their beck and call and to work heavy overtime, because the male worker will have a wife at home to deal with the children and care for his needs.

2. Wage structure. Instead of the *nenko/satei* wage structure that is so important in Japanese auto plants, where increases are determined both by seniority and by supervisors' evaluations, the North American plants opened with the flat wage structure that is industry standard here.[2] Japanese managers knew that it would be politically impossible to start up a union plant where the wage spread could reach two-to-one. Even the non-union transplants have not yet attempted it, probably for fear of unionization.[3] However, Toyota is introducing a larger number of pay grades in its Kentucky plant. And at least one report promoted by the President's Commission on the Future of Worker-Management Relations (the Dunlop Commission) emphasizes that linking promotion and employee compensation to performance appraisals is a central part of the new "High Performance Work Practices" approach.[4]

back" area;

—team members had not received ample time off for RSI recovery;

—the requirement of 14 workers and 1 floater had not been realized.

...There were two occasions where they had no choice but to stop the line as there was no manpower available to allow workers to leave the line to go to the restroom.

Management should now be aware that Health and Safety is not the problem of an individual but is the concern of teams collectively...

• **Define team leader as pro-worker**

One of the most important elements in turning the team into a solidaristic group is the team leader. He or she must see the job primarily as defending and advancing team members rather than as managing.

At all three plants, management clearly viewed the team leader as an assistant supervisor—a transmission belt from management to workers. While the initial procedures for selecting the team leader varied slightly from plant to plant, management had the final say. Anger at team leaders and the leader selection process, along with charges of favoritism, were widespread.

At NUMMI, workers' complaints forced management to modify its leader selection procedure to be more objective, to give union leaders a role in evaluations, and to make seniority a tie-breaker.

In 1992, CAMI workers won the right to elect team leaders, in a one-year experiment. At Mazda, electing team leaders was a key issue in the 1991 contract campaign. The union found that the effect of instituting elections was not so much turnover of team leaders; rather it forced team leaders to shape up. Now at AAI, team leaders are elected annually and serve one-year terms. In 1994 the union resisted the company's demand to pick team leaders by seniority.

Language in the AAI contract makes it clear that the team leader is not in any sense a supervisor or responsible for supervisor administrative duties. An "understanding" specifically excludes attendance taking, overtime schedul-

---

The wage system is critical to maintaining the management-by-stress system in Japanese auto plants. Up to half a worker's annual wage is contingent, with a major part directly determined by his foreman and another part more indirectly decided by management through group bonuses.

Workers thus have a strong incentive to come in early, do set-up work during break, submit *teians* (suggestions), vote for the company-favored union candidate, and even sing the company song. Under this system, many if not most workers will volunteer for extra work and forego their vacations. Use of group or individual pressure tactics against foremen is far less likely. With a set, flat wage structure, UAW and CAW members in the transplants are partially protected from the pressure to prove oneself individually.

3. Union role. For historical reasons, the expected role of the current main auto unions in Japan is to help management implement the production system. In North America, of course, the union's expected role had been to represent workers in an adversarial relationship. While the transplant managements tried as much as possible to convince the UAW and the CAW to act like Japanese company unions, and while the contracts were written to promote this stance, the fact that workers naturally had different expectations helped the unions to establish greater independence.

Similarly, in Japanese auto plants, supervisors are part of the same unions as rank and file workers and tend to control the unions in management's interests. In North America supervisors are generally not part of the bargaining unit.

4. The ideology of workers' power. The official ideology of CAMI, Mazda, and NUMMI emphasizes workers' voice and respect for workers as the basis of the production process. The NUMMI contract, for example, states that the union and the company are committed to "provide workers a voice in their own destiny in decisions that affect their lives before such decisions are made."

In Japan, workers *participate* by making suggestions, but neither side speaks of workers as empowered. The concept of "empowerment" was added to the package in North America to attract workers who might be leery of the unfamiliar Japanese system.

This false advertising had consequences. After workers' initial expectations of control and equality were dashed, in some situations they turned the promises against management, appropriating the rhetoric of participation and dignity for their own demands.

5. The ideology of teams. Under the Japanese version of management-by-stress, "teamwork" means workers cooperating to meet management's goals. Workers are organized into quality circles to work on specific problems, usually on non-work time, but these circles are not units of production.

At CAMI, NUMMI, and Mazda, the notion of teamwork was used to help sell the production system. For one thing, the experienced auto workers at NUMMI had to be won to a system without classifications, in which jobs had no sharp boundaries and any worker could be told to do any kind of work. This was defined as "teamwork."

Again, the rhetoric had consequences. Union activists appropriated the idea of teams and gave it their own content. We describe below how fights over the nature of the team leaders—should they be pro-worker or pro-company?—turned out.

ing, and payroll processing.

At CAMI, early on the union prepared a handbook to "help Team Leaders in performing their Team Leader functions and be good union members." It reminded leaders, for example, that they did not have to work off the clock, take attendance, equalize overtime, or do counseling. It encouraged them to call the committeeperson (union rep) with any questions.

When the one-year experiment was up, however, CAMI management ended the elections and installed a leader selection system similar to that used as NUMMI. Leader candidates are now chosen under a point system: up to 24 points for leadership courses taken, 20 points for the score on leadership exercises, 10 points for an interview, 15 points for attendance, 6 points for seniority, 9 points for seniority on the team, and 6 points for the team members' preference.[5]

CAMI management is blunt about the built-in contradiction in the leader's role. In a bulletin to team members explaining why management was ending the experiment, Vice President Phil Johnston noted,

> There is an inherent conflict as the Team Leader tries to satisfy the team members, perform the duties to the satisfaction of the Area Leader, and meet the objectives of the production system.[6]

According to CAW Local 88 Vice President Dave Binns, CAMI changed the system because the company wanted team leaders to be its pool for promotion to group leader. When team leaders were chosen by the teams, "they weren't the kind of people the company would have selected.[7]

In the U.S., election of team leaders seems to have become a standard union demand at plants newly installing lean production, such as Ford's Wayne Assembly plant near Detroit.

• **Establish a mechanism to challenge production standards**

The 1991 Mazda contract for the first time included

What We Need

Workers shouldn't have to say, as they do in lean production systems, that they can't survive to retirement. Instead, the workplace should be characterized by a comfortable work pace—one that is sustainable. This requires four elements:

1. A recognition that a comfortable pace involves discretionary time and the possibility for workers to vary the job and the pace.

2. Adequate relief staff.

3. A regulated (negotiated) process for changing job content and job times...

4. A recognition that foremen must stop working so the real problems can be corrected, not covered up.

—Dave Yettaw, President

[From the *Headlight*, newspaper of UAW-GM Local 599 in Flint, Michigan, July 28, 1994]

---

language similar to that in most Big Three contracts: "production standards will be set on the basis of normal working conditions, with experienced operators, and with consideration for fatigue and the need for relief time." It contains a mechanism for the union to challenge the way production is organized. A Union Work Standards Representative was established. Problem resolution is to consider "all aspects of the job including, but not limited to, the proper mix, sequence, method, process, tooling, and line balancing to ensure suitable employee work allocations."

In 1994 the union won much of the language of the Ford contract. It includes "when a production standard is established...the element times shall remain unchanged and not subject to dispute unless and until the operation is changed as a result of change in method, layout, tools, equipment, material or product design." The company cannot increase the amount of work required because of absenteeism; the worker and union rep must be notified before a time study is conducted.

The union has a specific means to keep the company from speeding up work. On the trim and final lines, for example, the union enforces "constraints" such as "no more than two manual transmissions in a row" or "no more than three sunroofs out of five."

If a priority 1 constraint cannot be met, the company must place an empty carrier on the line. If a priority 2 constraint cannot be met, the company must contact the affected area in advance to find out whether there are extra workers available. If not, management must release an empty carrier between cars.

At CAMI the contract commits the company to consider the "reasonable working capacity of normal experienced operators" in timing the elements of jobs and creates a procedure to discuss union complaints about heavy workloads. The company also agreed to review changes to job elements with the worker before they are implemented; and not to increase the speed of lines "beyond the level for which they are adequately staffed, for the purpose of making up lost production."

All these changes go directly against the grain of management-by-stress, whose byword is for management to have complete flexibility for "continuous improvement" in workloads.

CAMI workers also use unsafe work refusals to deal with job overloads.

• **Require replacement workers for absentees**

Originally, Mazda employed a force of temporary workers who could be used at management's sole discretion for a few hours, a day, or many months. These workers had no guaranteed work, no job security, and no real union protection. Although they paid dues, the contract specifically excluded union representation for temporary workers on discipline and discharge. As a result, they made possible a key aspect of the management-by-stress system: as lean a core workforce as possible, with a second tier of workers to absorb the fluctuations in management's needs. These temporaries, called "Support

Members," were easily intimidated by management and pressed to work exceptionally hard if they hoped to be hired for a regular job. Management often abused the concept of temporaries by keeping them on regular jobs for months at a time.

The 1991 Mazda contract did away with this kind of temporary and instead created a pool within the regular workforce to fill in for absentees. The 1992 contract at CAMI created a similar "Production Support Group." This goes against the grain of management-by-stress, since these are regular employees, on the payroll every day

whether they are needed or not. (In practice, of course, management keeps the pool small enough that no one is twiddling thumbs.) Management's ideal, of course, would be for team members to take up the slack when one member is absent.

AAI still employs temporary employees to cover extra absences on Mondays and Fridays and to a lesser extent on other days. But they may be used only with the union's permission. This has given the bargaining committee leverage in dealing with the company on other issues. The contract now provides for temporaries and probationers to have union representation on discharges.

• Establish rules to replace management flexibility, such as seniority for job openings

Workers preferred clearly defined rights and procedures over "flexibility." At all three plants, language has been added to deal with management favoritism in job assignments. The locals won procedures for notifying the workforce of job openings and filling them. Seniority has become the primary determinant for transferring to another job, and at CAMI and AAI, the right to move into openings by seniority has been extended to "secondary" openings (those created when a first opening is filled).

At AAI, plant-wide rather than departmental seniority became the determining factor for all openings in a unit. The definition of openings was broadened to include ones resulting from leaves or newly created jobs. In addition, the company's right to force an employee onto a different shift for quality purposes was reduced from 90 days to 14. Stronger notification requirements for scheduled overtime were included, and the company's right to change the time of lunch and other breaks was restricted.

The company often used favoritism in deciding who got temporary assignments and who got kaizened out of a unit. In 1994, the Temporary Assignment Pool was abolished. The union won the right to "canvass high, force low": the most senior worker would get the choice of taking the assignment; if no one wanted it, it would go to the lowest seniority worker.

• Train workers to use their rights

At CAMI the union trained workers in their rights under Ontario's safety laws. The union passed out wallet-size cards with step-by-step instructions for how to refuse to do unsafe work. The number of unsafe work refusals went up dramatically after the cards were handed out—including refusals by whole teams (see the union newspaper article on "Changing the Definition of Teamwork" above).

• Make job rotation a worker right, not a management right

At all three plants, workers quickly found that management had no particular interest in having team members exchange jobs on a regular basis. In fact, management tried to limit rotation, as its solution to quality and short-staffing problems. Management only wanted workers to *know* all the jobs in the team in case they were needed to fill in. Many workers, on the other hand, wanted rotation as a way to deal with strenuous jobs or to break the tedium.

Rotation is a continuing arena of struggle, with management unwilling to relinquish formal authority and teams striving to establish, in practice, their right to set up their own rotation schedules. At AAI, by mid-1993, management was allowing teams to determine how much and when rotation would take place. When necessary, district committeepersons intervened with supervisors to help teams secure this right.

At CAMI, the contract mentions "regular rotation" but does not specify what this means. Members try to enforce this right by calling for ergonomic assessments and

by using the health and safety language.

• Give members flexibility in taking time off

In 1991 Mazda workers won four days per year of personal leave (PAA), which could be taken in four- or eight-hour increments. It was only necessary to notify (not ask permission of) the supervisor before the start of the shift, or during the first part of the shift in order to be absent the second part. This provided an enormous sense of freedom and dignity, especially for single parents who were often faced with family emergencies.

• Give members tools to equalize power with supervisors'

Perhaps the most important tool is language requiring job selection by seniority, as discussed above. Another example was the unexpected use to which Mazda workers put their Paid Absence days. They found that when several workers used their PAA days at once, they could get even with poor supervisors who abused workers and the contract. This made production next to impossible and the supervisor's day quite miserable. Similarly, CAMI workers have used the threat of safety protests to insure more cooperative management.

Another technique used in punishing poor managers is exposure and ridicule in the union newspaper. This technique is used regularly in the CAW local newspaper *Off the Line*.

• Establish the union's independence

In the original agreements to recognize the UAW, the company envisioned the union being the company's partner, as in Japan. Thus the in-plant union office was shared with company labor relations officials; in some cases union and company personnel shared desks, telephones, and clerical help. If a worker had a problem, he or she would call the union/labor relations office and both union and management representatives would approach the worker together.

In both plants, pressure developed for an independent union life. Workers objected to having to reveal a problem to management without first being able to talk it over with a union representative. At Mazda the union won separate offices. Workers were urged to file formal grievances if their problems could not be solved easily. For years the NUMMI union leadership defended the joint office arrangement, but more militant committeepersons separated themselves from their management counterparts when talking to workers about their problems and encouraged grievances. This encouraged a more independent stance by most of the committeepersons. Following the 1994 election and contract the NUMMI local won a separate in-plant office.

In 1992, the Mazda local took the unusual step of declining to support the company's request for a tax abatement from the town of Flat Rock. Noting that "Other companies are routinely granted these abatements. Ford has received 80 abatements for 80 requests in the last few years," President Phil Keeling wrote, "Mazda's biggest problem seems to be a credibility issue with our members and with the City of Flat Rock. Our members still remember all the past promises that were not kept and all the issues that remain unresolved on the shop floor.[8]

• Use the union's right to block "consensus" as a pressure tactic

In the U.S. at the Big Three, the UAW may strike at any time over health and safety, work standards, or some cases of contracting out.[9] This right to strike gives the union leverage in settling other, non-strikable issues between contracts, since the union can suggest that failure to reach agreement over the latter might make it more likely to strike over the former.

The contracts at Mazda and NUMMI forbid strikes during the life of the agreement. At Mazda the union looked for an alternative source of power. From time to time the company wanted a special dispensation to waive parts of the contact. For example, with the agreement of the union, restrictions on overtime can be lifted for emergency conditions or during model changeover. The union uses its ability to grant or withhold the waiver to gain leverage on a range of issues, and to force management to be more cooperative in general.

• Organize the unorganized

Local 3000 has organized four smaller plants that supply AAI with windows, seats, and stampings, all Japanese-owned. Besides solidarity, their self-interested reason is to help raises wages in the suppliers, and thus discourage Mazda from contracting out more work.

In each case, involvement of rank and filers from the Mazda plant was key. They showed up for support meetings and rallies and leafleted the plants: "HAVE NO FEAR. WE ARE THREE THOUSAND MEMBERS STRONG! COME JOIN US." The local paid lost time for members to work on the campaigns and invited workers from the target plants to their union awareness classes. A week before the 1993 representation election at Lenawee Stamping, a 150-car caravan traveled 50 miles from Flat Rock past the home of the plant manager to a union rally. Local 3000 supported the drive financially, opening an office near the Lenawee plant, and with home visits.[10]

HOW THEY DID IT

How did the local unions win the changes described above?

CAMI

At CAMI, Local 88 had the strong backing of the national CAW throughout. Within six months of the plant's start-up, the CAW Council had adopted a policy statement

---

'Just-in-Time' Gives the Union Power

The February 1988 strike by British unions against Ford Motor Co. had management thinking twice about "just-in-time."

The strike lasted only nine days, but it cost the company $927.5 million in lost production—which is why Ford was willing to settle.

Here's what the Wall Street Journal *had to say about the strike even before it ended:*

[The] walkout underscores how modern factories increase labor's power.

The costly strike against Ford Motor Co. in Britain is driving home a sober lesson to manufacturers throughout Europe: New factory techniques, far from weakening the region's restive unions, are enhancing labor's power to disrupt production and slow the badly needed modernization of European industry.

In recent years, Ford stood out in Europe as an advocate of cost-cutting manufacturing methods used in Japan. It computerized factories, slashed inventories and boosted productivity. The big U.S. auto maker linked diverse European factories into one giant car- and truck-making machine. Ford Sierras, assembled in Belgium, ran on French-made transmissions powered by British engines. Ford's market share grew, particularly in the United Kingdom's highly competitive market.

"The downside [of this modernization] is what we're seeing now," a spokesman for Ford's U.K. unit acknowledged.

PRODUCTION HALTED

Ford's European juggernaut stalled within hours of a walkout Monday by 32,500 British workers. Without U.K. parts, some Ford production lines in Belgium have shut down, with 2,500 workers laid off yesterday at one plant and 100 more at another....Analysts expect closures to spread quickly to other countries. Each day that Ford loses production of 2,930 vehicles, it sacrifices at least $34.1 million in retail sales.

The auto maker's troubles are sending a shudder throughout the board rooms of Europe's leading manufacturers. To many executives, the Ford dispute dramatizes the one great risk of the new manufacturing techniques: a strike.

Walkouts "will grind operations to a halt far more quickly" than usual, said [a consultant]. The new methods cut costly inventories, and without big stockpiles of parts, strikes immediately close assembly lines.[11]

Similarly, in 1994 a strike over outsourcing by one of GM's Indiana parts plant shut down 13 assembly plants in the U.S. and Canada in just three days.

"reject[ing] the use of Japanese Production Methods."[12] The union not only gave special help to the new local; as a condition for the agreement the union required access to the plant for a serious research project, so as to figure out what this new production system might mean for the rest of the union.[13]

In 1992 the local struck for five weeks over the contract. It was a time when the newspapers were full of GM's financial troubles and its need to ax thousands of jobs. By conventional wisdom it was a lousy time to strike and an impossible time to win.

But national CAW leaders used the fact that they represented workers at all General Motors plants in Canada. They told GM in no uncertain terms, "If you go to war with our union, you're going to war with all of us." The national union had 31,000 leaflets distributed at other Canadian GM plants; both a big rally and a dues assessment to support the strikers were planned.

GM apparently feared that if it stonewalled at CAMI, the union might picket other GM facilities or that those plants could see a rise in health and safety work stoppages.

The strike won a pool of replacement workers for absentees, a dispute mechanism for disagreements on workloads, union access to the company's time-study information, language to prevent management from disciplining a worker who pulls the stop cord, a plantwide job posting procedure, more union reps (including on health and safety), parity with the Big Three on pensions (including cost-of-living for retirees), a supplemental unemployment benefits plan, and parity on shift premiums and vacations.[14]

In August 1994, CAMI launched a new model, to great fanfare. At the ceremonies, attended by dignitaries of all varieties, Shop Chair Mike Ruiter warned CAMI: Our people want jobs; we want to build quality. You have our assurances that if management tries to make us build inferior quality, or use inferior parts, we will stop production.

Set the Record Straight

CAMI's recent corporate objectives meeting was another futile attempt by management to make us believe that we have input into the running of the company...

We would like to set the record straight once and for all for the benefit of our vice presidents: the hourly workers of CAW Local 88 are not part of your team. We are unionized employees of CAMI Automotive Inc., who are building vehicles for your company under a collective bargaining contract, and not a particularly good one.

However, we hope to remedy that situation to some extent in the fall of 1995 [when our contract expires].

—Ed Vandenberghe, Assistant Editor

[From CAW Local 88 newsletter, *Off the Line*, June 1994.]

NUMMI

At NUMMI, as mentioned at the beginning of this chapter, the union has been less united and less able to make changes. Nevertheless, there have been achievements. In 1993 and again in 1994, the members were able to stave off the company's and union officials' attempt to institute the ten-hour day/four-day week.

Members feared that if they accepted a ten-hour day they would be faced with mandatory overtime above and beyond that figure, including working on their days off. NUMMI insisted that without this "Alternative Work Schedule," it would stop investing in the plant. The UAW Regional Director wrote to all local members urging them to vote yes.

The People's Caucus opposed the plan strongly, and the plant was flooded with leaflets on both sides. Vice President Richard Aguilar argued that if the company wanted to run the plant more hours, it should work a seven-hour day with three shifts, as a St. Louis Chrysler local had won.

The members voted down the alternative work schedule two-to-one in June 1993. But threats from company and union officials—including the rumor that Toyota would pull out of the joint venture—panicked the membership into a re-vote. This time, the company claimed it only wanted AWS for two desirable sections of the plant, and that people could transfer out of those sections if they wanted to. Union officials promised that they just wanted to negotiate some form of alternative schedule in the next contract, not necessarily the ten-hour day. The permission passed 1,698-705.[15]

When union elections came round the next June, the tables turned again. Aguilar defeated Chairman George Nano, although the People's Caucus remained a minority on the bargaining committee and the executive board. The contract expired less than two months later. The company demanded the alternative work schedule plantwide and a free hand to change work rules and attendance policy during the contract.

Aguilar and the rest of the bargaining committee, with the backing of International officials, resisted. Bargaining continued past the contract expiration but the company's position hardened; management even informed members how to cross the picket line if they went on strike. The union called a walkout at midnight, an hour and a half before the end of the shift. The company folded. Some members believe the company caved in so quickly partly to preserve its reputation for harmonious labor relations.[16]

MAZDA (AAI)

The first union officers in UAW Local 3000 were appointed by the union's regional office and the first contract reflected Mazda's views on labor relations. In early 1989, some rank and filers put together a slate, the New Directions Coalition, to run against the incumbents. Arguing "we should not be treated as so many parts in their just-in-time system," they won the presidency, bargaining chair,

A cartoon from *Union Spirit,* newspaper of UAW Local 2488 at Diamond-Star Motors.

and control of the executive board.

The new officers' first term was only one year. They had to deliver on their promise to change conditions in a short time and without renegotiating the contract, which did not expire until after the next election.

They established a different mood in the local and a different approach toward the company. When management asked the local to ease restrictions on overtime to deal with a backlog of repairs, the shop committee used the opportunity to demand a different attendance program—replacing one that was rife with favoritism. The two American managers responsible for the attendance policy fiasco "resigned."

In the 1990 elections the new leadership retained many key positions and turned their attention to negotiating a new contract. Their strategy was "an energized, mobilized, organized shop floor," as Shop Chair Greg Drudi put it. One technique was the group grievance. Members were urged to contact their union coordinator to sign a grievance over management's abuse of temporaries. The coordinators distributed stickers, "Fighting for a Better Contract in '91," that most union members wore (in violation of the dress code).

The coordinators became the base of a Union Contract Support Committee. They attended classes conducted by labor studies instructors from Wayne State University, both on their own time and on lost time. They distributed and collected, one on one, 2,380 contract survey forms, out of a plant population of about 2,800.[17] The union issued Negotiations Newsletters to report on the results. The newsletter helped members understand that many problems were common and made it clear to management that the union expected to get some action.

The union committee summed up the survey results and comments:

> The overwhelming majority of Mazda workers believe that they will be "injured or worn out" before they reach retirement; a sizeable majority believe management has aban-

doned its promise of participatory decision making; and resent the favoritism and self-serving behavior of their unit leaders.

Among other things, the survey found that 84 percent of respondents did not like the current system of choosing team leaders (that is, selected by management), and favored election, rotation, or seniority.[18]

The union leaders knew that management believed the members would not back the union in a strike. So, at the suggestion of UAW Regional Director Bob King, they decided to take the risky approach of holding the strike vote in the plant instead of at the union hall. The latter was traditional in UAW plants and generally produced a very large percentage in favor of a strike. But management would know that turnout was low. By holding the vote in-plant and making every effort to get all members to vote, the union could prove that both leaders and members were willing to strike to get what they needed.

In the strike authorization vote, 97 percent of the members voted, and 92 percent voted yes.

In negotiations, the union found that the "radical" and "militant" reputations of the local leaders were an advantage. Even though car sales were down and the political climate was conservative (this was during the Gulf War), a strike was a real possibility.

Changes in the new contract included election of team leaders, a separate in-plant office for the union, improvements in seniority rights, transfer rights, and overtime procedures, four paid personal days per year, a pool of regular employees to fill in for absentees, three additional district committeepersons, a second health and safety representative to cover the afternoon shift, and an ergonomics rep.

But there was no rest for the union in its dealings with management. In the summer of 1991 Local 3000 told its members: "It's time to face reality. We are not part of any partnership or cooperative effort... [We] are going to war."

The war developed from Mazda's attitude toward the four new personal days won in the April contract. No one had anticipated that the personal days would serve as a safety valve. Although they were supposed to be used over the course of a year, job pressures had built up so that workers were using their four days rapidly. In some areas enough workers exercised their rights that production had to stop on Fridays. Management was frantic.

The union indicated a willingness to make adjustments in the procedure, but also argued that insensitive supervisors and overloaded jobs—not absenteeism—were the real problems. As Shop Chair Greg Drudi put it, "If management weren't so insistent on running the place so lean, it wouldn't have so much trouble handling an unexpected absence."

President Phil Keeling summed up the situation: "Although this was not what we had intended in negotiating PAA [paid absence days], members found a powerful tool to pay back supervisors who messed with them. The PAA days gave the members some rights they could use. If the company wants to solve the problem, let them retrain their supervisors and check how hard the jobs are.[19]

The company offered hundreds of dollars in attendance bonuses and paid time off in exchange for what seemed to be small restrictions on use of PAA days. The officers, uncertain how the members would respond, agreed to put the issue to a vote. The union literature emphasized that "we have made it clear to Mazda that there can be no change in our Collective Bargaining Agreement without membership approval via the ratification process.[20] The union leadership remained essentially neutral in the vote.

To the surprise of management, the members voted down the proposal for more money by 77 percent, to protect a small but important right: to completely control their own time four days a year.

But Mazda's response was essentially to ignore the vote: management announced it would unilaterally restrict the use of PAAs.

This provocation raised the issue to a higher level. If workers had had some sympathy with Mazda's need to maintain production, it disappeared when the company made clear it had no respect for the contract or union democracy. The principle was now simple: Does Mazda have the right to alter the contract unilaterally?

The union leadership deserves credit: instead of taking the vote as a repudiation, they declared it working democracy and set out to carry out the membership mandate.

The union began legal action. But when the National Labor Relations Board deferred to arbitration, the union knew it could not wait for drawn-out proceedings: it began a work-to-rule campaign. In a leaflet, union leaders declared, "To hell with jointness and team work. We must continue to fight for a quality product, but now it must be done on our terms:

> Quality achieved through proper manpower and line speed.
> Build it right the first time. Take the time you need to do a good job and do it safely.
> Do what you are told and nothing more. Forget MQ circles, suggestion programs and pilot programs.

Many members took the initiative to insure quality production. Use of the pull-cord that stops the assembly line went up dramatically in some departments, from once or twice a day to dozens of times.

Friday, July 26, became union t-shirt day. Eighty to ninety percent of the workers wore union or message t-shirts. Wearing a union shirt was a serious decision, because Mazda workers were required to wear uniforms, and this requirement was strictly enforced. Management was in a frenzy, even though the plant apparently recorded high productivity and quality that day. Some workers say they cannot remember when morale was so high and work so much fun.

The union continued the campaign with demonstrations outside the plant. A photograph of a Mazda worker burning his uniform shirt made international news.

In the end, the two sides reached a settlement that included some restrictions on the total number of people who could use their personal days on Fridays and their half-days on other days. In exchange, workers received an additional holiday, a $1,000 bonus, and some other improvements. The membership approved the agreement by a 92 percent vote. Most important, they had made it clear that the union would not permit management to unilaterally change the contract.

SURVIVAL = STRONG UNION

In the "How They Did It" section above, the reader will notice that the three locals did not invent any startling new tactics. Union leaders put out leaflets to agitate for strong votes. They did contract surveys. Or members pushed their leaders into action. Workers held demonstrations. They worked to rule. They struck. Nothing new: *the way to survive lean production is to have a strong union.*

Just as in any other workplace, these sorts of mobilization take organization and membership involvement. Leaders must recognize that members will be involved at different levels. They use the structures that exist in the workplace—natural leaders, departments, perhaps the company's "teams." At Mazda, the union found the coordinators and built on them. Although working stewards like these are quite common in many unions, and had been in the UAW decades ago, at Mazda the union rediscovered the value of elected reps who are in daily working contact with a relatively small number of co-workers.

When an employer is able to organize the workplace around management-by-stress principles, that employer has some big advantages, summed up in the concept of flexibility. In the purest form of lean production, workers have few rights and the culture of the workplace reinforces management's ability to make changes at will.

Surviving lean production, then, means gaining collective power to restrict's management's arbitrary flexibility. In theory, this could happen either through changes in the union contract or through a change in the workplace culture that lets management know workers cannot be pushed around. In practice, it takes both.

The best contract provisions aren't worth very much if the union can't or won't defend them. And a united membership and a savvy leadership will find ways to extend the meaning of any contract, even one with few formal rights. For example: the right to rotate is vague in the CAMI contract, but members use their ergonomic rights and their power to refuse unsafe work to push management on rotation.

It's a cliche to say that the strength of a union is in its members. But under lean production, it's even more the case that the union leaders can't do it all themselves. Because of management's stress on gleaning workers' knowledge of the work process, and on using members to pressure each other, the workforce needs to be united in its understanding of the importance of what workers know, and how to use it to their own benefit rather than for management's speed-up. And they need to understand the "fragility" of the system, so that they recognize their own power to act in concert.

This means members who know how to act on their own every day, without marching orders. Their hand is further strengthened by democracy in the union: management must understand that if the union officers do not represent the members then the members will kick them out. Witness NUMMI.

This kind of membership democracy is not neat. When people get mobilized and angry at the company, as in some of the cases we describe here, they are not all satisfied at the same point. As a result some may get angry at the very union leaders who mobilized them for the battle. In the Mazda PAA struggle described above, the leaders took a lot of abuse from the members in the middle of the process. It wasn't pleasant for the leaders, but it was critical to making it clear to the company that the

members meant business, and it gave the negotiators the weight they needed to win the battle.

Similarly at NUMMI: much of the membership was so pumped up to strike over the 1994 contract that they denounced their officials for calling such a short strike and for not winning more. The newly-elected shop chair from the People's Caucus had to take a beating at a well-attended contract information meeting. But the local is in a much stronger position to carry on in day-to-day dealings with NUMMI than if the members had quietly lined up behind the settlement. Leaders who don't take membership uproar as a personal affront are the ones who equip their members to deal with management-by-stress.

For unions, grappling with lean production is the wave of the future. We encourage readers of this book to let us know the tactics and strategies they discover; we'll pass them on.

Notes

1. See Jacob M. Schlesinger, "Shift of Auto Plants to Rural Areas Cuts Hiring of Minorities," *Wall Street Journal*, April 12, 1988; Robert E. Cole and Donald R. Deskins Jr., "Racial Factors in Site Location and Employment Patterns of Japanese Auto Firms in America," *California Management Review*, Fall 1988, pp. 9-22.

2. The UAW made important concessions on the solidarity wage structure during the 1980s and 1990s: a new production worker at both the Big Three and the transplants now hires in at 70 percent of base rate, reaching full pay after three years. And there is other nibbling at the principle of equal pay; some plants have instituted "pay for knowledge" systems that allow very small differentials. But compared to Japan's the wage structure is still objective and flat.

3. Several researchers have reported statements by upper management in Japan that the desire to avoid unionization was the principal reason for their flat wage structure in the U.S. For example, Harley Shaiken, in a presentation to a conference on "Lean Production and Labor," Wayne State University, May 22, 1993, reported that this was Toyota management's frank explanation.

4. Mark A. Huselid, "The Impact of Human Resource Management Practices on Turnover, Productivity, and Corporate Financial Performance," *IMLR*, Rutgers University, May 1, 1994. See also U.S. Department of Labor, *High Performance Work Practices and Firm Performance*, 1993, p. 10.

5. CAMI, "Production Team Leader Selection and Review Process," July 1994.

6. May 13, 1994.

7. Interview, August 10, 1994.

8. "News Around the Local," *UAW Local 3000 Guide*, July 1992, p. 1.

9. In Canada, unions may not strike during the term of a contract.

10. Steve Babson, "'Come Join Us': Volunteer Organizing from a Local Union Base," *Labor Research Review* #18, pp. 61-71;

Norm Kujawa, "Michigan Mazda Workers Win Big at Japanese Parts Supplier,"*Labor Notes* #175, October 1993, pp. 5, 10.

11. Richard L. Hudson, "Strike at Ford shows problems of new methods," *Wall Street Journal*, February 10, 1988.

12. "CAW Statement on the Reorganization of Work."

13. "The CAMI Report: Lean Production in a Unionized Auto Plant," by the CAW-Canada Research Group on CAMI—David Robertson (coordinator), James Rinehart, Christopher Huxley, Jeff Wareham, Herman Rosenfeld, Alan McGough, and Steve Benedict, September 1993. This excellent study contains more detailed, on-the-ground information about the workings of a managed-by-stress factory in North America than any other publication. It is very thorough in describing the effects on workers and their responses.

14. Jane Slaughter, "A Big Win for Auto Workers—in Canada," *Labor Notes* #165, December 1992, pp. 1, 13.

15. Caroline Lund, "G.M.-Toyota Plant Backs Down on 10-Hour Day," *Labor Notes* #173, August 1993.

16. Caroline Lund, "Union Beats 10-Hour Day at NUMMI," *Labor Notes* #186, September 1994, p. 7. The local media continued to buy the notion of harmonious labor relations at NUMMI. A local newspaper, *The Tri-Valley Herald*, headlined "Agreement averts strike."

17. Steve Babson, "Lean or Mean: The MIT Model and Lean Production at Mazda," *Labor Studies Journal*, Vol. 18, No. 2, Summer 1993, pp. 3-24. This article does an excellent job of debunking the benevolent model of lean production, and reports in detail on the union's survey.

18. Babson, "Lean or Mean," p. 16.

19. Mike Parker, "UAW Goes to War as Mazda's 'Teamwork' Fails," *Labor Notes* #150, September 1991, pp. 5-6.

20. "UAW-MMUC P.A.A. Proposal," UAW 3000 leaflet, June 1991.

Working Smart:
A Union Guide to Participation Programs and Reengineering
Labor Notes • 7435 Michigan Ave. • Detroit, MI 48210 • (313) 842-6262

Chapter 37

The Collective Bargaining Model: UAW Local 909

Workers in one quality team imposed their own rules for their participation. They caucused among themselves, worked out any differences beforehand, and approached the team as a united group. They refused to accept management's "solution" to raise productivity, and insisted on their own, which preserved jobs.

by Alan Benchich

THE WORKERS AT THE General Motors Powertrain-Warren plant outside Detroit have a history of viewing joint programs with suspicion. After all, these members of United Auto Workers Local 909 had turned down a local agreement five times in 1987-88 because it included a team concept approach.

So when management wanted to include hourly workers from the channel plate department in a Quality Network program to "improve the quality and productivity of the department," they were less than enthusiastic. (A channel plate is part of a transmission.)

Nevertheless, we did participate, and we used some tactics and principles that should be helpful to others in the same situation:

1. The union assigned experienced union people to participate.

2. The union participants met among ourselves, without management. We did this both before the training started and during the sessions. If there was something we needed to talk about, we just said, "Excuse us..."

3. We adopted a "collective bargaining model." Rather than going into "brainstorming" and "consensus" in the QN sessions as individuals, we worked out any differences among ourselves and approached management as a united group.

4. We made it clear from the beginning that we would not consider any solutions that eliminated jobs, nor do any time-studies.

5. We involved the workers who would be affected by any changes.

ELIMINATING WASTE

Quality Network is a jointly-administered program in the UAW-GM National Agreement that claims to involve the union in "continuous improvement" and "eliminating every form of waste." It trains workers, both in the classroom and on the shop floor, in how to improve the layout of the workplace and to look for unnecessary motion and excess stock. The agreement allows the local parties to negotiate a re-deployment plan to provide "meaningful" work for those displaced by implementation of QN "improvements."

Workers on the channel plate job had already seen how this program worked in reality. The first QN training in the plant had consisted of management personnel only, including the plant manager. The union had declined to participate because management refused to negotiate a re-deployment plan.

As part of their training, the QN team went out on the shop floor, clipboards and stopwatches in hand, to observe an operation in the department next to the channel plate job. The result was the elimination of two jobs.

UNION PICKS GROUP MEMBERS

When management began to ask workers on the channel plate job to take part, the union realized that management was going to include hourly workers with or without the union's participation. So the shop chairman agreed to let workers participate, with the provision that the commit-

---

Alan Benchich is a pipefitter and formerly vice president of United Auto Workers Local 909.

teeman (steward) and myself, a skilled trades
worker from the area (who also happened to be
the vice-president of the local), be included in
the training.

That led to a class composed of six union
workers, two department supervisors, and a
plant engineer.

Before the first training session began, the
union participants sat down to talk about how
we should approach it. The workers knew that
the department was under a microscope. The
area had been poorly laid out—workers had to
drag parts 30 feet to where they were used. At
the same time, by hustling, workers could meet
the production standard for an hour in about 35
minutes. The workers felt that some changes
were inevitable.

A COLLECTIVE BARGAINING APPROACH

Three of the workers said that they didn't
really want to participate. They felt the program
would be used to eliminate jobs, and they didn't want to
be identified as the bums who helped management
eliminate them.

After a lot of discussion, we agreed that the most important thing was to act in unity and not get divided. We
agreed to use a collective bargaining approach: if we had
any differences we would work them out among ourselves
and deal with management as a group. It was the traditional way the union dealt with management. We agreed that
we would negotiate as we went along.

To let management know where we stood, we informed the instructors that we would participate in the
training but, since management refused to bargain a
redeployment plan, we would not look at any solutions
that eliminated jobs.

They looked at each other and didn't quite know what
to say. The Personnel Director said we should give the
program a chance and "trust the process." We reiterated
that we would not be a party to any plan that eliminated
jobs. We would quit the training and go back to work if
they tried to force us to do so.

The program began with several days of training in
how to look for wasted stock, space, and motion. The
"wasted motion" was the first stumbling block. We were
supposed to use a stopwatch to time our fellow workers,
to determine their productivity.

We took it on ourselves to call for a caucus to talk it
over. We didn't ask for the "right"; we just assumed it.
The union members felt that this was a time-study and
wanted no part in it. When we came back to the classroom, we told the instructors and management that we
would continue the program, but would not be involved in
anything that involved time-studying fellow workers. After
some discussion, we agreed that the supervisors in the
group would handle any time-study that took place.

MANAGEMENT STEERS TOWARD A SOLUTION

Early in the training it became clear that management
had already figured out the solution they wanted on the
channel plate job. The job of the engineer was to help
guide the group to that conclusion. We found out that engineers had already studied the area a year earlier; they
had designed a small hand press to aid in installing the pis-
tons and springs. In fact, they had already had the press
built, but it had sat in a storeroom for a year.

The engineer had also redesigned the layout of the
larger bearing presses to allow two workers to run four
presses, eliminating two workers. Two more jobs would
be eliminated by having a person on the line assemble the
channel plate canister and insert it directly into the channel
plate, instead of having the canister assembled off-line by
one person and inserted into the channel plate on the line
by a second person. Management seemed to expect us to
agree that this was the most logical plan to make the
department "competitive."

FINDING DIVISIONS IN MANAGEMENT

Once again some of the workers wanted to walk out
of the class, and once again we decided to caucus. But this
time the two supervisors asked if they could join us.

They too were reluctant to eliminate jobs. They felt
this would hurt their ability to provide different model
channel plates to the main transmission assembly line
when the main line unexpectedly changed to a different
model transmission. This happened quite frequently.
These supervisors gave us information we would not otherwise have had, such as the fact that management was planning to raise production schedules.

We knew that if we walked out, management would

300 • Chapter 37   Working Smart

THE FUTURE OF SHOPFLOOR HUMOR...

"So this one human says to the other human...."

implement their plan and eliminate the jobs anyway. We decided to use their process to come up with our own plan that would protect the jobs. We agreed that if we came up with a collective decision and management implemented their plan anyway, then at least we would be able to tell people that we did our best to protect the jobs. We drafted a letter to the Personnel Director, telling him that our continued participation depended on the fair resolution of our concerns.

KEEPING IN TOUCH WITH OUR BASE

One of our requests was for a meeting with the workers in the department from both shifts. At first the plant manager said we could meet, but on our own time. We insisted, however, and got them to agree to let us meet separately with each shift, on company time.

We let the workers know what we were doing and got some input from them, such as an ergonomic problem they wanted help with. They told us they trusted us and to do the best we could.

The engineer's plan had not taken into account several situations. First, sometimes there were not enough assembled channel plates at the beginning of the shift to keep the main transmission assembly lines supplied. At other times, because of a sudden model change, a different channel plate was needed and there were not enough on hand. As it stood now, the department had the ability to produce extra channel plates to keep the main assembly lines from shutting down.

The engineer's plan was not flexible enough to deal with such situations. It would cause the main lines, with over 100 people each, to shut down for lack of parts. His plan also did not take into account that production schedules were set to increase in the next few months.

By the time we were scheduled to make our presentation to upper management and the union bargaining com-

mittee, we had come up with an alternative plan: to rearrange the work layout for a more efficient flow of parts into and out of the department. We moved the raw stock closer to the work and the off-line jobs closer to the line, to minimize extra movement. Excess stock was eliminated, which saved money. The group even designed a small platform to allow a short woman to press the canister together in a more ergonomically correct manner.

Our plan entailed no loss of jobs. We showed how the anticipated rise in production could be handled by basically the same number of people: from 5,500 pieces produced by 17.5 people per shift to 6,400 by 18 people (an increase from 314 pieces per worker to 356). We explained how management's savings would increase when they raised production even more. The changes meant that more production could be run with only a small increase in people—8,600 pieces with 20 people.

To our surprise, the superintendent of production seemed elated with our plan and promised to begin implementing the changes right away, which he did.

The channel plate workers were glad to be able to stay in their area, where they could still get a little extra break time. Although they had to make more parts, they no longer had to drag parts across the floor or go pick up stock to bring to their work tables.

However, at a follow-up meeting one month later, the engineer was still pushing to rearrange the larger presses so that one person could work two, eliminating two jobs. So far, over a year later, we have managed to prevent that from happening.

IT DOESN'T ALWAYS WORK

A second QN class, with hourly workers from the transmission case job, did not fare as well. They too found that management had a pre-planned solution. This time, however, management did not buy the workers' alternative plan. Management implemented the plan it wanted, eliminating several jobs. Since this episode, there has been no further QN training.

Our group was justifiably proud that we were able to protect jobs by maintaining a strong union position. And the union was right in refusing to participate in a joint program in which the union did not have an equal voice. When that happens, we must maintain the process that gave us any power that we do have—the collective bargaining process.

At the same time, we realize that even this was not a perfect solution. We gave the company increased productivity if they expand production, thus protecting our jobs. But if the company does not increase total production, our solution might be used in whipsawing between plants. This points to the need for more contact between unions at the plant level.

Working Smart:
A Union Guide to Participation Programs and Reengineering
Labor Notes • 7435 Michigan Ave. • Detroit, MI 48210 • (313) 842-6262

Chapter 38

Asserting Union Independence: IAM Local 1293

This chapter, written in July 1994, represents a snapshot of a union local one year into serious involvement in a company participation program. Their techniques for building union independence include "hostaging," "solidarity schooling" for all members, caucusing during joint meetings, screening all work team suggestions, and a union definition of "what we need to produce quality products."

By Ed Miller, Rick McKim, and Roberta Till-Retz

BACKGROUND

IAM Local Lodge 1293 is an amalgamated local in IAM District 105, representing members of five different bargaining units in Fairfield, a small town in southeastern Iowa. One of the bargaining units is a plant in the Automotive Division of Rockwell International. Today all but four of the 381 workers belong to the union, a remarkable achievement in a right-to-work state.

The plant produces drivelines and universal joints for off-highway vehicles, and drivelines for marine engines. Rockwell is one of the auto and truck industry's largest independent component suppliers. It has 20,000 employees, half of them overseas. Of the 18 North American auto division plants, 12 are unionized. In recent years, 17 plants, all unionized, have been closed.

In a letter attached to its 1992 collective agreement, the local lodge agreed to look into moving into a high performance work system (HPWS). At the time, the local knew little about what the company intended, or indeed, what a "high performance" work system would entail.

There was and is a great amount of cynicism in the union and among members about the HPWS. Over the years, the company has tried a number of programs aimed at improving production and involving employees, including Quality Circles, statistical process control, cell concept, operator process control, and a task force in one department. Would this be one more "flavor of the month"? With this history in mind, the union cautiously allowed the company to proceed with initial start-up of committees and teams.

In early 1992, the union agreed to the establishment of a joint 14-person high performance steering committee. It included plant department heads and six union members—the bargaining committee plus Ed Miller, Directing Business Representative (chief officer) of the District Lodge. The committee's task was to oversee and approve changes in plant design that would be proposed to it by a joint Design Team. The steering committee agreed that decisions would be made by consensus rather than majority vote.

In April 1993, the Design Team was formed and received its first training. It was made up of the same union officials and 15 company personnel. This imbalance in membership was protested by the union, and by September, the company agreed that each side would have 11 members. In October, joint sub-groups of the Design Team were named to collect data from various areas in the plant over a six to seven-month period. These teams met one or two days per month.

Ed Miller is Directing Business Representative of Machinists District Lodge 105. Rick McKim is President of IAM Local Lodge 1293 in Fairfield, Iowa. Roberta Till-Retz is Program Coordinator at the University of Iowa Labor Center and a member of AFT Local 716.

By mid-1993, the company set out a time frame for implementation of its "redesign" process, which it said would take one to three years. At that point, the local and district union officers recognized that the company was apparently serious about the program. The company was very anxious for the union to "buy into" the program and help it convince workers to support serious changes in the work process. Ed Miller and Local Lodge President Rick McKim sat down to strategize a union response that would protect the contract, preserve seniority, and build the union among the members. Above all, the union leaders were concerned that the company would propose to change the contract in 1995 negotiations, to make "high performance" an integral part of the union-management relationship.

Over a period of one year, the local has achieved some important protections, which are outlined below. However, the approach is still very much one of guarded skepticism and an insistence that management consistently and concretely demonstrate good faith in all its dealings with the union.

UNION INDEPENDENCE AND UNION RIGHTS

A UNION FACILITATOR

McKim and Miller asserted early on that the local would need a full-time union-appointed facilitator for the program. The company agreed, and they chose one of the most strong-willed union supporters in the plant. The facilitator, Bill Cline, has taken sixteen hours of union "solidarity schooling" along with the management training and is in close contact with the bargaining committee and the Business Reps at all points in the process.

A UNION CONSULTANT

As the company training was beginning, McKim and Miller decided they needed an independent source of information on high performance and what it might mean for the union. They contacted the University of Iowa's Labor Center, a state-wide labor education program with long ties to the District Lodge and the local.

After two meetings with a program coordinator at the Center, the union requested that upper management at Rockwell meet with Labor Center staff to discuss their proposal that the company pay for a Labor Center staff person to serve as a separate, union-oriented consultant and teacher. The union representatives were able to persuade the company that since the union had only committed to "look at" HPWS, in order for its investigation to be impartial and fully informed, it required an independent perspective from someone who had only the interests of the union at heart.

The union consultant, Roberta Till-Retz, has over the last year conducted a series of activities to help the union develop an independent strategy toward High Performance. She met with the design team to develop a union

mission statement (the union "givens," below) and a union code of conduct. She has sat in as observer on a company training session for design team members and provided a written critique to the union. Most importantly, she has conducted Solidarity Schooling for the union, planned in consultation with Miller, McKim, and Don Brown, Assisting Business Representative.

THE UNION 'GIVENS'

The union observed that the company had written its own set of "givens," or assumptions about the program, without union input. In the summer of 1993 the local developed its own set of "givens" to set the parameters of its involvement. The union givens, modeled loosely on the mission statement of IBEW Local 336 (a telephone local in Illinois), emphasize the union's commitment to the "security, dignity, and solidarity" of its members and express its "healthy skepticism" about the company's program (see Appendix 1).

At first, management tried to get the union to merge its givens with those of the company, arguing that separate "givens" or missions would be incompatible with a High Performance system. However, the local held firm, and the company has accepted the existence of separate company and union mission statements, even printing the union statement along with its own "givens" in its official "Direction Setting Package" of April 1994.

SOLIDARITY SCHOOLING

Recognizing the need to educate participants in the dangers as well as potential opportunities of HPWS, the local from the outset insisted on paid time in the plant during work hours for what it calls "solidarity schooling." There have been three phases:

a) 16 hours of schooling for union members of the Steering Committee and Design Team, September 1993. The company agreed that this could be repeated when needed for a refresher.

b) 8 hours for any interested union members of all joint sub-committees, starting October 1993 and continuing through the present.

c) 8 hours for any interested union members, with a goal of educating all members by contract expiration. Classes have met once a month with 20-25 participants, October 1993 to the present. This phase of the schooling is what the union is perhaps most proud of—a unique opportunity to get the union message out to the rank and file.

This schooling is conducted by the union consultant. It discusses unions' experience with employee involvement programs, including the threat to jobs, solidarity, and the quality of work life, and the possible emergence of "enterprise unionism." It touches on labor history, developments in the U.S. economy, and threats to labor standards from the growing use of contingent workers. It contrasts lean production with Swedish models and "sociotechnical" systems.

**DESIGN TEAM MEMBERS:
FORGING A UNION IDENTITY**

Above all it focuses on the need for union solidarity at every point in the process, so that the fundamental union mission of protecting and representing members' interests not be compromised, and that it in fact be enhanced.

The idea is to drive home the concept that the teams and committees can and should be used for union-building purposes. The union insisted that there be no management input into the course. Management was given a general outline of the curriculum but no detailed description of course content. The union was also insistent that there be no management presence in the classroom.

The union consultant prepared a "Sourcebook on High Performance" based on company materials. This manual excerpted key passages on the values, methods, assumptions and possibly problematic aspects of the company's model, organized by topic. This served as a basis for class discussion and a foundation for the union to get a handle on the company's model.

The company has paid all costs associated with the schooling, including participants' lost time, and the Labor Center costs (which, including the participant manuals, run to approximately $400 per class). The company also paid the Labor Center fee for an off-site class on High Performance for the local union.

In an initial meeting with the union consultant, the union members of the Design Team identified possible outcomes of the redesign process, what they called "the good, the bad and the ugly." They included such hopes as more satisfying work and a better quality product, and such fears as a weakened union and loss of work rules.

They also identified six assumptions to guide their involvement in all joint activities, such as the sanctity of the contract and that "workers need a strong union which is independent of management." Perhaps the most unusual was, "We see the union-management relationship as a continuum, not one which can be fragmented into redesign-cooperation on the one hand and collective bargaining and contract administration on the other." This principle had consequences for the union's actions later on.

The members also articulated their "vision and mission as trade unionists":

> The mission of the union is different from the mission of the company, though there are areas of overlapping congruent goals.

> The union's primary responsibility is to secure the dignity, security and solidarity of the members through representing and defending their interests at the bargaining table,

in the workplace and in the redesign process.

To achieve these ends, there must be a strong independent union.

USING THE COMPANY MODEL: SOCIO-TECH VS. LEAN

At the union's request, Rockwell provided information on the model it intends to pursue: a socio-technical system, which places emphasis on the "social" or human side of production along with the technical demands of the process. The information on this model has given the union some leverage in discussions over specific changes in the production process.

At one point, the plant manager was stalling on committing to extra hires needed in one area where members were working 12-hour days on a regular basis. McKim confronted management: "This sounds like lean production, not social-tech, and we're not having it!" The company has since agreed to hire additional workers in the department. Union members who have gone through the Solidarity Schooling have been educated on lean production techniques and are forming a strong core of opposition to working lean. Earlier attempts to install trouble lights (*andons*) met a wall of union resistance and were discontinued—an achievement the union points to with pride.

"HOSTAGING"

From the beginning this local's participation has been characterized by a "healthy skepticism" about the program, coupled with an insistence that management concretely demonstrate its good faith across the entire spectrum of labor-management relations. Consequently, several times over the last year the union has put everything on hold in order to set something right. They have pulled out of steering committee meetings and even called the members off the teams and sub-committees.

Most consultants in the field condemn this behavior as "hostaging." They argue that holding partnership programs hostage to resolution of other, supposedly separate labor-management issues is to erode the foundation of the joint relationship. To Local 1293, however, there is but one labor-management relationship, and it is one to which the company must demonstrate its good faith on a daily basis. Every instance of hostaging seems to make the union stronger.

At one point the local pulled out of the joint program to fight a new, very strict absence control policy, arguing that the policy "didn't represent the spirit of cooperation." At another point, the occasion was management's unilateral imposition of a "quality pledge" employees were asked to sign, and again when a supervisor reneged on a promise to pay overtime to workers whose call-in for night work was cut short by a power outage. Ed Miller wrote: "We pulled out of the program when it became apparent the union was not being treated fairly. However, we continue to participate in the program so that we will be able to intelligently negotiate in this process in bargaining at the end of the year."

USING THE FAIR LABOR STANDARDS ACT

A key point at which the local drew the line was the company's attempt to get workers to work on projects on their own time. This very common practice in joint programs often requires the union to ignore contract provisions on distribution of overtime.

Local 1293, fearing a precedent, stood on the principle that "seniority is sacred" and insisted that any workers who had the overtime coming would be paid their time.

McKim also investigated the applicability of the federal Fair Labor Standards Act to insist on pay at time-and-a-half for any activities beyond a 40-hour week. The company (and even some affected workers) argued that working on joint projects such as a company Open House was not "work." McKim pointed out that the Act defines work as "physical or mental exertion, whether burdensome or not, controlled or required by the employer and pursued necessarily and primarily for the benefit of the employer and his business," and that "even voluntary overtime work may qualify for coverage if: activities are for the predominant benefit of the employer, and the employer has knowledge of the activities and acquiesces in them."[1]

McKim informed the company that the union would file charges with the Department of Labor and with the NLRB if necessary to preserve the contract and the principle of seniority as a basis for overtime.

This issue continues to arise, as when the company suggested that schooling take place on a Sunday at straight time pay, rather than during the week as had been agreed. "You know how we feel about the Fair Labor Standards Act," McKim has warned.

So far the union's stubborn insistence that its contract and its independence be protected within the High Performance experiment has paid off. The company has been willing to listen to union proposals and has retreated on many points. On several occasions, officials from corporate headquarters in Michigan got involved locally to help keep the program going. These incidents demonstrate to the local that union participation in any joint program will be a continuous struggle for union rights across the entire spectrum of labor relations issues.

UNION APPOINTS COMMITTEE MEMBERS

From the beginning, the union has asserted its right to name all union members of joint committees. This is a precondition to its participation and rests on a clause negotiated in the 1992 contract,[2] though the union is prepared to assert a legal right as well.

The local opted for a "first come, first named" selection procedure, to avoid the appearance of favoritism. This method has some disadvantages: it is not always possible to select those the bargaining committee feels would be the strongest union advocates, nor has the local been able to achieve much balance on the teams with regard to gender, shift, or other criteria.

The method was tested, at one point, when McKim pulled out of the process and asked all union members to withdraw from their committee and team assignments. They all did.

RIGHT TO CAUCUS DURING JOINT MEETINGS

This right was raised several months into the process, after the teams had been meeting for a while. The goal was—and remains—that union members be allowed to take paid time to meet *prior to* the joint meetings, to prepare. Thus far the company has not been willing to allow this right. However, the right to paid caucus time during the joint meetings has been asserted and is beginning to be used. Caucuses are usually called by the union president, who wants members to get used to using this right.

THE UNION "SCREEN"

The union has asserted the right to have the bargaining committee screen all problem-solving and productivity-enhancing suggestions that work teams produce. The committee would screen proposals for their possible adverse effects on union solidarity, jobs, contract violations, safety and health, and then pass those that posed no threats over to the joint Design Team for consideration and implementation.

At this point management has only partially accepted this idea. Management suggests that the screened-out ideas be brought to the steering committee. Since the union has a veto on implementation at that point, the idea might win acceptance. The issue is still under discussion.

UNION PRESENCE AT ALL JOINT MEETINGS

The local has asserted the right of bargaining committee members to be present at all joint design and sub-committee meetings, as well as the right of the Business Representatives, Ed Miller and Don Brown, to attend any meeting. The company agreed that all meetings would be held to accommodate the schedules of the Business Representatives. This has proven to be a right that needs to be constantly re-asserted with the plant-level management.

UNION VETO OF COMPANY TRAINING

The union president attended a consultant-provided week of training in Atlanta to evaluate its potential impact on union members. He returned convinced that its high-powered psychological techniques were not compatible with the union approach to HPWS. He therefore vetoed sending any additional members to that training.

SOLIDARITY-BUILDING ACTIVITIES

The union members of the Design Team developed a union code of conduct[3] for members involved in the new work system. Both it and the management and union "givens" are discussed in the union schooling (see Appendix 2).

The union president regularly uses the union bulletin board to communicate--often through cartoons pointing out the dangers of a lack of solidarity.

The union has distributed four letters on high performance to the members, informing them on where the union is in the process. The letters are handed out to members in the plant by the stewards, who are on the design team and have received Solidarity Schooling.

Participants in the classes have produced a union vision of quality, which contrasts starkly with the emphasis on elimination of waste and forced speed-up that some consultants teach (see the box).

AREAS TO WORK ON FOR THE FUTURE

This local sees clearly that the HPWS, if entered into, will pose continuing sharp challenges to its ability to carry out its mission.

With contract expiration January 31, 1995, the local lodge is expecting to encounter proposals from the company to implement HPWS. The challenge is to educate all members on the union values involved and to develop a strategic plan.

Potential areas to bargain on HPWS:[4]

• Protection of union independence and rights: getting contract language on the rights described above. Expanding union rights.

• Union rights to shared decision-making on production processes, including new technology design and implementation and choice of a technology which is worker centered and skill-based.

• Union rights to jointly determine strategic business directions, including plant location, product, and market planning.

• Provisions for continuous learning opportunities focusing on skill enhancement and "training beyond the job"—learning more than narrow job skills, including technology, history, and economics.

• Job security, including stronger language on sub-

Quality Criteria

The Solidarity Schooling classes have produced a union vision of quality, which contrasts starkly with the emphasis on elimination of waste and forced speed-up that some consultants teach.

What we need to produce quality services or products:

• Good equipment, properly maintained
• High quality supplies and materials
• Design—job or product is designed well
• Training adequate to the job—and beyond
• Adequate personnel and staffing to do the job
• Enough time to do the job
• Proper environmental conditions
• Good labor-management climate characterized by respect for worker knowledge and skill

contracting.

• Increased employment opportunities and a commitment from the company to reinvest a portion of Fairfield earnings into the Fairfield facility.

• Protection of the rights and opportunities of individual members in the HPWS, including rights to have their views heard, and to be assured dignity, privacy, and movement within the plant.

Maintaining a high level of union commitment and understanding among bargaining unit committee and team members will be a continuing challenge. Members who have been through the Solidarity Schooling are responsive to the union materials distributed in the workplace and to the president's admonitions about strict observance of contractual protections. The difference is noticeable with those who have not yet been through the schooling. How to institutionalize opportunities for the union spirit to be constantly refreshed remains a question.

The local and district union leaders are aware that there is much work ahead if the union and its members are to benefit from High Performance. The challenge of achieving "continuous improvement" in wages and conditions of work and in the "security, dignity, and solidarity of our members" remains this union's clear goal.

Appendix 1
'The Union Givens'

IAM&AW Local 1293 and District Lodge 105 recognize that we are among the finest workers in the manufacture of drivelines. As per the January 31, 1992 contractual Letter of Understanding on High Performance Systems and our dedication to serving our customers, Local Lodge 1293 is willing to participate in the redesign process. This participation is contingent on equal involvement of the interested parties and the demonstrated good faith of the company.

We acknowledge that some employee involvement activities offer real opportunity to participate in the decision-making process of the company. We look toward these efforts, in the spirit of mutual gains, to keep the company forerunners in the industry, and our members among the best trained and best compensated workers in our field.

We approach each of these activities with good faith and an open mind, looking forward to our share of mutual gains for our extra efforts. We maintain a healthy skepticism to that end.

We also remain ever vigilant that employee involvement will be geared toward the personal growth of our members, while applying their skills to improve the position of the company in the marketplace, within the confines of our collective bargaining agreement, and with the security, dignity, and solidarity of our members foremost in our minds.

Appendix 2
Union Code of Conduct

Union members shall not:

1. circumvent the contract
2. circumvent the grievance procedure
3. participate in the disciplining of bargaining unit members
4. support or encourage job elimination
5. discuss union business in front of or with management
6. complain about union members in front of management

7. negotiate contract changes individually with management
8. engage in sexual harassment or discrimination against any group.

Union members shall:

1. display loyalty and solidarity with other union members at all times
2. insist on democratic procedures when involved in HPWS or redesign committees.

Notes

1. William L. Richmond and Daniel L. Reynolds, "The Fair Labor Standards Act: A Potential Legal Constraint upon Quality Circles and Other Employee Participation Programs," *Labor Law Journal*, April 1986, p. 249. 29 USCA 207.

2. "There shall be a Shop Committee composed of not more than five (5) Committee-persons. All such Committee-persons shall be elected by employees of the Bargaining Unit in a method determined by the Union...*In the event there are any other joint committees or Bargaining Unit committees, the shop committee shall select those bargaining unit members.*" (emphasis added)

3. The code of conduct was modeled on that of IAM Local 1125 as written up in *A Union Strategy Guide for Labor-Management Participation Programs*, Mike Parker and Jane Slaughter, Labor Notes, Detroit, 1992.

4. These are areas outlined in the IAM International's white paper "High Performance Work Organization Partnership," 1994.

Working Smart:
A Union Guide to Participation Programs and Reengineering
Labor Notes • 7435 Michigan Ave. • Detroit, MI 48210 • (313) 842-6262

Chapter 39

Teamsters Turn Pepsi Right Side Up

This Teamsters local started in a weak position, but found that responding to a company participation program was an excellent opportunity for the union to rebuild itself overall. Although the union started with a neutral position on the participation program, it soon recruited rank and filers to an oversight committee, and some saw themselves as "infiltrating the teams." Another tactic was a survey of the membership that rated managers' competence.

by John Kobler

IN JANUARY 1992 PEPSICO headquarters rolled out its new "Right Side Up" philosophy at a managers meeting in Dallas, complete with the latest jargon:

> We will be an outstanding company by exceeding customer expectations through empowered people, guided by shared values...

Pepsi began setting up Right Side Up committees. The initial meetings were mandatory with threats of discipline for workers who did not attend.

Teamsters Local 792, which represented roughly 350 drivers, vending, and production workers at the Burnsville, Minnesota Pepsi plant, was not in a strong position. Years of "servicing model" unionism had left its mark: the members were not involved in the union.

But the local was changing. The union leadership got together a group of Pepsi workers and union officers to try to decide how to respond to Right Side Up. We started out trying to deal with a particular management program, and ended up strengthening the union on the shop floor.

We decided that the most reasonable approach to Right Side Up was to accept that the program would exist in one form or another and that our initial job as union representatives was to contain it and neutralize the anti-union aspects.

But, more importantly, it was an opportunity for the union to rebuild itself, by working closely with the members to avoid falling into the traps that these plans set for workers.

John Kobler is a member of Teamsters Local 792 and works on the QWL staff of the International Union.

WHAT WE DID

1. We defined the role of the local. We decided to start with an officially neutral posture. At the same time we made it clear that we intended to monitor the program to insure that it did not conflict with the collective bargaining agreement or in any way harm the interests of the membership. To that end, the union placed a steward at all team meetings as an observer.

We wanted to avoid two traps:

a) We did not want workers participating in the program because they believed it had the union's blessing. When management inevitably started restructuring jobs, these workers would feel betrayed by their union. Further, at this point we wanted to protect our rights to file an unfair labor practice complaint, which we could lose if we appeared to agree to the program.

b) At the same time the union did not want to get into the position of appearing to oppose all change. The company's arguments that they are improving employee relations can be very attractive. Often QWL initiatives are accompanied by minor improvements in working conditions. Employees resent feeling that the union is denying them the right to make up their own mind.

At this very early stage we also wanted to make it clear that the union's response to Right Side Up was going to be determined by the members. Not only was it a question of the union representing the interests of the members; it would be the members who would identify problems and in their actions would largely determine the union's response.

Leaflet from IBT Local 792's campaign around "Right Side Up" at Pepsi.

2. Education of the union representatives was critical. Stewards and business agents needed to be knowledgeable in kaizen, TQM, and continuous improvement theories. Union representatives should be able to tell the difference between harmless and dangerous aspects of these programs. Unions lose credibility when they fail to differentiate between an employee alerting the company about defective machinery, and having employees determine qualifications of other workers.

It was important for the union to identify those aspects of QWL that presented positive opportunities for workers. Improving customer satisfaction is an admirable goal as long as workers aren't penalized for it. And we didn't want reps to sweat the little stuff while missing the big picture. If the company wants to show workers how to make graphs it's no big deal. If the company wants the graphs to evaluate workers, it's time to put your foot down.

3. Very early on, the local looked for members who were interested in the issue, and encouraged them to get involved. Some members, with union encouragement, put out unofficial literature raising questions about how Pepsi's new philosophy really worked. Humor was part of their arsenal.

One leaflet titled "Lemmings are a Team" compared Pepsi management to the rodent known for its march to the sea. Stories of how management acted in practice, as opposed to their rhetoric, fed into this "Upside-Down Company" theme and logos.

Leaflets used by other unions, sections of Labor Notes books, and academic articles were widely distributed so that members and reps would understand the experiences of other unions and the pitfalls of similar programs. The idea was to get the members thinking and talking about Right Side Up from a union point of view.

4. Local 792 leadership developed some guidelines for membership participation in Right Side Up. Secretary-Treasurer Bill Urman sent out a letter to all members of the bargaining unit:

> Only time will tell how this will affect you...These programs often increase efficiency at the expense of the workforce. These plans can weaken or destroy seniority rights, wreck the job bidding process, cause the loss of jobs, increase employee workloads.
>
> Local 792 would never endorse or embrace anything that could hurt our members. We will attempt to negotiate safeguards ...[and] with your help we will fight any part of this program that threatens the well-being of our members.
>
> ...To do this the Union will be forming an oversight committee composed of a business agent, stewards, and most importantly rank and file members.
>
> What can you do right now?
>
> First, get a copy of the basic guidelines for participation from your steward...Second, if something is going on at the team meetings that makes you uncomfortable...get hold of a steward immediately...Third, join the oversight committee.[1]

5. The union encouraged the members who were participating to think of themselves as protectors of union interests and not just as individuals. The idea was to make sure there was a union presence in the teams and to push the union agenda. The members were the union—not just the officers. Some union members who wouldn't have participated otherwise saw this as "infiltrating the teams."

Some members on the teams saw this as making the program live up to its claims. They demanded that management prove their trustworthiness by modifying existing work rules that employees didn't like. They proposed that jobs previously held by low-level management should revert to the union workforce, and demanded that the ratio of managers to workers be reduced as a cost-saving measure.

Union-minded members used teams to point out foremen who treated workers badly and question why they weren't following the program. They looked for ways to increase productivity that negatively impacted management jobs.

The goal was to have the teams vote for improvements they wanted, and if management refused to cooperate, make sure the whole shop floor heard about it.

6. We worked on reconnecting the members in the plant to the local. Most important were the regular offsite meetings that combined socializing and discussion with local officers.

7. The organizing committee worked on providing a union agenda for improving relations in the plant. When management tried to use surveys to determine workers' attitudes, the organizing committee urged members not to participate in those surveys and did a survey of its own on management style. There were no employee responses to one management survey, and only two responses to the second. However, there were 131 out of 146 responses to

the union's survey on management.

The union's survey asked both general questions about how the plant was run and for ratings on specific managers. The union then distributed the results of the survey, complete with percentage tabulations and graphs.

The survey revealed that less than two percent felt relations with management were good. Only two percent wanted the union to endorse Right Side Up, while 15 percent wanted the union to oppose it outright and 78 percent wanted the union to "protect the members."

The survey also revealed that workers considered certain key managers (including the plant manager) incompetent, at the same time indicating a lot of respect for other managers. The fact that the survey results differentiated so greatly between managers gave it credibility, and caused a lot of discussion among managers as well as bargaining unit people.

Gathering the survey helped build the union, and the results gave support to the union's stance and tied it closer to the membership. Not too long afterwards the plant manager was unceremoniously transferred, which gave the membership a new sense of its power. Managers would have to be more careful about how they treated bargaining unit people in the future.

8. We worked to rebuild a general union organizing committee composed of workers from all the shifts that could deal with Right Side Up and also other issues. The union oversight committee became an internal organizing committee and began a campaign to prepare for the April 1994 contract.

IBT 792 Guidelines
(abbreviated)

When To Participate
Participatory management is only real when employees are allowed to make and execute their own decisions. However, if all you are allowed to do is make suggestions that management must approve, then...

Union members should have equal rights in putting topics on the agenda.

Meetings should be held in a democratic fashion. If management ignores a member because he is not saying what they want to hear...then the team should be abandoned.

When Not To Participate
When meetings make accusations about employees' work.

When meetings encourage snitching on other employees.

When meetings could result in the elimination of jobs.

When meetings encourage violation of seniority rights.

When meetings start to put peer pressure on members.

RATING THE UNION

Again the survey method was one of our chief tools. Not only did we ask about the standard stuff—contract issues—we also asked people to rate the functioning of the union and the union representatives. We surveyed what members knew about union procedures and activities to find out what areas the union had to do a better job in communicating to the members. (For example: "Do you know where the union hall is?" "Do you know what the Teamster Service Bureau does?") Finally, we asked members if they would like to participate in different ways in the union or on the Organizing Committee.

The approach bore fruit. Three years previously, the membership had been intimidated and passively voted for a substandard contract. This contract round was different. Members got actively and imaginatively involved.

The union had great posters—one featuring a shark ("Teamsters Bite Back")—and designed buttons on issues (the company was demanding a flexible work week). When managers aggressively tore down our signs, members made posters with pictures of their kids, with the caption, "Your greed for profits doesn't just hurt workers." Managers didn't dare tear these down.

The result was a mobilized and united membership. The first contract offer was turned down unanimously and the second overwhelmingly. The company was forced to make significant improvements in wages, shift premium, and early retirement.

But as important, the members got the sense of themselves as a union. The organizing committee got too large to meet in people's homes. Pepsi workers had a joint meeting with Coke workers—supposedly our competition—and we traded ideas. (The militancy spread to the Coke plant—but that's another story.)

★ ★ ★

Management started Right Side Up to win the hearts and minds of the workforce. They expected little fight from the union; our local had been absent from the shop floor for years.

Management became a lot less enthusiastic about Right Side Up when the union's discussion of it started to loosen the control they had over their workforce. They are not so fast to hand out extra work when they find out it may intensify shop floor activity, particularly at the next round of wage negotiations.

We were able to rebuild shop floor presence at Pepsico, and at the same time neutralize this management initiative.

Notes

1. Letter to Pepsico members of Local 792, September 30, 1992.

Working Smart:
A Union Guide to Participation Programs and Reengineering
Labor Notes • 7435 Michigan Ave. • Detroit, MI 48210 • (313) 842-6262

Chapter 40

Rail Union
Just Says 'No'

In one rail union, members have successfully boycotted participation programs. The leadership's education campaign on the dangers of participation was part of a larger mobilization against the railroads' and government's attacks that also changed the union's direction. As a result, members are ready and willing to walk away from participation programs.

by Martha Gruelle

THE BROTHERHOOD OF MAINTENANCE OF WAY EMPLOYEES has about 50,000 members repairing and maintaining railroad track, bridges, and electrical equipment in the U.S. and Canada. Major sections of the union have successfully boycotted labor-management cooperation programs. Below we look at how that happened on two railroads.

Education on cooperative programs was part of a membership mobilization campaign from within that also changed the union's leadership and direction. Since a natural part of the campaign was talking to members about the contrast between managements' team-building talk and their anti-worker actions, boycotting cooperative programs was a logical, though not automatic, outcome.

In 1987, BMWE's then-president Geoff Zey invited two railroads, the Burlington Northern and the CSX, to join "experimental" quality programs, launched at union expense. (The union hired a management consultant to design the programs, who happened to be Zey's next-door neighbor.)

But Zey was forced by members' reaction to withdraw union support of the programs in 1989, and then lost his presidency in 1990, partly because of the programs.

The bigger context for railroad quality programs in the late 1980s to early 1990s—and for Zey's ouster—was the national contract bargaining which ended with government intervention on the side of management.

Bargaining began in 1988 and stalled in 1990. George Bush appointed a Presidential Emergency Board which recommended a contract based largely on management's demands. Unions could not accept it and struck nationally in April 1991. That prompted Congress to declare a national emergency and order unions back to work under the terms written by the Emergency Board.

The contract was devastating for pay, job security, and work rules for all the crafts. It allowed companies to send many maintenance of way workers thousands of miles away from home to work for weeks at a time, gutting seniority rights to more local work. Other work rule protections were eliminated along with thousands of jobs, while real wages were cut by 15 percent.

Such major concessions demanded and won by highly profitable railroads tended to give cooperation rhetoric a hollow ring. Corporate actions provided real life examples for BMWE leaders' education on the goals and effects of the programs.

Railroad unions generally are organized into sections designed to represent workers on a particular railroad (though corporate mergers and spin-offs have scrambled this structure). Leaders of these sections develop policy and bargaining strategy for the union.

Below, we look at how boycotting the programs played out on the Burlington Northern and on Conrail.

BURLINGTON NORTHERN

Shortly after losing union support, the BN initiated its own quality program: the Quality Improvement Process. A "Vice President for Quality" was charged with setting

Martha Gruelle is a staff writer for Labor Notes who covers railroad unions, Teamsters, health care reform, and other issues.

up Quality Improvement Teams throughout the company.

But according to Paul Swanson, then General Chairman of the Burlington System Division of the BMWE, "The company's timing was always bad," when they pushed the teamwork message.

For instance, while hyping the new quality program in 1990, the company announced plans to cut 1,100 jobs. At a national meeting of local officers—organized by the Intercraft Association of Minnesota, a cross-union coalition of railroad workers—attenders circulated a button depicting a casket marked "1,100 jobs," with the caption "BN's Quality Program Pays Off." The same button was distributed among Burlington Northern rank and filers in several areas.

Since contract bargaining and the Board's recommendations meant high turnout at union meetings and increased interest in union activities, newsletters and discussions that criticized the quality program got members' attention.

And the terms of the government-imposed contract, and other contracts modeled on it, had an immediate negative effect on the quality of members' lives—more and harder work, more time away from home, less pay and job security. Union leaders on the BN who were against quality programs used the imposed contract to show how much management cared about union members of the "team."

While newsletter articles, cartoons, and speakers at union meetings consistently criticized the quality program, no formal boycott was called in 1991. But the educational efforts made a difference.

In Alliance, Nebraska, an entire Quality Improvement Team, members of several unions, resigned, saying, "In light of the Presidential Emergency Board's recommendation, which was influenced by Burlington Northern's management, [and] clearly reflects Burlington Northern's attitude toward its scheduled employees...As union members, we feel we can no longer participate in a process...that would profit Burlington Northern Railroad Company at the expense of the union employees."

Swanson says the vast majority of BMWE members on the BN—all those who would honor a picket line—stayed out of the quality program during this period. "Members could see that only the company hacks bought into the program."

In 1992, the BN revamped the program and seemed to make some headway. Union leaders still opposed the program, but saw some of their members joining.

Again, the company's timing was poor. That summer they joined with other railroads in locking out union workers, in response to a strike against the CSX. Congress again stepped in and imposed a contract modeled on the national language of 1991.

The lockout and Congressional intervention made rail-road workers furious, and union leaders aimed some of that anger at joint programs. The headline in the August 1992 BMWE Burlington System Division's newsletter linked the imposed contract with the company's propaganda: "BN and Congress Give Quality Treatment to Rail Workers."

BMWE activists helped spread their opposition to the other 15 craft unions on the BN. Mid-level union leaders from all the rail unions form the BN General Chairmen's Association, which has a standing Special Projects and Education Committee.

This committee organized a debate on quality programs at a GCA meeting in September 1992. After the debate, the general chairmen voted to urge members to leave the BN quality program unless the company would negotiate on it. They assigned the Special Projects and Education Committee to prepare a model quality program agreement.

The committee then met with labor educator Chuck Davis, of the University of Minnesota, and developed an ideal (from the union's viewpoint) quality program. In January 1993, they presented the program to BN management for negotiation.

The BN GCA's program included two conditions: no loss of jobs due to changes out of the quality program, and equal sharing of all financial benefits of the quality program with all employees.

The BN refused to negotiate.

The members got the point; they left the programs, and even started walking out of joint safety committees when the company began injecting "quality" questions into those, according to Swanson.

By summer of 1994, participation in the Burlington System Division had shrunk from about 20 BMWE members (out of 2,400) to none.

ON CONRAIL: 'THEY KNOW WE CAN PULL OUT AT ANY TIME'

Conrail operates in the northeastern and midwestern U.S., and sponsors several cooperative programs: Safety, Labor/Management, and Continuous Quality Improvement committees.

One of the two BMWE affiliates representing workers on Conrail, the Pennsylvania Federation (or "Penn Fed"), is a hotbed of internal reform in the union. The BMWE Direct Election Committee started in the Penn Fed; the committee advocates direct election of international officers and of top officers on each rail system. They've won direct election in the Penn Fed and several other similar bodies.

Officers of the Penn Fed have shown by example that membership mobilization works. In 1988, they chose to bargain locally with Conrail, and got a better contract than the national one imposed by the government in 1991.

They have also led on the question of cooperative programs, including campaigning against international president Geoff Zey when he sponsored them.

During the summer of 1993, each local union representing members employed by Conrail held a meeting to discuss and vote on whether to withdraw from the programs. The vote was 3,250 to 750 in favor of boycotting.

During the same meetings, votes were taken to authorize a strike over eleven different grievances. So, like on the BN, Conrail workers were debating the cooperation programs in the context of management's respect for contract rights. The strike vote passed by the same margin.

In September 1993 the top BMWE officers representing Conrail workers sent a letter to members asking them to withdraw from all cooperative programs in light of the membership vote. "...this action should in no way be interpreted negatively towards our brothers and sisters who have been active in these programs," said the letter from Jed Dodd (General Chairman of the Pennsylvania Federation) and James P. Cassese (General Chairman of the Consolidated Rail System Federation). "Many of us were only active in these programs because the Union asked us to be active."

According to Dodd, the union had always placed some of its most active and reliable members on the joint committees. This helped guard against participants becoming too tied to the committees or placing that participation above the union. They were ready to resign when the union voted to boycott.

In fact, after months of meetings, discussion, and votes, the union leadership had enough membership support that they could threaten discipline against the couple of members who stayed in the programs, without fear of backlash.

Conrail was unhappy with the union's stand—so unhappy they asked a federal court on two occasions to order the union not to boycott the programs. Each time they withdrew the request, once under pressure from a coalition of rail unions that supported the BMWE in strike action.

The BMWE decided to strike Conrail, in May 1994, over safety issues. Four members had been hit by trains in

the preceding six months, resulting in two deaths. By striking, the union won a court order for enforcement of Conrail's own safety procedures. They also strengthened the rail union coalition that helped force Conrail off its no-boycott position.

The court did order the union to give 30 days' notice before declaring a boycott and disciplining members who participate. The union agreed to rejoin the programs if negotiations over how they function are successful.

But the BMWE on Conrail is steadfastly maintaining its right to give 30 days' notice and withdraw members, which Dodd says they will not hesitate to do.

Dodd thinks the union can take advantage of what the company is willing to give on joint programs, and still be able to pull out if the programs start to threaten the union. "We'll negotiate joint safety committees in the next round of negotiations [starting late 1994]. I'm against jointness in principle, but we'll be able to have people running around on company time documenting safety violations by the company."

The union is in a position of strength on this score, because of the high level of organization shown in the boycott of cooperation programs and in the May 1994 strike over safety. As Dodd says, "They know we can pull out any time."

Working Smart:
A Union Guide to Participation Programs and Reengineering

Labor Notes • 7435 Michigan Ave. • Detroit, MI 48210 • (313) 842-6262

Chapter 41

Resources for Unions

Following are some aids for unions that want to take an active, independent stance toward participation programs.

In addition to what's listed here, you should check into resources from your own union and from unions dealing with similar employers. Be aware, however, that some unions have simply appropriated and reprinted the advice of various pro-participation consultants. Take advantage of meetings of councils or the like within your International to do some informal cross-local brain-picking. Investigate the labor studies program at your local college or university as well.

See the endnotes to the preceding chapters for more books and articles on participation programs, both pro and con.

Prices include postage.

INTERNAL ORGANIZING

A Troublemaker's Handbook—How to Fight Back Where You Work—and Win! by Dan La Botz. Filled with first-person accounts that highlight the steps of internal organizing, ranging from work-to-rules to corporate campaigns. A Labor Notes book. See the ad at the end of this book.

Mobilizing for the '90s. CWA Education Dept., 1925 K St. NW, Washington, DC 20006. Phone 202/728-2300. $4.

Creative Persistent Resistance (CPR): A Primer for Unions Taking the Strike Inside, by Michael Eisenscher. 207 Edinburgh, San Francisco, CA 94112. Phone 415/469-7235. $4.

The Inside Game. Inside strategies. AFL-CIO Industrial Union Dept., 815 16th St. NW, Washington, DC 20006. Order on union letterhead. $5.

How To Do Leaflets, Newsletters and Newspapers, by Nancy Brigham. UAW LUPA, 8000 Jefferson Ave., Detroit, MI 48214. $5.95.

Union News: A Basic Newsletter Course for Union Editors and Activists. Canadian Auto Workers Education Dept., 205 Placer Ct., North York, Willowdale, Ontario M2H 3H9. Phone 416/497-4110. $8.

BOOKS AND ARTICLES ON PARTICIPATION PROGRAMS

A Union Strategy Guide for Labor-Management Participation Programs, by Mike Parker and Jane Slaughter. A Labor Notes pamphlet, 1992. See the ad at the end of this book.

Inside the Circle: A Union Guide to QWL, by Mike Parker. Analysis and strategy advice for participation programs. A Labor Notes book, 1985. See the ad at the end of this book.

Total Quality Management, by Trudy Richardson. A 200-page handbook. Although focus is on the health care industry, much material applies to TQM anywhere; includes a strategy for the union. From United Nurses of Alberta, (a registered nurses' union), 9th Floor, Park Plaza, 10611 98th Ave., Edmonton, Alberta T5K 2P7. Phone 403/425-1025. Fax 403/426-2093. Free.

Don Wells, "Are Strong Unions Compatible with the New Model of Human Resource Management?" *Relations Industrielles/Industrial Relations,* Vol. 48, No. 1, 1993.

Participating in Management—Union Organizing on a New Terrain, Labor Research Review #14. Midwest Center for Labor Research, 3411 W. Diversey, Suite 10, Chicago, Il 60647. $8.

Jointness at GM—Company Unionism in the 21st Century, by Elly Leary and Marybeth Menaker. New Directions Region 9A, P.O. Box 2221, Woonsocket, RI 02895. Fax 617/364-6238. $3.

Total Quality Management: Should Unions Buy Into TQM?, by John Anderson. TARP, Ontario Federation of Labour, 15 Gervais Dr., 2nd Floor, Don Mills, Ontario M3C 1Y8. Free.

BOOKS AND ARTICLES ON LEAN PRODUCTION

Patient-Focused Care, by Trudy Richardson. 53 pages. Reengineering applied to the health care industry (longer version of chapter 11). United Nurses of Alberta, see above. Free.

Steve Babson, ed., *Lean Work: Exploitation and Empowerment in the Global Auto Industry,* Wayne State University, Detroit, Spring 1995. Papers from a conference on lean production held May 1993.

Steve Babson, "Lean or Mean: The MIT Model and Lean Production at Mazda," *Labor Studies Journal*, Vol. 18, No. 2, Summer 1993.

David Robertson and others, CAW Research Group on CAMI, "The CAMI Report: Lean Production in a Unionized Auto Plant," 1993, Canadian Auto Workers—Work Organization and Training Dept., 205 Placer Ct., North York, Willowdale, Ontario, M2H 3H9. Phone 416/497-4110. Fax 416/497-6552. $5.

Christian Berggren, *Alternatives to Lean Production: Work Organization in the Swedish Auto Industry*, ILR Press, Ithaca, New York, 1992.

Nelson Lichtenstein and Howell Harris, eds., *Industrial Democracy in America: The Ambiguous Promise*, Woodrow Wilson Center Press, Washington, D.C., 1993.

Joseph J. Fucini and Suzy Fucini, *Working for the Japanese: Inside Mazda's American Auto Plant*, MacMillan, New York, 1990.

Choosing Sides: Unions and the Team Concept by Mike Parker and Jane Slaughter. A Labor Notes book, 1988. Analysis of management-by-stress in the auto industry, with many case studies. Out of print, but available in many libraries.

Lean and Mean Production System...Speed-Up, by Dave Yettaw, President, UAW Local 599. Three-page review of what lean production means to auto workers, from the local's newspaper. Write to Dean Braid, UAW Local 599 Education Director, 812 Leith St., Flint, MI 48505. Free.

LABOR NOTES SCHOOLS

Once a year or so, Labor Notes holds an intensive, four-day, cross-union school for union activists and labor educators, about participation programs, management-by-stress, and what to do about it. The school covers much of the material in this book—but is enriched by the first-hand experiences of the union members/students. Call Labor Notes at 313/842-6262 to find out whether a school is scheduled soon.

Labor Notes also holds a large cross-union educational conference, in odd-numbered years in the spring. This conference deals with a host of union issues, in a mix of practical workshops and inspiring speakers. Labor-management participation is always covered extensively. It is difficult to describe this conference in one paragraph; let's just say that most of the 1,100 1993 participants will be back for the next one. The next conference is scheduled for April 28-30, 1995, in Detroit. Write or call Labor Notes for more information.

Finally, Labor Notes sometimes puts on one- or two-day seminars for unions. Call to discuss availability and particulars.

CONTRACT LANGUAGE

Negotiating New Work Systems: Contract Language to Protect the Union by Roberta Till-Retz. A collection of existing and suggested union contract language, by category,

including both positive and negative examples. Labor Center, Oakdale Hall, University of Iowa, Iowa City, IA 52242. Phone 319/335-4144. $5.

LEGAL QUESTIONS ABOUT PARTICIPATION PROGRAMS

All by attorney Ellis Boal. Order from Labor Notes for $4 each.

Amicus brief in *Ona Corp.* (1987), the first case heard by the NLRB in which a company was found to have used a modern participation program against a union organizing drive.

Labor Notes' amicus brief in the 1992 *Electromation* case, in which the NLRB ordered a company to dissolve company-dominated employee "action committees."

"The Independence of Labor," paper submitted to the Commission on the Future of Worker-Management Relations and cited in its Fact Finding Report.

A detailed analysis of the Commission's May 1994 Fact Finding Report, concentrating on the employee participation material.

Short summaries of all modern NLRB employee participation cases.

TRAINING

See the list at the end of chapter 35. Also, for an analysis of the problems with training as a solution, see "Into the Dark: Rough Ride Ahead for American Workers", by Jack Gordon, *Training* magazine, July 1993.

COMPANY UNIONS

"Polaroid: When Is a Union Not a Union?" by Dick Monks. The company dominated its Employees' Committee for 45 years until one feisty representative tried to reform it. January-February 1994 issue of the *Labor Page*, 335 Lamartine St., Jamaica Plain, MA 02130. $2.

"International Harvester," by Toni Gilpin. During the 1920s and 1930s, Harvester workers decided to organize against management's "Works Councils," and founded a real union. Spring 1992 issue of *Labor's Heritage*. George Meany Center, 10000 New Hampshire Ave., Silver Spring, MD 20903. $5.50.

JAPAN

The Asian Pacific Workers Solidarity Links—Japan Committee (APWSL-Japan) is an organization of grassroots union activists in Japan. The committee is part of a growing network of solidarity throughout the Asia Pacific region. Publishes an English-language newsletter with up-to-date labor news from Japan. To subscribe write APWSL-Japan, Kato Bldg, 4-21-7, Shinbashi, Minato-ku, Tokyo, Japan. Phone 81-3-3433-0375. Fax 81-3-3433-0394.

The Japanese Auto Industry: Is Lean Production on the Way Out? by Ben Watanabe, National Union of General Workers. 20 pages. 1993. Order from Labor Notes. $4.

*"Since we're all one big family here...
Can I use the plant as collateral on my car loan?"*

VIDEOS

We are Driven. 60 minutes. Originally broadcast on PBS January 23, 1984. About Nissan in Japan and at its Tennessee assembly plant; shows how Nissan management broke the union in Japan. UAW Solidarity House, Education Dept. Film/Video Library, 8000 E. Jefferson Ave, Detroit, MI 48214. Phone 313/926-5474. Fax 313/926-5609. Rental $7.50 per week plus postage.

Exorcising Labor-Management Cooperation. Greg Poferl of the American Postal Workers Union and labor historian Peter Rachleff discuss the historical context and pitfalls of labor-management cooperation. 40 minutes. LaborVision, P.O. Box 63234, St. Louis, MO 63163. Phone 314/773-0605. $16.50.

The Battle for Hearts and Minds. Shows union members at several workplaces grappling with participation programs. Footage of union education programs; a strategy debate among union officers. Canadian Labor Congress, Educational Services, 2841 Riverside Dr., Ste. 301, Ottawa, Ont. K1V 8X7. Phone 613/521-3400. $6, plus tax/shipping.

Working Lean, produced by Laura Sky in 1993. Includes footage and interviews with workers about lean production at CAMI and Air Canada. Canadian Auto Workers, Work Organization Dept, 205 Placer Ct., North York, Willowdale, Ontario M2H 3H9, Canada. $10 (Canadian) for either version (58.5 minutes or 31 minutes).

PERIODICALS

Labor Notes. Monthly magazine for union activists, and publishers of this book. Covers not only labor-management cooperation but labor news of all kinds. Slogan:

"Let's put the movement back in the labor movement." See the ad at the end of this book.

Labor Research Review. Semi-annual publication; each issue addresses a particular labor issue in depth. Midwest Center for Labor Research, 3411 W. Diversey, Ste. 10, Chicago, IL 60647. Two-year subscription is $25.

FROM THE HORSE'S MOUTH

We could fill a library with management's views on participation programs and lean production. See the chapter endnotes. Some current favorites:

W. Edwards Deming, *The New Economics for Industry, Government, Education*, MIT Center for Advanced Engineering Study, Cambridge, Mass., 1993.

James P. Womack, Daniel T. Jones, and Daniel Roos, *The Machine that Changed the World*, Rawson Associates, New York, 1990.

Michael Hammer and James Champy, *Reengineering the Corporation: A Manifesto for Business Revolution*, Harper Business, 1993.

The *Wall Street Journal* ran a series in March 1993 titled, "Down the Up Escalator: Why Some Workers Are Falling Behind." Contains a wealth of facts, statistics, and analysis of corporate downsizing and reengineering. See "Workplace Revolution Boosts Productivity at Cost of Job Security" (March 10); "Workers Are Forced To Take More Jobs with Few Benefits" (March 11); "'Reengineering' Gives Firms New Efficiency, Workers the Pink Slip" (March 16).

Working Smart:
A Union Guide to Participation Programs and Reengineering
Labor Notes • 7435 Michigan Ave. • Detroit, MI 48210 • (313) 842-6262

Index

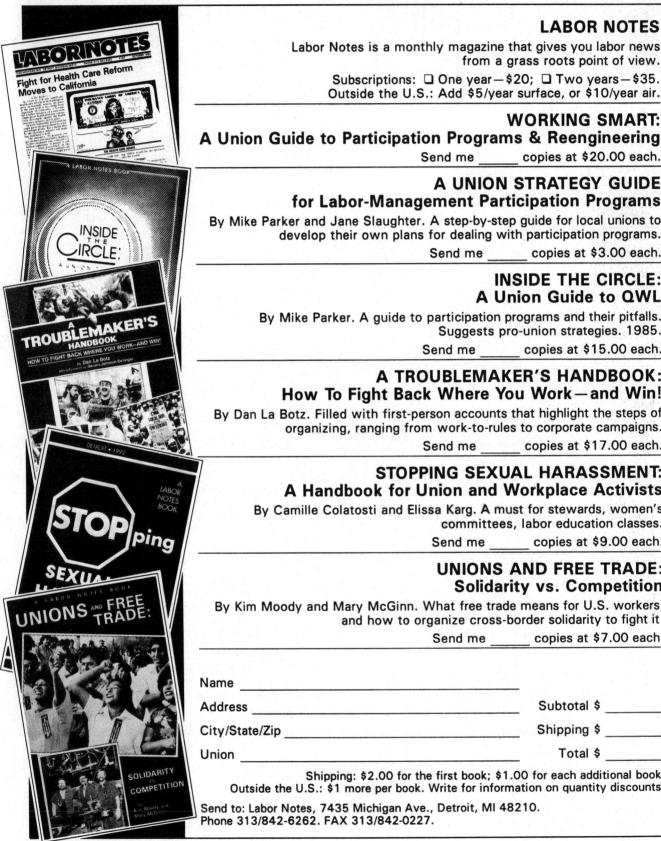

$3.00

A Union Strategy Guide
for Labor-Management Participation Programs

by Mike Parker and Jane Slaughter

A Labor Notes Publication

A Union Strategy Guide for Labor-Management Participation Programs

Dealing with labor-management participation programs—Total Quality Management, Employee Involvement, quality circles, team concept, Quality of Work Life—is one of the 1990s' most difficult challenges for unions.

The guide we present here is a plan to help the union figure out its needs and develop its specific strategy. It raises the key questions that unions need to answer and suggests a range of alternatives to choose from.

We cannot stress how important it is for unions to develop their own specific strategies, because:

1. Management's plans are usually flexible enough to go after the union's weak spots and avoid the strengths.

2. Going through the process of developing your own strategy will itself create a leadership and union which is more united and better understands the issues. The union will then be able to respond quickly when management shifts attack or changes the ground rules (which it surely will).

You may be tempted to skip the beginning stages of this process and get right to the tactics outlined in parts 8-13. We advise against this. The process of carefully considering your options and building a united union attitude is half (or more) of the game. For this reason we have included at the end of the guide a special section on strategic planning for unions.

The advice in this guide also assumes that the local union leadership can be united around the program—that you don't have two or more factions with different goals. If there are factions, you will have to add internal union politicking and assessment of the strengths of the various groupings to your agenda.

The guide draws on the experience of many local unions in the U.S. and Canada. For more help with strategies, see three Labor Notes books: *Inside the Circle: A Union Guide to QWL, Choosing Sides: Unions and the Team Concept,* and Chapter 5 of *A Troublemaker's Handbook.*

Sorting Out Participation

Management's offensive under the heading of "labor-management participation" has two parts: the cooperation apparatus and management-by-stress (MBS). You can think of the *cooperation apparatus* as the special events away from the job,

with company propaganda about quality and cooperation, and the *production system, MBS* issues as the things which affect what you do on the job most of the day.

The Cooperation Apparatus

The cooperation apparatus includes:

a. Special committees (quality circles, task forces, joint labor-management committees) and new positions (full-time facilitators, coordinators, trainers).

b. A new set of management policies. These include particular definitions of quality, competitiveness, the needs of the customer, and worker participation and dignity. They are usually accompanied by a propaganda offensive.

Both the new committees and the attitude training are outside the regular production process.

In this guide we have used the term *circles* to describe groups of workers meeting with management as part of the cooperation apparatus. An example would be volunteers brainstorming ideas about productivity or quality in a Total Quality Management program.

Management-by-Stress

In the 1990s there is one dominant management model for the ideal production system (the methods for organizing production of goods or services). We call this model system management-by-stress or MBS.

Others call it the lean production system, Toyotaism, Japanese production methods, synchronous production, world-class production, or team concept. It includes standardization and speedup of work, "just-in-time," elimination of job classifications, subcontracting, and a two-tier workforce. When management is able to implement this system fully, productivity is enhanced, jobs are lost, most of the remaining jobs are much less desirable, and unions are weakened or eliminated.

In this guide we use the word *team* to refer to the work groups created under the management-by-stress system, where the group is a central part of the day-to-day work organization.

The end goal of the cooperation apparatus is to introduce management-by-stress. This has become more and more apparent over the years, no matter how much management wraps its package in benevolent rhetoric.

In many workplaces, pieces of these two aspects of new work relations are often introduced at the same time. Management wants to abolish classifications. They justify it with circle meetings to present facts and figures about competitiveness. Management holds Statistical Process Control classes to lay the basis for doing away with inspectors and adding those jobs onto other workers. The cooperation apparatus often assists the reorganization of production by reducing resistance, weakening union and worker power, and providing the necessary attitude adjustment.

1 Form a Special Union Committee

You need a special committee to deal with the participation program. Give it a good name which indicates its purpose (here we'll call it a Solidarity Committee).

The selection of this committee must be done with particular care. While it can be changed as necessary, this will be the committee to guide the union in developing its strategy and implementing its policy. It will be the union body of experts. As can be seen from the checklist, different people will be on the committee for different reasons and perhaps carry out different functions. That's fine—that is true teamwork.

At the same time the committee should be kept small enough to be workable. The committee may visit other plants and spend time researching programs. Keep in mind the union's finances for lost time and travel. But even if finances permit, when a committee gets too large it loses its ability to discuss and work effectively. We recommend a committee of between four and 12.

Some union officers may view the committee as interfering in their turf, so it is important to have the committee's job defined carefully at the beginning, with its purpose written down and its powers spelled out. Remember that while it may seem easier to restrict the committee's power to avoid conflict, it will be a sign of unity if everyone gets behind the committee to give it sufficient authority to do its job of investigating and, later, leading.

Follow your union bylaws for special committees. In whatever form required, the committee should be explained at, discussed by, and confirmed by a membership meeting.

The first meeting(s) of the committee should make sure that all members understand its goals and functions and set rough timelines for accomplishing key tasks.

Checklist
* Include key officers (president or shop chair).
* Include people who are respected by sig-

nificant sections of the union (by work area, political caucus, seniority, race, sex, attitude or involvement in participation programs). This will be important in developing as much unity as possible for the union's program.
* Include the rank and file. Remember that participation programs are billed as giving a voice to the regular worker (as opposed to the union officials). You don't want to start out giving management a sledgehammer to drive this wedge in. Particularly look for rank and file members with leadership, writing, or research skills.
* Include one or two people who can devote a lot of time to the committee, to organize its work, do extra research, and serve as committee chair and/or secretary.
* Include union facilitators/coordinators from the participation program, unless they have been brainwashed by management.
* Be clear from the beginning on the committee's goals, responsibilities, authority, and limits.

2 Gather Information

The committee should find out as much as it can about the program itself and management's motives and plans. Take the time to research these

---

Cooperation Leads to MBS

The "Building Team 2000" plan of B.C. Hydro, the British Columbia electric utility, is an example of the blending of a cooperation apparatus with MBS objectives.

On page two, B.C. Hydro says that a main objective is "to be one of the best employers in British Columbia" and lists its values as "integrity, innovation, commitment, teamwork, and empowerment." There is much talk of meeting employees' needs and respecting the environment. As you read on, however, you find that the specifics of Building Team 2000 include:

* Forced retirement to achieve a younger workforce
* Contracting out
* Management flexibility to transfer workers to any part of the province
* Broadening classifications and bargaining unit boundaries
* "Abandoning outdated and unnecessary work practices"
* Job-specific training
* Speedup ("The new business environment is very demanding. In recognition of the increasing demands being placed on our employees, we will create a flexible working environment whereby employees have the opportunity to lead a balanced lifestyle [through] job sharing, sabbaticals and working from home.")

A UNION PLAN
for
Participation
Programs

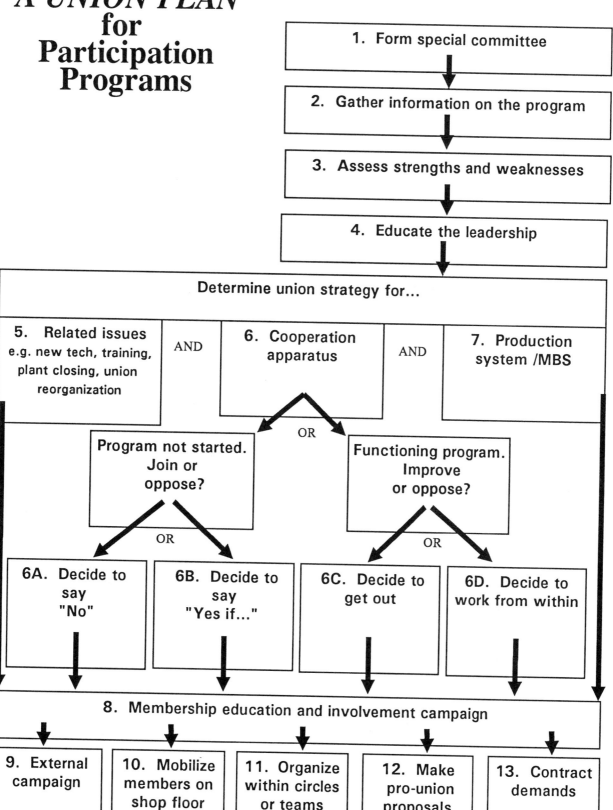

1. Form special committee

2. Gather information on the program

3. Assess strengths and weaknesses

4. Educate the leadership

Determine union strategy for...

5. Related issues
e.g. new tech, training, plant closing, union reorganization

AND

6. Cooperation apparatus

AND

7. Production system /MBS

OR

Program not started. Join or oppose?

Functioning program. Improve or oppose?

OR

OR

6A. Decide to say "No"

6B. Decide to say "Yes if..."

6C. Decide to get out

6D. Decide to work from within

8. Membership education and involvement campaign

9. External campaign

10. Mobilize members on shop floor

11. Organize within circles or teams

12. Make pro-union proposals

13. Contract demands

questions carefully. Enlist the aid of a labor educator at your local university if appropriate.

Get information from other unions, and from your International. Make contact with other unions, especially other locals in your own union, who have had experience with the same or similar program. Find weak links in management who are also not happy about the program, or office workers who can feed you information.

Check with organizations that have experience with different unions, such as Labor Notes, Midwest Center for Labor Research, American Labor Education Center, Labor Institute, Corporate Campaigns, Inc., Labor Resource Center. Labor Notes may be able to refer you to a labor educator in your area.

Questionnaire for Solidarity Committee

1. What does the program involve?

   a. Is it supposed to be about improving the quality of work life or is it specifically limited to productivity/quality?

   b. Does it involve group meetings separate from production or is it a reorganization of production?

   c. Are team members or task force members appointed or elected, or are they volunteers?

   d. Is the program accompanied by major changes in working conditions or contract items? What are they?

2. Where else, either in your company or elsewhere, has this program been introduced? What have been the results?

3. Who is the consultant management has hired to implement the program? What can you find out about the consultant's other activities (for example, helping a non-union company in an anti-union campaign)?

4. What is management trying to achieve through the program? List all possibilities.

5. What level of management is pushing it? Do they want the program mainly in name (because higher management insists on it)? Which elements do they want and which are window dressing?

6. Has management begun to introduce changes which will lead to a new production system?

7. How will these changes, or ones you can foresee, affect fundamental union issues such as job security, seniority, job classifications, contracting out? What other issues are at stake?

8. Who will the system help? Who will it hurt?

9. What sections of the contract are affected?

10. Which items does management indicate they are willing to bargain about and which do they consider management's rights?

If the program is already operating, the committee needs to gather detailed information on:

- What members feel are program successes.
- What members feel are possible future benefits from the program.
- How participants feel about the program.

The committee also needs to compile lists of:

- Ways that circles have violated the contract.
- Ways that circles have been turned against individuals or groups.
- Ways that circles have been induced to speed up or cut jobs.
- Times circles have been lied to about their decision-making responsibilities (e.g., management said they could choose a new machine but it was already purchased).
- Management actions which run counter to the spirit of trust and respect.

3 Assess Strengths and Weaknesses

The union should not approach a participation program as if it were the only thing going on in the union's life. In fact, one of the big dangers of these programs is that the union may end up so preoccupied with them that they do not respond to major management offensives on outsourcing, new technology, or work reorganization. You need to step back and put the program in the bigger picture, by understanding the union's strengths and weaknesses and the external threats and opportunities you are facing.

This is part of a process called strategic planning. Actually, most local unions badly need to do this sort of analysis. A new participation program can be the motivation.

See the Strategic Planning section at the end of this manual for a step-by-step guide. One tool described there is called "SWOT Analysis," for Strengths, Weaknesses, Opportunities, and Threats. Keep in mind that sometimes the same condition creates both a threat and an opportunity.

Opportunities and Threats —Some Sample Questions

1. What are the economic trends in your industry? Growing or shrinking? Profitable or unprofitable? What about your company? What are the changes on the horizon? What is your management doing about them?

2. What are the trends for the occupations of your members (e.g., keypunch operators are a disappearing breed, office workers must now have computer skills)?

3. What is happening in the community where your workplace is located?

4. How does the structure of your company

affect the union? Any changes there?

5. What relevant legislation is in place or pending?

Add your own questions.

Union's Strengths and Weaknesses —Some Sample Questions

This assessment can be difficult to do—especially for incumbents. But a frank, non-blaming assessment of your resources—positive and negative—is necessary.

1. How much control do members feel they have over their daily work? Is participation in decision-making an attractive idea to many?

2. How much power does the union have on the shop floor? Are contract protections enforced on a daily basis by union representatives *and* members? Does the presence of the union give members more feeling of control (rather than the union being merely a bargainer of wages and benefits)?

3. What do members think of the union? Is the union just the officers, or does everyone feel a part of it?

4. How is the company reaching members?

5. What are members' reactions to the program? Do different groups react differently (for example, low seniority vs. high, skilled vs. production)?

6. How good is the union's communication with members now?

7. If this system were in place, how would it affect the union's ability to communicate with members?

8. How easy is it for members to bring problems to the union?

9. How easy is it for members to become involved in union activities?

Add your own questions.

4 Educate the Leadership

The Solidarity Committee should organize a special seminar for the bargaining committee, executive board, and stewards if appropriate (depending on the size of your workforce). You may want to invite outside experts: a labor educator, someone from your International, or someone from another local which has already experienced the program.

The Solidarity Committee should meet with the experts for assistance in planning the meeting. But the ultimate responsibility for the meeting should stay with the Committee. This seminar should explain thoroughly not only the particular program you are faced with, but also give the bigger picture of where management is likely to head with it.

We recommend that this seminar be a two- or three-day off-site meeting. The first part should be strictly education organized by the Solidarity Committee. The second part could be the beginning of Step 6: brainstorming, formulating possible strategies, and hypothetically walking these through various scenarios.

Determine Union Strategy

Whatever union body is appropriate—the executive board, the Stewards Council, the membership—should decide the union's initial strategy for dealing with the program. It should be made clear to everyone that you will probably have to adopt several different types of activities for dealing with the different components of the program. Some may involve immediate decisions, some may not involve decisions until contract time. Some may be assigned to a committee for further work, and some can just be noted and postponed.

5 Strategy for Related Issues

Almost certainly your research and your SWOT Analysis will reveal related problems the union needs to deal with. Some will be from external factors like new technology or non-union shops opening up. Others may be serious internal weaknesses such as poor communication (no or poor union newspaper) or significant sections of the membership feeling alienated. The leadership needs to determine which of these to start on immediately with action or more research and which can be postponed. Probably these should be assigned to different committees or individuals.

6 Strategy for the Cooperation Apparatus

Here is where you make some crucial decisions about direction. Your position can change if events change, but clarifying the position and the reasons for it is vitally important.

Either your participation program has already begun or it has not yet gotten off the ground. In either case, you now need to decide whether to **just say no** or to **work from within** (see the chart on page 3).

Program Has Not Yet Started:
- Keep it from starting, OR
- Shape it to union needs.

Program Is Already Functioning:

- Get out, OR
- Shape it to union needs.

There will be a great deal of overlap in the tactics used in the four situations. For example, even if you are going to **say no** from the get-go, you still may want to put forward some positive proposals of your own (see section 12). And if you are going to **work from within,** you had better be sure you explain to the members management's true goals for participation programs (section 8).

Below, we have described the conditions which might lead the union to choose that option.

Management's Program Hasn't Begun

You can:

6a. Say no. You want no part of the company's program and will try to keep it from happening. You state your reasons clearly.

You may also want to put forward proposals of your own. For example, if management says the program will improve quality, the union can put forward its own ideas for improving quality which do not include a participation program.

Reasons to Choose This Option:

- The union is relatively strong and union leaders believe that members can be mobilized against the program.

6b. Say "Yes if..." The union says it wants to participate fully in the program and has its own ideas on how to make it work.

Reasons to Choose This Option:

- Management is open to input from the union.
- The union feels it must participate because:
  * The program is mandated in the contract.
  * Your International insists on it.
  * Your workplace will not be eligible for certain work if you do not participate.
  * Special circumstances: for example, for federal employee unions, such programs may allow the union to discuss issues that the Administration refuses to handle in bargaining.
- Management is very weak or divided and under great pressure from above; they are willing to give the union almost any content the union wants as long as management can have the program by name.

The Program is Already in Place

You can:

6c. Get out. Explain why management betrayed the stated goals of the program or why the program was structured solely to benefit management.

As in 6a, you may want to make your own pro-union proposals about how to reach the program's stated goals. See Appendix A for the withdrawal strategy followed by one local.

Reasons to Choose This Option:

- It is clear to all or most members that the program is working against their interests.
- The union is relatively strong and union leaders believe that members can be mobilized against the program.

Examples:

a. Inform management of specific union demands and that management lack of action in these areas is contrary to the supposed spirit of the participation program. The union will continue in the program only if improvements in these areas are made (examples: action on grievances, an end to contracting out—whatever is appropriate for your situation). Give a deadline by which the union must see some specific actions by management.

b. Inform management of particular supervisors who are acting contrary to the spirit of worker participation and demand corrective action, with a deadline.

c. Inform management that if the program is to continue the union needs to negotiate strong job security language, including a base level of jobs.

(The above three actions will not usually result in substantial change from management. If they do, so much the better. If they don't, you've made it clear to the membership that you have given management every chance to act in the true "win-win" spirit.)

6d. Work from within. Go on the offensive to force changes in the program; bargain changes through collective bargaining channels.

Reasons to Choose This Option:

- There is significant support in the membership for the program.
- It is mandated in the contract.
- Your International insists that you participate.
- You inherited the program from a preceding administration.
- Your workplace will not be eligible for certain work if you do not participate.

In either case the union should pay careful attention to the program's facilitators. They may be an excellent resource for the union because they understand the program and can see the dangers firsthand.

Or they may have been converted to management's thinking. The union should decide whether to replace facilitators, or insure that they are responsible to the union leadership and work with the Solidarity Committee.

What Stance to Take

Deciding what stance to take involves your analysis from earlier steps, decisions about organizing members, and internal union politics.

- What is the union's history of self-organization?
- Is there anything in the program to work with?
- What are levers to use against the company?
- What are the chances the company will accept your conditions?
- Is the membership scared? Is it mad?

As you make your choice, remember that working from within always seems to be the easiest initial choice, but *it is the hardest strategy to carry out successfully* and also the hardest union policy to reverse.

Working from within always creates a group within the union which has some vested interest in the program continuing, no matter how bad it gets.

At the same time, if you do have any success in making the program benefit your members, management is likely to shut it down or change it to reassert its own control.

Some union leaders believe that it is possible to have a public position and a private position: publicly we believe the program is a good thing (who could be against quality?), but privately we think it is garbage.

The main effect of this is to confuse the members, not fool the company. If the union is going to use the "work from within" option, it has to be honest about the dangers of the program but also clear that it wants to get in with both feet. The union leaders' message to members, management, and outsiders might be:

1. The history of these programs indicates that they hurt unions.

2. We have yet to see the proof in action that this program will be different.

3. However, many members would like to try.

4. Therefore, despite our skepticism, we will do all we can to make it work, until and unless the company shows that it has different intentions.

5. We will agree to participate if ...

6. And we will be watching for ...

7. We will evaluate and review ...(when), with the option to change our position.

7 Strategy for the Production System/MBS

Management may or may not give the union the same opportunity to participate in a new MBS production system as it usually does in a new cooperation apparatus. Often management just begins making changes in the production system without asking for union input.

On the other hand, sometimes management makes those changes as bargaining demands. Or the MBS changes may be thoroughly intertwined with the cooperation apparatus changes. You will have to determine for yourself at what stage of the strategy process outlined above you can jump in.

You will want to pay special attention to the sections below on organizing within the teams (11) and contract demands (13). Do not neglect education, however. The problems with MBS can be overwhelming to most members. Often they know they are unhappy, working too hard, uncomfortable in their jobs—but are not clear who or what is responsible.

If the union does not analyze the system and offer solutions, they may identify the causes of their problems incorrectly (as the system is designed to promote). They might place the blame on the worker next to them for not keeping up or for being absent. They might think the new problems are the fault of a couple of bad supervisors, or "the Japanese" in general, or the American managers. It is hard for an individual to identify the whole system as the problem.

It is a big mistake for the union simply to let things happen and then grieve individual contract violations as they come up. The union must try to anticipate management's moves and be prepared with its own plan (be proactive, in the participation jargon).

• • •

After a period of research, discussion, and decision-making, you are ready to begin the more action-oriented part of your campaign.

8 Membership Education & Involvement Campaign

Whether the participation program has just been announced or whether it's been around for a while, the key is to see your actions as a *campaign* which mobilizes the members.

The next step is to unify the local behind the campaign. Now is the time to make sure that all the leaders of the local not included in your initial seminars and discussions are brought on board. "Leader" here is very broadly defined: not only elected officers but also the opinion-makers on the shop floor. Supervisors are now being trained to go after these natural leaders. The union needs to draw them into greater union involvement.

- Education of the entire membership is critical. A union leadership cannot have much effect by itself.
- Because participation programs appeal to the worker as an individual, much one-on-one education will be necessary.
- The membership education campaign will have to explain the myths about participation programs, the honeymoon period, and the end goals that management is really driving at (management-by-stress). For help in your education plan, see *Inside the Circle* and *Choosing Sides*. See also the leaflets in this notebook for examples of arguments and cartoons that other unions have used.
- Once the membership is educated, many mobilization tactics you would use against any management offensive are suitable. (See *A Troublemaker's Handbook*.)
- You will have to keep coming back again and again, perhaps fighting new programs with new names.

Membership survey or questionnaire

This will gather information on members' ideas/fears about the participation program and other management initiatives. (See Appendix B.) Its advantages are:

- Promotes one-on-one contact.
- Starts the membership thinking about the issues.
- Reveals which issues the membership feels are most important plus problems the leadership has not thought of.
- Can be used to show membership support for the leadership's demands.

Face-to-face

- "Map" the workplace to show where opinion leaders work, who they influence, in which departments different opinions are prevalent.
- Make sure the Solidarity Committee has "operatives" in every department.
- Plan one-on-one communication by stewards or Solidarity Committee to members, especially members who are participating in existing programs. Each person is responsible for a specific number of members to talk to and for reporting back on their results.
- Hold lunchtime meetings by department.
- Call members out of work for classes on lost time.
- Sponsor an educational at a union meeting.
- Hold a special workshop on the weekend, with video or outside speaker.
- Have local officers or members of the Solidarity Committee visit circle meetings.
- Use management's own techniques, including brainstorming, team-building icebreakers, flipcharts and the rest.
- At a class, divide members into teams and try a management brainwashing technique

---

Vision Buster

In IBEW Local 2373 at a Square D transformer plant in Oshkosh, Wisconsin, management had implemented a program called "Vision Mission." The local wanted to get rid of the program in negotiations. As part of a program of membership involvement in bargaining, they held a Vision Buster Day. The message was that the Vision propaganda was poison, a hazard that had to be removed from the plant. A member in a toxic waste protection suit went around the plant collecting the Vision pennants and Vision graduation certificates.

The next week, on Vision Dump Day, all members were asked to bring in their Vision Mission coffee cups and smash them in the dumpster.

Both days, according to President Galen De Voe, got members involved who "are normally blended into the background."

on them, so they'll be prepared (for example, a "Lost in the Desert" exercise).

- Try an exercise that shows members what's going on behind a supposedly neutral technique, such as "cost/benefit analysis."
- Have members brainstorm their own ideas of worker control. The sky's the limit. Publish the results.
- Have members write a Union Code of Conduct which spells out how responsible union members should behave. (For example, no one makes suggestions which eliminate jobs.) See Appendix C for a sample code.

Written materials

- Use your own union newsletter or start a new one.
- Do special leaflets.
- If the program is already in operation, print examples of how it has undermined the union or caused speed-up, or where promises were violated.
- Invite participants to enter an essay contest on what they think of the program.
- Get firsthand testimonials from people in other workplaces who have experienced similar programs.
- Reprint newsletter articles or leaflets from other unions.
- Contrast management's statements about teamwork with other, anti-union actions they're taking, such as job-cutting. Run the statements on one half of the page and the actions on the other half.
- If management has hired a consultant, publicize his or her previous activities if they are anti-union.
- Copy material from *Choosing Sides, Inside the Circle*, or *A Troublemaker's Handbook*.

Informational hotline about the program and the union's campaign

9 External Campaign

Your International

- Make contact with relevant departments in your International, either to get their support or to neutralize their opposition.

Other locals

- Form a united front with other locals in your company, union, or community; pledge to deal with the program together.

* Exchange columns in your respective local newsletters.
* Invite spokespeople to each other's union-meetings.
* Exchange workplace tours.

Public support

- Get publicity. Rent a billboard. Take your case to the local newspapers. Buy a radio ad. Call a press conference. One OCAW local working under the Deming system erected a billboard on the Interstate that read "First in Productivity, Last in Appreciation."

Legal options

- In a few cases where management has ignored the union in implementing circles and where the union has protested to the National Labor Relations Board, the NLRB has found the programs to be illegal "company unions." Warning—this tactic will work only in some cases, will take a long time, and *cannot* be your only tactic. This area of the law may be changing rapidly. See Chapter 5 in *Choosing Sides* and Chapter 5 in *A Troublemaker's Handbook*, but consult an attorney for more complete information.

10 Mobilize Members on the Shop Floor

These tactics work both for opposing a program and for putting pressure on management to change it.

- Circulate a petition against the program or for changes you want.
- Collect pledges from members not to volunteer or participate in other ways; give copies to management.
- Have a t-shirt day, armband day or button day. Use a slogan like "We're on the Union Team."
- Publicize the Union Code of Conduct (see Section 8) and encourage members to think of creative ways to enforce it.
- Organize members to boycott activities such as surveys, personality testing, or meetings to launch the new program (organizing a boycott can be difficult; assess your influence carefully).
- Organize members to attend meetings but remain completely silent. See the "Just Say Nothing" leaflet in Appendix D and the letter in Appendix E.
- Organize members to take on management or the consultant at meetings. Pick out key

people and make sure they're prepared to speak. Use the arguments from your written materials. Have pointed questions to ask, such as, "Why did you promise this program was going to give us a say, but then you arbitrarily raised the quota in Department 10?"

- Organize members under each supervisor to personally make their feelings known to the supervisor, one member each day.
- Organize a mass resignation of facilitators. Dramatize it—facilitators march through the shop and go into the program director's office together to resign, for example. Or hold a mass clipboard burning in the parking lot.
- Hold a membership vote on what to do about the program.
- Union officers stop attending joint steering committee meetings.
- File grievances over contract violations. (For example, management may be changing job descriptions unilaterally or appointing jobs which should be bid.)

11 Organize within the Circles and Teams

Circles

Elect an informal "circle steward" for each circle, to work closely with the existing stewards and make sure the Union Code of Conduct is known and respected.

See the ideas for rights of circles under Section 13, Contract Demands.

Teams in an MBS production system

Too often, union leaders who oppose management's version of teams have wished they could just ignore them. When they do, the results are often disastrous—management has a free hand to propagandize, stir up jealousies, and promote their own favorites.

Although the teams were initiated by management, the union should view them as units of shop floor organization. To do so, you need to pay attention to the *team leaders* and establish a system of *team stewards*.

Team leaders

Team leaders (hourly workers who direct and assist other workers) are a key part of the MBS system. Management does all it can to co-opt team leaders to its side, and they are often a prime target of resentment from other team members. Too often, team members blame team leaders for their

problems rather than the MBS system as a whole. Therefore, within each team, the union needs to fight to get the most union-conscious person (rather than the apple-polisher) chosen as team leader. The team leader should see herself or himself as an advocate for team members to management, not a middle-person *between* workers and management. The union must be sure to define the role carefully.

Usually, the best way to get good team leaders is to insist that they be elected. This makes the leader most responsible to the members and least to management. Seniority and rotation are also possibilities; appointment by management is the worst option.

Team leaders' terms of office should be relatively short, and team members should have the right of recall by majority vote. The team leader should have the right to resign at any time. (See the contract language in Section 13.)

Team meetings should be turned into mini-union meetings, which workers use to organize for their point of view.

If necessary, union leaders should encourage proven shop floor leaders to run for team leader. Union leaders will need to pay attention to what is happening within the teams and be on hand to help solve problems.

Team stewards

Team stewards should be elected to represent members on daily problems with the immediate supervisor. A good ratio is one steward for every supervisor (each supervisor may boss two or three teams). Even if you cannot get management to recognize the team stewards officially (see the contract language in Section 13), they should still function informally as the members' front-line representatives. You may need to change your union bylaws as well as the contract.

Ideally, as in the situation described above, team leaders and team stewards should work very closely together and perform some of the same functions of advocating for the membership with supervision. (The steward would not, of course, perform any of the team leader's job-related functions such as giving breaks.)

But good rapport will not always be possible, for instance, in a situation where management appoints the team leaders. The union should elect team stewards in either case.

- If necessary, encourage particular people to run for team steward.
- Give team stewards union training.
- Use the team stewards as the union's eyes and ears on the shop floor, and for instant communication with the membership.

- To avoid tension and suspicion from higher-level union reps, educate them on the need for more shop floor, close-to-the-members reps under the team system. Spell out the duties of team stewards and how they are to work with higher-level reps.
- Establish a stewards council, which includes all reps, that meets monthly.

12 Make Pro-union Proposals

The union can put forward proposals of its own. These could range from specific ideas about improving quality, job security or worker rights up to a complete union-controlled participation program. You can put together a plan of your own using the suggestions here, or you can take a plan already designed and modify it for your own use. One plan that has been endorsed by the Machinists union was drawn up by labor educators Andy Banks and Jack Metzgar (see Appendix F).

Note that most of the activities under Section 10, Mobilizing on the Shop Floor, can be used to pressure *for* these sorts of union proposals, not just against management's.

Examples:

a. Management has said that the program will improve job security. The union makes its own job security proposals:
- A base level of jobs.
- Management commitment to investment in a type of equipment that will increase jobs or insource work.
- Program to enhance quality to the customer (not just reduce waste).

b. Management says that the program will enhance worker dignity. The union makes its own proposals:
- Innocent until proven guilty in the grievance procedure.
- Members may take personal and sick days off without providing documentation.
- Workers will have the authority to remove supervisors by majority vote of those working under that supervisor.
- Time off for community service.

c. Management says that the program will allow workers to have more control over their jobs. The union makes its own proposals:
- Reduction in number of supervisors.
- Worker ergonomics committee in charge of all job and equipment design and purchase.
- End to time-study.

Managers will not usually respond well to such proposals. If they do, take them up on it. If not, at least you've made it clear that you've given them every chance to act in the "win-win" spirit.

If Classifications Must Be Changed
Worker Bill of Rights

One problem that unions have with participation programs/MBS is management's demand to do away with classifications. In many workplaces, classifications form the basis of workers' rights—right to transfer, right to move to better jobs by seniority. Classifications give workers the means to resist management adding work onto their jobs, using favoritism in assignments, or arbitrarily moving people around.

At the same time, unions often have to admit that sometimes certain classifications are outmoded, perhaps because of technology changes or other changes in the work process.

The union should examine the classification system. In some cases new classifications may be required in order to develop new skills to meet new technology. But where the union finds that classifications are in fact outmoded, it could propose doing away with the old system only in exchange for a new system of worker rights, including some or all of the following, as appropriate:

1. Right to bid on individual jobs by seniority.
2. Right to a regular job (i.e., a job that is your job rather than assigned by management whim).
3. Grandparent clause protection for those who do not wish to participate in the new arangements.
4. Right to refuse any job that the worker believes to be unsafe (Canadian workers have this right by law).
5. Right to refuse any job which the worker believes causes stress.
6. Right to refuse any job for which the worker believes she or he has inadequate training.
7. Right to refuse any job where inadequate equipment, supplies or procedures result in poor quality.
8. Right to be treated as a mature adult who takes her/his job seriously but who has other responsibilities and goals. This means allowing workers to take personal days off with notice only, without a doctor's note or having to explain to management.
9. Right to have non-bargaining unit jobs filled by fair procedures negotiated with the union.

---

13 Contract Demands

Most of the suggestions in Section 12 are contract demands which the union could press whether it is facing a participation program or not. Following are demands that deal specifically with the cooperation apparatus or MBS.

Contract Demands for the Cooperation Apparatus

Voluntary

Participation in the program is voluntary, for individuals and for the union. Individuals or the union as a whole may withdraw at any time.

Rights of individuals

- No invasion of privacy.
- No forced overtime to replace someone who is working on a circle.
- No personality testing.

Rights of circles

- Circle may request a union representative to attend any meeting, and union reps may come to circle meetings on their own.
- Circles may hold meetings with other circles.
- Union members of the circle have the right to call a separate caucus.
- Union members have the right to their own planning time for circle meetings.
- Circles should include more than one or two union people.
- Circle meetings will take place on-site and on company time.
- Circle meetings will not be held at lunch or break time unless the circle chooses. For meetings held during those hours, overtime will be paid.
- Union members of circles will choose a spokesperson.
- Secretary of circle will be elected.
- Minutes of circle meetings must be approved by circle.
- Minutes must be posted for all employees.
- Union has veto power on projects.
- Management pays for everything.
- Agendas will be circulated in advance; changes may be made at the meeting.
- Circles will receive all financial and planning information pertinent to their projects.
- Union will receive all production, financial and business plan information available on the facility.
- Economic benefits of circle's work will be shared equally by all hourly employees.
- Quarterly meetings for all circles together.

Choice of circle members

If the number of circle participants is to be limited, then one of these procedures will be agreed on by the parties:

- Union members to be chosen by union, OR
- Union members to be elected by department, OR
- Union members may volunteer to participate in circles, with seniority governing.

Training for circle members

- Voluntary.
- Participants paid regular pay for training.
- Done on-site.
- May not be required outside of participant's normal working hours.
- No forced overtime to replace someone being trained.
- Training is jointly designed by union, OR
- Union has equal time to present its point of view in training, OR
- Some proportion of training is presented by the union only.
- Union veto power over training materials.
- Records kept of training.
- Training monitored by union—union reps have right to attend.

Circles will not be involved in

- Monitoring or evaluating work performance or ability.
- Hiring, firing, disciplining or transferring.

Union independence

- No union officers or facilitators may become supervisors while the program lasts, to prevent conflict of interest.
- Union is sole bargaining agent.
- No language committing union or individual workers to submit suggestions or to adopt company goals.
- Union may withdraw from program at any time.
- Program cannot circumvent contract.

Facilitators

- Appointed by or elected by union.
- Removable by union.
- Responsible to union.
- Receive training from union separate from company training.

Consultants

- Union has veto power over consultants.
- Union hires consultant at company expense.

No 'living agreement'

Any changes desired during the course of the agreement must be negotiated by the union bargaining committee and brought to a membership ratification vote.

Saving jobs

- All suggestions coming from circles will include an evaluation of the impact on jobs.
- All circle recommendations will be evaluated by the union for their impact on jobs and working conditions. Union has veto power over recommendations.
- No employee will be laid off as a result of the program.
- Any recommendation which decreases jobs must be compensated for by creation of new jobs or reduction of work time.
- No layoffs during the life of the program.

Governance

- Program will be overseen by a steering committee with equal numbers of union and management members.
- Equal numbers of union and management must be present at any steering committee meeting to constitute a quorum.
- Meetings of the steering committee will take place on-site and on company time.
- Union members of the committee will have the opportunity to adjourn and caucus.
- Steering committee minutes and decisions will be posted for the membership.

Contract Demands for MBS Production System

Selection of team leaders

- Team leaders will be elected by team members for six-month terms by secret ballot vote, without the supervisor present.
- Supervisors may not attempt to influence the team leader election.
- Team leaders may be recalled by majority vote.
- Team leaders can resign at any time.
- There should be a specified method for determining what job a defeated or resigning team leader will return to: his or her old job; the former job of the new team leader; the job within the department or team that he or she is able to bid on by seniority.

Team stewards

The teams under each supervisor will elect, without the supervisor present, a steward who has the authority to represent members with the supervisor. Team stewards will receive a specified number of hours off the job per week to perform these duties. They will also receive union training (not team training) on company time.

Rights of teams

- Union members may ask supervisor to leave the team meeting.
- A team may request a union representative to be present at any meeting.
- Union reps may attend team meetings on their own initiative.
- Teams may hold joint meetings with other teams.
- Management will honor the team's request for a new supervisor.

No forced participation in ''pay-for-knowledge,'' ''multiskilling'' schemes.

Management must employ regular workers as replacements to fill in for absentees.

If a ''just-in-time'' system is used, there must be sufficient ''banks'' so that workers can pace their own work to some extent. Decisions about the amount of work in progress between operations must be approved by teams and by a union representative to insure that workers and teams can sufficiently control the pace of work and have time to deal with normal breakdowns.

Proposals for improvements which result in a reduction of the number of team members must be approved by the team and a union representative.

Worker/team approval before any change made in standardized work.

Right to strike over health and safety and work standards. The right to strike over work standards goes to the heart of MBS. It is a mainstay of the system for management to have the right to change (add to) work standards at any time. Getting this clause would increase union leverage significantly.

Keep Union United in Quitting QWL Program

by Mike Parker

In October 1985, United Steelworkers Local 1033 at LTV's Chicago South Works withdrew from Labor-Management Participation Teams (LMPT), the cooperation program in the steel industry. The local's executive board took the action after four months of intensive discussion within the union and after management's rejection of proposals to put the program on a solid basis.

An LMPT program had been operating in the plant since 1983. But by 1985 many members were concerned that management was taking advantage of the union and using LMPT for its own ends. In May the grievance committee presented a petition to the executive board asking that LMPT be stopped if management closed the 10-inch and 21-inch mills.

The executive board decided not to withdraw at the time but to see if problems could be solved. The leadership began what President Maury Richards describes as a "period of intensive study and involvement in LMPT." The union replaced one of the full-time LMPT coordinators and increased union representation on the LMPT joint review committee. On July 25 the entire executive board, grievance committee, and top management held an all-day meeting with Sam Camens, who was in charge of LMPT for the USWA International.

Union Proposal

At the meeting union leaders made clear that company professions of cooperation in LMPT were meaningless while the company was refusing to answer grievances, continuing to contract out work, and combining and eliminating jobs. The union was not against cooperation but could not urge members to give ideas to management when management was using those ideas to eliminate jobs.

Following the meeting, the union drafted a proposal setting forth conditions for continued LMPT in the plant (see box) and gave the company 30 days to act. The company did take some action to reduce the backlog of grievances, but after almost two months, it was clear that the company had no intention of cooperating on job security. The union officially withdrew from LMPT.

From the time the issue came up, the union leadership made sure that the membership was brought into the discussion and that the union acted in a unified way. Individual officers made their views known in the union newspaper. Union leaders, particularly concerned about the 200 workers who were participating in LMPT groups, went to group meetings to explain the issues.

Debate

After the union officially withdrew, management called large meetings of LMPT participants to try to mobilize them against the union leadership. The leadership went to these meetings. At one, members,

top management, and union leaders participated in a three-hour debate on the problems in the plant.

There was some strong opposition in the local to withdrawing from the program. A number of the LMPT participants liked the program and did not want to see it connected with the issue of how the company was dealing with the union. The original LMPT coordinators tried to organize opposition to the union's position.

Nonetheless, Richards feels that most of the members supported the action. "We went to the membership every step of the way," he said. "When it was necessary we were able to make a clear break instead of dragging it out."

Local 1033's Conditions For Continuing LMPT

We do not believe that open communications, trust between labor and management, and the sharing of information, which is the basis of LMPT, should be confined to the program itself.

These types of improved relations must extend to all areas of Labor Relations in the plant if the program is to survive.

The Labor Agreement must be respected and its provisions lived up to...

I. Contractual Obligations

1. Resolution or processing the backlog of [grievances]...

2. The cessation of contracting out our work...

3. Open communication and an end to any obstacles that have prevented Grievers from meeting with superintendents...

II. Labor Relations

...the union will submit a list to the company of supervisors whose attitudes and behavior we consider to be detrimental to good labor relations... We expect the company to take firm action to correct the attitudes of any member of supervision incompatible with labor relations in the 1980's.

III. Job Security

If Labor-Management Participation is to succeed...steelworkers [must]...be able to go to work without the threats of job elimination or combinations hanging over our heads. The Union proposes that a Base Force Agreement be mutually negotiated...

Such an agreement would establish protected crew sizes in addition to work force levels based on normal levels of production...

New Mazda Contract Eases 'Management-by-Stress' System

by Mike Parker

The new contract at Mazda's Flat Rock, Michigan plant shows that it is possible to make gains in a bad bargaining environment and that there *can* be union life after team concept. The contract made gains in dealing with issues that arise in plants using so-called Japanese management techniques.

The changes included: election of team leaders, increased union independence and representation, and steps to reduce the impact of the management-by-stress system on workers' mental and physical health and personal lives. The contract was ratified 2,102-433 by members of United Auto Workers Local 3000 on March 13.

The contract was negotiated under conditions which reduced the union's bargaining clout: the company had a 260-day supply of Ford Probes, five times the desired level. The Michigan media was filled with news of extended layoffs at other auto plants.

But strengthening the union's hand was the fact that most of the current officers had been elected two years previously criticizing a cozy relationship with the company. The company was well aware of their militant reputations and knew there was no way they would agree to concessions.

The bargainers were well prepared and unified, and felt that they had strong support from UAW Regional Director Bob King.

CONTRACT CAMPAIGN

"The key in our bargaining was an energized, mobilized, organized shop floor," says Shop Chair Greg Drudi. One technique was group grievances, such as one over management's misuse of temporary workers.

A Contract Support Committee collected over 2,400 surveys and issued Negotiations Newsletters to report on the results. These indicated a marked difference between the way things are claimed to work at Mazda and the reality. Some examples:

Q: My Unit Leader (first-level supervisor) can be trusted to implement the Mazda philosophy.
Rarely/Never—42%
Only sometimes—44%

Q: In my team we rotate jobs fairly.
No—50%

Q: My programmed work sheet [step-by-step instructions for doing a job] has been changed without my consultation.
Never—19%
Several/Many Times—74%

Q: The change in my programmed work sheet made the job...
Easier—6%
Harder—67%

Q: At the present work intensity I...
Can stay healthy and make it to retirement—26%

The campaign focused on getting a very high strike authorization vote to send the company a message. The leadership chose to risk holding the vote in-plant rather than at the union hall. Although the hall vote would certainly have produced a high percentage, the leadership felt it was important to show that the whole plant was united.

Coordinators and committeepersons went "one-on-one" to get out the vote, and gave out paste-on stickers, "Fighting for a Better Contract in '91." As the voting went on, these made clear to all the plant's sentiment. The result: 97% voted, with 92% in favor.

TEAM LEADERS ELECTED

The new provision to elect team leaders touches the core of the Mazda system. One hourly person on each team of four to ten workers is the team leader, paid an extra 50¢/hr. Job responsibilities include relief for absent workers, assisting with difficulties, and training.

Management tries to turn team leaders into assistant supervisors by getting them to take attendance, administer overtime scheduling, etc.

Originally the team leader was selected by management. Under pressure from the union the selection system has evolved to include some consideration of seniority.

The new contract more clearly defines the team leader as a part of the union team. Elections by team members will be used to fill any vacancies. Every six months, if two-thirds of the team members petition, a new election will be held. The contract specifies that attendance, payroll and overtime responsibilities are management's.

The election provision is popular. Although most Mazda employees say that "bad" team leaders are a small minority, most have had experience with one who acts like a boss or plays favorites. In some other team concept plants, activists have been able to elect team leaders who resist unreasonable management demands.

Some present team leaders strongly oppose elections. They argue that the union is letting other members vote on whether they get to keep their desirable jobs and pay. "We do not have members vote on who gets to work in Quality or Maintenance. Why should we vote on team leader? This just opens the job up to popularity politics. It should be done by seniority," says team leader Gurnie Stout. Other team leaders have suggested that it may be hard for women and minorities to get elected.

Joe Ditz, a team leader and editor of the local's paper, agrees that these problems need to be addressed but says, "I would still rather put my trust in the employees than in the supervisor. Your team leader has too much influence over your conditions of work not to be held accountable."

The union won the right to have a separate in-plant union office. Until now, union representatives shared office space with their management counterparts, making it difficult for members to get help in private. For Mazda, this arrangement symbolizes the idea of enterprise unionism, where the union's main job is to assist in carrying out company policy.

PARITY WITH FORD

The contract achieves wage parity with Ford. Layoff language remained unchanged: Mazda will not lay off unless forced by "financial circumstances so severe that its long term...viability is threatened."

The very high membership mobilization and expectations which provided an important part of the pressure to achieve the gains also led to some demoralization when those expectations were not fully met. The company held its own or won on some issues, such as toughening up the attendance plan and establishing several "jointness" programs which, depending on implementation, could undermine the union.

Perhaps most important, the union demanded but did not win a change in the no-strike clause. Unlike Big Three contracts, health and safety and work standards are not strikable at Mazda.

Local leaders will continue to press for this. President Phil Keeling explained, "Without a right to strike if necessary at Mazda we lack the means to effectively enforce the contract in these critical areas. We are still working under the Mazda team concept system and there is a lot more we need to do." □

[Mike Parker is co-author of *Choosing Sides: Unions and the Team Concept*.]

UAW MEMBERSHIP SURVEY

Dear Brother/Sister

In preparing for the upcoming contract negotiations, your UAW Negotiating Team is encouraging and respectfully requesting your personal input.

Please complete the UAW Membership Survey and return it to the Union Contract Support Committee member who presented it to you.

Your confidential answers will help guide us in determining our bargaining priorities. SOLIDARITY and active membership participation will strengthen our bargaining powers. Please feel free to include any additional comments.

Your cooperation in this matter will be appreciated.

In Solidarity,

YOUR UAW NEGOTIATING TEAM

DEPARTMENT_____ SHIFT _____ NAME (Optional) _____

1. My workload is

    _____properly balanced _____heavy, but acceptable _____too heavy, I can barely keep up

    Comments: _____

2. In my team, we rotate jobs fairly

    _____yes _____no
    If not, what is the problem? _____

3. a. My Program Work Sheet has been changed without my consultation

    _____never _____once _____several times _____many times

    b. The change(s) made my job

    _____easier _____harder _____no difference

    Comments: _____

4. On average, I work _____hours of overtime per week. This is

    _____too little _____acceptable _____too much

    Comments: _____

5. If the present level of work intensity continues:

    _____I can stay healthy and make it to retirement.

    _____I will likely be injured or worn out before I can retire.

    Comments: _____

6. In terms of considering workers' needs and interests, my Unit Leader can be trusted to implement the Mazda Philosophy

    _____always _____only sometimes _____rarely _____never

    Comments: _____

7. Team Leaders should be chosen according to

    _____present system _____election by the team _____rotation

    _____seniority _____other _____

8. Compared to Mazda's promises to train us, the actual training that I have received is

    _____excellent _____fair _____poor _____none received

    Comments: _____

9. To protect our rights during the contract, our members need to have the right to strike
(Indicate one or more)

_____on health and safety issues _____on work standards issues

_____Quality _____none of the above

_____other issues _____

10. From the following list of bargaining issues, indicate your **top five priorities**, with number
one being most important, number two the next most important, etc.

_____Job Security   _____Health & Safety

_____Wages & Benefits   _____Seniority Rights
          & Bonuses
                                     _____Attendance Policy (with
_____Child Care   paid personal days)

_____Work Standards   _____Outsourcing/Outside
                                               Contracting
_____Penalties for Company
          Contract Violations   _____Job Classifications

_____Transfers/Job
          Bid System

_____Other _____

11. I believe that my job security will be best protected by:

_____the company's continued usage of SMP's

_____the company's **promise** of no lay-offs

_____definitive contract language based on the principles of seniority and
          income/job protections.

Comments: _____

12. a. Have you ever had reason to go to the Health Center?

_____yes _____no

b. If yes, did you have problems wlith any of the following:

_____Restrictions   _____Medical Treatment

_____Job Placement   _____Workers' Compensation

_____Salary Continuation   _____Project Re-Entry

Other _____

13. Additional Comments:
What other issues/concerns are important to you?

_____

_____

_____

_____

THANK YOU FOR HELPING TO BUILD OUR UNION!

Appendix C

LOCAL LODGE 1125

International Association of Machinists

AND AEROSPACE WORKERS

MACHINISTS BUILDING   5150 KEARNY MESA ROAD   SAN DIEGO, CALIFORNIA 92111

summary

I. The afternoon sessions of both the Steward and Leadership Seminars was a strategy session. The aim was to lay the foundation for a unified union plan for dealing with TQM. Here is what came out of those sessions shown side by side.

STEWARD SEMINAR

1 Code of Conduct for Union Members

Union Members Shall Not:
- undermine the contract nor give up anything that ~~that~~ makes us a union
- allow violations of contract at TQM meetings
- particpate in the discipline of other union members
- pass on skills and knowledge to mgt.
- snitch or participate in programs or behavior that will hurt other union members
- take any oaths of secrecy
- negotiate contract items directly with company

Union Members Shall:
- display loyalty solidarity with other union members at all times
- insist Union Steward presence at all TQM meetings
- insist on democratic procedures when involved in TQM committees
- maintain written minutes of all TQM meetings attended and uphold open disclosure of items discussed
- take problems to the union steward

2. Education Plan for Members
- written communications (newsletter, handbills, stewardgrams, mailers)
- steward networking in-plant
- lunch time meetings in plant
- union surveys and questionaires
- union videos, T-shirts, buttons, mottos
- hotline
- organized investigations of TQM
- form Union TQM strategy Committee
- one on one canvassing w/members
- circulate results of steward seminars
- circulate educational materials
- develop TQM fact sheets for members
- encourage more ethnic participation with bilingual materials
- family education

LEADERSHIP SEMINAR

1 Code of Conduct for Union Members

Union Members Shall Not:
- circumvent the contract
- circumvent the grievance procedure
- participate in the disciplining of union members
- support or encourage job elimination
- discuss union business in front of mgt.
- complain about other union members in front of mgt.
- negotiate contract changes individually with mgt.

Union Members Shall:
- practice solidarity with other union members at all times
- take notes at TQM proceedings and report to steward or BA
- promote union point of view
- support democratic procedures at all TQM functions

2. Education Plan for Members
- educate stewards who then educate members
- develop a union point of view about TQM with participation of members
- use training seminars, newsletters, handbills, mailers to members' homes
- distribute books and reprints
- develop a video
- use surveys to find out where members stand on important issues
- hold shop floor meetings
- invite guest speakers to union mtgs.
- research other plants who have TQM
- union orientation for new members
- promote union pt of view (T-shirts, buttons)

STEWARD SEMINAR

3. Role of Shop Steward under TQM
    :ducate and inform members about TQM
- inform members of rights and responsibilities
- monitor TQM activities in area (investigate and report)
- grieve TQM violations of contract
- question mgt. decisions
- continuous improvement of union plan
- show special concern for members' problems
- build solidarity and union morale
- communicate with stewardgrams
- show leadership, challenge mgt tactics
- be visible and active
- update addresses and tel.nos of members
- wear union emblems
- listen to members, solicit their opinions
- organize in dept.
- encourage participation by members
- facillitate communication between members and leaders
- help members with problems outside of plant
- respect all members and mediate roblems between members
- protect members' confidentiality
- protect members' health and safety

4. Contract Language needed in response to TQM
- job security, no layoffs due to TQM, restrict offloading and subcontracting
- new technology language, retraining, advance notice impact on jobs & health and safety
- maintain seniority classifications and labor grades
- modify "rights of mgt" clause
- union input into training programs
- anti-monitoring language
- language to control operation of TQM cttes, make participation voluntary
- job posting
- inplant labor EAP representative
- Chief Shop Steward
- open BA access to plant
- strengthen grievance procedure increase share of profits

LEADERSHIP SEMINAR

3. Role of Shop Steward under TQM

(NOT COVERED)

4. Contract Language needed in response to TQM
- new tech language protecting jobs
- provisions for retraining
- $$ compensation for increased productivity
- union have 50% decision making power including veto power over all TQM projects
- post minutes of all TQM meetings
- right to caucus for union members on TQM cttes
- pre-planning for union caucus on co. time
- right to quit cttes
- union steward presence at all TQM meetings
- save custodians and inspectors
- no job loss due to TQM
- early retirement w/full benefits
- job impact evaluation for every TQM solution proposed
- no discrimination due to union affiliation
- no oaths of secrecy

STEWARD SEMINAR	LEADERSHIP SEMINAR
5. Guidelines for Union Members involved on TQM Cttes.	**5. Guidelines for Union Members involved on TQM Cttes.**

Steward present at all TQM ctte meetings
- union decide method of choosing union members for ctte.
- 50% union input & joint control of ctte (co-chair ctte.)
- union keep own minutes
- union input into agenda for meetings
- no secrecy
- union members on ctte right to caucus during TQM ctte meetings
- right to veto
- right to call meetings
- right to select consultants

(NOT COVERED)

II. BELOW IS A SUMMARY OF SOME OF THE MORNING WORK DONE IN THE SEPTEMBER 1 & 12TH STEWARD SEMINAR. THIS WORK INVOLVED DEFINING CERTAIN TERMS WE ALL HAVE BEEN BOMBARDED WITH OVER THE PAST FEW MONTHS IN RELATION TO TQM: GOALS, QUALITY, IMPROVEMENT.

THE LESSON LEARNED HERE WAS THAT ALL THESE TERMS, AS WELL AS MANY OTHERS W[ ] WILL BE HEARING A LOT FROM, MEAN DIFFERENT THINGS TO DIFFERENT   INTERESTS. BELOW IS A LIST OF THE MEANINGS THESE TERMS HAVE FOR THE   UINION AND THE COMPANY. WE MUST INJECT OUR DEFINITIONS INTO THE DEBATE.

MANAGEMENT GOALS
more work for less pay, higher profits, control of workplace, short cuts/cut corners, suppress complaints, reduce classifications, steal worker knowledge union busting, destroy worker esteem, lower injury claims, cut costs by cutting wages, zero inventory, eliminate   seniority, reduce benefits, speed-up.   assign responsibility without giving   authority

UNION GOALS
job security, improved working conditions, worker pride, skill retention, equality in the workplace, strong grievance procedure to protect workers' rights, stress free workplace, improved wages and benefits, eliminate harrassment, improve health and safety, reduce costs by eliminating top heavy mgt., protect seniority, improve communication, maintain job classifications and labor grades

MGT DEFINITION OF "QUALITY"
cheapest acceptable, reduce inspection, meet minimum standards, speed, quick turnaround, meet schedules

UNION DEFINITION OF QUALITY
pride in workmanship, enhanced self-esteem on the job, low on the job stress, proper training and tools to do the job, safe and healthy work environment, sufficient time to do a good job, fair treatment on the job, respect and recognition

MGT. DEFINITION OF "IMPROVEMENT"
quicker, cheaper, eliminate jobs automation, workers own company attitude, more control of workplace, lower   compensadion costs, lower absenteeism, weaken union, weaken contract, offload and subcontract work

UNION DEFINITION OF "IMPROVEMENT"
safer workplace, more jobs, more time to do work, better tools, correct tools to do job, guidance not dictatorship, job security, reduction of stress, better understanding of work process, more say in how work gets done, better rights in shop, training and advancement

Nothing can stop Q1!

The Q1 program at Thilmany is under way, and there doesn't seem to be a way to stop it. Shouting at Joe Bergomi doesn't stop it. Talking about the strike in DePere doesn't stop it. Having discussions about our premium pay doesn't stop it. But there is something that can defeat the Q1 program. Nothing.

When you are forced to go to the Q1 meeting, do nothing. Don't write down "what you expect to get out of Q1". Don't "count off" when they ask you. Don't fill out the "Inner Customer" posterboard. Don't argue with the facilitator. Don't watch the videos. Don't complain about the food. Nothing.

Doing nothing takes courage and will power. When you hear some of the outrageous statements they make, you'll want to shout, scream, and argue. Don't. That is what they want. They're trying to open a "dialog", and consider it "good for Q1". They're not counting on one thing. Nothing.

What <u>CAN</u> you do? Wear your red shirts to show them your Solidarity in this battle. Doodle. Bring some popcorn to munch. Look out the window. Keep your mouth shut, and settle in for a long, boring day. Other than that... Nothing.

We're not asking you to "Just Say No" to Q1.
We're asking you to "Just Say <u>Nothing</u>".

UAW LOCAL 2114

P.O. BOX 6416
BROADVIEW, ILLINOIS 60153
(312) 681-4370

INTERNATIONAL UNION, UNITED AUTOMOBILE, AEROSPACE & AGRICULTURAL IMPLEMENT WORKERS OF AMERICA-UAW

819 SOUTH MANHIEM ROAD
WESTCHESTER, ILLINOIS 60153
(312) 681-5661

January 20, 1986

To All Members of U.A.W. Local 2114:

As you all know, on January 15, 1986 your Executive Board took a position on the Crosby College Quality Strategy. This is the so called "Quality" system that management has had meetings which they call "Quality Meetings" with employees.

The Executive Boards official position was printed and handed out to all members on January 16, 1986.

On Sunday, January 19, 1986 at our regular monthly meeting the Crosby College Quality Strategy was discussed. The Membership of U.A.W. Local 2114 then voted, UNANIMOUSLY, to support the Executive Boards official position.

What this means is that no member will voluntarily give any input into a so called "Quality Meeting". We will not say anything. We will not write anything. We will not accept the Crosby College Quality Strategy!

If you are taken into a so-called "Quality Meeting" and asked to take notes, give input, or check off items on their list and ect., say NO. If you are ordered to take notes, answer questions or check off items on a list and ect. say OK and at the same time ask for your committeeman. When you are ordered you then must answer so you will not be disciplined for disobeying a direct order. Remember this when you are Forced to answer, management cannot make you understand the questions! And consider this, they may be the real cause of their problems!

By voting to support the Executive Board, the membership has said, until such time as we are directed to do otherwise by the U.A.W. International Union, We the Members of Local 2114 will not participate in any way, shape or form in the Crosby College Quality Strategy.

WE STAND UNITED!

Chairman Shop Committee

Al Winkler

President

James R. Thielman

Participating in Management

[Following is a summary of the participation model outlined by Andy Banks and Jack Metzgar in Labor Research Review #14 (Midwest Center for Labor Research, 3411 W. Diversey, #10, Chicago, IL 60647; $7). For our evaluation of the strengths and weaknesses of the plan, see "Dealing With Good Management" in that same issue.]

Reject the idea of a neutral consultant. Management and union should each have their own. The union's resources for consultants and lost time should equal management's. The union will need at least one full-time coordinator, plus shopfloor facilitators.

The union must have its own strategy prior to any joint meetings. The union should draw up its own proposals and then bring them to the joint labor-management committee.

Exclude Management

The key is the structural exclusion of management from a direct relationship with the rank and file. This allows members to hide their knowledge from the boss. It keeps management from screwing up the program, and it clearly identifies the participation program as the union's, not as a joint program.

By keeping these programs away from both company supervisors and neutral facilitators, the union can eliminate potential for the kind of cooperationist attitude adjustment that many managements are after. Moreover, management will not be able to offer workers a structure which encourages them to bypass the union and go to management directly.

The program represented in the diagram is the periodic joining together of two separate programs, the union's and management's. Each half of the program has its own constituency, and each party retains its exclusive access to that constituency.

The union steering committee is composed of the top officers of the union. It reviews all proposals from the union side before they are presented to the joint union-management steering committee. The joint committee is composed of the union steering committee and a management committee with an equal number of the enterprise's top managers. The union has a full-time coordinator who acts as the staff of the union steering committee. It is his or her job to arrange for training and to assure access to information for the various union participation groups.

Jointness Only at the Top

With this model, the Area-wide Union Committee (AUC) solicits ideas from the workforce and develops them into proposals for change.

There is a sifting process on the part of the union leadership—the AUC members, the union coordinator and the union steering committee—before any proposal is presented to management. Jointness in this kind of program occurs only at the representative level, in joint committees, and only after the union has thoroughly explored the negative and positive potential of any workplace change.

But while the union thereby maintains control of the participation process, the proposed changes can be implemented only if management agrees.

Dealing With Bad Proposals

One thing that can go wrong: workers participating in the program may develop a cost-saving proposal that is bad for the union. In this case, the union coordinator would educate members on how their proposal could hurt and how it could be reformulated to meet cost-saving and union goals.

In the event management tried to sneak by the proposal at a joint meeting, the union would be able to exercise its veto.

Another problem that can be expected to crop up is that management will find that cooperating with a strong worker participation program is very stressful.

Management might withdraw its cooperation at any time. If so, the union might grieve the issue, or it might decide the best strategy is to do nothing until the contract expires, and raise the issue of mismanagement at that time.

A union-empowering worker participation program requires a level of internal union organization and membership participation that is rare today. But it also provides a concrete way to generate a high degree of organization and participation.

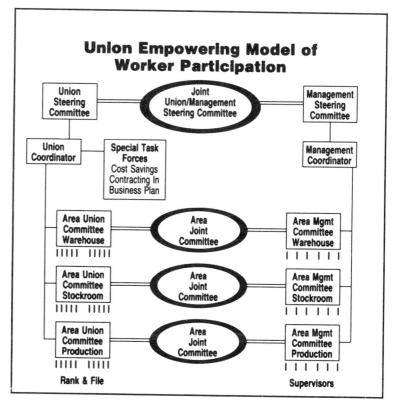

Union Empowering Model of Worker Participation

Strategic Planning for Unions

This section is excerpted from Labor Notes' **A Troublemaker's Handbook: How to Fight Back Where You Work—and Win!** *by Dan La Botz.*

We hope this guide has given you some ideas and you're anxious to use them. But wait. To make them work best, they have to be part of a well-thought-out, long-term *strategic plan*. You—that is, the collective you, the union as a whole—have to decide where it is you want to go and how you're going to get there. You need a plan.

Most local unions plan around their regular business: handling grievances, contract negotiations, strikes from time to time, regular union meetings, elections, conventions. These activities provide the regular rhythm of union life. Having too few resources to deal with them all properly, local union officials often find themselves overwhelmed with these day-to-day activities. They do not find the time to scan the horizon for internal or external developments which may change the entire context in which they are operating.

What Is Strategic Planning?

All too often unions simply react to management initiatives or seek only short-term tactical objectives. Strategic planning means analyzing your situation to develop long-range goals, and then working out the specific steps to get from here to there.

It is best to engage in a strategic planning discussion at a time when the union is not embroiled in a strike, an election or a convention, but rather at a moment when it is possible to sit down and think.

Strategic planning for unions is based on a "power analysis" or calculating the balance of forces. Such a calculation of the balance of forces must take into account the entire environment in which labor and management exist, as well as the relative strengths and weaknesses of the union and the company themselves. Such a power analysis must look not only at the situation of the moment, but especially at the changes taking place—the dynamics which are driving the society, the industry, the company, the union and the rank and file in various directions.

Let's say that your local is ready to set up a strategic planning session. There are certain important ingredients besides information and intelligence. These include:

The planners themselves. Think broadly about who should be in on your local's strategic planning sessions. You want elected officials, but there may be others who can contribute as much or more. There are many natural leaders and intelligent members who never run for union office. In addition, you need to have everyone who will be involved in implementing the plan on board from the beginning—those left out of the planning process will be less interested in carrying out the resulting strategy.

Think in terms of constituencies represented and different political followings. And also invite people with a range of skills—financial, creative, detail work, writing, big picture thinking, dealing with management. Even those who are not activists can be brought in through department meetings and questionnaires.

Go off-site. This is for two reasons. You need to be away from the day-to-day tasks which keep your nose to the grindstone and keep you from thinking long term. And you need to get across to the participants the idea that this meeting is something different, a chance to change old habits of thinking.

Use the brainstorming method. (See box.)

Use some of management's tools. A flipchart and a felt-tip marker to record everyone's ideas as you brainstorm will make a big difference from the usual free-for-all discussion. It will also help to keep traditional leaders from dominating—or others from deferring to them.

For space reasons we have presented the questions in this section in a condensed form. We recommend that you retype them with lots of blank space for writing in answers. For some reason a piece of paper with some white space on it seems to get many people's creative juices flowing. You'll want a page for a Mission Statement, for Key Goals, for a Strategic Analysis, and several for the Strategic Plan itself, including a timeline .

Consider using an outside facilitator. A neutral person experienced at drawing others out and moving the discussion along can help a lot. Perhaps someone you've met from another union in town would give you a hand.

There are essentially six steps to strategic planning:

- Agree on a mission statement.
- Pinpoint your key goals for the coming period (say a year).
- Analyze the balance of forces.
- Make a detailed plan for achieving your key goals.
- Carry out the plan.

- Evaluate how well the plan is working; make changes if necessary.

Write a Mission Statement

A mission statement is a clear statement of the purpose of the union. Why does the union exist? What does the union want to accomplish in the broadest sense? That is its mission. If this has not been discussed in your union for some time—in some unions it has not been discussed since the union was founded in the 1890s or the 1930s—then it may be worth some debate.

Rules for Brainstorming

1. Clarify and agree on the discussion topic.
2. Allow a minute of silence for people to think individually.
3. Be sure everyone has a chance to speak by going around the table to each person in turn. Take one idea at a time.
4. People may pass.
5. People may build on previous ideas.
6. Do not discuss or criticize ideas until they are all recorded.
7. People may add new ideas once discussion starts.
8. Encourage the widest range of ideas possible: far out is good.

Decide on Key Goals

Key goals are "got-to-haves," those two or three elements that distinguish success from failure for your union in the coming period.

For example: a union of electrical manufacturing workers is facing a trend toward the opening of non-union plants in the area, leading to a depression in wages. It might decide that organizing those plants is its most important key goal.

At the same time, the local leaders are aware that its older U.S.-born workers are rapidly retiring, while for the last two years the employer has hired only Latinos and Asians, the fastest growing immigrant groups in the area. The planners might decide that strengthening the involvement of the Latin and Asian workers—who represent the future of the union—is another key goal.

Another local union, this one in a multi-plant company, might determine that the greatest threat to the local is the employer's attempts to "whipsaw" it against a sister plant in another state—trying to get each to underbid the other for new work. This union might decide that building strong ties to the sister local and making a pledge to resist concessions together is a key goal.

Make an Analysis

To make a strategic analysis you must assess the external and the internal, the environment and the union. This is sometimes called a SWOT Analysis, for Strengths, Weaknesses, Opportunities and Threats.

Analyzing the Environment

In looking at the environment, you look not only at the current situation. You ask, what developments are taking place, and, even more important, what are the *trends*?

You may feel that you, as a group, are already very familiar with these facts and trends. But write down your answers and compare them. Discuss them. Add more questions to those here.

Economic Questions: What is the state of the industry? Of the company? Of your local workplace? Is the industry booming? Or is it on the way down? Is the company profitable? Is your workplace important for the company, or is it marginal? Is it profitable? Who are the company's owners? Any changes there? What about its managers? What is the company's market share? Who are its customers? Its suppliers? Is the company maintaining the facility, the equipment? How is new technology affecting your workplace? Is your employer keeping up with the pace of developments in the industry?

What is your company's overall corporate strategy for survival and growth? Within that, what is its strategy toward unions? What is the strategy of local management at your workplace? How are global economic changes affecting your workplace?

Social Questions: Is the workplace in an industrial, commercial or residential area? What are things like in the surrounding neighborhood? Are there important community institutions such as churches? Neighborhood organizations? Block clubs? What are race relations like in the area? What is the unemployment situation? What is the community's attitude toward the company? Toward the union? List all the union's current and potential allies and highlight the important ones.

Political Questions: What is the political situation in the city relevant to the labor movement? Are the mayor and city council pro- or anti-union? What about the police chief? What are their ties to this company? What are their neighborhood ties?

How are political trends in the country affecting your industry or members? What legislative decisions are affecting you?

Analyzing the Union

In analyzing your own organization, whether a local union or a rank and file group, you have to look at your own strengths and weaknesses.

Again, you will want to look at the *trends*. Add more questions to those here.

- What are the basic statistics of your organization? How many members do you have and what proportion of the total workforce does that represent? What is the demographic make-up of the workforce: Male? Female? White? Black? Latin? Asian? Immigrant? Documented? Undocumented? What is the age make-up of the workforce? How many are retiring and when? At what rate is the company hiring? How is the workforce organized and deployed into crafts, job titles, grades or other distinctions? In what direction are all these statistics changing?

- Take inventory of your financial resources: Union treasury? Strike benefits? Credit?

- How broad is the leadership of the organization? Does the entire executive board play a leadership role? What about the paid staff? Are all the stewards active? Do you have rank and filers who are active in the union? How many people come to union meetings? Department meetings? Are there other ways to measure membership commitment and participation? Are the official leaders of the union also the actual leaders? Are there potential leaders who have not yet been incorporated?

- How active is the rank and file? How many participated in the last strike? How many participated in the union's last major activity? How many voted in the last union election? How many calls are there to the office each week? How many visits by stewards with members, by business agents with stewards and members?

- Are there good or bad relations among the union's members? Is their any ill will among various groups (racial, sexual, craft or other)? Are there any historic problems that need to be dealt with? For example, "X group scabbed on the last strike," or "Y group got a bigger raise than

Z group." Are there differences of opinion in the union? Over what issues? What is the state of democracy in the union? Do all groups get a chance to make their feelings known? Is the leadership tolerant of dissent?

You may want to review goals and revise them in the light of your Strategic Analysis.

Look at the Big Picture

In doing the analysis above you will do best if you locate both the union and the employer in their larger setting.

For example, instead of seeing the shop as having 300 members or the local union as having 800 members who are arrayed against an employer which is a local company, those "facts" should be placed in their proper context. The 300 members at the shop have an average family size of four members, so we are talking about 1,200 people associated with the union and living in the community who are concerned about this shop directly. The union's 800 members represent 3,200 people in the community who have ties to this shop indirectly through the local union.

The union also has actual or potential connections to churches and neighborhood groups, to other unions in the Central Labor Council and to other locals in its International. Placed in their

context, the facts take on a new meaning: those 300 workers in the shop represent the possibility of mobilizing thousands.

The union's potential allies are only one part of the context, of course. Equally important is the context for your local management's moves—the situation in the industry, global competition. These are not as easy for a local union to affect, but they must be considered.

Mineworkers' Strategic Plan

Here's an example of a union which looked at the big picture and made a strategic plan.

For a decade or more, the United Mine Workers saw their power in the bituminous coal industry decline as more production moved west to non-union open pit mines. Furthermore, the employers themselves had gotten bigger as energy conglomerates bought up the old coal companies. Encouraged by these trends, employers began leaving the industry's collective bargaining arm, the Bituminous Coal Operators Association, and breaking with the pattern contract. Long industry-wide strikes in 1978 and 1981 had not stopped this trend and had cost the union dearly. The union was in danger of extinction.

In the early 1980s the union decided it was in need of a new strategy to stem the tide. The strategy included a proposed merger with the Oil, Chemical and Atomic Workers, which bargained with many of the same energy conglomerates and could bring greater combined resources. The UMWA also developed a new approach to strikes. First, the union would strike only companies that tried to break away from the national contract. Second, the strike itself would no longer be a simple withdrawal of labor. It would become a mass movement.

The new approach was first applied in 1984 when A.T. Massey tried to break with the pattern agreement. The union conducted a world-wide corporate campaign against Royal Dutch Shell, which was a major owner of Massey, emphasizing Shell's role in South Africa.

The union also used mass non-violent civil disobedience tactics. The new tactics were only partially successful in getting Massey to conform to the master contract, but the mine workers had learned about changing the balance of forces.

In 1988 1,700 coal miners in Virginia were faced with similar union-busting by the Pittston Coal Group, a large multinational conglomerate. The odds looked uneven. In line with their plan, miners knew 1) that keeping Pittston in line was key to preserving the union and 2) that they would need a strike based on a grassroots movement.

Again the union looked at the larger context: the miners' family members, laid-off and disabled miners, retirees, friends, other unions, potential support from other cities and states.

When the confrontation came in April 1989, Pittston faced not only 1,700 strikers but a totally mobilized community in southwestern Virginia and an even more impressive series of mass actions than Massey had faced. High school students struck in sympathy. Women, organized as the Daughters of Mother Jones, sat in at the company's regional offices. Tens of thousands of miners and supporters from dozens of unions came to "Camp Solidarity" in Virginia and participated in rallies and mass civil disobedience. The community came to see the union's cause as its own.

To most observers assessing the situation in 1980, it would have seemed impossible that the UMWA—a shrinking union in a changing industry—could survive so well for so long. The UMWA has not stopped the coal operators' union-busting plans once and for all. But for now, its strategy is working.

Make A Strategic Plan

It is crucial that the union's leadership broadly speaking (executive board, stewards, union activists, staff) be involved in developing the Strategic Plan, and that the rank and file be kept informed and periodically participate in helping to evolve it. If not, the union leadership may find itself having to "sell" a program for which it has failed to organize support as it went along.

While your key goals are somewhat general, Strategic Plans are very specific. Within the Plan, the objectives should be "SMART":

- Specific—specifies a key result.
- Measurable—so you can know whether you've succeeded or not.
- Assignable—specifies who will do it.
- Realistic—but still represents a change and a challenge.
- Time-related—specifies the amount of time needed or a deadline.

Let's create a hypothetical example. The leadership of a local union, a garment workers local made up mostly of women, decides that a key goal is strengthening the involvement of its growing numbers of Asian and Latin members. It decides that some measures of progress toward this goal are:

- Higher attendance of Asian and Latin members at union meetings.
- Involvement of Asian and Latin members on union committees.
- Greater number of grievances written by Asian and Latin members.
- Asian and Latin candidates for office.

The Strategic Plan must be made up of specific tasks. For example:

- Print contracts, union by-laws and constitution in Spanish and Korean.
- Arrange for translators for union meetings and department meetings.
- Place articles by and about Asian and Latin workers in union newsletter.
- Appoint two Asian and two Latin workers to fill vacant steward positions until next election. This will give them experience and make them viable candidates.
- Appoint Asian or Latin workers to fill vacancy on local executive board.
- Hire Asian or Latin woman organizer.
- Union officers visit Asian and Latin organizations and churches in the area.

Tasks must always be attached to times. A plan must have a time frame in which to accomplish its goals. Let's say the time frame is one year. There must also be a timetable—things to be done each month, week, and even day.

The filling of the vacancies can be done at once, the translation and reprinting within three months. The articles in the newsletter can begin with the next issue in one month.

Tasks must also be attached to individuals (perhaps committees) responsible for carrying them out. The local president will make the appointments to the executive board and the steward positions. The secretary-treasurer will see to arranging the translation and printing. The newsletter editor will see to getting letters by and about Korean and Salvadoran workers. A temporary search committee will be appointed to find the new organizer, and the executive board will approve her hiring. A new Outreach Committee will be recruited to visit the local community groups and report back on potential allies.

Strategic Plans have to be realistic. For example, if the local of electrical workers mentioned earlier under Key Goals has few members and a small treasury, and the electrical industry in the area involves scores of plants, then it may not be possible for that local alone to set itself the task of organizing the industry in the area. A more reasonable plan might be to convince other electrical workers' unions to join together to organize the non-union plants.

Evaluate & Be Flexible

In our garment workers example, the executive board might want to evaluate the process in three months. How have the Asian and Latin workers reacted to changes so far? Is attendance at union meetings higher, for example? How are non-immigrant workers responding to union initiatives?

The plan must be flexible. Perhaps there was an unforeseen layoff and a fall in dues income immediately after the plan was adopted, making it impossible to hire the new organizer. How will you compensate? Is it possible to set up a volunteer organizing committee?

Or it may turn out that production expanded rapidly and management began to hire more immigrants, this time from Haiti. It will be necessary to rethink the plan and come up with new tasks, specific individuals to carry them out, and a new time frame and timetable.